pulse

pulse pulse pulse

THE COMING AGE OF

SYSTEMS AND MACHINES

INSPIRED BY LIVING THINGS

Robert Frenay

FARRAR, STRAUS AND GIROUX
New York

Farrar, Straus and Giroux
19 Union Square West, New York 10003

Copyright © 2006 by Robert Frenay
Distributed in Canada by Douglas & McIntyre Ltd.
Printed in the United States of America
First edition, 2006

Portions of this work were originally published, in different form, in *Audubon* magazine.

Grateful acknowledgment is made for permission to reprint the following previously published material:
Material from talks given at The Bioneers Conference: "Practical Solutions for Restoring the Earth," October 31–November 1, 1997, copyright © 2006 by Collective Heritage Institute. Used by permission of Collective Heritage Institute.
Excerpts from *When Corporations Rule the World, Updated and Expanded Edition*, by David C. Korten (Bloomfield, CT, San Francisco, CA: a copublication of Kumarian Press, Inc., and Berrett-Koehler Publishers, 2001).
Excerpts from *The Third Culture* by John Brockman, copyright © 1995 by John Brockman, reprinted with permission of Simon & Schuster Adult Publishing Group.
Lines from "If the GDP Is Up, Why Is America Down?" in *The Atlantic Monthly*, October 1995, by Clifford Cobb, Ted Halstead, and Jonathan Rowe, copyright © 2006 by Redefining Progress. Used by permission of Redefining Progress.

Library of Congress Cataloging-in-Publication Data
Frenay, Robert, 1946–
    Pulse : the coming age of systems and machines inspired by living things / Robert Frenay.— 1st ed.
      p. cm.
    Includes index.
    ISBN-13: 978-0-374-11327-8 (alk. paper)
    ISBN-10: 0-374-11327-0 (alk. paper)
    1. Bioengineering. 2. Bionics. 3. Human-machine systems.   I. Title.

TA164.F74 2006
620'.0042—dc22

2005022285

Designed by Patrice Sheridan

www.fsgbooks.com

1 3 5 7 9 10 8 6 4 2

for Hanya

light is working in the stems' cells,
drawing up, adjusting, soft alignments
coming true . . .

A. R. Ammons

contents

9. Town and Country   237

part three: global designs

10. Industrial Ecology   285

11. The Real Conservatives   325

12. Feedback Culture   391

     Notes   457
     Index   521

acknowledgments

It has been said that having a writer in the family means the end of the family. If that has not been the case with mine, or with the many close friends I think of as my extended family, it's due to the forbearance, support, and numerous courtesies they have shown me during the eight years of this book's making. Add to those the time taken by all the professionals who talked with me about their work, and then read parts of the manuscript to help ensure its accuracy. Any attempt to thank them all runs the risk of sounding like one of those speeches by an actor who can't seem to leave the podium after getting an Academy Award. Still, this book would not be what it is without them.

I'd like to thank my two brothers: David, for instilling in all those around him a love of nature, and Gary, a songwriter, for our lifelong dialogue on the creative process. I'd also like to thank their wives—Carol and Jackie, my sisters—for their many kindnesses, and their great kids, Erica and Travis, Rob and Nick, who brighten not only their lives but mine. I owe a lasting debt of gratitude to my parents for the faith and guidance they showed me throughout their lifetimes, also to them and their numerous friends—so many of them rural storytellers—for their dry humor and dauntless good spirit, and for setting the best example I know of for how to live.

Among the thoughtful talks I had with sources for this book, conversations with Murray Gell-Mann, Rodney Brooks, Stewart Brand, Brian Arthur, William McDonough, Michael Braungart, and Richard Levine were particularly helpful in forming the ideas presented here. I'd like to express my appreciation for the time they took away from busy lives to talk with me, often repeatedly, about this subject.

I'm also grateful to those whose work is discussed here and who offered to review parts of the manuscript. They include Brian Arthur, Peter Barnes, Mark Bedau, Stewart Brand, Galen Brandt, Michael Braungart, Lynn Caporale, Patricia Churchland, Robert Costanza, David Crockett, Bruce Damer, Murray Gell-Mann, Paul Hawken, Dee Hock, Wes Jackson, Léon Krier, Christopher Langton, Richard Levine, William McDonough, Susan Oyama, Norman Packard, Rosalind Picard, David Pines, Thomas Ray, Mitchel Resnick, Joel Salatin, Clive Stannard, Wouter van Dieren, and Julian Vincent. Their generosity sharpened and improved in many ways the text that follows.

I would like to emphasize that while individual sources may have corrected parts of this manuscript, the larger synthesis of their work—and any mistakes or distortions resulting from that effort—are mine.

In the interest of full disclosure, I should note that some of the people mentioned here are friends or acquaintances. They include Peter Barnes (chapter 11), Lynn Caporale (chapters 6, 7, 8, 12), Peter Henry (chapter 7), Stephen Farrier (chapters 1, 5, 8), Dean Santner (chapter 3), and Todd Zimmerman (chapter 9). Additionally, some passages used here were first published in my regular Envirotech report in *Audubon* magazine and in a two-part feature that ran there. I'd like to thank my colleague Mary Sidney Kelly for consenting to let me draw on material that we coauthored in *Audubon*.

My work benefited greatly from the help of two organizations. First, I want to thank Della DeTore and her staff at the Sullivan Free Library—in the very small town of Bridgeport, New York—whose unfailing courtesy, professionalism, and ability to acquire obscure books from even more obscure sources has never ceased to amaze and delight me. Second, the overall structure of this book came together during a stay at the magical Mesa Refuge writers' retreat, in Point Reyes, California. My thanks to Peter Barnes, its founder; to Margaret Solle and Pam Carr, who made us feel like more than guests; to Beth Livermore, who referred me; and to my housemates Ami Chen Mills, Judith Helfand,

Dorothy Larson, and Kimi Eisele for all of the lively conversations and good cheer.

I would especially like to thank Mike Robbins, my former boss at *Audubon*, whom I have the good fortune to call a mentor and friend, and who sets a standard most of us can only aim for. Thanks also to another mentor, the distinguished author Leo Deuel, for all the guidance and good humor, and the many years of challenging and stimulating discussions across the tables of restaurants all over Manhattan. I'd like to express my deep appreciation to Barbara Murray, who put me on the path. Thanks to my friend Charles Platt for his frequent help and patient counsel through the course of several decades, and to my friend and FSG colleague, David Hajdu, for his astute suggestions on literary matters. I'm grateful to Paul and Suzanne Siegel for their support, and for our many years spent enjoying life's passing parade; and to Nick Banta for his thoughtful advice and for providing crucial motivation. My appreciation to John and Sherry Neish, to Pete and Michele Henry, and to their families, for a lifetime of encouragement, good company, and free meals, and to Travis Frenay for the essential deadline soundtrack. Thanks to Pat Mullins, old friend and counselor in matters personal and professional, and to another old friend, Carol Fierman, for being there through it all. Thanks to Evan and Debbie Ross for their faith and support, also to Debbie and her sister-in-law Lisa Ross for the beautiful walnut library table on which a number of these chapters were written. Thanks to Marc and Robin Abrahams, the well-known professional smart alecks, for their unique perspective and advice. I'm grateful to my lifestyle advisers, Russ and Cate Howell, who have raised the bar high, and to Russ for his always lucid take on complex problems. Special thanks to Celeste Moore, to Mickey and Tim McDaniel, and to their families for their resolute encouragement.

I'd also like to express my appreciation to Walt Sondheim for his hospitality and help during my visits to Santa Fe; Humberto Santos and his uncle, the bestselling author Lair Ribeiro, for their friendship and guidance during my time in Brazil; Michael Braungart, for his aid in setting up interviews in Germany and the Netherlands; Léon Krier, for taking me to see Port-Grimaud during my visit to talk with him in France; and Michael Trevillion and Sharon Horlor, for their many acts of generosity in London, not the least of which is Mike's photo on this book jacket. I'm grateful to Anita Fore of the Authors Guild for her patient advice on the many legal questions that emerged during this project. And thanks to Harry Salon and Andres Soto for granting grace when it mattered.

A number of people made direct contributions to my text. Chris Chang and Joanna Samuels did extensive work on the *Audubon* features that led to this book. They helped lay a sound foundation for what has followed. I'd also like to thank Chris, a know-it-all's know-it-all and now senior editor of *Film Comment*, for the years of frequent and illuminating digressions. I want to acknowledge my substantial debt to the talented editorial staff at *Audubon* during the time I was there—Roger Cohen, Bruce Stutz, David Seideman (now the magazine's editor in chief), Linda Perney, and Mary Powell Thomas. I learned important lessons from them all. In addition, working with Ted Williams there was a constant schooling in what it takes to be a great reporter.

Eben McLane, Yasuyo Uehara, Deborah Kreuze, Erica Frenay, and William Brayman did supplemental reporting for this book; their input was invaluable. Two interns, Brent Horton and Eric Gillin, were a great help. My thanks to David Salati for his hard work and diligence in the initial fact-checking. I'd like to acknowledge the indispensable contribution of the late Marion West, who brought intelligence and wit to the difficult task of transcribing the several dozen interviews conducted during my initial research. I'd also like to express my special thanks to Michele and Elissa Henry, who volunteered their help in making last-minute transcriptions under difficult circumstances. Pam Hall brought a reassuring ease and professionalism to the large task of transcribing excerpts and footnote data from the thousands of individual clips and book passages that inform the core of my text.

Many friends and family members have read parts of this book's proposal or manuscript, or have provided helpful perspective and suggestions. Among them are Alexa Brayman, William Brayman, Ami Chen Mills, David and Carol Frenay, Erica Frenay and Craig Modisher, Gary Frenay and Jackie Lewis, David Hajdu, Judith Helfand, Peter Henry, Russ and Cate Howell, Robert Kane, Deborah Kreuze, Beth Livermore, Peter London, Patrick Mullins, Michael Robbins, Paul Siegel, and Tom and Alex Stites. I'm grateful for their time and valuable contributions.

My interest in business reporting stems from an extended stint as a freelance researcher at *The New York Times*, at what was then its "Business World" magazine supplement. Working with the editor in chief, Marylin Bender, and her very capable staff—including Linda Lee, Tim Race, and Bob Woletz—was a formative experience. Special thanks to Bob, who showed me the ropes, and to Linda, for introducing me to my wonderful agent, Mary Evans.

During my eight years of work on this project, a few friends have gone beyond all obligations of friendship and taken it as their own. I owe more than I can say to Dean Santner, my lifelong collaborator, and to his beautiful and talented wife, Sally Maxwell Geer. Their strong interest and support, their many key suggestions, and their constant good humor have had a tremendous influence on this book, not to mention its author. I want to thank Dean for taking the time to read each chapter of the manuscript and for his frank critiques. In addition, I'd like to thank him for his camaraderie, good counsel, and moral guidance these many years.

Another old friend, Stephen Farrier, has made more direct contributions to this book than anyone save its author. I'd like to express my gratitude here for all the ways he has helped to make it possible. He has been a sharp and insightful reporter, contributing many of the citations from *Nature*, *Science*, and *The Economist* that are found here. Stephen's wide knowledge and ongoing interest, his constant support, and his rigorous criticisms have played a crucial role in this book's development. While he won't agree with everything included here, it's a much better book for his involvement.

I also owe a special debt of gratitude to my agent, Mary Evans, who has played such an important part in making this project a reality. She helped with the proposal, found distinguished publishers for the book here and abroad, read early chapters and the final manuscript, offered salient critiques and suggestions, and has stuck by it through its extended progress from seminal idea to finished work. Mary brings to her profession not just a sharp eye for business but also a high regard for quality. I hope this effort meets that standard, and I'd like to thank her sincerely for all she has done. I'd also like to express my appreciation to Devin McIntyre, of her office, for his many courtesies in helping to keep everything on track.

My deepest thanks to John Glusman, my editor at Farrar, Straus and Giroux, for his many insights, for his patience, and for his graciousness during the long evolution of this manuscript. Through every stage, John provided sure and vital guidance in the shaping of a large, unwieldy subject into readable form. Every writer knows the difference a good editor can make, and on this book I've been privileged to work with one of the best. To be at FSG is to be in the hands of thoroughgoing professionals. Lisa Silverman's thoughtful production editing and Ingrid Sterner's copyediting and sharp final fact-checking, on a tight deadline, have made this book a great deal clearer and more accurate. The elegant design of the book is thanks to Patrice Sheridan. Its striking and beautiful jacket is by Lynn Buckley. Also at FSG, Aodaoin O'Floinn brought intelligence and a fine eye to her editing and coordination, and did so with amiable good humor. Corinna Barsan has continued on in that spirit, offering valuable advice and crucial support in the book's final phase. My appreciation for their help and for making the whole process seem a pleasure.

Finally, I would like to thank my muse, Dr. Hanya Wozniak-Brayman, a slender, elegant woman with a keen mind, gentle manners, and a warm, lively sense of humor. Companion, lover, first critic, and abiding friend, her support and inspiration give meaning to my life. As Blake once said, "The soul of sweet delight can never pass away." What is best in this book comes from her.

introduction

Many will see this book as a visitor's guide to a brave new world of cutting-edge advances and gee-whiz technologies. So I should probably point out that there are no new ideas in the chapters that follow. True, the extraordinary developments outlined here will be mostly unknown to the casual reader, but the ideas that inform them are nearly four billion years old. What we *are* witnessing, and what this book charts, is a profound shift in the underlying concepts that shape virtually all human endeavors, or at least those in the industrialized world. As new insights into the workings of biology spawn fundamental redesigns of other fields, we can now watch the twin arcs of human culture and technology as they move to conform ever more closely to the underlying profile of living processes.

This is, at the same time, a big step past those reliable old machine age notions that have guided much of the world for centuries. And with that will come changes in the way we live. Many of them are going to be exciting and beneficial; some will be problematic, even dangerous. Either way, there is no question that they are well along. Because biological concepts are transforming so many different and seemingly unconnected fields at once, I believe those transformations are significant, evidence of a larger sea change.

What will be described here as the "new biology" draws from recent discoveries in biology to create machines and other systems that mimic the dynamics of life. Referred to technically by words like "biomimetics," "ecomimetics," and "bionics," those efforts have spawned an ever-growing list of dazzling innovations that even now are moving out of the labs and into our daily lives. I should add that adopting lessons from nature is nothing new. The machine age itself was an early attempt to do just that. Unfortunately, it stopped short in its understanding of nature, basing our industry and eventually much of our culture today on concepts from the physics of the seventeenth and eighteenth centuries. Still, time has shown that getting things even half right was a powerful advance. After some three centuries we see the fruits of its success all around us. The problem is that evidence of its shortcomings is also on the rise. And that problem remains unsolved because the machine age approach—the underlying philosophy—now guiding efforts to correct it is actually its cause. There are good reasons for how this situation came about, the main one being the lack of any broad, viable alternative. But things are set to change. The new biology is that alternative, a more effective and realistic basis for the conventional wisdom that guides our decisions in every area of life.

This book might be called a current history. After the centuries-long run of machine age outlooks and practices, it describes a brief period of roughly a decade in which a new idea of the world has snapped into focus. The start of that accelerated period of change can be marked approximately by the 1994 founding of the World Wide Web Consortium, also known as W3C, a standards-setting body established by the Web's inventor, Tim Berners-Lee. That action formalized the connecting of business, science, politics, art, design, philosophy, and a growing base of curious home users through the Internet. At the time there were only a few hundred thousand computers involved, but over the next ten years, through the meandering and ever-multiplying links of the Web, hundreds of millions more would be added. With that spreading network of connections, fields as diverse as genetics, cell biology, brain structure, and ecology would meet and mingle with other fields ranging from materials science, robotics, artificial intelligence, and artificial life to agriculture, town planning, manufacturing, and economic theory.

One result of this unprecedented exchange, among the sweetest fruits it has borne, is the deeper integration of our culture with the natural world. But unlike the romantic feelings that inspired earlier turns to nature, this new esteem for life stems from a sense of wonder at the vibrant dynamics we now see unfolding at its heart. It is those principles—and our dawning awareness of their practical superiority as a guide for human design—that hold out the promise of a new era.

My own love of nature comes from a childhood lived on a dirt road along a rural lakeshore in upstate New York. It was an idyllic beginning, and the careless hours I spent as a boy fishing and wandering through open fields or wondering about the distant stars have remained a touchstone throughout my life.

The genesis of this book was an ongoing series of conversations with Mike Robbins, my editor at *Audubon* magazine, where I worked in various capacities from 1991 through 1997. It was a formative experience, not least because of Robbins, then the magazine's editor in chief. An award-winning journalist, Mike combines intellectual rigor and openness toward new ideas to a degree rare even in top editors. And the energy and ease he brought to his work made it an inspiring time to be there.

I wrote a small column for *Audubon* during this period, focused on the interface of nature and culture—in particular, on positive developments in technology. A hunch that ecosystems and economic systems might have parallels eventually took me to the Santa Fe Institute. There, Stuart Kauffman and Brian Arthur had been working on that question for some time, using computers as a kind of translation device between their two disciplines. The economics angle ended up as a sidebar to two long stories on the environmental promise of biologically inspired design; they ran in *Audubon* during the fall of 1995 and winter of 1996. This book has grown from them, and in the process has become a much broader project. To the best of my knowledge it is the first to bring under a single cover the full range of different fields being transformed by the biological approach.

Someone once said that in order to have "interdisciplinary," you first have to have the disciplines, and this overview would not have been possible without the more specialized treatments that have preceded it. There are the classics like D'Arcy Thompson's *On Growth and Form*, Ian

McHarg's *Design with Nature*, Gregory Bateson's *Mind and Nature*, and Christopher Alexander's *A Pattern Language*. Since then there have been a number of books aimed at lay readers. They include *Lessons from Nature* by Daniel Chiras, Michael Rothschild's *Bionomics*, Bruce Mazlish's *The Fourth Discontinuity*, and Kevin Kelly's *Out of Control*. A more recent wave of titles has included *The Sand Dollar and the Slide Rule* by Delta Willis; James Hogan's *Mind Matters*; John Elkington's *The Chrysalis Economy*; and Janine Benyus' *Biomimicry*; also *Darwin Among the Machines* by George Dyson; *The Third Culture* by John Brockman; *Natural Capitalism* by Paul Hawken, Amory Lovins, and Hunter Lovins; as well as Douglas Robertson's *Phase Change*. And the list continues to grow. As this book was in its final stages, William McDonough and Michael Braungart added to the list with their *Cradle to Cradle*, as did Christopher Meyer and Stan Davis, with *It's Alive*. All these efforts chart the rising influence of biological principles as a guide to human design. In doing so, many of them draw from yet more specialized discussions by writers such as Murray Gell-Mann, Robert Costanza, Stuart Kauffman, Christopher Langton, Richard Neutra, Steven Vogel, Robert Socolow, Wes Jackson, Masanobu Fukuoka, Dee Hock, Steven Levy, and an ongoing list of others—whose work in turn is rooted in personal experience and research, in scientific journals and proceedings, and in the trade periodicals of design and engineering.

In reviewing these works, I found it remarkable that the writers on this list have tended to focus on either environmental issues or the evolution of computers, but have rarely looked at the rapid converging of the two (Kelly is a notable exception). What's more, during my interviews I was surprised to learn how few of the leading figures I talked with were aware of the extensive work being done to adopt biological principles in fields unrelated to their own.

While even experts may be unaware of how widespread the new biology has become, it's already so broad and diverse a subject that any attempt to describe all that's going on would require an encyclopedia. In this one volume there are more things left out than included. I have nevertheless tried to cover core developments in the United States, Europe, and elsewhere in order to give a broad picture of where things stand today and what the future holds. Each chapter focuses on a separate field where the insights of the new biology are having a major impact: nanotech and materials science; robotic limbs and senses; artificial intelligence; complex adaptive systems in computers; complex adaptive systems in nature; agriculture; community planning; industry; economics; and democratic systems. Within each chapter, the problems caused in that field by machine age logic are outlined, too. While I've taken an international approach through most of the book, limitations of space and time have dictated the focusing of my final chapter on the United States. Still, the issues in question here have wider relevance, as a warning and a worst-case metaphor for other countries, and due to American influence on the global situation now playing out.

Having said that, I should reemphasize that this is first and foremost a book about ideas, and above all about timeless ideas. Its many stories describing new technologies and other innovations are also meant as parables, to illustrate those deeper themes. In line with that, names and dates, which dot the text of most science books, here have often been transferred to the notes along with passages of technical detail that may be of less interest to lay readers. In many cases I've assumed that with the wide availability of Internet search tools, just providing a few reference points in the text is enough to serve readers who'd like to track things further. In the interests of readability, I've also worked to blend the many different background materials—personal interviews, quotations from magazines and newspapers, excerpts from books and Web sites, writings in professional journals—so that they will appear to the reader as a single conversation with each source. The major sources were given the opportunity to review those passages before they went to print.

My initial readings and interviews for this book were done in the late 1990s and 2000, although my conversations with some of those quoted here—Murray Gell-Mann and his colleagues at the Santa Fe Institute, also Michael Braungart, David Crockett, Paul Hawken, Richard Levine, Bill McDonough—go back over a decade. To keep the manuscript as current as possible, I gave it a gloss of updates drawn from later research and follow-up conversations with my sources shortly before it was finalized in 2005.

Even so, much will change before this book reaches wide distribution. Most of the fields described here are advancing rapidly. During the course of my writing, individual companies have come into or gone out of existence (and sometimes both); people have moved from one organization to another, from one project to another. In the eight years of this book's genesis that has been a continuing process. Readers interested in the work of a specific individual or company should look to the notes; when it seemed called for, I've included more recent information there.

A broad overview ("coarse-grained" in the current phrase) like this book is necessarily rough. No one person can master all of these different fields; and there may even be disagreement among experts within a single field on key points. My hope is that specialists, critics, and other interested parties will treat this book as a starting point, and see fit to clarify and extend the concepts that this text only gropes toward defining.

Certain basic assumptions and shorthand usages inform the arguments presented here. For instance, although the word "nature" necessarily includes both physics and biology, I've often used it here in the popular sense, as a shorthand for biology. And in referring to our species—*Homo sapiens sapiens*—I've used the term "modern humans." Anthropologists guess our origin as being somewhere between 100,000 and 200,000 years ago, with the most typical estimate now in the vicinity of 130,000. I've chosen the more conservative number not to take sides but as a means of emphasizing in simple round numbers how very recent our appearance is—to give an order-of-magnitude impression. I also mark the advent of culture at 50,000 years ago. While it can be argued that earlier human types, and even other animals, have had cultures of a sort, it's nonetheless safe to say that only ours has developed a computerized international economic system. In this sense, modern human culture truly is a thing apart.

The theory of evolution, and how that process affects our own continuing development, plays a large role in the arguments presented here. This inevitably raises the question of evolution and religion, a matter widely misrepresented today in media coverage—where it's often cast in sensational terms as a war between fundamentalist believers and scientific atheists. There is a legitimate debate between atheists and those fundamentalist (or "literalist") Christians who take the Old Testament story of Genesis as a factual account of creation. But the larger truth is that religious believers constitute the greater numbers on both sides of the debate (even after the many scientists who are religious are removed from the equation). What this means is that the main conflict over evolution is actually between those of faith who support a literal reading of Genesis and those of faith who don't. These last are in some ways a new silent majority, but their influence was felt in a modern U.S. court decision that supported teaching evolution as the most scientific account of human origins (*McLean v. Arkansas Board of Education*, January 5, 1982). In it, those signing on in support of evolution included Arkansas bishops of the Roman Catholic, United Methodist, Episcopal, and African Methodist Episcopal churches, along with the chief official of the Presbyterian Churches in Arkansas, and other United Methodist, Presbyterian, and Southern Baptist clergy. On that list, too, were the American Jewish Congress and two other Jewish organizations, representing large numbers of people who also ground their beliefs in the Bible.

It bears noting here that the American founding fathers George Washington, Thomas Jefferson, and Tom Paine were privately Deists, a religion that readily allows the concept of evolution; it's no accident that the U.S. Constitution has so many references to nature. And there are the numerous other world religions that see no conflict between scientific accounts of evolution and their own creation stories—viewing the latter as concerned essentially with meanings, an area in which the former has no competence. In the interest of full disclosure, I should say my own view is that human minds and senses are too limited to fully comprehend something infinite and transcendent—and that the attempt to contain the divine in mere words necessarily reduces the concept of God. On first seeing the locomotive, Native Americans famously called it an "iron horse." They lacked the understanding to truly describe what they saw, and so had to use the words available to them. Can we expect to do better in the face of life's deepest mystery?

I first came across the term "new biology" in the subtitle to a late edition of *Out of Control*, science writer Kevin Kelly's wide-ranging summary from the 1990s, a fact that deserves acknowledgment here. (Also, the word "neobio" occurred to me as this book was going to press. I'd like to suggest that it is another apt term for this subject.) Early on, a remark by the writer and entrepreneur Stewart Brand was also influential. What he said to me was, "The environment is an inherently conservative issue. The fact that it's become divisive is due to our failure to clearly define the issues." And I'd like to thank architect and planner Richard Levine, who first impressed on me the importance in nature of processes over goals, an insight that laid the groundwork for a major theme in what follows, the key role of realistic feedback in nature and in culture.

This book is a catalog of such ideas—a description of nature not as a place we visit or a focus of concern but as a system, a philosophy, a guide for our thinking and solutions in an increasingly complex world. Thinking in those terms has political implications as well. Today, positions of the right or of the left tend to be frozen in amber—with the issues on either side bound together in a sort of ideological kinship. In this arrangement, support for any one of the views in that kinship implies acceptance of the rest. Consequently there are those on the political right who will portray this book as a liberal polemic, due to its critique of multinational corporations and today's global trade practices, and to its numerous calls for increased environmental awareness. Meanwhile, because this book sees promise in a reformed globalization, and speaks approvingly of private property, technology, capitalism, and a return to the gold standard (or something like it), there will be environmentalists and others on the left who brand it a closet right-wing polemic. All of which misses the point. True, this is a polemic, but not for liberal or conservative dogmas in any sense that they are understood today. What it calls for is an outlook that doesn't yet exist—or, more properly, that we have only begun to comprehend.

Just how far from reality today's right-versus-left debates have strayed can be illustrated in a quick example: among those things that the new lessons from nature reveal is a love of contradiction—an ecological mandate for balancing paradoxical tendencies one against the other—so that cooperation and competition, community and individual, top-down and bottom-up, stability and change, are not either/or choices, but instead are closely linked elements in a larger mix. In that mix neither of these incompatible tendencies ever wins. What's more important, neither is meant to. Nurturing a dynamic tension between them is one of the keys to life's vitality. As that lesson filters into culture, it may bring a measure of humility to rigid ideologues of every stripe. Given human nature, we can only hope.

Certainly this book does not provide all the answers. Hopefully it will inspire a new generation of questions—questions that help us to look at nature with a clear eye, to learn from it with an open mind, and to leave behind the outdated political and environmental arguments of the twentieth century.

—————

Nature in full is complex beyond our understanding. But its under-lying patterns—the fluid metabolism and feedback cycles, the constant self-renewal and metamorphosis—look to a deeper simplicity. The word "ecology" is just shorthand for those basic rhythms and turnings, the topic of old songs sung by poets to celebrate the shifting tides, the changing seasons, the rise of living forms that move and eat and breathe for a time, then fall back into dust.

This book charts our fast-advancing insights into the science of that poetry. They foretell an age that reconnects us to those simpler, bucolic patterns, if in a wholly new way. Cultural evolution? An Arcadian tech-nology? The door stands open before us.

pulse

one

the new biology

It started with a tendency, something like desire. Random elements drifting together formed bonds, and then a jumble of connections. Nearly four billion years ago that union came alive. First there was the cell, the basic form. For a very long time that was all—just countless cells floating and reproducing in the ooze of ancient seas, using energy from the sun to draw materials from air and water.

Eventually came cells that released oxygen to the sky, seeding change in the world around them. Then a microbe with a novel skill took shelter in a larger cell. The guest provided energetic molecules its host could use for fuel, which made ambitious larger life forms possible. Cells soon joined together into vast mats of underwater plants, the beginnings of modern grass, trees, and flowers. They also formed animals that propelled themselves around and had a clever new feature called brains. That innovation powered the intelligent hunt for food. And more food meant more energy, to fuel larger and more complex brains.

Now, long after animals crawled out of the sea and began their walk on land, modern humans have added (varying degrees of) consciousness to the mix. We've existed in our present form for something like one hundred thousand years. Even so, it's just ten thousand since we worked out how to get more food energy by grouping plants into farms. Farming made possible the cultural and intellectual hubs known as cities, which in turn gave rise to industry. And with each step—the rise of farming, the growth of cities, the industrial revolution—a radically different culture emerged. Now we're entering another great transition.

The new biology is humanity's future. But few know that because it's not the future we've been led to expect. For instance, the new biology is not biotech: it's not genetic engineering, at least not as it's typically practiced today, and it isn't cloning either. Most biotech treats nature as if it worked like a machine. The new biology makes machines that work like living things.

More than that, it brings organic principles to all of human design. This wasn't possible before. We didn't know enough about how the old biology works. But in recent years, as fundamental breakthroughs have transformed life science, experts from other fields have watched and learned. Now insights once the province of ecologists, zoologists, and cell biologists are laying a new foundation for everything from materials science and medicine to farming, from robotics and artificial intelligence to community planning, from industrial design to the global economy.

The twenty-first century will mark a sea change in human affairs, one unlike any that has gone before. Soon to come are computers with emotions, ships that learn from fish, and "soft jets" that flex and twist like swooping birds. Fabricated arteries will pulse and contract just as they do in life. Industries will reabsorb waste, like fallen leaves fading into the earth, while a new kind of money looks to energy cascades in nature. These are not blue-sky dreams. Work on them is well advanced.

Pulse

A pulse is a sign of life. All living systems answer to a beat. In the future, in ways we've only begun to see, our culture and technology will take up that beat—and with it the energy cascades, feedback cycles, and other dynamics that drive evolution.

A pulse is also a seedhead, carrier of the design for a new generation. For two centuries in the industrial West, culture has carried to each new human generation a message of faith in machines, and in the narrow cause-and-effect logic they represent. We've even learned to think in mechanical terms. But just as plants can evolve and release seeds better adapted to their settings, the seeds of a more advanced culture are today being sown. Using lessons drawn from nature, a new generation of designers, scientists, engineers, academics, farmers, philosophers, city planners, business leaders, and public officials from every continent is quietly, and with no common plan, creating a global revolution.

The culture that now surrounds us and shapes us was itself shaped by the machine age. Its success is without precedent, but it's becoming clear that machines as we know them are just a subset of biology, and a primitive one at that. The great leap in knowledge that created them, and that spread them across the planet, was no more than a halting first step out of the murk of history.

The machine age is about to meet a superior challenge. This doesn't mean the end of technology. There will be more of it now than ever. But our best innovations will no longer be like those that sparked the industrial revolution. In the future they will increasingly be like living things. Not life in the traditional sense, but a biology that has been consciously crafted by humans—a new biology.

The New Biology

Just as there is no clear definition of life, there can be no precise definition of the new biology. But how important it is can be seen in how many different fields it's affecting at once. They range from microscopic realms to vast global systems. At the deepest levels, for instance, biocentric methods are guiding the assembly of molecules into a range of materials and structures, including synthetic human chromosomes and artificial muscles and bone. The military has developed battle armor based on insect carapaces, and "bioskins" are being "grown" to filter biological-warfare agents and as self-repairing surfaces for space probes.

In robotics, swimming robofish teach ships the natural tricks of propulsion, roboflies carry communications gear, and designers have adapted bird wingtips to planes and penguin contours to racing bikes. There are now tiny, primitive robots that can reproduce. Meanwhile, life-size robotic legs will soon walk like real legs, computerized eyes have already helped the blind to see, and there are important new developments in haptics—remote touching.

Computers, the pivotal tool in the shift to a new biology, are getting smarter as scientists learn to model them on the brain's neural patterns and structures. They now enliven robots that teach themselves how to navigate the world. The effort to develop emotional computers has birthed a series of biotoys, like dolls that interact with people in increasingly lifelike ways.

Artificial intelligence has opened the way to new fields of research—with names like "emergence," "self-organization," "complexity." They center on the growth of virtual life forms that compete, reproduce, and evolve inside computers and on the Web. With "virtual worlds" a new interactive realm has also established itself there, a stable and enduring 3-D electronic reality in which the sole inhabitants are "avatars," prosthetic extensions of human operators. Online Web conferences like the annual Biota now promote the birth and release of artificial life forms.

The complexity and interactivity that give rise to Web-based worlds are a central element in all complex systems, living ones, too. Our failure to understand ecological connections in nature has led to many of the problems facing us today. By challenging a global agriculture modeled on machine age logic, the new biology enters the outside world in force. Can grazing increase productivity of the land? Can farmers learn from prairies? Can forests save their nurse logs?

In all these fields there is a movement toward organic ways and means. The same is true for where and how we live. Urban ecology reintegrates communities and nests them more skillfully into natural systems, to mend the fracturing that came with modern subdivisions. State-of-the-art computer programs create virtual-reality urban models that twenty-first-century planners will use to track the flow of energy and materials through real cities. Materials will cycle and recycle through products designed for disassembly. In industrial ecosystems the waste products from one factory serve as raw material for another, just as in nature waste from one organism is food for another. A global effort now aims to convert the industrial world to hydrogen power, a key fuel in living cells and fuel cells.

Some of these changes may look expensive compared with our current system. That's a false comparison. Our current system uses unrealistic pricing; it's based on a machine age model that externalizes much of the real cost incurred. Today we call such externalized costs pollution. To new biologists they're a form of inefficiency. Cutting-edge schools of economic thought now show how an economy is not a big machine, as our present model holds. It's more like an ecosystem, with myriad interlocking feedback loops and a rough metabolism within limits. Powerful new computers now make it possible to model those dynamics, and to create money that mimics natural energy flows.

Democracies mirror the feedbacks in a natural system via their many cultural feedbacks, which serve to maintain a healthy society. By looking to nature we see the importance of keeping those feedbacks clear and accurate. The corporate distortions of media feedback that have come with consolidation and deception, voter feedback by corrupt campaign financing, and scientific feedback via the funding of biased research, all impede the vitality of culture. Restoring the credibility of those feedbacks is a key to cultural evolution.

The new biology heralds fundamental change. But that just makes it equal to the machine age. Its superiority lies in how, even as it brings great change, it integrates smoothly and at every level with nature. Human culture first emerged from hunting into farming, which then gave rise to cities, which in turn produced our industrial world. The new biology marks the start of yet another phase. In virtually every field of human endeavor—from materials science to robotics, from artificial intelligence to artificial life, and from Web-based worlds to farming, community planning to industry, and economic theory to democratic processes—the logic of ecology is morphing into social forms.

As with any major shift, all this can breed resistance. The machine age has enormous vested interests; much of the world's economic infrastructure today is based on it. Beyond that, over time we've also taught ourselves to think like machines. This means narrow, linear logic and a mechanistic mind-set often guide how we appraise new options. And because the new biology is so fundamental, there are dangers, too, dangers we'd be wise to keep in mind. Still, doing things as nature does them can mean real progress, not only for humans and the society we depend on, but for the natural systems that our society depends on.

Coming at the end of a turbulent century, and at the dawn of a millennium, the rise of nature into culture is real news. The quality of the minds the new biology attracts, the rapid growth and excitement it generates, its broad influence as a unifying concept, and its potential for reshaping culture all suggest we're at the brink of a historic transformation.

The Machine Metaphor

Drastic change is a rule of thumb in history. But it can be hard to see coming—or to accept when it arrives—because every culture has unquestioned ways of doing things, a set of intellectual blinders that shape how people think about the world. That cultural philosophy becomes a guide for what's right and natural in much of what we do.

The logic of the machine age is ours. During the course of two centuries of industrial revolution we've enshrined the mechanistic thinking that made our world possible, converting industrial-era logic into an all-purpose metaphor. As a result of that *machine metaphor*, our popular speech is littered with terms like "gear up," "fine-tune," and "on track" which reinforce the view that people and our affairs can run as smoothly and predictably as machines. That view took hold some three centuries ago with the scientific revolution, which was spurred by the ideas of the mathematician and philosopher René Descartes.

Among those ideas he championed that still shape our thought is a dualistic view of humans. For Descartes, the world outside of us was just a vast and intricate machine. But, he held, in each of our minds there is a kind of inner sanctum, a conscious awareness disconnected from that mechanistic outside world. He believed that inner realm houses the human soul, which makes conscious reason and free will possible. There were implications in that for other creatures, too. Because they lacked our consciousness and free will, Descartes said, animals were just bundles of reflexes, responding automatically to whatever stimuli the world presented. As he put it, they were nothing more than complex watchworks (and if a watchwork dog can be considered alive, say today's heirs of that view, why not computers and robots?).

During the centuries since then, as the concept of "world as mechanism" increasingly shaped how people thought, it shaped the culture they created. That's also true of "reductionism," another potent concept put forward by Descartes. Aided and abetted by the writer, philosopher, and statesman Francis Bacon, he pushed the view that nature's so-called watchworks can best be understood by breaking them down into parts.

Isaac Newton built on this outlook (now referred to as Cartesian) to lay the foundations of classical physics. He showed that important properties of the physical world can be discovered through reductionism, and by a linear, $1 + 2 = 3$ analysis of direct causes and effects. He then went on to show how reliable mechanical systems could be designed with that approach.

After centuries of medieval mysticism, all this came as a revelation. By the dawn of the nineteenth century, Newton's successors had explored hydrodynamics, electricity, and the smelting of iron, and developed standardization and interchangeable parts. With the invention of the steam engine, the industrial revolution was on its way. As mathematician Alfred North Whitehead later observed, it was around this time, too, that "the mechanical explanation of . . . nature finally hardened into a dogma of science."

The story of that time and of the machine age that followed is actually a great many stories—of rapid advances in science and industry, of the coming of public education and democracy, of destructive world wars and the rise of a global economy. But beneath all that another drama was unfolding, one now poised to have an even larger impact on our world. This was the rise of a complex view of nature, one recognizing that life is more than a big machine.

Just as with the new biology now, the machine age in its own time was an effort to use lessons learned from nature as a guide for human design. And over the course of two centuries its growing power made clear just how solid and well-founded the mechanical view of life is. For the new biology to subsume that, it has to show how the machine age view is incomplete, to demonstrate that a fuller understanding of nature is possible. This is a fundamental contest, one that's been developing for centuries. Throughout that time, as machine age methods spread across the globe, the alternate view of nature posed a rising challenge. The ongoing twists and turns of that debate help illustrate the ideas behind the new biology, and to reveal its deep roots. They also make a good story—one of brilliant, sometimes headstrong personalities and the rough-and-tumble clash of two great ideas.

Metamorphosis

The criticism began soon after the start of the machine age. Faith in mechanism and reduction had gained the high ground in science, but doubts were being raised in philosophy and the arts. Jean-Jacques Rousseau was notable among the skeptics. So was William Wordsworth, who wrote:

> *Sweet is the lore which Nature brings;*
> *Our meddling intellect*
> *Mis-shapes the beauteous forms of things:*
> *We murder to dissect.*

The philosopher Immanuel Kant added his voice to the dissenters, pointing out what he saw as a disconnect between mechanical explanations and how living things really work. In both systems, he said, the parts interact; but in organisms the parts also create one another. Which means that a life form, as he put it in his *Critique of Judgment*, is "both an organized and self-organizing being." This is arguably the first appearance of the term "self-organizing" in a description of living systems, a term now prominent in the most advanced speculations on the subject.

As the eighteenth century drew to a close, the great Romantic poet and philosopher Johann Wolfgang von Goethe made a major contribution to biology with his concept of "morphology." He suggested that all the parts of a plant are just manifestations of a single deeper pattern, one apparent in its leaves. In his view, that pattern moved through a series of transformations as different structures—leaves, flower petals, stamens—came into being. The process, he said, was similar to the changes an insect goes through during metamorphosis. Goethe saw that as evidence of nature's "moving order." His insight anticipated by two centuries the current view of life forms as coherent patterns through which energy and materials flow.

City of Light

The French Revolution unleashed a ferment of energy and ideas that, by 1800, made Paris the center of excellence in the sciences. There, at the famed National Museum of Natural History, the gathering forces that would shape biology in the coming century collided—personified in three extraordinary characters.

It was Jean-Baptiste de Lamarck who coined the term "biology." Among his many other contributions, he was the first to divide the animal kingdom into vertebrates and invertebrates. He also proposed a theory of adaptive change, an early version of evolution. "Nature," he wrote in 1809, "has produced all species of animals in succession, beginning with the most imperfect or the simplest, and ending her work with the most perfect, so as to create a gradually increasing complexity in her organization." This stood on its head Saint Augustine's dictum from *The City of God* that the "more perfect" can never be generated by the "less perfect." It didn't make Georges Cuvier happy either.

Lamarck was the museum's renowned zoologist, Cuvier its star anatomist. Cuvier was a brilliant champion of the machine metaphor. Vain, arrogant, authoritarian, he was seen as second only to Aristotle, Europe's vaunted first biologist. It was said that Cuvier could recall in detail the contents of all twenty thousand volumes in his library, and he was famous for describing whole animals after seeing only single bones from their skeletons. Among his many contributions to anatomy, he was the first to classify fossils for use in that study.

Until Cuvier, when a species disappeared, everyone thought it had just wandered off somewhere else. He turned up evidence that some species, like the mastodon, had actually become extinct. But he was no evolutionist. Following Descartes' line, Cuvier believed all species were like animated gears in a great machine—that they were fixed and forever unchanging.

This view was in marked contrast to Lamarck's notion of gradual adaptation and change for species, what he called "transformism." Compounding Cuvier's anger was the theory Lamarck used to explain those transformations, and for which he is largely remembered: the inheritance of acquired characteristics. Lamarck believed, for instance, that giraffes grew longer necks by stretching them to reach for leaves in trees, and then passed that trait on to their offspring. That explanation was later trumped by Charles Darwin's natural selection—in which giraffes that just happen to have longer necks are more likely to survive and reproduce—but aspects of Lamarck's theory still raise questions today.

It's not hard to see how the Paris feud began: two towering figures, treading on each other's toes in the museum's musty bone rooms, both with their eyes on history and committed to mutually exclusive theories. Lamarck was laid to rest in 1829. By then the rancor ran so deep that Cuvier used his memorial lecture for Lamarck as a chance to denounce him.

But Cuvier's problems weren't over. He was soon challenged by yet another museum colleague. Étienne Geoffroy Saint-Hilaire was, like Lamarck, a zoologist, and in a broad sense an evolutionist. He was also a leading supporter of the Romantic German *Naturphilosophie* school, which added animals to Goethe's vision of elemental organic patterns common to all plant forms. As might be expected, this was viewed with something less than enthusiasm by Cuvier, who lived very much in the stable, mechanistic world of Newton and Descartes. Where Saint-Hilaire saw common patterns shared by many different species, Cuvier saw only nature's adherence to mechanically functional forms.

Their dispute came to a head in a cause célèbre, a notorious debate at the museum, which serves as an early demonstration of the potent social effects of biocentric logic. At the time, 1830, the tension between the French Revolution and a resurgent monarchy was very much alive in the streets of Paris, and was being closely watched by the remaining crowned heads of Europe. In the superheated atmosphere, Cuvier's never-changing "fixed" species were seen to represent the unchanging royalist *ancien régime*. Saint-Hilaire's adaptation and unity suggested that the Revolution's upheaval and egalitarian ideals had legitimacy in nature.

The press pictured the event as a scene of angry debates, with women fainting and the museum's halls swarming with intense activity. In the end, the more eloquent Cuvier was judged to have won, but his victory was fleeting. The theory of evolution would revive soon enough with Darwin. Goethe's last writings were devoted to defending Saint-Hilaire. And some 150 years later, biologist Walter Gehring—discoverer of the "homeobox," a key body-plan gene that he found in virtually all animals—would write that the genetic patterns guiding development "are much more universal than anticipated," and that "our speculative hypothesis was proposed as early as 1830 by Étienne Geoffroy Saint-Hilaire."

The Frankenstein Effect

At the start of the nineteenth century, ideas like those of Goethe, Lamarck, and Saint-Hilaire were viewed by most scientists with distrust and even mockery. Airy notions of constant adaptation and fluid change seemed lacking in rigor to the champions of a mechanistic universe, one where definite causes had predictable effects. But in the arts, the assault on the machine metaphor continued.

In 1813 Percy Bysshe Shelley, writing of subservience to power, pictured it as transforming the human frame into "a mechanized automaton." Five years later his mate, Mary Wollstonecraft Shelley, tossed off her gothic alert on the larger dangers of treating nature as a machine.

In her classic tale, when the young protagonist Victor Frankenstein decides to use his knowledge of chemistry and anatomy to make a human being, he is at first optimistic, saying, "I prepared myself for a multitude of reverses . . . yet, when I considered the improvement which every day takes place in science and mechanics, I was encouraged." But the experiment goes horribly wrong, and after years of desperate wandering the creature eventually returns to demand a bride. When Frankenstein refuses, fearing they'll spawn a race of brutal subhumans, the enraged monster threatens to destroy all that is dear to him. "You are my creator," it warns, "but I am your master."

One by one, the creature kills those closest to Frankenstein, including his intended, Elizabeth, who was "the living spirit of love to soften and attract," and his best friend, Henry, who "was a being formed in the very 'poetry of nature.'" Toward the end Frankenstein, the daring scientist, is haggard and focused only on destroying his creation. "Learn from me," he laments, "how dangerous is the acquirement of knowledge."

In England by the middle of the nineteenth century, the "spirit of love" and the "poetry of nature" were fading fast. Labor exploitation was rampant, and yearly coal production, no more than ten million tons at the century's start, had grown to sixty million tons as the pace of industry quickened. Vast areas of pastoral countryside were transformed into ruined landscapes of belching chimneys, slag heaps, and streams full of wastes. Whole cities disappeared under palls of smoke.

The 2nd Law

Into that world stepped Nicolas Carnot, a military engineer interested in heat dissipation. While tinkering with steam engines he discovered a principle now recognized as central to all living things. Formalized by the physicist Rudolf Clausius, it became known as the 2nd Law of Thermodynamics. The thermodynamic 1st Law holds that energy is never lost from the universe. The 2nd Law shows that while energy isn't lost, it does dissipate from concentrated to diluted form—losing its ability to perform useful work as it flows from one physical system to another—and that when energy leaves a system, that system tends to degrade. As one writer puts it, "All fire will die, all variety goes bland, all structure will eventually extinguish itself."

This handed a challenge to the Lamarckian view, in which life was seen as becoming always richer and more diverse. How could that happen if everything was winding down?

One response among natural philosophers, as biologists were then called, was the theory of "vitalism." Life was animated not just by mechanical processes, they said, but by a kind of divine energy—a vital force that counterbalanced the 2nd Law's dissipation. Vitalism would continue as a scientific theory until early in the twentieth century and remains a force today in its current form as the new age movement. At the time, though, despite real concerns about the 2nd Law, another development was about to steal the spotlight.

Darwin's Daring Debut

Evolution is the keystone of modern biological theory, and all biology during the nineteenth century stands in relation to Charles Darwin. It's true that before he published *On the Origin of Species* in 1859, the basic concepts of evolution were in the air: from Erasmus Darwin, Adam Smith, Thomas Malthus, Lamarck, Saint-Hilaire, Robert Chambers, Herbert Spencer. It's also well known that Alfred Russel Wallace was the theory's codiscoverer. But it was Charles Darwin who became its most effective champion, who compelled what was by then called the scientific establishment to look at it plainly.

Although the popular response to evolution was and remains fractious—so far it's the only scientific theory ever judged by the U.S. Supreme Court—Darwin's ideas were welcomed by his peers. For them, the theory offered a practical description of how diversity and complexity arise in nature. It's worth noting that a key element in Darwin's credibility was his use of fossil evidence. Ironically, that was available largely through the efforts of evolution's great opponent, Georges Cuvier.

Darwin's theory also reached back to economics. In the previous century Adam Smith's *Wealth of Nations* argued that decentralized markets, individual action, and competition can bring collective benefit. Then came Thomas Malthus, who in his 1798 *Essay on the Principle of Population* described how population expands exponentially while food supply only grows arithmetically. He said that creates a necessary check on population growth through things like impoverishment, disease, war, and crime. Darwin drew on Smith's notion that individual competition could bring collective gain. He also recognized in natural systems the same tension between growth and limits to growth described in Malthus. He then combined that observation with his stockbreeder's notion of the "pick of the litter"—that is, natural selection—to show how nature profits from the tension.

On the overproduction of offspring in nature he wrote, "Every organic being naturally increases at so high a rate, that if not destroyed, the earth would soon be covered by the progeny of a single pair." That was no hyperbole. Without environmental constraints, for instance, a single

E. coli bacterium, in just twenty-four hours, would reproduce itself into a mass equal to all the living things on earth.

In a famous passage, Darwin wrote of how that impulse to expand is restrained and shaped by environmental limits: "As more individuals are produced than can possibly survive, there must in every case be a struggle for existence, either one individual with another of the same species, or with individuals of distinct species, or with the physical conditions of life."

The result, he said, was natural selection. "Owing to this struggle for life, any variation, however slight and from whatever cause . . . if it be in any degree profitable to an individual of any species, in its infinitely complex relations to other organic beings and to external nature, will tend to the preservation of that individual and will generally be inherited by its offspring." Those offspring, he concluded, then have a better chance of surviving and continuing the line. This was "Nature, red in tooth and claw," as Tennyson put it. Often overlooked, though, is the fact that when introducing the term "struggle for existence," Darwin added, "I should premise that I use this term in a large and metaphorical sense, including dependence of one being on another."

What all these effects produce are branching lines of offspring gradually separating and expanding through time—each shaped differently by the limits of its environment—to produce the kingdoms, phyla, classes, orders, families, genera, and species familiar to biologists today. Though that is commonly referred to as the tree of life, the various crossings and connections typical of nature in the wild are more like the "tangled bank" of shrubbery often found near a body of water. It was Darwin's tireless champion Thomas Huxley who described that as "the web and woof of matter and force interweaving by slow degrees."

Probable Cause

Darwin helped to move things a step away from the Cartesian world of mechanical certainties in science. His theory meant that species once seen as fixed and immutable were instead somehow fluid and malleable. He also disavowed clear distinctions between them, being aware, as science historian Bruce Mazlish writes, "that a finch in one territory could breed with those slightly different from it in an adjacent territory, and that that second finch could breed with its next-door neighbor, and

so on until at some farther remove, the original finch could not breed
with its nth neighbor." Rejecting Descartes on another front, Darwin
also held that animals had feelings and could experience pleasure and
pain, saying, "There is no fundamental difference between man and the
higher animals in their mental faculties."

Darwin's belief that absolute truth was unavailable to science upset
some critics even more than his views on the link between humans and
apes. His own theory was valid, he said, not because it was certain but
because it was productive. Simply speaking, it made sense. Writing to a
friend in 1861, he noted, "The change in species cannot be proved,
and . . . the doctrine must sink or swim according as it groups and explains [disparate] phenomena." Uncertainty permeated Darwin's view of
nature. In Newton's universe, causes predicted effects in a linear progres-
sion. In Darwin's world, as one writer describes it, "no elegant equations
could predict the future of even a single organism."

The disapprobation of mechanists had other targets, too. Changes
were afoot in the "hard" sciences, where work in topology and set theory was replacing elemental certainties with broad, statistical measures.
And widespread consternation ensued when the mathematical physicist
Ludwig Boltzmann together with James Clerk Maxwell—arguably the
century's leading physicist—claimed that probabilities were okay for an-
alyzing thermodynamics. But they were on the right path, and with
their work a door was opening that would add new complexities to our
understanding of the world.

Increasing levels of complexity were also being noted in what
would soon be called ecology. In a rarely noted passage from *Origin*,
Darwin relates a story told to him by a Colonel Newman:

> The number of humble-bees [*sic*] in any district depends in a great mea-
> sure upon the number of field mice, which destroy their combs and
> nests . . . Now the number of mice is largely dependent, as everyone
> knows, on the number of cats; and Col. Newman says, "Near the villages
> and small towns I have found the nests of humble-bees more numerous
> than elsewhere, which I attribute to the number of cats that destroy the
> mice." Hence it is quite credible that the presence of a feline animal
> in large numbers in a district might determine, through the intervention
> first of mice and then of bees, the frequency of certain flowers in that
> district!

Larger Patterns

Zoologist Ernst Haeckel coined the term "ecology" in 1866. He took the word from the old Greek *oikos*, meaning "household." Haeckel called ecology "the science of relations between organisms and their environment." In some ways he was also an early proponent of what today is called the new age. For instance, he was a vitalist who wrote popular books declaring that humans and animals share a common status and that the universe is one great balanced and unified organism.

It was Haeckel who first said "ontogeny recapitulates phylogeny"— that is, the development of an embryo in the womb mirrors the overall evolution of the species—a phrase that, while not precisely true, remains an intellectual chestnut. He guessed correctly that the key to heredity lay somewhere in the cell's nucleus. He also believed that our sense of duty is rooted in biology and that society should be reorganized using nature as a guide.

With that in mind Haeckel was a forceful proponent of "social Darwinism." Also called eugenics, this was a philosophy Darwin himself disavowed but that would inform the worst episode of the twentieth century. If the Paris debates were an early lesson in the power of biocentric logic, eugenics made clear its great potential for danger.

The Soul of a New Machine

Mary Shelley's *Frankenstein* had warned against treating nature like a machine. As the rampant advances of the machine age joined widening speculation on natural selection, writer Samuel Butler turned that concern inside out. In 1863, under the pen name Cellarius, he published an essay called "Darwin Among the Machines." In it, and in his subsequent novel *Erewhon*, he described machines as advanced evolutionary species. Butler was considered an eccentric, but with the publication of *Erewhon*, which went through eight editions in his lifetime, his ideas gained wide popularity.

He also wrote numerous pamphlets, in one of which he makes a typical argument:

> As the vegetable kingdom was slowly developed from the mineral, and as in like manner the animal supervened upon the vegetable, so now in these last few ages an entirely new kingdom has sprung up . . . It appears to

us that we are ourselves creating our own successors . . . giving them greater power and supplying by all sorts of ingenious contrivance that self-regulating, self-acting power which will be to them what intellect has been to the human race.

Germination

If that sounds a little exalted, it was. It's worth noting that until Karl von Baer's seminal work in the 1820s, biologists still thought the first stage of an embryo was just a tiny person. While Butler pontificated about the next species, we had only begun figuring out how this one works.

Progress was being made, though, and beyond the cascade of insights in morphology, evolution, and ecology, important work was being done in cellular biology. By the early part of the century it was generally accepted that organisms are made of cells. By 1850 we knew that cells come only from other cells. With better microscopes, biologists got their first look at a cell nucleus in 1870. A rough early description of DNA was published by Friedrich Miescher in 1871, and by the 1880s the idea that chromosomes carry heredity had been advanced independently by four different researchers.

One of them was August Weismann, and work he did in the following decade would have a special impact on the theory of evolution. In the course of his research, Weismann had cottoned on to the idea that as ancient single-celled life forms first joined into more complex organisms, they began to form specialized groups to handle different parts of the work. Some focused on reproduction while others took on the job of getting food. That led him to suspect a fundamental division in all embryos. On one side of that division were the sex cells, which carry heredity. On the other side lay those that would become the body.

He spun that into a remarkable insight on the reason for death. Given that the *sex* cells (the *germ-line* cells) in sperm and eggs are virtually immortal, he wondered why it is that all the other cells, those used to make bodies, have to grow old and die. His answer was natural selection. Death, he said, is a secondary characteristic "acquired as an adaptation." The expendable bodies of each new generation—first the parents, and then their offspring—grow up around the immortal germ line in order to nourish and protect it. As they grow, age, and then die off in turn, that succession of temporary bodies gives each new one a fresh chance to adapt to any changes in the world around it. As Samuel Butler put it, "A hen is only an egg's way of making another egg."

This had other implications too. For if there was a wall separating the cells that make babies from those that make bodies, there was no way for Lamarck's "acquired characteristics" to be transmitted back inside— from the environment to the organism's body, and then from there into the immortal germ-line cells that would create its offspring. No matter how far hungry giraffes stretched their necks, their young would always have to start again from scratch. All of which looked like the end for Lamarck.

That was okay with Weismann. A strict mechanist, he emphasized his point in a famously controversial experiment—by methodically cutting off the tails of rats through twenty generations and watching to see if any were born with shorter tails. None were, but the counterattack by neo-Lamarckians was immediate and heated. The playwright George Bernard Shaw, deviser of a "scientific religion" based on evolution, led the charge, saying the result was something "any fool could have told him beforehand." What was lacking, said Shaw, was a way to convince the rats that the fate of their world depended on losing their tails.

Perhaps not surprisingly, that argument was overlooked in the scientific community. Weismann was more persuasive. And we know now that while every cell in the body has a full genetic complement, in most animals there remains that crucial separation first described by him. The immortal germ-line cells carry genes in fully active form from one generation to the next, but in cells that are meant for growing body parts, only the relevant sections of each gene are active. While that distinction would not be clearly understood for decades, Weismann's so-called barrier—which separates the germ-line cells from those used just for growing bodies—survived. It remains an important factor in debates about how embryos develop into adults.

Material Evidence

In the tug-of-war between the machine metaphor and a more ecological concept of nature, the mechanical view was gaining ground. As the twentieth century began, Henry Adams—scion of the old New England political family that had produced a leader of the American Revolution and two presidents—was taken by a friend to the Paris Exhibition to see the hall of the electric dynamos. Standing there, as he later wrote in *The Education of Henry Adams*, he realized that the genteel eighteenth-century tradition his family had upheld for so long was gone forever, that "man had translated himself into a new universe which had no common scale of measurement with the old."

"To Adams," he wrote of himself,

> the dynamo became a symbol of infinity. As he grew accustomed to the great gallery of machines, he began to feel the 40-foot dynamos as a moral force, much as the early Christians felt of the Cross. The planet it-self seemed less impressive, in its old-fashioned, deliberate, annual or daily revolution, than this huge wheel, revolving within arm's-length at some vertiginous speed, and barely murmuring—scarcely humming an audible warning to stand a hair's-breadth further for respect of power . . . Before the end, one began to pray to it.

By the time Adams had his epiphany in Paris, the machine age—and the machine metaphor—was in high gear. Within a decade the Wright brothers would fly, J. P. Morgan would form U.S. Steel, and Henry Ford would begin flooding the world with cars—adding standardization to Descartes' mechanism and reductionism, as the third great premise of the machine age. Also during that period, a novel concept came to England in the form of speed limits, and in America something called a weekend gained popularity. Mary Pickford became the first film star, as Bakelite plastic and neon lights also made debuts.

In 1909 a new art movement idolizing speed, aggression, and the power of machines burst upon Europe with the publication of F. T. Marinetti's "Futurist Manifesto." In it he bade farewell to the whole classical ideal in art and culture, saying, "A roaring motor-car, which looks as though running on shrapnel, is more beautiful than the *Victory of Samothrace*."

With due respect to ancient Greece and its famed statue of "winged victory," the effort to limit the impact on culture of machines was no longer a real contest. Whatever else may be said of Marinetti, he was right about the future. A popular echo of the winged victory survives today as a Rolls-Royce hood ornament.

The Twentieth Century

The vivid blue waters of Crater Lake fill the cone of an ancient volcano in southern Oregon, along the crest of the Cascade Range. The rich blue comes from the scattering of sunlight in the lake's tremendous depths, nearly two thousand feet, and the purity of its water, which it receives entirely from rainfall and snowmelt. Today it remains largely as it was when a prospector stumbled onto it in the spring of 1853, a natural wonder of the North American landscape. The five-mile expanse of the lake's surface still mirrors piney slopes thick with ferns and wildflowers, marmots, bears, and deer, as golden eagles glide overhead. That is due in no small part to its being one of the national parks declared during the tenure of Theodore Roosevelt, the first U.S. president elected in the twentieth century.

A tireless outdoorsman, hunter, naturalist, and explorer, Roosevelt came to office in 1901 and remained a champion of nature throughout his eight-year term. Building on the efforts of groups like the Sierra Club and the National Audubon Society, he saw to the creation of five national parks, of reserves for moose and bison, and of over fifty bird refuges. He was also deeply involved in forestry issues, wrote extensively about his observations of nature, and in 1908 held the first National Conference on Conservation at the White House.

Roosevelt was emblematic of a coming shift. Until the twentieth century, the science of biology had been shaped primarily by the machine metaphor. As the new century progressed, that model would give way to another view of how living systems work. This involved an opening outward of awareness, a seeing beyond the narrow confines of those simple $1 + 2 = 3$ linear connections. In the age-old tension between figure and ground, between parts and wholes, Roosevelt's broader scope meant focusing a little less on individuals and more on their environments, less on the figure and more on the ground. This mirrored a rising tendency in physics, biology, psychology, and other fields—a trend toward looking at things in context. With that also came a turning away from Descartes' old program of reductionism and clockwork logic.

The struggle between the machine metaphor and the ecological view of nature would test the finest minds of the coming century, and to some extent continues even now. Mechanistic theory still guides our economic system, and by extension steers the worldwide industrial culture it supports. The machine metaphor informs much of what we see as common sense, too, affecting our lives in constant ways. But the leading edge of science has moved on. Where once biology was viewed as a big machine, we now know it involves concepts like self-organization, emergence, coevolution, and succession. In our understanding of life today, matter and energy don't just link mechanically; they flow through food chains and webs, cycling by way of myriad feedback loops that interlink in fluid, endless, metabolic networks in search of homeostasis— of that elusive sweet spot between impulse and restraint, competition and cooperation, chaos and order. Just as the machine age once took shape and direction from the machine metaphor, the twentieth century would see a new world forming on these notions.

Time's Flies

As the century began—although there was broad acceptance of Darwin's view that natural selection produced gradual evolution—a nagging problem remained. The theory was incomplete without an explanation for heredity. Into that setting burst the rediscovery of Gregor Mendel.

Working in obscurity some fifty years before, the patient monk had tracked inherited traits in generation upon generation of pea plants. If his methods were simple, their impact would be nonetheless vital. For the first time, basic principles governing heredity were laid bare. And one of those principles seemed to be that change occurred in discrete jumps, not by Darwin's gradual evolution. This was a problem for Darwinists.

In the new century, Mendel's champion was William Bateson. A zoologist, Bateson coined the term "genetics"—though no one yet knew what genes were—and worked to extend Mendel's insight into animals. To that end he culled examples of what were later termed "hopeful monsters." Those were cases where, for instance, a fly's wing might grow where a leg should be. His aim was to prove that, just as in peas, hereditary change in animals advanced in sudden small jumps. The appearance of one of those jumps was first documented in New York, in a Columbia University lab—the famous "fly room" of Thomas Hunt Morgan. Patiently tracking heredity through many generations of black-eyed fruit flies, Morgan witnessed the sudden appearance of one with white eyes. With time he would go on to establish that there were in fact genes; that whatever they were, they were located in the chromosomes of the cell's nucleus; and that they were the carriers of heredity.

While this was important work, not everyone was pleased with Morgan's flies. They would relegate supporters of Darwin's "gradual change" to something like obscurity for the next two decades. The view of nature as a machine was once more on the rise.

Mysteries of the Organism

If Darwin was under assault, the twentieth century was nonetheless a time of real progress for the ecological point of view. For one thing, the familiar mechanisms of classical physics were themselves being challenged. Early on, Albert Einstein coupled space and time, then went on to show that mass and energy are just different manifestations of the same thing. With this, he shifted things still further from the narrow verities of machine age thinking.

Three others who contributed to that shift were the physicist Henri Bénard, the mathematician Jules-Henri Poincaré, and the naturalist D'Arcy Thompson. At this time, the 2nd Law of Thermodynamics—which rules that energy always dilutes and structures always degrade—still challenged any notion that the natural world could have evolved to higher states. Bénard's work was the first to suggest an answer to that challenge. He was studying heat transfer in thin layers of liquid. When he applied heat slowly and evenly from below, the warmth behaved as would be expected, simply moving from bottom to top. As he gradually increased the temperature, though, a ghostly pattern emerged. Evanescent hexagonal cells like those in a honeycomb formed in his liquid. Further study revealed that the cell walls were carrying cool liquid down as heat upwelled through their centers. The formerly chaotic molecules had self-organized into efficient structural patterns.

At around the same time, Poincaré developed a new school of mathematics called topology. Sometimes referred to as "rubber sheet geometry," topology demonstrates how different shapes that can be stretched into one another are equivalent. For instance, in theory a square can be stretched to form a rectangle or triangle, even a circle. More complex shapes can be equivalents, too. A coffee cup can't become a pancake but it can become a doughnut, with the hole in its handle becoming the doughnut hole.

Those two discoveries opened the way for Thompson. In his classic book, *On Growth and Form*, he described patterns that connected Bénard's hexagonal cells to the way energy and materials flow through living systems. Those self-organizing hexagons, he said, recalled the microscopic cell structure of rapidly growing tissue. In a later chapter on related forms he also built on the rubbery patterns of Poincaré, bringing the principles of topology to living creatures. For instance, after drawing a rabbit's skull on a grid, he then stretched and deformed the grid to show a relationship between the rabbit's skull and that of a horse. In a series of these brilliant "transformations," he established like similarities between other species, in groups ranging from crustaceans to primates.

The work of those three reached not only toward the future but back in time. After more than a century, Kant's "self-organization," along with Goethe's "moving order" and his belief that every living thing "is but a patterned gradation of one harmonious whole," was once again becoming current.

Jazz Ecology

Those developments were a hint of what was coming. Ecological thinking—with its fluid dynamics, its approximations and gradations; with its self-organization, shifting patterns, and awareness of widespread interconnections—would emerge full-blown in the 1920s. They were expansive years. World War I had ended. The economy was booming, women were newly emancipated, and people everywhere were ready to kick up their heels. Big bands set the jazz age in motion as they propelled a dance craze across the U.S. and beyond. Talkies arrived, and in European cities the air was charged with Dada and surrealism. The world, it seemed, was opening to new possibilities.

By this time, the machine age had become larger and more powerful. And with that the machine metaphor held sway on a broader stage. It was now a central concept in industry, politics, and daily life. But in other realms an ecological crosscurrent was visible. This move away from simple mechanics found rich expression in Werner Heisenberg's work with quantum physics. It was Heisenberg who authored the well-known "uncertainty principle." Quantum physics shows that, at the deepest levels, matter manifests in wavelike patterns spreading out in space— and through interactions that can only be described in probabilities. "The world," he wrote, ". . . appears as a complicated tissue of events, in which connections of different kinds alternate or overlap or combine and thereby determine the texture of the whole."

The new trend of putting things in context didn't stop with quantum. In psychology, a movement called Gestalt arose to challenge the behaviorists—who traced their lineage back to Pavlov's salivating dogs and beyond, all the way to Descartes and his watchwork concept of animals. "Gestalt," from a German word for "organic wholes" (integrated patterns), holds that the brain is more than just mechanical reflexes. It says that in order to make sense of the world, we structure information from our senses into larger wholes, into broad and complex patterns.

The rising ecological view sparked fresh interest in metabolism. Work done earlier had pointed out that even as life forms move through a dynamic outside world of constant change, they still have to maintain a stable internal environment for their organs and tissues. Physiologist Walter Cannon now took things a step further, saying that life forms are dynamic on the inside, too. Far from being like watchworks, he said, organisms maintain only a rough internal balance between order and chaos, an equilibrium within tolerance limits. He called that "homeostasis."

As the twenties progressed, the intellectual ground shifted rapidly. The difference between living and nonliving blurred in 1926, when geologist Vladimir Vernadsky pointed out how thoroughly the two interpenetrate. In his book *The Biosphere*, he described the earth's organic surface layer as "a continual migration of atoms from the inert matter to living matter and back again." As Vernadsky saw it, plants and animals are just conduits for the movement of vast quantities of minerals through this biosphere. That notion helped shape another theory. Frederic Clements was a "community ecologist" who said that whole ecosystems have to maintain internal metabolisms, just like individual life forms, and that the resemblance didn't stop there. He described an ecosystem as a "superorganism"—a single integrated being that "arises, grows, matures, and dies . . . comparable in its chief features with the life history of an individual plant."

Systems ecology, another development, was led by the mathematical biologists Alfred Lotka and Vito Volterra. The best way to understand a natural system, Lotka said, is by looking at how energy flows increase the amount of matter cycling through a system. With a nod to the 2nd Law, he called the evolutionary competition among species a "general scrimmage for available energy." Working independently, he and Volterra published equations to describe that view. One result of their work was a description of how predator and prey populations can fall into stable, pulsing patterns of oscillations. For example, take the contest between Alaskan snowshoe hares and the young birch and willow trees they use for food. Every ten years or so the population of snowshoe hares reaches a peak. With thousands of the hares eating bark and twigs, the trees are devastated. But the trees fight back by exuding a resin that kills digestive bacteria in the hare's gut. So the more resinous bark a hare eats, the nearer it comes to starvation. With each succeeding year, in response to the feeding hares, the trees put out higher and higher concentrations of the resin. Eventually the hare population crashes, the plants stop making resin, and the cycle starts again.

Emergence

Through the early part of the twentieth century, increased attention was paid to context and large patterns. Then in the thirties, scientists began exploring how those patterns work. One outcome was "general systems theory." At about this time, philosopher C. D. Broad introduced the term "emergent properties." Lotka, too, had been wondering if there might be something interesting in the way that new and higher levels of complexity keep emerging in natural systems. Biologist Ludwig von Bertalanffy and his colleagues formalized those ideas, proposing not only that there are emergent layers of complexity in nature, but also that different qualities arise with each new layer. Science writer Fritjof Capra describes them:

> At each level of complexity the observed phenomena exhibit properties that do not exist at the lower level. For example, the concept of temperature, which is central to thermodynamics, is meaningless at the level of individual atoms, where the laws of quantum theory operate. Similarly, the taste of sugar is not present in the carbon, hydrogen, and oxygen atoms that constitute its components . . . According to the systems view, the essential properties of an organism or living system are properties of the whole, which none of the parts have. They arise from the interactions and relationships among the parts. These properties are destroyed when the system is dissected.

By this time the growing accent on whole systems had already shown the limits of cause-and-effect logic. Systems theory took the insurrection further, by breaking with reductionism—the belief that natural systems can be fully understood by simply looking at the parts.

But the matter was far from settled. The mechanical view of nature still had powerful advocates and was preparing another assault.

Genes Like Machines?

At heart, the study of life is the study of eating habits, waste streams, and sex. While the new ecologists focused on the first two parts of that formula, another group began to focus on the last.

Earlier in the century, Thomas Hunt Morgan's discovery that genes in flies evolve by sudden jumps had shouldered aside Darwin's belief in gradual change. Now the mechanists welcomed Darwin back to the fold. New math tools gave rise to a statistical way of looking at the problem. "Population genetics" tracked the distribution of gene traits not just in individuals but through whole populations. The use of statistics showed that even when *individual* advances came in small jumps, gradual change in *species* was possible. In 1937 Theodosius Dobzhansky, a former student of Morgan's, published *Genetics and the Origin of Species*, which outlined the new consensus. Ultimately—through a great interdisciplinary effort—new discoveries in genetics, mathematics, and paleontology, along with the widening focus on populations, were brought into correspondence as Mendel and Darwin made peace to produce what is known today as the "modern synthesis."

That movement, also sometimes called "neo-Darwinism," offered safe harbor to another doctrine, too—that the still-mysterious "genes" carrying heredity must be like tiny machines. This view picked up speed with some of the early discoveries in molecular biology, for if the genes were a mechanistic blueprint, now there were what looked like mechanical parts for the construction of living things.

In related work during this period, Morgan shored up Weismann's concept of a barrier that insulates the immortal germ-line sex cells—transmitters of genetic heredity—from the cells used for making our expendable bodies. To most biologists of the day this was the last hurrah for Lamarck. It meant that no matter how many times giraffes stretched their necks to eat leaves from tall trees, their genes could never learn from the experience. From this point forward the central dogma of the neo-Darwinist modern synthesis would claim not only that genes are like machines, but also that heredity radiates just one way—from genes outward into the body. Never the reverse.

Jumping Genes

From Darwin on, heredity was thought to be carried in units variously labeled gemmules, form-building elements, nuclein, determinants, or, finally, genes. Morgan had shown that heredity is transmitted by factors inside the cell's nucleus, within still-smaller structures called chromosomes. But chromosomes were themselves a grab bag of even smaller structures including proteins (molecules of fantastic complexity) and DNA (which was made of only four basic units that just repeated in various sequences). Everyone assumed that something as complex as heredity would have to be carried by the proteins.

As we now know, everyone was wrong. In 1944, work at the Rockefeller Institute established that heredity is transmitted through DNA. That breakthrough, by Oswald Avery, Colin MacLeod, and Maclyn McCarty, was followed within a decade by the celebrated unveiling of the structure of DNA by James Watson, Francis Crick, Rosalind Franklin, and Maurice Wilkins.

This historic development was at first interpreted through the eyes of the machine metaphor. As such, it served another big challenge to the ecological view. The mechanistic modern synthesis was based on the central importance of the gene, which could now be grounded in what seemed to be a stable, machinelike double helix. The statistical distribution of traits—another leg of the modern theory, the one that had reconciled Darwin and Mendel—also seemed secure. But there were those who viewed that synthesis as less a theory than a treaty.

The rebels found a handy weapon in new tools enabling the study of one-celled life forms (in place of flies or other larger bodies). By mid-century their work showed that some aspects of heredity were not carried in DNA. Instead, they were located in the *cytoplasm*, which fills the area of a cell between its nucleus and its outer membrane. That meant they were outside its nuclear DNA, which in turn meant they were operating outside the barrier Weismann had said walls off heredity from feedback by the larger world.

During the many skirmishes that followed, the acclaimed geneticist and protozoologist Tracy Sonneborn carried the flag for the rebels. It was in Sonneborn's University of Indiana lab that the study of one-celled organisms in the U.S. began. By looking at those simpler life forms, he believed, researchers could see life "stripped to essentials."

Over the next two decades he would do research that challenged the modern synthesis on its most basic terms. A classic experiment involved ciliated bacteria, one-celled creatures whose bodies sprout curved, hair-like arms they use for propulsion. Sonneborn removed a patch from the bacteria's outer cell wall, rotated it, and reattached it—so that a small group of cilia were curved in the opposite direction. When the bacteria reproduced, their offspring somehow inherited the backward cilia. How could this happen, he asked, if all heredity was carried in the nuclear genes, and if those genes were walled off from outside influence by Weismann's barrier?

That work was received warmly by scientists in Germany and France. A focus on ecological patterns, including the influence of environments on genes, had continued there since the days of Goethe and Lamarck. In 1945 Boris Ephrussi, Sonneborn's French counterpart, got a letter of support from an American friend, saying, "I suspect that the cytoplasm will now begin to play its proper part in our thinking." The letter was from Barbara McClintock, a geneticist who made her career studying corn. Though few realized it at the time, she was about to hand the modern synthesis its hat.

McClintock showed that genes aren't what the neo-Darwinists said they were, which is to say they are not machinelike units that change only with mutation, or in the fusion of egg and sperm. Far from it. Her work revealed that genes actually jump around. Mobile control elements constantly shift whole blocks of genes from one location to another. And in the process novel patterns of expression appear. What McClintock saw was so unexpected, so different, that scientists are still sorting it out today. But by the time she received her Nobel Prize in 1983, the staid and stable foundation of classical genetics would be gone, replaced by her vision of a "dynamic genome."

Loops and Flows

During much of the 1940s the all-too-real battles of World War II eclipsed the academic fray between mechanists and ecological thinkers. That period nonetheless saw the arrival of another major player in the debate. The sophisticated weapons systems developed for the war effort, and for the Cold War that followed, showed Washington the importance of science and technology. From then on, U.S. government funds would flow increasingly to the research community.

Among the many scientists riding that tide was mathematician Norbert Wiener. He was a prodigy who had begun to read at age three, earned his doctorate from Harvard by the time he was eighteen, and a year later was studying with Bertrand Russell. At Harvard Medical School he went on to study brain structure.

Wiener was interested in feedback loops. These self-correcting elements of nature had, in various forms, held the attention of Darwin, Malthus, Ampère, and Maxwell—who did the math for the early steam engine governors. Wiener's great insight was to show how rough, elemental feedback loops could be used to create precise self-correcting systems. His original work was funded by the Army, and used to improve artillery targeting during the war. Wiener called his theory "cybernetics," from the ancient Greek term for "steersman," and his book *Cybernetics; or, Control and Communication in the Animal and the Machine* later became a modest bestseller that spurred the introduction of electronic control circuits in manufacturing.

By mid-century, ecologists had learned their cybernetic feedback lessons from Wiener, along with the more complex lessons of systems theory. During that time, G. Evelyn Hutchinson fitted notions of metabolism more elegantly into ecological studies. And in the 1950s his student Howard Odum would begin the work of actually mapping energy flows through natural systems. Odum's brother, Eugene, made a study of "succession"—those higher levels of organization that emerge in living systems over time. Soon the population biologists Paul Ehrlich and Peter Raven would coin the term "coevolution" to describe how reciprocal changes evolve among interacting species.

As the modern synthesis was attacked at its heart by scientists like McClintock and Sonneborn, and pressured by outside developments in ecology, the definition of nature seemed to be loosening up. At about this time the ghost of Frederic Clements' ecological superorganism also drifted back into view. It had since become clear that ecosystems weren't organisms. But complex natural systems clearly did have qualities, like metabolism and intricate energy paths, that are common to all life forms. Who was to say that natural selection wasn't at work on ecological systems, too?

George Williams, for one. A distinguished evolutionary biologist, Williams published his *Adaptation and Natural Selection* in 1966. In it he argued forcefully for the view—later reflected in popular books by zoologist Richard Dawkins—that there's little sense in looking for the effect of natural selection on large-scale systems if all of their characteristics can be explained through the evolution of individuals. The study of natural selection, he said, is the study of genes. Williams' "ultra-Darwinist" argument had a chilling effect on the idea that evolution worked on ecosystems in the same way it did on organisms. And it was the beginning of a larger swing as the mechanical view of nature once again gained force.

It was supported by a curious development. By this time the Atomic Energy Commission, the AEC, had become the largest funder of ecosystem research in the United States. There were a number of reasons: Ecologists like Howard Odum, with their emphasis on energy flows through complex natural systems, were thought to be on a parallel path with the AEC engineers, who were then at work on complex engineering systems. Ecologists also promoted AEC research tools like radionuclides, by using them as tracking devices in their research. Those studies then showed the way to tracking exposures from nuclear power plants and weapons. More generally, the AEC had a notion that "ecosystem engineering" could contribute to its goal of a technological, nuclear-powered society.

The International Biological Program, with its "big ecology" and with its hierarchical ranks of researchers structured into corporate or military-style organizations, followed soon after. Its goal was to develop a unified theory of ecology, using computer models that could predict the behavior of ecosystems and assist in their management. In the late sixties the U.S. government poured more than $40 million into ecosystem studies.

Cyberbiology

In big ecology's mechanistic, top-down, command-and-control methods, there were clear parallels with the military influence on those programs. But as the decade turned, the seventies brought yet another reversal in the ongoing contest of ideas, highlighting forces in ecology that work from the bottom up. That development was fostered by computers.

Throughout the sixties computers had played a growing role in re-search. But their primitive sequential processors meant that machine age linear logic was built into the artificial intelligence programs being used. It wasn't until late in the decade that the advent of parallel processing made really complex calculations possible. The interactions of living sys-tems are so intricate and tangled that until then, any effort to describe them mathematically was too clumsy and approximate. Now scientists could begin to model what was actually going on in organic processes like genetics and evolution.

Computers would quickly take their place as the vital key to the new biology. Through their use, the mathematical probabilities that had found voice in Maxwell and Boltzmann, and become more pronounced with quantum, would flower into a bizarre and beautiful world of pat-terns within patterns and self-organizing structures that take shape around "strange attractors." Call it fate, hard work, or dumb luck, a very different kind of machine was evolving, and as a result something new and profound was coming into view.

Avoiding Equilibrium

During all this time a broader superstructure of theory was forming. The flapping wings of a butterfly in Rio de Janeiro, said meteorologist Edward Lorenz in his now-famous invocation, can cause a windstorm in Texas. With that, "sensitivity to initial conditions" became a catch-phrase.

The linear logic of classical physics is reversible. One plus two equals three; three minus two equals one. Water freezes into ice; ice melts back into water. But while direct relations like those are an obvious part of nature, they are also always contained in the larger dynamics of living systems. And those dynamics are ultimately nonlinear. There, not only do multiple and simultaneous outcomes emerge from any one action, but the layering of those outcomes—their accumulating history over time—gives rise to developments that can't be reversed. This unpre-dictable and irreversible nature is compounded by the feedback loops af-fecting everything alive. They amplify subtle distortions picked up as they cycle through a system again and again, modifying it to fit a con-stantly changing environment.

In the view of classical physics, things always move toward equilib-rium, much in the way a pendulum sooner or later comes to rest.

Organisms are different. For them equilibrium is death. They must avoid it at all costs. New light on life's ability to not only do that but thrive in the process was shed by Ilya Prigogine. In work he did during the sixties and early seventies, Prigogine brought those tendencies into correspondence with the always-problematic 2nd Law, with its mandate that all energy eventually dilutes into uselessness.

A life form, he said, is a "dissipative structure." By that he meant an organism is an open pattern—absorbing energy from the sun and matter from the earth, both of which flow through it and then back to the environment in degraded form as waste. But that constant dissipation, he said, is counterbalanced by life's ability to swim upstream on solar energy. So life remains in a state of profound imbalance. And the more the better. For the further it strays from equilibrium, the more diverse and complex it becomes. In this way, he argued, order "floats in disorder." In 1977 he received a Nobel Prize for developing nonlinear equations to describe that view.

We Contain Multitudes

In only a few decades, the staid world of biology had become a wonderland of fantastic processes and effects. And there was more to come. As one scientist put it, "What we call organisms are themselves communities of previously autonomous creatures that have become integrated into higher-level functional units."

The classic example of that is a one-celled creature called a slime mold. When food is scarce, thousands of individual mold cells mass together to form a larger body that "slimes" across the ground in search of greener pastures. Eventually the collected mass of cells differentiates into two tiers, a base and a "fruiting body," which then bursts, scattering spores for new generations.

Closer to home is the groundbreaking research of the cell biologist Lynn Margulis. Working in the mid-sixties, Margulis had pulled together a number of separate strands in developing a radical new theory of how we came to be.

She focused on cell structures called *mitochondria*, the power plants for cells in higher life forms. Like every other living thing, we're powered by a slow chemical "fire," which burns as long as we're alive. In us that fire is fueled by hydrogen extracted from fats and, more readily, from carbohydrates—sugars—in a complex process involving oxygen and other factors. It's why athletes practice carbo-loading before a contest, and why eating sweets will bring a familiar surge of energy. Mitochondria—vast numbers of which live in every cell in our bodies—are at the heart of the process.

In 1963, it had been discovered that mitochondria have their own genes. That led Margulis to suggest that somewhere back in the mists of time, mitochondria were free-roaming bacteria that somehow took up residence inside larger cells. Those new boarders, she said, received protection and greater mobility while paying the rent with the excess energy they gave off. When the relationship proved stable, the two types coevolved into one symbiotic unit. From that partnership came an ambitious new cell that would, over the course of time, become the basic building block for complex life forms—from frogs, blue jays, and roses to writers and readers of books.

The science establishment welcomed that thought with a collective cold shoulder. Margulis sent her paper to more than a dozen journals before it was accepted. But she had the last word. Her *symbiogenesis* is now taught in standard textbooks and considered a seminal insight. In fact, today it's widely accepted that at least two structures in our cells originated this way, and she suspects more.

As Margulis sees it, the great source of separate species isn't that of new types branching off from a single ancestor. Rather, she says, the great transformations in evolution occur in just the opposite way—through mergers as separate species converge to form a greater whole. This means, in her words, that "biologists must begin thinking of the cell as a complex community." Or, as the astrophysicist Carl Sagan put it, "We are not single organisms but an array of about ten trillion beings, and not all of the same kind."

Taken together with other work now being done, this paints a picture of us as dynamic self-organizing patterns swimming upstream into a current of energy. We use that energy to cycle matter through our systems, pulsing it into ecologies of internal life forms that are moving as we move, feeling as we feel, and continually burning with a slow cold flame.

Natural Logic

Near the shore of Lake Como, not far from where the monster came searching for Frankenstein's beloved Elizabeth, William Wimsatt sits in a quiet sunlit room looking out across the gardens. Like so many people on the frontiers of natural science these days, he's concerned about how—as the vast power of the machine age is harnessed to the new insights of biology—we can make sure that some even more frightening creation doesn't overtake us.

Wimsatt is a philosopher of science from the University of Chicago whose primary interest is biology. And he is here, at the Rockefeller Foundation retreat in Bellagio, Italy, to work on a collection of essays. His studio is part of a former ducal palace, and there was a time when the old duke had sixty-four gardeners to maintain the landscaped grounds. He could be seen mornings addressing his troops, uniformed gardeners lined up all in a row. While the formal gardens they maintained are still in flower, the image of nature that holds Wimsatt's attention is of a different sort.

Aristotle, the first biologist, said, "If one way be better than another, that way you may be sure is nature's way." Even to his keen mind, however, the inner workings of life remained mysterious. Some twenty-three hundred years later the dynamics of nature's logic are finally becoming known.

We understand that life is a process, one that involves energy from the sun animating matter from the earth. We can't prove how life started, but in the concepts of self-organization and emergence we have suggestive leads. We know that due to the 2nd Law of Thermodynamics—in which energy always dilutes from concentrated into useless form—all life forms have to swim upstream on solar energy. And that they tend to increase in complexity and diversity as they proceed.

The full process of life is intricate beyond human understanding, but the broad dynamics are being sorted out. There are certain patterns, like branching structures, that tend to repeat at the smallest and largest scales. It's clear that life evolves in complex interactions among organisms of every size and type. It's also clear that life thrives on tensions—between impulse and restraint, bottom-up and top-down, figure and ground, competition and cooperation, chaos and order.

In that context, individual competition produces macro cooperation to form ecosystems. They compete and grow and change even as the species within them compete and grow and change, and change each other. Those changes in turn shape and are shaped by the larger environment, which is going through the same thing. But the idea that our planet is a single life form is a charming misconception. No organism can feed on its own waste.

As life seeks out the sweet spot between chaos and order, impulse and restraint, it nestles in those areas where matter and energy flows are rich. That "food" is absorbed by forms that convert the energy it carries into a cold fire, which drives them until it fades and has to be renewed. While energy dissipates, matter recycles, creating intricate webs and chains that loop through connected species again and again. In the process, everything gets eaten by something else. All predators are prey.

Those loops shift and intersect with other loops in ways that are ongoing and simultaneous to create a self-regulating feedback with the environment, a metabolism within rough limits. If other forces disrupt it, side effects ripple through the system, and on into other systems that it meshes with. When ecosystems grow, they move through successive stages of self-organization as each new level of complexity emerges. Growing embryos do the same thing. And with each new layer of complexity come new properties, qualities not found in its predecessors.

Nature is flexible and resilient. Nature likes redundancy and dispersion. It is approximate and deals in gradients. All boundaries are permeable. Nature nests small systems like molecules within larger systems like cells, which in turn are nested in systems called organs, organisms, ecosystems. We grew from ancient one-celled ancestors. Nature likes mergers: we contain multitudes of other life forms within us. We stand at the crest of four billion years, bacteria molded into wondrous form, burning with a slow fire and about to take the next step.

Pulse

On the lush floors of tropical forests around the world, small colonies of leaf-cutting ants have for eons gathered plant fragments from the forest and carried them back to their nests to feed a mold that, in turn, is food for the ants. In a similar way, humanity is married to the peculiar apparatus we call technology.

The machine age was just a preliminary sketch of what human technology will become. The real work is now beginning. With the help of computers we find ourselves unfolding plans for the most complex, resilient, and dynamic system ever known.

And as computerized technology accelerates nature into culture, bringing new solutions, we're faced with novel problems, too. How will the industrial forces that brought us this far fit with the world now opening before us? How do we make the transition to a new foundation for everything in our lives? As Bill Wimsatt asks, how do we rebuild the lifeboat while we're still in it?

That first involves repairing the well-known breach between those who revere nature and those who design technology. That divide grew from the incompatibility of natural systems and machine age methods. But with insights fostered by computers, things are changing. Today an ecological view of life guides the best work of both groups, and a broad convergence is under way. An effort to define and expand their common ground will be the central dialogue of the twenty-first century.

In the end, what we are witnessing is the rise of a new cultural philosophy, a new conventional wisdom. Philosophical news is the most important kind of news. That's because when philosophy changes, everything changes. The machine age was based on a view of how nature works, and we got it half right. As the new biology subsumes the machine age, gathering its best features into a larger, organic scheme, the gee-whiz technologies and debate over methods will command attention. But behind the headlines, the real contest is between two great ideas. At the deepest level, the world is changing the way it thinks.

In the coming century we will be called on to see things in a fundamentally different way. Those who can make that transition will have better solutions, and so become the new leaders. A pulse is a sign of life. All of nature answers to a beat. A pulse is also a seedhead, carrier of the design for a new generation.

part one

and feel **look and feel** *look and*

two

building blocks

Surf washes onto a rocky coast in the fading light of day. With each pulse of a rising tide, waves reach farther up the shore, pouring fresh seawater into small tidepools scattered among the rocks. Tidepools are miniature worlds, natural stone basins vibrant with life. Some have bottoms carpeted with fluorescent algae that glow pink and orange, red and purple. There, white barnacles crowd around channels where the nutrient flows are rich, like buildings huddled on a downtown street. Near those channels there are also mussels, anemones, sand dollars, and a halo of other life forms that wait for food to come to them. The rising sea is just that, a rich bath of microscopic plants and small ocean creatures like shrimp, crabs, and baby fish. And when that waterborne feast pours in each day, tidepool inhabitants respond. The bony miniature towers housing barnacles lift their tops as fine tendrils reach into the flow, echoing strands of seaweed that wave and drift in the current overhead. Anemones open their flowerlike mouths. Crabs scurry and hungry fish dart and gulp. Meanwhile, a marauding sea star wraps its arms around a mussel, prying open the shell for dinner.

Organisms in a tidepool live there because it's a source of water and food. But in a deeper sense what they want are the atoms that make up both the water and the foods that seawater brings. Some of those atoms are used for energy. Others are building blocks that then pass up through the food chain, where DNA information shapes them into progressively larger and more complex forms.

A tidepool's vibrant biology is made the old-fashioned way: it grows there. As we identify life's most basic parts and processes, though, a new biology is emerging. Can we build our own molecules? Make our own chromosomes? Fabricate bone, muscle, and other tissues? In fact, each of the above and more are coming from a research lab near you. This presents something radically new in the course of human affairs, with implications beyond the familiar environmental or health concerns. We draw a sense of stability from the physical world. The metals, woods, and other materials we use to make things are staid and familiar. The same plants and animals reproduce each spring. Our children look more or less as we do. And there's little confusion about where biology leaves off and human design begins.

All that is changing. And any discussion of that change employs terms that fall below the radar of daily life. Most of us recognize words like "atom" and "molecule." Along with others like "gene," "chromosome," and "cell" they tend to get tossed in a mental bin labeled "too small to see." But our nonchalance toward small things is set to change as well. The microscopic realm is a universe unto itself, and as that subliminal world begins to flex and shift around us, the time has come to understand how it works.

Building Blocks

The old saw that an infinite number of monkeys with an infinite amount of time will type the works of Shakespeare is hard to dispute. But starting with no more than a barren, suffocating rock, nature evolved Shakespeare himself in just four billion years. And one can only wonder how long it would have taken him to produce his works if he'd thought just with random individual letters. Instead he combined them to form words, phrases, sentences, and passages, in expanding levels of integration. That linking of small parts into successively larger structures echoes a deep tendency in nature.

In practical terms, atoms are nature's fundamental parts. As far as we know, in all the universe there are only some one hundred different kinds. So everything is made of them—from rocks to seawater to the glowing pink algae in tidepools. All of these stem from the first interesting thing about nature: the social tendency of atoms, the fact that they like to bond. When two or more atoms bond, they form a molecule. To use a familiar example: a water molecule is made of two hydrogen atoms bonded to an oxygen atom. Larger groups are possible; some link hundreds, even millions of atoms in fantastic arrays. Molecules can bond with one another, too—for instance, to form larger molecules like amino acids, which our bodies then fit together to make the huge protein molecules we use for building cells. A cell is the basic life form.

The term "building block" is useful mental shorthand for atoms, molecules, and the larger structures they unite to form. But it bears stating that the clear boundaries we imagine between them are never more than approximations. From atoms to molecules, then on up the scale to cells, tissues, organs, organisms, and even to ecosystems like a tidepool, each is a dynamic, complex system nested inside larger systems.

What's more, the atoms that join to make the nutrients found in seawater don't change as they're absorbed first by simple life forms, then passed up food chains into increasingly complex forms—algae, then mussels, then sea stars—only to be reabsorbed one day by the sea. This interpenetration of the organic and inorganic is so intimate that science has never been able to draw a clear line separating them.

The new biology emulates living dynamics. And just as there is no strict definition of life, there can be no strict definition of the new biology. Its interest necessarily begins with the atoms and molecules that mysteriously join together to form the basic building blocks of life.

El Nano

Looking back on human events, it is often said that we stand on the shoulders of giants. If that's so, it is equally true that they stand on the shoulders of subvisible assemblies of atoms. In 1959, physicist Richard Feynman gave a seminal talk at the California Institute of Technology in which he suggested a new way of working with that invisible world. Called "There's Plenty of Room at the Bottom," his talk suggested that we might be able to build things atom by atom, using machines that are constructed to make smaller machines, which would make still smaller machines, and so on. The new field he described is known today as "nanotechnology."

Not much more was heard of Feynman's little scheme until 1986, when K. Eric Drexler, a young chemical engineer from the Massachusetts Institute of Technology, published a book called *Engines of Creation*. His argument was simple: If you start with the basic building blocks of nature, you can make pretty much anything. The book described his vision of a microscopic world of nanomachines assembling everything from furniture to molecular surgeons to new generations of self-replicating nanomachines, just by putting them together atom by atom. Drexler's vision soon captured the hearts and minds of other researchers. Within four years he could testify before the U.S. Congress—to the Subcommittee on Science, Technology, and Space—that IBM's Almaden lab had succeeded in spelling the letters "IBM" with thirty-five carefully arranged xenon atoms. By then scientists at DuPont had also joined the fray, precisely joining hundreds of atoms together to build a brand-new protein molecule.

Nanos is Greek for "dwarf." A nanometer is one-billionth of a meter, or the length of several atoms placed side by side. How small is that? A million of them would fit into the period at the end of this sentence. Since everything is made of atoms, most are plentiful; the challenge lies in their assembly. Theoretically that's doable. After all, in nature atoms constantly self-assemble to form molecules. Some *organelles* (the organs inside cells) assemble them to meet specific needs. A *ribosome*, for example, is an organelle for assembling the building blocks we call amino acid molecules; they are then snapped together to make the wide variety of proteins tailored to our bodies' changing needs. To supply ribosomes with those amino acid building blocks, our bodies also have molecules known as enzymes, which snip apart the existing proteins we take in as food. We call that process digestion.

"Atoms don't wear out," Drexler points out, "they're recyclable." Which means that with nanotechnology we can "break down materials to simple molecules and build them back up again." Drexler is the field's virtual creator and irrepressible advocate, founder of the Institute for Molecular Manufacturing and of an advocacy group, the Foresight Institute. His book *Unbounding the Future*, written with his former wife, Christine Peterson, and Gayle Pergamit, suggests that nano-assemblers could capture and recycle carbon atoms from what he calls atmospheric garbage—excess CO_2 thrown away during our "primitive" manufacturing processes. By doing so, he says, atomic assemblers could provide material for human construction and manufacturing needs without having to strip the earth of its resources.

Feynman's concept, as promulgated by Drexler, has now achieved critical mass, with researchers scrambling toward this rapidly diminishing new frontier. Advocates predict their work will bring revolutionary new kinds of buildings and other structures, fabrics that are stronger than steel, precision drug delivery to cells, "smart dust" sensor webs, and fantastically small computers that will interface directly with our brains.

In buildings, for example, engineers foresee a time when smart molecules embedded in structural material will allow it to evolve in response to continuing stress—so it can grow thicker in some areas while diminishing in others, as the stem of a plant does in response to prevailing winds or when it grows toward the sun. Architects such as Michael Weinstock of London's Architectural Association envision dynamic buildings that are no longer stolid, passive structures. Instead of requiring that we design in tons of extra mass, as we do now, to offset every possible impact, they would simply grow more mass when and where it was needed, changing their conformation in response to whatever new stresses came along. Architect John M. Johansen explores this subject in his book *Nanoarchitecture: A New Species of Architecture*.

While architects employ nanotech to make buildings that are more like living things, scientists explore its use in actual living bodies. One U.S. researcher seems to have found a nano–fountain of youth. She kept rat neurons alive for six times their typical life span by using nanoparticles to strip away free radicals that cause tissue aging. Japanese scientists have modified proteins to make hollow nano-cages, handy carriers into which they can push other materials—like medical molecules or genes for therapy—for delivery through the bloodstream to highly precise locations. In a related development, some years back a Cornell University team announced the first self-propelled "nanobot." They attached one end of an energy-carrying molecule to a metallic substrate and stuck the chemical equivalent of a propeller on the other. The tiny propeller "started to move and ran for 40 minutes before it was shut off." How will nanobots be refueled? Another group has developed a microbial power source that, when hooked to a nano–fuel cell, converts 80 percent of the available electrons in sugar to electric power. And the list goes on. Genome guru Craig Venter and his team recently assembled an actual working virus and have since launched ambitious plans to fabricate a living cell. The emerging nanosphere has even spawned a new field of science. Called NBIC, it is the convergence of nanotech, biotech, information technology, and cognitive science.

Despite this activity and more, Drexler's vision of commercially assembling atoms into molecules and self-replicating nanomachines remains elusive. Most advances so far have come at great expense, or by modifying existing molecules, or through arranged marriages between them. One stumbling block is that whatever looks solid to us is, at the atomic level, actually in a state of constant agitation. All atoms pulse, and that doesn't stop when they link to form a molecule. Instead, they just vibrate in harmony. They also vibrate in response to thermal noise and other forces buffeting them. Because of that, any device used for manipulating atoms has to be exceptionally stiff—since its own atoms will be vibrating, too. Many researchers think that need can best be filled with diamonds, which top the list of things they want to make.

Ralph Merkle, a leading advocate in the field, has claimed that just as there once were Stone and Bronze ages, we're about to enter a "Diamond Age." Merkle is an alumnus of the famous Xerox PARC (the Palo Alto Research Center), where he was known for his adventurous ideas. Among the latest of those is his prediction that nanotech assemblers will allow us to build inexpensive diamond fibers and mold them into any shape we want, even that of a passenger jet. A diamond jet would weigh a small fraction of what today's planes do, he says, be just as strong, and, because it's lighter, save on fuel.

The Nobel laureate Richard Smalley saw more prosaic returns coming from nano-research. Smalley got his Nobel for chemistry in 1996 for codiscovering *Buckminsterfullerenes*—or Buckyballs—which are nature's third basic form of carbon after diamonds and graphite. He was director of the Carbon Nanotechnology Laboratory at Rice University in Texas, where that group makes elongated Buckyballs called "nanotubes." Like diamonds, nanotubes have remarkable properties. They are one hundred times stronger than steel, at one-sixth the weight. And they can serve as electrical superconductors or as semiconductors, depending on how they're produced. Smalley saw them being used to harvest solar power, pointing out that the sun each year provides more energy than we need now or will in the foreseeable future. With nanotube technology, he believed, we can make solar cells and power-storage devices that catch a good percentage of that. Make materials out of them and we can also build space probes with strong, self-repairing nanotube skin.

If the more fervent nano prophets are right, all this is just the start of our shrinking prospects. In testimony before Congress, Merkle has predicted that molecular assemblers will one day supplant our whole manufacturing base with a new, radically less expensive, radically more precise—not to mention flexible—way of making things. As Merkle put it, "The aim is not simply to replace today's computer chip-making plants, but also to replace the assembly lines for cars, televisions, telephones, books, surgical tools, missiles, book cases, airplanes, tractors, and all the rest. The objective is a pervasive change in manufacturing, a change that will leave virtually no product untouched." And the government is listening. According to Mike Roco, a senior adviser at the U.S. National Science Foundation, "Because of nanotechnology we will see more change in our civilization in the next thirty years than we did during all of the twentieth century."

Those expectations have not escaped the notice of industry, and companies around the world are now gearing up to think small. Nanotech is unquestionably the hot new field in engineering innovation. IBM, Intel, and Hewlett-Packard are deeply involved in nano-computing research. L'Oréal puts nano-capsules in beauty creams, to help them penetrate more deeply into the skin; Wilson Sporting Goods makes longer-lasting tennis balls with nano-enhanced cores. General Motors uses nanoparticles to strengthen plastic running boards, while the glassmakers PPG and Pilkington use them for self-cleaning glass. Not to be outdone, Eddie Bauer now sells stain-resistant Nano-Care khakis, with fibers by Nano-Tex, a division of Burlington Industries.

That activity is mirrored in Europe and throughout the Asian Pacific Rim (as well as in Australia and, now, eastern Europe). The EU's Europractice, a research program aimed at fostering nano start-ups, was founded in 1995 and has since been involved in more than a dozen of them. Meanwhile, private industry and university labs across the EU are picking up the pace. Taiwan, Singapore, and Malaysia all have burgeoning programs. Taiwan is even working with China, at the just-completed Nano Sci-Tech Industrial Park, in a northwestern province there. The joint venture is based in the ancient capital city of Xi'an, now becoming a center for advanced technology.

By 2002 Japan was spending more on small-tech research and development than any other country, but the race for microscopic supremacy was clearly on: Between 1997 and 2002, nanotech R&D spending in China and Australia grew from none to $40 million; and in Taiwan and

South Korea it grew from none to $70 million and $100 million, respectively. During the same period it increased 175 percent, to over $350 million, in western Europe and by 40 percent, to $604 million, in the United States. Meanwhile Japan multiplied its investment by 525 percent, to $750 million. For 2004, U.S. federal funding rose to $847 million, and the recently passed 21st Century Nanotechnology Research and Development Act spreads another $3.7 billion over the four years beginning in 2005. U.S. officials see the sale of nanotech products reaching $1 trillion by 2015. Small wonder that when the European research firm CMP Científica released a nanotech market analysis in 2002, they called their study "a snapshot of an explosion."

Much of the U.S. funding flows through agencies ranging from the Department of Energy to NASA to the Environmental Protection Agency. But additional large sums pass through the Department of Defense, especially its high-tech brain trust DARPA—the Defense Advanced Research Projects Agency—which is a major developer of such fields as distributed nano-sensors for battlefields and civil defense, nano-filters for biowar agents, nanoscale computers, and biomolecular body armors. The book *Nanotechnology and Homeland Security* tracks the flow of funding downstream from federal agencies as it pours into the many government and university labs now involved, from UCLA's Institute for Cell Mimetic Space Exploration to MIT's new Institute for Soldier Nanotechnologies.

Toward the end of his life, Smalley warned that military involvement in nanotech opens a new frontier of risk. "Technology that turns out miniature computers could also be used to create miniature weapons," he said. And that will give rise to threats we are only beginning to comprehend. If we can program invisible nanobots to scrub plaque from arteries, for instance, they can also be programmed to kill. One expert worries that nano-computers that can lodge inside our brains could make us all love Big Brother. (This is not out of the question. For example, there are parasites that lodge in fish brains with similar effect: they cause the fish to behave in ways that make them vulnerable to a predator crucial to the parasites' life cycle. Other research has shown that nanoparticles placed in a human nose soon find their way into the brain.)

Of more immediate concern is a study in which DuPont researchers injected nanotubes into the lungs of lab rats. The animals soon began gasping for breath, and 15 percent of them died. An alarm has also been raised by a University of Liverpool pathologist whose work suggests that how small a particle is will play a much greater role than the material it's made of in determining whether it's hazardous. Says Pat Roy Mooney, executive director of ETC, a technology watchdog group, "Particles of that size can go anywhere they please. They pass the entire immune system. They can pass the blood-brain barrier; they can go into the spinal cord." Real concern is warranted, if so far largely unaddressed. Of the roughly $1 billion spent on nanotech R&D in 2003, less than 1 percent went for the study of toxic side effects.

And there is the infamous "gray goo" scenario cherished by sci-fi fans. In that scheme, self-replicating nanomachines get out of control and proliferate wildly until they blanket the earth. Regarding gray goo, writer Paul Marks notes, "Many might argue that a self-replicating nanoscale machine—human DNA—is already doing its damnedest to suffocate the planet." This notwithstanding, a gray goo catastrophe is unlikely anytime soon. In fact a number of scientists, Smalley prominent among them, have expressed doubts that assembling things atom by atom will ever produce self-replicating devices, or commercial products of any kind. Controlling things at atomic scale, they say, will simply cost too much and take too long. Michael Gross of Oxford University's Centre for Molecular Sciences joins them, raising the specter of the 2nd Law. "Assemblers can't just crawl around the nanoworld ordering atoms in the way we want them without creating some disorder in the exchange," he explains. "The natural tendency toward a disordered state would make this very difficult."

Beyond, or perhaps beneath, such concerns there are philosophical issues that also need resolving. Drexler, Merkle, and many of the people they work with envision nano-devices that are still based very much on the machine age model. Those devices, while extraordinary, are not all that different in spirit from nineteenth-century steam engines. The effect the machine age has had on the natural world should give us pause about a nanotechnology guided solely by the machine metaphor.

On the other hand, what if we can do as nature does? All apples, for instance, are the product of molecular assemblers. And they cost virtually nothing. Any apple can make more apples; it needs only soil and good weather. "The structural biology of the cell will be the most important input into nanotechnology," claims Gross, "definitely more important than positioning atoms. The cell never bothers about putting atoms into place." It employs what he calls "the modular design principle"—using a set of small molecules that come together like Lego bricks to build something larger, a big molecule like a protein or DNA. That modular principle can go a step further, Gross adds. "Even macromolecules can be building blocks." And the payoff is that they organize themselves: they have the right shape and binding preferences to form into even-more-complex structures. "The protein factory of the cell," he notes, "can self-assemble almost magically from a mix of more than fifty different molecular units."

The idea of mimicking a living cell's assemblers brings with it limitations. One is that cells tend to function only in water. Using organic parts, Smalley noted, "would greatly limit the range of materials that could be built" while at the same time imposing on the assembler "a long list of vulnerabilities and limitations to what it can do." But if that point is well taken, it's also true that the conceptual dynamics of natural logic can have broad application. Duke University's Steven Vogel, a leading new biologist, says, "The smaller the scale [at which bio-mimicry is conducted], the better the prospects for emulation." And Philip Ball, writing for the journal *Nature*, remarks:

> Fundamental research on the character of nature's mechanisms, from the elephant to the protein, is sure to enrich the pool from which designers and engineers can draw ideas. The scope for deepening this pool is still tremendous. It is at the molecular scale . . . that we will surely see the greatest expansion of horizons, as structural studies and single-molecule experiments reveal the mechanics of biomolecules. If any reminder is needed that nanotechnology should not seek to shrink mechanical engineering, cogs and all, to the molecule scale, it is found here.

On the other side of this debate are Drexler, Merkle, and their allies, who remain convinced they have the future in their grasp—a future of nanomechanical devices that can assemble materials into any shape and that will be cheap, easy to make, and inexpensive to operate.

Keeping his feet on what at least for now remains solid ground, Gross says, "I think the brave new world of infinite wealth is still a dream. But even if . . . a few more generations have to work in traditional factories instead of delegating their work to nanorobots, it would still be helpful if we could develop molecular motors as efficient as our muscles, and data storage devices as compact as DNA." Nature, he says, has taught us that these can be achieved.

The Cell

A cell is the fundamental living form. It's here that molecules like DNA, chromosomes, and proteins all come together. To begin with, information inherited through genes is stored in the familiar double-helix DNA molecules. Those DNA strands are wrapped in protective protein to form a chromosome (we have forty-six of them, which together hold some three billion genes). In complex organisms such as plants and animals, this delicate system is further enclosed in a nucleus, essentially a separate room at the heart of the cell.

In this system, parts of our genetic information are copied as we need them, with the copies then being ferried out of the nucleus and into the larger inner world of the cell. There they are used to guide assembly of the many different kinds of proteins our bodies use. That process takes place on a minuscule scale—imagine the cell as a domed sports stadium and protein production as marching bands parading around the infield.

The messengers used to make the transfer are called RNA. They transcribe and transport the data, just as an athlete might scribble notes from a playbook to carry out on the field while leaving the book itself safely behind. At the end of that journey, the instructions an RNA molecule carries are fed like punch tape through a microscopic decoder— the *ribosome*—where they guide the assembly of amino acids into fresh proteins.

The twenty different amino acids are combined in a variety of ways by life forms to make the assorted proteins they need. Those proteins are crucial building blocks, used in nearly every function of the body. When we eat the bodies of other organisms, our digestive enzymes snip their proteins apart. Those disassembled parts—now once again loose amino acids—are transported to our cells. There, our ribosomes reassemble them to make new proteins tailored to our own special needs.

If there's a cheerleader inside the cell, it's ATP, adenosine triphosphate, the energy-bearing molecule made by mitochondria. ATP spurs activity with the help of an internal cell framework called a *cytoskeleton*. The old notion of the cell as a big sac with the nucleus and other parts sort of floating around inside is obsolete. The interiors of plant and animal cells are actually laced with a threadlike gossamer scaffolding. That scaffold serves a dual function: It anchors the cell's organs—the *organelles*—such as the nucleus and the ribosomes. It's also part of a transport system. ATP powers protein molecules that serve as cargo carriers, pushing them along the cytoskeleton's rails.

On the outside surface of each cell membrane, on the roof of the stadium dome as it were, there are craterlike receptors into which lock only specific molecules that come floating down the bloodstream, such as hormones or specially flagged proteins. When that happens, they trigger a signaling cascade, like a section of fans in the bleachers doing "the wave." The end result could be the start of transcription for a given protein, or a muscle might contract, or blood vessels might dilate to allow greater flow. Certain dilation receptors are activated by sex drugs like Viagra. They contain molecules focused—much like the front page of a supermarket tabloid—primarily on a single function of the body.

Evolution Inc.

In the flood of information conveyed to us each day about sex, it's easy to forget that sex is itself a way of transmitting information. The data that sex transmits is then stored in the genes of our DNA. Since all organisms unfold from DNA, it's through changes there—in the merger of two parents, or via mutation—that new varieties spring forth to try their luck in the outside world. Those that succeed get leading roles in life's evolutionary drama. But life takes its time; species tend to change very little over millions of years. In view of that, impatient humans have developed a much speedier form. It's called "directed evolution," and new generations of its rapidly evolving progeny are now springing forth in labs around the world.

The method is simple in theory. Start by picking some eligible DNA. Use any of a number of available techniques to reproduce them and encourage mutations. Load each mutation into its own bacterium or yeast cell. Then grow the cells into populations. Out of those select the ones that are best at doing whatever it is you want done. Then repeat the process as many times as needed to evolve the final product. In principle it's a lot like breeding cats or horses. But directed evolution will bring changes far beyond those imagined by traditional breeders.

It all began with RNA, the molecule that usually serves as the cell's information processor. In the early 1980s, Thomas Cech and Sidney

Altman independently discovered that a rare RNA molecule could also behave like an enzyme. (An enzyme is a molecule that usually either merges or "cleaves" other molecules—as when our digestive enzymes cut up the proteins in food, separating them back into their amino acid building blocks.) A decade later, in 1992, Gerald Joyce and his colleague Amber Beaudry took up that discovery in their lab at the Scripps Research Institute in La Jolla, California. They were curious about what else RNA might do. Specifically, they wanted to see if they could breed it to cleave DNA. Being able to cleave DNA at a precise location—in order to remove a damaging mutation, for instance, and patch in a healthy replacement—is a crucial step in genetic therapies.

RNA is not alive. The Scripps team couldn't just mate various RNA strands and wait for nature to take its course. So they used standard recombining techniques to get a population with something like ten trillion variants, then turned them loose on a DNA target. To their amazement, a vanishingly small number of them, something like one in one billion, did split the DNA.

The team quickly used those successful RNA as the basis for a new generation, and so the process moved forward as they tested each new cycle to see which variants were more effective, then discarded the rest and started again. By the tenth generation, they had evolved individuals that were sixty times more efficient than their ancestors. After a few dozen cycles the artificially selected cleavers could do in five minutes what had taken those rare members of the first generation an hour.

Joyce saw something else he found interesting while watching this process: the mutations seemed to be competing with one another. A kind of survival-of-the-fittest contest was going on between parts of the molecules themselves as they evolved. It began when he noticed two different mutations that were ineffective at DNA slicing on their own. If they occurred together, though—within the same RNA molecule—they were highly effective. When he graphed their accumulation, it looked like two spires, so he called them the "twin towers." Next he discovered another promising mutation, located right next to the site of the towers. It worked only in those versions where the towers had fallen away. In RNA with the twin towers, the neighbor was suppressed; then, when the neighbor occurred, the towers were suppressed. "They were mutually exclusive," he said. Joyce came to see this as a horse race between competing factions. Generation after generation, he watched as one or the other pulled ahead. For a while the twin towers surged. Then, by the eighteenth cycle, things reversed: the towers were down and the neighbor was up. By the twenty-seventh generation it reversed again but with a twist—one tower came up with its own fresh mutation.

"Today's loser may turn out to be tomorrow's winner," Joyce joked at the time, adding, "That's evolution." But he went on to make a more serious point. We are, he said, "beginning to see that evolutionary traits are highly dependent on each other. You can't simply say, 'Here's a gene, it does this. Here's another gene, it does that.' It's more how they interplay with each other—synergistic effects, mutually exclusive effects." By that he meant to sound a note of caution for the practice of gene-splicing. "It's not known what adding or removing one gene in a whole system of genes will do. It all depends on how its effect plays out in a network of interactions."

With what we know today about gene networks, Joyce's thoughtful early warning was well advised. But it's being lost in the shuffle of a present-day race in which some outsize players jockey for position. A first generation of commercial operations is now looking to evolve genes, too. With names like Applied Molecular Evolution, Celltech Chiroscience (formerly Darwin Molecular), and Maxygen, they are flush with venture capital and looking for new markets. As those companies emerged from the labs, one front-page story trumpeted: "Mother Nature at Warp Speed."

Does that sound like a good idea? A number of serious people are persuaded that it is, and are taking pains to show why. They cite numerous potential benefits to industry and health, and point to such feats of traditional genetic engineering as the bacteria that now produce human insulin.

The first "evolved" product to actually make it to market was a new stain-fighting enzyme for laundry detergents, which was launched by the Danish industrial-enzyme giant Novo Nordisk in 1998. Since then, the field has expanded in a number of other directions. Maxygen, one of the largest and most assertive of the new directed-evolution firms, is using what it calls "gene shuffling" to develop a complete product line ranging from crops to medicines. Diversa, a San Diego biotech, has evolved new human antibodies to fight cancer and infectious and autoimmune diseases. Applied Molecular Evolution, another San Diego company, has evolved a drug called Vitaxin, which blocks the growth of blood vessels in tumors. According to the company's CEO, "Initial human trials showed actual decrease in the size of some tumors." The drug is currently licensed to the Gaithersburg, Maryland–based biotech MedImmune, which has advanced it to Phase 2 clinical trials for the treatment of prostate cancer, melanoma, psoriasis, and rheumatoid arthritis.

Directed evolution is itself now evolving at a rapid pace. Caltech's Frances Arnold, a pioneer in the field, remarks on how quickly a once-obscure area of research has been transformed into a billion-dollar industry. Says Arnold, "Now it's the standard paradigm—it's not science fiction anymore."

Optional Genes

Something like that sentiment echoed in another field when news of the first human artificial chromosome, or HAC, surfaced in 1997. It was created by a team at Ohio's Case Western Reserve University, led by the geneticist Huntington Willard and working with the Athersys corporation. The HAC was successfully taken up by a single human cell and passed down through 240 generations.

The human genome is contained in twenty-three pairs of sausage-shaped units called chromosomes. At the heart of every chromosome is a double-helix strand of DNA twirled around ball-shaped proteins called *histones*. Then the whole business is wrapped in a shell of *chromatin*—still more protein. The Case Western replica was roughly a tenth the size of a typical human chromosome. When it was placed inside a nucleus, it was welcomed into the natural sequence of chromosomes and wrapped up in chromatin. Melissa Rosenfeld, speaking at the time for the National Human Genome Research Institute, described the effort as "an important landmark."

When evolution tries out a mutation that seems to reduce fitness, it's labeled a genetic disease. Some of them are terrible, and we have good information on the causes. But to insert therapeutic genes requires a delivery system that the nucleus will accept. Until now the available vectors—modified viruses—have been so dangerous and imprecise that it's had a restraining influence.

All this changes with HACs. They are larger than viruses, and so can carry bigger genetic payloads. They aren't inserted in the body's DNA but are added on, as a separate chromosome. They are less likely to provoke immune reactions. And they don't have to be "disarmed," as viruses do, so there's no risk that the disarming might fail and cause a serious disease or even death. The availability of HACs as a safer delivery cart will mean a steep rise in the number of attempts at gene therapy. That has profound implications. Beyond concerns over modifying a fundamental system that we don't fully understand, the deeper issue HACs raise involves the ease with which they can permanently alter the human gene pool.

Germ-line cells are sperm and eggs. As they combine and grow into the earliest stage of an embryo, the body sets aside the cells meant to make more sperm and eggs—directing them along a line that is separate from those other cells that grow into organs in the expendable body. This is August Weismann's famous barrier between cells for making babies and those for making bodies. The genetic modifications that are allowed today are made to cells that have already passed through Weismann's barrier. Since they will only grow into body parts—skin, a heart, an eye—the results from any modification are contained within that body alone. But germ-line cells are for reproduction; genetic changes to them will be inherited by offspring. HACs increase the plausibility of engineering the germ line.

As with directed evolution, even though the implications here are radical, there is strong support for doing it. Most of that support focuses on health issues. In dealing with a genetic disease, for example, the advantages are clear. Where there is reason to suspect an inherited disease, instead of having to treat all the cells affected in an adult organ, doctors can head off the culprit at its source. Responding to one science magazine straw poll, a group of gene researchers described human germ-line engineering variously as " 'irresistible,' 'morally questionable,' or 'dangerous.' " But they all agreed that "germ-line engineered humans are likely to become a reality." Gregory Stock, a UCLA biophysicist and outspoken proponent, claims the technology is unavoidable. The prospects, he says, are simply too bright. In his book *Redesigning Humans*, he describes a future in which parents pick their children's features as they would options for a new car. Far from discouraging germ-line modifications, Stock argues, we should manage them in a "free market environment with real individual choice, modest oversight, and robust mechanisms to learn quickly from mistakes."

There's little question that HACs could allow the loading of customized gene sequences into human germ-line cells. There is even speculation about building in genetic "switches" that would be activated only in specific tissues, or by a drug the patient takes later. Some historical perspective is in order here, involving the "Beltsville pig"—or No. 6707, as he was known to the USDA researchers who created him. The animal was genetically engineered some years ago to produce human growth hormone that would make it grow faster and leaner. The result of that work, according to Andrew Kimbrell in his book *The Human Body Shop*, was "a tragicomic creation. Excessively hairy, lethargic, riddled with arthritis, apparently impotent, and slightly cross-eyed, the pig could hardly stand up." The engineers had spliced in a switch intended to activate the hormone only when the pig ate large amounts of zinc. The switch failed.

A more basic problem stems from what Gerald Joyce found while racing his competing RNA mutations. Genes often work in concert, either activating or suppressing other genes. The problem comes when gene splicers treat them like pop-it beads that can simply be snapped apart or stuck back together at will. And with human germ-line engineering, any blunder will literally take on a human life of its own. By inserting HACs into germ-line cells, one writer notes, "the changes we make to our DNA are passed on to our kids, and our kids' kids, and so on down the line." In essence, designer chromosomes—with the genes they carry—could enter the human gene pool.

A Council of Europe convention banning germ-line procedures has been signed by twenty-three countries, and the U.S. Food and Drug Administration has vowed not to approve them without extensive public comment. The President's Council on Bioethics has released a report stating, "The human body and mind, highly complex and delicately balanced as a result of eons of gradual and exacting evolution, are almost certainly at risk from any ill-considered attempt at 'improvement.'" Environmentalist Bill McKibben takes a philosophical view:

> If you genetically alter your child and the programming works, then you will have turned your child into an automaton to one degree or another; and if it only sort of works, you will have seeded the ground for a harvest of neurosis and self-doubt we can only barely begin to imagine. If "Who am I?" is the quintessential modern question, you will have guaranteed that your children will never be able to fashion a workable answer.

Despite these formidable objections, many experts believe we'll have designer babies toddling around in little more than a few decades. Victims of some incurable disease like cystic fibrosis, which is inherited and is relatively simple to fix, will likely be the first to receive germ-line treatment, because successful therapy would cure not only the patients but all their future offspring. And how long after that will parents resist the temptation to endow their progeny with cheerfulness, intelligence, courage, sexual preference, athletic ability, or physical beauty—for all of which genetic origins are now being touted?

Aquarium fish engineered to glow in the dark are already being sold in pet stores. Writer James Gorman imagines a future where genetic mod-shops dot the urban landscape like tattoo parlors. If we could pay to have genes for glowing in the dark inserted into our bodies, he asks, "How many glowing teenagers would there be?"

Princeton biologist Lee Silver, in his book *Remaking Eden*, depicts a new human species that won't want to, or even be able to, mate with its "gene poor" cousins. As Stock has said, "Evolution is being superseded by technology, and the time scale will be far more rapid." The argument against enhancement, he claims, simply denies the reality. "It's what we want. We want to be healthier. We want to be stronger. We want to be smarter. We want to live longer. It's obvious."

Chromos Molecular Systems of Burnaby, British Columbia, recently announced that mice it engineered with artificial chromosomes had succeeded in passing them on to their young. It was the first time, said a company spokesperson, "that an artificial chromosome has ever been shown to be inherited in any mammal."

The engineered mice were mated with natural mice, and the Chromos replicas were inherited along with the animals' natural chromosomes. Chromos is now developing "blank" chromosomes with targetable integration sites that can be used in a variety of different species. "We can insert genes onto the blank chromosome," says Joseph Zendegui, the company's VP of business development, "and then transfer them into the cell." This, he says, means a safer and more predictable way to carry out genetic modifications. The new chromosomes will work in humans, but will be used only in conventional gene therapy. As Zendegui puts it, "We are in control of the technology and we are not interested in germ-line gene therapy."

Strutting

In the early 1970s a small company named Dome East was formed on the North Shore of Long Island, New York. The Port Jefferson start-up made geodesic domes and was, in a larger sense, an outgrowth of the enthusiasm of that time for the ideas of R. Buckminster Fuller. The company's design was one of the more elegant materializations of his concept; it featured a soft white-plastic internal membrane suspended from a silver lattice of geodesic aluminum struts. Dome East and the genial longhairs who ran it disbanded long ago, but a picture of one of their domes turned up in 1998 in *Scientific American*. The article was authored by Donald Ingber, and listed him as president of Molecular Geodesics, Inc.

Ingber has a notable background. He holds five separate degrees from Yale, ranging from a master's in philosophy to an M.D. He is a pathologist at Harvard Medical School, an associate at Children's Hospital in Boston, and a member of the MIT Center for Bioengineering. What's more, his zeal for Fuller's work may exceed that of its earlier allies. Ingber brings all these perspectives to bear on his central interest, the cytoskeleton—the loosely geodesic structure that serves as a flexible, multifunctional scaffold inside our cells.

In describing geodesics, he can't talk for long without mentioning their fractal nature. Whether one speaks of the elegant Dome East structures or the grouping of sixty carbon atoms in a microscopic Buckyball—the molecule named for Fuller—Ingber sees the same pattern. "Viruses, enzymes, organelles, cells, and even small organisms," he explains, all exhibit geodesic properties.

Intrinsic to that is a related fractal that Fuller called *tensegrity*. By way of explanation he notes how the structural dynamics of most buildings come from stacking one part on top of another. "They're stabilized mainly by gravity," Ingber says. "If you hit them from the side, they fall apart like dominoes." But natural structures, he adds, get their stability by a "continuous tension" between the parts, by a tendency to contract like rubber bands. If there were nothing but that, of course, they would just pull themselves into tight balls. So in nature that tendency is opposed by a countervailing force. The contracting elements—what he calls "cables"—are attached to parts that resist contraction, the "struts." That balance of forces is self-stabilizing, a constant push matched against a constant pull, which is what Fuller meant by tensegrity.

It's a "pre-stressed system," Ingber explains. "A bow used to shoot an arrow is one example, as are Fuller's own geodesic domes." The constant tension between push and pull is how natural structures keep their shape and their strength. Toward the large end of the scale, for example, the skeletal bones in our bodies are the struts, while our muscles are the cables that keep those struts under tension. At the microscopic level, he says, proteins and other key molecules are stabilized by tensegrity, too.

Turning to the cytoskeleton, he points out that it has another function beyond supporting organelles and providing rails for protein cargo carriers. It's also a flexible tensegrity structure. This allows the cell and its many internal parts to adjust as the cell is pushed or pulled or flattened, in response to the various movements and pressures from our bodies. In fact, looking outward to the next level of integration, the cell itself resides in a tangle of fine support fibers called the extracellular matrix. Here again, it all links together, in this case to form our tissues.

As Ingber explains it, the constant internal push and pull of tensegrity is a factor at each level, holding together everything from molecules through cells to bones and muscles and tendons. In his view it's the only mechanism that explains how, every time you move your arm, "your skin stretches, your extracellular matrix extends, your cells distort, and the interconnective molecules that form the internal framework of the cell feel a pull."

Molecular Geodesics, Inc., or MGI, was founded in 1996 to apply those principles in the design of custom-made materials. The company also developed software for use in evolving materials based on those principles—for instance, in the creation of filtering devices. If one wants a material that allows a lot of air through it—say, 95 percent porosity—Ingber says, they could "just tell the computer to build it." Typical instructions might call for varying a tetrahedral shape, as well as the width and the height of each strut. "In three minutes the computer goes through three million possibilities," he says. "Of those, three hundred thousand fit the shape, and maybe twenty-one of them have 95 percent porosity." Then comes the interesting part, he adds. "Some of them have huge, thick struts and are almost all air. Some have tiny little struts but thousands of them. Each model would have the same porosity, but with very different surface areas, different mechanical properties."

MGI received a DARPA contract to develop those concepts into synthetic biomimetic materials for use in protective masks, battle dress, and artificial bioskins (high-porosity layers designed to hold chemicals or enzymes that could neutralize any biological warfare agent passing through them). MGI's plan was to develop them with a rapid prototyper. That is a kind of 3-D lithographer in which, for instance, a liquid polymer is infinitesimally solidified—microscopic layer by microscopic layer—using a precision laser beam guided by a computer model.

Rapid prototyping allows quick construction of intricate three-dimensional models, but the MGI team ran up against an engineering barrier. They couldn't tweak the existing technology to produce structures at a fine enough scale for their aims. That was the end of their work for DARPA. But prior to that the company had also been working on orthopedic applications, on the creation and manufacture of "porous scaffolds that mimic the precise microstructure of living materials." The aim there was to design components that would "induce new tissue growth and regeneration" and that were fully biocompatible and resorbable. One early brochure even showed a mock photo of an off-the-shelf, complete "Left Leg Kit (Male)."

Under a new name, Tensegra, Ingber's team successfully developed a synthetic vertebral disc. But on the eve of a crucial fund-raising effort, the terrorist attacks of September 11, 2001, put most new venture capital activity on hold. A short time later, the company closed its doors. Ingber remains in his other positions, and as a consultant to industry. He also continues to publish research on tensegrity and the function of the cytoskeleton, including his theory that through it, forces outside the cell can affect the nuclear DNA by mechanical means.

Stretching Out

One of the novelist Honoré de Balzac's "three most beautiful things" is a galloping horse (the others are a ship in full sail and a woman dancing). There is something nearly magical about the way horses run. In fact, new research confirms that. Not only are they earth's most efficient runners, but their "apparent efficiency" is 110 percent. That's 10 percent higher than the amount of work their oxygen intake should allow.

No violations of the laws of physics are involved. What this seemingly impossible equation leaves out is the energy stored—during each stride the animal takes—in its stretched-out muscles and tendons. That stored energy helps a horse leverage how much work it can do with each breath.

Carried out at Milan's Institute for Biomedical Technologies, the study shows that a galloping horse stores energy in three ways, all of which bear more than a passing resemblance to elements in a tensegrity system. The first is by stretching out its elastic tendons, another is by bending its spine like a bow, the third is by the constant tension that muscles exert on tendons even when they aren't being stretched. This also ties in with some nice work being done by Daniel Urry, formerly a professor of chemical engineering and materials science at the University of Minnesota and now head of his own company, Bioelastics Research.

Urry's specialty is contractile protein, by which he means protein that changes its shape as part of its function. In his work he has developed a model of a rubbery protein called *elastin*. That's the stuff that forms the big ligament on the back of a grazing animal's neck—as in a cow—connecting the base of its skull to the join of its shoulders. The ligament is a strong elastic band, which counterbalances the weight of the head and the neck more or less in the manner of the spring balancing an overhead garage door. Elastin's function is to allow the animal to raise and lower its head, alternately grazing and looking for predators, while spending a minimum of energy.

As in the legs of a running horse, the energy is saved through a microscopic chemical process. The proteins in elastin fold, and that folding is the key. "In nature, elastin functions by having been mechanically stretched," Urry says. Whenever it is stretched, "it stores that stretching energy, and then provides the recoil. And the primary ligament in the cattle is a beautiful example of this." But for Urry there are more pertinent examples— for instance, the aortic arch and descending aorta. Those two are the first sections of the large artery that extends from the top of the heart, looping around in a broad curve to carry blood down into the body.

Two-thirds of the protein found in the aortic arch and descending aorta, he points out, is elastin. And when the heart contracts, pumping its contents out into the artery, those sections swell with the increased pressure. As that happens, the heart valve slams shut so that the blood can't back up. Next, the stretched elastin in the artery begins to contract in the same way that a stretched rubber band wants to contract. As the artery wall squeezes back down to its original size, it pulses the blood still farther into the body.

Urry uses chemical synthesis or modified bacteria to assemble his molecules. They are *polypeptides*, junior proteins made with just a few amino acids, and they closely resemble the real thing. Natural elastin stretches out and stores energy; then, as soon as the force that causes that stretching is relaxed, the molecule folds back into its original shape. Urry's new elastin does the same thing, and responds to a range of stimuli.

His team has developed synthetic elastin sheets that respond to temperature. If the temperature is lowered slightly the sheet will expand, and if the temperature rises slightly it will contract. They can hang a weight on it, and when it contracts it will pick up the weight. In essence, adding thermal energy causes a physical contraction. And when those molecules contract they can exert a good deal of force—some lift more than a thousand times their dry weight.

"This is what sustains life," says Urry, "these contractile proteins that can convert available energy into the kind of energy needed to sustain a living organism."

It was Seymour Glagov at the University of Chicago who back in the 1970s did the early work in this area, discovering the elastin layer beneath other cells on the wall of anterior (near the heart) arteries. He scraped away the cells, down to the basic elastin, then started putting some of them back. What he found amazed him. When he put a pulsing pressure through the artery—the kind of pulse a heart would exert—the cells started to self-assemble themselves into what looked like the flesh of a normal artery.

"As the wall stretches, those cells get stretched," says Urry. And cells are connected to each other by microtubule fibers. When you stretch those, he notes, "they trigger chemical signals—which play a part in the release of phosphates and ATP and all the other things that are turning on genes and turning off genes and so on." As a result, the cell produces materials that will make the arterial walls elastic enough to sustain that force. Urry calls this adaptive restructuring.

You see it in terms of exercise, he observes, where you build bone mass—so that in the next go-round the bone has become stronger. It happens in brain development, too. "In the case of children born with cataracts," Urry says, "it used to be that we wouldn't take the cataracts off for a couple of years. By then the child was absolutely blind. But if you let the light in early, so the cells in the brain can receive that light and actively restructure, they will make synapses and networks. Then the next time the light comes in, they can see it even better, and they can get the images better."

That is adaptive restructuring in response to an energy input, he concludes. "And that's what, to me, is unique about a living system—the capacity to take the energy input that drives a function, and then adapt in such a way that it can even better receive that energy input. It's what makes living systems living."

Urry sees his new biology sheets of elastin as potential patches for use in the repair of artery walls. "For these patches," he says, "in the protein sequence we've designed, we can put in cell-attachment sequences. So the cells can colonize a tube made of artificial elastin, and attach to it just like when they are in a natural artery. And when that tube is stretched out—when the blood pulse goes through it—the artery senses exactly the force it has to sustain and responds to it. The cells then remodel the synthetic scaffolding and integrate it into the natural arterial wall.

"So that is our concept," he says. "What we put in is ultimately degraded and remodeled. It disappears, and the natural artery simply replaces it." In response to a question about tissue rejection, a common problem in transplant operations, Urry says, "This is terrific stuff in that regard. The basic sequence is so innocuous that the host doesn't even know it's there. The material we introduce is made of amino acids. During the remodeling process the amino acids are eventually degraded—broken down and reincorporated back into new proteins. We talk about a temporary functional scaffolding," he says, "that the host does not know is foreign. In that context we use the term 'handshake.' We make our material so much like the natural material that the handshake is complete."

The team has confirmed this concept by making an artificial bladder from elastin sheets. When they pulsed it by filling and emptying it, they could see local cell types colonizing and absorbing the scaffold.

Urry calls their work "soft tissue restoration." Their start-up company is based in Birmingham, Alabama, and there's a subsidiary in Japan. For now they're concentrating on soft tissue, but eventually they may make bone as well.

Another term Urry sometimes uses to describe their work is "consilient engineering." He borrowed the term from Harvard biologist E. O. Wilson, whose popular book *Consilience* calls for a unity of all knowledge. Urry likes the word because the mechanism he is working with—which causes the protein folding—makes possible not only mechanical work but chemical work and electrical work and other kinds of work in the body. There are, he says, all kinds of energies being interconverted in living organisms by that single means.

Commenting on the importance of natural logic as a replacement for the machine metaphor, he likes to quote from Wilson's book, which in the final chapter says, "What does it all mean, this is what it all means: To the extent that we depend on prosthetic devices to keep ourselves and the biosphere alive we will render everything fragile." There are now, Urry points out, operations in which pigs' heart valves are introduced into humans. These are very sophisticated surgeries, "but then people wander around for the rest of their lives worrying about blood clotting and rejection. They have to take a drug that prevents rejection, and another that prevents the clotting. But then there is a risk of hemorrhage. And so they become very fragile."

His point, and Wilson's, is that natural systems are resilient until we introduce mechanistic interfaces—with all their necessary adjustments and compensations—as a means of sustaining ourselves. Those interfaces not only isolate us from nature but at the same time create systems that are brittle and delicate.

Resilience

That's not the case with hedgehogs. You wouldn't want to actually bounce a hedgehog, Julian Vincent says. But the point is that you could. They fall out of trees all the time without getting hurt. The reason is something to which Vincent has given a lot of attention. Director of the Centre for Biomimetic and Natural Technologies at the University of Bath in southwest England, Vincent is one of the more persuasive thinkers and doers in the rapidly changing world of materials science. In the case of the hedgehog, what he and a former student, Paul Owers, found was that the sharp hollow spines protecting it from attack are also exceptionally good shock absorbers. So much so that the late James Gordon—Vincent's mentor and a major figure in this field—once designed a puncture-proof car tire by ringing a wheel with a bristling fringe of hedgehog spines.

The hedgehog's secret is that the cores of its hollow spines are filled with a natural honeycomb. That core prevents the tubes from collapsing like crimped drinking straws when they're bent by an attacking predator, or by the ground moving toward it at unusual speed.

"Every organism is a bag of solutions to problems posed by the need to survive," Vincent says. And he believes we can learn from that. It's a common engineering trick to stiffen hollow tubes with foam; it's often used in the suspension struts for race cars, for example. If we can learn to make an internal honeycomb as nature does, he says, we'll have support structures of all kinds that are at once lighter, cheaper, and stronger.

At ease in his cluttered office, Vincent is a thoughtful, good-natured man with an ample reserve of wonder for his favorite subject. One of the things he finds most extraordinary is the surprisingly few components from which natural materials are made. "For their ceramics," he notes, "most organisms use one of two calcium salts." Or occasionally silica. He goes on to list the rest: "Organic fibers in animals are largely collagen, a protein. In plants they are mostly cellulose, a sugar polymer." Chitin, a strong fiber related to cellulose, turns up in arthropods—insects, spiders, crabs, prawns—and some plants and fungi. And then there are the keratins, another protein family, which figure in various guises as nails, horns, hair, and feathers, not to mention hedgehog spines.

Summing up, he counts them down: Broadly speaking, nature probably has no more than two main types of ceramics, two fibrous sugar polymers, four fibrous proteins, and some globular structural proteins. Beyond those lie a lesser assortment of fillers and lubricants, and the fatty molecules called lipids that are used in cell membranes.

Compare that, he says, with the surfeit of artificial materials we've come up with: ten main types of ceramics, fifteen plastics, ten fibers. Many of those require toxic ingredients and vast amounts of energy during production, then can't be disposed of without poisoning other systems. Given the subtlety, economy, and infinite variety of nature's designs, he says, and how simple and clean her methods are, we still have a lot to learn.

In looking to nature for lessons, Vincent likes dandelions, whose flowering stems are only 7 percent solids and yet grow nearly a foot tall and withstand all kinds of weather. A good example, he suggests, for lightweight buildings and aerospace design. Or consider how a spider handles one of the toughest problems in engineering—attaching one kind of material to another at a right angle. When a spider glues the main support for its web to a leaf, it does so with one hundred tiny threads that it generates "by dropping its bottom on the ground twice for about half a second." In that brief moment it achieves a near-perfect adhesive joint, of a quality equal to what you might find at the terminus of a well-designed bridge.

Vincent's preferred approach to learning from nature is abstraction, borrowing structures or mechanisms from biology and using them to create new materials. An example is the discovery at the University of Reading (his former base), by James Gordon and George Jeronimidis, of what makes wood so tough.

As preface, Vincent tells a story about the attempt by Rolls-Royce in the 1960s to design exceptionally strong jet engine blades using high-tech carbon fiber. The company spent untold sums and the engine was fully developed before they discovered that while the new blades held up well under the intense vibration and fierce heat conditions normal inside a jet engine, they couldn't withstand collisions with birds—something that can happen to any aircraft. That kind of impact shattered the blades to pieces. The reason was that while carbon fiber is very strong, it's also brittle. Wood, on the other hand, Vincent points out approvingly, is tough.

He describes how miners prefer wooden beams in their tunnels because the wood "talks to them." That peculiar characteristic—the creaking and groaning of wood long before it reaches a breaking point—comes from its internal structure.

Wood is basically a thick bundle of hollow tubes carrying water through the body of the plant. The walls of these long, narrow tubes—more properly, tubules—are made of microscopic fibers of cellulose wound spirally, like a compressed spring, and then solidified with a gluey substance called *lignin*. When wood grain is stressed—for instance, in a support beam of a mine shaft—those coils are gradually pulled open. With that, the lignin begins to fail and miners hear the familiar groaning and cracking. By that mechanism, instead of breaking abruptly—as carbon fiber does—wood gives way only gradually, with the coils unwinding lengthwise for some time before they snap. Miners say that for as long as the wood is talking to them, they know they still have time.

Based on its discovery, the Reading team developed a wood analogue using glass fibers embedded in resin. First they made large flat sheets of that material, with the fibers in each sheet running in a single direction just as fibers in wood grain do. They then layered three sheets together into something resembling corrugated cardboard: a sandwich composed of top and bottom layers separated by a rippled center layer.

Their trick was to angle each of the three layers a little differently, so the direction of the fibers in one layer was shifted alternately some fifteen degrees from the next. Once those were cemented in place, the corrugated channels in the center layer were like tubules. And the slightly varying directions of the grain in each layer roughly mirrored the circular spiraling that creates the tubules found in actual wood. The result? Says Vincent, "Under impact, weight for weight, it is the toughest artificial material known."

In a footnote to this tale Bill Clegg, an engineer at the University of Cambridge, developed a new generation of super-tough jet engine fuel burners based on his studies of mother-of-pearl, the nacre commonly found inside mollusk shells. Although mother-of-pearl is 95 percent chalk, he says, due to its peculiar composition (millions of chalk microplatelets randomly layered, then cemented with small amounts of protein glue) it is three thousand times tougher than chalk.

With all this activity, it probably comes as no surprise that the military has turned its sights on organic materials research. In both the United States and Britain, defense agencies—and defense dollars—loom large in the effort to learn from biology. The British army has shown a lively interest in the wood analogue described above, which has potential as a shield against shrapnel and other battlefield hazards. Among the other defense contracts Vincent can talk about, and there are many he cannot, is the effort to design tougher helmets by studying nutshells and antler bone.

Then there's a project looking at pinecones and transpiration methods in leaves in order to design military clothing that adapts to different weather conditions by changing its "breathability." A study of the cockroach's excellent sensing mechanisms, for use in fighter aircraft, is paralleled by a scheme to use beetle carapaces as models for light, superstrong body armor. Another looks at how insect wings unfold as a clue to designing deployable arrays for space missions.

One day we may even gaze up at a sky traced by shape-shifting jets that twist and flex through the air like birds in flight. British military plans for a soft jet that would do just that were lofted in the 1990s, then promptly dropped from sight for reasons that remain obscure. Something very much like it is now in the works in the U.S. at NASA's Langley Research Center, as part of a program called the Morphing Project. The NASA engineers imagine a plane with wings that change their shape in reaction to changing flight conditions just as those of birds do.

A key to those next-generation jets will be "shape memory" and other smart materials that furl and torque and bend in response to electric currents. Says the project's manager, Anna McGowan, a smart-materials specialist, "To make this technology possible, you would need to distribute . . . actuators and sensors throughout the wings. That's similar to how the human body operates. We have muscles and nerves all over our bodies—so we are aware of what's happening to our bodies and we can respond to it in a number of ways." Will jet wings ever change their shapes as easily as the wings of a living organism? The U.S. government is betting they will, with $30 million per year in funding. NASA is now working with the Air Force and Boeing to develop an "active aeroelastic" wing. Informed observers predict the flight of a small, unmanned model in less than a decade.

As all this work moves forward, Vincent applauds it while maintaining the skeptical realism of any good engineer. Back at his office in Bath, he raises some cautions about treating nature as the answer to every question. Many of the materials used by nature, he points out, are effective only within the fairly small temperature ranges inhabited by the plants and animals that create them. Spider silk is a good case in point: synthetic versions are avidly being sought due to its tremendous strength, but it degrades above 80 degrees centigrade. Also, when nature makes materials, it takes its time. There are trees a century old. Simple creatures like mollusks may need years to form their shells. Still, even where there are limits in nature's processes, Vincent believes, there may be important lessons to be gained from natural principles.

For instance in a broad sense, a major difference between human creations and the way nature does things lies in our overall approach to design. Taking a linear, machine age approach, we are normally concerned with finding a specific answer to some specific question. But a living thing, he points out, is a complex answer drawn from nature's response to a multitude of questions—and from the need to answer them all at once. That process is an ongoing interaction, pitting the strengths and needs of the organism against the various limits and resources of the world in which it lives. Holding up a picture of a swallow, Vincent says, "This bird can fly and it has a good visioning system, and coordination for capturing prey, and it digests food, and it reproduces. Then this very small creature can travel thousands of miles, migrating to the south and back north again.

"That's quite an extraordinary thing when you think of it," he remarks. "It's that integration of many different systems, the optimization of all those systems, that is the really impressive thing about nature." Our problem, he adds, is that "the methods we use now for engineering aren't well adapted to that kind of optimization."

When people first tried to make flapping wings to help them fly, for example, they failed for that reason. Looking in a linear way for a single answer to a single question, they studied wings but overlooked the fact that breast muscles in an adult bird can be nearly half its total weight, and that skeletal bones in birds, such as pigeons, are mostly hollow—not only having no marrow but in some cases conveying oxygen. Those early flight engineers also overlooked certain physical scaling laws and the limits of metabolism, which mean the larger the bird, the less able it is to fly by merely flapping its wings. Compare the tiny hummingbird—hovering in one spot to extract nectar from a flower—with the great albatross as it searches the sea for fish, calmly soaring thousands of miles on ocean thermals.

That's true at every level. In order to evaluate any part of a natural system, we have to consider the interdependencies. Atoms are nested into systems called molecules, which nest in large molecular systems like amino acids. They are then nested into still-larger systems called protein molecules, which in turn nest into the systems called cells.

Then at that point—where materials science is embodied in living form—a dynamic new interdependency arises: organisms are nested in environments, which they constantly alter and are altered by, like marauding sea stars crawling through a tidepool. In something like the push and pull of tensegrity, that interaction is marked by the contrasting tensions between figure and ground, between individual drives and environmental limits. Tension keeps the interface between them lively. So much so that it has given rise to some of nature's more dramatic innovations—things like mobility, and senses. That lively interface and the wonders it has wrought are fueling the next chapter of developments in the new biology.

three

figure and ground

One thousand miles in from the Brazilian coast, at the heart of a vast and fertile basin, two rivers—the Rio Negro and the Solimões—meet to form the legendary Amazon. Near the point where they join lies the city of Manaus, an improbable outpost of civilization surrounded by jungle. The moldy, ramshackle buildings that line many of the narrow streets here have a raffish air. But at the city's heart, like a sign of some great and improbable dream, rises a brilliant-pink Grand Opera House resplendent in its Italianate style.

Offshore, where the black water of the Rio Negro collides with the yellow water of the Solimões, there is the famous confluence, or lack of one, in which the two different waters flow alongside each other without mixing.

Manaus represents another kind of failure to interact. The city's proud opera house was built in the nineteenth century, and since then there has been no shortage of grand schemes to exploit the region's natural resources. There was Fordlandia, the huge rubber plantation that Ford Motor Company spent millions on. There were gem mines. There were gold strikes. And today there still hovers over the city a sense of boundless dreams. It may be the setting. The turgid waters of the river spread for miles from bank to bank, ripe and thick, moving slowly in the sweltering heat. And the surrounding jungle seems endless, the largest tropical forest on the planet—although that forest is threatened now, by the nightmare dreams of international timber companies, even as slash-and-burn agriculture gnaws away at its edges.

All this is more than local history. It is a resonant symbol for the failure of individuals to integrate with their environments. But lately there are promising signs, some from Manaus itself.

The city rests on a long peninsula, which separates the Rio Negro from the greater river. Toward the base of that peninsula, beyond the noise and spreading suburbs, one man has followed a different sort of dream, the dream of a business that exists on equal terms with the natural world. He calls his jungle retreat Terra Verde, and with it aims to preserve twenty thousand acres of unique virgin rain forest.

Getting there is like a primal journey. The trip upriver in one of the long narrow boats used here is punctuated by frequent stops and starts. Water levels can vary dramatically in this region. It's February now and the water is low—the trees onshore show a high-water mark a good twenty feet above the surface. On all sides the insistent life of the jungle surges into the receding river, making it dense with greenery. Every few minutes the guides have to halt the boat and lift the prop out of the water, to pull off clumping vegetation.

In the flat calm and blazing heat of the river's surface, in the general torpor, the frequent stops and starts take on a pulsing quality that is in keeping with the jungle's exuberant fertility. The river's pink dolphins, says a local legend, can transform themselves into men. Then, "dressed in white like charming creatures, they leave the water and seduce women."

A garáa bird calls overhead, soaring low, following the path of the river, then veering off along a tributary. After a time the boat veers off, too, as the channel narrows and eventually leads to Terra Verde. On a narrow strip of cleared land along the river stands an old masonry plantation house. It is flanked by straw-roofed cottages to the left and, on the right, an open-sided pavilion. This is the forest enclave of Zygmunt Sulistrowski.

Sulistrowski is a big, square-framed man in his seventies, solidly built with long hair and pale eyes that show a sharp intelligence. He came to the Amazon in 1976, as an award-winning filmmaker then working for Warner Brothers. While flying the area looking for locations, he spotted an old Portuguese plantation house down along a river. It intrigued him and he approached the owners, who eventually succumbed to his repeated offers. He has lived here ever since.

It is a special place, and not only geographically. The very different chemistries of the two rivers on opposite sides of the peninsula give rise to quite different ecologies on their separate shores. Then inland, at the peninsula's center—where those two different realms collide—they produce a riot of intermingling life forms that makes even the abundance of a rain forest seem politely restrained.

"Once I had a chance to walk around in the forest," Sulistrowski says, "I fell in love with it." Little wonder. There are trees on this peninsula that twenty people with arms stretched wide could scarcely girdle. Black and multicolored jaguars live here, along with some two hundred varieties of birds. It is an area unique in all the Amazon basin for its diversity—a fact attested by the Smithsonian Institution's National Museum of Natural History, which has commended Sulistrowski and acknowledged the importance of the forest his work preserves.

While he sees his main work as saving the forest, he also encourages research on the area's biological and genetic diversity. Beyond that he tries to be a force for good locally. He encourages fishing methods, for instance, that don't involve dynamite, and agriculture that doesn't involve burning trees. And he works to promote, he says, "a better knowledge of the splendor and importance of the Amazon and of the need to preserve its ecology," adding that the best way of doing that is "not by building a Chinese wall around it but by living in harmony with nature, by harvesting the fruits of nature without destroying her."

Sulistrowski thinks ecotourism is one such solution. With that in mind he has joined forces with another facility an hour upriver to create the world's largest ecotourism resort. Called Ariaú Amazon Towers, that other site is quite different from his. Where Terra Verde is very much on the ground, integrated with the forest through paths leading from shoreline into deep forest shadows, Ariaú is essentially a collection of tree houses strung through the high canopy, interconnected by a rambling network of skywalks.

Closing the door quickly behind visitors, a staffer there smiles and explains, "The monkeys are very wicked." In fact the monkeys are everywhere, whole troops of them swinging through the trees and hanging out by the various cabins and facilities of the Ariaú complex. People who leave clothing out to dry on a windowsill may find it gone in the morning. If someone has a camera that looks interesting, one monkey may act to distract him while another grabs the camera and hightails it into the bush.

Ariaú is owned by Brazilians. No trees have been cut down to build it, waste is carefully isolated from the environment, and 90 percent of the staff are locals. Its ramshackle charm has drawn prominent visitors from around the world to see the Amazon. Ranging from bestselling Brazilian author Lair Ribeiro to Jacques Cousteau and Bill Gates, from Isabel Allende to Presidents Jimmy Carter and Bill Clinton, they come to be harassed by the monkeys, go piranha fishing, or take moonlight boat rides to view caimans, the small crocodiles that live in the Rio Negro's tepid waters.

Ecotourism has grown rapidly in popularity in the past few decades. Throughout the world there are now agencies and destinations specializing in it. Some observers complain, and justifiably, of the effect a resort like Ariaú has on such things as the natural habits of the local monkey population, or of the polluting jet travel typically involved in getting people there and back. But compared with the vast and ruthless violation of the forest by timber companies, or with a slash-and-burn death by a thousand cuts, ecotourism marks a hopeful step forward. It's a more interactive view of the relationship between individuals and their environments.

The expansion of Manaus into the fertile Amazon basin is the story of machine age logic in the jungle, but it symbolizes a deeper relationship, too: the elemental tension between figure and ground, parts and wholes; between active elements and the larger patterns they act within. That tension is at the heart of work by Sulistrowski and a generation of activists like him, who feel we have to be more responsive to the natural world that surrounds us, and from which we draw life.

Wherever they carry that argument, beyond pragmatic issues, they also run up against the popular image of heroic individuals conquering their environments—a notion ingrained in our culture. For that reason, while it may be just a coincidence, it is nonetheless an interesting one that a similar contest of views underlies theories about what happens during the growth of a fertilized egg.

Understanding Eggs

There may be no more magical transformation than that of information from microscopic DNA unfolding to become an adult living thing. If there's any place where nature is telling us something fundamental, it would seem to be there. With that in mind it's hard to overemphasize the importance of the great debate about how embryos develop—not only for biology and evolution theory, but for any serious effort to draw lessons from nature.

In the classical view, the information needed to create an adult organism was contained entirely within its embryo's nuclear DNA. This view held that the nucleus developed much as Manaus and its population have traditionally interacted with the Amazon basin—which is to say without much in the way of feedback from its surroundings. Embryo growth and development were thought to be just the mechanical expression of a predetermined plan.

During the past century and more, from the time of August Weismann on, this view had great authority. It gained influence by its correspondence to the genetic "central dogma," the belief that evolution unfolds from a DNA that is inviolate and unperturbed by feedback from without. In this view, only mutations in an embryo's nuclear DNA, or the genetic combining of traits from multiple parents, can introduce variations into evolution. In other words, genetic information flows only one way—from the center outward.

But by the end of the twentieth century it had become hard for champions of that view to ignore the mounting evidence that there were other factors involved. New studies show that a growing nucleus is also shaped—and in profound ways—by forces outside an embryo's nuclear DNA, that it is shaped by exclusively maternal forces that act on it through the cytoplasm of the egg.

Hard-nosed captains of industry as well as admirers of new age goddesses may both prefer not to hear that the maternal egg is nature's finest example of capitalism at work. An egg is a single cell, swollen immensely by an accumulation of nutrients in its cytoplasm (which fills up the space between an egg's DNA-packed nucleus and its outer membrane or shell). The nutrients found there are drawn from throughout the mother's body and are meant to be invested in the growth of an embryo.

But the egg does more than accumulate capital for a new venture. Factors in the cytoplasm also shape a developing embryo from the moment of conception. Far from being just an expression of the plan found within its own nuclear DNA, the eventual form an embryo takes is the product of constant interaction between that DNA and the surrounding character and constraints of the egg.

One effect transmitted this way comes via mitochondria. They were once free-roaming bacteria that had the neat trick of using oxygen and hydrogen to generate a cold chemical "fire" that produces surplus energy. Long ago they took up residence in the cells of larger organisms, and ever since have paid the rent by supplying energy that makes complex life forms possible. Because of this, they are densely packed into the cells of organs where energy requirements are high, such as our eyes, pancreas, liver, nerves, and muscles. Mitochondria make up one-third of the total volume of a typical heart muscle cell.

As formerly independent life forms, mitochondria have their own genes. And they inhabit the cell's cytoplasm, which is to say they live outside of that cell's nuclear DNA. Moreover, mitochondria are inherited largely from the mother. In a developing mouse embryo, for example, those inherited from the mother outnumber the father's by a ratio of ten thousand to one. But as mitochondria are drawn into the earliest stages of an embryo's development, something that affects it in major ways can happen.

Development begins with a process in which there is no actual growth. What happens instead is that the egg is repeatedly cleaved into a ball of increasingly smaller cells, each of which is complete and has its own copy of the nuclear DNA. These are the embryonic stem cells of recent debate.

As that process reaches its end, a dramatic new set of changes called *gastrulation* begins. In it, separate zones of cells form, which will with time become the different organs, and those zones begin to migrate to an early approximation of where they'll be in the body. This extraordinary involution—in which various zones dive into the center, roll to the surface, or shear into layers—is akin to a ball turning itself inside out. "It is not birth, marriage, or death, but gastrulation," says biologist Lewis Wolpert, "which is truly the most important time in your life."

This is no less so because it's then that a damaged mitochondrion—which can get shunted into specific cells during cleavage—may then become endemic to specific cell zones. Later, once those zones develop into organs, like the eyes and pancreas, their damaged mitochondria cause the disease called diabetes. Or so recent studies claim. In the past two decades, geneticists have suggested hundreds of links between mitochondrial mutations and specific human problems. Along with diabetes they include deafness, speech defects, shortness, mental retardation, and strokes. And in every case their origins stem from mitochondria, which, as noted, are separate from the embryo's nuclear DNA.

But the egg cytoplasm has another, more significant influence on development. That influence is coded in patterns the mother lays down there, and to which the growing embryo conforms. Nuclear DNA is often described as a kind of blueprint, but that's fundamentally misleading. As Wolpert puts it:

> A descriptive program, like a blueprint or a plan, describes an object in some detail. A generative program describes how to make an object. For the same object the two programs are very different. Consider Origami, the Japanese art of paper folding. By folding a piece of paper in various directions it is quite easy to make a paper hat or a bird from a single sheet. To describe in any detail the final form of the paper, with the complex relationships between its parts, is really very difficult, and not of much help in explaining how to achieve that. Much more useful and easier to formulate are instructions on how to fold the paper. The reason for this is that simple instructions about folding have complex spatial consequences. In development, gene action similarly sets in motion a sequence of events that can bring about profound changes in the embryo. One can thus think of the genetic information in the fertilized egg as equivalent to the folding instruction in Origami—both contain a generative program for making a particular structure.

In lower life forms such as fruit flies, the embryo's nuclear "generative program" expands out into the surrounding cytoplasm (whereas in mammals the nucleus and cytoplasm both cleave to form the start of an embryo). In either case, as an embryo accelerates through the wrenching transformations of cleavage and gastrulation, and begins the process of forming actual organs, it is also being shaped by structures found only in the cytoplasm of the egg.

For instance, all complex life forms have in common the tendency to take shape around an axis. Plants have tips and roots, animals have head (anterior) and tail (posterior) ends. The development of fruit flies—the workhorses, so to speak, of embryo research—illustrates a principle common to most developing animals. Maternal genes and proteins are transmitted to various regions of the cytoplasm by the mother fly. That happens as the egg is being formed. And these set a pattern of "positional information" that then triggers certain genes inside the expanding embryo.

As those genes are activated, a cascade effect takes place in the embryo. First, three broad domains form. Then—as the cascade continues and new genes are successively brought into play—smaller domains form within those three. Conceptually, these come to resemble a row of zebra-striped segments across the body's axis. That axis is another characteristic set by genes and proteins in the cytoplasm. The axis appears to be oriented by a gradient there, the various shades of which determine what will become the anterior and posterior regions of the body. Among the proteins found in the anterior region of the cytoplasm is one called *bicoid*. In a study that sounds less like science than fiction, bicoid was injected into various locations of developing eggs. Wherever it came into contact with the embryonic fly's developing body, that's where the head grew.

The influence from mitochondria and the shaping of overall body plan are just two in a growing list of ways that factors outside an embryo's nuclear DNA can affect its growth and form. Those factors also seem to pace the rhythm of each new pulse of cell divisions during cleavage and to guide the migration of cell zones in gastrulation. Biologist Mae-Wan Ho has called the development process "a true communication channel" between the environment and nuclear genes. Maternal and cytoplasmic effects, Ho adds, provide that link. The cytoplasm is both a "carrier of heredity," quite apart from the nuclear genes of the developing embryo, and "the necessary interface between [those] nuclear genes and the environment, in the coordination of developmental and evolutionary processes."

Until recently those were fighting words among specialists in these fields. They signaled a fundamental shift. Received wisdom since the 1930s had coalesced around the neo-Darwinist view, the dogma of unfettered nuclear DNA authority. But as one critic has pointed out, if development is nothing more than the outgrowth of nuclear DNA, "it would be the only example found in nature of a biological process devoid of feedback."

Loose Behavior

The use of counteracting forces is one of nature's favorite tricks. The tension between individuals and their environments isn't unique to Manaus and the Amazon basin; it's as old as life itself. In embryo development it means, on the one hand, aggressive growth and a dynamic game plan for the nucleus and, on the other hand, the shaping force of factors imposed by the cytoplasm. How is that tension resolved? The answer lies in a sweet spot.

In developmental terms, being "robust" means being able to resist change. For a growing embryo, it's the ability to withstand disturbances and emerge from the prenatal process as normal and healthy. Another phrase to describe robustness would be "dynamic stability." And in this concept lies what could be the most remarkable thing about development.

A growing embryo is a roiling mass of transformations—in just forty-eight hours a fertilized frog egg becomes a free-roaming tadpole; human fetal brain neurons grow at a rate of 250,000 per minute. Through all that the embryo is, as Kant pointed out over a century ago, "both an organized and self-organizing being" whose growing parts at the same time also have to produce one another. Add to that ongoing convulsion the effects of skewed signals from genetic mutations at its core, and of environmental pressures buffeting it from without, and there's a certain wonder in the fact that anything recognizable emerges, much less a complex and fully functioning life form.

The developing embryo is by definition always changing, moving forward through biological time on a kind of trajectory. So maintaining stability by the use of static means is not an option: dynamic sequences cascade through fields of interacting networks; nested systems of multiple, transient causes and effects advance as they coevolve. Robustness is the result of nature's ability to channel the developing embryo—in the lingo, to "canalize" it. The biologists' metaphor is that of a landscape. Developmental valleys provide equilibrium pathways, hills offer gently rising resistance.

And therein lies a lesson. The concepts of adaptation and evolution are the linchpins of modern biology. At heart they are expressions of the tension between figure and ground, between the individual and its environment. Mutation in an individual, without environmental constraints, would just produce genetic chaos. On the other hand, if constraints from the environment were too tight, the individual would lose all identity.

Nature's solution to this dilemma is a sweetly funky one: it favors a "loose coupling."

Philosopher of biology Susan Oyama outlines the paradox of natural processes, in which "flexibility gives rise to exact consequences." Development, Oyama points out, can appear quite rigid, in that parents reliably produce similar offspring. And yet, she says, the developmental process manages that accomplishment "only by having a substantial amount of play in its workings."

Play is the key. The lesson is that along that boundary where the push of individual initiative comes up against the shove of environmental constraint, nature finds a sweet spot—a vibrant zone where the tensions between figure and ground are resolved in dynamic interaction.

This interplay happens between the nucleus and the cytoplasm in development; it then occurs again in the outside world, along the boundary between the fully grown individual and its environment. Through this constant interplay, animals evolve tools to negotiate that boundary: tools such as senses and mobility.

Liquid Logic
When a fish swings its tail, it leaves behind a swirl of spinning water. As the tail swings back, it stirs another eddy. Each stroke sends a liquid swirl spinning in the opposite direction. Though that seems commonplace, research now shows that fish use their tails to arrange those swirls in precise patterns, and that this behavior is a key to their exceptional speed and mobility. Each swirl reduces drag from the wake even as it provides something for the fish to press its tail against on the return stroke, giving it more power.

One of the new biologists responsible for that insight, Michael Triantafyllou, is a naval architect and a professor of ocean engineering at the Massachusetts Institute of Technology. With his colleagues he has designed a model that wriggles through water with an efficiency near that of living fish.

Walking alongside the tanks in his lab, Triantafyllou points to a container of particles that fluoresce when they are thrown in the water and illuminated with laser beams. "We throw thousands of particles in here," he says. "When we shine the laser it's like looking at the night sky, with thousands of little stars. Any motion is immediately reflected. Then we take photographs of that, which give us the velocities and what's happening in the water around the fish."

The MIT fish is a five-foot-long model tuna, with an aluminum skeleton and joints sheathed by a smooth skin of latex foam covered with Lycra, the material used for swimsuits. The many joints let it undulate back and forth much as real fish do. The Robotuna team employed directed evolution to refine its design through some two thousand generations. Computers also figure in a feedback system now in development that will help it to adjust to changed conditions in the water.

Robotuna approaches the swimming efficiency of a living tuna, which reaches speeds of up to forty knots. A comparably powered research sub, driven by propellers and lacking fishy streamlining, might reach six knots. That could be one reason funding for this work comes from the National Oceanic and Atmospheric Administration and the Naval Research Laboratory. Someday schools of swimming robofish may sample ocean nutrients or probe volcanic vents, test for toxic spills or go exploring through sunken wrecks.

Fly Spies

Scientists elsewhere are looking at how flies manage to fly. At first glance they shouldn't be able to. The aerodynamic lift forces used by planes and birds don't work for small insects. They have relatively large bodies as compared with their wingspans. And at their scale, the air's viscosity makes the act of flying more like swimming in molasses.

With that in mind, Michael Dickinson of the California Institute of Technology suspended a bird-size pair of model insect wings covered with sensors in a drum of mineral oil. What he and others doing similar work discovered has interesting parallels with the MIT fish tail.

When an insect sweeps its wings forward and back, at the end of its return stroke it rotates each wing to create a backspin. This causes lower pressure above the wing and a momentary lift. Then, as the wing sweeps forward, it creates a rolling "leading-edge vortex" on top of the wing, which provides more lift. And at either end of the stroke, the wings also play off those front and back vortices in much the way a fish's tail presses against the whirlpools it creates. It's by using these tricks that insects can do things like take off backward and land upside down.

More remarkable, flies do all that with brains the size of poppy seeds. "A fly has, on average, 350,000 neurons," Dickinson notes (we have 100 billion). "Most of them [are] dedicated to processing sensory information." As much as three-quarters of its brain is devoted to just the eyes. Yet "when a fly breaks out of its pupa, it can fly as well as it ever will." Dickinson is interested in how the fly's brain works, he says, in how it's possible for relatively few neurons to produce such complex behavior. "Brains evolved integrally related to bodies," he notes, "and bodies evolved in the physical world."

The Caltech team relies heavily on computers for modeling and tracking its flies. They also use an exotic array of computer-linked machines with names like Robofly (the fly simulator), Fly-O-Rama (flight path recording chamber with video inputs), Rock-n-Roll Fly Arena (flight recording chamber that pitches and yaws, with variable light arrays), FlyBall (neo fly eye), and the perhaps inevitable Bride of Robofly.

Dickinson is working with Ronald Fearing—a colleague from the University of California at Berkeley—on the development of a micro-mechanical flying insect. They have fabricated a diminutive robot thorax, and wings that will beat 150 times a second. A prototype that can hover in still air is their goal, but that's only the start. The possibility of roboflies was first raised in a 1992 Rand Corporation study for the Pentagon. Several million dollars in funding for their development has now been awarded to the Dickinson-Fearing group and to such places as the Georgia Tech Research Institute in Atlanta. Robofly funding comes from the Office of Naval Research and the ever-present DARPA—the Defense Advanced Research Projects Agency.

The military envisions a new class of reconnaissance device called a MicroFlier, which individual personnel can carry and release. Once the operator gives a robofly general instructions about where to go, it will quickly disappear from sight and complete the mission by itself. It will be programmed to compensate for obstacles and wind drift on its own.

Ride the Wind
The work at MIT and Caltech is lively and creative, but it is hardly unique. In labs around the world, scientists and engineers who study the boundary dynamics of living systems are asking new questions and getting new answers. Whether it's the seminal work in England of James Gray at Cambridge and R. McNeill Alexander in Leeds; that of Robert

Full at UC Berkeley; or of Steven Vogel, Stephen Wainright, and Charles Pell at Duke, they're looking at the way things navigate the world around them. How does a bug walk? How does a fish swim? How does the shape of a pelican's head affect the impact on its spinal cord when it dives in the water to catch that fish?

One of the earliest researchers in the field was Ingo Rechenberg of the Department of Bionics and Evolution Technique at the Technical University of Berlin. A trip to Rechenberg's lab involves driving near the former site of the infamous Berlin Wall, once both a symbolic and an all-too-real boundary between the city of West Berlin and the larger Soviet world. Then it was a barren corridor through the city's center, a no-man's-land of empty lots filled with barbed wire and guard posts. Today that boundary has been transformed. The guards are gone, the wall is gone, and green grass grows on open lots where children laugh and run, playing soccer.

The sound of children playing nearby is appropriate, since Rechenberg works in one of the world's great toy boxes. He himself is a cheerful, grinning man whose longish hair has the windblown look of someone who spends a good deal of time standing in front of wind tunnels. The lab is a largely open two-story room filled with outsize equipment, spiral staircases, hanging balconies, and scientists working with him on a number of different projects, all of which are moving forward at the same time.

Rechenberg first came to prominence in the early 1960s, when he devised an evolutionary way to reduce the wind drag across a jointed series of metal plates. Using dice to create hundreds of random "mutations"—slight changes in the angles of the joints—his tests eventually showed that the most efficient shape wasn't the flat surface that common sense suggests but a mildly planar curve, like the upper surface of a plane's wing. His group still uses evolutionary techniques to solve engineering problems, though the process is now computerized. And they haven't stopped there.

Talking and gesturing as he wanders across catwalks and down stairways, Rechenberg has an enthusiasm that is infectious. He fires up an enormous wind tunnel and as the whining of the engines accelerates he shows photos of a bird in flight. When its wings flap, a small group of feathers on each wingtip is clearly visible. They are spread wide and seem to be playing some kind of role. He trundles a cart with an enor-

mous pair of stork wings into position in front of the wind tunnel, and
as the breeze intensifies, the wings lift and the same effect is clear—at
their ends, feathers move apart like spreading fingers.

"On the upper side of a wing," says Rechenberg, "is low pressure,
and below it is high pressure." The end of the wing, he continues, is
where those low- and high-pressure zones collide. For that reason, on
airplane wings that zone is a region of chaotic air drag. But not for birds.

"These are the fingers," Rechenberg says, pointing to the spreading
feathers. He goes on to explain that where the low- and high-pressure
zones meet at the end of a stork's wing, each of those fingers produces
an air vortex that trails along behind it. "On the wing we are looking
at," he says, "there are three separate feathers. So in this instance there
are three vortices." He shows a diagram of how the vortices coil back
from each feather. Ultimately they spiral together, much like a DNA
double helix. He says that inside the core of that spiraling tunnel the
headwind is accelerated to produce thrust, which offsets drag.

"The drag of this zone on an ordinary airplane is 40 to 50 percent
of the total drag on a wing," he continues. But in their best experiments
with wingtips that have fingers, "that drag can go to 10 percent." To exploit this effect, Airbus and other manufacturers are now looking into
using split ends on the wingtips of their aircraft.

His colleague T. K. Mueller picks up the conversation as he demonstrates an experiment set up at another wind tunnel. Here the matter at
hand is stall. One of the most dangerous times for aircraft of every kind
is the point at which a plane is landing and loses speed. It's then that the
balance between the high- and the low-pressure zones above and below
its wings can become unstable and cause a stall. If that occurs the plane
can drop abruptly from the air—something that has happened in a number of commercial air disasters.

Showing film of a bird landing, Mueller points out how, as the bird
slows, a separate layer of feathers on the top surface of its wings begins
to lift. The layer forms a gentle, rippling pattern. By turning on the
wind machine and gradually angling a wing in front of it, he produces
the same effect.

What happens in a stall, he says, is that "if the airspeed gets too low
or the angle of attack too steep," the lift that comes from air moving
across the top of the wing weakens as that air fails to reach all the way
back to the wing's trailing edge. When this happens, an eddy begins to

creep up from that edge, advancing forward along the top of the wing. The eddy works its way beneath the air that's rushing back, separating that airflow from the wing. "When that flow is lifted off the surface," Mueller points out, "it does not produce lift anymore." As a result, a feedback loop forms in which the eddy propagates faster and faster and the lift gets weaker and weaker until all lift fails. "Most airplane accidents," he says, "happen because of a stall.

"Now we look at birds," he continues, "and we find that they have a solution." Pointing to the rising layer of feathers along the tops of bird wings, he calls them "smart" devices. "They sense when the eddy is spreading forward," he says, "and as that happens, they lift up, to separate it from the air coming back from the front edge. So there is a wedge effect going on." A slender, rippling wave of feathers rules out a failure of lift.

The Rechenberg lab has worked with the German glider company Stemme, which tested a similar system of flaps on its plane wings. It worked, says Mueller. "We have tried out the flaps and the pilot says that he could not get into a stall that easily. He went up to one thousand meters and tried to stall or tried to tumble, and he felt a real difference."

As Mueller talks, far above his head a clear plastic tunnel that is about three feet in diameter and filled with water can be seen extending across the lab. Another scientist in the group, Rudolf Bannasch, propels life-size models of penguins through it while filming them. Says Bannasch, "We have studied the energetics of penguins swimming in the Antarctic. These animals spend most of their lives in the water of the cold ice sea. They had to learn how to use their energy in an ergonomic way—how to spend as little as possible for swimming."

Bannasch has been looking at how the penguin's body contours affect the water in which it swims. And he has found something quite similar to how the stall effect occurs on wings, although in this case it works to the animal's advantage. Rather than being one smooth contour from head to tail, a penguin's body has small undulations—subtle ridges around its circumference—which raise the speed of the water passing over them. Behind those undulations the passing water slows and curls in on itself. This creates a roller effect that separates the water flowing past it from the animal's body, dramatically reducing friction.

Penguins feed on krill, a small crustacean, Bannasch says. "We analyzed their energy consumption and found that they need only one kilogram of krill to travel about a hundred and thirty kilometers in the sea." That's the equivalent, he translates, of using a liter of gasoline to travel about fifteen hundred kilometers in that water.

Back at his desk, Bannasch displays with some pride a photo of an athlete dressed in brightly colored shorts and T-shirt, standing next to an unusual-looking bicycle. It's enclosed in a streamlined white shell that looks oddly like a penguin. The bike is a racer, and the light fiberglass shell was formed in a Mercedes-Benz lab. They have raced it, he says, and with impressive results.

Run, Don't Walk

At Waseda University in Japan, scientists have for some time now been working on humanoids—which is to say, robots that walk like people. Shigeo Hirose at the Tokyo Institute of Technology—where there's a major lab focusing on this kind of work—has built a number of legged robots, including quadrupeds. He also has a line, called Titan, which they sell to other research labs. The automaker Honda has spent $30 million developing Asimo, a beautifully engineered biped that even looks like a human, albeit a moonwalker encased in white armor, as it trots around booting a soccer ball. Their design strategy involved filming an actual person, then engineering his joint angles and movement characteristics into the robot. Korea's full-bodied walker, HUBO, takes things a step further, with individually moving fingers. Scientists at Carnegie Mellon University are developing an Anatomically Correct Testbed hand. It has bones and joints that mimic ours, and is controlled by emulations of the neural signals coming from our brains. So far the group has completed one finger. Engineering departments at schools across the U.S. now routinely feature robotics programs, though perhaps none focuses more intensely on this subject than MIT.

There, one finds a science fiction junkyard bounded by vague walls, overworked snack machines, and desks submerged under slurries of paperwork. At first glance it appears to be inhabited by machines that almost resemble living things: tall ostrichlike birds, oversize bugs, humans with their top halves missing. This is the leg lab. Closer inspection reveals a sparse population of real humans bent over obscure tasks. One of these, graduate student Jerry Pratt, sits poking what could be a screwdriver into something that might be a femur but looks more like a spare part for the Terminator.

"One of the nice things about robots now," Pratt says, "is that they've gotten to the point where it's not painful to watch them move. You know, like fifteen years ago, there were robots but when you watched them you got bored. Now they go on the order of human walking. So they're a lot more exciting and a lot more practical." A main goal for designers of legged robots is what Pratt refers to as "biological looks." By that he means they want to make it look the way a natural organism looks when it's moving.

As it turns out, walking is a "hard problem"—a term of art that mathematicians use meaning, essentially, that they can't figure out how it works. But important progress is being made. That progress comes in no small part due to the work of the lab's founder, Marc Raibert, one of the world's most prolific roboticists. Raibert has since left MIT to form Boston Dynamics, a leader in the human simulation software used to create lifelike movement in humanoids. But during his tenure here he was interested in balance. An early project was a single-legged hopping machine that behaved like a ten-year-old on a pogo stick. It worked partly by using a gyroscope similar to the sensors in our inner ears.

"From that single-legged machine," says Hugh Herr, now director of the lab, "he learned how to stabilize the bouncing height and tension of the machine and how to control the speed. Then he applied those principles to machines with two legs, and then with four legs. He eventually developed bipeds that could run and even do flips, really amazing feats." According to Herr, a Raibert robot holds the land speed record for an artificial biped, thirteen miles per hour—which approaches a four-minute mile.

That's a fast pace for any biped, though in the end it is the act of walking that presents the bigger challenge.

"One thing we find," says Pratt, "is that walking is actually harder than running. The difficulty is that you always have to be balanced." One way of looking at how running is easier than walking, he says, "is if you are walking and you're about to trip and want to recover, the way you recover is by running a few steps."

With this principle in mind Herr worked out a system in which a robot's legs moved through their arcs as if they were spokes on a wheel. "Even though it was a funny wheel," he says, "with the spokes being elastic and changing length, I still applied that principle. It turns out that when you do that, it just balances and doesn't require any information on its orientation in space. And it balances a lot better than a lot of the more sophisticated machines." What that implies, he says, is that "when a horse is trotting or galloping along steadily, it's not actively using its inner ear to balance. There is no active balance. It is stable by its very nature."

Roboticists, says Pratt, "are starting to find that when you talk about artificial intelligence or creature intelligence—the intelligence we're interested in, the intelligence of a cat running around, for instance—you need to think more in terms of dynamical systems than of classical AI stuff like logic. The classical AI approach . . . and the figuring out and solving of logical equations that way . . . nature doesn't operate like that. A living creature is a dynamical system with a bunch of state variables, which are constantly changing.

"In a brain, for instance," he says, "each neuron might have ten state variables, where the state of the neuron changes with the input from other neurons. So what you're getting is a network with billions of these, thousands of millions of interconnections between each one . . . and based on the structure of the system and the physics behind it, they're all changing over time."

Seeing Is Connecting

Whether it's penguins adapting to icy seas or single neurons connecting with webs of other neurons, in nature individual elements and the larger patterns that contain them are always linked. They interact in that strange and wondrous process through which individuals change the world around them even as the world around them changes them. Something like that holds true as well in the formation of senses, another of nature's innovations along the boundary between figure and ground.

When early work in robotics and artificial intelligence at MIT, at Stanford, and in Edinburgh, Scotland, explored the interface between television cameras and computers, one of the more obvious things the research found was the fundamental importance of world knowledge. The incoming data had to fit into a context.

The minute we're born, our senses begin sending information to our brains. As that happens, patterns of neural connections and the strengths of those connections are constantly modified by experience. As mentioned earlier, if a child has a cataract on one eye at birth and corrective surgery is delayed, the eye will fail to form essential connections with the brain. In "the more subtle types of response" that we call learning, writes Enrico Coen in *The Art of Genes*, "as when the cell interactions in the brain are modified by being exposed to language or objects around us . . . we might equally say that it is simply a more plant-like form of development, in which the organism modifies its internal patterns in response to variation in its surroundings."

Tomaso Poggio, a brain and cognitive sciences professor at MIT, studies the behavior of neurons involved in vision. He describes the area he works in as "between computers and brains." Poggio was originally trained as a physicist. There, he says, "we look at machine analogies. But the understanding of molecular biology is of a different type than the theory we know of in physics." It is not just descriptive. "How does our brain see?" he asks. As it turns out, in the brain specific neurons respond to motion, or to color, or to other kinds of stimuli. And what Poggio does is focus on that learning process. He calls his work "computational neuroscience."

One of the questions he and his colleagues look at is how a 3-D model is represented in the brain. Is it like a CAD (computer-aided design) model, or is it more like a series of snapshots? With CAD there is a complete if virtual 3-D model that can be turned in space and viewed from different angles, much in the way you would turn something held in your hand. The second possibility is more like having a number of closely related snapshots, each taken from a slightly different angle, with one after the other stored as static images.

Tests done with human subjects suggested the snapshot method. Then research with monkeys showed the same effect. "Monkeys," he says, "could recognize objects only if they had seen them up close from a similar angle. They couldn't infer familiarity from a different view. It's the snapshot approach."

When they mapped the brain response of monkeys during those tests, they also found that different neurons responded strongly to different views of the same object. And those neurons would respond nearly as strongly to a reversed view—as if the image had been flipped in a mirror. That was another indication, Poggio says, that the snapshot theory was right.

There seem to be on the order of four hundred cells tuned to a single view. "So it is not one neuron, and it's not millions." With a computational neuroscience model, he says, "it's possible to program that connectivity and plasticity so it recognizes things in the same way as does the brain."

Poggio and his colleagues at MIT aren't the only computer scientists looking closely at how we see. Carver Mead and Christof Koch at Caltech are using neuromorphology as a guide to building chips that imitate the neural properties of the human retina. And that work takes shape against an international background of efforts, some of which have moved beyond research.

But Now I See

At age sixty-two, "Jerry" had been blind for nearly three decades when his doctor, William Dobelle, first connected him to the computer. The device itself was essentially a pair of sunglasses with a pinhole camera linked to an image processor. This translated the camera's pictures into patterns the brain can understand. From there the information pulsed through a small wire array to a contact on the visual region of Jerry's brain.

Wearing the unit, he was able to walk across a room, locate a black cap hanging against a white wall, then bring it back and set it on a mannequin's head. According to Dobelle, who heads a medical device company in New York, Jerry could also make out a two-inch-high letter from a distance of five feet. That event is considered the first meaningful demonstration of artificial vision. Dobelle has since made numerous advances with his device—making it more portable and improving resolution to the point that one patient could drive a car, if only in a parking lot. On four continents there are now a dozen teams moving ahead with sight-related devices. Among them, Mark Humayun at the University of Southern California is developing an artificial retina, and Richard Norman at the University of Utah makes implants that actually hook into the visual cortex (Dobelle's contacts rest on its surface).

Work on the other senses has advanced to a similar degree. Growing out of basic research by George Dodd at the University of Warwick in England, electronic noses have been on the market since the early 1990s. They're used now to monitor things like batches of beer, but will soon provide everything from medical diagnoses to airport security. Artificial retinas are also being developed at the University of Pennsylvania. A Caltech group has done insightful work on the hearing of owls. Haptics— from the Greek *haptesthai*, meaning "to touch"—is the theme of research at places like the MIT Touch Lab. There, work on the problem of remote tactile interaction is well under way, with what eventual implications for the Internet one can only speculate.

Figure and Ground

The machine age outlook has often led humans to act on the biological world in ways that are harmful to it. So there's some irony in the fact that the mechanical world we have surrounded ourselves with is now impinging on human biology. This fact is an incentive for the rapidly growing field of ergonomics, which looks to improve the interface between individuals and their environments in the design of everything from car seats to staple gun handles.

The interface between users and their computers has become a major ergonomic focus. A $5.8 million damage award in 1986—against the Digital Equipment Corporation, for repetitive strain injuries caused by its keyboards—marked the start of a series of large jury awards for health problems caused by poorly designed environments. Dean Santner, a furniture designer based in Alameda, California, has worked for much of his life in the field. His company, Navigator Systems, designs adaptable, ergonomic desk arrays that have been prescribed to patients by doctors. "When people sit down to a task," he says, "my job is to see that they don't have to work in order to get to their work." What interests Santner most about ergonomics is how it "brings together statistics, medicine, physics, biomechanics, anthropometry, kinesiology, engineering, and psychology" in the effort to integrate people more effectively with their environments.

One Stanford University study turned up an amusing example of psychological ergonomics. A group of computer users, who had been asked to score the performance of their computers, adjusted their answers in a surprising way. When required to respond through the monitors of their own computers, the subjects gave much more positive evaluations than when they answered the same questions through other computers or on paper. Says Stanford's Clifford Nass, "Our participants automatically and unconsciously made an attempt to ingratiate themselves to a computer."

Associated Press newswire item: "Issaquah, Wash.—A 43-year-old man was coaxed out of his home by police after he pulled a gun on his personal computer and shot it several times, apparently in frustration."

This story went on to reveal that the man shot his computer four times through the hard drive and once through the monitor, and that he had been taken away for mental evaluation. Some, though, suggest it's the computer that should have been removed and tested for antisocial behavior. According to Neil Gershenfeld, author of *When Things Start to Think*, it's a mistake to assume that a computer interface happens "between a person sitting at a desk and a computer sitting on the desk."

"The speed of the computer is increasingly much less of a concern," he says, "than the difficulty in telling it what you want it to do, or in understanding what it has done . . . As smart as computers may have become," he adds, "they are not yet wise."

Artificial intelligence pioneer Marvin Minsky once remarked that computers lack the common sense of a six-year-old. That's not surprising, Gershenfeld replies, "since they also lack the life experience of a six-year-old . . . A blind, deaf, and dumb computer, immobilized on a desktop, following rote instruction, has no chance of understanding its world."

The importance of perception to cognition, he points out, can be seen in the way we are wired. "Our senses are connected by two-way channels: Information goes in both directions." This lets us "fine-tune how we see and hear and touch in order to learn the most about our environment."

In nature the link between figure and ground is just such a two-way channel. Much of life is defined by the contest between freedom of action for individuals and the integrity of larger patterns. Each represents a fundamental principle in living systems. Nature likes dynamic opposition, in some sense "wants" the tension between them, but also wants it to be animated by active play along the boundary. All of which has led to nature's most extraordinary innovation at the boundary between the individual and its environment—brains.

four

thinking

The first human delegation to the moon included Buzz Aldrin, who was a graduate of MIT. Radar was developed at MIT. Digital computers are possible because of the magnetic-core memory invented here, and MIT pioneers like Marvin Minsky steered the birth of artificial intelligence. Another of the school's pioneers, Phillip Sharp, codiscovered the split-gene structure of higher life forms, an important insight for genetic engineering. With that he became one of MIT's many Nobel laureates, working in an atmosphere where faith in and knowledge of mechanics have strong foundations.

MIT is a world leader in engineering, and, like its inhabitants, the campus is inclined toward pragmatism. Although the old main building features the typical pillars and a dome, the resemblance to other schools mostly ends there as a crowded hodgepodge of functional structures fans out behind it. But while the predominant color scheme at MIT is variations on gray, the building that houses its biology department is a notable exception. In these surroundings its multifaceted green-glass facade looks like an exotic plant. If Manaus in the Amazon symbolizes the entry of Western mechanization into the richest organic environment on earth, MIT's biology building stands for the inverse—the entry of organic logic into the very heart of the machine metaphor.

When it opened in 1994, the $70 million structure was the biggest and most expensive building ever constructed at MIT, and in the time since then biology has become the school's second-largest undergraduate major. "There's a growing awareness of the importance of this science in the future of many other activities," says Sharp, who currently heads the department. As evidence of that he points to the fact that all MIT undergraduates are now required to take courses in molecular and cell biology, and to the rising attendance at summer courses he offers for instructors from other disciplines. "So the campus is sort of beating with a pulse," he says, "that every day sees more emphasis on life science." That emphasis is nowhere more evident than in an even larger and more costly structure just completed at MIT: its dramatic new home for the Computer Science and Artificial Intelligence Laboratory.

Smart Machines
All this is a far cry from what Joseph Weizenbaum found when he arrived here in 1963. Flush with military dollars from the newly formed DARPA, the Defense Advanced Research Projects Agency, the group he joined was a small but forceful exponent of the command-and-control style of artificial intelligence—the linear, top-down, mechanistic model of computing introduced in 1956 at a legendary Dartmouth conference. For inspiration that approach looked to the then-prevailing school of psychology, "behaviorism," which traced its roots back to Pavlov, and beyond him to Descartes' belief that animals are machines. That fitted well with the Cartesian view of higher intelligence as a form of symbol processing, which in turn linked neatly with the linear, serial-logic processors used for that research. Another behaviorist notion also dovetailed with these—that what goes on inside the "box" (inside the brain of an animal or even that of a person) is less important than knowing which outside stimulus produces which measurable response.

The theory of artificial intelligence (AI) that grew from this held that symbol manipulation was the essence of mind, and that the kind of machinery producing the symbols—the underlying architecture—was incidental. In other words, if a machine behaved in a way that resembled human intelligence, that *was* human intelligence. This approach would come to be known as classical AI.

Weizenbaum didn't buy that, but the possibility of mimicking intelligence intrigued him, even if it seemed no more than a clever ruse. To that end in 1966 he joined with Stanford psychologist Kenneth Colby to produce a program they called Eliza. They took that name from the spunky ragamuffin Eliza Doolittle, who learns to speak like a grand lady in the George Bernard Shaw play *Pygmalion*, later made into the musical *My Fair Lady*. Their Eliza learned to talk, too, but with a crucial difference. She talked like a psychologist.

Their method was simple. The program Weizenbaum wrote just inverted sentences or added prefixes to echo the vague phrases used in certain forms of therapy. "I am" became "you are": a sentence like "I am frustrated" became "I'm sorry to hear you are frustrated." Mention of the word "mother" triggered a question about "your family." Now and then, for good measure, it would say, "Tell me more about that," or ask, "Why do you think so?" or add a general embellishment to something that had been mentioned earlier. The results could border on the spooky, as in the following exchange with a young woman, in which Eliza's responses are capitalized:

Men are all alike.
IN WHAT WAY?
They're always bugging us about something or other.
CAN YOU THINK OF A SPECIFIC EXAMPLE?
Well, my boyfriend made me come here.
YOUR BOYFRIEND MADE YOU COME HERE.
He says I'm depressed much of the time.
I'M SORRY TO HEAR YOU ARE DEPRESSED.
It's true. I am unhappy.
DO YOU THINK THAT COMING HERE WILL HELP YOU NOT TO BE
     UNHAPPY?
I need some help, that much seems certain.
WHAT WOULD IT MEAN TO YOU IF YOU GOT SOME HELP?
Perhaps I could learn to get along with my mother.
TELL ME MORE ABOUT YOUR FAMILY.
My mother takes care of me.
WHO ELSE IN YOUR FAMILY TAKES CARE OF YOU?
My father.
YOUR FATHER.
You are like my father in some ways.

WHAT RESEMBLANCE DO YOU SEE?
You are not very aggressive, but I think you don't want me to notice that.
WHAT MAKES YOU THINK I AM NOT VERY AGGRESSIVE?
You don't argue with me.
WHY DO YOU THINK I DON'T ARGUE WITH YOU?
You are afraid of me.
DOES IT PLEASE YOU TO THINK I AM AFRAID OF YOU?
My father is afraid of everybody.
WHAT ELSE COMES TO MIND WHEN YOU THINK OF YOUR FATHER?
Bullies.
DOES THAT HAVE ANYTHING TO DO WITH THE FACT THAT YOUR
   BOYFRIEND MADE YOU COME HERE?

Eliza quickly became a hit at MIT. Weizenbaum, a trickster at heart, was amused by all the people calling for appointments to talk with his computer, and by incidents like the time someone logged on to Eliza by mistake, thinking they were chatting online with him. But he began to wonder the day his secretary asked him to leave the room so she could talk privately with Eliza about personal matters. When his partner Colby suggested the use of computer therapists to help people with real problems, Weizenbaum stopped smiling.

The computer wasn't really thinking, he kept saying, it was all just sleight of hand. But no one was listening. Writing a decade later, in his book *Computer Power and Human Reason*, he still hadn't gotten over how "extremely short exposures to a relatively simple computer program could induce powerful delusional thinking in quite normal people." But normal people were only a part of his concern. That those outside his field might be taken in was at least conceivable. But how to explain why top computer scientists were doing much the same thing?

Weizenbaum's doubts just caused exasperation among his AI colleagues. But support for his critique came from an unexpected quarter—philosophy. If Western philosophers had labored twenty-five hundred years without producing a final definition of what thinking was, they could at least say with some clarity what it was not. Hubert Dreyfus became the first to join the fray. A physicist turned philosopher, he had expressed strong doubts about AI as early as 1961. Three years later he was hired by the Rand Corporation, the military think tank, to evaluate AI and came back with a scathing denunciation titled *Alchemy and Artificial Intelligence*.

In that report and later writings Dreyfus maintained that the approach then being used for AI would never work—that, like climbing a mountain to reach the moon, it was based on a naive theory. In the empty symbols being shuffled around in linear-logic processors, there was no larger awareness, he argued, of the complex background knowledge that confers meaning to the symbols used in human thought. There was also no tolerance for ambiguity and no appreciation for the kind of "likenesses" that give power to metaphor or help us identify members of the same family. Dreyfus condemned the failure to recognize such oversights as inexcusable and argued that AI was the least self-critical field in science.

Whatever the merits of that charge, there was no shortage of criticism for Dreyfus. Among others, Herbert Simon and Allen Newell—the Carnegie Mellon scientists who had come up with the first working AI program—lobbied Rand to suppress the report and nearly succeeded. It wasn't published officially until 1967. Marvin Minsky and Seymour Papert, who were heading the AI program at MIT, launched another counterattack with a refutation by Papert titled *The Artificial Intelligence of Hubert L. Dreyfus*.

As support for their claims, Minsky, Papert, and the other champions of classical AI pointed to how well Eliza and similar "expert systems" were doing in the Turing test. That was something suggested in 1950 by famed mathematician Alan Turing, who first conceived what would become the modern computer. In his test, a human operator types questions that are answered by unseen correspondents in separate rooms. One of them is a person; one is a computer. When an operator can't tell from the responses which is which, the computer has passed.

In the matrix of Cartesian and behaviorist notions then shaping AI, the Turing test was seen as ultimate justification. What came out of the box was all that mattered. The underlying architecture—how things worked inside the box—was beside the point.

Pressure mounted on Dreyfus, who was then teaching at MIT. He became isolated and eventually moved on to the University of California at Berkeley as classical AI's stock kept rising. Throughout the 1960s and '70s private corporations and the military poured enormous sums into the development of expert systems. It was believed that they would eventually dispense generations of accumulated wisdom and experience. But things didn't work out that way. Instead, it soon became clear that they had to be upgraded whenever conditions changed, which was constantly. The problem was that they couldn't learn on their own. As Weizenbaum and Dreyfus had tried to show, they didn't know how to think.

In 1980, Berkeley philosopher John Searle published his "Chinese room" parable, which would become the classic debunking of classical AI. In it he assailed the Turing test by asking the reader to do the following:

> Imagine yourself sitting in a room, provided with a list of Chinese symbols and rules to match them. Your only connection to the outside world is a slot. Through this slot, you receive input in the form of certain Chinese symbols. According to your lists, you replace the incoming symbols with others and pass them back through the slot as output. For the people outside the room, the input was a question in Chinese, and the output was a reasonable answer to it also in Chinese. They would be justified in supposing that a Chinese speaker is inside the room.

But, Searle asked, would you yourself say that you understood Chinese? Clearly not. It was just as clear, he went on to say, that regardless of whether they could pass the Turing test, classical AI programs didn't know what they were doing.

Berkeley computer scientist Lotfi Zadeh added that in order to confuse a machine in the Turing test, you need only ask it to summarize what you tell it. "No machine will be able to pass this test," he said. "You need no other test, just ask the machine to summarize what you said or typed."

By the end of the 1980s the AI landscape was like a beach littered with empty shells, the remains of bankrupt AI companies. As Minsky would later concede, "The main problem seemed to be that each of our so-called 'expert systems' could be used only for some single, specialized application . . . None of them showed any signs of having what we call common sense." In the early 1990s DARPA announced that it was shifting $500 million in research funding away from classical AI and awarding it instead to a new approach—parallel distributed processing. That approach looked to how information is actually processed in the brain. It was there that the next advances would come.

The Architecture Matters

"If we do not know how the brain works," says Patricia Smith Churchland, "then the structure and organization is likely to provide indispensable clues." Churchland is a professor of philosophy at the University of California at San Diego, where she is part of the cognitive science program. Her interest is in how neuroscience impacts the philosophy of mind, and what it can tell us about such things as consciousness, knowledge, free will, and our sense of self. Her 1986 book, *Neurophilosophy,* remains a classic in the field.

The San Diego program is a leading center for the study of living minds. To that end it unites computer science with a broad spectrum of related fields: psychology, linguistics, philosophy, anthropology, and the various neurosciences. The members of that group view organic thinking as a tumult of interweaving processes all advancing along parallel lines. Says Churchland's husband, Paul, who carries the same title at San Diego and shares similar views, "If you want to do things in real time as mice and birds and creatures who have to live in the real world do, then you have to go to massively parallel architectures. The architecture does matter profoundly, even to do the job at all."

Stanford University cognitive scientist Terry Winograd, a former student of Minsky's, points to another consideration. The structures of the nervous system, he says, aren't uniform interconnections of similar elements. Instead, they are "a complex architecture of different kinds of cells with different kinds of cells, connections, layers, and so on." The way we think, he adds, "is in some sense a function of that complexity."

"The brain is not just the hardware; the brain is the hardware *and* the software," notes Terrence Sejnowski, who teaches neuroscience in the San Diego group and has a lab nearby at the Salk Institute. "In fact," he says, "it is almost impossible to separate the two. The very concept of software has to be modified, I think, when you come to the question of how the brain is programmed." Most of the things we know or do, he points out, are learned through experience. And not only does that come in a great variety of ways, but "what happens in this process is that the actual circuitry of the brain is being modified; it is as if the hardware itself is changing."

All these factors are born of interaction. If how fish swim or bees fly is the result of creative play along the boundary between animals and their environments, that play and the lessons learned from it are also embodied in the complex structures and internal interactions of brains. That's how brains came about—and why they work so well. As one observer has put it, "Until we try to emulate living systems artificially, we don't appreciate the stupefying excellence of biological nervous systems that can coordinate the movements of a cheetah cornering at speed or of a hawk coming in to land."

Just as nature combines basic building blocks called atoms, then molecules, and then cells to make organisms, so, too, it assembles basic mental structures to make our brains. In the course of eons, each of those structures has formed over and to some extent subsumed its evolutionary precursors. At the deepest level, at the top end of the spine, is a small bulb sometimes called the "fish brain." It regulates basic body functions like pulse. Over that is the R-complex, which first evolved some sixty million years ago in reptiles. And above that is the more recent limbic system, or "mammal brain." These deep structures feed raw mental energy—the instincts, drives, and feelings referred to by psychologists— up into the newer layers of the brain, to the cerebral hemispheres and their cortex.

Each of these structures lends different outlooks, abilities, and inclinations to the overall mix we call mentality. And to that we also have to add the often-contrary urges spurred by the release of various hormones. A picture emerges of mentality not as coherent but as a multitude of competing tendencies that we constantly balance against one another. Just as it is a key to ecology and so many other aspects of natural systems, that counterbalancing tendency is how most of the brain's structures and processes function. In the introduction to their influential book, *Parallel Distributed Processing: Explorations in the Microstructure of Cognition*, David E. Rumelhart and James L. McClelland, founders of the San Diego group, write, "The currency of our systems is not symbols, but excitation and inhibition."

All of those mental systems are dense with neurons, the elongated cells—some as long as three feet—that transmit electrochemical messages throughout the body. By far the densest concentration of neurons in the brain is found in the cerebral cortex, the thin grayish pink carpet of cells that overlays the hemispheres. In that eighth-inch-thick layer enfolding a structure no larger than a grapefruit, there are some thirty billion neurons. The words "density" and "complexity" fail spectacularly in trying to describe the actual density and complexity of the brain. If all the neurons in just one human brain were laid end to end, they would reach to the moon and back, and then to the moon again.

But the brain's complexity only begins there. It's further multiplied by the fantastic number of possible connections among its synapses: Each neuron is excited or inhibited by data it receives from other cells, and from chemical messengers in the bloodstream. It converts that information into signals that course through its elongated body at a rate of some one hundred pulses per second. At one end of the neuron there are thousands of *dendrites*, feathery tendrils that reach out to receive signals from other neurons. At its opposite end there is a corresponding number of *axons*, similar arrays that send off the neuron's own signals. As they flash out through the axons, those signals are converted into molecules called *neurotransmitters*. These then leap from the axons' sending synapses out across a gap to connect with the receiving synapses on nearby dendrites.

With these transmitters leaping among so many potential receiving synapses, the versatility of that interplay leverages the number of possible synaptic connections in the human brain to a figure quite literally beyond imagining. Some suggest it may exceed the number of atoms in the universe. What's more, the system is in constant flux—its connections shifting and strengthening and weakening as it responds to changing signals from the world around it. Little wonder the attempt to equal all that with a linear processor failed.

Connecting

In broad terms, algorithms are mathematical formulas that build on themselves. For instance, just multiplying times three over and over can produce a simplistic algorithm like 3, 9, 27. But the algorithms used by programmers to write software code are variable and highly complex. They are in essence recipes for making a computer do something, a sequence of steps that leads it to process words when we type them, or find the best route through a network, or manipulate an image in a computer game.

It was John Holland who devised the first "genetic algorithm," which employs evolution to do the hard job of writing code. Working in the early 1960s at the University of Michigan, he imagined how an array of algorithms could compete against one another to solve a problem. In that array, as Holland saw it, each string of numbers would evolve within a set number of steps, until one produced the best solution—in essence until it met a "fitness standard." The winner was selected much as genes are in evolution. It was a striking idea, but it meant running parallel arrays of evolving variations, and at that time there were no true parallel computers to run them on. The big dollars were going to what would become classical AI.

Then, in 1969, a student of Minsky's at MIT—W. Daniel Hillis—devised the first real PDP, or parallel distributed processor. It was an unwieldy beast, with sixty-four thousand processors all hooked together into something no one was at first quite sure what to do with. But building on foundations laid by Holland, Nils Barricelli, and others, Hillis gradually defined a working approach to the programming.

By the mid-seventies his Connection Machine was increasingly recognized as an important development. In 1983 he cofounded a company, the Thinking Machines Corporation, to commercialize it. The motive for the parallel approach was as simple as it was ambitious. "Clearly," said Hillis, "the organizing principle of the brain is parallelism. It's using massive parallelism. The information is in the connection between a lot of very simple parallel units working together. So if we built a computer that was more along that system of organization, it would likely be able to do the same kinds of things the brain does."

The PDP approach was a notable departure, and not only because it looked for inspiration to the brain's neural networks—an approach that came to be called "connectionist." Beyond that, as the top-down approach of classical AI faltered, the new concept represented a polar opposite. By combining parallel architecture with genetic algorithms and "neural net" software—in which connections are strengthened or weakened, depending on how often they're reinforced—it fostered the emergence from the bottom up of something more like real thinking. As noted science writer John Brockman later observed, "Hillis's work demonstrates that when systems are not engineered but instead allowed to evolve—to build themselves—then the resultant whole is greater than the sum of its parts." As Hillis himself would put it:

> I have programs that have evolved within the computer from nothing, and they do fairly complicated things. You begin by putting in sequences of random instructions, and these programs compete and interact with each

other and have sex with each other and produce new generations of programs. If you put them in a world where they survive by solving a problem, then with each successive generation they get better and better at
solving the problem, and after a few hundred thousand generations they
solve the problem very well. That approach may actually be used to produce the thinking machine.

The connectionist approach was taken up with enthusiasm by the
San Diego group. Its members had been frustrated with behaviorism—
the idea that since what went on inside the brain couldn't be modeled,
it wasn't worth considering. Parallel distributed processing freed them
from the many constraints of working with the linear, classical AI machines. It opened the door to exploring new models of how thinking
works. And in that work a principal tool was the genetic algorithm. Said
Sejnowski, "Parallel algorithms are now being discovered that were totally overlooked but are now practical, because the Connection Machine
with 64 thousand processing units can efficiently implement them."
John Koza first taught genetic algorithms how to have sex. A Stanford
University computer scientist and former student of Holland's, Koza
noticed that an evolving formula might not solve a whole problem but
could nonetheless have a component that worked well for part of it. He
came up with a method that encouraged formulas to "interbreed,"
swapping segments and improving until one came out on top. Other researchers noticed that evolving formulas would sometimes begin cen-
tering on half solutions and get stuck there, like mountain climbers who
had successfully scaled a midsize peak but didn't know how to get back
down from there in order to ascend a larger one. The problem was solved
by introducing occasional mutations—random backward steps—into
even the most successful formulas.
As software programs had grown increasingly complex, a related
concern arose. With that complexity, coding errors had become harder
to detect. A space probe to Venus was lost because a single comma got
left out of a crucial line of code. Hillis used PDP to produce a system
where that couldn't happen. To help evolve a multimillion-line naviga-
tion code for airplanes, he developed tiny parasitic programs that he
turned loose on it to try to crash it. His experiments showed that parasites sped up the evolution of a robust, error-free program. Assessing that
success, he said, "Rather than spending uncountable hours designing

code, doing error-checking, and so on, we'd like to spend more time making better parasites!"

As might be expected, solutions arrived at by these means look nothing like the pure, precise, highly distilled equations of formal mathematics. In fact they're a mess, just as they are in nature. Researchers looking at the patterns of natural neurons in a crayfish tail, for instance, reported how amazed they were at the scrambled, inelegant Rube Goldberg contraption they uncovered. Surely, they concluded, human efforts could come up with something more economical. Natural circuits are redundant and circuitous. Rather than remove an error, they detour around it or put in a counterbalancing tendency. But they work; they have far fewer errors. And when errors do occur, they have a quality called "graceful degradation": unlike with the Venus probe, no single small malfunction causes failure of the system.

It's no coincidence that that is one of the real strengths of PDP, as are physical coordination and areas where pattern recognition is key— like hearing, vision, and speech. (This is why Hillis was once hired by the Disney animatronics group to help develop more-lifelike robotic creatures for its films and theme parks.) Other scientists have used distributed arrays to process information in a pattern similar to avian brain circuits in order to localize sound the way a barn owl does.

Varieties of parallel distributed processing also now guide numerous human systems where sheer complexity makes conscious direction infeasible, as in phone networks and financial webs. A DARPA bulletin announces the deployment of artificial neural nets as target-recognition devices in Comanche helicopters, and astronomers use them to parse the vast amount of telescope data streaming in. They are also the key to "data mining," in which, for instance, PDP pattern recognition is linked to databases to extract demographic profiles—to make mailing lists used in direct-mail promotions, to amass credit agency files on individuals and companies, and the like. Agencies that collect these huge centralized stores of private information are coming under increasing fire for their careless practices in disseminating it and their lax security. PDP data mining is also central to the proliferating numbers of surveillance systems being deployed in response to terrorism. And with its ability to recognize faces, even personal gaits, as well as to sift through the enormous quantities of personal information now available on everyone in a wired world, this raises privacy concerns of a kind never before imagined. In a rare public misstep, DARPA floated plans for a Total Information Awareness data-mining system in the United States following the September 11, 2001, terrorist attacks. Those plans were apparently shelved in response to an outcry from liberals and conservatives alike, but continue to spur debate on the thorny question of how to protect people from terrorism while also guarding democratic rights.

Meanwhile, scientists are still tinkering with PDPs in the lab. If they can't yet be said to truly think, they are clearly doing something. One of Koza's programs, by itself, came up with Kepler's Third Law. On his personal Web page at Stanford, Koza describes his efforts to genetically evolve a "result that is publishable in its own right."

Science writer James Hogan, in his thoughtful book *Mind Matters*, has described how distributed networks can exhibit the same kinds of errors in learning that people do. While being trained in English-language verb tenses, one Connection Machine was fed a small list of verbs of the kind children learn early on. At first, the system could only regurgitate what it had been told. But as learning continued, Hogan said, two notable behaviors emerged:

> First, at some point, the network begins generating the standard "ed" past-tense ending for verbs it hasn't seen before. Second, once it has grasped this generalizing principle, it will over-apply it by incorrectly regularizing irregular verbs it had previously completed correctly, such as "goed" instead of "went," and sometimes blending a correct irregular past tense with the regular ending, for example, "camed." Such tendencies strikingly mirror the trial-and-error learning observed in young children.

Compared with classical AI, parallel systems are better at recognizing likenesses between things. They also do better at pulling up references based on associations rather than sorting through strictly defined lists and categories, and they're good in situations where a number of differing constraints have to be considered all at once. They do, however, have trouble with some things that classical AI does well. For instance, if a PDP system is told that "Mary is having a sandwich" and that "John is having a sandwich," it has difficulty understanding they're not the same sandwich. Classical AI also shows better aptitudes for symbol processing, and with rule-based schemes like language or any logic of a systematic nature.

One concern with traditional PDP systems has been that they are uniformly interconnected. Human intelligence includes elements where that is the case, but it also counterbalances very different kinds of systems, and links some more closely than others. The rough beginnings of a solution to this problem can now be seen in hybrid PDP systems that bring the serial-logic processing of classical AI into the mix.

Thinking Machines stopped making PDP computers in 1994. In a sense those first machines were victims of their own success: The parallel concept they advanced had by then expanded outward, to encompass large arrays of individual computers simply wired together over local networks. Then, as major companies like IBM, Hewlett-Packard, and Compaq leaped into networking, the parallel concept expanded outward once again—this time by an order of magnitude. Through the Internet, it is about to encompass the globe. The basic technology is now in place to put the combined processing power of the world's largest supercomputers into the hands of anyone with a Web link.

The Grid

The first big test of what is now called "grid computing" debuted at a San Diego supercomputing conference in 1995. There, eleven high-speed networks were lashed together for three days to create a single meta-computer. Through it conferees could, among the many cool tools on display, try out a working ecosystem model of the Chesapeake Bay and watch spiral galaxies collide. As one of them recalls, "It was the Woodstock of the grid—everyone not sleeping for three days, running around and engaged in a kind of scientific performance art." The project was called I-Way, and it launched what many feel is a major step forward in the evolution of the Internet. In that view, the first step came when computers were hooked together by wires to produce the Internet. The second step was the World Wide Web, which created a common interface, a way of sharing information over the Internet. Now with the third big step—Internet grids—we can share processing power itself.

Just as with the World Wide Web, grids rely on a common interface—in this case the Globus software designed by Ian Foster, a senior scientist at Argonne National Laboratory, and Carl Kesselman, who heads the Center for Grid Technologies at the University of Southern

California (this work was funded by DARPA). Their decision to make Globus open-source—to publish its code for free on the Web—has spurred the rapid rise of grids around the world.

And that rise is truly rapid. Globus was released in 1996. Just three years later in the U.S., the National Science Foundation and the Department of Energy set up their Access Grid—to serve large, multiple-site meetings online—while NASA deployed its Information Power Grid for aerospace and planetary science. Ensuing years brought NSF's Grid Physics Network, Germany's Unicore, the U.K. National Grid, the European DataGrid, and the International Virtual DataGrid Laboratory—the first true global grid, linking supercomputing centers in Europe, the U.S., Japan, and Australia into one behemoth processing entity.

The power of grids is growing, too. In the United States the new, $53 million TeraGrid links four supercomputing clusters into a transcontinental PDP that can process twenty trillion mathematical operations per second. A project called Enabling Grids for E-science in Europe will build the largest international grid so far, linking seventy institutions into a twenty-four-hour grid service with power that equals twenty thousand large computers combined. And the new power is being used: for efforts in climate modeling, gene research, high-end physics, brain studies, even earthquake modeling. It's also being taken up by business.

The drugmaker Novartis recently created an in-house supercomputer by linking twenty-seven hundred of its desktop computers into a private grid for use in drug design. It worked so well that the entire corporate network—seventy thousand personal computers—is now being hooked in. IBM is a major player here. Big Blue is involved in Openlab, the Euro equivalent of TeraGrid. It also built the national grids for the U.K. and the Netherlands, and is grid-enabling many of its own servers. Computer makers around the world are following suit. Software designers, too. Microsoft will build the Globus Toolkit into a version of Windows XP. Meanwhile, IBM, Sun, Hewlett-Packard, and Intel have thrown their weight behind the nonprofit Globus Consortium, which aims to make grid computing more accessible.

The top-down advances put in place by governments and big business are being joined now by a countersurge of development, one emerging from the bottom up. That move employs available downtime on home and business computers, which have been enlisted into meta-networks. "There are 100 million machines hooked to the Internet," says James Gannon, "all of them doing nothing a lot of the time." Gannon is an officer at Parabon Computation, one of a lengthening list of grid start-ups that includes United Devices, Avaki (formerly Applied Meta-Computing), KnowledgePort Alliance, and the San Diego–based Entropia. These companies link idle home and business computers, sometimes vast numbers of them, into parallel distributed systems. Within eighty days of its initial offering, Parabon had enough clients signed up to rank its system among the top one hundred supercomputers in the world.

Informed observers predict that within ten years the combined processing power of the entire world will be melding into one "seamless computational universe" that anyone can tap at any time. This portends real change. As Globus' coinventor Kesselman puts it, "The ultimate goal is a fundamental shift in how we go about solving human problems."

With the grid, we now stand where the Web was in 1994, says Larry Smarr, director of the California Institute for Telecommunications and Information Technology. "What we are seeing," says Smarr, "is the emergence of a new infrastructure upon which first science, and then the whole economy, will be built." Smarr believes the effects of that change may even dwarf the great Internet boom of the 1990s. In his words, the emergence of the grid is "completely transformational."

Save the Robots

While parallel distributed processing made dramatic advances, another aspect of natural intelligence was taking hold on a different front. It sought to address a problem that many had with AI from the start. As Terry Winograd has described it, "The main problem area is one that you can label in different ways: commonsense reasoning, background, context. It is the way in which thinking and language are shaped and affected by the sort of broader, imprecise context of what you know, what is going on, and what is relevant . . . This is not modeled in a straightforward way by rules or algorithms." Addressing the same concern, John Searle has pointed out, "Just as one cannot take a molecule of water and say, 'This one is wet,' so we cannot pick out a single neuron and say, 'This one is thinking about tomorrow's lecture.'"

Where does conscious awareness come from? How do we know if something's relevant? What is it that gives meaning to the obscure sparking of neurons in our brains—that accounts for the pleasure of pleasure, the blueness of blue? Those qualities somehow emerge from underlying structures that seem almost disconnected from the wonders they produce. If we still have no clear fix on how those occur, we do know they arise from the interactions between figure and ground, between individual life forms and the worlds they inhabit. We act on the world while the world acts on us. Without that, words like "relevance" and "awareness" have no meaning. As Searle has pointed out, such things as "a nice day for a picnic" are not inherent features of reality. What we call "a nice day for a picnic," he says, "exists only relative to observers and users."

"The world is its own best model," says Rodney Brooks, the reigning intelligence at MIT's Artificial Intelligence Lab. "Explicit representations in models of the world simply get in the way." By that he means that just programming things in misses the point. Real minds are programmed by engagement with the world. Or, as Brooks put it in a statement that shook up the world of computerized intelligence:

> I wish to build completely autonomous mobile agents that co-exist in the world with humans, and are seen by those humans as intelligent beings in their own right. I will call such agents Creatures . . . I have no particular interest in demonstrating how human beings work, although humans, like other animals, are interesting objects of study in this endeavor as they are successful autonomous agents. I have no particular interest in applications . . . if my goals can be met then the range of applications for such Creatures will be limited only by our own (or their) imaginations. I have no particular interest in the philosophical implications of Creatures, although clearly there will be significant implications.

Creature Features

Brooks' research looks to ethology, the study of how animals interact with their worlds. It sees animal behavior as shaped first by inborn tendencies, and then by what happens when those tendencies meet the influences, obstacles, and rewards of the outside world. After Brooks became director of the AI Lab in 1984, ethology textbooks started turning up on students' bookshelves there. Brooks' strategy was simple: Stop trying to force-feed human intelligence into machines. Just give them a few basic rules, turn them loose in the world, and see what happens.

It seemed to Brooks that the basics, the simple things any two-year-old can do, were actually the hardest part. "Evolution took three billion years to get from single cells to insects," he points out, "but only another 500 million years from there to humans." Culture, reason, abstract thinking—the stuff we're so proud of—took some 100,000 years more, a blink of the eye in evolutionary terms. Which explains why the greater part of the brain is given over to just running the body. Basic skills like mobility and perception, the ways we interact physically with the world, were much more difficult to achieve. Once they were in place the rest was comparatively easy—critical thinking is just a high-level add-on.

Brooks proposed a bottom-up approach to building intelligence. "It is soon apparent," he said in his seminal 1991 paper, "when 'reasoning' is stripped away as the prime component of a robot's intellect, that the dynamics of the interaction of the robot and its environment are primary determinants of the structure of its intelligence."

That insight is nicely illustrated in a passage by the ecologist Paul Shepard. "Terrain structure," he writes, "is the model for patterns of cognition. As children we internalize its order as we practice 'going' from thought to thought, and learn to recognize perceptions and ideas as details in the sweep of larger generalizations." Because minds have the patterns of place imprinted on them, Shepard says, "we describe excursions, like this essay, as a ramble between 'points,' the exploration of 'fields,' following 'paths,' and finding 'boundaries,' 'wastelands,' or 'jungles,' of the difficulty of seeing forests for the trees, of making mountains of mole hills, of the dark and light sides, of going downhill or uphill."

Using the world as its own model can bring surprising results. Ethological studies show that even elemental life forms exhibit what seems like complex, goal-directed behavior by following only a few simple rules of interaction. The coastal snail *Littorina*, for example, has five reactions called variously *dark*, *up*, *bright*, *darker*, and *stop*. The first, *dark*, steers it from the light sandy bottom to dark masses of rock, which are likely to be near the shore. Arriving there, *up* urges it to crawl against the pull of gravity. But when, and only when, the snail finds itself upside down, *bright* kicks in—leading it toward the sky. Once it emerges from the water, *darker* comes into play, guiding it into ever-darker areas, crevices where algae may be growing. If the snail finds itself completely dry, it has gone too far inland, and *stop* brings it to a halt while it waits for a wave to wash it back to sea.

Brooks and his students began making robots with layers of simple instructions like those. Each layer had its own relationship to the world and operated independently of the others. For instance, a first layer might work to avoid bumping into things, while a second sought out distant places to visit. As the second layer guided the creature toward some new vista, the first would continue working independently to veer the creature away from obstacles. Ultimately the second layer would achieve its goal without ever being aware of obstacles, or of the efforts made by the first layer to avoid them—that was all being handled at a lower level of control.

It's now known that when we walk, for instance, similar principles are at work. In reality, walking is so complicated that if we had to be conscious of everything involved there would be far fewer people chewing gum. That in turn has implications for our notions of perception. Rather than being a single unified awareness, as was long believed, perception is now known to be an aggregation of many different kinds of sensibilities, located in a variety of systems and subsystems—with many of them being virtually independent of conscious awareness or intent.

One of the more appealing creatures the AI Lab devised was called Herbert. It was built by graduate student Jon Connell, using ethological studies for inspiration. In particular, Connell had become fascinated by one showing that baby seagulls developed attachments to a rough mockup of a parent gull's head—as long as there was a crucial marker, a red spot, on the end of the mock beak.

Herbert didn't eat fish, though; he collected soda cans. Building on earlier work, Connell gave Herbert obstacle-avoiding reactions and a desire to wander, along with a more specific interest in exploring certain kinds of spaces. A laser-guided soda can finder steered Herbert to a spot in front of a can. When he came to a stop, a searching program activated his arm. It might grope out along a desktop until feeling something that was the shape of a can, then close his hand around it, weigh it to make sure it was empty, and remove it. Finally he carried the can back home for deposit. Many people in the lab had links to Danny Hillis and his Connection Machine, so Herbert was quickly dubbed "the collection machine."

Prior to Brooks, experiments with mobile robots had tried programming them with internal models of the world in which they operated. Largely as a result of that, they were confined to highly simplified environments. Herbert, on the other hand, had no internal model. In fact he had no memory to speak of. What's more, he was just turned loose to wander through the AI Lab, with people walking around, watching him, and deliberately trying to confuse him. But with nothing more than the interaction of a few basic sets of rules, he *seemed* to be doing things that all the earlier attempts had tried to do and failed—things like path planning and map building.

While the grail of higher intelligence necessarily involves learning and education from the top down, in this and in later attempts at more sophisticated creatures Brooks and his students have shown that building from the bottom up is an equally vital process. Along the way they have also supplied evidence for the argument that intelligence is not a single unified process but the interaction of different elements—each with its own character and qualities.

And as work at MIT's AI Lab pushes the limits of simple reactions, across campus Rosalind Picard works on another mental factor.

Motivational Program

"When you have a complex set of goals that a system needs to achieve," says Rosalind Picard, "and there is limited time, and you have limited resources, and the inputs are unpredictable—with the model constantly changing, so you can't just model the space once and solve the problem—then you need regulatory mechanisms to help the computer decide what to do next." Moreover, she adds, a computer needs to know whether "if it is doing one thing, it should drop that and try something else, because there are other things more important." In short, it needs judgment, something to guide its behavior. And human judgment is informed by emotion, says Picard, who heads MIT's Affective Computing Group. "If we want a computer to have those abilities, we are going to have to effectively give it an emotional system."

In his thesis, "Natural Intelligence in Artificial Creatures," Swedish computer scientist Christian Balkenius makes the point that when Pavlov did his famous study—in which dogs salivated at the sound of a dinner bell—he didn't test dogs that weren't hungry. Since a dog won't salivate if it isn't hungry, Balkenius points out, Pavlov's results are compromised. He didn't control for motivation.

Until recently, Picard and her group focused on making computers more responsive to the feelings of humans, but now she's calling for a major new initiative. One of her inspirations for that is the work of Antonio Damasio, whose book *Descartes' Error: Emotion, Reason, and the Human Brain* describes his experience treating emotionally impaired patients. Those patients, who seem strangely unemotional, suffered from a marred rational decision-making that Picard found oddly similar to the brittle expert systems of classical AI.

Discussions at MIT rarely go far without reference to science fiction. Picard alludes to the popular television show *Star Trek: The Next Generation*, in which the android Commander Data can turn his emotions on or off at will. Says Picard, "He clicks off his emotion chip and he functions better than anybody on the ship, right? And then he clicks it on only when he wants to write poetry or be more human. That's wrong. If we click off our emotion 'chip,' so to speak, we become like Damasio's emotion-impaired patients—who instead of being more rational actually have trouble with day-to-day decisions such as when to schedule an appointment. They invest in the wrong things and lose all their money, and keep doing it. They behave irrationally."

"What we don't see," says Picard, "is that emotions inside us are regulating and biasing the rational decision making in everything we do, coloring all of our information . . . If we really clicked off those emotions, we would have some serious problems." Through her reading of Damasio and the work of others in neuroscience, cognitive science, and psychology, Picard came to the view that learning, flexibility, and creativity in thinking can be seriously hampered by a lack of emotion. Looking back, she recalls, "Basically what I said when reading it was, 'Gosh, this is just what computers do. They malfunction in the same ways as these people whose emotions are disconnected.'"

That's one reason why "most of these machines make terrible assistants," she says. "They are fine for use as a hammer or direct communication tool, but when you want to have them do some autonomous task for you, they're terrible . . . We've erred on the side of building these neurologically impaired patients."

Emotion clearly does play a role in mentality. Nature retains few useless features, and the parts of our brains responsible for feelings are still very much alive and kicking. We also know now that they are part of the mental energy that fuels higher cognitive operations. But could there be too much of a good thing? Harvard sociobiologist E. O. Wilson has said,

"If chimpanzees had the atom bomb, we'd all be dead in a matter of weeks." And what about teenagers?

"Yes, for sure," says Picard, "especially if you just think we are giving these machines the ability to have temper tantrums. But that's certainly not what this is about . . . None of us wants to wait for the computer to feel interested in what we have to say before it will listen to us." It's not a question of one or the other, Picard says, adding, "I think balance is the real issue here. I wouldn't hire a secretary because she's more emotional, right? But I also wouldn't hire one that didn't have emotions. That would be just as disastrous . . . What we're looking for is the sweet spot between two extremes."

While the ultimate nature of emotion remains a subject of controversy, work is proceeding. Writes Juan Velasquez, a graduate student who worked with Picard and laid some essential groundwork, "We model affect as a network of reactive emotional systems which represent a basic emotion family such as anger, fear, or disgust. Each of these systems has several sensors, organized into four different groups—neural, sensorimotor, motivational, and cognitive—that represent different kinds of both cognitive and non-cognitive elicitors for the emotion family represented by that particular system."

A charming outgrowth of this work is Kismet, a robotic face and head assembled by Cynthia Breazeal, a grad student in Rodney Brooks' lab, with Picard helping out as an adviser. The project serves as a test platform for behaviors intended for a more elaborate robot named Cog. In building Kismet, Breazeal sought to create a face that actually expresses feelings. Her attempt employs a collection of roughly human features—cartoonlike big blue eyes with eyelids, lips that open and close, pink ears and bushy eyebrows—all hung from an open framework and looking like a symbiotic merger between an Erector set and Mr. Potato Head. Although her features are rudimentary, Kismet still manages to display a certain goofy allure as she works the crowd, trying to elicit emotional responses from those around her.

"Kismet takes advantage of the way we are programmed to interact with small children," Breazeal says. If "shameless" is a word that can be applied to a robot, Kismet is all of that. Left alone, she pouts, but when someone comes along to play, her face lights up—the eyebrows rise as her eyes open wide and ears perk. But should her human companion just repeat the same game over and over, she gets bored and her face droops.

Kismet has a repertoire of nine expressions: anger, fear, happiness, sadness, calm, interest, tiredness, disgust, and surprise. Those are in turn motivated by a set of interacting drives—whose intensities increase or decline based on Kismet's level of satiation. When she's left alone, her social drive increases. When she detects a face nearby, she focuses on it and starts socializing. As she plays, the expression on her face becomes happier while her social drive decreases. But if the interaction becomes too demanding, she scowls with displeasure. "These drives are always changing in time," says Breazeal. "When one need becomes very strong, behaviors such as facial expressions that act to satiate that need become active."

Artificial Behavior

Robotics programs that look to biological models are a familiar presence now at schools with engineering programs. But people like MIT's Mitchel Resnick see that as only the beginning. Resnick is a tall, lanky scientist with a big grin and an engaging manner. With his curly hair, oversize glasses, and rumpled demeanor, he looks a bit like an overgrown kid and in some ways is. But when he talks about the computer toys he designs, he is clearly a thoughtful man. "My academic degree is in computer science," he remarks, "but I have always been very interested in educational issues.

"I want to help get these ideas about biologically based thinking—or what is sometimes called decentralized or ecological thinking—out into the broader culture," he explains. "Because, for me, I'm excited about not just when these ideas start influencing researchers but especially when they enter into the lives of children . . . I think the types of models and metaphors you have for understanding the world as you grow up are very much going to influence the way you see the world later on."

Resnick's group developed the ideas used in the Mindstorms toys now being marketed by Lego—the Danish firm that, with the help of small children, has distributed billions of sharp little plastic blocks beneath the bare feet of yelping parents around the world. "With traditional Legos," he explains, "kids build structures and they build mechanisms but they can't build behaviors. We want to let kids build behaviors." Taking two small gadgets he calls crickets, he places them so that they face each other. "When they see each other, they're so happy they do a little dance," he says, demonstrating. "Now, if I stop them from communicating, they stop dancing. When they see each other again, they start dancing.

"If kids can give simple rules to different robotic creatures and then see the patterns that form through their interaction," Resnick says, "they have to start thinking about that." The Lego Mindstorms series allows children to build robots with some three thousand different programmed behaviors. They can also post their own software creations on the Lego Web site for other kids to try.

With all that, he adds, "ideas about feedback and control—which have traditionally been taught in university-level courses—all of a sudden become accessible to fourth graders. Before, if you went to a school and said, 'We want to add the concept of feedback to the fourth-grade curriculum,' they would say, 'No way. That's an advanced concept. You can't do it here.' But the idea is not an inherently difficult one. It's just been seen as an advanced idea because in the past the only way we could study it was through advanced mathematical formulations. Now we can study it in a way that is accessible to fourth graders."

Resnick boots up a program he calls StarLogo on his computer. By playing with StarLogo, he says, kids can learn about concepts like decentralization and swarm behavior, and about the importance of randomness in creating order. "Now, again," he says, "high school students don't necessarily talk in those terms, but they have learned that in an intuitive way. At a traffic jam, you see the jam, but the constituent parts are changing all the time—if you come a little later, it's a different set of cars. A lot of biological things are that way, even our own bodies. Our cells die off and are replaced by other ones. We are still sort of the same person even though some of the particular parts are changing over time. So that's an important idea."

The number of robotic toys is growing rapidly, though not all of them arise from such mindful concerns. In a spread on the opening page of a section devoted to electronics, *The New York Times* once showed a photo of a small girl with her arms crossed, scowling down at a metallic robot pup. The headline read: "What Do You Mean, 'It's Just Like a Real Dog'?"

The subhead stated, "As Robot Pets and Dolls Multiply, Children React in New Ways to Things That Are 'Almost Alive.'" In the article that followed, developmental psychologist Jean Piaget was cited, and there were comments by Sherry Turkle, a psychoanalyst specializing in how people relate to their computers. The story concluded that since children at play can imagine virtually anything as being alive, it's too soon to say how toys that are "almost alive" may affect them. One thing is clear, there will be no shortage of opportunities to find out.

If Lego Mindstorms was among the earliest and most thoughtful of the new biology toys to reach mass markets, it is hardly alone. Following on the success of Tamagotchis and the cuddly Furby came Sony Corporation's Aibo—a $2,500 robodog that instantly sold out. In short order a pack of clones appeared: Puppy Magic, Tekno, i-Cybie, Me and My Shadow, Poo-Chi, and Rocket the Wonder Dog, as well as Big Scratch and Little Scratch, even a cat called FurReal. The technological mutts feature behaviors ranging from pet tricks to scratching, belching, wiggling, panting, and snuffling. One answers only to its master's voice and looks hapless when it's scolded. Another has magnetic fleas. In Japan now, there are robot aquarium fish.

With all that, could babies be far behind? Enter Mattel's Miracle Moves Baby, a living doll with her Flex-Soft skin, naturalistic movements, twenty sensors, and "personality matrix" capable of expressions ranging from hunger to happiness to sleepiness. Cindy Smart, by Toy Quest, sees, tells time, can do simple math, and speaks in five languages. Not to be outdone, Hasbro has My Real Baby, designed at iRobot—a company cofounded by Rodney Brooks. My Real Baby can scrunch up her face, grumbles when her diaper needs changing, and has language skills that evolve over time. "The kind of software that we use offers a dramatic complexity because it has emergent behaviors," says Helen Greiner, iRobot's president. "We think that makes toys more interesting. They don't entirely do the same thing each time you play with them."

It's ironic that a new generation of toys has been made possible by the military, which is a primary funding source for research in the new biology. From the development of parallel distributed processing to Brooks' lab full of meandering creatures, DARPA dollars are at work. One of the fruits of that labor can be seen at the iRobot shop. DART is a robofish based on the work of Michael Triantafyllou and featuring sophisticated AI guidance for seagoing reconnaissance. Ariel is a waterproof robot that moves like a crab—the prototype for a class of military devices meant to be released in a swarm underwater before the invasion of a hostile shore. The Ariels' mission is to crawl around detecting underwater mines, then detonate them before human personnel make a landing.

In a related development, Marc Raibert's Boston Dynamics is working on a robotic mutt called Big Dog, meant to serve as a pack animal for soldiers in the field. These developments are only the start. The U.S. Congress has mandated that a third of all military deep-strike aircraft and ground vehicles must be robotic by 2010. And according to a 2005 news report, "The Pentagon predicts that robots will be a major fighting force in the American military in less than a decade, hunting and killing enemies in combat." That effort is backed by the largest military contract in U.S. history—a $127 billion project called Future Combat Systems.

The military hasn't figured out yet what to make of Mark Tilden's robots, but he has an office at Los Alamos National Laboratory, near Santa Fe, New Mexico. It's piled with the spare parts from discarded Walkmans, calculators, and other electronic detritus that he uses to build them. Tilden's approach is unique in a couple of ways. For one thing it's cheap. Much of it involves hot-rodding scrap parts that any hobbyist could afford. Also, it's analog. Where the great majority of work in computers and robotics today uses digital processors—with their streams of ones and zeros, binary bits flipping on and off—Tilden's robots run on waves.

His first-generation critters are no more than four inches long and skitter around like insects. They're powered by the solar cells he rescues from busted calculators and have little in the way of programming, beyond a tendency to move toward the light. But they are nonetheless remarkable. Tilden sets a tray of them near a window awash with brilliant daylight. The bugs quickly become animated, forming a pile of scurrying parts as they clamor over each other trying to get near the sun. It's a peculiar and unsettling sight. Early efforts to retail the bugs failed. "They crawled off the shelves," he observes drily. But toy giant Hasbro marketed his next product, the Biologically Inspired Organisms, or "BIO toys." These ready-for-prime-time versions were a foot long, came with sleek carapaces, and featured a variety of different colors and behaviors. The Wow Wee toy company released the third generation of robobugs in 2001, and its technology was later stirred into their Robosapien toy.

As the use of natural principles makes robots more economical, industry has found uses for them, too. Back at iRobot, a thirty-foot tubular worm called MicroRig has been developed to slink on its own down into oil wells. Greiner holds out her hand to display a Holon, which resembles a toy octopus with tentacles made from strands of beads. Like the Ariel, it is, she says, a multiple "redundant mechanism." First spreading its tentacles, then drawing them to one side, then curling them in a ball, she demonstrates all the ways that Holons can move. They're used in Japan to carry sensors into risky areas of nuclear plants. Though it's not from iRobot, the Japanese also have for some years now had a spider robot with sixteen legs that creeps across the surfaces of fuel storage tanks looking for cracks.

Back on the home front, iRobot's Roomba Intelligent FloorVac—which looks like a Frisbee on steroids—uses lessons learned from Herbert, the soda can "collection machine," to navigate around a room as it vacuums the floor. It can be purchased at conventional retail outlets throughout the U.S.

Evolutionary Robotics

When the makers of gear that employs silicon chips build a prototype, or ship a new product, they assume that bugs in the system will turn up. Because of that, early versions of electronics products are sometimes made with a chip called a field-programmable gate array, or FPGA. These contain arrays of gates (the "and"s, "or"s, and "not"s that lie at the heart of a logical system) as well as input and output feeds, which can be reprogrammed in the field. FPGAs are slower than chips designed for a single purpose, but their advantage lies in the costs saved by not having to manufacture new chips once the inevitable problems arise.

When scientists working with genetic algorithms saw all those switchable elements, they made the obvious connection: here was an evolvable hardware. An Australian named Hugo de Garis was the first to imagine the possibility of evolving chips in response to specific tasks by using genetic algorithms. The concept was later confirmed by Japan's Tetsuya Higuchi. Then, in 1995, working in England, Adrian Thompson was the first to generate an evolved hardware control circuit for a robot.

In a 2000 book, *Evolutionary Robotics*, Stefano Nolfi and Dario Floreano of the National Research Council in Rome documented the evolution of robot evolvability. They described studies in which robo-insects taught themselves to walk, robosalamanders taught themselves to swim, and a robodog taught itself to walk more efficiently than it could with a program designed by humans. Their book culminated with a look down the road at the next frontier—evolvable bodies. In that context they mentioned promising experiments by Jordan Pollack and Hod Lipson of Brandeis University in Waltham, Massachusetts.

In the summer of 2000, Pollack and Lipson delivered on that promise by creating the first robot able to design and build other robots. They published their results in the journal *Nature*, a leading science forum. Their team managed the feat by hooking a PDP system to a 3-D rapid-prototyping machine—the device used for creating 3-D plastic test models. They gave their PDP a list of parts it could use, basic information on friction and the laws of gravity, and a goal of moving across a level surface. Then, providing it with plans for two hundred nonworking designs, they turned the system loose.

After several hundred generations its genetic algorithm program evolved a working design and the prototyping machine began fabricating odd, small creatures that look vaguely like crabs made of plastic triangles. Although humans had to be employed to install the motors and download the new programming into them, the robot offspring were otherwise developed without human interference or control. Says Pollack, "They were not engineered by humans, and they were not manufactured by humans."

Although the robots created were nowhere near as complex as the equipment that begat them, they struck many as evidence of yet another hurdle overcome in the narrowing gap between real life forms and artificial ones. As one news report put it, the Brandeis project "revives concerns that computer scientists could eventually create a robotic species that would supplant biological life, including humans."

Those concerns were not allayed by news, the same year, that the roboticist Stuart Wilkinson had created a device named Chew Chew that gets its energy by eating food. Wilkinson, of the University of South Florida in Tampa, equipped his "gastrobot" with microbial fuel cells that digest carbohydrates, converting them to electrical power. He envisions vegetation munchers that run off the lawn grass they clip, or that are programmed as "ecological antibodies" that eat kudzu and other alien species. A parallel effort by a team in England is developing a robot that will feed on garden slugs—a more nutritious form of pest. And once there's a flesh-eating "slugbot," some wonder, can a meat eater be far behind?

For those who need still more to worry about, the software engineer Peter Bentley, writing on self-evolving and self-healing software, reports a breaking development in evolvable hardware. "One of the most promising innovations," he says, "is the modular transformer robot (M-TRAN) built at Japan's National Institute of Advanced Industrial Science and Technology . . . It comprises many modules with joints that can stick together in different ways, just like real cells. The robot can dynamically form legs and walk, then rebuild itself and squirm along the ground like a worm. Recent work has used computer evolution to control the robot. There is every chance that the use of developmental process with such hardware could produce the first self-designing, self-building, self-repairing robots within two years."

In 1950 Isaac Asimov wrote *I, Robot*, a collection of stories that included "The Three Laws of Robotics"—a guide for how to program robots so they can do us no harm. Over the years his laws became a protective invocation for people concerned about the growing numbers and power of robots. The laws were reassuring in their simplicity:

> 1—A robot may not injure a human being, or, through inaction, allow a human being to come to harm. 2—A robot must obey the orders given it by human beings except where such orders would conflict with the First Law. 3—A robot must protect its own existence as long as such protection does not conflict with the First or Second Law.

But there's a problem with Asimov's laws. They are designed to deal with robots that will do what we tell them to—which is contrary to the main thrust of research in artificial intelligence today. "It seems to me," says Rosalind Picard, reflecting the opinion of most cutting-edge scientists in her field, "that to get really smart machines, you sort of have to let them control themselves."

Even ten years ago it was becoming clear that big changes are on the way. Speaking at the time, Danny Hillis said, "We're beginning to depend on computers that use a process very different from engineering, a process that allows us to produce things of much more complexity than we could with normal engineering. Yet we don't quite understand the possibilities of that process, so in a sense it's getting ahead of us. We're now using those programs to make much faster computers so that we will be able to run this process much faster. The process is feeding on itself . . . We're analogous to the single-celled organisms when they were turning into multicellular organisms. We're the amoebas, and we can't figure out what the hell this thing is that we're creating."

It is haughty of us, Hillis said, to think we're the end product of evolution, and he was not alone. Philosopher Daniel Dennett counseled, "If we are to make further progress in artificial intelligence, we have to give up our awe of living things." Visionary roboticist Hans Moravec predicted that "by 2040, the robots will be as smart as we are." Ray Kurzweil, the famed inventor, agreed, as did futurist Vernor Vinge, who said, "Within thirty years, we will have the technological means to create superhuman intelligence. Shortly after, the human era will be ended." Responding to the many skeptics those pronouncements have aroused, George Dyson, in his book *Darwin Among the Machines*, replied, "The emergence of life and intelligence from less-alive and less-intelligent components has happened at least once."

Asked if computers will succeed us, MIT's Rodney Brooks turns the question on its head. "You can't know, because it's so hypothetical," he says. "But I think to a certain extent we're going to have to face issues like this a lot earlier than we think. But it's going to be the cyborg, the melding of silicon and living things. That's where these issues are going to occur first. It's not going to be purely intelligent robot versus current existing life form . . . It's going to be humans mixed with silicon, and the basic intelligence is still going to be human intelligence.

"So mind you, once we get through that, if we get through that, or how we get through that, who knows what it's going to be later on? Because just that is going to be such a shattering debate for what humankind is. It's going to transform the whole landscape so much, and it's coming.

"The intelligent robot that is as good as a human, or supersedes a human, I don't think I'm going to see that. I'd love to, I mean that's what my life's work is dedicated to. But realistically I don't think I'm going to see that . . . Not that we won't have really intelligent machines, but they aren't going to be introduced into this world. They are going to be introduced into a transformed world that we can't even begin to imagine."

Toward that end a UC San Diego team, led by physicist Henry Abarbanel, has connected lobster neurons to a circuit they made using $7.50 worth of parts bought at RadioShack. According to Abarbanel, the living cells and electronic circuit worked smoothly as a single unit. That work is supplemented by advances in "neurocomputing" by Georgia Tech's Steve Potter and others. The University of Florida's Thomas DeMarse has taught a dish filled with 25,000 living rat neurons laid on a grid of sixty electrodes to fly an F-22 fighter jet simulator. And at Arizona State University in Tempe and the Neurosciences Institute near San Diego, researchers have implanted electrodes in the brains of monkeys, who can now move a robotic hand and a cursor on a computer screen with only their thoughts. Companies with names like Advanced Bionics, Cyberkinetics, and Neural Signals (led by pioneering neuroscientist Philip Kennedy) are working with human paralytics, aiming to give them similar abilities.

With all this activity, can Brooks' cyborg mind meld be far off? A group at Cornell has used DARPA funding to develop a bio-silicon Hybrid Information Appliance that instead of relying on batteries can be fed with sugar in the field, and DARPA has awarded millions to the Brain-Machine Interface Program.

As artificial intelligence continues to evolve, it feeds into yet another new field: "complexity." If AI aims to mimic the dynamics of individual minds, the science of complexity looks to a broader dynamic—that of large numbers of individuals interacting in complex systems. How do order and chaos work together in sustaining life? Why do higher levels of organization keep emerging in nature? At places like the Santa Fe Institute, out in the rugged landscape of the American Southwest, scientists are coming up with provocative new clues.

five

interacting parts

Traveling on the mile-high plateau around Santa Fe, New Mexico, is like roaming the floor of the universe. The ancient volcanic land spreads out in great dry vistas that crack suddenly into gorges, and the sky seems to rise up forever. Beyond the city limits, the human imprint is slight. Dirt roads fade away toward the hills. Old pickup trucks baked and bleached by the sun rattle among enduring small settlements of one-story adobe buildings. Older still are the pueblos, graceful structures that might have emerged from the ground itself.

The human landscape here is a complex mix of cultures. With the mystical Zuni, Catholic Penitentes, Buddhist adepts, and assorted new age apostles, as well as the particle physics wizards in Los Alamos and artificial life experts at the Santa Fe Institute, few regions boast so many different kinds of seekers. The most quixotic search among them may be a scientific effort—one to track how raw matter emerged into the complex structures and interactions of life.

That search begins with a crucial gap in our knowledge. At the most basic level quantum theory offers persuasive, if curious, explanations for the conduct of particles and atoms. At the high end of the scale, biology gives good descriptions of life forms and their functions. But the magical and elemental question remains.

The tendency of matter to self-organize into life forms, and of life forms to join into ever more complex and ever more interactive systems is one of the enduring mysteries. How do groups of molecules assemble into the ribosomes that build proteins? What makes cells self-organize into the structures in organs, or the walls of arteries that pulse? How do individually dumb social insects like ants attain such high communal intelligence? Why do all organisms link up with whatever other organisms are handy to form ecosystems?

The study of evolution began with the relationship between figure and ground, with the interaction between a single organism and its environment. The larger study of living systems—what are termed "complex adaptive systems"—adds a new dimension. It looks at how the many dynamic parts in those systems interact and how higher levels of organization emerge from their interaction. The results suggest there are other principles at work—beyond natural selection—in the development of life. With that, words like "emergence" and "complexity" have taken on new meaning.

Getting Organized

"If we can discover organizing principles in biology other than evolution, it means we will be able to make living systems in the laboratory," says David Pines. A physicist at Los Alamos National Laboratory, near Santa Fe, Pines is a codirector of ICAM, the University of California's recently formed Institute for Complex Adaptive Matter. ICAM's researchers are looking at what Pines calls the "mesoscale," the realm of matter just below the threshold of life. In that world the predictable equations of atomic physics enter into the more complex realm of self-organization, of dynamic processes that resist easy measure or description. As Pines and a group of ICAM colleagues put it:

> The miracles of nature revealed by modern molecular biology are no less astonishing than those found by physicists in macroscopic matter. Their existence leads one to question whether as-yet-undiscovered organizing principles might be at work at the mesoscopic scale, at least in living things. This is by any measure a central philosophical controversy of modern science, for a commonly held view is that there are no principles in biology except for Darwinian evolution. But what if this view is just a consequence of our inability to see?

We don't know much about the mesoscopic realm because we don't have tools that can see it. Atoms and molecules can be viewed with today's scanning-force electron microscopes, which makes them useful in nanotechnology. But they disrupt the delicate, shifting interactions of the mesoscale. And conventional optical microscopes see little beneath the level of cells and their organs. Says Robert Laughlin, a physicist at Stanford University and an ICAM member, "We are blinded to the area where self-organization is happening."

What little we have managed to learn about that supple world is remarkable. For example, it has long been thought that when a chain of amino acids folds into one of the complex molecules we call proteins, the same amino acids always make the same protein. By using data inferred from nuclear magnetic resonance experiments, ICAM scientists have clarified that a specific chain of amino acids can fold itself into many different proteins. Stranger still, a single type of protein can be created by any one of a dazzling variety of amino acid chains.

How that could be remains something of a puzzle, one that illustrates the magnitude of the challenge. Even so, most ICAM researchers resist the temptation to fill in gaps in their understanding with theoretical computer models. That they lack hard experimental data to form theories might be a weakness, Laughlin concedes. But, he adds, "admitting it is a strength."

Complex Adaptive Systems

Scientists at the Santa Fe Institute, or SFI, approach that question from the other side. Theoretical computer models are primary tools here, and few of the world's research centers have employed them with more effect.

It was in 1984 that a group of senior scientists affiliated with Los Alamos conceived SFI. That group included Pines, as well as chemist George Cowan, who became the institute's first president, and the physicist Murray Gell-Mann, who became its chairman of the board. A Nobel laureate and one of the world's leading particle physicists, Gell-Mann believed the deterministic program he had come to dominate was only one part of the puzzle. Through a series of informal meetings the group eventually settled on the notion of a cross-disciplinary center. Gell-Mann pushed for making it as broad as possible, with an emphasis on theory and the use of computers.

Like the ICAM effort, research at the Santa Fe Institute tracks the emergence of complex systems, of individual parts interacting to produce higher levels of organization. But beyond its emphasis on computer models, it also differs from ICAM in its broader scope: encompassing physics, mathematics, molecular and evolutionary biology, ecology, neurobiology, psychology, linguistics, economics, anthropology, and—it sometimes seems—the pet subject of anyone interesting who walks in the door. As one resident has put it, "This place *is* a complex adaptive system."

In the two decades of SFI's existence, its open, adaptive structure has drawn a host of luminaries through that door. Pines is on the science board, along with genetic algorithm creator John Holland and Caltech's Frances Arnold, the directed evolution pioneer. So are MIT's Mitchel Resnick and Rodney Brooks. Chaos theorists J. Doyne Farmer and Norman Packard passed through here before going on to form a company that forecasts the probability of financial market fluctuations, and they are still involved. Stewart Brand has been an adviser for more than a decade. Stanford economist Brian Arthur has long been affiliated, as has Stuart Kauffman, the well-known theoretical biologist. It was here that computer scientist Chris Langton helped to spawn one of the new biology's more exotic fields—artificial life.

At first glance Gell-Mann, the ace reductionist, would seem an unlikely champion for SFI's broad and inclusive "crude look at the whole," as he calls it. His lean, hawklike visage and penchant for biting remarks are known throughout the scientific community. Acknowledging that he's "one of the great thinkers," AI expert Marvin Minsky adds, "Murray has developed one of the best inventories of put-downs that exists." Whatever the truth in that, there's little doubt that having a brilliant and notorious skeptic like Gell-Mann at the helm has lent credence to the often controversial work of SFI scientists.

Moreover, in lending his formidable intellect and reputation to the institute, Gell-Mann pointed the way for a new generation. Says the astrophysicist Martin Rees, "Particle physicists have often been ultra-elitist, regarding their subject as being the highest paradigm, toward which all other sciences should strive. Murray is now emphasizing clearly that many other sciences are equally difficult and challenging, because of complexity."

That emphasis is yet another step in the shift away from a strictly mechanical outlook. Belief in the deterministic character of classical physics—that it represents the foundation of reality—is a cornerstone of the machine metaphor. Some five hundred years ago the scientific revolution that launched our modern world was founded on that belief, and on the ensuing conclusion that natural systems were best understood by reducing them to their parts.

In that view nature was just a big machine. Once we knew the parts and how they worked, their collective behavior was predetermined. That view was forcefully stated in the dictum of eighteenth-century mathematician Pierre-Simon Laplace. As he famously claimed, to an intellect that knew all the laws and elements of the universe, "nothing would be uncertain for it, and the future, like the past, would be present to its eyes."

Not so, says Gell-Mann. "Even if the initial condition of the universe and the fundamental law of the elementary particles and their interactions are both exactly known," he explains, "the history of the universe is still not determined. Instead, quantum mechanics gives only probabilities for alternative histories of the universe." That means we each owe our existence not only to underlying laws but to "the relentless operation of chance."

Natural selection gives form and direction, Gell-Mann says, but no certainty. And research in complex systems provides another reason we can't just add up the parts to understand the whole. That's because "higher-level phenomena" can emerge from the interaction of simpler parts—as when inert molecules assemble themselves into the structures of living cells. This suggests other effective organizing principles at work. Some in the field speculate that there may be a critical mass of complexity, at which those systems become adaptive. Could that be, they ask, how life first took form?

Putting the Pieces Together

Those who ponder complexity may be unsure of just how that transformation happens, but, as the running gag has it, at least they're perplexed on a higher and more significant level. And there are provocative clues. Gell-Mann describes one of them. He points out how a system that is highly random, with virtually no regularities, has little or no complexity. Nor, he adds, does one that is completely regular. Complex adaptive systems "function best in a regime intermediate between order and disorder." Mathematician Stephen Farrier uses a metaphor to describe that. "Imagine a set of letters that is completely ordered—all *A*s, followed by *B*s, followed by *C*s—to one side," he says, "and a different set of letters that is scattered in a completely random sequence on the other. Then, between them, the works of Shakespeare."

What does that mean for organisms? Writes SFI's Kauffman, in his book *At Home in the Universe: The Search for Laws of Self-Organization and Complexity*:

> To engage in the Darwinian saga, a living system must first be able to strike an internal compromise between malleability and stability. To survive in a variable environment, it must be stable, to be sure, but not so stable that it remains forever static. Nor can it be so unstable that the slightest internal chemical fluctuation causes the whole teetering structure to collapse.

Briefly put: life exists in the sweet spot between order and chaos.

Kauffman—a MacArthur "genius award" recipient—first arrived at SFI from the University of Pennsylvania, where he had taught biochemistry. Before that he'd studied philosophy at Dartmouth and Oxford, then gone on to a medical degree. But his interests have always included theories of the origin of life. While at Penn, Kauffman developed computer models of how random collections of molecules self-assemble into coherent structures. He calls the outcome of that process "order for free."

By that he means the reverse of that tendency for all systems to disorganize (as in the 2nd Law of Thermodynamics). He also means the reverse of that sensitivity to initial conditions found in chaos theory—as when the flapping wings of a butterfly in Rio de Janeiro set off escalating patterns of chaos that result in windstorms over Texas. He's talking instead about convergence, as in the ICAM experiments, where very different amino acid chains can each somehow fold to make exactly the same protein.

No organism can create itself, but what Kauffman's controversial models suggest is that if everything in a pot catalyzes at least one of the reactions needed for life, together they can give rise to a whole that's greater than the sum of their parts. As he puts it, "If you have complex enough systems of polymers [like amino acids] capable of catalytic action, they'll self-organize into an autocatalytic system and, essentially, simply be alive." Darwin's great insight was to recognize how natural selection imposes order on nature. But if there's order for free, Kauffman says, "then some of the order you see in organisms is not due to selection. It is due to something somehow inherent in the building blocks."

There are broad implications in that. "Not only does metabolic life begin whole and complex," he writes in *At Home*, "but all the panoply of mutualism and competition that we think of as an ecosystem springs forth from the very beginning. The story of such ecosystems at all scales is the story not merely of evolution, but of coevolution. We have all made our worlds together for almost four billion years."

Going Through a Phase

If Kauffman is right, his concept implies that this pattern is consistent for every scale at which elements interact—from the molecules that combine to make cells to the life forms that combine to make ecosystems. It means that the spontaneous emergence of order from the interaction of random parts is a basic property of life. In that view, life manifests a kind of phase shift—from randomness into coherence—which can be seen in *all* complex adaptive systems at *every* level. The flocking of birds and the schooling behavior of fish are loosely structured examples. A traffic jam—which keeps its shape and location even as some cars leave the front and more cars join from behind—is another. As computer scientist Mitchel Resnick has described it, in his book *Turtles, Termites, and Traffic Jams*:

> Ant colonies, highway traffic, market economies, immune systems—in all of these systems, patterns are determined not by some centralized authority but by local interactions among decentralized components. As ants forage for food, their trail patterns are determined not by the dictates of the queen ant but by local interactions among thousands of worker ants. Patterns of traffic arise from local interactions among individual cars. Macroeconomic patterns arise from local interactions among millions of buyers and sellers. In immune systems, armies of antibodies seek out bacteria in a systematic, coordinated attack—without any "generals" organizing the overall battle plan.

The same holds true elsewhere in our bodies. New cells are created from the fresh energy and building blocks we take in as food, even as older cells are broken down and their parts cast off as waste. Yet despite that ongoing flow of energy and materials through us, we continue to be relatively stable, coherent entities for as long as we're alive.

Emerging Trend

The effort to model complex adaptive systems, in all their diversity, has also been informed by the study of artificial life. "My background is a mongrel, mainly because I was sort of following a scent," says Chris Langton. An undergraduate in philosophy and anthropology, he went on to take his master's and Ph.D. in computer science at the University of Michigan, in the department that was also home to John Holland. There, his adviser was editing and completing some aspects of John von Neumann's work. The computational descendants of von Neumann's so-called cellular automata—the interactive computer programs he developed in the 1950s at Princeton's Institute for Advanced Study—are now part of an effort to model one of the unifying principles in life.

Langton was involved in that effort early on. His epiphany came after a hang glider accident; he broke multiple bones, then spent months in bed thinking about the big questions. Little more than a decade later, Langton had become a pivotal figure in the study of "artificial life," a term he coined.

The line connecting von Neumann to Langton is a serendipitous one. After the initial work at the Institute for Advanced Study (IAS), scientific interest in cellular automata languished. In the late sixties, famed University of Cambridge mathematician John Horton Conway used them to create his Game of Life, based on the ancient Asian board game Go. But the next real attention to them came in the 1970s from Stephen Wolfram, the cranky, eccentric child prodigy who coasted through Oxford as a teenager and had received his doctorate from Caltech by the time he was twenty. From there Wolfram joined the IAS group, where he shrugged off other promising career paths to pursue the study of cellular automata (even though they were then looked on by most scientists as irrelevant). An IAS colleague named Norman Packard shared his interest and they began working together.

Growing up in the Southwest, Packard and his friend Doyne Farmer had invented a concealed computer system. It was hooked to a minicam hidden in eyeglasses and to unseen switches in the soles of their shoes. Their goal was to predict the behavior of those shiny steel balls spinning around Las Vegas roulette wheels. In the end, their winnings were limited by casino security measures, not to mention the unpredictable nature of the problem. But the effort awoke in both of them an interest in the chaotic behavior of physical systems. Farmer eventually turned up at Los Alamos, where he worked at the Center for Nonlinear Studies and later set up the Complex Systems Group. In 1985, Packard joined his old friend there to cochair a conference called "Evolution, Games, and Learning."

Sounding a note that is a recurring theme for the new biology, in their opening comments they told the audience they would "bring together the study of adaptive processes in nature and their implementation in artificial systems." Among those listening was Langton, who had come there as a postdoc. At Los Alamos two years later, on September 21, 1987, Langton opened the first conference on artificial life.

Imitation of Life

The study of artificial life, or A-Life, as it is frequently called now, involves three interrelated efforts. For convenience' sake they are generally termed "soft," "hard," and "wet." Wet artificial life aims to create actual living cells from nonliving matter and is currently in a nascent stage. Efforts at producing hard A-Life are somewhat more developed, as in the evolutionary robotics described in chapter 4. Soft A-Life has seen the most progress. It is the design of software entities that act out virtual "lives" inside computers. These include everything from Karl Sims' charming "blocky" creatures (in which separate "chunks" program themselves into odd and whimsical combinations that swim, lumber around, and jump in the air) to Tom Ray's evolving complex system Tierra and beyond. It is through those software efforts that A-Life offered its first blush of insights into living processes.

Soft A-Life involves a number of loosely related concepts—among them genetic algorithms, chaos theory, attractors, phase shifts, and fractals. But near its heart are cellular automata. That system, developed by John von Neumann with his colleague Stanislaw Ulam, and later Nils Barricelli, is a gridlike checkerboard of squares (the cells), each of which can change in response to changes in neighboring squares.

To imagine that, picture a grid in which all the squares are blue but are programmed to turn yellow whenever a neighbor does. With that simple rule the introduction of just one yellow square into the grid sends a wave of phase shifts rippling across the board as each square in turn blinks to yellow. More complex rules can send striking and intricate patterns unfolding across the grid. Still, comparing those first cellular automata to their current offspring is like comparing a game of tic-tac-toe to what happens when a chess grand master takes on the latest number-crunching behemoth from IBM.

Chris Langton soon found his way to SFI, where, with a program called Swarm, he and his colleagues freed digital creatures from the rigors of the grid. "It's like cellular automata," he says, "except that you can put pieces on the game board that will move around and change neighborhoods. Or new ones can come and old ones die out. So it's much more dynamic." To demonstrate that, he displays a computer screen dotted with glowing red lumps: "warm" spots that are gradually dissipating heat. Wandering randomly among them are small green "bugs" whose programmed goal in life is to maintain a given body temperature. The bugs, like any living thing, also dissipate some heat. Because of that, when they run into one another, they tend to stay together. As the situation evolves, a higher-level behavior emerges: they eventually form up into jostling flocks at a comfortable distance from the glowing red spots—like moths around a flame.

While such nonlinear experiments can sound exotic, Langton demurs. "Stan Ulam said that calling this the study of nonlinear systems was like calling zoology the study of non-elephant animals," he says. "The point is that most of the world and nature and the physical universe is fundamentally nonlinear . . . It's changing all the time; it has dynamics. Most of mathematics wants to compress dynamics out of the system and just give you the stable point. But for things like economies and evolution, for ecosystems—and for a lot of other interesting things—you're not going to see a stable point."

Using tools like Swarm, computers have now given rise to complex virtual ecosystems in which digital creatures compete, reproduce, and evolve. And unlike the artificial selection that takes place with directed evolution—where the goal is to evolve things like medical molecules or AI circuits for some specified use—the evolution of A-Life is open-ended by design. This approach was an effort to mirror the real world, where "a strategy doesn't have intrinsic value; it has value only in the context of an ecology of other strategies." For the most part, Langton says, "Nature has learned how to bring about organization without em-

ploying a central organizer . . . In fact, natural systems didn't evolve under conditions that particularly favored central control. Anything that
existed in nature had to behave in the context of a zillion other things
out there behaving and interacting with it." This is "a very distributed,
massively parallel architecture."

The Sweet Spot

These artificial worlds take shape from the bottom up. They are also
transient. It was Norman Packard and Chris Langton who first spotted
the tendency of digital ecologies to emerge in the "zone between order
and chaos." Langton then noticed that as a system approaches that region—the sweet spot of greatest adaptability—it tends to slow down, as
if trying to surf along on a wave. Soon Kauffman was suggesting that
evolution might select for systems better able to do that.

Travels with My Ant

If there's a poster child for the artificial life community, says Mitchel
Resnick, it is the ant. Pictures of ants decorate announcements for conferences and illustrate articles. Ant colonies are subjects for research on
complexity and emergent behavior. *The Ants*, a standard reference work
by Harvard professors Bert Hölldobler and E. O. Wilson, has become a
kind of A-Life cult classic.

   Emergence, in this sense, is the phenomenon by which one ant isn't
very smart but a colony of them somehow is. Early on, Chris Langton
had been impressed with a comment by AI pioneer Herbert Simon. "An
ant, viewed as a behaving system, is quite simple," Simon said. "The apparent complexity of its behavior over time is largely a reflection of the
complexity of the environment in which it finds itself." This begins to
explain the often amazing communal intelligence of ants—for instance,
as they create a bridge with their bodies from one tree to a second so others can scurry across. As science writer Kevin Kelly observes:

> An army of ants too dumb to measure and too blind to see far can rapidly
> find the shortest route across a very rugged landscape. This calculation
> perfectly mirrors the evolutionary search: Dumb, blind, simultaneous
> agents trying to optimize a path on a computationally rugged landscape.
> Ants are a parallel processing machine.

Examples like this have given rise to the theory that all interactions of organisms with their environments, even those of bacteria, are in some sense cognitive. Moreover, a colony of social insects like ants can be seen as a single, distributed organism—with freely mobile "cells" that are linked not by neurons but by chemical signals.

For instance, in many ant species, when an individual finds food, it drops a pheromone trail as it carries a particle back to the nest. Then, as other ants come across that trail, they follow it to the food, reinforcing it as they return home with their own particles. In a short time, there's a strong chemical trail with marching columns of ants transporting the new food source to the nest. Only ants carrying food leave pheromones, so when the food is used up, they no longer reinforce the trail. It begins to evaporate and the ants stop following it.

But that's only one element of a colony's foraging strategy. Ant researcher Jean-Louis Deneubourg of the Free University of Brussels points out that ants don't follow pheromone trails perfectly. A typical percentage of them will always stray off course and wander aimlessly away. Deneubourg doesn't see that as a defect, though. He views that randomness as adaptive behavior. To demonstrate why, he and his colleagues set up an experiment. They put a poor food source near a nest and a rich one farther away, then watched to see what would happen. The ants found the near source first and rapidly formed a trail, but some kept wandering off it. Eventually those lost ants stumbled onto the rich food source and formed an alternative trail leading there. The pheromones an ant leaves indicate the quality of the food, so as increasing numbers of ants switched over, the trail to the richer source soon became the stronger of the two.

For the ants, disciplined following of the trail to a food source is the key to its exploitation, but randomness is the key to new exploration. This mirrors early work done with genetic algorithms, which would often evolve to a modest adaptive peak, but then got hung up there, unable to descend into a valley of lower efficiency so they could find a new and potentially higher peak. In that case, programmers found they had to introduce random mutations into even the most effective programs, to prevent them from locking into a less-than-optimum feedback loop. They saw that randomness as kin to the mutations that occur in living genomes.

So it's significant that—at a higher level of organization—the same is true for the ants. Perfect adherence to a single path could delay, or even prevent, them from stumbling across a better food source. Total randomness would fail to deplete even the first one. Between order and chaos, the colony has found an interactive sweet spot in which the ants can thrive.

Bugs in the System

Ants are thriving electronically, too. Their foraging strategies have attracted the attention of major telecom companies, which have started using digital pheromone trails to steer traffic in overburdened networks. Phone systems work through myriad nodes, each of which employs a routing table to determine how best to steer each signal on through the network. In the new approach virtual ants are continuously sent down possible routes. Where the ants find congestion and delay along their way, they leave fainter trails—as numeric signals—in the nodes that might route calls through that area. But if the ants find a clear channel, they leave a richer signal. Just as in nature, the trails fade away if they aren't reinforced, so when a new route becomes congested, the system quickly adjusts.

Several phone companies are either using or exploring this approach, including France Télécom and BT (formerly British Telecom) in Europe and MCI in the United States. In the long run the Internet may become the ultimate virtual ecosystem for virtual ants. Traffic is especially unpredictable there, and numerous tests have shown that ant-based routing is superior to the protocol now in use. Some A-Life experts have voiced concerns that turning loose vast populations of digital ants to wander around on their own through the Web may spawn unpredictable emergent behaviors—a natural worry, given how computer viruses have found a home there.

Contagious Concepts

The first predatory digital organisms were created at AT&T's famous Bell Labs in the 1960s. Based on von Neumann's automata theory, they were in essence digital gladiators in a game called Darwin, which the Bell scientists invented to amuse themselves. One of the players, Robert Morris, developed a cyber-warrior that won consistently by using adaptive behavior. It not only learned from its battles but passed those lessons on to offspring.

The self-replicating fighters of Darwin never left the bowels of Bell Labs. But in 1983, a graduate student named Fred Cohen took things another step into the future. A computer theory and robotics major at the University of Southern California, Cohen became the father of the modern computer virus when he released his thesis project into the UNIX environment of the university's VAX 11/750 computer. Although he had the school's approval for the experiment, it's doubtful they grasped the implications of what Cohen would ultimately describe as "a program that can 'infect' other programs by modifying them to include a possibly evolved copy of itself."

Any doubts about the potential of online viruses were put to rest in 1988. That's when a Cornell University student named Robert Morris, Jr., son of the Darwin game champ, turned loose what would come to be known as the Internet Worm. The infamous virus infected thousands of academic and military computers, crashing databases and causing a national uproar. Spurred by DARPA's Computer Emergency Response Team, antiviral strategies were quickly devised. Congress mulled a Computer Virus Eradication Act while other agencies proposed a Center for Virus Control, to be modeled on Atlanta's Centers for Disease Control. In that single year the number of known viruses increased from seven to thirty. One late-night comedian warned computer users to "remember, when you connect with another computer, you're connecting to every computer that computer has ever connected to."

None of this was lost on A-Life exponents. Langton's 1987 conference had spurred interest in digital life forms, and computer viruses looked like a candidate. Biological viruses are just strands of DNA or RNA in a protein wrapper—essentially, naked germ lines. They can't reproduce on their own, so they invade a host cell and commandeer its reproductive functions, redirecting them to make more viruses. Because viruses can't reproduce themselves, most biologists stop short of calling them alive. Even so, many A-Life researchers felt that with digital viruses they had found entry into the big tent of biology. There was no denying the interesting parallels between their viruses and nature's. But there was also an important difference—unlike the digital warriors of Darwin, early Internet viruses didn't know how to evolve.

Virtual Evolution

Leave that to Tom Ray. He began his career in the tropical forests of Costa Rica as an unassuming Harvard grad student, digging ant colonies from the jungle floor and shipping them back to Cambridge, to renowned entomologist E. O. Wilson. While tracking ants through the forest, Ray came across something that awoke his interest in natural interactions. He noticed that as army ants swarmed across a landscape devouring the animals they met, clouds of escaping insects rose up from the foliage along the way. And because of that, the ants were being followed by birds who had learned to feed on the insects. But that wasn't all, for the birds in turn were followed by an obscure species of butterfly that fed on their droppings, a rich source of the nitrogen it needed for egg laying. Ray watched in awe as the motley procession of nomads— ants, insects, birds, butterflies—careened through the underbrush like a circus on parade.

He was struck by the complexity of that movable feast. How, he wondered, did all those interacting parts ever come to link up—how did they coevolve? By the time he received his Ph.D., his interest had shifted away from the fruits of evolution and onto evolution itself. He had a problem with that, however. There was no way to actually watch things evolve. Evolution works over millions of years. To a scientist with less than a century for observation, it seems to be standing still. Then one day a hacker friend mentioned it was possible to write self-replicating computer programs. As a result of that, Ray eventually "stopped reading novels and started reading computer manuals."

If Gell-Mann was an unlikely champion for the wide-ranging biological work at SFI, Tom Ray—botanist, bird-watcher, insect collector—was an equally improbable cybernaut. But he soon made himself familiar with the work of von Neumann, Barricelli, and the rest. In that, he was a good example of the broad connections emerging in the cross-disciplinary world of the new biology. Before long, he would make his own contribution to that world: he called it Tierra.

In an A-Life Hall of Fame, Tierra would have its own room. From the Spanish word for "earth," Tierra took the notion of a digital life form to a new degree of sophistication. All by itself, for instance, Tierra invented parasites. Then it invented sex.

In the beginning, Ray programmed a variety of digital organisms so they could replicate and turned them loose inside his computer. As they interacted and the dynamics of their virtual ecosystem took shape, something unexpected happened. One of his creatures shed almost half its code and started using the reproduction code from its neighbors in order to duplicate itself. Because it had less information to copy, the new parasite was able to reproduce much more quickly than its hosts. Ray hadn't programmed that; it simply emerged on its own. But there was more to come.

Soon the hosts evolved defenses, and the parasites and hosts settled into Lotka-Volterra cycles. In the 1930s those ecologists were the first to show how populations of predator and prey species waxed and waned in inverse proportions to form stable oscillations—as with the populations of arctic hares that fluctuate inversely with the young trees they feed on. First the hare population grows, decimating the trees. Then the trees produce increasing amounts of toxic resin in their bark, ruining the hares' digestion and reducing their numbers. As the hare population tails off, the plants stop producing the toxin. Then the whole cycle begins again. Neither side ever wins. What Ray saw on his computer screen had interesting parallels with that. Said Ray, "The parasites cannot displace their hosts from the [computer] memory, because they depend on them for critical information."

Early on, Ray had programmed mutation into his organisms. And whenever the computer's memory was full, his Darwinian operating system killed off the older or deficient ones. With the ability to crank up the speed on their activities, he soon found he was able to do what he'd long hoped for, to watch a kind of evolution in progress. But one day, after turning off the mutation function, he noticed that the creatures on his screen were somehow still evolving. Puzzled, he looked more closely and discovered a primitive sexual relationship taking place. In "real" life, sex is a much more potent source of change than genetic mutation. It brings together the codes of two different parents and combines them into a new descendant. What Ray discovered was that sometimes, when parasites were reproducing themselves in dying hosts, a mix of old and new codes was being taken up in the following generation. These were in essence "wild" combinations. Cybernetic offspring. Babies.

As Tierra evolved, with new generations unfolding one from the other—and with each generation adapting to whatever changes were taking place in all those other species that it interacted with—another provocative feature appeared. The changes Ray was seeing didn't progress in simple, orderly fashion. Instead, periods of relative stasis were followed by bursts of rampant transformation. In that, there was a parallel with the theory of punctuated equilibrium, a leading view of how evolution occurs in nature.

Ray and his A-Life colleagues began talking about what evolutionists call the Cambrian explosion. Simply put: Although life has existed on earth for nearly four billion years, it was limited to one-celled organisms until just beyond 500 million years ago. Then, during the Cambrian Era, there came a sudden flowering of diversity that has populated the earth with many of the life forms we see—and which see us—today. Multicellular creatures, nervous systems, brains, in all their wondrous variety, all have come since then. Our challenge, said Ray, is "to engineer the proper conditions for digital organisms in order to place them on the threshold of a digital version of the Cambrian explosion."

Real Artificial Life

Despite such great expectations, by the turn of the century the work of pioneers like Langton and Ray had reached an impasse as the creativity of their systems seemed to plateau. But their work laid the foundation for a new round of attempts. Today's A-Life research is at once less abstract and more ambitious. According to Mark Bedau, editor in chief of the journal *Artificial Life*, "One thing happening now is that people are connecting the results from virtual worlds with real world data." That is in part now possible due to work by Bedau and Norman Packard, which compares statistics on the creativity of artificial life forms with statistics from the real-world fossil record, and from human patent files. According to Bedau, this indicates that "the biosphere—as reflected in the fossil record—shows a kind of creativity that no one has captured in an artificial life system." In the first generation of A-Life programs designed by Langton, Ray, and others, the creativity of the system does eventually reach a plateau and stop. Says Bedau, "We still are missing some insight."

Advances made with those programs are nonetheless potent. They inform directed evolution. They've aided research on how normal cells become cancerous. They have been used to model immune system processes, in the effort to counteract Internet viruses and worms. Physicist Stephen Wolfram, in his highly controversial book *A New Kind of Science*, claims that insights gained from cellular automata can explain the origins of the universe. Their ability to convert elementary rules into cascades of wildly increasing complexity suggests that there may be no more than a half-dozen basic rules guiding the creation of everything, from stars to raindrops to the way we think, Wolfram maintains. The book holds up his "Rule 30," which produces an unusually diverse cascade, as a window into that possibility.

Meanwhile, research continues to move ahead in other areas. Ray has joined with virtual-reality visionary Jaron Lanier, and a board of other luminaries, in the Darwin@Home project. It preserves and extends the concept of linking private computers through the Web, as a habitat for experimental new A-Life creatures. A recent international conference—combining the Seventh European Conference on Artificial Life, in Dortmund, Germany, with one held jointly at Los Alamos and SFI—featured a new generation of "soft" A-Life programs. Steen Rasmussen and his group from Los Alamos showed one in which succeeding layers of entities evolved higher-level emergent properties that, in turn, evolved still-higher-level emergent entities, and so on. Bridging the gap between "soft" and "wet," Takashi Ikegami of the University of Tokyo presented a software model that generated the "spontaneous formation and reproduction of cell-like structures."

Numerous efforts in the quest to create "wet" A-Life (the assembly of an actual living cell from nonliving matter) are also in evidence. The one most likely to bear fruit soon is that of the radical genomicist Craig Venter, in partnership with Hamilton Smith, at the Institute for Biological Energy Alternatives. Theirs is a top-down strategy. Says Packard, "They're basically gutting an existing cell and inserting their own genome in it." For that purpose they have chosen *Mycoplasma genitalium* (the bacterium with the simplest known genome).

More challenging is the bottom-up approach now being widely pursued, in which cell-like structures are essentially built from scratch with nonliving chemistries. Toward that effort the Programmable Artificial Cell Evolution project—directed by John McCaskill (Fraunhofer-Gesellschaft, Germany)—is spending $10 million over four years, at nearly a dozen research centers in Europe. Its aim is to develop the technology needed for the effort to create an artificial living cell by directed evolution. That approach is also being taken up by private companies like Packard's start-up, ProtoLife. From whatever source, these fabricated protocells, as they are called, may turn out to be much smaller than normal living cells and could differ from them in other ways as well. All of which raises an old and dicey question: What distinguishes a system that is alive from one that is not?

If any local system of molecules can draw matter and energy from the environment into a cellular structure, can regenerate and reproduce itself, and can retain information and evolve, most scientists today would consider it alive. One paper at the 2003 conference pointed up another difference between life and its absence. Nonliving chemical reactions that are driven by thermodynamics (heat) explore the possibilities open to them in an ergodic fashion—that is, by a process in which every exploratory sequence is the same. Life, on the other hand, explores its possibilities through evolution. It accumulates information—first in genes, then in memory—to help guide its search down narrower and more productive paths. This insight follows on Humberto Maturana and Francisco Varela, who in the 1970s made the case for treating *all* life forms as being somehow cognitive.

As these perspectives merge, much of A-Life seems itself to be narrowing in on a common theme: How and when did information come to dominate the energetic processes of the physical world, and in doing so give rise to life?

Bedau points out that if the ability to cope with a complex, dynamic, and unpredictable environment is a defining feature of intelligence, it "implies a fundamental similarity in the key mechanisms behind living and cognitive systems." This brings things around to Rodney Brooks and his primitive machines bumping their way through the MIT AI Lab. In fact it was Brooks who first suggested that the futures of both artificial intelligence and artificial life hinge on understanding the transition from nonliving to living matter. "If Brooks is right," Bedau says, "then we can expect 'wet' artificial life to become inseparably intertwined with 'soft' and 'hard' artificial life, and we can expect all three to merge with cognitive science."

Virtual Worlds

In some respects software, hardware, and wetware are already merging on the Web, which has become the platform for a vast experiment involving another realm of complex interactions. At present the virtual worlds phenomenon is not widely understood. But if its partisans are right, and they may be, it is poised to make the text-based Internet as antiquated as a dial telephone. Over the long run, they say, it could also mark the emergence of a new, "higher-level" reality.

Virtual worlds were born in the convergence of three loosely related areas: First among them was computer games, especially the cyberspace meeting grounds called MUDs (Multi-User Domains), where players from remote locations interact. The second area encompassed graphic software programs like Richard Dawkins' Biomorph Land, which evolves complex and often lifelike images onscreen. And finally there were "bots," which are simplified AI agents that humans use to represent themselves in MUDs, or elsewhere online. From those three roots sprang Web-based inhabited worlds. Many of the same interactions that take place in real communities occur in virtual worlds, too. But since virtual worlds are so divorced from the physical laws and limits of "normal" reality, those interactions can play out in novel ways.

Virtual worlds are an emerging phenomenon; there's still some disagreement in defining them. Sometimes included are highly sophisticated software programs like the Brookings Institution's Sugarscape and the popular SimCity, with its immediate offspring. But they're more of a kind with cellular automata and are aptly grouped with A-Life programs. Online virtual worlds and their inhabitants are different; they represent the interaction of living, breathing humans sharing their thoughts and desires.

Following on the heels of the earliest interactive computer games, the first MUD was created by two London graduate students in 1979. As the notion of inhabited places "within" the Internet was established by MUDs—and by similar online meeting grounds like the WELL and the Internet Chat Relay network—those places began receiving visits from bots.

A bot—slang for robot—is a common online stand-in for its operator. At first the average bot was a simple AI program that was sent out onto the Internet by a human. It was just smart enough to provide the passwords for entry into various discussion groups and then—once inside—post messages, issue invitations, broadcast opinions or rants, and otherwise make its human operator's presence felt.

The original bots inhabited a purely text-based Internet. As that environment became more complex with time, bots evolved, too. A primordial virtual world called TinyMUD saw the birth of Julia—a kind of smarter but snide younger sister to Eliza, and one of the Internet's first chatterbots. In following years the number and variety of bots proliferated. Then came the advent of the World Wide Web, which opened another frontier. By the end of 1994 the Web was doubling in size every two months.

Web pages featured something new: images. And as the Web expanded, the graphic tools for generating images were improving, too. It was in 1985 that the prominent zoologist Richard Dawkins had developed a pictorial program mimicking the evolution of trees. But he was surprised to find that it not only evolved images of organic branching forms but continued on to "grow" myriad insects and other unlikely creatures beyond his wildest hopes. Called Biomorph Land, his was among the first of the new generation of graphics tools that also included those used in early computer games like Doom and Quake.

In the same year of Dawkins' first Biomorphs, a new kind of interactive environment named Habitat made its debut online. Within Habitat, visitors employed visual incarnations, imaginary versions of themselves. These Avatars—from an ancient Sanskrit word meaning "God's embodiment on Earth"—were descendants of bots. But they were also a good deal more. These were being operated in real time. And now they were dressed for success.

Things came together in 1995 with a community called Worlds Chat. There the "avatars"—rapidly evolving digital personae representing live people from around the globe—could interact with one another while wandering through a 3-D virtual space station. Microsoft's graphics-rich V-Chat premiered the same year. Inhabited worlds soon spread across the Internet. As a result—while most denizens of the Internet were still figuring out how to use desktop icons, e-mail, search engines, and Web pages—by the turn of the century a new generation was maturing online. These were the iGeneration kids who grew up playing computer games. And they were accustomed to navigating in a very different kind of cyberspace, to moving through complex 3-D environments rife with unexpected challenges and interactive behaviors. For them the Internet wasn't just a communications tool. For them cyberspace had become a world unto itself.

Consider AlphaWorld, which was also founded in the summer of 1995. It drew 200,000 "citizens" during the first year and a half of its existence. Today, along with its five hundred sister worlds, AlphaWorld features some fifty million virtual objects arrayed in sprawling 3-D cityscapes, all built by home users with ordinary computers and modems.

Another platform, The Palace, is a "community of worlds" whose backers include the Sci Fi Channel and writer Michael Crichton. It describes itself as building "the first real-time, interactive rich media network by packaging content, audience, advertising and e-commerce." To that end The Palace provides its users with the tools to "create and grow the Internet's most-compelling communities."

Touring the labyrinth of virtual worlds in The Palace is like rambling around in humanity's collective unconscious: There is a guru chat room cheek by jowl with Cuddles 'n' Kisses, a site where "tasteful" nude avatars are welcome. Tradition-minded couples may decide on a visit to the Wedding Chapel. At CyberPowWow one can "wear a Native American Avatar and hang out in an electric blue teepee." Further along is Edge of Heaven, "a sanctuary filled with friendship and love," where avatars "visit a celestial paradise, relax near a calming waterfall, and experience the thrill of a spring thunderstorm." Beyond those individual environments, the Palace Arena offers film festivals and music concerts. Other large events there range from avatar costume balls to a chance to interact with Miss Teen USA delegates. When all else fails, visitors can shop at a site offering "high quality Avatars and props" along with the motto "If You Can Dream It, You Can Do It."

Today vast numbers of users also interact through massively multiplayer games on the Web. EverQuest—a sword and sorcery game—currently hosts a continuous online population of some 100,000 players. And to that number add the millions of players in other games like Star Wars Galaxies, Second Life, Sims Online, Ultima Online, Dark Age of Camelot, City of Heroes, Legend of Mir, Final Fantasy XI, Lineage, Lineage II, MU Online, Ragnarok Online, Kingdom of the Winds, RuneScape, Playdo, Habbo Hotel, and dozens more. Microsoft's Xbox Halo 2 game cleared $125 million on its first day of release (selling 2.38 million units in twenty-four hours).

Add, too, the proliferating AI bots and biots that also populate those games and that—as one gamer notes—"are getting pretty crafty." In a remarkable development, an in-world protest was organized by players unhappy with the skills available for one of the game avatars in a world called There. More than a hundred of those avatars marched in-world for five hours, from a city called Hope to the headquarters of the "Interstellar Confederation of Corporations." In recognition, Funcom, the game's maker, even turned the sky black overhead. Protests may be in the offing elsewhere, too, now that the McDonald's fast-food chain has opened an in-world kiosk as a part of the Sims Online world, and a new advertising agency called Massive is placing ads in other virtual worlds.

But gamers aren't opposed to all business activity. They have developed sophisticated online economies of their own, where they mine ores, smelt them into metals to make armor and weapons, sell them for gold coins, and then use that money to buy other goods—all in-world. A recent study estimates that the current economic productivity of such virtual activities in all multiplayer games (not including subscription fees) exceeds the population and per capita GDP of the nation of Namibia. Meanwhile, the number of players keeps growing, along with their sophistication. A twenty-two-year-old gamer known as Deathifier, in the multiplayer Project Entropia, has paid $26,500 to buy an "island" in its virtual landscape. He expects to turn a profit by selling the mineral and hunting rights on his land.

On another front, as the U.S. military becomes ever more remote-controlled, it is adapting the architecture of multiplayer worlds like Doom and EverQuest for use as "virtual distributed training environments." Avatars in mufti were deployed in Qatar prior to the U.S.-led invasion of Iraq. There, the headquarters of Gen. Tommy Franks—commander of the U.S. forces—conducted Operation Internal Look, a computer-generated interactive world that modeled the looming conflict. The Army's simulation technology center, in Orlando, Florida, is also setting up a virtual Afghanistan that could network hundreds of thousands of computers. "The intent," says the center's director, Michael Macedonia, "is to build a simulation that allows people to play in that world for months or years, participate in different types of roles and see consequences of their decisions." In one of the largest multiplayer games in existence today, America's Army takes players through basic training and the entire military experience, eventually ending up in realistic battles involving modern tactics and weaponry. The real U.S. Army spent $12 million developing the game, which now hosts five million registered users in various stages of training and deployment.

Avatars have been called "personalized online representations of people" and "visible alter egos." They can also be strikingly beautiful. The

Avvy Awards are part of a yearly conference held by the Contact Consortium—a nonprofit group central to the development of virtual worlds. Past Avvy winners have included "Summer," designed by Victoria D'Onofrio and Rody Galeano. Summer is a lithe, lovely young digital woman dressed in little but strategically placed butterflies, with flowers in her hair and a friendly rabbit curled under one arm as she strides along. Compared with Summer, the Barbie doll is clearly from another era. A prize also went to "Genius." By Planet 9 Studios, Genius looks to have emerged from the scrambling of genetic codes for Albert Einstein and Mark Twain. In one year the overall winner was a graceful and authentic geisha. In another the prizewinning Chrome Angel was a science fiction fantasy, a figure floating in space and draped in gossamer, with geometric structures drifting behind it that vaguely suggested wings.

The rise of interactive avatars takes things beyond the emergence of life forms from random molecules, beyond the emergence of communal intelligence from individual ants, and beyond the rise of evolutionary behavior from digital creatures. In virtual worlds a new interactive reality has emerged among people. It is a stable, ongoing, 3-D electronic realm in which the sole inhabitants are prosthetic extensions of the human psyche.

Virtual worlds pioneer Bruce Damer and anthropologist Jim Funaro founded the Contact Consortium in 1995. Damer—referred to in-world as DigiGardener—is one of those advocates one senses just isn't going to take no for an answer, or at least not for long. Inhabited cyberspace, "in glorious three dimensions and occupied by thousands of people at the same time," he is quick to point out, "is a place, not just an interface." As he describes it:

> Little kids are building enormous 3D cityscapes on the Net. Thousands of them congregate and build these floating cities. The Virtual Worlds are where they live. There has been a merger between all those high-end, virtual reality systems that we've seen over the last ten years where people are sort of goggling into these realities, where doctors are operating on virtual patients and pilots training in virtual aircraft. All of those very serious uses are merging with what used to be just gaming engines like Doom. You are getting this strange, new hybrid in the case of the Virtual World that isn't really a game . . . It's a new creature.

The occupants of these virtual worlds, he says, "know they are true pioneers of a new medium of human contact, a medium that will have as profound an impact on the 21st Century as the telephone, television or film had on the 20th."

The Persistence of Memory

One of the revolutionary qualities of virtual worlds is that they are "persistent." If you leave them and return, everything is still there, just where you left it. That feature has made them attractive for applications in which the Web was, before now, just an information delivery vehicle. Business is one area where Damer sees major changes on the way. The Contact Consortium, for instance, has no office beyond a post office box. Instead, he says, "We have hundreds of square miles of virtual real estate, twenty-four hours a day, with teams here, in Canada, and in Europe, Australia, and Japan." They interact in virtual conference rooms through their avatars—using virtual PowerPoint presentations and with virtual notes pinned to the virtual walls, all of which can be left in place for future use.

Virtual worlds may have an even larger impact on education. In 1996, Stuart Gold, a partner in Contact Consortium, was involved in setting up TheU, a virtual university supported by a number of schools. With Jan de Bruin, a policy scientist at Tilburg University in the Netherlands, Gold later wrote of creating "a learning space appropriate to a 3D online inhabited virtual world." TheU is no longer active, having now been superseded by VLearn3D, another consortium project. It draws support from Cornell University, Indiana University, and the University of California at Santa Cruz. Event producer Galen Brandt, Damer's wife, has also worked with New York's Fashion Institute of Technology and a Canadian school on Ratava's Line. Students made conventional 2-D fashion sketches and transposed them into 3-D virtual garments, which were then modeled online by fashion avatars in virtual space. The project culminated in a fashion show at FIT. There, students wore real versions of the virtual garments while interacting with projected images of their avatar selves.

In another educational display, virtual worlds developer Bonnie DeVarco, working with the University of California at Santa Cruz, set up the experimental Virtual High School. It's an elegant integration of online worlds with other Web-based learning tools. Here avatars inhabit generous spaces with broad corridors, beautiful gardens, and windows looking out on fine prospects. In addition to real-time interactions among students, the school features easy access to select Web sites. Students in Spanish class, for instance, can click on a Spanish-English dictionary whose icon hangs on the classroom wall. Or the whole class can "tele-port" to a virtual Spain for a field trip together. In the science lecture hall, clicking on a wall photo of Einstein brings up his bio page. A student giving a presentation there might display her personal Web page selections to all those assembled in the hall—moving from basic information about carbon, for example, to large 3-D models of Buckyballs that her fellow students can walk around in, and then on to discussions of NASA experiments aimed at using carbon nanotubes for storing hydrogen in the space program. Teachers also arrange sessions for tutors and students, who may live hundreds of miles apart but can meet to work together in real time in a virtual classroom. DeVarco has more recently set up LinkWorld. It serves hundreds of high school students in Southern California with college prep and course-related activities.

Digital Bonfire

Each year the Contact Consortium holds its international conference entirely in digital space. And each year the meeting ground is constructed on a theme. In past years visitors have found themselves in an environment best suited to a Hobbit, or in a beautifully rendered recreation of the spaceship from *2001* (with HAL asking, "What do you think you're doing, Dave?" each time they clicked on a portal).

In 2004—with U.S. Mars rovers wandering the surface of the red planet—the conference was called AvaMars and featured a "Drive on Mars." For the conference, NASA supplied detailed background data from the actual rover. So the Drive on Mars was a complete digital recreation of the rover and its environment. In that mirror world, all of the actual features were present: the rocks on the ground, the rim of the crater, the howling wind. As the sun passed overhead from morning to night through each Mars day, the shadows on the rocks and crater walls lengthened or retracted just as they do on Mars. What's more, the rover itself could be driven about and its robot arm deployed, all without the twenty-minute delay that NASA scientists had to deal with when operating the real rover. During the conference, visitors could take the rover for a spin. Among them was a classroom of schoolkids, the first step in a plan to expand access to other schools as well as to planetariums and science exploratoriums.

Environments like AvaMars, VLearn3D, The Palace, and the rapidly evolving worlds of massively multiplayer games are unique mediums of interaction. But they foreshadow even more exotic possibilities. Says Tom Ray, "In a typical virtual world we move about in a street lined by buildings. We approach a building and click on the door to enter. Inside we find conventional rooms and objects." Because that approach is familiar, says Ray, new visitors don't need much training. But he compares it to the first movies—before the nature of cinema was understood—when they were just films of plays taking place onstage. The same is true of the way we now use digital media, he says. "It is as if we feel compelled to take our bodies with us into cyberspace, when in fact cyberspace is for the mind, and does not need to be limited to the kinds of spaces we are familiar with in the material world."

Damer brings another perspective. Today's virtual worlds, he points out, "sit on a pinnacle of technological development going back thousands of years, to the beginning of language and symbolic representation." And where "computing used to be about numbers, about computation," he says, "now it's also about creating social spaces." These online social worlds "involve every aspect of computing: networks, databases, graphical 3-D rendering engines, artificial intelligence and artificial life, all the software and all of the hardware reaching back to the abacus. Then they also bring in the skill sets needed for making theme parks—like Disney imagineers—as well as the abilities of sound designers, social mavens, and crowd managers." With all that, Damer says, virtual worlds "are probably the largest design space in technology right now." They also represent, he believes, the turning of a deep cycle, one reaching back to early humans:

> Our primitive ancestors would gather around the light of a fire. There were dancing shamans wearing masks and the cave walls were covered with visual representations like human handprints and paintings of wild animals. That was an immersive experience—what we call a suspension of disbelief—where they forgot about the outside world for a while. If we could go back in time to experience that, the way early humans did in the Caves of Lascaux, we would be more involved, more overwhelmed, than we are when we're watching the best Hollywood movie today. But the drive toward that kind of immersion is still one of the strongest we have, and

with virtual worlds we are in a sense climbing back to that experience. So the whole ten-thousand-year buildup of technology—the slow accumulating of layers of invention over time—has brought us around to something very basic and primal, but in this new and really extraordinary way. And in the avatar-inhabited, multiuser online worlds, the drive of our species to create and live in immersive spaces has also spawned the richest of all the Web-based ecosystems. It's like some kind of digital primordial soup. Virtual worlds feature complexity, selection pressures, diversity, and dynamism. And in the end, hundreds of thousands of young minds are going to produce something no laboratory could ever come up with.

Interconnecting

There are partisans of the new cyber frontier who sound a lot like the futurists, the art movement that deified the power and speed of machines at the start of the last century. "Professional synergist" Charles Ostman is among them. He was for a time science editor of *Mondo 2000*—a wild and often brilliant San Francisco–based magazine that effloresced and faded with the 1990s dot.com bubble, and that routinely pushed the boundary between cyber science and visionary fantasy. Ostman is prone to such statements as "There is a state of change at hand, the rate and complexity of which is an acceleration vector never before experienced in human history." He sees the Internet as an embryonic organism, and one of his repeated exhortations is, "We are becoming immersed in an irreversible human/Internet symbiosis."

In countries like the United States it's already true that, as one writer notes, "children born today will grow up to live in a world where computers outnumber them." One way or another that will have its effect. But there are reasons for entering this brave new world with care. Thomas Jefferson once observed that whatever government can do for us it can also do to us. With apologies to the former president, the same holds true for symbiotic integration with a macro-synthetic nervous system.

Connectivity is a case in point. It has become a kind of grail among many of those closest to the new interactive technologies. There is even speculation about a "singularity," the point at which the Internet becomes so densely interconnected that it "wakes up." But work done by Stuart Kauffman at the Santa Fe Institute has raised questions about how much connectivity is productive for us.

While experimenting with massively parallel A-Life programs, he found that adaptability in his virtual networks peaked at a fairly low number of interconnections per member. Too few connections made the system stagnant, because too sparse a network didn't do a good job of transmitting innovations. Then, as he increased the number of connections per member to ten or so, he saw the systems increase in adaptability and resilience—innovations flowed rapidly through the networks, and they bounced back strongly from disturbances. But when he raised the density of connections still further, bureaucratic gridlock set in. Now there were too many agents tugging against one another. The lesson: beyond an optimum number, more connections actually slowed down adaptation. Things worked best near the center. Kauffman's network had zeroed in on the sweet spot.

Science writer Kevin Kelly has described that in prosaic terms. "In the long run," he has said, "an overly linked system was as debilitating as a mob of uncoordinated loners." From that, Kelly drew a simple conclusion: "We own the technology to connect everyone to everyone, but those of us who have tried living that way are finding that we are disconnecting to get anything done."

Could there be a sweet spot lying somewhere between the old world from which we came and the hyperconnected futurist vision of today's more avid prophets—a cultural zone of maximum evolvability for humans? Says MIT's Neil Gershenfeld, "Evolution is the consequence of interaction, and information technology is profoundly changing how we interact; therefore, it's not crazy to think about an impact on evolution."

And where will that take us? There is no shortage of predictions. But according to Tom Ray, we can't know, because our imaginations are bounded by our preconceptions and by the limited knowledge we have to build on. "As a thought exercise," he says, "imagine that you are standing in a pool of microorganisms, at the threshold of the Cambrian explosion. Your only knowledge of life is single-celled bacteria, algae, protozoa, and viruses. With no prior experience of complex multicellular life, you probably could not imagine the forms of life that are about to emerge. Thus you could not have imagined in advance the applications that humans would derive from organic evolution: rice, corn, wheat, chickens, pigs, cows, silk, mahogany, mink, cats, dogs, cotton, etc." We are, Ray suggests, in the same situation now with our rapidly evolving digital information processes.

In that comment, Ray reflects a point of view that grew from evolutionary theory, is informed by research into chaos, and has come into something like full flower with the rise of complexity and emergence as fields of study.

In each of those areas, the increasing power of computers and networks has brought dramatic advances. And due in part to them, the new biology is moving our notions of computers and what they can do beyond an early reliance on machinelike models of intelligence. Elsewhere, though, the machine metaphor remains entrenched. Those who lift their eyes from their computer screens still have to deal with how that legacy is affecting "real" biology—the genetic data points that constitute actual plants, animals, and other living things.

At every level of matter and in every area of life, computers are now central in our quest to better understand how natural systems work. And that understanding has in turn revolutionized how we design and use computers. Now the influence of that learning feedback loop is spreading outward—as computers become central to the application of nature-based solutions in agriculture, industry, community planning, and economics. With that, the new biology leaves the limited realm of labs and computer screens to enter the outside world in force.

And it's there that it will have its broadest effect. The practice of managing domestic crops and livestock as if they were machines has meant vast problems for the natural systems they inhabit. Those problems are compounded by the mechanistic design of our industries, our communities, and even the economic theories that support and guide them.

In order to understand that impact, and appreciate just how fundamentally our world is about to change, we need to know something of how large-scale systems in nature work. That study is called ecology, and it is key. For it's within ecology that the dynamic interactions of all the molecules, of every gene, of all the parts of bodies, and bodies, and groups of bodies on earth are somehow pulled together into one vibrant fabric. When we speak of ecology, we're talking about real complexity.

part two

natural connections

six

ecology

In an old northern forest, a brief summer shower ends and the sun comes out again. Rainwater slowed by layers of foliage drips to the floor as shafts of light pierce the canopy. One strikes an ancient, mossy log that glows green where it lies half-sunken in a slope. Water has pooled on its uphill side, forming part of a small-scale landscape—one that seems still and quiet until a closer look shows that it is teeming with life.

Mushrooms compete with puffballs, seedlings, flowers, and slime mold for a footing in the moist rot of the old tree's body. Beetles tunnel toward its heartwood, opening a path for mites and nematodes. Termites gnaw on it as parasites in their guts digest it for them. Slugs inch their way across the carpet of moss while crickets leap from place to place overhead. A salamander darts for a worm as, in great lurching gulps, a frog devours a butterfly. Woodpeckers land and start digging for ants. A snake glides under loose scraps of bark, not far from where a mouse and her young huddle in a shady gap.

"Earth knows no desolation," said the poet George Meredith. "She smells regeneration in the moist breath of decay." Downed trees can take a century to decay. Some need more than a thousand years. During that time a web of interacting species centers on them, which is why biologists call them "nurse logs." Since nurse logs offer habitat that is stable

for centuries, many of the creatures coevolving there are flightless; their
history doesn't include dealing with frequent disruptions. While a nurse
log is being decomposed, the thousands of different species that feed on
it or on each other also die and decompose. When they do, the carbon,
nitrogen, and other nutrients they've extracted are laid down around it
in successive mats of rich new soil. A fresh generation of trees and other
plants will draw food from that soil for growth. Then they, too, die and
are decomposed into soil.

This basic loop is where topsoil comes from. It was zoologist Jean-
Baptiste de Lamarck—the man who coined the term "biology"—who
first suggested that. At the start of the eighteenth century he wrote,
"Complex mineral substances of all kinds that constitute the external
crust of the Earth . . . forming lowlands, hills, valleys, and mountains,
are exclusively products of the animals and plants that existed within
these areas of the Earth's surface."

Lamarck was right. When we leave tracks on a forest floor or sift
rich, loamy farmland through our fingers, we're in touch with uncounted
millions of life forms that came before us. Soil is the common ground,
a transition in the loop connecting decomposers like mold or beetles
with what ecologists call producers—those flowers, crops, trees, and other
plants that draw directly on the sun's energy for life.

The loop of plants, decomposers, and new soil is our foundation.
All that we are and all that we have start there. Despite our many advances it remains at the heart of civilization. Without it the world we
know would cease to be.

New Roots

The story of how human culture rests on the birth, death, and recycling
of plants is inseparable from the story of ecology, of the dynamics that
govern natural systems. They have shaped us intimately, and we answer
to them in ways that are just as critical. The full intricacy of nature is beyond us, but the general outline is emerging. We can now see beyond
the simple machine model that shaped our view of nature for so long.

Ecology is our tool for understanding how complex systems in
nature—called ecosystems—work. As human population continues to
grow and our impact on the world grows with it, the need to understand ecology and work within those principles increases. Crucial hu-

man enterprises such as farming, housing, logging, and industry now blanket the globe. This has meant widespread entry into the vast, seamless network of webs within webs and cycles within cycles that makes life on earth possible.

There are clear benefits in looking to nature for guidance in that. Just as materials modeled on nature are tougher, just as artificial intelligence modeled on real minds is smarter, and just as digital organisms that reproduce and compete are more adaptive, lessons from ecology can strengthen our most basic life supports.

Heart of Grass

Why bother? After all, the world provides food, shelter, and freshwater to a vast and rapidly expanding number of people—a number that was unthinkable only a century ago. Even with that expansion, in countries that have Western-style economies the abundance is historic. And there are global efforts to extend it to all nations of the world. If the system isn't broke, why fix it?

The reason is that we are feeding and sheltering six billion people with a kind of parlor trick that involves pulling the rug out from under our own feet. The power and effectiveness of industrial methods have done a lot to persuade us we're standing on solid ground. But now that ground is quite literally slipping away.

With that, our comfortable world of abundant food, shelter, and freshwater is slipping away, too. As the next chapter will show in detail, this is no longer subject to realistic debate. It's already happening, although for now the symptoms are being treated with increasingly harsh medicines. Unpleasant news is unwelcome news. That's one reason the term "sustainable" has become a political football. But pragmatically speaking, it stands for the most basic question we face in choosing how to support ourselves: "Will this last?" "Does this have staying power?" "Can we count on it in the future?" One of the hardest truths confronting us today is that the industrial methods we've used to create a doubling of world population in just fifty years won't last. They can't be sustained.

That wasn't the plan. Those methods were put in place with the best of intentions, and they have brought better lives to vast numbers of people. But now, to continue growing ever-larger populations with a system we know will fail is to be reckless with hundreds of millions of lives.

How could we get something so essential so wrong? The short answer is that virtually no one understood ecology. In designing the support systems we depend on, we looked to the mechanistic principles we knew best. That was a fundamental error. Natural systems do make use of the linear logic that guides machines, but it's just one element in a larger and highly interactive design.

Ecology is the system of systems—linking all dynamic processes that govern life on earth. Any living system that can't mix with ecology won't last. It is where we began, and working within it is our only sure bridge to the future.

To grasp how serious things are—and how the new biology can help—we need to have a feel for ecological ways and means. For business and political leaders, as well as people in every walk of life, that means getting acquainted with food chains and webs, with how succeeding layers of complexity form, and with the interacting feedback cycles that link all life. It also means knowing about some essential ingredients—sunlight, foods such as nitrogen, and of course water.

Just Add Water

The earth is covered with water, but only 3 percent of it is fresh. And of that small portion more than 99 percent is unavailable—locked in glaciers, in ice caps, or deeper in the ground than any well can reach. The myriad life forms trying to get by above sea level have to divide up what's left— no small concern given that everything alive is at least 75 percent water.

Freshwater connects all the parts of a healthy forest. Water itself is made of hydrogen and oxygen, which plants extract for growth. As water falls from the sky, soaks into the soil, and is drawn up into plants, it also carries crucial foods like nitrogen with it into those plants. Excess water then transpires from their leaves back to the sky. Dead trees and other plants that litter slopes create dams. They slow the runoff of excess water, holding it for the forest and curbing erosion. The freshwater that nurse logs absorb—as much as twenty times that soaked up by the ground—creates a fertile habitat for the millions of creatures that decompose them into soil.

Because nurse logs hold water during dry periods and in dry climates, they're also home to fungi that aid in the strenuous search by plants for food. Mammals like voles and deer eat the fungi off logs and spread their spores around the woods in their droppings. Water then carries those spores into the soil, where they colonize the roots of forest plants. Once in residence there, the fungi send cord-like feelers out through the dark soil searching for nutrients, including the rare deposits of usable nitrogen. When they sense one, a structure of fine thready hairs fans out to contact and absorb it, then feed it—with water—back to the root.

Aboveground, every aspect of a forest slows and captures water like a sponge. With its many layers of foliage and its ground littered with porous debris, an old forest is nature's best filter—producer of the finest-quality freshwater. That water then flows from wooded slopes out to the larger world. It courses through streams and rivers into lakes, out across open plains, and then is filtered again in marshes and deltas before pouring into the sea. Over the eons it also seeps down through the soil to fill vast underground aquifers. These lie beneath many regions of the world. Created largely by runoff from ancient forests, they are the world's main reserves of freshwater.

The Big Fix

One of the more critical cycles in a plant's life involves nitrogen, which it uses to make DNA, RNA, and the proteins they create. Other vital nutrients like carbon are easy to find. But for plants, nitrogen is like money. They all need it but there's rarely enough to go around. Not that there's any real shortage. Our atmosphere is 78 percent nitrogen. But it has to be "fixed"—chemically linked to oxygen, hydrogen, or carbon—before most plants can accept it. Otherwise it's like trying to use a bar of gold bullion as payment at a highway tollgate.

Solving that problem isn't easy. In the atmosphere, nitrogen atoms pair together in a strong bond. Lots of energy is needed to split them so they can be linked instead to oxygen or hydrogen, the forms that plants like best. Bolts of lightning can do it. Lightning storms mix nitrogen with oxygen to make nitrate, which then falls to earth with the rain. A very few microbes can do it, too. They live mainly in water or healthy soil and create ammonia—which is a compound of nitrogen and hydrogen. In nature, most of the nitrogen used by plants comes (directly or indirectly) from them.

Because it's both essential and rare, the amount of fixed nitrogen available in a landscape limits everything else, including us. We don't need much of it, but our lives depend on the plants that do. With unintentional irony, ecologists group humans in a class they call "consumers." By that they mean we're among those animals that consume plants, or consume other animals that do (or in our case both).

Theoretically at least, we're not necessary to the more basic loop of plants, decomposers, and soil. Yet the size and diversity of human populations, along with those of all our fellow land-based consumers, rest upon that loop. And in the wild, the vitality of that loop rests upon the health of a few species of nitrogen-fixing microbes.

Those microbes make their homes largely on the roots of plants called legumes. Each plant spoon-feeds sugar—carbohydrates that it makes using energy from the sun—to its own personal microbes. They return the favor by supplying the plant with fixed nitrogen as ammonia. In a year's time the legumes in a healthy forest host the production of hundreds of pounds of fixed nitrogen per acre, which is drawn up into their roots and then deposited by their decomposing bodies in the soil around them. They provide that indispensable service all over the globe.

It is one of nature's true wonders that so much of the vast nitrogen cycle, which is crucial to life and involves one of the more abundant elements on earth, must pass through the needle's eye of microscopic life forms on the roots of a single kind of plant—the legume. The seedhead of that plant is called a pulse.

The Young and the Restless

Imagine a pond in a country meadow. The runoff from a spring shower brings with it a few specks of algae searching for new frontiers. In the still, clear waters of the pond they find ample sunlight. Basic nutrients are plentiful. So the algae take up residence and begin what is an ancient strategy of colonization: they eat and reproduce as fast as they can.

For a while life is good. The water takes on a reassuring green tint as the alga population expands. But with the abundance of food and water their numbers soon grow so large that the water becomes murky with them. Then things start going wrong. They've filled the pond to its boundaries, and now there's not enough freshwater to go around. As they form a scum on the pond's surface, the sun no longer reaches those algae below it. Meanwhile, other nutrients begin running out. The algae respond by doing what they always do: eating and reproducing as fast as they can. But where once that meant success, it now means large quantities of dead algae falling to the bottom, where their decomposition steals oxygen from the water, accelerating the destructive spiral.

Algae are what ecologists call pioneers. They are simple life forms whose secret of success is rampant reproduction. We can all sympathize with that, and the truth is we still have a lot of the pioneer spirit in us— the tendency to seek out new frontiers and start filling them up with others like us.

Dare to Succeed

Living things tend to outgrow their food supplies. That's how evolution works. The natural bias toward overproduction means only the better-adapted members of a species survive. This is what Darwin meant by survival of the fittest.

That underlying tension—between sun-powered expansion and earthbound limits—shapes life into ever more sophisticated forms. Over time, restless young pioneers such as the algae in a pond, or the simple weeds and grasses that first move onto open land, provide support for increasingly elaborate layers of growth. First come larger and more complex plants, then consumers like dragonflies or raccoons, all accompanied by growing armies of decomposers. As each new layer succeeds the last, the size and diversity of the system eventually top out in what is called a climax community. Simply put: it's as much life as a particular habitat can carry.

For that reason a climax community can be large or small. It's what we see when we walk through acres of tall grass in a native prairie, with graceful stems waving high overhead in the sun as insects buzz among the flowers. But it could also be a few gnarled plants in a pocket of soil near the tree line on a cold granite peak. A mature tropical forest, dense with tangled greenery and birdcalls, is a climax community. So are full-grown ocean tidepools.

Climax communities are as different from pioneers as a coral reef is from a pond full of algae. Instead of focusing all their energy on the heedless exploitation of resources, the myriad different life forms of a mature system spend it in ways that share and recycle those resources. That means more density, more diversity, and slower growth. It also means greater energy efficiency and nutrient conservation. In this sense energy efficiency draws living systems toward complexity, by what might be called natural seduction.

"Succession" is the process by which higher and more complex levels of organization emerge from simpler predecessors. It's not unlike the progressive stages of growth in an embryo. It also parallels the emerging complexity seen in A-Life computer programs. Nature is unimaginably more intricate than those programs, but in them, as in nature, simple elements acting with a few basic rules give rise to higher and more elaborate layers of growth.

Succession is the process by which flowers that make nectar, birds that eat bees, cats that hunt birds, dogs that chase cats, and people that breed dogs all somehow emerged from restless young pioneers. It is central to how natural wonders like a forest come about.

Climax communities are more stable than those of pioneers, but no ecosystem is permanent. When a mature system such as a forest is disturbed—by fire, for instance—it can revert all the way back to the simple grasses and weeds of the pioneer phase. With that, the soil it has made for centuries starts washing away. Given time, if it's not interfered with, succession will regrow the network of plants, animals, and fungi that create and shelter soil. But it won't re-create the same forest. Just as death and birth give rise to better-adapted individuals, the destruction and regrowth of large systems adapt them to changing factors such as weather or disease. That slow pulse is part of the deeper rhythm of nature—a rhythm in which, says ecologist C. S. Holling, "chaos emerges from order, and order emerges from chaos."

You Are What You Eat

"There is a continual migration of atoms from inert matter to living matter and back again," said the geologist Vladimir Vernadsky. The channeling of nitrogen and other atoms through the nurse log cycle of plants, then decomposers, and then soil is a notable case in point.

Life is an ongoing negotiation between energy and matter, a process in which energy from the sun animates matter from the earth. Or as ecologist Paul Shepard nicely puts it, the members of an ecosystem "are engaged in a kind of choreography of materials and energy and information."

The sun makes that dance possible. Virtually all energy on earth began with the sun. Atoms may recycle endlessly through live systems, but that's not the case for energy. Like shafts of light piercing a forest canopy, energy moves in just one direction—from the sun into plants, and from them on through each member of a food chain. Plants do the grunt work of converting solar energy into chemical forms such as fats or sugary carbohydrates. Then, with each transition—as a mouse eats a plant and a hawk eats the mouse—most of the energy in each one dissipates. There's no escaping that; the 2nd Law of Thermodynamics decrees it. If the sun didn't come up again each morning, the music would soon stop.

This is what the great American ecologist Aldo Leopold meant when he called an ecosystem "a fountain of energy flowing through a circuit of soils, plants, and animals." The constant press of energy from the sun pushes life into ever more specialized nooks and crannies. As a result, new species develop in order to take advantage of the different kinds of food available there, or the different ways it is available. We talk about complexity in A-Life programs, but nature is truly complex. For instance, researchers studying a mature Norwegian beech forest found more than four thousand different microbial species in a single crumb of soil.

In the end, diversity is a genetic record of nature's long, patient exploration into a habitat's "carrying capacity"—the kinds and quantities of life a location can support. As succeeding layers of growth appear, with each one being more complex than the last, the efficiency of their energy and resource use continues getting better. That, in turn, increases the carrying capacity.

It takes both cooperation and competition to make all that happen. Neither by itself will do. Danish botanist Eugenius Warming pointed out over a century ago that competition is strongest among members of the same species, because only they compete for exactly the same resources. In that way, competition drives evolution. When two different species compete for the same limited resource, many ecologists now believe, one of them will die out unless it can adapt to a slightly different niche. As species diversify to occupy different ecological niches, they no longer compete head-on. So they can develop mutually sustaining relationships—cooperation.

Cooperation in this sense is not the buddy system. Simple cooperation does occur in nature, as among ants in a colony or wolves that hunt in packs. More commonly, though, it involves separate species that channel energy and nutrients in mutually beneficial ways. One case of that is the nurse log cycle, where the waste from a dead tree serves as food for millions of other life forms. And there are others.

For example, cowbirds in the American Great Plains stopped competing with their cousins for the same foods by adapting to eat pests off the backs of roaming bison. But that created another problem. Because cowbirds had to trail the wandering herds, they couldn't stay in one place long enough to hatch and rear their young. So they laid their eggs in the nests of their cousins—sparrows, finches, warblers, cardinals, and other species—who for many thousands of years now have been tricked into nurturing cowbird chicks while the real parents wander.

Ecologically, by removing themselves from local competition, cowbirds increased the food supply for other bird populations, helping them to grow. Cowbird numbers grew, too, as a result of their finding a new food source on the bison. In a clever twist, the cowbirds then reclaimed some of the extra food they had freed for the cousins, by channeling it through those hapless birds back into their own chicks.

Ecologists' somewhat hard-nosed view of cooperating also includes being eaten by something else. That makes food chains the most common form of cooperation among species. In a food chain, nutrients and energy flow from one organism to the next, with every step in the chain being one step further from the sun. Here, the 2nd Law of Thermodynamics makes itself felt: as energy flows from plants to herbivores to carnivores, the 2nd Law limits the amount available to the organisms at each succeeding step. This is why top predators like hawks have such large hunting grounds. It takes a hundred kilograms of prairie grass shoots to feed the ten kilograms of field mice needed to nourish one kilogram of red-tailed hawk.

But as the amount of energy diminishes, there's a corresponding increase in the quality of its use. Gram for gram, hawks are more energy efficient than mice and have a much greater influence on the ecosystem.

Because many animals feed on a variety of prey, food chains tend to cross-link into webs, with energy and resources flowing and branching through them. As one writer describes it, those flows of matter and energy through ecosystems are a "continuation of the metabolic pathways through organisms." This is an example of the self-similar patterns within patterns that recur throughout nature at every level and scale— including in hawks.

Red-tailed hawks aren't just elements in an ecosystem; each one is an ecological community in itself. Like ecosystems, hawks take in fresh energy and building blocks to grow new cells, even as older cells are broken down and cast off as waste. Complex, higher-level behaviors emerge in them as a result of interactions among simpler internal parts. They also contain whole populations of smaller, interdependent life forms: gut bacteria, parasites, mitochondria. And just as in ecosystems, with the constant flow of energy and materials through them, hawks grow in succeeding stages, reach maturity, then continue on in roughly stable form for as long as they survive.

Sooner or later all living things die. Individuals are just temporary examples of an ongoing genetic pattern. But because individuals both reproduce and interact, they are a biological crossroads—the point at which life's internal genetic memory and its outside ecological priorities intersect. By generating new individuals, genes test the water, so to speak, so they can adapt to a changing outside world. Over the course of nearly four billion years that connection has gradually pushed one-celled pioneers to coalesce into ever more complex structures.

In essence, life forms are templates for channeling energy and matter, templates that evolve through time as they move upstream into the flow of free energy from the sun. A red-tailed hawk soaring high over a valley is all of these things—a striking emblem of an even more extraordinary process.

Cycles Within Cycles

If there's anything more remarkable in nature than its complexity, it's how gracefully it is organized—that such an unimaginable number and diversity of life forms somehow behaves as a coherent system.

The fresh energy that comes with each sunrise and that drives living things forward is directed by four basic steering mechanisms. They unite all of life and keep it aimed for the sweet spot of maximum resilience and adaptability. First among them are habitats, which put local limits on the amount of sunlight, space, water, and nutrients available for life to exploit. Then the still-mysterious process of self-organization charts a course between order and chaos while giving rise to higher levels of complexity. Next, genes carry survival lessons from the past, mix and mutate to adapt, and provide the templates for future generations. Finally, there are feedback cycles.

By linking habitat, self-organization, and genetics through a web of interacting cycles, large systems act in concert. For instance, a species is a gene pool. The broader the pool, the better that species can survive in a changing world. When a growing forest expands to its natural limits, that means support for more and larger gene pools. As a result, all of the flowers, trees, frogs, birds, and other life forms benefit. In turn, their greater numbers and diversity make the forest more resilient. Like the age-old symbol of the uroborus—the snake eating its own tail—the forest and its parts are united in a feedback cycle, a cycle that feeds on itself.

All the procedures of nature are linked through cycles, and cycles within cycles. The vast nitrogen cycle moves from the atmosphere through plants and then back up into the air when they die. But within that, nitrogen also moves through the smaller nurse log loop of plants, decomposers, and soil. And within that, nitrogen figures in still-smaller feedback loops among individual organisms. All of those hook into added networks of cycles involving weather and other nutrients. Millions of feedback cycles large and small then link them with still more cycles involving myriad invisible microbes living all around us.

When one cycle is disrupted, it sets off a cascade of effects as the network seeks a new balance. But any balance or stability in nature is transient. All cycles link with each other intimately or through endless intermediaries. So changes are always rippling inward and outward between local systems and global systems. Just as the rhythm of the tides moves through all the world's oceans, ecological effects wash through all of its living systems.

The Whale and the Otter

In a distant sea, in a time not so long ago, one story of how changes cascade through a system played out in vivid terms. It began as scientists noticed a startling decline in the numbers of otters along the Alaska coast. In one five-hundred-mile stretch they decreased by 90 percent in just a decade. In some areas they simply vanished. It turned out they were being eaten by orcas, killer whales.

That puzzled everyone who knew the whales. They usually feed on seals and sea lions, which insulate themselves with rich layers of fat, a high-octane food. Otters insulate themselves with fur. As one whale expert put it, "For them, switching from seals to otters is like changing from steaks to popcorn."

Researchers from the U.S. Geological Survey eventually came up with an explanation for the mystery. They suspect that an ecological cascade began with the displacement of rich, oily fish such as herring and ocean perch by a less nutritious species called pollack. The cause may have been human predation, climate change, or a decline in plankton-eating whales (which freed up more food for the plankton-eating pollack). In any case, that shift led to a decline in the seal and sea lion populations, which feed on herring and ocean perch. With fewer seals and sea lions to eat, marauding killer whales started cruising coastal waters, devouring whole populations of otters.

The widening cascade of effects didn't stop there. As the otters disappeared, one of their favorite foods—sea urchins—underwent a population explosion. Vast new armies of hungry urchins soon began devouring their own favorite food, kelp forests. Now a host of fish species dependent on coastal kelp forests are affected. This in turn affects fish-eating predators like bald eagles. And those link to still more cycles, as the ripples continue to spread.

Superfluke

As the story of the whale and the otter shows, there's no way to know the full consequences of an ecological cascade. But the complexity of nature doesn't end there. The actors at work in even a single food chain can be equally hard to fathom. Consider the mighty fluke *Euhaplorchis californiensis*, whose eggs fall from the sky into the Carpinteria Salt Marsh—near Santa Barbara, California—in the droppings of waterbirds.

The eggs are eaten by horn snails that feed on those droppings. A first generation of flukes soon inhabits the snails, castrating them and laying eggs for a new generation that swims away to find the fluke's second host—the California killifish. Entering the fish through its gills, the flukes work their way up fine blood vessels to a nerve that they then crawl along to reach the fish's brain. There they spread out, carpeting the brain's surface.

A team of scientists studying Carpinteria's ecology looked at that and wondered what was going on. They eventually discovered that the infected fish have a peculiar habit—they shimmy and flash their bellies near the surface, which makes waterbirds thirty times more likely to hunt and eat them. Once that happens, the flukes take up residence in their third home, waterbird stomachs, in which they fly around while feeding and preparing for the next turn of the wheel. "Could we have so many birds out there if it were 30 times harder for them to find their food?" asks Armand Kuris, a University of California at Santa Barbara marine biologist who was on the team. "Parasites don't just modify individual behavior," he says, "they're really powerful—they may be running a large part of the waterbird ecology."

Flexing

Life on earth is shaped by vast numbers of intimate and often invisible interactions. The quiet vistas in a pastoral landscape are misleading. There is no real stability in nature, just the ongoing dynamics of metabolism. Not only do feedback cycles link and shift, not only are food chains warped by unseen actors like parasites, but even the specific relations between parasites and their hosts can flex—in ways that inject yet another level of complexity and interaction into a system.

That's no small consideration. The species of parasites on earth so outnumber all other living things that some scientists claim the study of life is mainly the study of parasites. It will come as no surprise that the people saying that are parasitologists, but the point remains. Beneath the surface of what we do see, there is a lot going on that we don't.

In Panama, for example, fig tree wasps are hosts to a minute roundworm that becomes more virulent or less so depending on the size of the wasp population. When figs are plentiful and times are good for the wasps, the roundworms spread horizontally through the wasp population, infecting large numbers of the insects and destroying their eggs. But when figs are in short supply and the wasps are in decline, the roundworms become less virulent and transmit only from female wasps directly to their offspring through their eggs.

This predator-prey pattern was first described in the Lotka-Volterra cycles uncovered by those 1930s ecologists. It's also the pattern that Tom Ray's A-Life Tierra creatures fell into, between his parasitic digital predators and their hapless digital prey. Evolution balances the effectiveness of predators against their need to preserve their prey. Grasping that principle has helped scientists better understand how to deal with one of our own parasites—the bacterium *Vibrio cholerae*, or, as it's more commonly known, cholera.

Cholera spreads in two ways: through water, or in food handled by people who are carriers. Evolutionary biologist Paul Ewald of Amherst College, in Massachusetts, reasoned that any cholera passed through food would be milder, because it required living humans as a link. After all, if it were fatal to its hosts, they wouldn't be able to prepare the food it needed for further transmission. So natural selection should favor a less virulent strain. But waterborne cholera, Ewald figured, wasn't limited by that concern. It wouldn't care if its hosts lived or died so long as their wastes entered the water supply. In that case natural selection would favor maximum reproduction, regardless of its effect on us.

He tested his notion by examining samples of cholera bacteria that had been preserved from the South American epidemic of the 1990s. During that disastrous period tens of thousands of people died or were made seriously ill. But Ewald noted that in Chile, where there were adequate measures to protect the water supply, there were few serious cases. The tragedy seemed to focus on countries like Peru and Guatemala.

When he and his team examined the samples, their tests showed a link between toxicity and virulence in the disease—the faster it reproduced, the more toxic it seemed to be. They also established that at the start of the epidemic there were highly toxic strains in all of the countries affected. But by 1994 there was a shift. The strains in Chile had become milder, with about one-tenth the toxicity. Ewald concluded that cleaning up the water in Chile not only eliminated many bacteria, it caused others to evolve to a less virulent form. And because they then stimulate the immune system without causing serious disease, they act like vaccines. Said Ewald, "The ones that are left end up protecting people."

The Rebound Effect

Like the young and restless pioneers that first settle ecosystems, simple organisms tend to have very brief lives. That means as a species they can adapt quickly.

In essence, every life form on earth centers on its own coil of DNA. But while members of a species share the same genetic traits, there are subtle differences from one individual to the next. We see that even among people in the same family. While resembling one another in basic ways, brothers and sisters often differ slightly in height, weight, intelligence, temperament, and physical stamina. The tendency to produce related but somewhat differing individuals holds true throughout nature, from complex life forms like people all the way down to bacteria.

That subtle but persistent variety is where the Darwinian rubber of genetic adaptation meets the hard road of environmental limits. In the impartial eyes of evolution, the death of an individual is no misfortune—it's a steering mechanism. So long as the gene pool is big enough for survival of the species, nature treats individual deaths as useful feedback. Like a fading ant pheromone trail, they mark a less viable path.

In humans and other complex life forms, the lessons of that feedback are not always easy to parse. As with an old forest, our size and internal complexity make us highly resilient in the face of threats. So there is often more than one cause for death, or the ultimate cause may not be readily apparent. But in the simple worlds of creatures like insects, worms, flukes, and bacteria, things are more direct. There, a sudden reduction in the food supply, or a big change in the weather, or the introduction of a toxin can rapidly cause large die-offs.

This is where the subtle varieties in a species have their effect. As those unable to handle the threat die away, their hardier kin go on doing what simple life forms always do: they eat and reproduce as fast as they can. Bacteria have stronger defenses, since they can swap genes or activate dormant genes to help themselves adapt. But the end result is the same. Any hazard that doesn't stamp out an entire species serves only to select for those members strong enough to resist it. Even when just a small percentage of them survive, their next generation is better adapted to withstand the threat. And in each generation that follows, the next wave of survivors is stronger and more numerous. Because they have such short lives and reproduce so quickly, they soon grow around the problem. That's the rebound effect.

The rebound effect flies in the face of the machine age view of nature, which has long guided how we deal with parasites and other unwanted pests. In that view, if we come up with a way to destroy 90 percent of a parasite population, it only remains for us to go out and get the rest. Nothing could be further from the truth.

The story of penicillin is a good case in point. In 1942, virtually all strains of the bacteria *Staphylococcus aureus* were affected by penicillin. While the emergence of a penicillin-resistant bacterium is rare—literally one in a million—bacteria can reproduce at a rate of one million cell divisions in twenty-four hours. That helps explain why today more than

95 percent of staph infections are resistant to not only penicillin but also ampicillin and other more recent varieties of the drug. As fast as we develop new medicines, our targets develop resistance to them. That ongoing arms race is why public health officials have now launched a worldwide campaign urging doctors not to prescribe antibiotics that aren't crucial, and warning patients to finish the full course of their prescriptions.

The rebound effect is natural selection on fast-forward. It is a vivid example of how nature uses death and gene variance to hone a species to its environment. As one observer puts it, antibiotics or pesticides are a form of "evolutionary pressure" which "actually selects over time for a population of organisms that is increasingly resistant to the very measure intended to kill them." To put it another way: what kills them makes them stronger.

Drug resistance is a growing and far-reaching concern. But as the following chapter will show, the intersection of machine age logic with the rebound effect has given rise to a problem of even greater magnitude—a destructive feedback cycle in which we pour ever larger and more toxic quantities of poison on our food supply to breed everstronger populations of pests.

Genetic Ecology
Creatures like insects, worms, flukes, and bacteria are among life's simplest forms. But there's an even more basic realm where scientists now see ecological principles at work. Genes lie at the heart of the living world. Virtually every life form has at its core a twist of DNA—in complex life forms many—which guides design and construction of the proteins and other molecules we're made of.

It's hard to imagine an area where the new biology is more crucial than it is for genetics. Ecologists recognize how dynamic all living systems are, with their emerging levels of complexity, their vast networks of food chains and webs and feedback loops, with the nearly incomprehensible intimacy of their relationships. And there's the added flexibility selection brings as it hones the genes of individual species, and with that alters the evolution of other species—sending the whole vast network of interlinking cycles off in new directions. But somehow, despite those insights, the machine age view of DNA as a tiny mechanical Tinkertoy remains. With the coming of biotechnology, as humans start to monkey with the genetic heart of life, the implications are both obvious and profound.

To claim that means danger is to understate the case. But the cavalry is coming. And leading the charge is a thoughtful, dedicated scientist named Lynn Helena Caporale. It was Caporale who some twenty years ago wrote an insightful paper suggesting junk DNA—the long stretches of code that Tinkertoy geneticists see as useless—and other regions might interact with other parts of the strand to regulate their mutation rates. It was Caporale who, with Nobel laureate Werner Arber, pulled together an auspicious conference—"Molecular Strategies in Biological Evolution"—at New York's Rockefeller University in 1998. There she spurred on the rumpled academic ranks now clearing a path for the view that genomes, like the rest of life, are dynamic systems. And it was Caporale who opened the conference with a gracious reference to Barbara McClintock as perhaps the most important biologist of the twentieth century.

Most people have never heard of McClintock. But starting in the 1940s, she quietly and methodically laid the groundwork for a revolution in our concept of the genome, one only now coming to pass. During thirty years of subtle and insightful experiments focused on corn, she did what great scientists always do: she uncovered aspects of nature with vast general implications. She was the first to suggest that there were genes she called "transposable elements," which "jumped" from one location to another within DNA. She also showed for the first time that one genetic region could affect the behavior of another. But her ideas and influence went beyond that. As one writer observed, in an obituary for her in 1992, "Standard theories are still framed in terms of independent genetic units, whereas McClintock thought of the genome as a complex unified system exquisitely integrated into the cell and the organism." It wasn't until 1983 that she was belatedly awarded her Nobel Prize.

To growing numbers of informed observers, it's clear that McClintock's fluid genome is replacing the Tinkertoy model. That even today the old view holds, despite all we now know about nature, serves to demonstrate how much power the machine metaphor still exerts on even the brightest minds.

That wasn't the case at the Rockefeller University conference. There, an international group spent two and a half long days swapping arcane information that few outside their fields would comprehend. But over time its ramifications promise to be broad, for it sanctions a view of the genome as a highly interactive system.

Caporale described how genomes can vary the mutation rates of different sequences within their DNA, and explained why evolution would select for that. As she later put it in her book *Darwin in the Genome*, "It really isn't correct to make the assumption that mutations are random in the sense that they are equally likely at every spot along the DNA. Some changes are more likely than others." An easy way to picture this is to think of it in personal terms. We probably wouldn't object to mutations that might make our fingers longer. But much chancier would be those that could introduce random changes into the process of cell division, or the Krebs cycle—which is used by all complex life forms to generate the energy that makes us possible.

As the conference proceeded, more evidence piled up. James Shapiro of the University of Chicago spoke of "rapid genome restructuring guided by biological feedback networks." Takashi Gojobori from Japan's National Institute of Genetics referred to the genome's "plasticity" and described it as "a complex, self-regulating, and integrated system." In a nice mirror of the principle advanced by the Santa Fe Institute's Stuart Kauffman, Nina Fedoroff from Pennsylvania State University talked about how genomes internally negotiate a sweet spot between stability and adaptation.

In all this—as in so much that is ecological—there are what begin to sound like philosophical lessons, not only for species but for the new biology: Interaction is key and change is ongoing. But in the process hold fast to what is crucial and experiment with what isn't. If you confuse the two, nature will replace you.

Genome Space

Just as nature doesn't focus on single lives but looks instead to larger patterns, a new wave of geneticists is looking beyond the earlier focus on single genes, which they now know can change activity with a shift in context. They've begun to study coordinated networks of thousands of genes.

One of the more remarkable concepts to come out of the Rockefeller University meeting was Takashi Gojobori's notion of "genome space," which he defines as "the entire set of genomes of all living organisms."

It is in itself a striking idea. But more than that, as scientists have deciphered the genetic codes of increasing numbers of life forms, they've been surprised to find many of the same genes at work in all of them: whether in fungi, sponges, or plants, on through flies, frogs, birds, even humans. Over the course of some four billion years—as new and more complex life forms emerged from their simpler predecessors—tried-and-true genetic parts were being kept on and stirred into new forms.

At first glance, the notion that we share genes with lettuce can be a little disconcerting. But knowing that adds a dimension of wonder to everything we see while walking through an ancient forest. It's extraordinary to think that the many and diverse life forms all around us—from the restless young algae in a pond to the lustrous green moss on a nurse log, from bees droning in the sun to birds chirping in the trees—share bits of the same DNA. Nature just works them into fresh contexts. Each then becomes a unique dynamic system in its own right—in one case a milkweed plant, in another the monarch butterfly that feeds on it.

Seeding the Future
Whether we focus on the genome or the vast diversity of an old forest, it's clear now that—at every level and scale—nature uses ecological rules. There is in that what Sim Van der Ryn and Stuart Cowan, in their fine book, *Ecological Design*, call "a rich kind of design competence."

The scientists, engineers, and planners who have taken up the new biology as their standard are charting the path to a very different world. Of potentially even greater importance is that coming soon is a generation of ordinary people now absorbing the lessons of ecology as children. For them it will no longer be an exotic and difficult subject that flies in the face of machine age logic. For them ecology will be common sense, conventional wisdom.

The following is a homework assignment by Claire Kinnell, a third-grade student in a rural American elementary school. Remarkable for its sophistication, her paper also neatly summarizes many of the principles at work in ecology:

ECOLOGY—CLAIRE KINNELL
1. *Community*—a place where plants and animals *depend* on each other.

2. *Energy source*—a *source* of food for a plant or animal.

3. *Herbivore*—an animal that eats *only plants*.

4. *Carnivore*—an animal that eats *only meat*.

5. *Omnivore*—an animal that eats *both plants* and *meat*.

6. *Camouflage*—helps an animal *blend in* with its surroundings.

7. *Producer*—*plant* that makes food.

8. *Consumer*—an *animal* that must *find food* to eat.

9. *Prey*—an animal that is being *hunted by another* animal.

10. *Predator*—an animal that *hunts another animal* for *food*.

11. *Habitat*—where an animal or plant *lives*. (home)

12. *Shelter*—a place that *protects* an animal.

13. *Food chain*—a *path-way* for *energies* movement from one living thing to another. Always starts with a plant.

14. *Food web*—*food chains connected*.

"Out of the mouth of babes," as the old psalm puts it, "hast thou ordained strength." The emergence of the human race has brought with it remarkable new developments, and a more extraordinary future awaits us. But to pursue it we first must accept that ecological standards are fundamental—that they are among those things to which we must hold fast. The machine age was an experiment, a largely successful one. But it also enhanced our feeling of separateness. That's in part an illusion. We are different from other life forms in obvious ways, but throughout the long centuries of the industrial era, the intimacy of our connection to the rest of nature never really varied. And because there are so many of us now, our impact on the interconnecting webs and cycles that link all natural systems is washing through them on a vast new scale.

Environmentalists justly raise concerns about endangered species and habitats. Those are real and necessary cares. But ultimately it's no contest. Individual species may come or go but nature always wins in the end. The big question is whether it will feel the need to replace us.

The natural world isn't bigger than we are because it occupies more ground. It's bigger than we are because our existence is predicated on its systems, on its processes. They are inviolable, and they are first, last, and always ecological. In recent years the word "ecology" has been given political connotations. But it's worth bearing in mind that no matter what we call them, those processes are a bedrock reality. The machine age was a great and historic achievement. But like algae in a pond, we have now begun pushing up against our habitat limits. It's time for a more complex and efficient culture to emerge.

Can the new biology change the design and construction of our communities, of our industries, of the economic system that guides so much of what we do? The answer is that work is well advanced in each of those fields. But first must come agriculture, where machine age methods have seriously degraded the loop of plants, decomposers, and soil that is the basis for all else in human civilization.

seven

growing problems

In the remains of a clearcut industrial forest, a brief shower ends and the sun comes out again. Muddy water slices channels through a stubble of naked tree stumps. The rain's impact isn't softened by succeeding layers of foliage and there are no dead logs left on the ground, to slow the running water now washing away topsoil created over centuries. Unfiltered and unrefined, that muddy water has instead become a slush that clogs the local streams and watery habitats. The lack of nurse logs on the forest floor also means that no new soil is being formed. It means the millions of decomposers that once digested dead logs into soil have waned for lack of food. So the birds and other animals that feed on decomposers have moved on. All this contributes to a destructive feedback cycle. The spiraling decline in diversity drives a corresponding decline in stability, as the snake's mouth gradually releases its tail.

Our shelter, our food, and our freshwater are keyed to the growth of plants. Their continuing health is at the core of the drama between nature and machine age logic, and that contest is far from over. Machine age ideas continue to guide our great endeavors: in community planning, in industry, in economics, the power of industrial methods and the sway of mechanistic thinking still close minds to the need for new solutions—to even the notion that they might exist. But the deepest effect those old ideas have is on the loop of plants, decomposers, and new soil that supplies a crucial life support. We can and should be concerned about nanotechnology, proliferating robots, and invasions of privacy by artificially intelligent agents. Suburban sprawl, industrial waste, nonrenewable energy, and unrealistic economic feedbacks are parts of the problem, too. But the ancient loop of plants, decomposers, and new soil is the heart of the matter; and industrial agriculture is now thwarting it on a global scale. Because that loop is so fundamental, there is no other area of life where the machine age legacy poses such a threat to our future.

That's not how it was meant to be. The world now shelters, feeds, and provides freshwater for some six billion people. In the West, industrial methods have produced historic abundance, and there are efforts under way to extend our system to all nations. That approach has brought better lives to billions of people. We see now, though, that it has also brought a profound new vulnerability. Even as we look for ways to expand our comfortable world, its foundations are eroding.

That's because we didn't understand ecology. In designing our agriculture, we looked to solid mechanistic principles. But those methods are inappropriate to the management of living systems. Life does make use of simple mechanics, but they're just one aspect in a larger design. As life rose from the primordial ooze, it drew them into much more complex wholes. The machine metaphor is a primitive subset of biology. It can't be a governing principle.

That fact is beyond sensible dispute. The need to ingrain it in our culture should be, too. Still, putting aside industrial agriculture is no simple matter. It's entrenched by conventional wisdom and practice, by the weight of huge capital investments, by long-established political and educational support structures. And now the whole process is being computerized, programmed into the global digital nervous system. Moreover, billions of human lives now depend on it. For all these reasons, widespread evidence of failure in our current approach to agriculture is being masked with extreme measures, or by incomplete reporting.

Clearcut Problems
The many problems born of industrial logging don't stop at a forest's edge. Like all ecological change, they ripple through neighboring systems, interrupting other cycles, too. As topsoil from a newly cut forest

washes away, it's deposited in streams. The sediment then clogs spawning grounds for salmon, trout, and other species. Where overhanging trees have been cut away, sunlight heats the water, reducing how much oxygen it holds and making life still harder for the fish. Since all woody debris is removed during harvest, there's none left to float downstream, where it can lodge in streambeds and make habitat for fish. There is also none for rivers to carry out to sea, where it plays a vital role in the food chains supporting deepwater species like salmon in their adult phase.

When wild salmon populations fail, human populations linked to salmon fisheries suffer. Moreover, the loss of a forest may upset local weather patterns, affecting farmers in the region. And as industrial "monocultures" of single-species, same-aged trees spread across huge areas, they bring a global loss of diversity—not only for the trees but for the many other life forms living among them. Even when industrial forests regenerate, that lack of diversity makes them poor habitat. So they grow no new soil. Because they lack the resilience of wild systems, they're also more vulnerable to damage by wind and disease.

Until recently, timber companies could at least pace their cuttings, to make sure new trees were grown as fast as others were harvested. Back in the days when 3 percent financial rates of return were a sufficient yield on investment, the trees grew fast enough to keep up. That's no longer so. When inflation and interest rates rose in the 1970s (after the U.S. dollar was unlinked from any pretext of a gold standard), timber firms started pushing their assets for rates of return that were nearer to 10 percent. Combined with the rising demand for shelter from a booming human population, that brought about a fundamental shift. By the mid-nineties Maine forests of red spruce—a prime commercial species— were being cut at some four times their rate of growth. Now it wasn't only birds and other forest creatures losing basic life supports. Loggers were endangered, too.

So were the timber companies, which were fast depleting their main resource. As political resistance to cutting more forests in the U.S. stiffened, the timber companies looked elsewhere—to equatorial Brazil and Indonesia, where great tropical forests remain. Because of this, and the expansion of farmland needed to feed rising populations, more than half of the earth's natural forest cover is now gone. Thirty percent of the remainder is either degraded or fragmented. The endgame here is apparent, and with it will come huge ecological paybacks.

A cascade that forces killer whales to devour whole populations of otters is barely worth mentioning next to what the harvesting of forests on a planetary scale will bring. And if our maturing ecological insights teach us anything, it's that we can't separate ourselves out from the seamless network of webs within webs and cycles within cycles that connects all of life. That's the first lesson of the new biology. To the degree that machine age logic distorts key natural systems, it's not practical. For all living things, including us, biology comes first.

Why don't free market economies make unsustainable logging too costly? After all, isn't that what free markets are for? Why doesn't the loss of a crucial resource push prices higher and spur alternatives? The answer is simple. Today's pricing systems—modeled on narrow, linear machine age accounting—don't reflect all the damage being done. They externalize many of their costs. As ecological forestry advocate Jim Drescher has written, on the practice of clearcutting forests as if they were cornfields:

> It is more profitable to clearcut. The community, present and future, will pick up all the spinoff [external] costs, which include a decrease in land values, soil erosion, stream siltation, damage to public roads and bridges, disruption of surface-water flow cycles, species extinction, damage to fish stocks, reduction of recreational values, and loss of local employment. Until the clearcutters are assessed and charged for *all* the costs of their harvesting, they will continue to clearcut; our society is subsidizing them to do so.

This was not a conscious decision. When those practices took form, we were simply unaware of the centuries-long cycles at work in keeping a forest healthy. In our neat, mechanical worldview, soil had always been there and always would be, and nurse logs were just one more thing to trip over in the woods. We didn't know that a nurse log might have to lie undisturbed in one spot for a hundred years in order to feed the trees around it.

We also didn't know that even a local watershed needs to have thousands of tons of rotting wood scattered around in its drainage basin— that without those natural dams to slow running water, the soil that trees grow in washes away. For similar reasons, we didn't see how important those natural dams are in capturing freshwater for our own use. And we viewed fish and water as little more than components: just put them together and let nature do the rest. Few understood the exquisite interfacing of species and habitat that grows four thousand different kinds of microbe in a single crumb of soil. Life is complex. We can't just put fish in water and expect them to thrive. When we look back now, there seems an almost childish naïveté in thinking it could be otherwise.

That naïveté has led to rising consequences from the mechanistic forestry now spreading across the globe. But as large, and real, as those problems are, they pale in comparison to the risks being taken in the vast industrial farming systems we use to feed ourselves.

Feeding the World

"The grass was the country, as the water is the sea," novelist Willa Cather wrote of the American Great Plains. That image connects to the evolution of humans on the open savanna. With the rise of agriculture, we've planted much of the world's open land with crops, but Cather's primal vision still runs deep. From amber waves of grain to the verdant green of rice fields, the promise of an abundant harvest comforts us in ways that few sights can.

Farming was invented some ten thousand years ago. During the long stretch from then until about fifty years ago, global human population reached 2.5 billion. In just the five decades since, that number has doubled. The expanding multitude of humans now on earth is also better fed. This is because world grain harvests have more than doubled. Today the number of us eating fewer than twenty-one hundred calories a day, which is a standard cutoff for malnutrition, has fallen by 75 percent.

That historic feat is due largely to the "green revolution," which grew from the work of scientists at two global research agencies—the International Maize and Wheat Improvement Center (known by its Spanish acronym CIMMYT) and the International Rice Research Institute (IRRI)—along with efforts by other affiliated labs in the sixteen-member Consultative Group on International Agricultural Research (CGIAR). Their efforts came out of work done in Mexico and were funded largely by private institutions, in particular the Rockefeller Foundation.

The green revolution fought its good fight on two main fronts. The first made use of traditional crossbreeding methods to raise the percentage of a plant's biomass that it converts into grain. With rice and wheat, "dwarf" varieties were bred that doubled their proportion of the cereal grains we and our domestic animals eat. When dwarf strains of maize (corn) proved too shady to flourish, alternate types were bred that could be planted more densely.

The second front in the green revolution made creative use of fossil fuels. Oil-based pesticides and herbicides were employed. And the scientists chose plant strains that respond well to the uptake of chemical fertilizer, with its high nitrogen content. (Nitrogen is key. The scarcity of fixed nitrogen in nature is a main limiter of growth for wild plants.) That fertilizer was manufactured using fossil fuel. Then, to hold farm labor costs down, gas- and diesel-powered equipment was brought in to run the pumps used to irrigate the enormous new farms and for the mechanized plows and reapers used to cultivate them. The results of all that work changed the world. Soon row upon endless row of genetically identical "super" strains were spreading across whole nations, a vast flowering banquet waving in the sun.

Rising Inputs

If it once seemed true that what was good for industry was good for America, the machine age logic of that simpler time also implied that what was good for industry would work for nature too. And for several decades that outlook was borne out. The U.S., as the center of industrial farming, was soon producing more food per unit of labor than anywhere else in the world. But by the end of the twentieth century unforeseen problems had arisen.

For one thing, humans weren't the only species eyeing the green revolution banquet. It turned out that those vast monoculture farms were unusually tempting feasts for crop pests, whose dining habits are less constrained than ours. In 1970 an uninvited strain of corn blight ate much of the U.S. crop. In 1986, warding off the hungry Russian wheat aphid cost America's industrial farmers nearly a billion dollars for insecticides and other defenses. Today the widely monocropped Cavendish banana—favored by European and American consumers—is under assault and headed toward the fate of the once equally popular but now-extinct Gros Michel, which the Cavendish had replaced.

Extensive monocultures weren't the only thing that brought new

problems. It also turned out that a wide range of crop pathogens—
including viruses, bacteria, and fungi—actually cause more damage where
inputs of nitrogen are high. We hadn't foreseen that nitrogen fertilizer
doesn't just feed the plants; it also boosts the nutritional value of their
sap. That helped grow more and stronger pests, like the brown planthopper, a rice symbiont that quickly overran Southeast Asia. The net result was that in whole regions, damage from the increased numbers of
pests outstripped the gains from fertilization.

Moreover, as Peter Kenmore, then head of pest management in Asia
for the UN's Food and Agriculture Organization, described it, trying to
control those insect outbreaks with insecticides was "like pouring kerosene on a fire." All over the world, the simple life forms we call pests
continue doing what they've always done: eating and reproducing as
fast as they can. No sooner do we depress their numbers with poison
than the survivors rebound around it. What kills them makes them
stronger.

The statistics are sobering. At mid-century, the U.S. used fifty million pounds of pesticides a year and lost 7 percent of its preharvest to insects. Today, harvests have more than doubled. But pesticide use has
increased nearly twentyfold—to a billion pounds a year—and that flood
of poison hasn't stopped the bugs. On the contrary. Where once they
got just 7 percent of our crops, now their take is 13 percent. One of the
more disturbing aspects of this is how fast and how far pest adaptations
can spread. In 2002 a team from England's University of Bath analyzed
fruit flies to discover a basis for the resistance they had formed to DDT.
The scientists found that a jumping gene in the flies' DNA had moved
to a new location, near a gene that codes an enzyme used for chewing
up harmful chemicals. That change caused the target gene to produce
one hundred times more of the enzyme than usual. More striking is
what the team found when it looked at seventy-five different lab populations of fruit flies originally collected from across the globe, from
every continent except Antarctica. All of the fruit fly populations had
developed resistance to DDT, and in each case that resistance was due to
precisely the same mutation.

To think ecologically also means to understand that there are side effects beyond the bugs. In the Philippines, for example, during the war
against the brown planthopper and other pests, two-thirds of the country's rice fields became chemically degraded.

Despite these and many other problems, the industrial farming system has for half a century met most challenges with the same answer: more inputs. Annual world use of pesticides overall is now more than 5.5 billion pounds. Fully 70 percent of the antibiotics produced in the U.S. are administered to farm animals—such as chickens, hogs, and cattle—that are raised in cramped quarters that put them at constant risk from contagious disease. The amount of land under irrigation has doubled, and with that some two-thirds of all the freshwater we draw from lakes, rivers, and aquifers now goes to agriculture. Fertilizer use has also risen, more than 600 percent.

And one way or another, all of this has fed a growing demand for oil. More than a decade ago Cutler Cleveland of Boston University's Center for Energy and Environmental Studies made the case in clear and simple terms:

> The revolution in agriculture of the past 30 or 40 years, which we've often heard referred to as the green revolution, is really another aspect of the industrial revolution of the last 150 years. That is, learning how to use fossil fuels more cleverly to do various tasks—in this case to grow more wheat, more maize, or whatever the crop may be. And wherever we look across the world—in the industrial world of western Europe, Japan, and North America—high rates of production and food exports are very closely tied with increases in the amount of fossil fuel used.

Current estimates are that on American farms, the petroleum energy put into them now equals ten times the amount of food energy we get back. The effects of this artificial efficiency are many. By the mid-1980s—due to the spreading green revolution—nations in the developing world were using as much fertilizer as the industrialized countries of the West. By midway through the 1990s, they were using more. And as the bill for oil and chemical inputs rises, poorer nations in places like Africa feel the squeeze.

They're not the only ones. Small farmers in the West feel it, too. In 1900, when an American farmer spent a dollar on farm inputs, he got back four dollars' worth of crops. Today, Peter Henry, who runs a three-hundred-acre family farm in Chittenango, a small town in central New York, spends more than two dollars to get back four. His situation is typical. If other factors like labor are included, U.S. farm production costs have risen from half to more than 80 percent of gross income. Says Henry, "In some years, if it wasn't for the subsidies, you'd be lucky to make ten dollars on an acre."

Where does the money go? Most of the returns in agriculture—the world's largest business—today go to suppliers of pesticide and fertilizer inputs, and to the related companies that sell seed to farmers or purchase their grain. Swollen by rising cash flows, those companies have expanded into multinational giants. Ten companies now control nearly 40 percent of the world's seed market. Six handle 85 percent of its grain. Eleven large firms control 81 percent of all agrochemical sales. Sophisticated ad campaigns paired with global aid programs have fostered a booming growth market for chemical inputs in developing nations. This is big business. The world agrochemical market by itself is worth $30 billion a year.

Save the Dirt

The full-page ad in *The New York Times* proclaimed, "Too bad 'save the dirt' doesn't have that catchy ring to it." The ad was run by a life science corporation, Monsanto. "Look closer at big problems," Monsanto advised, like the billions of tons of "topsoil lost to erosion last year. The topsoil that food comes from." The ad pointed out that a main cause of erosion is the age-old custom of plowing to limit weeds. But Monsanto, it said, has developed a way to make crops resistant to a herbicide that controls weeds with far less plowing: "So the farmers can grow the crops in a more sustainable manner, by practicing what's called Conservation Tillage." The ad closed with the message, "Look closer and you find hope."

What the ad didn't say is that the new resistant plants mean doses of herbicide so high they would kill conventional food crops, or that farmers who use the new Monsanto plants are also required to buy Monsanto herbicide. It also didn't say that those higher doses burn the life from the soil.

"The living earth" is not a poetic metaphor. Rich, healthy soil can contain as much life below the ground's surface as it does above. The thousands of different kinds of microbes in each square inch of soil are only the beginning. As writer Douglas Chadwick has described it in this lively picture of soil organisms in a Midwestern prairie:

Now imagine . . . tribes of mites, insect larvae, earthworms, and microscopic, wormlike nematodes, the most abundant multicellular animals of the prairie. Together, they nearly match the weight of whatever large creatures are grazing overhead on the same acreage, and because the little beasts' metabolic rates are substantially higher they have by far the greater biological effect. In their myriad roamings, tunnelings, and turnings, these invertebrates break apart clays; pass enormous quantities of dirt through their guts; granulate the soil; enrich it with urea, amino acids, and other nitrogenous waste readily absorbed by plants; aerate it; and fashion pathways for root hairs and fungi to follow . . . Fungi-devouring herds of nematodes keep the [fungi] in balance while depositing yet more excretions into the humus. And on the process goes, generation upon generation.

Each of those life forms has a role in the dark lacework of underground givings and takings that create fertile soil. Monsanto is right to point out that when we tear the soil with plows, erosion follows. But it stopped short of naming another big cause. Pouring large volumes of herbicides, pesticides, and fertilizers on that lacework triggers a cascade of interacting effects that leaves soil degraded and unbalanced.

As populations of soil organisms crash they retain less moisture. With that, the large-crumb structure that lets air and water permeate soil breaks down into fine granules that easily wash away. The toxic destruction of delicate root structures and fungi networks accelerates that effect. Dying soil compacts more easily, so new roots can't penetrate as deeply. And with time, there are fewer nutrients for food crops to absorb.

On many industrial farms, repeated chemical dosing has caused a plight underground like that aboveground in industrial forests—the decline of diversity is paralleled by a decline in resilience and stability. Where farms are irrigated, that effect is exaggerated by salinization, in which evaporating water concentrates destructive salts in the soil. Some 20 percent of irrigated farmland worldwide has been damaged by salinization.

All this has contributed to soil loss on unprecedented scales. Around the world, erosion is now carrying topsoil away far more quickly than nature can replace it. Even with real improvements in conservation methods since the 1980s, the U.S. still loses nearly six tons of soil with every ton of grain it harvests. One-third of its original topsoil is gone, and much of what remains has been degraded.

The loop of plants, decomposers, and new soil is the foundation of our civilization. All we are and all we have emerge from that. Harvests today surpass any the world has known, but in the constant effort to raise more crops, we're pulling the rug from under our feet. The soil that our crops need for growth is gradually slipping away.

In his book *Grassland*, Richard Manning described what he called "pedestals carved by the plow." These remnants of unfarmed, original prairie exist as raised areas scattered throughout the farmlands of the American Great Plains. The crowns of those pedestals were once level with the plowed ground. Now that ground lies several feet below them. As one of the more thoughtful critics of industrial farming, the geneticist Wes Jackson, has said, "Modern agriculture has failed to produce a system that sustains its own capital."

Collateral Damage

When the soil is gone, we can't just crumble up asphalt and sprinkle it with fertilizer. But that's just a part of the problem we face. The destructive effects at work in soil decline reach beyond farms. As with all ecological change, they ripple out through other systems.

When topsoil loses its hold on moisture, more water washes off the land and into streams, rivers, and lakes. That runoff carries with it degraded and granulated soil—so much that the amount of sediment in U.S. waterways has now doubled. The heavy sediment load in turn clogs spawning grounds, shrinks capacity in reservoirs, and narrows the channels of rivers, increasing their speed. The wetlands that it chokes would otherwise sponge up floods and serve as filters—purifying water before it flows into lakes and seas, or where it seeps down into aquifers. So even as the amount of water flowing into watersheds increases, their ability to handle it declines.

While washing away the topsoil, runoff water also carries with it the strange brew of chemicals applied to farm soil each year. And just as they degrade the life in soil, those chemicals degrade the food chains in waterways. They also leach into groundwater. U.S. tests have found residues of seventy-four pesticides and chemical fertilizers in the water of thirty-eight states. Among them is the herbicide atrazine, which is now present in virtually all U.S. water. It's in a class of common chemicals that mimic the female hormone estrogen. One of the more disturbing outcomes of that are findings that link such chemicals to sex organ deformities in animals ranging from frogs to deer to alligators. A University of North Carolina study has suggested a link between them and a dramatic lowering of the age at which American girls are entering puberty. Many today show breast development and pubic hair at the age of seven, it said, and 1 percent now do so at age three. The compounding effects of persistent chemicals like these in living tissue were examined in the 1996 book *Our Stolen Future.*

More even than pesticides, farm runoff contains nitrogen. The scarcity of fixed nitrogen in nature limits growth, so when we increase that flow it has real consequences. Our massive broadcasts of fertilizer up yields and help mask the decline of topsoil. But crops absorb only about half of what we apply; the rest flows on into other systems. Then there is the runoff from farm animals. Their total mass is currently twice that of humanity's and is an order of magnitude beyond that of wild mammals. Most of them are kept on huge factory farms where they're fed highly enriched diets that—like fertilizer on crops—they only partly absorb. What they don't absorb becomes the billions of tons of "superwaste" that have polluted thirty-five thousand miles of American rivers in the past decade. These and other nitrogen outputs from human culture now equal all of the naturally fixed nitrogen on earth.

This enormous runoff—a doubling of one of the most valuable elements in nature—quickly finds new takers. On land it fosters the growth of ecological pioneers, aggressive plants like quack grass that run wild in high-nitrogen environments and crowd out diversity. In waterways it becomes ten to one hundred times more concentrated than on land. Huge algae blooms grow as a result. And when those algae die and decay, they soak up aquatic oxygen, asphyxiating fish and other sea life. Farm runoff from the corn belt of the Midwest, concentrated in the Mississippi River, flows into the Gulf of Mexico. There it has created a dead zone that in some years equals the size of New Jersey. Similar effects are at work in European rivers such as the Thames, Rhine, Meuse, and Elbe. Australian runoff degrades the Great Barrier Reef, the world's largest coral reef. Farm runoff has been blamed for collapsing fisheries in the Baltic Sea. Excess nitrogen also feeds blooms of toxic algae, the red tides familiar to seacoast residents.

Genetic Erosion

Even as crop plants contend with the outside stresses caused by industrial farming, the genetic basis of those crops is also at risk. Among the fifty thousand species of edible plants, only some two hundred are now widely planted. And of those, just twenty major food crops provide virtually all of the nutrition we take from plants. Moreover, in the rice fields of Asia, where thousands of regional types were once the norm, just a few green revolution hybrids have largely taken their place. Most commercially grown tomatoes in the West today stem from an equally narrow genetic base, and that story holds for other important food crops. This loss of diversity in the fields is called genetic erosion.

Monocropping makes plants more vulnerable to pests and disease. In a memorable nineteenth-century example, when Britain's great coffee plantations in Sri Lanka (then Ceylon) were wiped out, they were replanted with an entirely different beverage crop. The result is still acknowledged by the British at about 4:00 p.m. each day.

The catastrophic Irish potato blight, which killed one million people, did its damage because Ireland's entire crop then consisted of just two varieties. The blight was stopped when scientists went back to the source—Peru, where some three thousand varieties of potato were still grown. There they found one that was resistant. In the U.S., the 1970 corn blight and the 1986 attack of the Russian wheat aphid were both halted by a similar approach, but with an important difference. In those cases the resistant strains came from seed banks.

It's the job of seed banks—now more often called gene banks—to save varieties no longer sown in fields. But even within those banks, genetic erosion has continued. For stored varieties to remain vital, they have to be germinated every few years to produce fresh seeds, and many types require special handling. Due to budget cuts, wars, and neglect—at facilities in the Americas, Europe, Asia, the Middle East, Africa, and Australia—large numbers of rare and irreplaceable seeds are being lost.

The good news is that there are now nearly fifteen hundred gene banks around the world (in the 1970s there were fewer than ten), and that the UN's Food and Agriculture Organization (FAO) and CGIAR are currently raising $260 million for the Global Crop Diversity Trust, which will upgrade and support them. That move aims to address the bad news, which is that in 1996, when the FAO surveyed the world's repositories, it flunked more than half of them, saying they were "perhaps incapable at present of performing the basic conservation role of a genebank."

This suggests the potential for more losses before the trust is in place. But those losses pale in comparison to what may already have disappeared. As an example of that, the survey cites an American report that analyzed historical USDA records from the nineteenth century:

> It revealed that most varieties . . . can no longer be found in either commercial agriculture or any US genebank. For example, of the 7,098 apple varieties documented as having been in use between 1804 and 1904, approximately 86 percent have been lost. Similarly, 95 percent of the cabbage, 91 percent of the field maize, 94 percent of the pea, and 81 percent of the tomato varieties apparently no longer exist. The processes of modernization and varietal replacement, well documented in the US, have now occurred in many other countries.

Continuing that trend will only weaken further the genetic basis for our food supply, opening the door wider for diseases, not to mention acts of bioterrorism. Clive Stannard, a high-level FAO official in Rome, notes that "food security depends overwhelmingly on a few crops . . . and on the diversity within those crops."

Topping Out

Despite all the difficulties, officials at the World Trade Organization, the UN, and other international bodies are cautiously optimistic that scientists will somehow repeat the gains of the first green revolution. Plant breeders are less sanguine. According to Robert S. Loomis, an agronomist from the University of California at Davis, "Maximum rice yields have been the same for thirty years. We're plateauing out in biomass, and there's no easy answer for it."

A more immediate concern is the problem of sustaining the yields we already have. According to a report by the Rockefeller Foundation—a primary funder of the first green revolution—"Recent data on crop yields and production . . . suggest a degree of stagnation which is worrying."

Tapping Out

From the 1950s to today is not much time for all that to have happened. And the next fifty years will bring even more change. By then our petroleum reserves will be seriously depleted; and the spread of violent conflict in oil-producing regions like the Middle East could threaten supplies sooner. In fifty years our reserves of phosphate—a crucial fertilizer found mainly in North Africa—may also be gone. But above and beyond all this is the concern that we are running out of water.

Humanity uses fully half of all the world's freshwater. Moreover, we devote two-thirds of that to irrigated farms (which grow 40 percent of our food). Like our topsoil, that water is being used faster than it's replenished. As a result, once-mighty inland bodies of water like Lake Chad in Africa and the Aral Sea in central Asia are being sucked dry, creating world-class environmental disasters. Elsewhere, India's self-sufficiency in food, hard earned over several decades, is now threatened by the siltation of reservoirs and by overpumping in the crucial Punjab region. So much water is taken from the Ganges that little reaches the sea. The same is true of the Nile. In the American West, states along the Colorado—epic sculptor of the Grand Canyon—have now parceled out more water on paper than there is in the river.

Lakes and rivers in semiarid regions aren't the only water supplies under stress. Aquifers, the vast underground reservoirs that were filled up during the course of eons, are disappearing, too. In the U.S. the Ogallala Aquifer—an ancient reserve the size of California—extends beneath the High Plains from Texas all the way to the Dakotas. Some 40 percent of American feedlot cattle eat grain made with Ogallala water. But it's being drawn down at a rate of from three to ten feet a year, and in parts of Texas is already mostly gone. In West Texas, where water disputes with Mexico have sharpened over the disappearing Rio Grande, former junk-bond kingpin T. Boone Pickens has declared mining the remaining Texas water reserves to be the next big thing.

Regional water disputes are an increasing problem for Israel and its neighbors, as they are among Turkey, Syria, and Iraq, and for Egypt, Ethiopia, and the Sudan. They're also a growing point of contention between farmers and cities everywhere. A short list of headlines taken from major news outlets during the first three years of this century tells the story. They are presented here in order of appearance:

"A RIFT OVER RIO GRANDE WATER RIGHTS: TEXANS CRY FOUL
AFTER MEXICO WARNS THAT IT WILL BREACH TREATY"

"LEASING THE RAIN: THE WORLD IS RUNNING OUT OF FRESH
WATER AND THE FIGHT TO CONTROL IT HAS BEGUN"

"WATER WAR: INDIA COULD SUCK PAKISTAN DRY"

"ATLANTA'S GROWING THIRST CREATES WATER WAR"

"AS MULTINATIONALS RUN THE TAPS, ANGER RISES OVER
WATER FOR PROFIT"

"CHINA WILL MOVE WATERS TO QUENCH THIRST OF CITIES"

"THE GREAT THIRST: DROUGHT AND DISEASE THREATEN TO SET
OFF A WATER WAR IN VOLATILE CENTRAL ASIA"

"ISRAEL WAITS FOR SEA OF GALILEE'S LOW TIDE TO TURN"

"20,000 FISH ARE DEAD IN RIVER WHERE WATER FLOW
IS DISPUTED"

"ARKANSAS RICE FARMERS RUN DRY, AND U.S. REMEDY SETS
OFF DEBATE"

"GRAND SOVIET SCHEME FOR SHARING WATER IN CENTRAL
ASIA IS FOUNDERING"

"U.S. TO CUT CALIFORNIA'S SHARE OF WATER FROM
COLORADO RIVER"

"FAILED DEAL IN CALIFORNIA CUTS WATER FOR NEVADA"

"A NEW FRONTIER IN WATER WARS EMERGES IN EAST"

"MILLIONS FACE WATER SHORTAGE IN NORTH CHINA,
OFFICIALS WARN"

"ACCORD IN WEST WILL GIVE CITIES FARMERS' WATER"

"WEST TEXANS SIZZLE OVER A PLAN TO SELL THEIR WATER"

In 1998, Canada—which holds 30 percent of the world's freshwater—
quietly passed legislation banning its export. The U.S. governors of
states surrounding the Great Lakes are now negotiating laws that will do
the same. Meanwhile, in the developing world, the World Bank has begun requiring countries that seek water-related loans to let their water
supplies be privatized, typically by multinationals.

Irrigation has made deserts bloom. But as Wes Jackson points out, un-sustainable water-use strategies are just a way of "padding the statistics." The day of reckoning no longer lies in the future. Irrigation is already being used in most of the places where it's practical, yet as human pop-ulation climbs above six billion, pressure is growing for the system to expand. That's an unsettling backdrop for a projection by a CGIAR water-management lab. It forecasts that within the next quarter century, as many as thirty-nine countries—including areas of China, India, and much of Africa—will be so short of water they'll have to *reduce* irrigation.

Countries with water shortages have to import their grain, but with the grain-exporting nations already supplying 260 million tons to world markets each year, and with the current system facing fundamental chal-lenges on several fronts, there is some question about their ability to meet larger demands. And larger demands are coming. According to *Vital Signs*, a tracking report published each year by the Worldwatch Institute:

> Three large countries that currently produce most of their own food—China, India, and Pakistan—are likely to be driven by water stress and other factors to join the ranks of the grain importers in the near future. China already has severe water problems in its agriculturally important Hai and Yellow River basins. The projected water deficit for these two basins is roughly equal to the volume of water needed to grow 55 million tons of grain. As much as one-fourth of India's grain production—some 45 million tons—is jeopardized by groundwater overpumping alone. Thus India and China could be headed toward combined grain imports of 100 million tons—more than the entire current U.S. supply of grain to world markets.

Taken together, the rebounding populations of crop pests, the rise in the costs of inputs, the continuous loss of topsoil, the damage from chemical runoff, the decline in supplies of freshwater, the genetic ero-sion of food crops, the topping out of crop plant productivity, and the exponential growth of human population are causes for real concern. Says Tony Fischer, a crop sciences program manager at the Australian Centre for International Agricultural Research, "When you add up everything that has to be done, and the narrowing range of options for how to do it, the challenge is dauntingly large."

Demographic Transition Theory

Habitat limits are hard limits. Even the cleverest creatures have to deal with them sooner or later. In ecology those limits are embodied in the notion of carrying capacity—of how much life a region can support. For most species that's a local question; that is, larger forests support more deer than small ones can. But as human population tops six billion, the carrying capacity of our planet has become a concern.

Carrying capacity is at the heart of evolution. Populations, Darwin said, always outgrow their food supplies. That overproduction means only the fittest survive, which is how natural selection works. But a school of thought called "demographic transition theory" maintains that humans are beating the system. That theory is based on the fact that in the industrialized West, as people have become more educated and financially secure, the birthrate has fallen below two for each childbearing woman. As Western values and economic prospects spread, it suggests, they carry that trend with them around the world. And in fact, according to a recent UN report, the global fertility rate is now down to 1.85 children per woman. This should bring a leveling off of population at just under nine billion by 2050, followed by a gradual decline. That is put forward as an important benefit of globalization based on the Western industrial scheme.

Have we outsmarted evolution? Will the leveling off and decline of human population mean our system respects the earth's ultimate carrying capacity? No, it does not. The problem with that view is that it's linear. It thinks big, but it doesn't think wide.

Demographic transition theory ignores the fact that humans are different from deer. Deer just eat, make waste, and reproduce. Humans have complex cultures. What that means is that for us humans, it isn't carrying capacity, it's "cultural carrying capacity": the per capita consumption that a given region can support. And per capita consumption in humans can vary dramatically. When anthropologist Napoleon Chagnon did his well-known study of the Yąnomamö, an isolated tribe living deep in the Amazonian forest, he estimated their combined numbers as ten thousand and their range at roughly eighty-thousand square kilometers—a ratio of eight square kilometers per person. How can they be equated with residents of a country like the Netherlands, where population density is more than one thousand people per square kilometer? Both are human populations, but their cultures—hunter-gatherer on the one hand, modern and industrial on the other—put very different per capita demands on the world around them.

Hunter-gatherers take a simple approach to survival, essentially just feeding off the local fruit of the land on which they live. Our Western industrial system is widespread and circuitous. We use fossil fuels to manufacture nitrogen, which we apply to distant farmlands treated with oil-based pesticides and tilled by oil-powered machines. Through those means, manufactured nitrogen is absorbed by crop plants. They in turn use it to make amino acids, which those plants then assemble into proteins. When domestic animals consume the plants, they concentrate them into higher grades of protein. We eat both of those, and the proteins we take in as food—still carrying industrial nitrogen—are broken back down by our digestive systems into loose amino acids. They are then reassembled in our cells to make whatever customized proteins our bodies may require.

It's an extraordinary process. With it we've accelerated productivity on fertile lands and grown larger human populations around the world. For instance, industrial fertilizer now accounts for half of all the nitrogen in China's food protein. That means it has been used to construct the cells in the bodies of some five hundred million people.

In this sense farming is an energy technology, and in modern farming oil is food. But the oil needed to keep all this going is essentially just solar energy that has been stored in rotted biomass, much as it might be in a big battery. Sooner or later it's going to run out. The only real question is, when? Writer Richard Manning brings some historical perspective to the question:

> Every single calorie we eat is backed by at least a calorie of oil, more like ten. In 1940 the average farm in the United States produced 2.3 calories of food energy for every calorie of fossil energy it used. By 1974 (the last year in which anyone looked closely at the issue), that ratio was 1:1. And this understates the problem, because at the same time that there is more oil in our food there is less oil in our oil. A couple of generations ago we spent a lot less energy drilling, pumping, and distributing than we do now. In the 1940s we got about 100 barrels of oil back for every barrel of oil spent getting it. Today each barrel of oil invested in the process returns only ten.

And, he goes on to point out, that calculation omits all the oil spent fueling military operations that secure access to oil in unstable parts of the world.

In light of realities like these, the idea that population may level off or even decline before it hits nine billion is irrelevant. We're already far beyond sustainable levels, and as efforts to extend the Western system to the rest of the world succeed, Western standards of consumption are spreading, too.

Cultural carrying capacity is key. Just how serious a question it is can be seen in two remarkable statistics. If, starting in 1984, energy use for the rest of the world's farms had been like that of farms in the United States, then agriculture by itself would have exhausted all known world oil reserves by 1996. Not incidentally, by that date human consumption of freshwater was growing at a rate two and a half times faster than the growth in population.

At Play in the Fields of the Lord

The fix we're in comes not from an absence of good intentions. It stems from an incomplete understanding of ecology, from a reliance on machine age views of nature. But even though the problems caused by that are getting harder to miss, the latest solutions for ending world hunger bring mechanical thinking to the ultimate new frontier: the genome. That frontier was opened in 1980, when the U.S. Supreme Court sanctioned a patented life form, a microbe engineered to eat oil spills. With that, multinational corporations swung their gaze to the elemental structure of life.

The results have often been impressive: Hawaii's papaya crop saved by a gene that wards off the voracious ring spot virus. Engineered proteins stimulating the growth of red blood cells for patients with anemia. Microbes gobbling up various toxins. But as with the green revolution, there are dangers here, too. That's because most of the new biotech corporations bring narrow, linear machine age logic to the business of engineering genes. As early as 1987, Wes Jackson was pointing out: "They are offering the 'specific problem–specific solution' approach. This approach assumes that everything outside the specific problem for which they intend to splice in a solution can be held still, that nothing else will wobble; or if it does, that they can splice in a correction for that, too."

That wobble can mean unforeseen problems for the organisms being altered. It can also mean unanticipated repercussions when they're turned loose to enter the interactive webs and cycles of life.

In the early days of genetic engineering, concern for that possibility was so great that research was limited to labs with negative air pressure.

Today some 200 million acres of farmland around the world grow genetically modified organisms under the open sky. That change came about
not because there's no longer any reason for concern. It was due to a
costly lobbying campaign in Washington and elsewhere, conducted by
multinational biotech corporations and led by Monsanto.

Monsanto is based in St. Louis, where Bill Lambrecht, a reporter for
the *St. Louis Post-Dispatch*, did a thorough and insightful job of tracking
the global drama that ensued. In the mid-1980s the White House agreed
to "adopt a framework that would operate with no new legislation. This
strategy assured that genetic engineering would, for the most part, remain out of the domain of the Congress."

One outcome of that understanding was that the Food and Drug
Administration was given no authority over genetically engineered
foods. This put primary oversight in the hands of the U.S. Department
of Agriculture. There, the influence of big biotech corporations was so
blatant that by the turn of the century top USDA officials were being
publicly branded "biotechnology shills." And not without reason. Of
the forty thousand field tests involving gene-engineered crops between
1987 and 2002, the USDA rejected the applications for only 3.5 percent. And those, according to the U.S. Public Interest Research Group,
were due mostly to incomplete paperwork or other minor errors. Meanwhile, top U.S. government officials were fanning out across the globe
to promote the new GM (genetically modified) crops.

The introduction of any novel species into a natural system is a risk,
even without genetic engineering. A Cornell University study has estimated that the introduction of alien weeds into the United States has
cost the economy $35.5 billion. The bill for alien insects is $20 billion,
the study said, and for human disease-causing organisms it is $6.5 bil-
lion. In addition, the study concluded that 40 percent of all the U.S.
species labeled threatened or endangered are at risk primarily due to
aliens. That would seem to raise a red flag for biotechnology. But as
Andrew Kimbrell of the Washington-based International Center for
Technology Assessment has pointed out, "We now have biotechnologists creating tens and hundreds of thousands of novel microbes, plants,
and animals, and releasing them into the environment."

Among the GM organisms causing concern are plants modified
with a gene from the *Bacillus thuringiensis* bacterium. "*Bt* corn," for instance, kills the corn borer and other pests without the use of insecticide.

The problem is that *Bt* sprays have long been used in small quantities and precise applications by organic farmers. They're now worried that *Bt*'s use in large monocropping systems will trigger widespread insect resistance as its target populations rebound around it. That could mean the permanent loss of an important defensive tool. Recognizing the threat, the Environmental Protection Agency has ruled that 20 percent of the acreage in *Bt* cornfields should be planted with unmodified corn. This practice provides a reserve for the insects, so they don't have to evolve resistance in order to reproduce. But a recent study based on USDA information—obtained under the Freedom of Information Act—showed that in three of the biggest corn-growing states some 19 percent of farms did not plant large enough refuges, and that 13 percent of those farms planted no refuge at all. The biotech industry itself admits an overall 14 percent noncompliance rate.

The problem of how insects develop resistance is mirrored by weeds, where there is the potential for "gene flow" among plants. That's because most crop plants were originally developed from wild types. When crops are genetically engineered and released, they can still breed with their wild cousins, thus radiating altered genes in unplanned directions. In the case of *Bt*, or with crops engineered to resist pesticides, they can even produce new strains of "superweeds."

Lab research has shown that *Bt*-modified oil seed rape (canola) can pass its resistance to a related weed called birdseed rape. The same transfer has been demonstrated from domestic to wild sunflowers. In another test, researchers tracked the spread of a jellyfish-fluorescence gene—which was engineered into rapeseed—to a relative, the wild turnip. In the area around the rapeseed field, 10 percent of the wild turnips were soon glowing in the dark. Gene flow has occurred on farms, too. In a Canadian case, an Alberta farmer planted three different genetically modified varieties of rapeseed in three separate fields. The plants had been engineered to withstand high doses of herbicide. Within two years he began finding resistant wild weeds among his crops. They appeared in every field. Now much more powerful herbicides are needed to control them.

In the U.S. between 2001 and 2003, the widespread planting of crops that are modified to survive higher doses of herbicides has brought an increase of seventy-three million pounds in the use of herbicides as existing weeds developed resistance or tougher species moved into fields.

Not all GM plants have the potential to spread. Many today are essentially hothouse varieties that would have little to teach their hardier cousins. But new problems are on the way. Says Allison Snow, an Ohio State University plant ecologist, "The genes that catch my attention . . . are anything that makes the plants bigger and healthier, or anything that would allow them to expand their range, like cold tolerance or drought tolerance or salt tolerance. These are all genes that people are working on now, and they're going to be available in five or ten years. Those could have some major ecological effects if they get into wild relatives and suddenly those plants could grow where they never grew before." Like alien invaders, they could become the transgene equivalent of kudzu or worse.

Elaine Ingham, one of the world's preeminent microbiologists, was involved in a case in which an actual doomsday scenario was narrowly avoided. In her Oregon State University lab, she and a graduate student, Michael Holmes, were looking at an engineered version of *Klebsiella planticola*, a bacterium found on plants. The GM version included an extra gene that caused it to produce large quantities of alcohol. The idea behind the modification was that plant debris would be gathered after harvest and put into vats along with the GM bacteria, which would convert it into fuel. Then leftover residue from that process could be spread back on the fields as fertilizer. The parent bacterium was a type commonly found in the fungus that inhabits plant roots.

The GM organisms had already received EPA approval for field trials—via a process that had subjected them to the same tests as those used for screening pesticide toxicity. But when Holmes introduced the approved bacteria to actual living wheat plants for the first time in his lab, the plants immediately died. Later analysis showed that the bacteria had migrated to the root fungi (which also help plants absorb nitrogen). There, the large amounts of alcohol it produced quickly and efficiently killed the plants. The implications of that are profound. As Ingham later summarized them, "It is inadequate to subject organisms to the [tests] required for non-living chemical pesticides, and conclude that there will be no adverse or risky effects from release of those organisms . . . With a single release, we know that bacteria can spread over large distances, probably worldwide. These bacteria would therefore get into the root systems of all terrestrial plants and begin to produce alcohol." She went on to a chilling conclusion: "This would result in the death of . . . corn, wheat, barley, vegetable crops, trees, bushes, etc., conceivably all terrestrial plants. It is clear, therefore, that current testing procedures required by US regulatory agencies are completely inadequate in assessing the potential risks involved with genetically engineered organisms."

A Roll of the Dice

One way or another, all these problems stem from how little we really know about what we're tinkering with. "You can't look at the genome of an organism and even tell how many legs it has," says Roger Brent of the Molecular Sciences Institute in Berkeley, California. That flies in the face of notions that DNA is just a mechanical lineup of independent units, with each one expressing some trait. According to the microbiologist Lynn Caporale, "Gene families should be analyzed as systems rather than as lists of related genes." The genes of all mammals—be they dogs, cows, or people—are pretty much the same. What makes them into different species, says the biologist and Nobel laureate Sydney Brenner, is how those genes are arranged. Another expert, the developmental biologist Scott Gilbert, observes that what any given gene does "depends on the context in which it finds itself." Genomes are networks, he says, where regulatory regions decide how and when specific genes are expressed. When things get shifted around, new networks—and new organisms—come into being.

The moving of gene regulatory "promoters," "enhancers," and "modulators" to unfamiliar territory can send unplanned changes rippling through the genome ecology and on out into the organism. The response to DDT by fruit fly DNA mentioned earlier is a case in point. If the jump of an enhancer gene in fruit fly DNA can spur a chemical-chomping enzyme to be produced at a hundred times its normal rate, it's not hard to imagine how inserting an enhancer in an abnormal position can disturb cell multiplication, thereby creating a malignancy in a human baby.

As the big new life science companies move forward with plans for a genetic green revolution, the intertwining ecological interactions of the genome should be high on their lists of things to bear in mind. Quite the opposite often seems to be the case. One of the newest of those firms is Maxygen, which on its Web site bills itself as "the leading supplier of directed evolution technologies known as Molecular Breeding for optimization of genes for the development of products in the areas of human therapeutics, vaccines, agriculture and chemicals."

Maxygen's breakthrough is its patented "shuffling" process for recombining genes, which was initially described by one trade journal as "cutting them all into small pieces and then putting the pieces back together in the right order but without regard as to which gene any particular piece came from." Those hybrids are then screened for desired traits and used as the basis for subsequent generations in the familiar process of directed evolution.

The company was founded in 1997 as a spinoff from the drugmaker Glaxo Wellcome–Affymax. Just in time for New Year's 2000, financial markets welcomed the promise of "a virtually infinite amount of novel, proprietary high-value diversity" by bidding its shares up 162 percent during a $110 million initial public offering. In an interview prior to that in *The Economist*, Maxygen's chief noted that until then the company's techniques could shuffle only genomes that had at least half their sequences in common. But he said he looked forward to mixing DNA from vastly different organisms soon.

Gene shuffling allows Maxygen, it claims, "to rapidly develop novel genes for commercial applications that would be difficult or impossible to develop or find through other processes." It also says that its technologies are efficient in part "because they require minimal understanding of complex underlying biological mechanisms."

An Even Greener Revolution

Is it possible that groundwater once contaminated can be purified, or once depleted refilled, that forests and topsoil once lost can be restored, that new and disruptive species once set loose can be recalled? In a world where historic feats and grand ambitions are everyday matters, even these slim prospects may be allowed. But no conservative would count on them. To anyone with knowledge of ecology it's clear that our agriculture—the essential loop of plants, decomposers, and new soil on which civilization is founded—has fallen into the hands of radicals.

Their solution to the problems we now face is to up the risks even more. In light of that it's worth recalling something Einstein once said: we can't solve today's problems with the kind of thinking that created them. Changing course won't be easy. Still, it will be impossible until we focus on the crux of the matter. Farmers and loggers aren't the problem. The existence of genetic engineering isn't the problem. While companies may misbehave, corporations aren't the problem either. Like a growing organism in nature, they're shaped by the system in which they operate. And for centuries now we've let the machine metaphor guide our culture.

That's the problem. Humans are biological; so are the foods we eat, which means our lives are bound to the rules of nature. Mechanisms are a legitimate part of life; the machine age itself was an effort to employ natural principles and we got it half right. But mechanism is a subset of biology. It can't be a governing principle.

The term "sustainable" stands for the most basic question we face in choosing how to support our culture: "Can we count on this to last?" A fleeting abundance is no measure of success. And the hard truth is, the industrial approach we've used to double world population in just fifty years is faltering; it's not a reliable path to the future. That approach looks like a winner only because we have, as Wes Jackson puts it, been padding the stats.

The notion that we can conquer nature and make our own way is foolish in the deepest possible sense. There is no other way, no other means. All habitats have limits. We can't make something out of nothing. There's only so much energy, and we must use matter wisely. Moreover, when we focus energy and resources in one area, the 2nd Law of Thermodynamics calls for a corresponding depletion and disorganization somewhere else. Then there are the ecological rules of engagement: what goes around comes around. Which brings around the question of population.

Conventional wisdom holds that populations are growing, so we have to feed them. But in the unrelenting logic of nature, they grow *because* we feed them. This reflects one of the central tenets of evolution: populations always outgrow their resources—that's how natural selection works. As the number of humans now presses up against earth's carrying capacity, Darwin's insight is no longer academic. It is a timely warning. But according to demographic transition theory, industrial cultures are smart enough to rein themselves in before they hit the wall of habitat limits. Agriculture is the ultimate test.

Computers will play a pivotal role in whatever comes. Just as they amplify today's problems—by automating machine age methods on a whole new scale—so, too, the biological insight and cultural flexibility they bring will be at the heart of any change. Corporations can help as well. Says Peter Raven—director of the famed Missouri Botanical Garden and codiscoverer of coevolution—"Multinational corporations are one of the best vehicles to achieve global sustainability." If we can reform the system that guides them, they have the reach and influence to carry new solutions across the globe.

There is no future for human culture without a sustainable agriculture. That is the first and fundamental challenge. And as the following chapter shows—in forestry, in farming, in all the areas where we manage natural systems—lasting solutions are at hand.

eight

the even greener
revolution

The "new forestry" aims to replace the widespread clearcutting that breaks down woodland cycles. Instead it looks for guidance to the weblike interactions of ecology. Within each commercial timber stand, it sets apart an unlogged heartland. That becomes a collecting ground for diversity, a genetic reserve where numerous species can survive and co-evolve. Also unlogged are densely wooded migration corridors that fan out like spokes to connect with other heartlands. Those spokes are genetic highways, conduits providing safe passage for wandering plants and animals through less hospitable zones. They offer passage into other regions, too. Some connect with wilderness areas, homes to big predators like bear. Others reach down into valleys—to riparian shores that serve as wombs for countless species. Seen through the eye of a high-flying bird, the dark green hubs and spokes of these systems form lush ecological webs that overlay rolling open pastures and settled areas as well as regions where timber has been cut.

From forested slopes to fruited plains and on through the teeming shallows of wetlands, all natural systems are webs of interacting cycles, conducting the flow of genes evolved over millions of years. Genes themselves are, in essence, information. They remember how energy can coordinate matter into living forms. Then, wherever life occurs, it constantly plays with those forms, adapting genetic information, shifting populations around, always seeking out the sweet spot that will heighten productivity in any given place. This deeper reality lies behind everything we see when we walk through a natural landscape—from the verdant carpeting of tree-covered hills to the endless munching of beetles on nurse logs, from the sea of grass on a prairie to a turtle swimming clumsily though a pond.

As science now unveils the living world to show its deeper workings, the effects of industrial agriculture are more apparent, too. And because the loop of plants, decomposers, and new soil lies at the heart of all we are and all we have, it's also where the new biology can have its greatest effect. That loop is our foundation. Keeping the door to our future open means going back to basics, reconnecting culture to the natural webs and cycles from which life comes.

Logging the Web

The famed anthropologist Gregory Bateson liked to tell a story about New College, in Oxford, England. The main hall there was built in the mid-seventeenth century with oak beams forty feet long and two feet thick. Recently they began to suffer from dry rot, and administrators couldn't find English oaks large enough to replace them. A young faculty member said, "Why don't we ask the college forester if some of the lands given to Oxford might have enough trees to call upon?" They brought in the forester, who said, "We've been wondering when you would ask this question. When the present building was constructed 350 years ago, the architects specified that a grove of trees be planted and maintained to replace the beams in the ceiling when they suffered from dry rot." Bateson's conclusion was "That's the way to run a culture."

What kind of foundation are we laying for the world of three centuries from today? Forests once covered nearly half of the earth's continental surface. We have reduced them to less than a quarter, and in the process degraded the life-support system of a planet. That's why new foresters don't clearcut whole tracts, why they take pains to thin the ecological structure without removing it. It's why they leave a few dead trees standing, as habitat for woodpeckers and other snag dwellers. It's why some dead wood is also left on the ground, to slow running water and become nurse logs. And it's why stream banks are lined by buffer zones of unlogged trees and shrubbery. In the new forestry, monocultures are discouraged. Road building and other disruptions are minimized. Where possible, timber is milled on-site with small portable units, creating local jobs. And rotations—how soon trees are recut—are geared to natural growth rates: fast-growing pines are cut often, while the harvesting of oaks like those for New College is paced to their centuries-long cycle.

There are also organizations now that certify ecological timber production, and the chains of custody that bring it to market. SmartWood—a Richmond, Vermont–based group formed in 1989—is the oldest and largest. The Forest Stewardship Council (FSC), based in Oaxaca, Mexico, was started in 1993. It sets world standards and certifies the certifiers. The FSC now sanctions over seventy million acres, an area that would cover all of Britain and more.

The new approach is not strictly speaking new. The Magnifica Comunità di Fiemme, in northern Italy—not far from Lake Como—is a forestry commune that has managed some fifty thousand acres since its founding in A.D. 1111. It uses many of the practices now gaining favor. And the U.S. president Teddy Roosevelt's progressive approach to forestry was borrowed from Germany, one of the first nations to recognize the value of replanting timber after a harvest to ensure future yields. In Germany today, the new forestry guides logging in all state-owned forests.

But Switzerland leads the world in sustainable forestry. The Swiss banned clearcutting on mountains in 1876, and expanded that law to all forests in 1902, while adding on more prescriptions for things like selective logging and controlled cuts. Today the Swiss Forest Legislation bans monocultures, along with pesticides and fertilizers, and guides the most sustainable logging system in Europe.

That comes at a price. Swiss production costs are nearly double those of other nations. But behind that lies another statistic. The industrialized Canadian forest sector creates three direct and indirect jobs for every twenty-five hundred acres it logs; a tract that size in Switzerland produces eighty-three jobs. That's a remarkable benefit for only a doubling of costs, and even the cost disparity could cease—perhaps even reverse—with the adoption of full cost accounting. Today's machine age accounting doesn't count all the real costs of industrial methods. As mentioned in chapter 7, they conveniently leave out "the decrease in land values, soil erosion, stream siltation, damage to public roads and bridges, disruption of surface-water flow cycles, species extinction, damage to fish stocks, reduction of recreational values, and loss of local employment."

In the end, this means that the price of ecological timber isn't high, it's accurate. The disparity stems from the fact that industrial timber prices are being kept artificially low. Because those pricing models externalize the collateral damage that industrial logging inflicts, they're based on incomplete data. Anyone who values the free market can see why that's a problem. Companies don't have to cook the books; the system is doing it for them.

In a world with realistic timber costs, the free market works as it should: Valid prices spur conservation and push new alternatives. Jobs are created, and quality of life improves in woodland communities. The use of waste products from mills to make chipboard products becomes a cost-effective alternative, and incentives to recycle increase. Related businesses—like salmon fisheries—benefit as well. And market forces replace the need for many of the government programs and controls now in place in those areas.

With all this there could come a day when high-flying birds look down on a vast new development. A landscape in which lush, skeletal webs of genetic hubs and connecting spokes have softened human impact.

Harvesting Information

We benefit from undisturbed tracts of forest, too. Their natural splendor is an ancient source of wonder. They are actors in many of the cycles we link to ecologically—as when they filter freshwater, or absorb the carbon from CO_2 and release the oxygen we breathe. They're also, especially tropical forests, among the richest genetic reserves on earth.

As such they are an important source for natural compounds that serve as medicines. There are today more than one hundred prescription drugs based on plants. Aspirin, one of the world's most popular remedies, is a synthetic based on willow bark. Then there are the antimalarial quinine; L-dopa, for Parkinson's disease; digitalis, for cardiac failure; tranquilizers like reserpine and scopolamine; and the cancer drugs Taxol and vinblastine—all of them derived from plants.

"The information of nature is not just beauty," says Cornell

University biologist Tom Eisner. And "harvesting the information of nature doesn't have to be as invasive as harvesting the minerals of nature." People tried making gold for many years, Eisner points out. Chemistry was born through the mistakes of alchemy. "But the new alchemy, basically resynthesizing the chemicals of nature, that's a realistic thing." Once you know a certain chemical, he says, "you can synthesize it and use it as a medicinal. And that generates jobs." Eisner is not just speculating. He was among those who worked to set up INBio, a pioneering project in which drugmaker Merck helped preserve large tracts of native ecosystems in Costa Rica. Local people received training on how to identify and collect plant samples, which were then forwarded to Merck labs for assay.

The effort to parse the great quantities of natural information being harvested has given rise to a novel kind of drug research. Following in the steps of Harvard's Richard Evans Schultes, scientists called ethnobotanists now interview tribal healers around the world to learn about traditional remedies that may have broader application.

"You need an ear for language and you have to know your plants cold," says Paul Cox of the National Tropical Botanical Garden in Hawaii. He was using both those skills while interviewing Epenesa Mauigoa, a traditional healer on the Samoan island of Savaii. When she mentioned a hepatitis treatment from the mamala tree's stem wood, his interest was piqued. In later tests by the U.S. National Cancer Institute (NCI), the wood was found to contain a phorbol ester that drives dormant HIV cells out of hiding so they can be attacked by other AIDS drugs. Because of the molecule's structure, it would otherwise have been dismissed as a potential carcinogen. But for reasons still unclear, it doesn't show that effect. Commenting on the discovery, NCI's Gordon Cragg says, "Chemists at the bench could never dream up what nature provides."

The new compound has now been licensed to a nonprofit organization that will also ensure that 20 percent of any profits from drug sales go to the Samoans. This addresses the long-standing problem of multinational corporations co-opting native research and development without thanks. For example, the neem tree was bred by farmers in India to make a natural pesticide. With no compensation to those farmers, it's now being patented and sold in other countries. During his time in Samoa, Cox ran into another common problem. He had to fight a plan to log the forest where mamala trees are found. Despite such complications, he still values the knowledge traditional healers impart. "Talking to them about the plants," he says, "was like talking to another Ph.D."

While some researchers tramp through the woods, still more are searching through a new and rapidly developing habitat for drug information: computers. It's hard to overstate the importance of data-crunching skills in drug discovery today, both in recording molecular data and in providing the means for searching through it. With the brisk growth in computerized libraries of compounds, huge volumes of them are being recorded. Even with that, compounds that might work for any one disease remain comparatively rare. Describing the value of digital search tools, Steve Kaldor, chief of the drug discovery company Syrrx, has said, "It's important to be able to sift through data from many simultaneous projects."

The process of transferring the information of nature into computer databases has just begun. It is now stored only in ecological systems. And there the sheer diversity of life forms, and of how they interact, defies imagination. "Look at insects," Eisner says. "If you ask an entomologist how many species there are, some will say there are five to eight million, others will say thirty million. And bear in mind that every insect probably has got its bag of parasites on the microbial level.

"One thing I know," he concludes, "there is no way that we're ever going to approach the limits of knowledge. And all these frontiers are out there left to be discovered." For Eisner, that's a critical argument for leaving old forests intact. "If we don't preserve the library of nature," he says, "that's going to be lost forever."

Sowing Change

With the spring rains, water floods downward from tree-covered hills and out across open land. There, as it flows through streams and into rivers, it runs past an ancient sight—farmers out sowing their seeds for the coming year's crop. "Agricultural plants are not natural. They have coevolved with people over long periods of time," says the seed search activist and "Bioneer" Kenny Ausubel. "When people stop planting them, that's how they go away. It's a partnership."

Ausubel is concerned about the genetic erosion caused by green revolution techniques. A company he cofounded, Seeds of Change, answers that concern by offering traditional seeds to gardeners and farmers around the world. That effort complements those of Gary Nabhan, who with his company, Native Seeds Search, scouts the world for seeds used in traditional cultures.

The variety of plants grown by those cultures is impressive. According to Ausubel, in even the driest parts of the American Southwest, the tribes tended 375 staple plants and, altogether, employed more than three thousand types. Nabhan's group also seeks out traditional knowledge of how crop plants interact—about which of them were planted or rotated together. For instance, over many generations a Hopi tribe may have worked out which legume works best in fixing nitrogen for blue corn.

Groups like Seeds of Change and Native Seeds Search have helped inspire larger efforts, too. A joint European program is being coordinated by major research centers in the Netherlands, England, and Switzerland. The project aims to hybridize modern crop types with traditional varieties. Those plants will be bred for flavor and nutrition, and to render good yields without the use of synthetic fertilizer.

Good Earth

They will also conform to the European Union's new laws for organic farming, which represents a full turn of the wheel. The modern organic farming movement began in Europe.

Back in 1940, in his book *An Agricultural Testament*, Sir Albert Howard wrote that nature is the "supreme farmer." He recommended that humans farm like the forest and nicely summarized a nature-based approach:

> Mother Earth never attempts to farm without livestock; she always raises mixed crops; great pains are taken to preserve the soil and to prevent erosion; the mixed vegetable and animal wastes are converted into humus; there is no waste; the processes of growth and the processes of decay balance one another; ample provision is made to maintain large reserves of fertility; the greatest care is taken to store the rainfall; both plants and animals are left to protect themselves against disease.

Howard's efforts paralleled work by Robert McCarrison, George Stapledon, and Rudolf Steiner. Howard and McCarrison sought to show that soil's health affects the quality of plants grown in it, and thus the health of animals feeding on them. Stapledon advocated bioregions.

Steiner was a vitalist—the founder of what he termed "biodynamic" farming—who spoke in mystical terms of the energy embodied in good soil. These strands came together in Lady Eve Balfour's 1943 book, *The Living Soil*, which was an effort to muster the best science then available on the subject.

An emphasis on soil health continues on organic farms today. Potentially harmful pesticides and herbicides aren't used. Grain crops are rotated with legumes like soy and alfalfa. These move fixed nitrogen into the soil. The soil is also protected by mulch and fertilized with organic compost, to feed the rich web of soil bacteria, fungi, earthworms, and other organisms interacting underground. They keep soil structure loose and open, so it holds more water and promotes deep root penetration. Cheryl Clough of Pike Agri-Lab Supplies—a compost supply company in Strong, Maine—summarizes: "Instead of trying to feed plants with fertilizer, you just take care of life in the soil, and let the soil feed the plants."

Although Howard and McCarrison raised early concerns about the nutritional effects of synthetic fertilizer, studies have repeatedly failed to show any difference between organic and synthetic nitrogen. But thinking ecologically, Lady Balfour outlined another cause for those concerns:

> Anything having an effect on root distribution . . . may have an effect on plant nutrition because it will influence the volume of soil explored. Thus, good soil structure in depth, such as is obtained in a biologically ac- tive soil, can improve productivity simply by increasing the depth of soil exploited for water and nutrients. There is now well-documented scien- tific evidence that fertilizer concentrations of N [nitrogen] and P [phos- phate] have an influence on localized root branching. They induce it at the expense of deep rooting exploration. This could well lead to luxury uptakes of N and P linked to inadequate uptake of other nutrients. There are implications in this for nutrient unbalance in the crop and thereby some risk of nutrient unbalance in the animals and humans feeding upon it.

For many, doubts about organic farming stem from the fact that it has long been championed by vitalists—now sailing under the flag of the new age. But in recent decades, organic methods have enjoyed growing support from science.

An exhaustive study published in 1989 by the National Research Council noted that "alternative farmers often produce high per-acre yields with significant reductions in costs per unit of crop harvested," even though "many federal policies discourage adoption of alternative practices and systems," and those farmers get "relatively little help from commodity income and price support programs." The report urged that federal programs be restructured to help farmers benefit from alternative methods.

In the following decade the journal *Science* published a study of sixteen adjacent conventional and biodynamic farms producing dairy products, livestock, fruits, and vegetables. After eight years of biodynamic treatment, the study showed, soils had "significantly greater organic-matter content and microbial activity, more earthworms, better soil structure, lower bulk density, easier penetrability, and thicker topsoil" in most cases. The research was done in New Zealand. A subsequent U.S. study in the journal *Nature* matched one conventional and two organic farms over ten years. It showed that while maize production and profits were similar, nitrogen loss in the soil was "about 50 percent higher in the conventional system."

A 2001 report by scientists at Washington State University, also released in *Nature*, compared test plots of Golden Delicious apples grown by organic methods, by conventional methods, and by an "integrated" approach that combined the two. "We kept track of everything that went in," says John Reganold, who led the research team. By that he means that on each plot they recorded the inputs of all the compost, chemicals, and fuel used. The six-year study showed that although it took longer to reach its optimum, by the end of that time the organic farm ranked first in energy efficiency and profitability, as well as sustainability. The integrated orchard ranked second and the conventional system placed last. Making victory all the sweeter, untrained tasters judged the organic apples to have the most flavor. Says David Tillman, an ecologist at the University of Minnesota in St. Paul, "This is one of the first well-replicated rigorous experiments that's looked at all the benefits and costs involved in an alternative farming practice."

The question of nutrient content is being looked at, too. In 2002, a study by British biochemist John Patterson found that organic brands of vegetable soup had nearly six times the salicylic acid of nonorganic brands. Salicylic acid is the anti-inflammatory ingredient in aspirin, and has been cited for its value in preventing heart attacks, strokes, and cancer. Plants produce the acid as a defense against disease and stress, a possible reason why higher levels occur in organic vegetables (which are not usually protected by pesticides). That same year an Italian study was released that found higher levels of vitamin C in organic peaches, and of polyphenols—natural antioxidants—in organic pears and peaches. Both papers were published in the *European Journal of Nutrition*. But these and other studies like them are criticized by Alex Avery, director of research at the Center for Global Food Issues at the Hudson Institute. According to Avery, they are biased and show insubstantial results. "I don't think you are going to find any health differences," he says. Avery's Center for Global Food Issues receives funding from Monsanto, Dow Agro Sciences, and Zeneca.

Marion Nestle of New York University's Department of Nutrition, Food Studies, and Public Health says, "I don't think there is any question that as more research is done, it is going to become increasingly apparent that organic food is healthier."

Serious federal rules for organic farming are now in place in the United States, but it took some doing. The first stab at setting organic standards was taken by the Department of Agriculture back when it was known by reporters as the "Department of Monsanto." Curiously, the standards proposed back then embraced genetically engineered crops. That announcement provoked the biggest public outcry in the department's history; it received more than 200,000 letters of protest. After what might be called a period of internal reassessment, it issued a new set of regulations that it described as the "most comprehensive, strictest organic rules in the world."

They are rigorous. The round, green-and-white USDA ORGANIC label—which debuted on October 21, 2002—denotes a process that bans genetic engineering along with virtually all pesticides, herbicides, and artificial fertilizers. Also ruled out are food irradiation and the use of industrial sludge on farm fields. Livestock have to be fed with organic produce, and the use of antibiotics is limited. Organic farmers nonetheless have concerns not answered by the new rules—for instance, the possibility of gene flow from genetically modified crop fields into nearby organic crops. Also, the new rules still allow plowing and large monocrop plantings while barring any labeling claims for methods superior to the USDA's. And they give no preference to locally grown and raised foods, a major focus for many in the organic movement. The trip from farms to American dinner tables typically ranges from fifteen hundred to twenty-five hundred miles. That favors crops bred for shelf life rather than flavor or nutrition, even as it consumes huge amounts of energy. And as this book goes to press, food-processing corporations have a bill before Congress that would further compromise the USDA standards.

Despite those real concerns, change is in the wind. McDonald's, the global fast-food burger chain, has asked its meat suppliers to cut back on the use of antibiotics (it buys 2.5 billion pounds of beef, poultry, and pork each year). Some of New York's finest restaurants now serve grass-fed beef, and the Italian "slow food" movement—begun by journalist Carlo Petrini in 1986—has become an international phenomenon. Agro giants like Dole, Gallo, Paramount, and Pandole Brothers are all reducing their chemical use. Mars, the candy company, has purchased Seeds of Change. Pillsbury now sells organic flour; Tyson sells organic chickens. Even Wal-Mart has begun to carry organic foods. As part of acquiring a one-third partnership in the organics producer Natural Selection Foods, California-based Tanimura & Antle—one of the world's largest conventional growers—agreed to shift fifteen hundred acres of its agricultural land to organic methods. That agreement stipulates that it convert its other holdings as demand requires.

There's no question that demand will come. In the ten years from 1990 to 2000, organic food sales in the U.S. boomed from $1 billion to over $6 billion. As the world stood agog at the yearly 15 percent growth rate of dot.com companies during that time, organic farmers were quietly but consistently outpacing them. Early in 2000, when General Mills announced its purchase of Small Planet Foods—a $60 million organics producer—General Mills' chairman and CEO, Steve Sanger, observed, "Sales of organic and natural foods have been growing by more than 20 percent a year over the last five years, and this strong market growth is expected to continue." Two years later, annual U.S. organic food sales were approaching $10 billion.

In Britain, the growth rate is equally swift. Reeling from mad cow disease—unleashed there by industrial farming methods that deemed it sensible to feed live cows with the ground-up remains of dead cows—consumers have turned back to basics in force. Not surprisingly, retailers have followed suit. Iceland Foods, which operates some eight hundred stores, was the first company there to exclude all genetically modified

ingredients and label its foods as such. Iceland now offers organic vegetables in its frozen food lines and with no price markup. That decision
was taken after polls showed that three out of four consumers would
buy organics if prices were competitive. Iceland's sales growth now
outpaces the industry average.

Overall, the sale of organic foods in Britain is increasing by 40 percent a year. A similar trend is under way on the Continent. At the current growth rate, more than 10 percent of Europe's farmland will be
organic by the end of this decade. Meanwhile, the European Parliament
has approved legislation that requires strict labeling for foods made with
genetically modified ingredients.

Pest 2 Pest

In a sun-drenched open field, a bee buzzes quietly among the flowers.
That's a familiar sight, but this bee carries unusual cargo. When it left the
hive, it walked through a tray of talcum that scientists had mixed with
the nuclear polyhedrosis virus—which is harmless to bees but dangerous
to certain crop pests. As the bee works its way from blossom to blossom,
it leaves traces of the virus for other visitors. Dispersed that way in tests,
the virus killed 75 percent of the corn earworm larvae in plots of crim-
son clover.

As agriculture is reinvented in nature's image, one of the more creative areas of change has been pest control. Beyond using a virus to pester
earworms, scientists have been looking at insect antennae. Insects often
use them in the search for food, and most bugs need to eat before they
mate. By removing antennae and metering them with electrodes, researchers can track which odors produce the greatest electrical response.
Those odors are then mimicked chemically and used to trap or divert
insects before they damage crops.

Beetle bait isolated this way from spud leaves was used in Maine potato
fields to triple the number of the insects caught in traps. A related strategy creates artificial pheromones—the sex attractants bugs, and humans,
use to find potential mates. Spreading a mimic of insect pheromone in
a field disrupts the reproductive cycle. Males can't locate sex partners.

Just as we have pests, our pests have them, too. The new approach
makes use of those antagonists—which provide a novel answer to the rebound effect (where pests mutate around any effort to control them).

With natural antagonists, the control evolves right along with the pest. But that means neither side ever fully wins. Says writer Martin Waterman, "The battle of the bugs is somewhat like the battle of the sexes; there is too much fraternizing with the enemy for any one side to be victorious."

Nor should it be. If all the pests disappear from a field, there's no food left for the organisms meant to control them. Then they die off, too, or leave in search of greener pastures, clearing the way for a new round of pests to move back in. According to plant ecologists Allison Snow and Pedro Moran-Palma, writing in the journal *BioScience*, "The goal should be to suppress insect populations to levels that result in economic benefits but still allow [target insects] to survive and reproduce."

This integrated pest management, or IPM, is not without problems. Environmentalists oppose introducing any new species in a region. That's because ecological effects can be so hard to predict. As farm ecologists Judith Soule and Jon Piper put it in their book *Farming in Nature's Image*, "An adult insect may be an important pollinator of one plant species, but its larvae may be devastating herbivores on another. Or a bird that eats prodigious numbers of damaging insects from a plant in the spring may eat that plant's seeds later in the fall." Before introducing what looks like a beneficial species for pest control, biologists now test it extensively. Those tests involve isolating the controlling species with near relatives of its target. The aim is to see if—deprived of a preferred food source—the control will adapt to feed on the target's near relative. Researchers also test the species to see if they will feed on other food crops.

Measures like that were taken before Cornell scientists imported two types of beetles and a root weevil to feed on purple loosestrife. That's the attractive purple plant now growing along most U.S. roadsides. It was brought here in the nineteenth century from Europe, leaving its natural predators behind, and has since infested wetlands in every part of the country. Among the many kinds of mischief it creates, purple loosestrife crowds out native vegetation that would otherwise offer shelter, food, and nesting sites for native waterfowl and songbirds. In test plots the immigrant beetles cut the loosestrife population by up to 95 percent. They are now being released by the millions.

Some of the most sophisticated IPM is practiced in Cuba. With the collapse of the Soviet bloc, the island lost supports for its green revolution farm base. In response, Cuba transformed itself into the world's first national economy based on scientific organic farming. Some 50 percent of its fresh vegetables and 65 percent of its rice are now grown organically. As part of that change, a network of over two hundred research stations monitors pest behavior on farms and deploys an array of bio-controls—including viruses, bacteria, fungi, and insects. The stations release flies that parasitize the sugarcane borer, and miniature wasps that feed on caterpillar eggs. Sweet potatoes are planted at the base of other food crops, to shade out weeds; then predator ants are sent out to eat the sweet potato weevils.

Cuba isn't the only nation to serve as a test bed for IPM controls. Indonesia banned more than fifty insecticides in 1987, in response to rebounding populations of brown planthoppers on rice paddies there. At the same time it began a program of educating farmers in IPM techniques. In only three years the overall use of pesticides was cut in half, farmland infested with planthoppers declined from 500,000 acres to 50,000, and rice yields were up 12 percent.

Another challenge to chemical pesticides has emerged in China, where ecological diversity is being tried at test farms on a broad scale. Monocultures are unusual in nature. Evolution doesn't encourage them, because the more concentrated and uniform a plant's distribution is, the more readily disease can spread through it. Diversity guards against that, just as it does against pest infestations. Because of the innate diversity in natural systems, pests have to spend a lot of their energy just getting around things they can't eat in order to find something they can. That obstacle course means fewer succeed.

The same principle is now being applied in one of the largest agricultural experiments ever conducted. In that test, thousands of rice farms in China's Yunnan Province have increased yields of a prized crop, nearly eliminated its most devastating disease, and done so without the use of chemicals or by incurring other costs.

The target of the study is rice blast fungus, a pathogen that each year costs rice farmers several billion dollars in crop losses. The test involves "intercropping" two plant types: a standard rice resistant to the disease and a much more valuable sticky rice that easily succumbs. Since rice blast travels by airborne spores, the study's aim was to see if the resistant plants could block those spores from reaching their glutinous cousins.

An international team led by Youyong Zhu, a plant pathologist at the Yunnan Agricultural University in Kunming, China, administered the project, which also included monoculture control plots. According to their report, published in the journal *Nature*, the intercropping strategy proved so successful that chemical fungicides on those fields were discontinued after two years. The study has now expanded to 100,000 acres, an expansion that has brought with it surprise benefits. As science writer Carol Kaesuk Yoon described them for *The New York Times*:

> Resistant plants did block the airborne spores in a field, but as more and more farmers became involved in the study, these positive effects began to multiply across the region. Not only were disease spores not blowing in from the next row, they were no longer coming from the next farmer's field either or the next or the next, rapidly damping the spread of the disease on a grand scale.

The Chinese research has turned more than a few heads in the life sciences. Noting the biotech industry's relentless push for genetically engineered monocultures, Columbia University ecologist Shahid Naeem remarks that the China study "shows how we've lost sight of the fact that there are some really simple things we can do in the field to manage crops." Comments Alison Power, an agricultural ecologist at Cornell, "People have said that these kinds of ecological approaches wouldn't work on a commercial scale. This is a huge scale."

Scientists are testing intercropping on other produce, too—for instance, barley in Europe and coffee in Colombia. And beyond the effect it has on pests, intercropping also seems to boost yields. An Iowa farmer who alternated rows of corn, oats, and soybeans saw corn yields rise by 25 percent and oat yields by 9 percent, while soybeans declined only slightly. Another study, done in Mexico, showed that intercropping maize, beans, and squash produced 1.7 times the total food yield per acre. Perhaps more remarkable is the discovery that with modern ecological management, larger—not smaller—numbers of cattle boost the productivity of pastures.

Greener Pastures

"There is no sense in trying to teach a pig to fly," says Joel Salatin. "He can't learn how to do it, and it makes him mad anyway." Salatin, who operates a small family farm in Virginia's Shenandoah Valley, likes and admires the other farmers who are his neighbors. But he knows they're set in their ways. That's why he keeps mum when he hears them explain that his cows have greener pastures because "they get more rain over there than we do."

When Salatin was a teenager, his family's ninety-five-acre farm couldn't support ten cows. "Today," he says, "it supports one hundred and we have extra feed. And we haven't bought an ounce of fertilizer in thirty-six years." It supports more humans, too: his family, his brother's family, salaries for two apprentices, and the mortgage on his brother's house.

One of the more novel challenges to emerge with the new biology is learning to think of farmers—with hayseeds in their pant cuffs and manure on their shoes—as at the cutting edge of science. But Salatin and large numbers of farmers like him clearly are. They've borrowed an insight about how grazing animals interact with the land and put it to work on their farms.

"We want to mimic the patterns in nature," he says. "If you look at any herbivore population in nature you will notice two things. One is that it is always mobbed up for protection. The other is that it is always moving to fresh forage. So mimicking that on a domestic scale . . . we just move them every twenty-four hours to a fresh patch."

He compares that to the difference between ten people and a thousand people trying to eat at a big buffet. If there were a thousand people waiting behind you, he points out, "there would be much less selectivity at the table because all the folks behind would push the people in front to get through, so you would grab what you could." The point, he says, is that "when you mob the animals up, they graze very aggressively."

That view draws on work by Allan Savory. While working as a wildlife biologist in Zimbabwe, Savory noticed that the great herds of native grazers moving across the savanna seemed to do no harm to the grasslands. But herds maintained by farmers on the same kind of land did. It was Savory who concluded that the influence of predators, which keeps wild herds bunched up and moving, also affects the plants on which those herds graze.

As Salatin explains it, a plant belowground "is a mirror image of what is above the ground." By that he means there is as much plant material below the surface as above. "Now when a cow comes along and eats a twelve-inch grass plant down, amazingly, the grass plant below the ground automatically eliminates the same amount of root mass." It does that, he explains, in order to put its energy into the plant's crown (the junction of the stem and the root)—"so it doesn't die maintaining those centimeters of root hairs when there is no carbohydrate station, no photosynthesis, occurring above the ground."

That puts a surge of energy into the crown, so it can send up new tillers (or shoots). As the plant regrows, Salatin points out, "the fresh tillers are yellowish. They're pulling energy up from the crown. As they get long enough for chlorophyll photosynthesis to set in, they turn green." Those of us who have lawns to mow (and who actually mow them) can see that effect if we cut the grass too short.

Herds that are free to spread out and eat at leisure eat only the tastiest plants—grazing them down to the ground and causing their root systems to shrink. With repeated grazing those species die off, upsetting the balance of plant types that makes for a healthy range. But when cows are kept moving in tight herds, they graze the pasture evenly. Their hooves also leave a dense pattern of indents that then traps water, seeds, and dung for the growth of new plants.

The constantly moving cattle on Salatin's farm stay on any single square foot of land for no more than six days out of a year. That means at any given time, most of the farm is at rest. Referring to how more complex layers of life can emerge to increase an area's carrying capacity, he says, "Succession is the most powerful force in nature, but until you get thirty thousand pounds of animal weight per acre at least once a year, you won't see succession go forward." He calls this approach "pulsing the pasture."

He then improves on it by borrowing another trick from nature. The manure cow pies left by cattle are magnets for flies, which cover them with eggs. Within two days the eggs reach their larval stage. That's when Salatin wheels in his eggmobile—a chicken coop on wheels. He turns loose the chickens and they devour the larvae, consuming the cow pies in the process. Then they scatter their own droppings evenly across the field.

With the use of natural methods like these, Salatin is able to feed his cattle without grain—they live on the perennial grasses that they help to grow. As a result, he keeps half of the income his farm generates, rather than passing most of it along to the giant agrotech input suppliers.

"Farmers all the time are complaining about Monsanto and Pioneer, you know, the big multinational corporations," he says, adding, "Hey, they don't even exist as far as I'm concerned. The stranglehold that the big bad corporations have, it's a joke. The only stranglehold they have is . . . in individual farmers' minds. It doesn't have to be that way. We don't have to destroy the agribusiness people and regulate . . . All we have to do is do what we know how to do and we've got it."

Game ranching is now a growth industry in southern Africa. And Savory has gone on from his work in Zimbabwe to show how those insights can restore arid parts of the American West—proving, as one observer puts it, "that much of the rangeland commonly considered overgrazed is actually undergrazed but grazed the wrong way." In a sure sign that the new forage ecology is gaining acceptance in the States, it now has its own acronym—MIRG (management-intensive rotational grazing). Between 1993 and 1997 in Wisconsin, a major dairy-farming state, MIRG operations grew to encompass some 15 percent of all dairy farms there.

Environmental benefits come with the new method, too. Nitrogen runoff from perennial grass pastures is dramatically less than from the industrialized fields that usually feed cattle. Natural grass diets—instead of the cheap corn feed that cows are not evolved to eat—also mean fewer methane emissions from the cows. Methane is a potent greenhouse gas that environmentalists have concerns about.

Because the new approach needs less land, it also impacts another greenhouse gas: carbon dioxide. When plants grow, they absorb carbon dioxide from the air. They then break it down, releasing the oxygen and using the captured carbon atoms to construct body parts like roots, stems, leaves, and flowers. That's why biologists talk of plant communities as "carbon sinks." It's also why they estimate that between 20 and 30 percent of the excess carbon dioxide in the atmosphere from humans is a result of tropical deforestation. An important part of that is due to what might be called "the hamburger effect." Since 1960, some 25 percent of Central American forests have been cut to clear pastures for cattle—due to the rising demand for beef in fast-food franchises. By the mid-1990s, according to the Rainforest Action Network, Central America was shipping eight hundred million hamburgers to the United States each year.

Whether burning down the house to roast a pig, or mowing down the trees to feed the cattle, the dynamic is largely the same—needless waste due to primitive methods. "Seventy percent of all the annual row-

crop grain grown in America goes through multi-stomach animals,"
Salatin points out. Forage ecology based on rotational grazing, he says,
offers an important alternative because it's a more efficient use of land.

To those environmentalists who would expel cattle from rangeland
he adds, "I don't think you will find any type of grassland area in the
world that didn't have huge herds. They go together. The coexistence of
herbivores and grasses has been a symbiotic one for centuries." The
problem is not that we have too many cows, Salatin says. "The problem
is that we don't have enough cows in the right place at the right time."

Late Bloomers
"There is lots of water in the desert," remarks Wouter van Dieren, senior statesman of European environmentalists. "Overnight, when the
desert cools off, you see to your surprise condensation. That means that
there is humidity in the air. The problem is to keep it there."

That's easier said than done. The cycle of plants absorbing moisture
from the soil and transpiring it into the sky—to form clouds that then
send rain back to the soil—can be broken by undergrazing, clearcutting,
and other human practices. When that occurs, a devolving feedback cycle sets in and the desert may spread. As van Dieren explains it, heat rising from the sand then sends a vertical column of warm air up into the
sky. And that column prevents clouds from moving in over the area,
clouds that would otherwise shade the sun and hold moisture down.

Van Dieren is involved with a project that curbs that effect in desert
regions by using stand-ins for the clouds. Along the edges of areas where
plants still have a hold, they set up a narrow border of silvery tentlike
tarps made of Mylar. The border permits ambient light but shades the
soil from the sun's direct heat. With that, existing vegetation starts re-
claiming land. He says the shade "allows the grass or vegetation to begin
to come in. Then we can move it farther and farther." And each time
that shining border moves a step farther into the desert, the process of
reversing the cycle takes another step toward reclamation.

All this sounds a little like eco–science fiction. But van Dieren, who
heads the venture, called Ocean Desert Enterprises, says not. There are
several sites under consideration around the world, and the first of them
is now up and running in Ensenada, Mexico. "I'm not talking only hot
air," he says, smiling. "It's all there."

Ecological systems for managing plants are themselves a growth area. Bill Mollison, from Australia, has pioneered "permaculture," a form of permanent agriculture that embodies many of the new biology's design principles. In Japan, Masanobu Fukuoka developed a "do-nothing" rice-farming method with impressive results. The Rodale Institute research farm in Pennsylvania has long been at the cutting edge of organic farming methods, and there are similar efforts in California, led by people like John Jeavons, Richard Merrill, Steve Gliessman, and Miguel Altieri. Some of the new systems are, like van Dieren's, highly innovative. Wes Jackson is breeding perennial food crops that mimic the natural ecology of Kansas prairies. In Germany, van Dieren's colleague Michael Braungart has designed a clever system that integrates the functions of a small farm into naturalistic cycles.

Braungart is a prominent voice for environmental concerns in Europe. Among his many projects and positions, he heads a nonprofit organization in Germany called the Hamburg Environmental Institute, which has designed a small-farm "biomass nutrient recycling" scheme now being tried in tropical and subtropical countries. It uses several organic cycles that intersect through a series of deep ponds. The ponds act as processors for local sewage and farm wastes, which aquatic plants and algae growing in the ponds absorb. The plants enlarge by drawing their nutrients from the water, and that cleans it enough to provide habitat for fish. The plants are then harvested to provide food for livestock, or are used with waste from livestock as fertilizer. Pigs feed on vegetables and snails that grow at the site. Ducks and geese consume algae and provide nutrients for the fish. And in the end, purified water passes from the ponds into the local watershed—from which it will be drawn again for irrigation and as drinking water.

According to Braungart, with these measures small farmers can trim production costs by as much as half. And, he points out, unlike with the existing green revolution methods, they won't be loading the soil and water with excess nitrogen from fertilizer. Instead, the system "feeds families and brings nutrients back into the cycle." Around the world there are now forty facilities based on that design. They exist in various guises in Madras and on the Bay of Bengal, in India; in China on the Zhu (Pearl) River delta near Hong Kong and inland of there, in Guangdong Province; and at sites in Brazil, Thailand, and Vietnam. Many of them have been in operation for a dozen years, adding as much as a thousand dollars annually to family incomes.

Another innovation is gaining ground in Japan. In his classic 1978 book, *The One-Straw Revolution*, Japanese farmer Masanobu Fukuoka wrote, "If farmers would stop using weak, 'improved' seed varieties, stop adding too much nitrogen to soil, and reduce the amount of irrigation water so that strong roots could develop, these diseases [stem rot, rice blast, and leaf blight] would all but disappear and chemical sprays would become unnecessary." He was talking about one advantage of his do-nothing approach to farming based on ecological and seasonal cycles. Fukuoka never fertilized, never used pesticides, and never plowed. In his system, as one observer puts it, "an elegantly conceived sequence of plantings provides the weed control, composting, and other services automatically, just by doing the right few things at the right time and in the right sequence." Science writer Janine Benyus describes that cycle, picking it up just before the autumn rice harvest:

> In early October, Fukuoka hand-sows clover into his standing rice crop. Shortly after that he sows seeds of rye and barley into the rice. (He coats the seeds with clay so they won't be eaten by birds.) When the rice is ready for harvest, he cuts it, threshes it, and then throws the straw back over the field. By this time, clover is already well established, helping to smother weeds and fix nitrogen in the soil. Through the tangle of clover and straw, rye and barley burst up and begin their climb toward the sun. Just before he harvests the rye and barley, he starts the cycle again, tossing in rice seeds to start their protected ascent. On and on the cycle goes, self-fertilizing and self-cultivating. In this way rice and winter grains can be grown in the same field for many years without diminishing soil fertility.

Fukuoka's system will produce twenty-two bushels (thirteen hundred pounds) of rice and another twenty-two bushels of winter grain from a quarter-acre field, enough to support "five to ten people, with each investing less than one hour of labor a day"—and with no loss of fertility in the soil. The yield is comparable to that of industrial rice farms in Japan, although those farms require substantial inputs of chemicals, petroleum, machinery, and human labor. Fukuoka's do-nothing method is now used widely in Japan and is gaining acceptance in China.

In a similar spirit, an American is exploring what might be considered the final farm frontier. His aim is to breed crops that essentially take care of themselves, by mimicking the ecosystem of the Midwestern Great Plains.

Four for Kansas

Viewed from a jet above central Kansas, the overlay of Cartesian logic on natural systems seems written on the landscape. During the great free land rush of the nineteenth century, the prairie here was broken into square-mile "sections" that remain a fixture today. Around Salina, a farm town near the heart of the state, dirt roads outlining them form a big checkerboard spread out in all directions under the midsummer sun. That grid overlays the undulating surface of the prairie and—with a notable exception—frames fields of corn that have a uniformity broken only by the snaking trails of deeper green along streams.

The exception is geneticist Wes Jackson's Land Institute. A dusty, sunbaked ride from Salina brings you to a compound of low buildings and sheds perched on a rise. These buildings don't look out over uniform rows of corn. They survey a broad native meadow that's home to plants like big bluestem, sage, snow-on-the-mountain, and daisy fleabane—shaded here and there by locust trees or hedge apples. And ranging through that pastoral wilderness is a lively assortment of skinks, skunks, possums, snakes, turkeys, swallows, larks, deer, chiggers, toads, grasshoppers, and field mice. The air is warm and still—quiet except for the drone of crickets and an occasional birdcall. Far overhead, hawks dip and slide through a clear summer sky.

To one side of the meadow, a small herd of Texas longhorns grazes near a stock tank. They've been chosen because they're similar in basic ways to the buffalo that once roamed these plains. They're also easier to manage. The cattle are on a rotational grazing scheme that moves them every few days, and are kept in a tight herd by a poly-wire electric fence running on a solar charge.

Down the road is a piece of cropland that looks a little like a shaggy cousin to a cornfield. Rows of huge bushy plants reaching well overhead are intercropped with rows of other plants less than waist high. In one corner of the field, chickens poke around the weeds beneath an old tractor bleached dull pink by years of sitting unused in the sun. Machinery is sometimes employed here, but this farm is fundamentally different. For one thing, it's seldom plowed—a practice common on farms, even the most organic of them. What really sets it apart, though, is that there will be no seeds to sow next spring. These crops don't need to be replanted.

Back at the compound, in a small shed that serves as his office,

Jackson is a large, burly man in his sixties. Dressed in worn overalls and work boots, he looks very much like the farmer he is. But his reputation precedes him. Author of numerous books, speaker at international conferences, deviser of the most advanced agricultural system yet conceived, he is widely regarded as a kind of agrarian sage.

"The idea of environment is really a bad idea," Jackson says. By that he means it perpetuates a view of the world we live in as something apart from ourselves—an old dualism reaching back through Descartes to the ancient Greeks and beyond.

Another separation Jackson objects to is the one we place between the organic and the inorganic world. He quotes ecologist Stan Rowe, who says, "Imagine if we were to make ourselves small enough that we could go into a cell. We would find as much in that cell that's not living as is living." Or, he adds, think of an oxygen molecule "out in the air, then in your mouth, and in your lungs, and then oxidizing sugar. At what point does it become you?" Jackson is talking about our failure to appreciate "the interpenetration of the nonliving with the living." This creates problems because it gives the impression that anything not alive is, as Rowe put it, "just sort of loose stuff lying around."

That's not how life works, Jackson says. For instance, "the spaces between plants are as important as the living material itself—that's where gas exchange occurs." And then there are the root microbes hard at work cycling nitrogen into plants all over the globe. "It seems to me when we talk about life," he observes, "first of all we have a hard time defining it, and second of all it may even be less than half the equation. To me a better term is 'ecosystem'—because the ecosystem includes both the living and the nonliving."

He likes to quote Alexander Pope: "In all, let Nature never be forgot . . . Consult the Genius of the Place in all." The term "consult," Jackson points out, is an inspired one. "It doesn't say absolutely obey. It's a consultation. It leads inevitably to a conversation with nature. You start with what was here. Then you move on to what is nature going to require of us here, and what's nature going to help us do here?"

Referring to the big checkerboard that contains so many Kansas farms, including his own, he says, "There's something very powerful in that grid that overrides a tendency to really look at the landscape and see what it will do." A lot of problems in the West, Jackson believes, come from the same thinking that produced the grid.

The dust bowl is an example. With the strong winds and low rainfall characteristic of the Great Plains, plant communities here evolved with most of their mass belowground—in a tangle of widespread and highly integrated stems and roots. The waving grasses of a prairie are actually just the branches of underground plants. That has the obvious value of guarding their subterranean bodies from the wind, but it serves other purposes, too. During the periodic droughts, those underground networks help the soil retain moisture. At the same time, they anchor it, protecting it from erosion by the wind. In that way, the soil protects the plants while the plants protect the soil. As plants die and are succeeded, their decomposed remains add still more soil to the base into which their offspring grow. Those many interacting processes have worked together over long periods of time—building on a rich bed of minerals that in some regions was eroded by wind and water from the uplift of the Rocky Mountains, and in others by glaciers carrying pulverized rocks down from Canada. The result is the American Midwest, layered with perhaps the deepest and richest bed of topsoil on earth.

In the 1930s drought returned to the prairie as it had periodically through history. But this time it found something new. The land's surface had been scored with rows of cuts that spread across vast areas of the landscape. Those furrows disconnected the anchoring network of underground root structures provided by native plants. Instead, the furrows made the way for food crops that were harvested each year and that leave no lasting roots in the soil. Some farmers were by then also using synthetic fertilizers, herbicides, and pesticides. These upset the metabolic balance among native plants and the uncounted millions of other life forms underground—from visible to microscopic—which give rise to the soil's richness and spongy, absorbent character. When the winds came, it all blew away.

In the Midwest, and elsewhere, the topsoil needed to grow our food continues to disappear faster than natural processes replace it. In response to that Jackson founded the Land Institute almost three decades ago. His aim was to breed an interacting ecology of food plants. Those crops would protect themselves from pests and fertilize the soil in the same way that plants in nature do. And they would grow from the kind of permanent root structures found in natural prairies. The eventual result of that effort would be the development of a "natural systems agriculture."

The institute began by acknowledging the reality of what Jackson calls "the ecological mosaic." But, he adds, "we have to be careful when we talk about a mosaic, because you can see a mosaic from ten thousand feet, and then you go all the way down to a cubic inch, and you've got a mosaic there, too. So where," he asks, "is homo the homogenizer free to roam—and put in crops of his or her design?"

In evolution, the sharpest competition is among members of the same species. That's because they're after identical resources. But different species can complement each other. Due to that, natural diversity often increases the productivity of individual plants, a process called overyielding. That principle is where the Land Institute team went looking in its search for a place to develop their crops. They soon identified four basic plant types that shape the ecological structure of the prairie. Certain legumes fix their own nitrogen and fertilize the soil. Cool-season grasses come up early. As spring yields to summer, warm-season grasses follow. And composites flower throughout the season.

A wide range of species fall into one or another of those four ecological niches. But with their differing heights, root structures, and seasonal patterns, those four basic types work together to make the prairie more resilient and productive than any one of them would be on its own. Mimicking that, the Kansas team turned to four crop plants—one for each niche. They have begun domesticating the tall Illinois bundleflower as their legume. Their cool-season grass is a domestic wheat being crossed with several wild relatives. They are also perennializing domestic corn and sorghum to serve as their warm-season grasses. And their composite is a domestic sunflower being crossed with a wild perennial called the Maximilian. In the end, all will be perennials.

From time to time the Land Institute kitchen tries using grain from some of these crops to turn out muffins and other baked goods. Don't look for them anytime soon at your local market. Part of the challenge will clearly be to breed perennials that match the taste and texture of the grains we enjoy today. Another question is whether perennials will be able to match the yield of annuals. The majority of food calories today— some 70 percent—come from annuals. They're bred to invest more energy in their seedheads, the part we like to eat. At season's end the rest of the plant just dies. Perennials, on the other hand, have to maintain permanent root structures. Because of that, some breeders question whether perennials can ever spare the energy needed to grow equally large seedheads.

Jackson calls that a misconception. "When you look at an ancient oak tree," he says, "the only life you see is a year old." By that he means to point out that while the roots, trunk, and branches of a perennial like an oak tree do endure, they are mostly dead matter. All the growth rings inside it, for instance, are dead accumulated carbon that the tree has "sequestered." And the same holds true for the bark. Those parts require no energy from the plant in order to survive. Actually, the only living parts are its cambium layer—just inside the bark—and the new ring being laid down beneath it, along with any new leaves, small branches, and roots. What that means, Jackson explains, is that long-term growth in perennials is mostly a buildup of dead carbon that incurs no new cost (since it's been paid for in previous years). So a perennial plant's root structure does not pull energy away from its seedhead. By contrast, he says, annual plants have to spend the energy needed to put down entire new root systems every year. The upshot? "We can breed perennials to increase the yield."

Keeping track of where the energy goes—and where it comes from—is a major focus here. There's something almost magical in how plants use energy from the sun to draw carbon out of the air as a way to enlarge their bodies. For modern humans the growth process is more abstract. We use solar energy stored in petroleum to make chemicals and to manufacture and fuel machines made with metals drawn from the earth to grow the plants that we then eat.

The 1st Law of Thermodynamics holds that energy is constant in the universe—it can never increase or decrease. The 2nd Law shows how more order in one system means disintegration somewhere else. As we focus larger amounts of materials and energy on growing food, the disruption of other systems is becoming hard to overlook. As Jackson wrote in his book *Altars of Unhewn Stone*, "We need economic models that will account for the cycling of materials and handle the flow of energy . . . in a safe and orderly manner. This model can be found in nearly all natural ecosystems."

In a large, ramshackle room at the Land Institute, Marty Bender sits near his computer at a nicked and scarred conference table poring over sheets of numbers. The floor is uneven, and one table leg is propped up on a book titled *Biochemicals, Organic Compounds, and Diagnostic Reagents*. The scene symbolizes both the rambling structure of a working farm and the scientific rigor that underlies this one. Bender has for the past decade been developing a computerized "energy audit" of an institute farm. This means carefully measuring the calorie count of food energy produced there, then comparing it with what he describes as the energy "embodied" in the inputs needed to grow that food. It's a daunting challenge, but one he says is necessary. "Economics can change according to technological developments, tax policy, or farm subsidies," Bender notes. That's why "energetics and ecological constraints are the place to focus."

Bender is a plant biologist who started here as an intern in 1978. He's a patient man, and needs to be. His work involves not only tracking the random and convoluted trails of energy expended each day on a working farm, but also looking back through the chains of enormously complex processes that went into creating each and every building or piece of equipment used. "Marty is looking at energy, materials, and labor," Jackson says. "And you take this all the way back to mining the ore in the Minnesota iron range to build a tractor. You have to know the embodied energy of a bolt."

With that in mind Jackson talks about the need to, as he puts it, "expand our boundary of consideration to overlap the boundaries of causation." Which is to say that—in farming on a square prairie plot, for instance—one has to draw a larger circle to encompass all the energy and materials that flow into the farm from outside that square. "What keeps the corn plants in a field going," he points out, "is mostly the stuff that comes in across the boundary." Stuff like fuel from petroleum and all the chemicals we manufacture with it. The full cost of those inputs is not counted by our current pricing system. And that makes for an uneven playing field. "To expect natural systems agriculture to play by a set of rules in which it acknowledges all the costs for food production, while [industrial farming] gets away with that theft," he says, "is not a fair comparison."

Can a new biology mimic of the prairie give good yields? Can it fix enough atmospheric nitrogen? Can it handle its own pests? Those questions are being explored on this isolated stretch of prairie deep in the heart of Kansas. It's going to take time, but at this point the indications are promising. Jackson notes that the Wright brothers could not have imagined where their efforts would lead. That's one reason he's arguing for the creation of a $130 million national program to support the development of perennial crops, with the Land Institute contributing expertise.

He sees this as a long-term effort. "The major environmental problems—global warming, soil erosion, what's happening in the oceans—have no short-term solutions." And breeding a perennial corn crop could take fifty years, because "in plant breeding, continuity is more important than ingenuity." To that end, Jackson is looking for individuals or foundations that are "willing to fund something the results of which they will not see in their lifetimes."

In light of the tax-funded subsidies now being pumped through industrial farms and into the hands of agribusiness multinationals—more than $20 billion each year—it seems like little enough to ask. The loop of plants, decomposers, and new soil is at the heart of everything we are and everything we have. Securing that should be the first obligation of any culture. And if Jackson and his team succeed, it could mean the start of a truly sustainable agriculture.

It will also mean that farm input costs—and the huge agro companies that feed on them—can be reduced to a manageable scale. In light of the heroic bungle we've made of industrial farming, Jackson offers the ultimate rationale. "In natural systems agriculture," he says, "we're talking about a system more resilient to human folly."

Thinking Wide

"It took endangered-species conservationists about a hundred years to shift from trying to conserve individual species to conserving habitats and ecosystems and watersheds and large landscapes," says Gary Nabhan, founder of Native Seeds Search. "We have to see the same kind of thing happen with agricultural conservation." Nabhan is talking about plants, but the same might be said of small farms. In the simple logic of the machine age, if farmers are under economic pressure, then subsidizing them makes sense. Wes Jackson sees a problem with that. A farmer isn't a separate unit, sitting off to one side and needing repair, he says. That's why it's a bad idea for policy to focus on the family farm. As it now stands, the farmer just "launders government money, called subsidies, passing it on to the suppliers of inputs and equipment."

Before farmers became root microbes in the big-money ecology of corporate agribusiness, that money flowed into rural communities. There it made a crucial difference in the health of small towns. More than a decade ago Dean MacCannell, a researcher from the University of California at Davis, took a look at that question. Although his study got little media attention at the time, it is of some importance to the subject at hand.

MacCannell began with a suggestion by the anthropologist Walter Goldschmidt. Comparing two farm towns in California's Central Valley, Goldschmidt had concluded that the structure of surrounding agriculture affected them. Small family farms, he said, appear to be crucial to the health of rural towns. MacCannell decided to test that notion on a broad scale—by comparing eighty Central Valley communities or one hundred Sunbelt counties. What he found both confirmed and refined Goldschmidt's suggestion. Quality of life improved as farm size increased, up to about three hundred acres. Then, where the size of surrounding farms grew beyond that, there was a sharp decline of conditions in the towns. It's not hard to see why. As rising input costs drive small farms out of business and the money stream shifts to multinational corporations, less of it is spent locally. There's an echo in that of the 2nd Law of Thermodynamics, where more energy and organization in one system mean depletion and disorder somewhere else.

If one actor in that drama bears a resemblance to the 2nd Law, waiting in the wings is another main principle of the new biology, ready to take the stage. As noted in chapter 5, in describing complex systems the physicist Murray Gell-Mann has pointed out that a random system has little or no complexity, nor does one that's regular. Complex adaptive systems, he said, "function best in a regime intermediate between order and disorder." Following on that, mathematician Stephen Farrier proposed a metaphor to describe them. Imagine on one side a set of letters that is completely ordered, he said—for instance, all *A*s, followed by *B*s, and then *C*s—and on the other side a different set of letters randomly scattered. "Then, between them, the works of Shakespeare." Three centuries ago the great composer Johann Sebastian Bach anticipated their comments when he wrote, "Not the autocracy of a single stubborn melody on the one hand. Nor the anarchy of unchecked noise on the other. No, a delicate balance between the two; an enlightened freedom."

Maintaining that "enlightened freedom"—finding the sweet spot between stability and change—is a key to success in evolution. Software designers came up against the same challenge in their early work with genetic algorithms, which AI programs use to "evolve" smarter solutions. Evolving programs would advance to modest adaptive peaks but then get hung up there. They couldn't descend to valleys of lower performance that would then make it possible for them to climb to new and higher peaks of effectiveness. The designers found they had to introduce random mutations into even the most effective programs, to prevent them from locking into less than optimum solutions. At a more complex level of organization, ant colonies do the same thing. While most ants will rigorously follow a pheromone trail to a proven food source, assuring survival of the colony, some ants always wander off in random directions. Their "pure research" makes the discovery of richer food sources possible. Between stability and change, order and chaos, the colony has found a sweet spot in which the ants can thrive. Then there is the loose coupling between the push of individual initiative and the shove of environmental constraint. That interplay begins between the nucleus and the cytoplasm and continues in the outside world, between adults and their surroundings.

The ability to make conscious choices is our great gift. Choice can also be a burden, though—one grown larger now that potent new technologies are being unleashed all around us, and unprecedented change has become a constant. The fact that machine age logic, which has brought us so far, has no clear vision for the future is no help either. In the running battle between corporate radicals pushing unmitigated change and ecological conservatives who oppose them at every turn, how do we find the sweet spot for a robust evolution in our own culture?

A fundamental clue comes from the genome, life's fundamental plan. At the Rockefeller University conference mentioned near the end of chapter 6, Lynn Caporale described how a genome varies mutation rates within its different regions—allowing change in some areas while conserving stability in others. If we view that in personal terms, it's easy to see why evolution would favor such a strategy. For instance, while we might welcome a gamble that could make our fingers longer, we'd be less likely to take risks with the Krebs cycle, which generates the cellular energy that keeps us all alive. In that spirit, the regions of a genome that guide basic functions like energy production are strictly conserved. What this says is that the sweet spot between stability and change is more than just a fifty-fifty compromise. It tells us to conserve what is essential and experiment with what isn't.

The loop of plants, decomposers, and new soil is our foundation—

the first energy technology and the basis for all else. For human culture to advance to a higher level, we first have to conserve that. Lady Eve Balfour put it well: "The criteria for a sustainable agriculture can be summed up in one word—permanence." Everyone involved in today's global agrotech industry knows that it can't meet that test. In fact, it's already failing. And now that failure is affecting our communities.

Communities have other problems, too. So while ecological concepts are being used to reform agriculture, new biologists are also using them to tackle the breakdown of human settlements brought on by machine age planning. Now just as materials modeled on nature are tougher and artificial intelligence modeled on real minds is smarter, just as digital organisms that compete are more adaptive and lessons from ecology can secure our food supply, so, too, natural logic offers guidance for those peculiar human ecosystems we call cities.

nine

town and country

From its hilltop site the ancient town of Todi looks out over Umbria. This province is the verdant heart of Italy, a quiet haven lying south of Florence, west of Ravenna, and just north of Rome. From earliest days here settlers occupied the hills that served defensive needs, and left the lowlands free for farming. A few steps from Todi's fine medieval plaza, one looks out on the valley of the legendary Tiber—onto a vista of small settlements and family farms changed little by the passage of time. The river remains a bright ribbon winding through the play of sun and shade on rounded hills. Along their slopes, forests have long blended into vineyards and the silver haze of olive groves, where goats and sheep and cattle graze. As it has for centuries, the valley floor offers up a lush mosaic of crop fields edged by dark green rows of trees.

It was in Umbria that Saint Francis, from nearby Assisi, made his famous pilgrimage, teaching a simple joy in the beauty of nature and identification with all living things. That message seems born of the landscape here, where human culture and nature exist in a harmony reaching back through antiquity. The communities have an elemental character, one with patterns common to enduring human settlements everywhere. There may be no finer example of that than Todi, an ancient small town on a remote Italian hill. That's why the Center for Sustainable

Cities hails it as a model not only of what is beautiful about the past, but for lessons that can help to guide the future.

Richard Levine is codirector of the center and a professor of architecture at the University of Kentucky, where it's based. In his view cities are organic wholes, the outgrowths of deep-rooted cultural and economic patterns. The purest distillation of those patterns is found, he believes, in the ancient hill towns of central Italy, where "narrow streets flow into public squares and . . . the city is perceived as a continuous fabric." One can, Levine says, walk through these towns and see things that don't make logical sense: "Many small connecting streets in one area, and no connecting streets somewhere else. Seemingly arbitrary changes in material or articulation. Majestic entrances to small courtyards and subtle entries to majestic spaces." And yet, he adds, "it all seems just right." What these towns share, says writer Carol Field, "is the way they grew organically in relation to the landscape with intimate narrow streets, runs of stairs, and open piazze creating a pattern as complex as medieval tapestries."

Much as Wes Jackson stresses the importance on a farm of the space between plants, Levine cites the value in a town of the space between structures—what he calls the "fabric of city space interwoven through the fabric of buildings." His point is that buildings serve not only their individual purposes; they also shape and characterize the public domain, and through it a town's "internal energy and information flows." Field describes those flows in prosaic terms as "the warmth and the sense of identity and community that draw us to the hill towns. The street and piazza become shared public space, the focus of life, where the community gathers to talk and do business, where the town market spills its provender under canvas awnings and umbrellas, brilliant colors undulating like waves in a great stone sea."

Todi is among the oldest towns of Umbria. Settlers have occupied this site since the Iron Age some three thousand years ago. The town was once an outpost of the Etruscan civilization that dominated central Italy before succumbing to the Romans, who called it Tuder, after an earlier Etruscan word for "boundary." Todi's great period was its rise as a city-state in the twelfth and thirteenth centuries. Then—along with nearby hill towns like Perugia, Trevi, and Spoleto—it bucked the medieval trend of rule by feudal lords. The city-states were run by a quasi-democratic system of trade guilds, a precursor to the modern era. It was then, too, that Todi assumed the form that remains today for the three thousand people who inhabit the town and the seventeen thousand or so others nearby.

People from the countryside still file through the gates of Todi's medieval wall, then on in past the ruin of the still older Roman wall and the even earlier remains of the Etruscan wall to follow cobblestone streets to the main plaza. There they find the market, the stately facades of their civic buildings, the mystery of flickering candles and incense in the cathedral. The scale and placement of those institutions—their relation to public space as well as to the informal shops and more modest facades of residential neighborhoods—both express and uphold the structure of public life. From this foundation, this urban core, the town has endured the shifting tides of history. And if that core gives continuity, it allows for adaptation, too. Says Levine, "The town is able to change in order to meet changing needs. Responsiveness is one of its qualities." Along with the small farms nourishing Todi, this combination of stability and openness has sustained it as a vital population center for seven centuries.

We tend to see ourselves as apart from nature, but we're not. Human culture is just a higher level of organization. First, cells combine to make the complex systems we call tissues and organs, which in turn make up those systems we call complex life forms. They then self-organize into the even more elaborate groupings labeled ecosystems. In each case, increasingly complex articulations of life emerge from and overlay the simpler forms that sustain them. The link between human culture and the natural systems from which we have emerged is nowhere more evident than in central Italy: in the vista of these medieval towns, each crowning its own hilltop and looking out on the cultivation of nature that surrounds it and has sustained it through the centuries.

Yet this ground once trod by Etruscan princes and Roman tribunes, by medieval friars and Renaissance traders, is under a new kind of stress. An agriculture that pays its own bills, like that of the Umbrian valleys, can't compete with the artificially lowered prices from industrial farms, which avoid paying so many of their true costs. In parts of Umbria the fertile blend of vineyards, orchards, olive groves, and grazing animals— along with the mix of tobacco, sunflowers, legumes, and various grains grown in small fields—is surrendering to large monoculture cropping systems. The region no longer depends primarily on farming, and farmers are leaving to find work in the cities.

That's not the case in Todi, at least not yet. Its location just sixty miles north of Rome has made it a haunt for weekending Romans and wealthy foreigners, who buy farms here to use as vacation retreats. And each year the region is a magnet for visitors who come from around the world to enjoy the view, to linger in the streets and courtyards, and to sample for a while the rich pleasures of life that residents take as their birthright. Despite such incursions, the basic pattern of life here still holds.

Levine sees in that pattern a model for the sustainable city of the future. His point is not that we should return to the Middle Ages. Far from it. With that era's primitive conditions, restrictive social strata, and limited options, he says, "It was a society in which none of us would be comfortable." But by looking at towns that were supporting themselves well before industrial methods were part of the landscape, he says we can learn something basic about how a sustainable community works.

First among those lessons is that we should avoid rigid ideology. The city on the hill has often served as a symbol of utopia—as a vision of a pure and ideal future. The hill towns of central Italy aren't like that, and are all the better for it, says Levine. In a sustainable city, "disorder, conflict, and mistakes are not things to be eliminated," he claims. "They're an essential creative process of the city, an inherent and integral part of the system. They input a healthy tension."

For centuries—through wars and conflict, expansion and decline, plagues and dark ages, peace and prosperity, sacred and secular rule—Todi has shaped and been shaped by the tumult of human interaction. At the heart of all that lies a fundamental urban pattern that has endured it all and may still serve to guide our best efforts. It favors neither rigid, sterile purity on the one hand nor anarchy on the other. Instead it has found a civilizing sweet spot between the structured order and the vibrant chaos of life.

Suburban Sprawl

That was once the case for all enduring cities and towns, but things began to change with the industrial revolution. The development of steam engines and railroads made it easy to locate factories inside cities, with their ready populations of workers. Along with that move came noise and pollution, as well as a population shift into those cities from farms. Then, as nineteenth-century cities grew noisier, dirtier, and more crowded, a countertrend emerged. Those who could afford it sought to get away while still remaining in touch with urban business and cultural benefits. Around that impulse grew a new idea of town planning. Cast as havens of greenery and quiet for the middle class, "suburban" communities began to appear outside major cities. John Nash created the picturesque Park Village, near Regent's Park in London. Frederick Law Olmsted designed Riverside, not far from Chicago. By the end of the century, the social reformer Ebenezer Howard would propose his "garden city" plan—a series of new towns surrounded by greenbelts, connected by mass transportation, and sharing a common cultural center. Residents, he said, "would enjoy all the advantages of a great and most beautiful city, and yet all the fresh delights of the country."

Such homely notions had obvious appeal. But they were soon swept aside by a radical new approach to the design of buildings and towns. With the 1930s came modernism—an architectural expression of the machine age. One of its most forceful exponents, the visionary architect Le Corbusier, called buildings "machines for living" and extolled a time when pure logic would define all. In line with that, he described a vision of utopian perfection in his proposal for an idyllic "radiant city." There, he said,

> you will live under trees, surrounded by limitless expanses of green lawns. The air will be pure and there will be scarcely any noise . . . At a great distance one from the other will be gigantic glass shapes sparkling in the sky and seeming to float in the air rather than touch the earth . . . Thanks to the magical properties of electricity these shapes will twinkle in the night. The roof gardens of the buildings appear to be golden bridges flung across the night from which one may discern the distant roar which comes from the ancient, time-encrusted districts of Paris.

Germany's Bauhaus school was at the center of that movement, which quickly captured the hearts and minds of a generation of designers. The austerity of industrial forms became the new ideal. Words like "apartment" and "house" were banned in favor of "cell," and books about older schools of design were purged from university libraries. Despite all this, Le Corbusier's radiant city never really came to pass. While sleek, elegant buildings were and still are built by modernists, the broader outcome of that movement was a manufactured uniformity that quickly became endemic.

That was a sharp break with the past. One critic, the architect
François Spoerry, noted how modernism "replaced the slow and continuous biological formation and growth which so characterized towns
and villages formerly." He complained that its top-down, analytical
methods divorced "those who conceived these ideas and those forced to
accept and live in them." Such critics notwithstanding, midway through
the twentieth century modernism had made a clean sweep of design
academies in the West. Old verities gave way to Zenlike pronouncements such as "Form follows function" and "Less is more."

By then the impulse to exit industrial centers had grown, but the
new suburbs born of mechanical methods would differ from their cozy
greenbelt ancestors, and nowhere more than in the United States. In the
three centuries leading up to 1950, the total number of Americans had
reached 140 million. Then, as industrial farming supercharged the baby
boom, population soared. Just twenty years later it was closing in on
200 million. Moreover, now those people were driving around in
100 million cars, and most of them were heading out of town. Machine
age planners tackled the problem with characteristic vigor. If the standardized farms of the green revolution could use cheap energy to grow
unprecedented new populations, the same industrial logic would provide them with nice, orderly places to live.

Seemingly overnight subdivisions of neat, standardized homes spread
outward from the cities into rural pastures. Levittown, the first manufactured suburb, was founded in 1947 on Long Island, just east of New
York City. It provided 17,400 affordable homes for the families of returning GIs. Many of those families today look back on that with gratitude and affection, but it was the beginning of a trend with unforeseen
consequences.

As suburbs spread across open areas, the cost of farmland was driven
up and rural taxes rose, putting pressure on farmers to adopt the more
"efficient" industrial methods. That interlocking expansion—of populations, of suburbs, of the demand for more food, and of the mechanized
farming meant to fill that demand—also saw the cutting and grading of
wildlife habitats on a historic scale. As ever-greater numbers moved to
the suburbs to be near the country, the country itself was disappearing
beneath them.

Wetlands, crucial incubators for disproportionate numbers of species,
were filled in as a matter of course. Forests were clearcut to provide

lumber for new homes, denuding watersheds that then eroded into streams and devastated fish populations. Fertilizer runoff from industrial farms compounded the problem. In some places those streams were also affected by toxic runoff from mines, as whole mountainsides were stripped away to provide coal for factories, and for the metal to make the cars that would carry people to and from their homes. In an effort to lessen the impact, rural zoning boards mandated lower population densities, which then made mass transit impractical. The spreading suburban populations were soon followed by businesses relocating into something the world had never seen—shopping malls.

During this time population statistics show a 15 percent differential in growth, with cities declining as suburbs rose. Retail sales growth tells a more revealing story. In suburbs it was double that of the cities. As the middle class exited the cities, it left behind only the rich and those who were poor and disadvantaged. Enter a generation of idealistic social engineers. Due largely to their efforts new freeways sliced through urban neighborhoods in order to link city centers with the suburbs. But as highways and cloverleafs spiraled into the countryside, they only helped to spur the outward trend. A time-lapse film shot from above a typical American city during this period would show its center collapsing as successive rings of suburbs spread out around it.

To deal with mounting problems in the inner city, a federal program called Urban Renewal spent some $10 billion between 1949 and 1974. Many of those projects were blocks of housing towers that made things even worse. That wasn't the intent. They were inspired by the design of Le Corbusier, whose drawings for his "city in a garden" show elegant towers rising from pleasant, landscaped grounds. But what inner-city residents got was a grim knockoff, and their neighborhoods were razed to make way for it. The age-old pattern of residential blocks clustered around traditional neighborhood centers disappeared. And with that went the familiar interactions both expressed in and reinforced by that pattern. In exchange, whole populations were isolated in poorly made industrial boxes. Little wonder that by the mid-sixties, when violent civil disturbances swept through inner cities across the U.S., they often centered in the "projects."

Writer Jane Jacobs raised a sharp protest against what was happening with her 1961 book, *The Death and Life of Great American Cities*. She turned a spotlight on the loss of urban neighborhoods, and on the monolithic developments replacing them. The billions spent on urban renewal, she said, created "cultural centers that are unable to support a good bookstore. Civil centers that are avoided by everyone but bums . . . Promenades that go from no place to nowhere and have no promenaders. Expressways that eviscerate great cities." As Milwaukee mayor John Norquist would later put it, "A lot of our problems are caused by solutions."

There were corporate and political agendas in the development of suburbs, and the subsequent damage to cities. But to a large degree the problems were brought on by thoughtful people with a real desire to improve life. A prime cause of those optimistic disasters was the harnessing of great power to headstrong idealism in the service of limited comprehension. Cheap energy was being used to supercharge a machine age approach to problem solving, a narrow logic that failed to grasp the larger context of urban life.

One result of that was a remarkable shift in spending. In 1901, fully a third of household spending by American middle-class families went for food. By the end of the century, their outlay for food had declined to only 15 percent. But during that same time the amount they spent on transportation rose from less than 2 percent to 20 percent.

Half of all Americans now live in suburbs. In just the five years from 1992 to 1997, more land was taken for development than in the preceding ten. And during those fifteen years some forty million acres of cropland, rangeland, and pasture were built over. Today, for every minute that goes by, the U.S. loses another two acres of open land, largely prime farmland, to development. And these facts link with the other essential pattern of modern suburban development. According to the Oakland, California–based organization Urban Ecology, from the 1970s until now America's population increased by 40 percent while the land area covered by its cities increased by 100 percent.

That sprawl is something new. The noted architect Richard Rogers says, "Just as the elevator made the skyscraper possible, so the car has enabled citizens to drive away from polluted city centers, and has made viable the whole concept of dividing our everyday activities into segregated zones of offices, shops and homes. As cities spread out, it becomes uneconomic to expand public transport systems, and they therefore fail to provide an adequate alternative to driving."

Like a forest that's been clearcut, that destructive feedback loop reinforces itself. In 2001 Congress spent $33 billion on highways and just $0.5 billion on passenger rail.

Beyond impacting transportation policy and the environment, the disintegration of urban centers has also affected the way many people relate to the world around them. Vacationers take trips to be close to nature, and they travel to great cities where the urban fabric is still intact. They also fly in from all over the world to walk the streets and public squares of Italian hill towns. But they don't go to see other suburbs. In the quiet, machinelike order of neat suburban homes and standardized zones of activity, there is little feeling of closeness with either nature or other people. There, the nearest thing to an urban center is the shopping mall, where people of all ages wander through the clutter of store displays and earnest artifice as if looking for a connection to something deeper.

What's missing is a sense of place. Like the ecological patterns in nature, the age-old patterns of urban life resonate with us. Long-standing population centers have distinct characters, which emerge from how local culture integrates with the land and climate of a region. In that, there is a sense of interaction and community we find deeply familiar.

Form Follows Form

"My ambition has been to produce a style of architecture that makes the heart sing," wrote town planner François Spoerry in his book *A Gentle Architecture*. Spoerry sees the industrial approach to design, and the built environment it has produced, as both "brutal" and "aggressive." As an alternative, he was an early and persuasive advocate of "vernacular architecture"—which mimics the forms of traditional local structures and communities.

His Port-Grimaud is a small waterfront town near St.-Tropez, along the azure southern coast of France. On a bright late-summer afternoon there the Mediterranean works its usual magic as sunlight glances off the waves from a light breeze. The wind stirs a chorus of low creaks and hums from the rigging of hundreds of sailboats that ring Port-Grimaud's many islands and peninsulas—fingers of land that interlock with fingers of blue water. Seen through the veil of swaying masts, the buildings of the town are an exercise in classical repose. Rows of town houses have similar shapes and facades, but each is a little unlike its neighbors, with different terraces or balconies, windows of varying heights, changes in doorways, subtle shifts in the pastel shades that color the walls and trim. The varied texture of those facades is capped by roofs that display furrowed rows of traditional Roman tiles, with their ochre and straw hues. A walk through Port-Grimaud takes one repeatedly over water, often by means of low, solid, arched bridges whose silhouettes are familiar throughout the region. Where the land opens up, there are small squares, occasionally also larger ones, bordered by a sizable public building, a church, clusters of retail shops. With the balance between similarity and diversity in its structures, and the scale of public life shaped by its plan, Port-Grimaud echoes many of the forms and patterns found in Todi and in towns that dot the sere hills rising from this golden coast. The big difference is that those towns are many centuries old; Port-Grimaud was founded in 1966.

Since then, Spoerry has gone on to build vernacular towns all over the world, including Puerto Escondido, on the Sea of Cortés in Mexico; Bendinat, near Palma, on the Mediterranean island of Majorca; and Port Liberty, an expansive development just across the Hudson River from lower Manhattan.

Spoerry doesn't reject modernism out of hand. He offers high praise for I. M. Pei and for the firm Skidmore, Owings & Merrill. He admires Eero Saarinen's famous gull-wing air terminal for TWA in New York. He also praises New York itself—for the "beauty" and "overall effect of all the many skyscrapers that tower over the city." But on the whole he believes settlements in vernacular form still serve most people best. As a student in the 1930s, he sailed among the Aegean Islands to document old Greek towns. He made a study of villages in Italy, Spain, and Provence before designing Port-Grimaud. In that design he used, he says, "a whole arsenal of . . . traditional shapes, all of which gave me the possibility of creating a homogeneous whole, while diversifying the details." As Spoerry puts it, these are "classic urban forms" that since time immemorial have represented the traditional town, forms "which to its inhabitants speak a known, safe, loved and familiar language."

A Pattern Language

Perhaps the bestselling architecture book of all time is one that most people have never heard of. *A Pattern Language*, first published in 1977, still sells more than ten thousand copies each year and has acquired an avid and diverse group of admirers. Reporter Patricia Leigh Brown, writing for *The New York Times*, called it "a wise old owl of a book, one to curl up with in an inglenook on a rainy day," the better to leaf through its "almanac-like entries that illustrate the warmth and harmony possible in buildings." Prince Charles invited its principal author—the architect Christopher Alexander—to serve as a trustee for his Institute of Architecture in London. Will Wright, creator of the popular computer game the Sims, regularly cites it as a major influence, and it has inspired a cultlike following among software programmers.

That's a lot for any one book to accomplish, and *A Pattern Language* can only nominally be described as a book. It was developed by Alexander—now a professor emeritus of architecture at the University of California at Berkeley—along with several colleagues, and is the second in a series. Nevertheless it stands apart, not just for its unusual organization but for its "vocabulary" of the patterns common to good buildings and vital urban centers.

That language consists of 253 commonsense verities for every aspect of design. For homes, its subjects range from large rooms to window seats to garden paths to the elements of a comfortable porch. The view is a recurring theme. One pattern instructs, "If there is a beautiful view, don't spoil it by building huge windows that gape at it incessantly. Instead, put the windows which look onto the view at places of transition—along paths, in hallways, in entryways, on stairs, between rooms."

The book's structure was revolutionary for its time. Auguring today's Web links, the description for any one pattern also lists others that typically link with it to make up a more complex whole. To that end, each description includes two separate sets of links: the first leads to those larger patterns that contain it; the second connects to the smaller patterns contained by it.

For instance, town planners in search of ideas for a public square begin with: "A town needs public squares; they are the largest, most public rooms that a town has. But when they are too large, they look and feel deserted." After a brief discussion, and photos or sketches to illustrate that concept, the section lists a set of links to larger patterns that a public square is part of: they're labeled ACTIVITY NODE, PROMENADE, and IDENTIFIABLE NEIGHBORHOOD. The section then also lists links to the smaller patterns that form parts of a viable public square. For instance, following the link to ACTIVITY POCKETS yields: "The life of a public square forms naturally around its edge. If the edge fails, then the square never becomes lively." HIERARCHY OF OPEN SPACE suggests, "Outdoors, people always try to find a spot where they can have their backs protected, looking out toward some larger opening." BUILDING FRONTS makes a case for eliminating setbacks, a standard feature of modern zoning plans. It argues that "building set-backs from the street . . . have actually helped greatly to destroy the street as a social space." STAIR SEATS describes how "Wherever there is action in a place, the spots which are most inviting, are those high enough to give people a vantage point, and low enough to put them in the action." SOMETHING ROUGHLY IN THE MIDDLE concludes, "A public space without a middle is quite likely to stay empty."

Given its hyperlinked structure, it's not hard to see how the book caught the eye of software designers, among whom it's credited with shaping the concept of object-oriented computing. They helped to put the book online, arguably its natural habitat, at a site called PatternLanguage.com. It has also inspired yearly conferences known as PLoPs (Pattern Languages of Programming). One takes place in the United States, at the University of Illinois. The others are held in Germany (EuroPLoP) and Australia (KoalaPLoP).

A Pattern Language is less a book than a tool. But the advice it gives is linked to the deep patterns of human settlement, to the shapes and forms of life in old places like Todi. After a few hours leafing through it, one can develop intelligent designs for everything from street cafés to town squares, from window seats to backyard gardens. In all of that it serves as a tool for reintegrating the basic structures of public and private life.

The New Urbanism

According to Léon Krier, the "functional fragmentation" of the city and the destruction of the countryside are one and the same thing. It is, he says, "the effective dissolution of the idea of town and country." His answer is what he calls the polycentric city.

Visionary architect and planner, author of numerous books, subject of an exhibition at New York's Museum of Modern Art, teacher at the Royal College of Art in London and at such American universities as Princeton and Yale, Krier is a leading voice in what has become known as "the new urbanism." Truth be told, there's little new about it. By expanding on the work of pioneers like Spoerry and Alexander, it articulates the qualities found in lasting human settlements. What is new are the growing number of efforts to revive those patterns in a standardized, machine age landscape that has long since lost sight of them. In that, the new urbanism is a popular corrective to the worst tendencies of modernism.

If cities don't look like nature, says Krier, they are in any case "second nature." But by ignoring the ecological imperatives of context, diversity, and intimate interaction, modern cities have tended toward what he calls "monofunctional overexpansion." In effect, their centers overexpand vertically, leading to "an excessive density of buildings, activities and users." Meanwhile, the outlying residential areas overexpand horizontally, "resulting in very low densities of buildings, uses and activities."

Krier likes to illustrate his points with sketchy and amusing cartoons. One, titled "3 Basic Modern Building-Types," depicts the Skyscraper (vertical box), the Landscraper (long, low, one-story box of the kind found in strip malls), and the Sprawler (row of tiny, identical boxes with peaked roofs). In another, huge cannon barrels have emerged from the roofs of Sprawlers and are lobbing dark shapes resembling cars through the sky at a nearby downtown. The caption reads, "Not the car but the suburban home is the deadly weapon."

In fact, suburbs have not been sub-urban for a long time. The nineteenth-century vision of compact, middle-class communities in rural settings, tied to city centers by light-rail links, has long since dissolved in a maze of cloverleafs, subdivisions, and malls. The sprawling bedroom communities of today are neither rural nor sub-urban, neither country nor town.

Although misuse of the term "suburban" is now anchored in common practice, the distinction is worth noting. That's because something like the original suburb is at the heart of Krier's polycentric idea. Instead of sprawl, it looks to a more organic kind of development—one like the fractal patterns in nature—with large, diverse, human-scale cities and towns giving rise to smaller, self-similar communities around them. In the Umbrian hills near Todi, for example, two or three kilometers out around the town there is a larger perimeter defined by several villages called *burgos*. They're agrarian centers that once also doubled as military outposts. As Krier puts it, "Just like a family of individuals, a city can grow only by reproduction and multiplication, that is, by becoming polycentric."

Krier and his musician wife live in an old Provence hill town half an hour inland from Port-Grimaud. As he talks in his quiet, tasteful study, his comments expand on the notion of urban environments as natural phenomena. Not only do they have definable forms, he says, but also definable boundaries. He speaks of a "cognitive radius" that seems to set the outer limits of ancient cities. Within that radius there are, he notes, also smaller natural perimeters, like the roughly ten-minute walking time that defines the size of virtually all urban neighborhoods. Such notions fly in the face of sprawl, and of the whole intellectual superstructure that views it as both reasonable and inevitable. "Maturity is the end goal of all growth," Krier writes in his book *Architecture: Choice or Fate*. "Excessive expansion just leads to exhaustion of the generative system."

Zoned In

"It's hard to fight the suburban model because it's zoned in," says American planner Andres Duany. He is speaking at a conference in the historic Biltmore Hotel in Coral Gables, Florida, a graceful planned community founded in the 1920s. The conference is sponsored by the University of Miami, where his wife and partner, Elizabeth Plater-Zyberk, is dean of the School of Architecture. "The problem is in the overall regional conception," he says. "Given sprawl, malls and office parks are *rational*." And at the heart of the problem is zoning. Duany explains that the first zoning codes just separated tenements from the smoky mills, "but now there may be thirty different zoning categories in a region." Zoning was a central factor as federal mortgage policy steered parents of the American baby boom into subdivisions. Those new commuters and the services that followed them were funneled into separate, standardized zones to a degree unequaled anywhere in the world. Far from creating polycentric communities, by the 1970s zoning restrictions had made the building of small towns in the U.S. virtually illegal.

Instead of aiding the "organic integration" of urban functions, says Léon Krier, "zoning imposes their mechanical segregation." Krier lays the blame for that on the 1931 Charter of Athens, a proto-modernist document, saying it made the breakup of town centers inevitable. In his view the advent of large, monofunctional zones—strictly segregated districts for homes, or education, or recreation, or business, or industry, or administration—now means that people "can accomplish only one function in one place at one time." That, he notes, makes modern life "extremely complex and wasteful in terms of transportation time" and "guarantees the maximum consumption of units of time, energy, hardware and land" for the execution of simple daily tasks.

Another problem caused by zoning, Krier says, is that "density, function, location, and, to a large extent, the form of these developments are decided before they land on the architect's drawing board." Zoning too large an area "leads only to uniformity and boredom, which you then try to liven up with kitsch and false diversity."

As a corrective to that, new-urban schemes come in three general types:

Urban Infill: restoring old neighborhoods and structures or creating new ones, within existing city boundaries.

Suburban Infill: grafting downtown centers into existing suburbs, typically in the sites of dead malls.

Greenfield Development: channeling rural population growth into new towns instead of sprawling subdivisions.

Despite their uphill battles with the zoning laws, new-urban projects are having an impact in the U.S. According to the trade journal *New Urban News*, there were 472 neighborhood-scale projects in 2002, a rise of 26 percent from the previous year. While they represent a small percentage of overall housing starts, their high success rate and the rapid growth in their numbers are evidence of a larger reintegrating trend. One sign of that is the recent shift in vacancy rates for commercial property: in city centers like Dallas, Atlanta, Portland, and Washington, D.C., there are now on average 8 percent fewer vacancies than in their surrounding suburbs.

Television and the Web are useful mediums, but the global village can't and shouldn't replace real villages. After decades of alienation for children who grow up with fresh air and open space but no sense of community, for stay-at-home parents living with social isolation, and for working parents who spend hundreds of hours each year sitting in traffic jams, all this may seem too little too late. New urbanists are nevertheless hopeful, and may yet have the last word. As Winston Churchill once remarked, "You can count on Americans to do the right thing after they've tried every possible alternative."

Back to the Future

The baby sports goggles and leans forward into the wind, tiny fingers clutching the front bar of the stroller. His mother, a smartly dressed young woman wearing Rollerblades, races them along a riverside promenade in a fast, sinuous weave through clusters of less animated pedestrians. It is of course New York, a place of famous and relentless energy and one of the few modern cities that new urbanists say good things about.

One reason for that is its extensive public transport system—a dense interlacing of trains, helicopters, ferries, buses, subways, car services, and cabs; not to mention the bicyclists, skateboarders, pedestrians, and occasional Rollerblading mothers with dauntless toddlers. New Yorkers are the only Americans who routinely go through life without driver's licenses.

Another reason new urbanists like New York is that most of its skyscrapers are designed to respect the urban fabric of the street. Still, many of the problems Krier points to are endemic here. With rush hour, the population of Manhattan nearly doubles each day. The congestion, stress level, and general combativeness of life in New York are the stuff of legend—it surprises few to hear that, per capita, the city produces more Congressional Medal of Honor winners than any other place in the U.S. Yet order and chaos remain in dynamic if precarious balance and New Yorkers remain, more or less, civilized. From great boulevards like Park Avenue through the hive of midtown to the tangle of old streets in the financial district, New York is the outstanding example of ancient urban patterns containing and shaping the modernist impulse.

Battery Park City is literally an extension of that—a new-urban infill development, and one of the finest—built on landfill in the Hudson River, at the foot of the former World Trade Center. The project was designed in 1979 by Alexander Cooper and Stanton Eckstut.

It was on Battery Park City's graceful riverfront promenade that the New York mother and child traced their rapid path, flashing south from where weekend throngs at sidewalk cafés surround a marina filled with yachts and where a great glass barrel vault arches above shoppers and free concerts, amid a handsome crowd of office buildings. Farther down along the river, residential blocks are punctuated by neighborhood parks and squares, a gym, a discreet restaurant.

The imprimatur of New York, with its prominence and pacesetting reputation, has spurred the development of new-urban infill projects elsewhere. Traditionally styled ballparks, squares, and marketplaces are appearing in cities across the U.S. Since 1993, the Hope VI program of the Department of Housing and Urban Development has spent $4 billion replacing failed modernist public housing with new-urban infills.

At Battery Park City, where residential blocks give way at its south end to a small cove bounded by informal gardens and a museum, there are vantage points for looking out across the harbor to the Statue of Liberty. Also visible from there is the broad expanse of François Spoerry's Port Liberty, his big new-urban infill project across the Hudson River. Spoerry recalls how he first noticed the location. In the early 1980s he was having lunch at Windows on the World, the celebrated restaurant at the top of one of the World Trade Center's twin towers. Looking down from 107 stories above the river, he spied an abandoned ship terminal on the far shore and hastened across that day to inspect it and secure an option. Ironically, a relentless critic of modernism was thus brought to his most ambitious scheme by one of the last great projects of the modernist International Style.

On September 11, 2001, in the deadly terrorist attack that collapsed the twin towers of the World Trade Center, Battery Park City was seriously damaged and is currently being restored. The larger job of overseeing a new master plan for ground zero and the financial district will be handled by Beyer Blinder Belle—a firm that specializes in major, tradition-oriented projects. Also advising will be the new-urbanist firm Peterson/Littenberg.

Suburban Infill

As cities add traditional neighborhoods or reclaim them with urban infill, a larger problem remains: the suburbs. One answer to that is suburban infill—which inserts brand-new downtowns into existing subdivisions, often into the sites of abandoned malls. A recent study shows that nearly 20 percent of the malls in the U.S. are either dead or dying. According to new-urban developer Robert Davis, "As investors admit they have a problem, they are beginning to reconfigure these places into centers of real neighborhoods." Malls are surrounded, he says, by plenty of "single-family rooftops." Realizing that, canny mall operators "are adding townhouses, apartments, offices, schools, and churches and public places, while reducing the quantity of retail."

Mashpee Commons, a complete village built on the site of a 1960s mall on Cape Cod, near Boston, was founded in 1986. The same approach is now being pursued at sites around the country, including Santana Row in San Jose, California; Park Commons in St. Louis Park, Minnesota; CityCenter in Englewood, Colorado; and Belmar in Denver. Market analyst Robert Gibbs points to a parallel trend. He notes the emergence of newly constructed malls—like Valencia Town Center, in California—that incorporate shops, offices, even housing around open-air main streets.

Gibbs sees the creation of as many as three thousand new, mixed-use town centers before the end of the decade. Reinforcing that shift is a change in traffic patterns. Commuting to inner cities is no longer the biggest source of mileage for suburban drivers. More than half of all miles driven in suburbs are now spent moving people around within them.

Real Suburbs

While infill projects—urban and suburban—are vital correctives, the ultimate problem lies elsewhere. In coming decades, as population growth continues, greenfield development—where new residential and commercial projects are built on open land—will send new subdivisions sprawling across tens of millions of acres. Says Andres Duany, "New urbanists do work in the inner city, and very effectively, but 95 percent of what is built in this country is built on greenfield sites."

Even if population growth won't be halted anytime soon, its impact on open country can be limited. Rather than spreading out in disconnected, monofunctional zones, populations can be focused into dense new-urban centers. When designing those, American planners look for guidance to the early part of last century. Speaking at the conference in Coral Gables—George Merrick's lovely old Mediterranean Revival–style community on the outskirts of Miami—Duany noted, "We measure our wealth by growth in housing starts, and yet people now resist them. Why? Because people no longer trust the planners." The great names of American real estate are from the 1920s, he said, when developers were known as town founders.

The point is well taken. Names like Myers Park, Coral Gables, Shaker Heights, Palm Beach, Beverly Hills, Princeton, and Forest Hills show the wisdom of an earlier approach to suburban development, one now honored by that highest of all American accolades: exorbitant prices.

Area Codes

The design of a new-urban town typically begins with a charette. This is an ongoing session in which the planners meet with local politicians, zoning boards, fire departments, public works officials, school boards, and others with a stake in the result. The planners then channel that input into a formal code, or pattern book, which lays down the ground plan for the town while mandating certain characteristic shapes and standards for the buildings, as well as for the materials used to build them.

Some codes are quite detailed. Andres Duany and Elizabeth Plater-Zyberk coded the roof slopes and eaves in their first town, Seaside, on the Florida Panhandle. Krier's master plan for Florence-Novoli—a fourteen-block infill in an industrial suburb of Florence—is comparatively loose and rudimentary. Different codes have different priorities. Planner Peter Calthorpe focuses on public transportation links. The code for Celebration—the celebrated town built in Florida by Disney—calls for a main street devoid of boutiquification by Banana Republics, Victoria's Secrets, and other franchise chains. Instead a national search scouted out quality local small businesses, which were invited to expand there.

As each town grows into a form defined by its code, a natural tension emerges, like the expansion of an embryo into the limiting and defining elements of an egg. As the town takes shape, its code has to balance the tension between individuality and community. Krier acknowledges something like that when he says, "The masterplan is to the construction of a city what the constitution is to the life of a nation." That outlook bolsters the views of Yale architectural historian Vincent Scully, who taught Duany, Plater-Zyberk, Calthorpe, and numerous others in the new generation of traditional town planners. "The International Style built many beautiful buildings," Scully says, "but its urbanistic theory and practice destroyed the city. It wrote bad law. Its theme in the end was individuality; hence its purest creations were [buildings that] celebrated the individual free from history and time. One could not make a community out of them."

The Price of Success

That's not the case at Seaside. If the ant is a poster child for the artificial life community, something like that is true as well for Seaside and new urbanism. This is the first big American greenfield project that was dis-

tinctly and unapologetically new-urban. While some buildings here
have a modern, even odd cast, the code ensures common qualities, too.
Public buildings are free from all but the most basic design controls, but
the differing residential neighborhoods are coded for roof slopes, front
porches, and other shapes and features drawn from Florida tradition.
"When buildings share a common vernacular," says Duany, "it's possible
to integrate them in great variety . . . without raising hackles." That formula clearly works at Seaside, where it has produced a streetscape that is
cheerful, lively, and gently offbeat.

Seaside began when developer Robert Davis' grandfather left him
eighty acres of open waterfront property on Florida's Panhandle,
roughly forty-five minutes west of Panama City. At the time, some two
decades ago, this was just scrubland on a stretch of beach so isolated
people called it the Redneck Riviera. Davis and his wife, Daryl, saw
things differently, and set off in their old red Pontiac convertible to study
the rural architecture of the Florida Gulf Coast. They eventually hooked
up with Duany and Plater-Zyberk, who were eager to try ideas inspired
by their time with Scully at Yale, and by a visiting lecturer there named
Léon Krier. With that, impulse met opportunity and an American icon
was born.

Twenty years later Seaside is a vibrant resort community of more
than three hundred homes. From narrow lanes of modest Rosewalk cottages to a boulevard fronted by grand mansions, the streets here come
alive each season with kids on bikes, retirees in golf carts, and young
parents pushing strollers, although the parents here generally do their
strolling without Rollerblades. Seaside's street plan arches around a larg-
ish town center, with the streets forming concentric rings of half circles
that open onto the beach and blue waters of the shore. At that junction,
each street terminates with a distinctive gateway that marks its connection with the shore. Inland, streets sometimes converge in small round-
abouts ornamented by gazebos or stands of trees. The street grid is
also supplemented by a fine web of sandy paths between backyards—
shortcuts for beachgoers in bare feet.

Can new urbanism revive the natural patterns of small-town life
found in places like Todi? Can the mixed-use, polycentric idea hope to
prevail over the standardized, monofunctional zoning that now shapes so
much of the industrial world? And don't most people, when all is said
and done, just prefer life in the suburbs? Suburbs certainly do look great

when the main alternative is disintegrating, crime-ridden cities. That's why commuters have put up with the endless drive time, with the cost of maintaining two cars (equal by itself to the yearly mortgage on a small house), and with living in a social netherworld of not quite isolation but not quite community, either. Now there's a truly sub-urban alternative to those pleasant, sprawling "anywheres"—namely, pleasant, traditional neighborhoods and towns with up-to-date wiring and plumbing. And buyers are beating a path to their doors.

As a result, over the past two decades a growing list of planners has created hundreds of new-urban towns in the U.S. and elsewhere. In Canada there are several developments in Markham, near Toronto, while Calgary features McKenzie Towne and Garrison Woods. Meanwhile, in Europe, there are projects like Spoerry's Port-Grimaud in France; as well as Krier's Florence-Novoli in Italy and Poundbury in England. Other planners have built Tacheles, Potsdam-Drewitz, and Karow-Nord in Germany; Pont Royal en Provence, Gassin, and Le Plessis-Robinson in France; and Las Lomas de Marbella and La Heredia in Spain.

All this activity represents more than civic spirit alone. The first cottages sold at Seaside, in 1983, went for $63,000 apiece. By the fall of 2004, the least expensive private home there was an eighteen-hundred-square-foot cottage on sale for $1.6 million. To a lesser degree that effect holds true in other new-urban developments. Row houses in Kentlands, a greenfield project in suburban Maryland, command a $30,000–$40,000 premium over comparable single-family homes in the area. What's more, according to market analyst Todd Zimmerman, 42 percent of the housing there is owned by families. "Kids love high density," he says.

The persistent price advantage of new-urban projects has also brought criticism—accusations that they're elite enclaves, geared only to upper-middle-class and wealthy home buyers. Duany answers that we just need to make more of them. "While they do not necessarily cost more to build, they do usually sell for more," he concedes, adding, "Laws of supply and demand drive up the prices of commodities that are better and scarce."

Royal Treatment

While the new urbanism is a main force in reintegrating communities, an often-noted weakness has been its lack of ecological awareness. Its planners look to traditional towns for their shapes and overall form. But the best and most enduring old towns—like Todi—express both urban *and* ecological patterns. In the deepest sense they are a product of that union. New urbanism has been slow to embrace green planning.

That began to change with Poundbury, the new town sponsored by Britain's Prince Charles. Poundbury was designed by Léon Krier and, as might be expected, shares certain basics with Seaside. Its quiet, intimate neighborhoods are densely woven and human in their scale. The buildings draw their design and materials from local vernacular—in this case handsome stone or brick houses with steep-pitched roofs and high chimneys, which cast distinctive profiles against the soft skies of the English countryside. There are pragmatic similarities, too. Cars, power lines, and phone wires are generally out of view. And like Seaside, Poundbury is built on inherited land, although in this case it has been in the family since 1342, and instead of the Redneck Riviera it's known as the Duchy of Cornwall.

Among other differences, Poundbury is larger, with an expected population of five thousand. It contains light industry and thoughtfully designed public housing. Rather than being built on a greenfield, it is an extension of the old market town of Dorchester in southwest England. And it looks out not on the Gulf of Mexico but across a broad valley, to the remains of an Iron Age fort called Maiden Castle.

But the landmark difference—the one that truly sets Poundbury apart—is that it was the first new-urban town to make energy efficiency and other green technologies a part of its code. Prince Charles is well known, and often assailed, for opposing modernism. Among European political figures he's also a leading advocate for sustainable development. Those two interests found mutual expression at Poundbury. Says Andrew Hamilton, the town's developer, "The prince wanted this to be a showcase."

He spoke more than he knew. For what Poundbury showcases is the start of a shift in awareness to a more fundamental understanding of how communities come to be. It recognizes that just as farming produces organic matter to feed human populations, the built environment also must be fed—with constant inputs of energy; with trees culled from forests, stone from quarries, metal from mines, plastics drawn from various feedstocks. So as human populations continue to swell they not only cover more ground; they also consume more energy and materials.

Some 40 percent of all sand, stone, and gravel; 40 percent of all processed materials like steel; and 25 percent of the wood harvest go into buildings. In the U.S., building materials, construction, and maintenance use up 40 percent of the energy production.

Any new-urban town has a head start on sustainability. Its smaller footprint means less habitat is destroyed. It means less energy and materials are needed for the construction of roads, water mains, and other infrastructure. That same density encourages walking instead of driving. Poundbury enjoys all these advantages, then goes further. Built in an existing population center instead of out on open land, it answers a major concern of environmentalists. That, along with its energy management systems, high-efficiency boilers, gray-water recycling, and other advanced technologies, signals the merger of new urbanism with another new strategy for town planning. Called "urban ecology," it focuses less on the structure of human communities than on integrating them with the ecological cycles and patterns of the natural world.

Urban Ecology

Richard Levine cites the venerable maxim "All politics is local," adding that one can likewise say, "All sustainability is local." As he sees it, "You can't think globally. No one can understand such a large system." But focusing on cities brings the global problem back to human scale. The city, he says, is the only unit both small enough to respond to local action and large enough to impact the global system.

According to Levine, just building urban infills won't suffice. We need to insert, to "implant" neighborhoods that are "big enough to be designed and ultimately planned as organisms, as urban ecosystems." Levine was a principal author of the influential Aalborg Charter. That document was signed in Aalborg, Denmark, in 1994 by more than one hundred European cities and towns, including Vienna, Lisbon, and Oslo. Those principles call for an "ecosystemic" approach to urban management that opens feedback channels to all citizens and interested groups, that doesn't "export problems into the larger environment or to the future," and that treats resources like air, soil, water, and forests as what economist E. F. Schumacher called "natural capital."

Levine is currently working with Vienna-based urban ecologists Oikodrom on a scenario-building project in rural China. With funding from the EU, and in cooperation with the Chinese government, they're studying villages that just decades ago had been unchanged for centuries. Although the quality of life then was elemental, he says, they were self-sufficient for all of that time while also maintaining the environment's ability to support them. That's changing now as modernization brings electricity, paved roads, machinery, TV, and consumer goods, along with a new economic dependency on the outside world.

As one part of their mandate, Levine's group designs scenarios that show how modern green technologies can be tailored to the needs and resources of each of the villages. The aim is to improve their economies while moving them once again toward sustainability. For the second part, the group will, in essence, ask: "What if we stop here and rewind the film, back to before the past few decades of development occurred, and then imagine a scenario for how modernization could have taken place here along fully sustainable lines?" This work, Levine suggests, could in the end have value for developing nations everywhere. In a nice complement to these efforts he has begun another project there, too, this one with Chinese academics. He says, "We're searching through all of Chinese mythology, religion, and culture—from Lao-tzu to Confucius, even Chairman Mao—to extract intellectual precursors for the idea of sustainability."

Among them could well be what was said of Li Ch'eng, the great tenth-century master of Sung landscape painting. It was claimed that he could no more paint a tree that looked wrong than nature could grow one that way, so attuned was he to natural process and spontaneity. In the West, architect Richard Neutra expressed a similar, if less elegant, formulation of that notion some fifty years ago. In his book *Survival Through Design* he wrote, "Design must always have an intimate kinship to the life processes." Moving beyond airy theorems, Neutra also tried to formulate pragmatic strategies for creating communities in harmony with nature. "The proper gauge of value" lies in "the aids and harms to the survival of a given biological community," he said. For that reason, "community planning is . . . in need of a large scientific advisory board, chaired by an expert in biology."

Neutra became famous for his spare, open buildings, but he constructed no towns. That remained for people like Judy and Michael Corbett. In the mid-1970s they became pioneers of urban ecology in America by developing Village Homes—one of the earliest modern green communities—on the outskirts of Davis, California. With its small clusters of reasonably priced homes sharing common playgrounds and orchards, its naturalistic drainage system, its photovoltaic rooftop arrays and "solar rights" manifesto (ensuring that no one structure blocks the sun from another), Village Homes was a decidedly odd duck when it opened for business back then. The Corbetts recall the experience in their concise and readable book, *Designing Sustainable Communities*:

> Solar technology was very new at this time, and local real estate agents knew little about it and trusted it less. They actively discouraged prospective buyers, disparaged the experimental features of the project, and raised concerns about resale value. We heard that Village Homes was the laughingstock of the local realty community.

Today, as with new-urban towns like Seaside, those modest structures are the most costly real estate in Davis, selling for eleven dollars per square foot more than the average home there.

By developing Village Homes, the Corbetts joined with Neutra, Levine, and the villagers of ancient China in a common understanding: in nature, sooner or later, the ecological bill comes due. The only economically secure strategies are ones that work within that reality. A dawning of that awareness for another group was made official in 1998, when the Congress for the New Urbanism—which sets guidelines for the field—centered its annual conference on sustainable city planning. Green planning continues as a major theme in its conferences, and the organization is now in talks with the Natural Resources Defense Council and the U.S. Green Building Council for a proposed joint venture to devise green urban standards.

These lessons would seem to be reaching the ears of China's leaders, who in 2005 announced their plan to build a huge eco-city the size of Manhattan on an island in the Yangtze River delta near Shanghai. The new city will be called Dongtan and will eventually house several million people.

Shelter from the Norm

Green cities and towns rest on the design and creation of green buildings. In the past, models from nature have often shaped human structures, from the organic forms of Antonio Gaudi through Buckminster Fuller's geodesic domes and the membrane-like tents of Frei Otto. The new green designers are turning instead to natural processes for inspiration, to see how energy and materials flow through buildings—and how buildings themselves evolve through time.

The Rocky Mountain Institute (RMI), one of the world's leading think tanks for alternative energy, has built a state-of-the-art headquarters that actually generates power from renewable sources and exports it to the grid. RMI has also published a guide: *Green Development: Integrating Ecology and Real Estate.* Many new buildings now employ sustainably harvested wood. Or reuse materials. The home near Seattle of Microsoft's chief, Bill Gates, was among the first large-scale projects built with reclaimed timber. The new approach recycles buildings, too. Adding on to buildings or converting them to new use is common in old towns like Todi, but the industrial mind-set has brought with it a throwaway culture of structures that are put up cheaply, then simply razed and replaced. When that happens, their materials and the energy embodied in them disappear into landfills. More sustainable, say the new designers, are buildings meant to evolve through time. A large private home may one day become a restaurant, or be divided into smaller apartments. As writer and entrepreneur Stewart Brand says in his book *How Buildings Learn,* "A building is not something you finish. A building is something you start."

The landmark example of a recycled, ecologically sophisticated building is the handsome New York headquarters of the National Audubon Society. Designed by architect Randy Croxton and Audubon's former science adviser Jan Beyea, it recycled a century-old eight-story structure in lower Manhattan. The building was first stripped to its shell and girders, then rebuilt from the inside out with materials carefully selected to be benign not only in the larger environment but for inhabitants, too.

The ultimate point of a building is of course to shelter residents from harm, but with the advent of industrial building and furnishing materials a curious inversion has occurred. The chemicals in them keep releasing low but persistent levels of toxic vapor into the air long after construction is done. This outgassing can affect the health of occupants—a development commonly known as sick building syndrome. Mindful of that, the designers of the Audubon building saw to it that the plywood underlayment for floors has no toxins in the glue, and that the carpets covering it are natural wool—that is, without chemical dyes or pesticides. Office furniture was chamber-tested for outgassing before purchase. Outdoor air is drawn into the structure at the roof level (as opposed to street side, the case in many large buildings), and on the roof the intake and vent are widely separated. Once in the system, the air is thoroughly filtered, and on every floor it's completely changed several times per hour. Those factors combine to produce what Audubon staffers call "the freshest air in New York."

Clean air is always a source of wonder for New Yorkers, doubly so when it's found in offices. Combined with the building's other innovations, that has brought economic paybacks in the form of lower absenteeism and higher productivity, which help offset the added costs of construction.

In the book *Natural Capitalism*, business activist Paul Hawken, with RMI's Amory and Hunter Lovins, cite another new approach to ventilation, this one introduced in Japan. It creates small variations in airflow. As described in the book, those systems "constantly vary temperatures over a modest range. Their microchip controls deliver air not in a steady stream but in seemingly random gusts. They may even inject whiffs of jasmine or sandalwood."

If the Japanese design is appealing, it could be because that pattern of minor variations around a norm has a pleasant and familiar feel. For instance, it mirrors the architectural pattern of subtle variations on a basic theme that informs traditional streetscapes everywhere. And both of those echo a deeper natural pattern—the subtle genetic variations expressed by individuals around the norm of a species, and then by various slightly differing species around the norm of a genus, and so on. In ways small and large, at every level of life the same pattern obtains: not chaos and not uniformity either, but a dynamic interplay of the two around a broadly defined theme. The machinelike standardization of today's uniform suburban homes and streetscapes flies in the face of that.

A still more basic balancing act of nature is how it links scarce energy from the sun with earth's abundant raw materials. This is another relationship being disrupted by our industrial scheme. In that scheme it's energy that is abundant today—never mind that it's being drained from the ground and will soon be all gone—while industrial raw materials are becoming scarce. Their scarcity is due mainly to the fact that we use them once and bury them, one of the more peculiar symptoms of linear thinking. But the upshot is that it makes our system a direct inversion of the natural order. In nature, energy is scarce and materials are abundant. For us, energy seems abundant and materials scarce.

Children of the machine age are now comfortably ensconced in a series of dynamics fundamentally at odds with nature, and no system out of sync with nature lasts. The question is, how do we reverse such a basic equation? It's an enormous challenge, one that green architects are helping to address. But that effort is hampered by their having to work within an unsustainable culture. There's not much a single building can do beyond serving as an example to others of how to slow the hell-bent velocity of the system.

The Audubon building does that through energy and resource efficiency. Recycled materials were used wherever possible. Its high-efficiency heater-chiller unit saves energy, as do adjacent systems like sensors that dim the lights whenever sunlight is available, and motion sensors that turn off those lights when there is no one moving around beneath them. (During late-night deadlines in the society's magazine office, writers who've let themselves get lost in thought can at times be seen waving their arms overhead to bring the lights back on.)

All arm waving aside, if the developer of one of these new high-performance buildings can reduce energy use by 70 percent or more, year after year, what is that worth in added construction costs? What is the value of a 15 percent increase in office productivity—or of the higher retail sales in stores—attainable with better light and air? One answer to such questions came at a new green 300,000-square-foot manufacturing center in Holland, Michigan, for Herman Miller SQA, the noted producer of sophisticated office furnishings. There, productivity gains brought a revenue increase of $1.5 million within two years. The building that encouraged those gains is framed with locally recycled steel and looks more like a vast greenhouse than a factory. Arrays of windows, skylights, and clerestories flood the offices and assembly floors with daylight. Native trees, grasses, and wildflowers cover the grounds, and there are wetlands thick with cattails. "This building is about connections," says William McDonough, the building's architect and a leader in the field. "People connecting with each other, people connecting with nature, and the building itself connecting with nature. Connecting to the whole is nature's way of staying healthy."

McDonough wrote the preface to *Big & Green*. That beautifully designed book highlights fifty green skyscrapers and other large buildings—from Frankfurt's 1977 Commerzbank, the first green high-rise and the tallest building in Europe; and New York's new Condé Nast Building at Four Times Square, currently the largest green building in the U.S.; to Ventiform, a lovely model by Foster and Partners for a white structure inspired by sand-eroded rocks, whose soft, curvy shape funnels wind to a huge, centrally positioned wind turbine.

In his preface to the book, which also served as the catalog for an exhibition, McDonough writes:

> The Earth's natural communities . . . thrive not by producing the same response worldwide but by fitting elegantly into a profusion of niches. Even nature's laws express themselves variously in different communities, as processes such as photosynthesis and nutrient cycling yield different forms from region to region. We could say form doesn't follow function, it follows evolution . . . The buildings featured in the exhibition represent small steps toward an ideal. They capture a moment in which we are striving to find a new way of living. None of the problems associated with large-scale building design have been solved, many issues remain. But this exhibition offers clues, a suggestion of possibilities. There are hints of an abundant future, a new engagement with the natural world, and better, more enriching places—by design.

The modernist tradition gave rise to many architectural stars, but McDonough is the first green architect to achieve media prominence. He's a gifted phrasemaker and much-sought-after speaker. He is profiled regularly in the press and was chosen to receive the first Presidential Award for Sustainable Development.

That prominence is grounded on an impressive résumé. Now based in Charlottesville, Virginia, he is former dean of architecture at the University of Virginia there. His 1986 eco-renovation of the Environmental Defense Fund's headquarters in New York anticipated the Audubon building by several years. He helped set up an early sustainable forestry plan, and when New York clothier Paul Stuart specified that he use oak paneling in renovating their Madison Avenue store, he made them plant new oaks to replace the trees being culled. When it was built, his headquarters building for the Gap, in San Bruno, California, featured the biggest living roof in the country; it's covered with an open field of soil, grasses, and other vegetation drawn from the region. That has now been superseded in McDonough's effort to green the Ford Motor Company's vast River Rouge plant—one of the oldest and most famous machine age manufacturing facilities. Today it supports a ten-and-a-half-acre habitat roof, the world's largest. McDonough is currently designing new eco-urban centers for a town and six major cities in China, including Beijing.

In most of his ventures he partners with Michael Braungart, the prominent German chemist and environmental activist. For instance, working for the office-fabrics firm Designtex, they developed a line of seating fabric so benign that when it's worn out, it can be used as mulch. In all of their projects they show a deep, even poetic awareness of natural processes and of how to integrate those insights into the built environment. At the close of their winning bid to design a green European headquarters for sport shoe maker Nike, McDonough said they would view the project as successful "when songbirds return to the site."

Chattanooga Turnaround

Songbirds are returning to whole cities now as urban ecology—which began with green buildings and small neighborhood developments—knits those factors into new urbanist schemes to create larger wholes. Chattanooga is a case in point. Today the skies here are clear and blue, and this city of 300,000, set in a looping bend of the Tennessee River, is, as one booster describes it, "a living laboratory" for sustainable development. But three decades ago it was officially the most polluted American city. The problem then was poor air quality, caused by the city's industrial base of smokestack factories. Their smoke was once so thick that people had to drive with their headlights on at midday and the soot clogged the government's air-monitoring filters solid. Then, in the seventies and eighties, manufacturing jobs began disappearing overseas as the global economy took form. With that, many companies cut back or closed down altogether, laying off thousands. As Chattanooga's economic infrastructure collapsed, the companies still there were hit with rising taxes even as growing crime rates, poor schools, and racial conflict contributed to a sense of urban decay.

During that time the city was also at odds with its setting. East Tennessee is a lush green carpet of ridges and valleys—the surface soil of several states scoured down from the Appalachians and deposited here when glaciers worked their way south ten thousand years ago. Due to that the hills surrounding Chattanooga are home to one of the most diverse temperate bioregions on earth. People here share a real love and respect for the natural beauty of those hills and hollows. That could be why, in 1984, residents answered a citywide planning initiative by saying that yes, they wanted good jobs and a strong local economy but that wasn't enough. They wanted clean air, too, they said, and somewhere to walk by the river. They wanted to go fishing without driving out of town, and to eat the fish they caught without worrying if they were safe.

By the time of a second planning session in 1993, Chattanooga's transformation had begun. And in that process the environment had become not just one item on the agenda but the goal that would drive all others. By then a private/public coalition had removed a clutter of derelict warehouses and piers blocking access to the river, replacing it with new fishing piers and Riverwalk, a shoreline greenbelt with trails and bike paths. A $45 million freshwater aquarium arose at the park's center, and nearby an old iron bridge across the river was restored for bike and pedestrian use. A company was formed to manufacture electric buses, which began running as free shuttles downtown. And riders on the shuttles could witness the renovation of landmark buildings and residential areas. With those efforts the city and surrounding county also drew nearly $500 million in new investment. At the center of all this activity were the local activist Mai Bell Hurley, then-mayor Gene Roberts, the designer Stroud Watson, and the Lyndhurst Foundation, which provided seed money.

Another local figure who rose to prominence then is David Crockett. Kin to the famed American frontiersman, Crockett is a big, voluble man with the easy manner of someone born and bred in rural East Tennessee. A city councilman at that time, he was and remains an articulate champion of the effort to put Chattanooga on a sustainable footing. To that effort he brings a pragmatic awareness of the broader problems facing cities today. "You don't have to be a member of some environmental group, you don't even have to be real good at math to see that things have to change," Crockett says. "We can't just go on consuming resources and dumping waste in holes. We don't have enough resources; we don't have enough holes in the ground."

Crockett was deeply involved in the process in October 1995, when a design charette was held to guide the city's next big effort. It focused on the downtown south-central district, a vast tract of abandoned industrial brownyards, razed blocks, and crumbling residential neighborhoods. It also brought to Chattanooga a who's who of the new biology. Among them were William McDonough, Paul Hawken, Peter Calthorpe, Amory Lovins, and representatives for John Todd, who designs plant-based waste treatment systems he calls "living machines."

Today you can visit the transformed south-central district and walk around on a large multicolored map of the city and its surrounding region. That map spreads out across the terrazzo floor in the lobby of the new $1.5 million Development Resource Center. The center brings to one site the many local and regional offices involved in development— building permits, utilities, the planning board, the air pollution control agency, and others—to foster cooperation between agencies and make it simpler for people with good ideas to get them built. It's also an aggressively green structure that rivals the Audubon building. And like Audubon, the center is an infill development, set into the blocks of renovated storefronts and restaurants that now cluster around Broad Street, the spine that connects the revived waterfront to a nascent clean-industry district. Nearby is the recently completed sports stadium, set below ground level and ringed by a grass-covered berm. Adjacent to that, the rusting hulk of an old hangar-like foundry has been stripped to its girders, cleaned up, and glassed over, and now serves as an open-air pavilion for a weekend farmers' market.

Nearby, the tracks of an abandoned rail line running past the stadium are being pulled up so that native trees can reclaim what will be a greenbelt urban forest, connecting the stadium to the university across town with bike and pedestrian pathways. The riverfront park today extends for some twenty miles and is linked with a nationally acclaimed "blueways" program that promotes water sports and other forms of recreation with a low environmental impact. Meanwhile, a "green necklace" of habitat and nature parks bordering the urban center preserves tens of thousands of acres.

Inside that circle, the city has recognized that some inhabitants need more than amenities. One of the most pressing cases has been Alton Park, an impoverished area on the south side. A century of industrial activity along neighboring Chattanooga Creek had produced what Crockett once described as "a toxic waste dump with a stream running across it." That problem was compounded by other toxic sites in the area, some near playgrounds and schools. According to a neighborhood resident, Milton Jackson, whose organization STOP (Stop TOxic Pollution) is a local force in lobbying for change, the creek has now undergone a major cleanup and the other problems are being addressed. In addition, a federal housing program—one that replaces failed modernist projects around the U.S. with new-urban infill—is set to spend $35 million in

Alton Park. There's more work yet to come, Jackson says, but "the city is doing a magnificent job."

Back in south-central, close on the new clean-industry district, another infill project has created blocks of modest homes, the first new housing in Chattanooga's inner city for many years. City boosters boast about the influx of new residents who have heard about the decent, affordable housing and walk-to-work jobs. They're not the only ones headed for Chattanooga. The city now receives a million visitors each year, among them representatives from cities across the United States and around the world, including delegations from all forty prefectures of Japan.

Chattanooga doesn't have all the answers. But more than most American cities it has begun the process of asking the right questions. In all this Crockett sees the emergence of a larger change. "If you look at the industrial age in this country and all the implications it had," he says, "It changed everything, from how we worked to family structure. Then along came cars, and they changed politics, agriculture, the environment, how cities grew. Now we have an age of computers, and you can see that it's changing things again. We believe that the next big shift will be the age of sustainability . . . We have started to recognize that we're at the doorstep of this great change, and that we should try to think of things in a different way. We have to look at the interrelationship of all things." That's because "in the end, the redesign of Chattanooga is not about the projects—the electric buses, the stadium. The real essence is the process of involving the community, of understanding fully how each piece affects everything else."

Crockett, in the spirit of his famous namesake, has carried his convictions to the fight for other cities around the world. Working with the Citistates Group—an organization of speakers, journalists, and political leaders who advocate new planning strategies—he has traveled to hundreds of cities in recent years. And the message he and his colleagues bring is that towns and cities are ecosystems, too, and it's time they start behaving that way.

The challenge they face is a daunting one. While the middle class fled Western cities for the suburbs, a countertrend was emerging in other parts of the world. Exploding rural populations displaced by industrial farming or environmental decline have been moving en masse to urban centers and in the process creating huge megacities. Due to that, roughly half of the world's people now live in cities, largely in the developing world. Within twenty-five years, they could have another two billion residents—with fully half of them living in shantytowns. If bringing sustainability to the old industrial centers of the West is an up-hill fight, how then to deal with those cities where the problems are so different, and where resources and infrastructure may be severely limited?

The Girl from Curitiba

On a narrow dirt road far inland from Rio de Janeiro's glittering coast, in the flat, dry outskirts of Curitiba, Brazil, more than a hundred people stand in a ragged line waiting patiently in the sun, their arms filled with household junk. Dogs poke around the dusty yards of makeshift struc-tures along the lane, shelters made of wallboard, cinder blocks, corru-gated metal, old timber, and whatever else is handy. A young girl at the front of the line grips a toy wheelbarrow piled with discards. When her turn comes she steers it to a waiting city garbage truck, where a man in green overalls unloads it. In exchange he gives her some paper tickets, which she takes around to a second truck. There they put a bag filled with fresh bananas, tomatoes, and cucumbers in her wheelbarrow, and she proudly trundles it back home down the lane.

This is garbage collection in Curitiba (pronounced "Coordicheeba"), in the shantytown, or favela, called Vila Trindade. Faced with the inabil-ity of its trucks to navigate the narrow paths and lanes of the favelas, the city instead rewards those residents for helping. For garbage it trades food, children's textbooks, or bus tokens good on its world-renowned mass transit system.

Like Chattanooga, this city of 1.6 million still falls short of full sus-tainability. In fact, it's doubtful whether any city can be truly sustainable in the context of a national economy that isn't. But the green programs in Curitiba predate Chattanooga's and are more comprehensive, and it rivals that city as a magnet for visiting delegations from around the world. Little wonder. A survey of urban residents conducted in the early 1990s found that 60 percent of those living in New York, the business and intellectual capital of the U.S., would move if they could (by 2002, after the World Trade Center attack, that was roughly the percentage of residents who wanted to stay). Some 70 percent of those living in São Paulo, the business and intellectual capital of Brazil, thought life would be better in Curitiba. More than 99 percent of Curitibans said they wouldn't want to live anywhere else.

Jaime Lerner, the architect turned mayor who in the 1970s put all this in motion, eventually went on to become governor of the province. Like Lerner, his successor, Cassio Taniguchi, divides his time between a downtown civic center and the mayoral "thinking office," a small lodge made of recycled utility poles and set in a forested city park. He also meets each month with residents at one or another of the "citizenship streets" found in each of the city's eight districts. Those are complexes that feature sports stadiums alongside roofed malls that house local offices for dozens of agencies—from child welfare to the phone company, from the waterworks to the secretary of education, from police substations to health clinics, and on down the list.

Back in his log cabin office, Taniguchi takes another sip from his mug—in Brazil one can't sit still for more than ten minutes without being handed a cup of coffee—as a blue jay pecks on the window. The sounds of a running stream and of birds and monkeys calling through the treetops drift into the room. In Curitiba, he says, an extensive library system is geared to the children of every neighborhood, and special programs teach them such things as how to test for polluted water or use the online reporting systems. That is key. "We must always educate," he says. In line with that, the environmental university, in yet another log structure in yet another city park, offers a free adult course that teaches about the sustainability programs. The city's cabdrivers have to take the course before getting their licenses.

Taniguchi is proud that while Curitiba has gone through explosive population growth—from 600,000 in 1980 to 1.6 million today—the standard of living for its poorest residents has risen, too. But as their per capita consumption has increased, cultural carrying capacity has become an issue. Recently, over the course of two years, he says, the total waste stream grew by 76 percent. In response, Curitiba's Garbage That Is Not Garbage program now draws from more than two-thirds of its households. An electronic sign in midtown also lists how many trees are being saved by recycling. It records more than three million so far.

The city favors companies using recycled material. It also fosters suburban infill, locating small businesses in areas that were once strictly residential. "Urban diversity is the key. If you have several functions mixed together, it's more stable," says Taniguchi, who is an engineer by training. "In nature, you cannot just plant one kind of tree. You must mix them. In the city we use the same conception, mixed functions. The more they are mixed, the better the quality of life." Curitiba zoning now mandates mixed use. It also concentrates density. High-rises are allowed along main bus routes only.

The city's renowned bus lines are like surface-level subways, with raised platforms for collecting fares and quick boarding, and switches in the drivers' cabs that let them change the traffic lights. Express and local lines run on parallel streets along five major arterials. Those reach out from the city center in a starfish pattern, with the five arms cross-linked at strategic points.

Those bus lines are privately run and turn a profit, but the city links their income to the number of miles served. This practice has spurred the extension of express lines to outlying towns, where multiuse and focused-density zoning also apply. As a result, those towns are a nascent realization of Léon Krier's polycentric city, which develops not by sprawl but by the "reproduction and multiplication" of urban centers.

If one looks down from a high tower over central Curitiba, the effect of the density zones is clear. Like a coastal tidepool—in which larger and denser accumulations of life cluster along the deep channels where energy flows are rich—the Curitiba skyline shows clusters of high-rise buildings growing up along the city's arterials.

Also visible is the extensive patchwork of parks, gardens, and greenbelts that cover nearly 20 percent of the city. In front of an old utility shed on a back lot in one of those parks, Laudelino Matoso sits sunning himself during his lunch break. Several years ago he was hired to mow lawns, but now he has a new civil service position: shepherd. It's a good job, he acknowledges of his duties watching the herd of thirty-five sheep that has replaced his mechanical mower. Now when the grass gets a little too high in one area he just drives the sheep in that direction. "I would rather fight with the sheep than mow," he says, smiling. They also provide good fertilizer, he points out, and as the herd grows, the extra sheep are moved to another park to start a new herd. Each year the city has its herds shorn and makes the wool into blankets, which it distributes free to the poor.

Pattern Recognition

The growth along Curitiba's starfish pattern of arterials brought new form to the city. It also suggests a nice fit with a larger pattern described by American planner Ian McHarg in his seminal 1969 book, *Design with*

Nature. Forests and other open land covered by plants, he wrote, "are distinctly cooler than cities in summer." Air passing over them and into the city "will bring cooler air" and "relief from humidity." It presents an opportunity, he said, for microclimate control, by creating "fingers of open space penetrating from the rural hinterland, radially into the city."

Or, as planner Eliel Saarinen put it, "Always design with the next larger context in mind." While polycentric strategies reshape urban expansions from the inside out, another new influence on development is reshaping them from the outside in. Seattle, with the highest U.S. growth rate, has not only stopped subsidizing sprawl; it now levies impact fees on new development. It has also surrounded itself with an urban boundary, separating town and country.

Whether the rallying cry is "support smart growth" or "stop dumb growth," the movement is clearly expanding. More than thirty governors have now addressed the question of sprawl in their State of the State messages. In that, they're led by the concerns of counties and municipalities, which feel the direct impact of sprawling costs. Farmers are affected, too, and are becoming vocal critics. "Agriculture pays $3 in taxes for every $1 it uses," notes Ed Thompson of the American Farmland Trust. "But residential development pays $1 in taxes for every $1.25 it uses." Why is that? "Cows don't go to school," he says.

Energy Web
Context is the key. For architects designing green buildings and for green neighborhood, town, and city planners, the final lesson of sustainability is that size matters. It's difficult for part of a system to be sustainable when the system it's part of is not.

The way we make energy to power communities is a good case in point. Today it comes from large centralized systems in which massive generators pulse electricity through the grid to distant users. This form of energy production mirrors the sprawling, monocentric patterns of modern population centers. And just as those waste energy in transporting people over long distances, monocentric grids waste energy in transmitting power over long distances. Some 7 percent of all the power they generate is lost along the way, and that doesn't include the additional amounts of energy spent setting up and maintaining those vast grids. No building, town, or city dependent on that system can claim to be sustainable.

While new urbanism works to reshape city centers and their sprawling suburbs into polycentric form, something like that is also happening with energy—as the "micropower" revolution challenges the big, centralized power stations and their far-flung grids. Rapid increases in efficiency for wind, solar, and geothermal power are a factor. And all of these work well at local scale. Microturbines and fuel cells are becoming viable, too. According to *The Economist*, "Even if the power they produce is more costly at the source . . . they do not suffer huge transmission losses when sending it to consumers. On top of that, the surplus heat they generate can be employed for useful purposes, such as warming buildings, whereas that of big generators located in the middle of the countryside is usually wasted."

Since 1995, venture capital investments in micropower (sometimes called "distributed power") have increased from $25 million to more than $800 million. That surge is fed by predictions that within this decade the market for micropower-generating technologies could reach $60 billion. Growth is also being spurred by military concerns. Weaning industrial economies from dependence on oil, so much of which comes from unstable sources, is now a matter of national defense. And the big centralized energy facilities of the twentieth century—large dams, generators, nuclear plants, tanker ports, and the fragile grid itself—look today like fat and ready targets for terrorists. The Internet was developed by the military as a decentralized means of ensuring communication in the event of attack. But how secure is an Internet powered by an antiquated grid that can black out the entire northeastern United States and parts of Canada as the result of a tree falling somewhere in Ohio?

The Electric Power Research Institute (EPRI)—the research arm of American energy providers—estimates that yearly losses due to power fluctuations and outages in the U.S. are $100 billion, or half again the total amount the country spends on electricity. More reliable, say experts, would be a power supply whose structure is more like the Internet itself. In short: distributed micropower. To help that transition along, EPRI has developed a converter that permits the "plug and play" connection of any micropower source to the larger grid. EPRI also advocates creating "premium power parks," electrified by private "microgrids," for the growing numbers of businesses (server farms, chip fab plants, hospitals, telecoms, call centers) that require higher reliability than a centralized grid can supply. One such park is already up and running as a test case at the University of California at Irvine.

Meanwhile, out on the grid, its old electromechanical switches are being replaced by solid-state controllers, embedded sensors, and intelligent agents. *Wired* magazine describes the emerging "smart grid":

> The smarter energy network of the future . . . will incorporate a diversified pool of resources located closer to the consumer, pumping out low- or zero-emissions power in backyards, driveways, downscaled local power stations, and even in automobiles, while giving electricity users the option to become energy vendors. The front end of this new system will be managed by third-party "virtual utilities," which will bundle electricity, gas, internet access, broadband entertainment, and other customized services.

EPRI's chief, Kurt Yeager, says, "Our society is changing more rapidly and more broadly than at any time since [Thomas] Edison's day. The current power infrastructure is as incompatible with the future as horse trails were with automobiles."

Micropower is also set to change the face of the developing world, where there is little infrastructure. *The Economist* notes that micropower energy sources "may now allow many countries to skip the giant-power-station stage altogether—rather as many countries are sensibly jumping over wired telephony and straight to wireless."

Cyber-Commuters

Undue dependence on cars is another legacy of our machine age cultural context. Cars are an emblem of the modern age, but at heart they're a somewhat outdated transportation concept. Often it's not the person that needs to be conveyed; it's his or her information. That's implicit in the development of telegraphs, radio, TV, phones, fax machines, and the new satellite newspaper kiosks—which, instead of importing and selling papers, just download them electronically and then print them out on demand. All these in turn link to that higher level of organization now emerging as the online world.

The terrorist strikes on the World Trade Center and Pentagon brought fearful human tolls, but the information flowing through those nerve centers was soon rerouted by decentralized online communications webs. The military long ago learned the value of decentralization, a key lesson from nature. It developed the Internet as a way to guard data transfer in the event of nuclear attack. The Internet's civilian incarnations—

the World Wide Web and other online systems—were no less a factor for the big financial firms in the World Trade Center attack. The trading house Cantor Fitzgerald was among the hardest hit. Yet in the heat of calamity central operations shifted quickly to its London office, and the company's online trading service, handling roughly half of all U.S. Treasury bond traffic, was up and running again in forty-eight hours.

Such stories have spurred a trend already under way. Companies have begun decentralizing through the Web. That shift also helps to advance the polycentric model for towns. Online shopping, tele-work, teleconferencing, virtual reality operations at a distance, personal avatars interacting in virtual worlds—all make it easier for the information, not the individual, to do the commuting. These trends will only accelerate as grid computing puts the power of supercomputers in the hands of virtually anyone anywhere.

Could this yield an even more pervasive kind of sprawl? That seems unlikely. Humans are social animals; we enjoy being around one another (given the usual exceptions). But during the twentieth century we stretched our notion of community in order to handle increasingly distant flows of materials and information. In the process we laid the groundwork for a human cultural ecology that's global in design. Unfortunately, in that process, we also found ourselves living in sprawling, monocentric twentieth-century schemes that created social alienation, ate up farmland and natural habitats, and wasted vast amounts of resources moving energy, materials, people, and information around. Now computerized Web-based systems offer better alternatives, which in turn could free human communities to retract to more natural, polycentric forms.

A circle seems to be closing. Decentralized energy technologies are linking through computers into microgrids and virtual utilities, which animate the computerized online world that is in turn a main factor in decentralization. With that, something like the forecast of MIT cyberneticist Rodney Brooks—that the physical linking of humans and computers is the next big step—is taking place at the level of human communities. As the blooming electronic overlay of sustainable energy sources and information technology spurs change in our work and housing patterns, it weds computers and communities into an ever-more-intimate congress. The notion of a cyborg brings with it obvious concerns, but the merging of green power, computers, sustainability, and traditional community design has all the earmarks of a natural fit.

Emerald City

A good example of that is a project now in development at the Center for Sustainable Cities. Richard Levine and the center's codirector, Ernest Yanarella, are working to integrate several data technologies into a single tool they call the Sustainability Engine™. Their effort stems from the concern that there is no research tool connecting all the data on efficiency in buildings to that on automobiles, on specific industries, and on the many other elements that come to bear in sustainable city design. "All of those are looked at as discrete research programs," Levine says. "Our argument is that you need to think in terms of linking them together."

Cities and other large systems are too complicated to understand fully, Levine concedes, but he adds that we don't fully understand our bodies either, or need to in order to stay healthy. What we need are the appropriate feedback mechanisms. That doesn't mean the current system has to be junked, just rewired—with feedback loops connecting causes and effects, to tell us when things move too far toward chaos, or too far toward order.

"We call this the information age, but we don't get the right information," he says, "or enough of the right information." In old hill towns like Todi, Levine points out, "causes and effects were intimately known. If some farmer was being lazy, or planting his crops in a way that lost too much soil, it showed up in the marketplace, and there would have to be a correction. If there wasn't, the carrying capacity of the town would decline and people would go hungry." The personal, political, and economic consequences of farm production rippled through the region, and in turn fed back into farming practices. Continuous feedback loops drove the system toward balance, just as they do in A-Life computer programs, just as they do in the cycle of plants and decomposers and new soil in ecology. For seven centuries in Todi, Levine notes, "the rate of change was slow but the feedback was perfect." Now, he says, "we're in a global economy, with multiple causes and multiple effects, and we're making changes very quickly."

The Sustainability Engine™ will one day interface with that reality (or lack of it) in comprehensive ways. Meanwhile, a seedling of their concept—which they call Emerald City: The Sustainability Game—is already being used by their students. It allows those students to game the interactions between various interested groups and parties in the virtual redevelopment of an old industrial site. By interacting through various kinds of strategies, they gain insight into the larger outcomes of their choices.

Emerald City takes inspiration from the computer game SimCity, which in turn looks to the hyperlinking structure of *A Pattern Language*, written by Christopher Alexander and his colleagues some thirty years ago. Another tool like that is Quest, developed by John Robinson, a geographer now at the University of British Columbia. His interest in sustainable planning turned to computers when he read the directions for players on the first version of SimCity, in 1989. They said:

> As long as your city can provide places for people to live, work, shop, and play, it will attract residents. And as long as traffic, pollution, overcrowding, crime or taxes don't drive them away, your city will live.

That sounded to him like good advice for planners, too, and he soon developed the first version of Quest. It modeled the Georgia Basin region around Vancouver, but the game has since been adapted to other regions, from Manchester, England, to Mexico City and Kuala Lumpur. Quest works by giving players choices between variables for transportation, energy use, waste disposal, different kinds of zoning—and showing how they will impact the larger system. Move residential neighborhoods away from industry? Okay, but that means more commute time. Spend more tax revenue on health care? Then there's less available to pay for garbage pickup. The game projects the outcomes of those choices through 2040. When that reveals unanticipated problems, as it often does, the players can then go back and begin again.

With programs like Emerald City and Quest we see the start of planning methods that can offer real insight into complex systems like cities. They provide, as one observer puts it, "a way of looking into the future." Building on them, Levine and Yanarella are proposing the endgame—integrating the whole spectrum of software planning systems into their single, all-encompassing engine.

At the heart of their concept lies a digital model of the city and its surrounding region. The model includes a 3-D virtual townscape rendered by CAD (computer-aided design) programs combined with geographic information system images of the landscape, and employing modified FM (facilities management) software. FM can track things like energy use and heat loss for every component in a building. They see the various programs in this model being linked to the CAD townscape much in the way spreadsheet software and SimCity now operate, so that any proposed change in one area distributes the resulting problems or benefits throughout the scheme.

Together those programs constitute the "city model," the first of three basic categories in their concept. The second major component is a "systems model" that tracks the material and energy flows available from the immediate region. Its third element is a library of "plug-ins"— modules keyed to specific industries, types of power, transport systems. Combining those three would make it possible to match highly specific information on material and energy demands against their local availability, while coordinating all that through a dynamic virtual model of the city and its workings. With this, the Sustainability Engine™ could run scenarios approaching realistic complexity.

That represents a radical break from most sustainable planning— those gradual improvements in energy or resource efficiency. Levine is critical of them, saying they just "pick the low-hanging fruit." Once the easy changes have been made, he says, each succeeding step just gets harder until economic or political back pressures grind things to a halt. At a fundamental level, that strategy misses the point. "Sustainability," he says, "is not a condition that you incrementally move toward. It's a process you operate."

And the Sustainability Engine™ could help to show how. "It's a utility, one that will let us do our experimenting quickly and cheaply by running multiple scenarios," Levine explains. "It creates a parallel reality for urban systems and their settings, so we can see how different approaches will work out before we actually build." After all, building things is a very expensive way to discover unanticipated costs, especially if we can let computer programs bump up against them for us. What's more, simulating these large-scale scenarios "will allow us to be creative at a higher level of complexity and responsiveness." And with time, he suggests, some evolution of the system may become a basic tool of government, "a step upward in what democracy means."

Sea Change

Complaints about the machine age and its industries tend to focus on greed. That's naive. People are no more venal now than they have been throughout the turbulent history of Todi or other old towns. What has changed is that our behavior now plays out on a scale so vast it elevates human choice to a Faustian level.

What the world needs now is a way to make smarter choices. The simplicity of the machine metaphor was always one of its strengths. Time has shown that it's also a weakness. Today's technologies are too primitive to integrate smoothly with the complex systems animating nature. Whether it's in materials science, robotics, artificial intelligence, agriculture, or in the way we build communities, the new biology offers better models.

What the rising generation of architects, planners, and developers advocate is at once new and ancient. A cyberspace planning engine is at the cutting edge of gee-whiz technology, but it represents something very old, and not just centuries old. It brings urban design into harmony with processes and patterns that have animated life for billions of years.

Those processes and patterns are at work on a rocky coast as waves crash and spray in the air. There, water running back to the sea drains through the tidepools formed by shallow basins in the rocks. That's how algae and other nutrients cycling through the world's oceans are fed into local communities of marine life. Just as urban density collects around downtown areas, where traffic and energy flows are richest, so, too, in tidepools brilliant multicolored suburbs of mold give way to crenellated towers of barnacles in those areas where water and nutrient flows run deep. The analogy goes further. From above human settlements the same pattern can be seen in the wider landscape, in how towns cluster around rivers and harbors, historic links for commerce with the larger world.

Levine notes that urban areas are where most products begin and where they end up. So as we learn more about how energy and materials flow through them, that's where the loop will be closed. In the future, he says—with products made for disassembly and recycling—cities will become more than the engines that drive economies. They will be the world's main sources of industrial raw material.

All of this points to a basic principle of the new biology: the interplay between local and global systems. There is no real stability in life, just the balance-seeking tendency we call metabolism. Local ecologies such as tidepools receive nutrients that wash through the world's seas. They in turn get nutrients from the countless tidepools and local systems found in every oceanic nook and cranny. That interplay is also at work in the human ecologies we call cities and towns, but with us there's a major difference. To the natural global flows of materials we've added our own. There is the widening spread of farm wastes, now overlaid with the vast streams of industrial materials and products that flow through our manufacturing systems. And with global manufacturing has come a burgeoning global economy. Those two great systems—industrial and economic—are among the final frontiers of the new biology, and where some of its most creative work is being done. Reforming them will open the way to a human feedback culture.

part three

designs **global designs** *global de.*

ten

industrial ecology

Sunlight washes across the earth as it turns, warming it against the chill of deep space. The cooler poles and mountaintops gleam with ice while carpets of green spread out on temperate lowlands. Rivers trickle through them into lakes and seas. Wherever there is water the sun gives rise to mist, which around the globe floats outward to form scudding layers of clouds.

Airstreams we call wind move clouds, dust, and flying creatures above the earth. Less apparent are the marine flows that carry swimming species, salt runoff from the land, and most of all heat in fluid conveyor belts that run on and beneath the surface of the world's oceans. These blue-water rivers course thousands of miles to loop through the Atlantic, Pacific, and Indian oceans, twisting and turning along continents and through archipelagoes, diving deep, and then upwelling to the surface.

They are driven by "salt pumps," areas where runoffs from surrounding land or evaporation by prevailing winds increase the salt density of the water, making it heavier and causing it to sink. That downwelling draws new water in along the surface. Runoff from the shores of Greenland and Labrador, for instance, joins a large subsurface waterfall from the Nordic seas to raise the salt content of the North Atlantic. Come winter, cold dry winds from Canada blow east across it, too; they concentrate the salt still more by causing evaporation. The heavier water these produce sinks deep beneath the sea, then flows along the ocean bottom for thousands of miles to skirt the South American coast. Suction from that pump—from that huge North Atlantic downwelling—then draws new water in at the surface. It pulls a warm oceanic river the size of one hundred Amazons up from the Tropics past the coasts of Spain and England. And there, as tropical water steams into the sky, it warms those cold Canadian winds before they pass across Europe. This is the source of Europe's temperate climate, which—due to its high northern latitude—would otherwise be as cold as Canada's.

Much as underwater rivers link the seas, atmospheric winds link distant lands. Sahara Desert dust rains on the Alps, the Caribbean, and Florida, even the Great Plains states. In a spectacular case in 1991, some fifty thousand tonnes of dust and pollen largely from Algeria fell on northern Scandinavia. And dust is not the only thing blowing in the wind. Industrial plumes from the Midwest cause acid rain in New York lakes. Chemicals from Asian factories fall on Washington State. One researcher has remarked that Mauna Loa, in Hawaii, "is effectively a suburb of Beijing each Spring."

Airborne matter plays a role in the greenhouse effect, which begins when natural outlets send carbon dioxide (CO_2) and other gases into the sky. Once there, they form transparent layers that trap heat like a car parked with the windows closed on a sunny day. That warming makes life as we know it possible. But global industries now release so much of those same gases that they may be raising temperatures further.

There is no doubt the earth is warming, and rapidly. Antarctica's glaciers have begun to slide more quickly to the sea. During the past century, alpine glaciers retreated 25 percent. In the Himalayas and on the Tibetan plateau they're melting even faster. Africa's famed snows of Kilimanjaro are all but gone. Northern lakes now freeze later in the winter and thaw sooner each spring. Butterflies across the U.S. and Europe range farther north. Warm-weather plant species climb South American mountainsides. In Alaska, the melting of permafrost (frozen ground) and the ice pockets it contains has caused thousands of miles of trees to sink at crazy angles—a phenomenon called "drunken forest." During the summer of 2000 it was discovered that the ice field covering the North Pole had simply melted away. Scientists now believe that within fifty years the entire Arctic ice cap will disappear each summer—the first time this has happened in fifteen million years.

The effects of global warming have been widely reported: rising sea levels, an expanding range for tropical diseases, drought and wildfires in what once were temperate zones. All of these are under way, and their increase is routinely projected through this century. The problem is that those projections are linear. The earth and its atmosphere are nonlinear systems.

A growing body of work now argues that the final effect of global warming may actually be an abrupt and dramatic cooling in large parts of the world. A central factor in that is the downwelling North Atlantic salt pump, which pulls warm water up from the Tropics along the coast of Europe. As the glaciers of Greenland and the Arctic ice cap melt, vast new quantities of freshwater flow into that pump, diluting its salt content. Weather effects from warming also cause rainfall and decrease evaporation there. With less salt to weigh it down, water in the North Atlantic sinks less rapidly. And with that, it draws less water north from the Tropics to warm those Canadian winter winds before they blow across Europe.

What would Europe be like if balmy, "southern" Rome were as cool as Chicago, which lies at the same, forty-two-degree latitude? What if the weather in Berlin were more like that of Moscow, just four degrees farther north? The implications are profound. Europe, with its temperate climate and long growing season, now feeds above 650 million people. Where will their food come from if the growing season is curtailed? The response by a group of powerful industrial countries to a dramatic decline in food supply could be calamitous.

A sudden cooling of Europe's climate would also trigger ecological cascades around the globe. In the end, even the Tropics might cool. These concerns are based on more than speculation. By studying cores of ancient ice along with pollen cores from old lake beds, we know that global climate flips have occurred throughout time, and that warming periods in the past have led to abrupt cooling, even without the effects of industry. At least twice, that cooling was related to a failure of the North Atlantic pump, with a subsequent halting of the warm-water conveyor belt that draws heat north from the Tropics. The so-called Little Ice Age—which plagued Europe on and off from the fourteenth century until the start of the industrial era—may have been due to that.

Available evidence suggests that another big climate flip is coming. Researchers from the Ocean Climate Group, at the Scottish Executive's Marine Laboratory in Aberdeen, reviewed some seventeen thousand measurements of salinity taken since 1893 in the seawater between Shetland and the Faroe Islands. They discovered that in each of the past two decades, the deep water flowing southward has lost 0.01 grams of salt per kilogram of seawater. "This is the largest change we have seen in the outflow in the last 100 years," says Bill Turrell, the group's leader. "It is consistent with models showing the stopping of the pump and the conveyor belt."

Today's computerized climate models are highly evolved descendants of John von Neumann's grid-like cellular automata. They expand his checkerboard of interacting cells around a virtual globe to parse climate patterns. With the rising power of computers (and now the coming of grid computing, which links supercomputers together to form mega-computers), the complexity and resolution of those models have increased. One thing they now show is that as a climate flip nears, there will be growing instability in the weather. Describing that process in an exhaustive look at climate change for *The Atlantic Monthly*, scientist William Calvin noted:

> Feedbacks are what determine thresholds, where one mode flips into another. Near a threshold one can sometimes observe abortive responses, rather like the act of stepping back onto a curb several times before finally running across a busy street. Abortive responses and rapid chattering between modes are common problems in nonlinear systems with not quite enough oomph—the reason that old fluorescent lights flicker. To keep a bi-stable system firmly in one state or the other, it should be kept away from the transition threshold.

Are we near a threshold? Ask insurance companies. Growing weather instability is affecting them around the world. In Europe, a summer of disastrous storms in 2002 was followed in 2003 by a sizzling summer of forest fires and parched crop fields. Fierce hurricanes like the one that recently devastated New Orleans are on the rise. The influence of long-term weather cycles on these events is still under debate, but one thing is clear: According to Thomas Loster of the reinsurance firm Munich Re, "The number of really big weather disasters has increased fourfold compared to the 1960s." Worldwide, violent storms caused $70 billion worth of damage in 2002, and a UN study released that year warned the insurance industry it could be facing yearly claims of $150 billion within a decade. In response to the growing trend, the industry has even begun working with the environmental group Greenpeace, to exchange ideas on the risks of global warming and ways to mitigate them.

At the heart of such efforts is the question of how much we're doing to push things to the brink. On that count, speculation has given way to increasingly persuasive evidence. Most credible scientists now believe we play a significant role. The Intergovernmental Panel on Climate Change, a worldwide body that includes hundreds of scientists, for a long time hedged its findings. It now concludes that human activities, especially the burning of fossil fuels, have "contributed substantially to the observed warming over the past fifty years."

As the evidence mounts, interest is turning to remedies. For the North Atlantic pump, a number of make-do fixes are proposed: redirecting meltwater from glaciers, seeding clouds over land to dissolve them before they can rain on the open sea, the use of surfactants to increase evaporation there. More generally, international pressure is growing for countries to slow the warming trend by capping their emissions. That effort is serious and well intended, and gets closer to the cause, but it often involves what are called "end-of-pipe" solutions, filters on exhaust stacks and other industrial waste streams. Those are expensive for business and in the end just concentrate waste that still needs to go somewhere.

That's not a real solution, according to William McDonough. He is the award-winning architect introduced in the last chapter—an intrepid reformer with a bow tie, a wry grin, and a knack for stating the lessons of the new biology in memorable terms. Beyond his architectural work, he has also become a prominent voice for reinventing how we make things. Says McDonough, "It's time to take the filters out of the pipes and chimneys and put them where they belong—in the designers' heads."

What's needed today are not just new solutions but new kinds of solutions. A central problem of the industrial world is the linear, machine age model on which it is based. That machine metaphor looks to principles from nature, but we now know that its idea of nature is incomplete. It employs the lessons of classical physics but fails to recognize how, in living systems, those principles are drawn into higher levels of organization—where they are subsumed by more complex dynamics. This is why so many machine age solutions end up causing more problems down the road. New biologists aim to ground industry in a fuller comprehension of nature, so a new generation can participate without qualms in what Ed Cohen-Rosenthal, the Cornell green industry pioneer, called "the power and magic of making new things in service to our larger society."

Flows and Sinks

Each spring in Washington, D.C., thousands of cherry trees bloom. They display a cloud of pink flowers against the white buildings and green lawns of the capital in a show that draws visitors from around the globe. That burst of color is more than a visual treat; it's an example of nature's tendency toward overproduction. The blossoms produce many thousands of cherries and seeds that, even without the restraining effect of groundskeepers, would give rise to only a few new trees.

As McDonough likes to point out, in nature, for each new cherry tree grown, vast amounts of material and energy are expended. But nature is a whole system. Flower petals that fall to earth are decomposed and absorbed by insects and microbes in the soil. Cherries that don't become trees serve as food for birds and other wildlife. Nothing is wasted. Moreover, nature sustains itself on solar energy. Compared with nature, our system leaks most of the materials we put through it. It also loses the vast amounts of energy embedded in their production. The waste heat alone that U.S. power plants send up their stacks is equal to the energy used by the whole Japanese economy.

George Bernard Shaw once said the mark of an educated mind is the ability to be deeply moved by statistics. If so, it's no wonder that informed observers around the world are having fits. The sheer magnitude of material flows in human industry is staggering. America alone consumes a million gallons of oil every two minutes, transforming much of it into carbon dioxide that then drifts up into the sky. Worldwide industrial flows of sulfur and nitrogen are equal to or exceed the earth's natural flows. For most metals the industrial flows are twice that of nature's, lead is eighteen times greater, and all of them are growing. At the start of the last century, Americans used about 1.8 tons of resources apiece over the course of a year. Now each American uses ten times that amount.

It doesn't seem so, because the products we buy are such a small part of that overall flow. Some 95 percent of the material involved in making them is discarded before they ever reach store shelves. Then the products are thrown away, too. "More than 90 percent of the stuff made in America ends up in landfill within one year of the time it's produced," says McDonough. "One year! Future generations will shake their heads and wonder, 'What were they thinking?'"

The size of our industrial flows would matter less if they were reabsorbed as nature's are. Instead we make piles of unusable waste—a novel human invention. Each year Americans handle nineteen billion pounds of polystyrene packing peanuts, virtually all of which are discarded. With the aluminum America wastes, it could replace its whole fleet of commercial aircraft every three months. According to one analysis, "Over the course of a decade, 500 trillion pounds of American resources will have been transformed into nonproductive solids and gases."

In nature, a "sink" is the destination of a flow. Since all of nature is united by cycles, sinks tend to be transitional: they not only receive flows; they're also the places from which flows emerge. For instance, cherry trees and other plants are a sink for carbon, which they extract from CO_2 in the air. Fossil fuel reserves (ancient underground stores of rotted biomass) are a sink for plants. Completing the cycle, the atmosphere is a sink for the CO_2 released by plant decomposition, or when fossil fuel is burned. As the writer and business activist Paul Hawken frequently says, "You can't throw things away. There is no away."

Carrying capacity means more than whether a habitat provides the food and water its occupants need. Its capacity as a sink—whether it can absorb their wastes—is just as important.

By draining fossil fuels from the ground at our present rate, we are depleting a sink that will take millions of years to replenish. Then, by converting it into the eight billion tons of CO_2 that we pump into the atmosphere each year, we overload another sink. Many are concerned that we're running out of the best fuels now used to fire industry. While those concerns are valid, they miss the larger problem. We have already run out of places to put the CO_2.

Industrial Ecology

Braden Allenby, vice president of environmental health and safety for AT&T, brings the real magnitude of the environmental question into focus:

Because of the increasingly tight coupling between human and natural
systems, we are now reaching a point where the dynamics of natural systems . . . can only be understood in relationship to the human systems
with which they are coupled . . . There are no "natural" systems anymore,
and the distinction between "human" and "natural" systems is somewhat
misleading in its superficial clarity. Clearly there are phenomena, primarily geologic—volcanoes and plate tectonics come to mind—that human
activities do not affect. But against this must be balanced the reality that
the dynamics of most fundamental systems—the nitrogen, carbon, phos-
phorous, sulfur and hydrologic cycles, the biosphere at various scales from
genetic to regional, the climate and oceanic circulation systems—are increasingly dominated by [human] activities . . . Difficult as it is to accept,
there is no natural history anymore. There is only human history.

That daunting prospect calls for new ideas. As Hawken points out, no
one wakes up in the morning and says, "Today I think I'll go out and
destroy the environment." The depletion of oil reserves didn't start in
Saudi Arabia, and the destruction of tropical forests didn't start in the
Amazon. Those problems began in places like Detroit, Stuttgart, São
Paulo, and Hong Kong—in the minds of people just going about their
daily business. Like so many of the modern world's ills, today's environmental problems are an outgrowth of flaws in what we think of as common sense.

A hard-nosed realism is the mark of any good business exec, but our
current system views it as realistic to cut down a tree in Alaska that took
centuries to grow, sell it for the price of a pizza, ship it three thousand
miles to Japan, where it's rendered into snack chip bags, then ship those
three thousand miles back to the U.S. for sale. Such practices are commonplace, but compared with the dynamic, resilient, energy-capturing
systems that nature has evolved, they are only superficially realistic.

In most of nature, carrying capacity is a basic equation. The demands that dragonflies put on habitat don't change much from one dragonfly to the next. Humans add a twist. Per capita consumption can vary
greatly from one person to the next, and from one culture to the next.
As a result, our relation to nature is defined differently. We have to consider cultural carrying capacity. The concept is simple: As per capita
consumption rises, the number of people a habitat can support declines.
Or, seen another way, as consumption rises, the size of the habitat they

need also expands. For instance, from 1969 to 1995 the number of cars in the United States grew six times faster than the population. That cultural change meant not only stripping ever-greater quantities of metal from ever-larger numbers of hills, but draining domestic oil reserves, too, and then reaching out to foreign sources (today more than half of America's oil is imported). It also means that just 5 percent of the world's population now generates 25 percent of its greenhouse gases.

The linear thinking that drove the machine age has linked unrealistic energy prices and a partial understanding of nature to bring a fleeting kind of wealth. Like trust fund babies dipping into principal, the industrial nations have depleted their natural capital at a furious pace. Today, although little more than 20 percent of the world's population, they consume 80 percent of its fossil fuels and 60 percent of its food, not to mention the lion's share of metals, wood, and other resources.

Such demands are much greater than those placed on nature by traditional ways of life, but global trade pacts are now spreading our lavish ways around the world. As astrophysicist Martin Rees has pointed out, if the whole world lived the way we do, it would take three more planet Earths to support everyone. Hawken responds, "The only good news in that is that it's impossible." In his book *The Ecology of Commerce*, he wrote that the question generally asked in this context is "How do we save the environment?" Ridiculous as it might sound, he adds, the real question may be "How do we save business?"

As Hawken sees it, "The first industrial revolution is over. It's brought us a long way but its day has passed. The time has come to give it a gold watch, a pat on the back, and send it on its way." In the first industrial revolution, Britain took a century to double its income. For the U.S., the lag was fifty years. Korea took less than twenty-five years. The Chinese doubled their income in nine. The pace of growth is quickening, and with that so, too, is the need for industries that mesh effectively with nature. That is industrial ecology, and it is coming. In the words of the *Harvard Business Review*, "Sustainable development will constitute one of the biggest opportunities in the history of commerce."

Waste Less Want Less

"A Rolls-Royce is the most sustainable car." That curious statement is all the more curious for its source: Wouter van Dieren, a business consultant and one of Europe's leading environmentalists. A gracious Netherlander with white hair and youthful features, van Dieren takes sly pleasure in making remarks like that as he sits in an easy chair in his study, at his home not far from Utrecht. With Mozart playing softly in the background, he says the reason for that seemingly outlandish claim is obvious. "A Rolls-Royce certainly can live one hundred years. In that hundred years you don't need new steel ovens, you don't need new aluminum smelters. Although it runs on a mile per gallon or something like that, in the long term it is well accounted for." In other words, he concludes, the total cost for energy and material needed to carry people around in a Rolls for one hundred years "is less than that needed for the twenty-five economy cars they would buy otherwise during that time," each of which involves producing another whole new car.

Doing that means making the factory equipment needed to make the cars, and the forges that make the iron and steel used to make the equipment, as well as the oceans of energy needed to mine the metals and to fuel those forges and factories. It requires the energy and materials needed to construct power plants, and the fuel they in turn consume— and so on in an ever-expanding web of extravagant ramifications. Engaging that process twenty-five times involves quantities of energy, materials, waste, and pollution so vast that the extra fuel consumption of a Rolls-Royce means little in comparison. As van Dieren puts it, in the end all this is not a technological question but a financial one. The Rolls "is very expensive in the beginning, but the curve of all-inclusive real costs goes down very rapidly," he says.

Whether it's a lightbulb burning, a CD playing, a cup of hot coffee, or a ride in a car, the point is to consider "the total amount of energy and materials that are input for each unit of service they provide." It is, he says, just a matter of looking at things differently.

Doing that lets us see through the artificial efficiencies of the present day. Van Dieren credits Friedrich Schmidt-Bleek of Germany's Wuppertal Institute with first articulating this approach. Following on that, Walter Stahel has founded the Institut de la Durée (roughly, Product-Life Institute) in Geneva. Amory Lovins of the Rocky Mountain Institute has long been a forceful voice for real efficiencies. McDonough cites the "dematerialization" of industry. Looking at the growing demand for energy and raw materials, Hawken says, "The world is moving from an era in which man-made capital was the limiting factor into an era in which the remaining natural capital is the limiting factor."

One of the first big efforts to make industry cleaner and less wasteful came through what is now called the World Business Council for Sustainable Development, founded by industrialist Stephan Schmidheiny. The group cites "eco-efficiency" as its watchword and includes dozens of major corporations like DuPont, Dow, Chevron, ConAgra, Monsanto, Johnson & Johnson, and 3M. In the case of 3M, for example, the company has saved more than $200 million as a result of various programs to reduce waste and pollution. Working behind the scenes to make such gains possible is a lengthening list of people like the international consultant Donald Huisingh, editor of the *Journal of Cleaner Production*. It promotes awareness of pollution as a form of inefficiency, an awareness that has also spawned a variety of plans to raise "resource productivity," which is the use of less energy and materials in making products. The Factor Ten Club, sponsored by the Wuppertal Institute, is one. Others are the Natural Step, from Sweden, and the Future 500. A scheme called Muda—from a Japanese term for "waste" or "purposelessness"—was developed early on and independently by Taiichi Ohno, author of the famed Toyota production system. As described in the book *Lean Thinking*, it is now being taken up in the West.

Today's environmental laws tend to reflect that outlook, but while van Dieren, Hawken, McDonough, and others see such moves as crucial for buying time, they also view them as no more than a partial solution. One problem is the industrial rebound effect. As van Dieren puts it, "What happens if cars become so efficient that now every family will buy four?" That question is more than academic. Over the past three decades the chemical industry has reduced its energy consumption per unit of production by 57 percent. But in the same period the industry more than doubled in size, so its total consumption continues to grow.

And there are other concerns. Community planner Richard Levine has warned that "picking the low-hanging fruit" is counterproductive in the long run, because once the easy efficiency gains are "picked," each succeeding step becomes harder until progress grinds to a halt. McDonough argues that dematerialization doesn't change the basic story, saying, "If they make twice as many boxes out of the trees in Indonesia, it's still good-bye Indonesia." As van Dieren puts it, while efficiency programs are crucial now, in the end they can't help falling short. "You are continuing a system that is ultimately unsustainable. The fact that you're moving in the same direction at a slower speed doesn't help the main question." At some point, he says, "You have to move in a new direction."

Waste Equals Food

Looking back to the cherry tree, William McDonough and chemist Michael Braungart write, "It makes thousands of blossoms, just so that another tree might germinate, take root, and grow. Who would notice piles of cherry blossoms littering the ground in the spring and think, 'How inefficient and wasteful'? The tree's abundance is useful and safe. After falling to the ground, the blossoms return to the soil and become nutrients for the surrounding environment. Every last particle contributes in some way to the health of a thriving ecosystem . . . Waste that stays waste does not exist." This builds on a favorite phrase of Braungart's. Of all the lessons we can learn from nature, he asserts, one is central: " 'Waste equals food'—the first principle of the Next Industrial Revolution."

Most recycling efforts today count the number of times a material is reused in its passage from cradle to grave. New biologists look beyond that. "Cradle-to-grave analysis is not enough," says McDonough. "As long as there's something called waste, as long as we're still designing in linear terms, we haven't solved the problem. Reprocessing old Clorox bottles into countertops and park benches won't do. That's just 'downcycling.' Sooner or later it's still going to end up in the landfill." We need recycling that completes the loop, he says. Not cradle to grave but "cradle to cradle."

As McDonough and Braungart see it, the best solution is clear. If nothing harmful goes into a process, it's easier to make sure that nothing harmful will come out of it. In that spirit they have, for the New York City firm Designtex, produced a line of compostable fabrics. Working with European chemical giant Ciba-Geigy, they vetted a list of three hundred dyes by using "knockout criteria": Is it carcinogenic, mutagenic, bioaccumulative? Is it an allergen, an endocrine disrupter? Does it contain heavy metals? Is it effective? The process yielded just sixteen acceptable dyes, which Designtex now uses to color a line of wool-and-ramie upholstery fabric. Water flowing out of the production plant is just as clean as the water flowing in, McDonough says, and when the cloth wears out you can toss it in the backyard to feed the soil.

Beer is the focus of another team's venture. The Zero Emissions Research and Initiatives, or ZERI, is a program headed by Gunter Pauli at United Nations University in Tokyo. Using the Internet, the program links more than four thousand researchers from a variety of disciplines in order to bring together "advanced process engineering and biochemistry." Their efforts have produced a system that organizes brewery waste flows into natural cascades, through several stages of an engineered food chain.

There are now ZERI breweries in Japan, Namibia, Sweden, and Canada. In a typical example, the process begins with spent grains from the brewing stage. These are rich in protein and fiber, so ZERI uses them as a bed for growing mushrooms, for which there's a ready market. Raising mushrooms in that bed leaves it more digestible and nutritious for its second use—as feed for the livestock that are also part of the system. Manure from the livestock and brewery wastewater are then both flushed into a digester, which produces biogas and a rich nutrient solution. The gas is stored in tanks for sale or reuse in powering the brewery. The nutrient flows into a shallow basin where algae digest it and multiply using photosynthesis. The algae are then channeled into a farther pond, where they're absorbed by yet another life form in the food chain, to become fish.

Magical transformations of that kind are routine in nature, and are now being tried by a whole new generation of engineers looking to apply ecological principles to waste streams from human communities. One of them is John Todd, a New England biologist with a lifelong commitment to clean water through the use of what he calls "living machines." These are different from ordinary machines, says Todd, in that "most of the parts inside them are alive." Coming upon a John Todd waste treatment facility can be a little like stumbling onto some new age hanging garden. In a treatment plant in the atrium of a Toronto high school, water moves through a descending spiral of large, translucent cylinders as it passes along a carefully designed food chain that begins with bright green layers of algae, then features tanks of bulrushes and other marsh plants, and finally moves on to fish.

Todd also designs large, open wetland systems. In that he's part of a flourishing movement. Hundreds of engineered wetlands are in use across Europe, where they were pioneered in the 1950s by Kathe Seidel at Germany's Max Planck Institute. In America, Donald Hammer was an early and forceful proponent, building on work done by Max Small at the Brookhaven National Laboratory in the 1970s. And a U.S. textbook for the wetland approach, *Natural Systems for Waste Management and Treatment*, first appeared in 1988. In it, another of the field's pioneers, Sherwood Reed, and his coauthors detail how to match the nutrient uptake of various plants to existing waste flows. Michael Ogden's Natural

Systems International has installed the largest number of engineered wetlands in the U.S., with sites now in nearly every state.

Beyond simple effectiveness, there are other reasons why these systems have spread rapidly. For one thing, they're cheaper to install than the tangle of expensive concrete and pipes used in the machine age approach. One Gulf Coast town faced with costs of $11 million to fix a machine age plant replaced it with a wetland costing $350,000. Engineered wetlands also tend to be odor-free.

Much of the work in natural waste treatment is done by symbiotic microbes on the roots of water-loving plants like duckweed and cattails, hyacinths and bulrushes. Some have roots that absorb the water all around them; with others their roots reach into gravel beds, through which gray water flows. As water is drawn up through a host plant—and then transpired from its leaves—it creates a subtle inflow that draws nutrient to the root, where it's broken down by the microbes. Their byproducts then pass upward to become the body of the plant.

Engineered wetlands often look like real wetlands. The resemblance is more than skin deep. In nature, one function that wetlands serve is to filter runoff before it reaches large bodies of water. So engineers typically use wetland plants in their designs. The result can be a magnet for wildlife. Wetlands are unusually rich habitat; they serve as wombs for living things of every kind. In America alone they're home to 500,000 different kinds of plants, 190 species of amphibians, and 270 species of birds, not to mention the many other creatures that spend parts of their lives nesting or hunting in them. But that fecundity has a downside. During the past century the loss of wetlands to development has had a disproportionate impact. Nearly half of all the threatened and endangered species in the United States are among those that depend on wetlands.

Helping to buck that trend is the twelve lush acres of calla lilies, water irises, arrowheads, and bulrushes in Benton, Mississippi, that now treat 200,000 gallons of wastewater each day. The system was designed by Bill Wolverton, a former NASA engineer who once planned natural treatment systems for moon bases. He went on to design systems for towns across the South. *Audubon* magazine described an early Wolverton system in elegiac prose:

One early summer morning purple martins and swallows sweep through the shrouds of mist rising from the two oxidation ponds of the rock-reed filter plant . . . A forest of giant bulrushes grows in the 15-acre rock marsh . . . a 5-foot alligator lay partially concealed in the grass on one of the ponds' levees, its glistening eyes the only hint of life within the still shape. A colony of red-winged blackbirds perched on the long stalks, filling the air with clucking and raspy beeping.

In many towns, waste systems are themselves going through a magical transformation. Once thought of as blights to be hidden away and avoided, they are becoming parks and recreation areas for hikers or for local office workers there to eat lunch and watch the wildlife. Orlando, Florida's twelve-hundred-acre waste treatment wetland is called Wilderness Park, and is home to rare white pelicans and bald eagles. Bird-watchers at the Arcata Marsh and Wildlife Sanctuary, a natural waste treatment system in northern California, have recorded more than two hundred species. It has become a tourist draw. And once wastewater has passed through its ponds inhabited by various bacteria, algae, mollusks, and fish—and then through its shallows thick with cattails, bulrushes, duckweed, and pennywort—water flowing into the bay is typically cleaner than the bay itself.

Ecosystems in nature link local and global flows and sinks. The push to mimic that can also have a global reach. In Japan an agency called the Research Institute of Innovative Technology for the Earth is working with the prestigious University of Tokyo, and with major funding from companies like Hitachi, Mitsubishi, and Kawasaki. It is developing absorbent bacteria and micro-algae for large-scale, organic devices that will soak up substantial amounts of CO_2. In the mid-1990s, the Dutch Electricity Generating Board began another long-term global effort. In the first of several such projects it paid a Malaysian forestry company on the other side of the world to replant five thousand acres of logged-over forest with native trees, to be grown as an emissions sink. The growing trees will absorb the CO_2 output from one large Dutch power station over its twenty-five-year life span.

Technical Cycles

Such feats, however striking, deal with only half the problem. Physicist Robert Socolow of Princeton University says, "We and the plants both speak organic carbon, but only we speak polychlorinated biphenyl." As McDonough and Braungart put it, "The ability of complex, interdependent natural ecosystems to absorb such foreign material is limited if not nonexistent . . . Unlike the waste from nature's work, the waste from human industry is not 'food' at all. In fact, it is often poison. Thus the two conflicting systems: A pile of cherry blossoms and a heap of toxic junk in a landfill."

While companies strive to make their factories cleaner and less wasteful, another problem is often overlooked. According to Jens Soth, who works with Braungart, "There is one emission that we do not have any clue how to deal with in terms of environmental management. This emission is just going through the outer door. And that is the product of the company."

Socolow agrees, saying that companies "get awards for being clean, but the products they make are still not clean." One case in point is a plastic that incorporates a widely used chlorinated organic molecule. Polyvinyl chloride—commonly called PVC or vinyl—is cheap and versatile, and used in everything from siding to flooring, from medical products to children's toys. One problem with it is that, according to the *American Journal of Public Health*, children who play on vinyl flooring have an 89 percent greater risk of bronchial obstruction. Moreover, because PVC plastics require so many additives, they are not easily recycled, so they often end up in incinerators. Heating the chlorine in PVC produces dioxins—one of the most potent carcinogens known. Dioxin plumes from incinerators settle in reservoirs and on produce. They are inhaled by livestock and people.

Another concern is with vinyl additives like lead, or the phthalates used as softening agents. Research has shown that a phthalate often found in PVC is hazardous to human fertility and development, and that it leaches out of medical IV bags, tubes, and other devices during use. Baxter Healthcare, the largest U.S. maker of IV bags, has now committed to phase out PVC, and other health care firms are following suit. In similar moves the European Union has banned the use of phthalates in children's toys, and Mattel—maker of the Barbie doll—is switching to vegetable-based plastics. New biologists anticipate a chemical industry no longer married to chlorinated organic molecules, one that makes plastics from bioproducts like carbohydrates.

Says Braungart, "You need to eliminate everything where you cannot afford to make a mistake, because the ability to make mistakes is one of the nicest things we have." Tall and lanky, Braungart combines a soft-spoken manner with fierce intelligence and an encyclopedic command of the facts. And he is relentless on his chosen subject. From his base in Hamburg, Germany, he heads a group that does complete toxicological breakdowns of everyday products. For instance, a typical silk tie, they found, contains up to forty grams of heavy metal, in order to make the silk heavier. According to their tests, there are more than four thousand chemicals in a television, and eight hundred outgassing from a video recorder. Many of those are hazardous and outgas when the appliances are running. A washing machine tested contained 1,200 chemicals, at least 180 of which are known to be dangerous—including benzene and toulene. "Is it fair," he asks, "to sell hazardous wastes to someone who only wants to wash his clothes?"

Braungart's great-grandfather was a cobbler. "They used oak extract to do the tanning process," he explains. "They produced shoes that were ugly, and they were very expensive. One pair of shoes was about half the monthly income of a worker in Germany. But those shoes were totally environmentally sound. You could throw them away and you could compost them."

"Today," Braungart says, "shoes are relatively nice. They're relatively cheap. But they are hazardous waste. About 20 percent of the world's chromium is used for leather tanning. And chromium is rare. In one kilogram of shoe waste there are about forty grams of chromium." It's foolish, he says, to get rid of chromium in that way. We need it for steel manufacturing. Should we use plastic shoe soles instead? "We have twenty-six thousand pounds of PVC being used for shoe soles each year in Germany, and . . . lead is used as a stabilizer for the PVC." The lead in dust from shoe soles is carried off by rain, then goes into the wastewater system and the sewage sludge—which makes it difficult to use sewage sludge for agriculture. As things are now, he adds puckishly, we may be better off driving cars than walking, since the rubber dust from tires is more environmentally sound than the dust from billions of shoe soles scuffling across the planet. "You can use [treatment] plants to take out the lead," he says, "but this is ridiculous. All instead of solving the design problem."

Many of the harmful emissions from appliances are caused by using cheap materials in their construction. Braungart points this out while noting that it doesn't have to be that way. Higher quality, less toxic plastics and chemicals could be used to make a video recorder—and with no general increase in cost—if it were designed for disassembly. The trick is to use those materials that can be banked and reused at the end of a product's life, instead of losing them to landfills.

That notion informs an idea for which he and McDonough have become international front men. While PVC and other major toxins should be phased out, they say, other materials are both useful and manageable, even though they're still not safe "food" for biological cycles. Can industrial products be designed so those materials—those "technical nutrients"—stay within industrial feedback loops? According to Braungart and McDonough, that's not only possible but necessary. Just as there are organic cycles, they say, we need to start thinking in terms of "technical cycles." Then make sure that organic and technical cycles don't mix.

Industrial Ecosystems

Beneath a pale northern sky, surrounded by rolling hills and flourishing small farms, the town of Kalundborg occupies the shore of a deep fjord along the Samsø Bælt, the "great belt" of cold water flowing through the heart of Denmark to connect the Baltic and North seas. It's a postcard town of twenty thousand, with an ancient cathedral and a pedestrian main street of storefronts painted in bright primary colors—the kind of quiet, friendly setting where groups of laughing schoolkids whir from place to place on bikes.

In 1990, three of those schoolkids were assigned to do an environmental report on the area's industries. They produced a model showing how wastes were being exchanged among several companies: a power plant, an oil refinery, a biotech pharmaceuticals plant, and a Sheetrock manufacturer. In each case, the companies receiving those wastes used them as raw materials. The children compared the system to food webs found in nature. That was news to Kalundborg's business leaders. Their "industrial ecosystem," as it's now often called, came about through no conscious plan. It evolved piecemeal over the course of three decades through informal talks among managers and CEOs with little more in mind than saving a few kroner.

It was just "good economy," says Mogens Olesen, the power plant manager. But the system they created is a complex interchange of water, energy, and solid wastes that goes beyond the old machine age notion of economy.

Kalundborg's industrial ecosystem begins with water drawn from a nearby lake. It enters the system at a Statoil refinery, which uses it for cooling, then pipes it down the road to the power plant, where it serves as coolant again. That plant, Asnæsvaerkert, burns coal to make electricity, but—as is typical with coal-fired plants—only some 35 percent of the energy released becomes power. The rest is thrown off as waste heat. But here, instead of just dissipating, much of that heat is absorbed by a coolant, and so produces steam. The steam is then pumped through pipes back to the refinery and on to Novo Nordisk, a biotech company. Both companies use it for power. Another pipeline carries more of this steam heat to large districts of the town, eliminating the need for some thirty-five hundred oil-fired furnaces. The power plant also draws salt water from the fjord and, after warming it, feeds it into the ponds of a nearby fish farm. The fish grow more rapidly in warm water, producing 250 tons of trout and turbot each year.

Meanwhile, back at the refinery, sulfur is being stripped from the waste gas, which is then used internally or piped as fuel to Gyproc, a Sheetrock maker, as well as to the power plant—thus saving it some thirty thousand tons of coal a year. The sulfur removed from that waste gas gets trucked to another company, Kemira A/S, which makes sulfuric acid. Meanwhile, the power plant cleans its stack emissions with a scrubber that converts 90 percent of its flue gas sulfur into calcium sulfate, also known as industrial gypsum. Gyproc now buys up to eighty-five thousand tons of it each year for use in making Sheetrock. That avoids the cost of importing mined gypsum all the way from South America.

Running east a mile or so from the power plant, like a new vine shooting out from a spider plant, a meandering pipeline painted light green to match the shrubbery takes live steam to the biotech firm. There the heat is used to make insulin and enzymes. Their fermentation vats also yield 700,000 tons each year of a thin, nitrogen-rich slurry that was once dumped in the fjord. Now it's piped free to local farmers who use it as fertilizer. The farmers in turn grow biomass for the vats, while yeast cake from the vats feeds rural Kalundborg's hogs.

Kalundborg shows that Braungart and McDonough's dictum—"waste equals food"—is a realistic goal for industry. In doing so, it has also opened a door to the coming world of technical cycles—the discrete feedback loops that are material cycles kept separate from those in nature.

As attention turns to the promise of industrial ecosystems, more are being found. For instance, one has been identified in the Austrian state of Styria; another along the Houston, Texas, ship channel. According to Paul Hawken, those examples show the wealth of exchanges possible between industries without design or preplanning. "Imagine," he says, "what a team of designers could come up with if they were to start from scratch."

In fact, that effort is under way. In 1991 the Global Change Institute convened a workshop that brought together social scientists and experts in natural systems. Called "Industrial Ecology and Global Change," the event was chaired by Princeton's Socolow and documented in a 1994 book by that name. It was an early session in what has since become a movable feast of conferences and workshops with sponsors ranging from guilds and academia to individual cities, national governments, and the United Nations.

And actual projects are in development. Consultant Ernest Lowe has one in Dalian, China, east of Beijing. The governor of the surrounding province there is also discussing plans for a recycling economy. Donald Huisingh worked on a major effort with Erasmus University, using computers to link up waste exchanges among hundreds of companies around Rotterdam harbor. In Nova Scotia, Raymond Côté of Dalhousie University has a similar project at the huge Burnside Industrial Park. Yale's Marian Chertow is assessing sites in Puerto Rico. Industrial ecosystems are under development in several American cities, including Londonderry, New Hampshire. "I find communities are very receptive to these concepts," says Lowe. "Most of this stuff is common sense. It's just that we've been in a departure from common sense for some time."

There are questions about "eco-industrial parks." Some observers wonder how many will have the diversity to absorb all their own wastes. Another concern is that, after the cooperating companies are locked into a network of material flows, the failure of any one company could disrupt the system—much as the disappearance of a keystone species does in an ecosystem. Both questions are being addressed by the rise of computerized waste-exchange webs. The Southern Waste Information eXchange, for instance, is one of the many regional clearinghouses that have sprung up in the past fifteen years to perform that function. On its Web site it posts other exchanges in thirty-nine states. These exchanges connect suppliers and potential users in their areas through computer databases, giving industrial ecosystems a regional diversity and stability.

That's just one of the trends driving industry to mimic ecological food webs. ZERI's Gunter Pauli points to the clustering of related companies that emerged twenty years ago with the "just-in-time" revolution, which focused on the delivery of parts and materials. That clustering was meant to reduce the money wasted on chronic overproduction, transport, and warehousing costs. Pauli believes it can now help stamp out the waste of materials by fostering their exchange. Writer and consultant Hardin Tibbs says that industrial ecosystems are a "mirror image of just-in-time." They simply add waste exchange to an existing local web of material flows.

Tachi Kiuchi, managing director of Mitsubishi Electric, and William Shireman, CEO of the consulting firm Global Futures, point to another development: "The sector that probably benefited most from the energy crisis was the emerging information sector: semiconductors, microprocessors, and the computers, screens, peripherals, printers, networks, and service industries that relied on them. High energy and material prices made information-based substitutes cheaper than ever." They see that move to computer-based systems paralleled by another major shift—the flattening of corporate structure:

> Where tall hierarchies served growth in the industrial era, flatter power pyramids often proved to enhance organizational success in the post-industrial era. Mass markets began to subdivide into more narrowly defined niches. Products began to diversify. Generic giants like General Motors fell on hard times and were forced to downsize or decentralize . . . Corporate conglomerates—accumulations of dissimilar businesses under uniform machinelike managements—fell apart or were torn apart in the late 1970s and 1980s.

In that shift from sheer size and vertical integration to decentralized structures, they say, economies of scale are giving way to "ecologies of scale."

Life Cycle Analysis

Japan is energy efficient but at the expense of using nuclear power, with its by-product of radioactive waste. Lighter cars use less material and get better mileage but raise safety concerns and encourage more use. Cloth diapers would seem an obvious choice over plastic disposables, but with the huge amount of pesticides employed to grow cotton, the energy spent for constant pickup and delivery from a diaper service, and the assorted costs of washing them with detergents, the choice becomes less clear. As Jens Soth puts it, "Complexity comes naturally." By that he means that unintended trade-offs are innate to complex systems. They're also a challenge for designers.

Life cycle analysis, or LCA, is an effort to deal with that complexity, to calculate the real costs of making, using, and disposing of products as they move through their useful lives from "upstream" to "downstream." It does that by using powerful computers to track the flows feeding into and emerging from the manufacturing process. By asking questions such as What does this deplete? How much does it pollute? What are the health effects? LCA aims to rule out the externalization of costs—the kind of artificial efficiency that says killing off fish populations with industrial toxin has nothing to do with the cost of making widgets.

LCA is in its infancy, but even in maturity it will never be a true science. It involves too many judgment calls. Who can set the value of fresh air, or a wetland, or a convenient way to get to work? But advocates believe with time and experience those judgments can be refined. In Europe, where landfill space is disappearing, some countries have passed "take-back" laws. They require manufacturers to reclaim and dispose of products at the end of their lives. Given how most things are made today, companies can now find themselves responsible for millions of tons of unrecyclable, often toxic waste. That problem has helped spur a race to develop LCA protocols. Now, with the coming of grid computing, enormous new amounts of processing power will be brought to bear on the problem.

LCA systems begin with complex software programs. They generate "process trees" depicting every aspect of a product's life cycle—from the mining and refinement of its raw materials to the energy production required for that, then through the many other stages of its manufacture and use, and so on to its end-of-life breakdown and reclamation. These "trees" can feature several hundred lines of intertwining environmental impacts, which are then parsed even further in later stages of the process.

Among manufacturers, the Swedish carmaker Volvo is an LCA leader. Its Environmental Priority Strategies, or EPS, were designed with the input of scientists, engineers, and economists from a number of different industries. The system rates materials and processes by "environ-mental load units." According to Sven Ryding, one of its designers, EPS can take into account such things as how much energy is used to make a given part from aluminum. It can even distinguish between the envi-ronmental costs of smelting that aluminum with coal, oil, or hydro-electric power. Using EPS, Volvo has culled thousands of problematic substances from its lines and set up a database of some four thousand chemicals and their impacts, to help designers and staff choose which are more benign to the environment.

Wouter van Dieren's organization was instrumental in the develop-ment of LCA and has worked to merge it with other environmental management systems and with ISO 14000, the current international standard for quality manufacturing. Their efforts are part of a growing awareness that beyond designing products, we now must begin design-ing product life cycles.

For McDonough and Braungart that means that instead of paper, the pages of their book *Cradle to Cradle* were made of a soft, waterproof polymer. Although it looks and feels like paper, the ink can be washed off and reclaimed, and the pages then reprinted with new text and im-ages. Someday they hope to see 800 numbers on all manufactured goods. When a TV is beyond repair or a rug wears out, you can call the factory. The maker comes to get it, then breaks it down and reuses the materials to make something new. Even a chemical could be tagged, with a nano-tech molecular marker, for reclamation at the end of its useful life. And if one turns up where it doesn't belong, there'd be no question of where it came from. In their view, increasing numbers of products should be leased rather than purchased outright, as they are now.

With that, a new approach to leasing is being championed in Europe by Braungart and the Product-Life Institute's Walter Stahel, among oth-ers. It challenges manufacturers to stop thinking of themselves as just sellers of products, encouraging them to instead become providers of services. That shift, to leasing "products of service," has several advantages. It returns things to their makers in the end, helping to close the loop of material flows. It also, as Stahel puts it, "creates a financial incentive for the company to increase the lifetime of the product delivering the service." At the same time it drives companies to reduce the materials and energy used to provide a service—whether in computers for crunching data, in cam-eras for taking pictures, or in vehicles for moving people.

All conservations devoutly to be wished, but is it practical? Will it turn a profit? Ask Ray Anderson, chairman of Interface, a $1 billion company and the world's largest maker of commercial carpet tiles. After reading Paul Hawken's *Ecology of Commerce* in 1994, Anderson had an epiphany. He decided to remake Interface into a company with no smokestacks, no sewer pipes, and a technical cycle of material flows that would loop through the system indefinitely. Now, instead of buying carpet-tile floors from Interface, customers lease them. When an area becomes worn, Interface replaces it. The spent tiles are then taken back, melted down, and used to make new tiles. Within four years of adopting that strategy, Interface saw its revenues double, its number of employees nearly double, and its profits triple. Interface is not alone. Xerox, General Electric, Dow, and other large firms are trying variations on that approach. An example familiar to tourists is the one-use camera, now sold by Eastman Kodak and Fuji, which is sent back to those companies for photo processing, then reloaded and resold at kiosks everywhere.

Closing the Loop

For every plant in nature there are myriad decomposers. They're part of the basic ecological loop; they feed on plant waste even as their own waste feeds the soil that feeds the plants. Animals are part of the cycle, too, eating plants and, when their lives are done, becoming food for decomposers—which break them down into raw materials for the soil and eventual reuptake by the plants. In that overall cycle, says Ernest Lowe, "as much as 90 percent of the energy goes directly into the system of decomposition, to continually renew the nutrients needed for ongoing life." That's why decomposers outnumber all other species. Without those fungi, bacteria, beetles, termites, nematodes, and other flora and fauna, he explains, "the world would be overwhelmed by waste."

With the advent of take-back laws and other ecological strategies, there is a growing emphasis on "design for disassembly," on making things whose materials will flow smoothly back into closed-loop technical cycles. As consultant Hardin Tibbs puts it, "We need to design industrial ecosystems with processes of decay and breakdown explicitly in mind."

Braungart calls that "design for reincarnation," and it is rapidly becoming big business. He has worked with several European appliance producers in the development of a washing machine made entirely of "technical nutrients," which can be recycled endlessly. He and McDonough, through their company MBDC, helped bring the same principle to Shaw Industries in developing its EcoWorx carpets. Shaw is among the world's largest carpet manufacturers. Xerox now reuses up to 90 percent of the materials that go into its document technologies.

Carmakers have a history of reclamation and reuse, which they're now expanding. A new sports car from BMW features a recyclable thermoplastic body that can be disconnected from its frame in twenty minutes. Audi has joined with Volkswagen and Preussag, the steel company, to set up a chain of auto-disassembly plants. With funding primarily from Ford, as well as from Xerox and GE Plastics, Carnegie Mellon University has developed ReStar—a software that analyzes disassembly tasks. McDonough and Braungart are working with Ford on another development, what they variously call the "buffalo car" and the Model U (that is, the next big step after the Model T). The ambitious goal is to design a production model in which every material can eventually be reused—much as the buffalo was by Native Americans. The first step in that process debuted at the 2003 Detroit Auto Show. It featured an interior made entirely of technical nutrients.

Small companies are emerging as decomposers, too. One example is Big City Forest in the Bronx, New York, which has taken a page from the original Henry Ford's book (he used lumber from shipping pallets as floorboards in Model Ts). It reclaims tens of thousands of shipping pallets each year, remanufacturing them or using their hardwood to make new products such as furniture.

As with the decomposers in nature, labor requirements for industrial decomposition and remanufacture are high. That has meant real growth for this new category of "green collar" jobs. U.S. remanufacturing firms are now a $50 billion industry that directly employs some 500,000 people.

Design for disassembly means, as Hawken puts it, that "productivity can go *down*, employment up, and profits increase." Moreover, it means leaving irreplaceable raw materials in the ground. Since urban areas are where most products end up, it also leads to a future where cities become the main sources of industrial raw material—as old products are continuously broken down and reconstituted into new.

Cities as nurse logs? Just as nature combines elements such as nitrogen, oxygen, and carbon to make a cherry blossom or a dragonfly—

then decomposes and reabsorbs them when their lives are done—
materials in a fully evolved technical cycle will take specific form only
to provide services like a car for transportation, a washing machine to
clean clothes, a phone for communications, before being absorbed back
into the web of industrial material flows.

It's the Energy, Stupid!

We can conserve material with closed loops like those found in nature,
but that still leaves aside a very large part of the industrial equation: energy is a separate question. As the 2nd Law of Thermodynamics shows,
through all the universe energy constantly dilutes. It may be captured in
ways large and small, and used more effectively, but it can never be recycled. Organisms survive only by constantly seeking out and channeling fresh energy flows into their bodies. In that they are essentially
swimming upstream on power from the sun, our cardinal energy source.
Virtually all food chains on earth sooner or later lead back to it.

Complex organisms like us became possible more than a billion years
ago, when single-celled creatures called mitochondria first took up residence in larger cells. Mitochondria remain at the heart of our cell metabolism today. They process the hydrogen needed to make the cell's key
energy distributors—molecules called ATP. Those are molecules into
which an extra phosphate has been packed, making them highly unstable and full of tension, like a jack-in-the-box before it's opened. When
they come near a site in the cell where energy is needed, a standard reaction pops the lid off the box. With that, the unwanted extra phosphate
jumps off, releasing the heat energy that keeps us alive. Those newly
separated parts are then cycled back through mitochondrial machinery
that once again packs the loose phosphate into place for another round.
This packing process—the stuffing of the jack back into the box—is
powered by a clever nanotechnology that's fueled entirely by hydrogen
ions. About nine are needed to fuel a single packing, and each ATP molecule cycles through this process three times per minute. In every single
human cell, at any given time, there are roughly one billion ATP molecules releasing energy.

In an interesting sidelight, as hydrogen electrons are drawn through
the mitochondrial machinery to fuel ATP packing, they leave behind
the hydrogen protons from which they were separated. The protons

have to be dealt with so they don't cause damage. Nature's solution is to combine them with oxygen to make water, which our bodies then use for other functions. The poison called cyanide, which acts very quickly, works by blocking this process.

Hydrogen is the most abundant matter in the universe, and its best energy carrier. Some 90 percent of all atoms are hydrogen. When you look out over the vast, glistening waters of a river, lake, or sea, two-thirds of what you're looking at is hydrogen. The sun itself is powered by the fusion of hydrogen. Through the ages, the ongoing use of hydrogen to fuel cell-energy processes has spurred the emergence of new levels of complexity, diversity, and higher organization in an ever-growing multitude of forms. That's one reason we're so fond of carbohydrates, those sugary blends of carbon, oxygen, and most of all hydrogen atoms. Our industries have evolved to use hydrogen-rich fuel, too—hydrocarbon (hydrogen and carbon) fossil fuels, the sinks of rotted biomass that lie beneath the earth.

Food contains sunlight transformed by plants into energy we can use. So does fossil fuel. Just as with living food chains, that industrial food chain leads back to the sun—although in this case it tracks back through the dark caverns of the earth before getting there. It was our good fortune to have that underground "storage battery for solar energy." By drawing on it we've made a conspicuous start. But as we burned all those hydrocarbons, leftover carbon molecules linked themselves to oxygen. With that we unknowingly soaked our atmosphere with CO_2, an oversight of historic proportion. The warping of global climate is an error so vast it challenges belief. For many, it just doesn't seem possible. It is occurring nonetheless—with glaciers melting, Arctic forests sinking into the ground, and once-temperate regions turning brittle and dry. If a climate flip cools large parts of the globe, our problems will get worse. It would deal a crushing blow to a food supply already suffering major strains.

Central to all this is the question of energy. We've begun to change how Western nations make it. And as developing countries around the world design and build new infrastructure, they need a better model to work from. Two billion people still live in rural areas beyond the reach of centralized grids. "Distributed power" from freestanding alternate sources is cost-effective in those regions. It also figures in the rise of microgrids—localized energy networks. As discussed in chapter 9, new computerized adapters let diverse new kinds of power inputs feed them, and can link them into larger webs. These considerations favor a shift away from large, centralized power grids, with all the unexpected interruptions and transmission inefficiencies they bring.

Distributed power builds on local ecological strengths. A town house on Manhattan's Upper East Side uses geothermal power, steam heat drawn from deep within the earth. A device on the Scottish coast reaps energy from the rising and falling tides. Various fuels can be extracted from biomass (although plants grown as fuel compete for space against plants providing food or habitat; they also deplete increasingly scarce water). Methane from farm waste and landfills shows more promise. Where it's breezy, windmills crown the ridgelines. They're also heading offshore. A new $12.4 billion project is putting wind farms off the British coast in three sites; they'll generate up to 7 percent of Britain's energy needs. Since 1995, worldwide installed wattage from wind power has been growing by an average of 33 percent each year. The harvesting of solar power directly from the sun, through photovoltaic cells, has expanded almost as fast. Japan currently leads the world, with 120 megawatts installed in 2001, and during that same year installed U.S. wattage rose by 50 percent. China has ambitious plans to develop twenty thousand megawatts of wind power by 2020.

This rapid growth is fueled by steady declines in the cost of alternative power. A common measure of output is a kilowatt-hour of electricity, which will run a hair dryer for an hour or a 100-watt lightbulb all night. A decade ago, solar cell power cost as much as a dollar per kilowatt-hour. Conventional solar cells now make it for twenty to thirty cents, and experimental types promise ten cents or less. Windmills currently do a better job. The windmills that today produce a fifth of Denmark's power do so at about five cents per installed kilowatt-hour. Employing lessons from aeronautics, models entering production can deliver unsubsidized power for nearly four cents.

By comparison, today's fossil fuel plants run for around five to seven cents per kilowatt-hour, nuclear somewhat more when the expensive permitting process is factored in. Those costs are possible only thanks to taxpayer subsidies like the oil-depletion allowance and in many cases are rising now with the sharp increase in oil and natural gas prices. Moreover, they do not include the costs to the environment of waste problems, or the amount of power lost when transmitting it over long distances from central plants. Nor do they reflect the great political and military costs of securing vital energy from politically unstable regions of the world. To those concerns we have now added the threat of domestic terrorism, with all the vulnerabilities innate to our centralized power plants and narrow supply chains (not to mention nuclear plants or the waste they generate, the storehouses for which some critics describe as plutonium depositories for terrorists).

Solar cells today are still the product of machine age design, but new biologists are at work on nanotechnologies that can mimic photosynthesis. That effort first saw light at Arizona State University in Tempe, where chemistry professor J. Devens Gust, Jr., along with Thomas and Ana Moore, heads a large team of scientists that continues to make advances. In the roughly twenty years since they published their early work the new field has become an international quest, with labs around the world pushing one another along. Copying photosynthesis marks another of those basic shifts now taking place in so many fields due to the new biology. In this case, the shift is away from our fiery machine age approach to generating energy, and toward cellular power produced by a molecular exchange, in the "cold fire" that animates all living things.

Such developments have stirred an undercurrent of excitement, but beyond concerns for cost they face another obstacle: their inconsistency. Power plants that run on fossil fuels—like coal, oil, or natural gas—can rely on that underground storage battery. Although our use of that battery has spawned a range of artificial efficiencies, and its depletion is a problem for the future, using it now ensures that our power won't go off when the sun sets. For as long as it lasts, we can convert it into usable form whenever we like.

Solar and windmills, the natural power schemes with the widest potential for the future, aren't like that. They both depend on the sun. Solar draws power from it directly; windmills depend on weather that it creates. All of this means they are less consistent sources of power. That in turn means their widespread use requires some replacement for the storage battery we use now, a replacement that will furnish power during night hours or at other times when those systems are down. Years of intensive battery R&D have yielded little promise on that front. Ultra-high-speed flywheels can help but have limited duration. Pumping water into reservoirs for later use as hydropower is highly site-specific and draws political fire. A consensus of engineers, environmentalists, and political leaders is now turning to one all-encompassing solution: use solar power to make hydrogen, then use the hydrogen to power fuel cells. These generate current through an exchange of protons and electrons, in a way that echoes what happens in living cells.

Hydrogen Rising

Can we replace today's underground petroleum "battery" by storing pure hydrogen instead, then using it as needed to drive fuel cells? Not right away. The cost of splitting hydrogen from its various feedstocks is high, and there are concerns over how to store it. Also, fuel cells are still primitive. But things are advancing rapidly. In the past decade a massive global research effort has pushed back problems of cost, power density (how big a cell must be to produce a given amount of power), and hydrogen storage. The foundations for a hydrogen-based economy are actively being laid.

The reasons for that refocusing aren't hard to grasp. Concerns about CO_2 and global warming have sharpened; the time that our remaining oil reserves can last is measured in decades; soaring demand from nations like India and China has increased competition for those reserves; and the need to import oil from areas where the industrial world is unwelcome has brought grave and costly security issues. All of those signal foreclosure for the petroleum era. Plus, as the engineering challenges are being met, it becomes clear that hydrogen is a superior alternative.

Fuel cells generate power in a way that echoes nature. Their only "exhaust" is pure water. They are silent and have no moving parts. Moreover, fuel cell efficiency is high, roughly twice that of today's internal combustion engines, and the power they create is electrical. That makes them a natural fit for electric motors, which are exceptionally efficient, too. Of the half-dozen varieties of fuel cell, some types throw off heat that can be used in localized ways—as hot water heaters and furnaces, for instance, or to drive auxiliary turbines—boosting overall system efficiency still more. In the long run, they could serve as micropower generators. Cars that aren't being used for transportation could plug in and feed energy into the larger grid.

All this has made fuel cells a bright star in the firmament of energy alternatives. By the late 1990s the fledgling industry's revenues, though modest at about $20 million, were increasing by 20 percent a year. And according to the marketing consulting group Frost & Sullivan, the fuel cell market is about to see compound annual growth rates of nearly 50 percent. Still more dramatic are the goings-on behind the scenes. There are now some sixty companies developing fuel cell technology, including dozens of brash start-ups as well as eight of the world's ten largest revenue producers. Among the core players—as recorded each month in newsletters like the U.S.-based *Hydrogen & Fuel Cell Letter*, the Fuel Cells 2000 *Technology Update*, and the *Hydrogen & Fuel Cell Investor*, as well as in Germany's *HyWeb-Gazette*—there is an incessant drumbeat of mergers, acquisitions, licensing deals, and joint ventures as they mix and match to exploit potential synergies.

While full commercialization is decades away, the number of pilot projects is reaching critical mass. In stationary applications in the U.S., the new green skyscraper that rises over New York City at Four Times Square employs fuel cells for power and heat. They're also being used in universities, at a health center in Texas, by a central mail-processing facility in Alaska, and in structures at Yosemite and Yellowstone national parks. In Germany there are fuel cells heating and lighting large buildings in Essen, Hamburg, and Berlin. In Fukuoka, Japan, they make electricity from the methane given off at a municipal waste treatment plant. In Chiba, near Tokyo, they draw electricity from a brewery's wastewater and feed that power back to the brewery.

The Royal Dutch/Shell Group is developing a large fuel cell power source for industry. The start-up Plug Power focuses on refrigerator-size units for home use; General Electric will distribute them. Another industrial giant, General Motors, is working to produce home units as well as larger systems for private microgrids, set up by users needing uninterrupted, premium power—such as the server farms, chip fab plants, hospitals, telecoms, and call centers mentioned in chapter 9. Alone among American automakers, GM is also developing its own fuel cells to power a radical new generation of cars.

Many of the world's carmakers have turned to one company for their fuel cell motors: the Canadian start-up Ballard Power Systems, a world leader in the development of light, compact fuel cells for transportation. Big chunks of the company have been acquired by DaimlerChrysler and Ford, and it has joint ventures or licensing agreements with a host of other firms. Virtually all major carmakers have prototype fuel cell vehicles in the works, and several—including GM, Toyota, Honda, Nissan, Ford, and DaimlerChrysler—are planning production models soon. Daimler-Chrysler has earmarked $1.5 billion for its program.

GM has already spent a billion dollars, and may triple that amount by 2010. It aims to have a fuel cell car on the market at the end of the decade and to sell a million of them by 2015—many in places like China, where no gasoline infrastructure exists. To meet that ambitious timetable, GM engineers have addressed the high cost of current fuel cell power by thinking wide. Knowing they couldn't bring that cost down anytime soon, they reconceived the rest of the car to make the overall system less expensive. With the AUTOnomy and Hy-wire concept cars, GM has moved toward a future in which different bodies simply snap on and off a standardized fuel-cell-powered chassis (the "skateboard"), transforming it as needed into a sedan, a sports car, a minivan, or even a truck. In that scheme the most expensive part of a car, the chassis—with the motor and other running gear now tucked into a low, sleek pod—is reduced to just three basic platforms: small, medium, and large. This saves billions of dollars in factory tooling costs by matching the stream-lined new cars with a streamlined manufacturing process.

Some hydrogen vehicles are already out on the streets. Fuel cell golf carts and buses ply the parks and streets of desert communities in the Coachella Valley, in Southern California. The buses gas up in Thousand Palms, at the twenty-four-hour "clean fuel mall." Ballard-powered buses are entering service in London and other European cities. They have for several years carried passengers on regular routes in Vancouver and Chicago. One Chicago newspaper photographed that city's mayor chug-ging down a glass of hydrogen fuel cell bus exhaust: pure water.

Students at Zurich's Swiss Federal Institute of Technology built the fuel-cell PacCar II, a 62-pound three-wheeler that runs at the equiva-lent of 9,023 miles per gallon of gas. The Rocky Mountain Institute, a leading green think tank, has developed a hydrogen-fueled, open-source prototype called the Hypercar. Says the institute's director, Amory Lovins, "Very exciting things are happening in the car business. It's just like the era when personal computers started to replace typewriters and it took a while to realize what was going on. This is going to be the biggest shift in industrial structure since chips."

Laptop computers need portable power, too, as do cell phones, video cameras, and the numerous other gizmos of an increasingly mo-bile age. Micro fuel cells are under development by companies like Motorola, Sony, and the start-up Manhattan Scientifics. Micro cells are typically no bigger than a pocket lighter and provide a lightweight, longer-lasting alternative to batteries. Medis Technologies, based in Israel, in a deal with French cell phone maker Sagem, is ramping up to produce fifty million micro fuel cells a year. It's also working with General Dynamics to develop portable systems for the U.S. military. As such it is one among many under similar contracts. As elsewhere, DARPA—

the Defense Advanced Research Projects Agency—is on the scene. According to Robert Nowak of that agency, U.S. soldiers now carry twenty to thirty pounds of batteries with them to run communications and other advanced battle data gear. Considering that, he says, "Fuel cells begin to look very attractive."

In other mobile applications, fuel cell bikes are appearing on the market. And scooters. Italy's Celco Profil is developing one. The Scoot, designed by the San Francisco start-up fuseproject, can be folded up and carried on your back. In large, advanced technology projects the U.S. Navy is looking at fuel cells for its new class of hydrogen-fueled, twenty-first-century destroyers. International Fuel Cells, a division of United Technologies Corporation, has long produced power for the American space program. Fuel cells drive the next Mars rover and a submersible set to cruise beneath the Arctic sea. AeroVironment uses fuel cells in its unmanned, high-altitude, solar-electric aircraft for NASA, the *Helios.* With them it can fly at altitudes approaching fifty thousand feet for days on end.

While issues of weight, power density, and cost are being addressed by fuel cell makers, fundamental problems remain: How will we store and transport the hydrogen used to charge them? Where will we get it in the first place?

Hydrogen in free form is virtually unknown in nature. It bonds so readily that it tends to link with other elements. A plant stores it by bonding it with carbon and oxygen in the form of carbohydrates. These have an absorbent structure and tend to soak up water, which makes plants relatively heavy. Plants rarely move about, so that's no problem, but mobile life forms had to come up with a lighter way to store their fuel. Their solution was to evolve fats, which are made primarily of hydrogen. That is why, when we eat more carbohydrates than we can burn, we grow fat—our bodies are storing the excess hydrogen for future use. Fat is also compact and lighter than water. Even the seeds that plants send out into the world store their hydrogen in fat.

Questions of weight and compactness are no less vital for cars and other fuel-cell-powered vehicles. Compressed-gas tanks are large and raise safety concerns. (It should be noted here that exaggerated safety concerns about hydrogen are unwarranted. It is arguably less dangerous than the natural gas now used to fuel homes and many vehicle fleets. While highly flammable, hydrogen dissipates upward quickly because it's so light. Moreover, it doesn't throw off white-hot carbon "soot" that adheres to surfaces, as gasoline and other hydrocarbons do. The famed conflagration of the *Hindenburg* was due to factors other than hydrogen [see note].) Another storage scheme absorbs the gas into metal hydrides, which release it safely in small amounts when they are warmed, but tanks of that type are still quite heavy. The eventual solution may turn out to be absorption of the hydrogen into carbon nanotubes—which are light and can release it as needed when they're warmed.

Fueling stations are also a problem. While vast amounts of hydrogen are now being produced for industrial use (it's combined with nitrogen, for example, to make ammonia for fertilizer and is used to boost octane in gasoline), there is no hydrogen-distribution system equal to the 175,000 gas stations that dot the U.S. Onboard reformers can extract hydrogen from most conventional fuels, but reformers are complicated and expensive, making each car into a miniature chemical factory. Larger, stationary units at existing gas stations and fuel depots are a better bet. They could be paid for by expanding the market; and the best way to accomplish that, many experts now agree, is by converting today's internal combustion engines to burn hydrogen. That conversion is fairly simple and would make them both more efficient and less polluting. How to make that hydrogen without using power from the old, polluting grid remains a concern.

As oil reserves wane and CO_2 levels rise, the world's oil companies have seen the writing on the wall and begun recasting themselves as energy companies. BP Amoco now says "BP" stands for "Beyond Petroleum." Royal Dutch/Shell has formed Shell Hydrogen. With DaimlerChrysler it is building a chain of hydrogen stations across Iceland, for a new fleet of eighty fuel cell buses. The government of Iceland is working to make that country the world's first hydrogen-powered economy.

With time, large-scale systems may be supplemented by home reformers that sit out in the family garage, making hydrogen for cars and other uses. At first they would split it off from conventional feedstocks like oil, natural gas, or methane. Teams in England and the U.S. have developed fuel cells that feed on sugar. Somewhere in the future lies the lodestar of the fuel cell economy—splitting hydrogen from water.

If using hydrogen from water to fuel a process that in the end just makes more water sounds like a scheme from science fiction, it's one that has drawn tantalizingly near. Wind-powered splitters can do the job using renewable power, and they have a price advantage, but closer to nature's way is direct solar. In 1972 Akira Fujishima at Kanagawa University and Kenichi Honda at the University of Tokyo were the first to use a solar cell to split hydrogen from water. That work was later extended by research done at the U.S. National Renewable Energy Laboratory (NREL). Since 1986 a public/private effort, the Solar-Wasserstoff-Bayern Project, has used power from solar panels to separate hydrogen from water for a liquid-hydrogen fuel station in Germany. BMW and the Munich Technical University are working on a design using solar power to separate hydrogen from seawater in Dubai. A solar-hydrogen-fuel-cell array powers an environmental information center in Stockholm. A device made by the Solar Hydrogen Energy Corporation employs reflectors to focus the power from sunlight. It splits water to make hydrogen that the company says is 99.999 percent pure. And at the Virginia Polytechnic Institute and State University, scientists have devised a supramolecular complex—a large hybrid molecule—that brings together units that absorb light for energy with others that combine with hydrogen in water molecules to split them into hydrogen and oxygen. The new nano-splitters are a breakthrough in efficiency and come as the result of a ten-year research effort.

While these developments represent real progress, they're just the start. "We would like to use green plants to split water into molecular hydrogen and oxygen," says Elias Greenbaum, a researcher at the Oak Ridge National Laboratory in Tennessee. "The hydrogen could then be used in a fuel cell to make electricity." Photosynthesis is the crucial link between the inorganic and the organic worlds, employing solar energy to draw matter into the plant forms that serve as fuel for other living things. As such it is a key process in life. Agriculture was our first controlled means of collecting energy through photosynthesis. Adapting it to power industry would be another major step.

Since the early 1980s Ingo Rechenberg, one of Europe's leading new biologists, has forayed from his lab at the Berlin Technical University to scour the world—from Japan to the Caribbean, Antarctica to the Sahara Desert—in his hunt for superior strains of a purple bacterium that can make hydrogen. Kazuhisa Miyamoto of Osaka University has developed a hydrogen-producing strain of a blue-green alga called *Anabaena cylindrica*. James Guillet from the University of Toronto has patented artificial duckweed—one of several nature-based strategies he sees producing hydrogen. The European Union has COST Action 841, a broad effort involving forty-five labs in fourteen countries to explore the potential of natural hydrogen metabolism.

At the University of California at Berkeley, a team led by the microbiologist Tasios Melis and backed by researchers at NREL has been working with an alga called *Chlamydomonas reinhardtii*, a.k.a. pond scum. What they've found is that the alga, which usually grows by photosynthesis, can be "switched" to an alternate mode by depriving it of sulfur. Doing that cripples its internal photosynthetic cascade. Unable to burn stored fuel in the usual way, the algae resort to an alternate metabolic pathway—one that releases hydrogen as a by-product. "They're utilizing stored compounds and bleeding hydrogen just to survive," says Melis. "It's probably an ancient strategy that the organism developed to live in sulfur-poor anaerobic conditions." The algae can continue in that mode for about four days. After that they have to be switched back to normal photosynthesis in order to bank more carbohydrates. Then they can be tapped again, to draw off the new hydrogen they have stored. According to a member of the NREL team, "The cell culture can go back and forth like this many times." They foresee a future when a small commercial algae pond will produce enough hydrogen to fuel several cars for a week.

That hope led Melis in 2001 to form Melis Energy, a start-up that will further develop their energetic swamp thing. One goal is to increase output by engineering the algae to express higher levels of hydrogenase—the enzyme that splits off the hydrogen from its carbohydrate feedstock. His company is also working to patent a sealed "tubular reactor" network for growing the algae and drawing off the hydrogen. The tube farms could contain anywhere from five thousand to ten thousand gallons of advanced pond scum.

Work like this is in the stage that solar power was a decade ago. Early demonstrations show promise; commercial applications are yet to come. But along with the many alternate technologies now reaching commercial status, they point to a systemic change, one in which a growing diversity of energy devices tap local ecological strengths. Someday we may even see a power system like nature's, in which water is a primary storage tank for our hydrogen. As in plants, that system would release oxygen as the hydrogen is culled. It would also make pure water as its by-product and—in a welcome change from the way we make power today—absorb CO_2 in the process.

The key to that is continued development of fuel cells. The molecular transactions now running them are far from the elegant cascades of nature. Still, the shift from hot flames to cold fire marks a major turning point in the evolution of human industry.

Completing the Picture

When fish swing their tails, they leave deft swirls of water. As their tails return, they stir up more. Each stroke sets new whirlpools spinning in the opposite direction. We understand now that fish arrange those swirls in deliberate patterns, a trick that improves their speed and mobility. The swirls reduce drag from wakes even as they offer something for fish to press their tails against on return strokes. That insight serves those who study propulsion, but it offers a larger lesson, too: until we understand the water and the whirlpools, we can't really understand the fish. They don't exist apart from their context. Neither do we.

That's what the community planner Eliel Saarinen meant when he counseled, "Always design with the next larger context in mind." It's what Richard Levine means when he says that a given activity or process "can take its place in a larger system only by seeking its balance within that more encompassing system." Interactions between organisms and the environment drive their overall dispersion and abundance. That is the essence of ecology. Industrial ecology aims to merge human interactions with those deeper patterns.

As Bill McDonough nicely puts it:

> Let's say we've got this planet that is just rocks and water. Add a little so-lar energy and all of a sudden you've got "physics meets chemistry," and you go to the single photosynthetic cell and get biology. Then that cell splits and things start to happen. I mean, that's the basis of our food chain. It's energy transforming into mass. So what ends up happening is the world fills up with diversity because the solar-powered engine fills niches, and the more niches it fills, the more potent the biology. Every time there's an opportunity for fecundity, current solar income gets translated into a development that wasn't here before. So that physical and chemical transformation—which results in biota that are richer all the time—that becomes the design model.

Preserving nature doesn't have to involve sacrifice and going without, he says. We can learn to celebrate, to emulate, life's fecundity and abundance.

Industries have so often been destructive to nature it's common to think of the two as opposites. Environmentalists protesting the activities of business make that assumption as often as business leaders protesting the activities of environmentalists. But it's not true. The machine model that shapes industry today was a largely successful effort to use nature-based logic. This is a crucial distinction. Our problems actually began, as so many of them do, with our own limited comprehension. We designed a system based on partial knowledge. Then, using our great gift for deliberate action, we took what we had and ran with it. The system that resulted is not some evil empire, and it's not failing because it is the opposite of nature. The machine age is obsolete because it's incomplete.

The new biology aims to build on the work begun by industrialization, not simply to do away with it. And large corporations can be the key to that effort. They are crucial springboards, with the resources and economic reach to spread new solutions around the globe. Corporations, says AT&T's Braden Allenby, are like people. We need to discourage their bad sides and encourage the good. That is especially true now as they face profound new responsibilities, for which nothing in the past has prepared them. As Allenby points out, the role of the firm "is shifting from being a developer and producer of products to being the manager, in the social sense, of new technologies with significant social and ethical dimensions . . . what can be seen as Earth systems engineering."

As humans take the reins of natural history, making choices that affect all life on earth, we do well to bear in mind that nature is implacable. In the largest sense it will prevail. If we make mistakes—like pumping too much CO_2 into the sky—nature will correct us with the same cold rigor it applies to any organism that exceeds its natural limits. Other life forms have learned to answer those limits with diversity, fecundity, and abundance. The new biology offers tools that can help us do the same. That is the challenge for our decade, and for our century. From this point forward, all technologies are old news unless they work within the frame of natural logic.

That doesn't mean the end of industrial maxims like standardization, or of large organizations. Atoms are standardized building blocks, as are the molecules they form. In that spirit, widely differing species, from lettuce to humans, share the same genes. With mitochondria, life has used the same standard energy device to power us and our ancestors through time. Large organizations and systems are another industrial touchstone that is in keeping with life. The new biology doesn't mean that only small is beautiful. Nature likes large systems. The larger and more complex they are, the more energy efficient—so long as they are truly responsive to natural feedbacks, and they can adapt to the fluctuating local diversity those encourage. Pound for pound, a red-tailed hawk is more efficient than the field mouse it hunts; a cougar more efficient than the hawk. As life fills out the niches in an ecosystem, it becomes more efficient overall.

That happens because natural feedback loops merge both large and small in a single, common web. Cascades of energy and materials pulse through linked arrays, from top down and bottom up, forming ever more complex and effective networks that connect on every side and at every scale. In this also lies our ultimate model for industry. It's possible now to imagine a world that integrates diverse cultures and business enterprises in a way not unlike how nature unites large and small—where individuals as well as local and global systems all process energy and matter by the same ecological principles. As Michael Braungart puts it, "It's not about respecting biodiversity; it's about supporting it—by feeding into natural cycles."

"The unique attribute of the living system, the magical ingredient we seek to borrow, is its ability to begin with a finite supply of raw materials, and yet evolve into a seemingly infinite array of forms, by cycling and recycling its resources continuously over time," write Tachi Kiuchi and William Shireman. Nature, they say, end-runs the 2nd Law's continuous dilution of energy not by adding on physically but by developing inwardly, increasing its design complexity. As that complexity multiplies, natural systems pass certain thresholds, "at which point whole new qualities emerge, qualities that enable the system to express higher-level functions while physically consuming nothing new." Looking over the horizon, the authors see that process continuing indefinitely. "Matter has evolved into forms that exhibited function, then life, then thought, and finally conscious volition. The increasing efficiencies and emergent qualities of a healthy ecosystem have no known limit."

All this foretells the rise of something altogether new: an Arcadian technology. We have only begun that shift, but it's coming fast. With nanotechnology and directed evolution we can mimic nature at the deepest levels of matter. Our robots now move like living things and have also begun to see as they do. Neural nets and biological components are transforming artificial intelligence. In artificial life and self-organizing systems we find echoes of our own evolution; with virtual worlds, a higher-level reality may even be emerging. After a failed marriage with the machine age, agriculture and community planning are rediscovering their roots in ecology. Throughout industry, ecological means are gaining ground. Many of these fields bleed into one another; computers play a growing role in all of them.

Beyond that, there is one overarching human system that drives and shapes the rest, whose sole purpose is to link the wants and needs of individuals with the exchange of goods on a worldwide scale. That system is economics. The rise of globalization, in all its manifestations, is an economic act. And at its core today lies an economic model based, like so much else in the industrial world, on a linear, machine age vision of nature. How good that model is has been attested by success. That it could benefit from improvement is also clear—from its failure to account for the depletion of resources, or the losses due to the accumulation of wastes like CO_2. By externalizing factors like these from free markets, today's economy isolates our purchasing decisions from realistic feedback about their impact on the world. For that reason our economic reality is a distorted mirror, one that doesn't reflect true costs. Inaccurate costs give rise to inaccurate prices. Without accurate prices, free markets don't work the way they should.

Can economies mirror ecology? Can globalization serve large and small systems alike? Can money mirror the 2nd Law of Thermodynamics? As one might expect, there are new biologists working on it.

eleven

the real conservatives

The ocean lifts and rolls beneath the sun. As waves slide across the water, shafts of daylight ripple undersea to fire a rich display of life. Among the many things found growing there are clouds of floating algae that eat calcium, which comes to them in runoff from onshore. They absorb it and transform it into miniature snowflake shells. As the algae die their shells drift down like falling snow into the blue depths. Over vast periods they layer the ocean floor with thick beds of chalky rock. Those beds then sink into earth's tectonic plates, moving with them as they slide and crash together, at times veering upward to form limestone outcrops like the famed White Cliffs of Dover. In the gray of dawn a snail works its way by inches across the edge of those cliffs, where plants extract calcium from the rock. The snail in turn draws calcium from them for its shell. Just like the algae before it, and like the plants on which it feeds, the snail is performing that most basic of economic acts—using solar energy to stir matter into new form.

In the ongoing cycles of nature the snail will one day return its calcium to the limestone cliffs, even as runoff from those cliffs will return calcium to the sea and to the clouds of floating algae that transform it back once more into delicate snowflake shells. Calcium atoms move from inert to living states when algae draw them from the sea, then again

when snails draw them via plants from the rock. We extract them, too—
from plants, from water, from milk—and transform them into teeth and
bones. As calcium is taken into living bodies, and then with time returns
to earth, it's just one of many atoms cycling in and out of life.

The seamless flow of atoms from inert to living form and back again
makes it hard for science to define what life is. We can say it uses energy
from the sun to draw matter into higher levels of organization, into new
and more complex patterns that grow and reproduce and then dissolve.
And we can say that at the heart of that process lies feedback. Natural selection is a feedback process. Feedback links organic patterns at every
scale, connecting figure and ground, parts and wholes, from molecular
to global, tying them into networks that evolve as the individuals within
them evolve. Ultimately, it is feedback that steers earth's limited supply
of atoms into endless, recycling loops, making possible life's rich abundance and diversity of form.

Feedback is also crucial on another front. As organisms use solar
power to stir matter into new forms, feedback spurs them to be thrifty
with the power that drives them. Since our energy ultimately comes from
the sun, and flows to earth at a limited rate, there's only so much to go
around. What's more, the 2nd Law of Thermodynamics means whatever energy we do get is always being diluted as it passes along from one
life form to another in food chains. It was feedback that evolved large
predators, which pound for pound are more efficient than small prey.
Feedback taught fish to use the dynamics of water in elegant ways to increase their speed. Feedback shaped snails to graze along white cliffs,
where they can extract the calcium for their shells.

Life has flourished despite the limited flow of power from the sun
and a limited stock of materials here on earth. Therein lies what may be
the central lesson for a new biology: all this is possible only because
manifold feedbacks drive life toward a sweet spot between figure and
ground, connecting the lives of individuals to those larger flows and patterns from which they emerge.

Without the measureless billions of sea algae that have gone on forming snowflake shells for one hundred million years, without the great
beds of chalky limestone they produce, and without the slow slide of
tectonic plates around the earth's core, there would be no white cliffs for
snails to graze on. The algae, the chalk, the snail, express how well natural feedback links the simplest economic acts to vast and often-unseen

global cycles. In this way a single snail absorbing calcium from the White Cliffs of Dover is an expression of how nature unifies local and global economies.

Applied Theory

If nature's economy is elegant, dynamic, and resilient across many levels, that's less true for the system we've devised. In fact, questions persist about its validity. One practitioner wryly admits, "Outside the circle of professional economists, statements implying that economics is a science do not meet with universal acceptance." More to the point, physicist Murray Gell-Mann tells a story concerning his trip to Stockholm to receive the Nobel Prize in 1969, the first year an award was given for economics. Describing the ceremony later, he shocked a colleague by mentioning the two winners of that award. "You mean," the man exclaimed in disbelief, "they sat on the platform with you?"

The dismal science remains so. "Every government in the world," writes one critic, "employs an army of economic advisors to counsel it on the plotting of a safe course through the battlefield of stock market crashes, budget deficits, trade imbalances, stagflation, currency revaluations, and the myriad other landmines and pitfalls of modern economic life. Yet by common consent, prospects have never been bleaker for a stable and secure global economic order."

However flawed our system may be, few question its importance. Economic schools of thought shape our farming, our communities, our industry. As such they are the guiding force by which most of today's six billion people find themselves populating earth. The Cold War, which brought humanity to the brink of annihilation, was a dispute over economic theory. As economist John Maynard Keynes once remarked, "The ideas of economists and political philosophers, both when they are right and when they are wrong, are more powerful than is commonly understood. Indeed the world is ruled by little else. Practical men who believe themselves to be quite exempt from any intellectual influences are usually the slaves of some defunct economist."

To most of us economics seems arcane. We are if not blissfully then at least mostly unaware of its deeper workings. While words like "atom," "molecule," and "chromosome" get tossed in a mental bin titled "too small to see," the word "economics" typically ends up in one labeled "too big to comprehend." Still, the truly big ideas in life are generally quite simple, and the Western economic scheme now spreading across the globe rests on a few basic notions: that if someone wants something it must have value; that the tension between what people want and its availability is a good gauge of its value; and that free markets do the best job of fixing value because consumers act knowledgeably and in logical ways.

Once we accept that, all we have to do is leave things alone and let the "invisible hand" of the market sort them out. Capital investments will be allocated wisely and the market will find its way to a state of equilibrium. In the end local and global will mesh effortlessly, and we'll all be as happy as snails eating calcium on the White Cliffs of Dover. Or so the theory goes.

Letting individual demand guide free markets seems in tune with nature, and in many ways it is. The great economist Alfred Marshall famously remarked that the mecca of economics is biology, and in general the classic laissez-faire approach concedes that nature rules. As noted, classical economics inspired Charles Darwin. Writing in the late eighteenth century, Adam Smith, in his *Wealth of Nations*, argued that individual action, competition, and decentralized markets can bring collective benefit. Shortly after, Thomas Malthus, in *An Essay on the Principle of Population*, described how populations grow exponentially but food supplies only arithmetically—which showed how growth and the limits on growth worked in constant opposition. Darwin saw in Malthus the essential device of natural selection, and drew on Smith's idea that competition between individuals can yield mutual gain.

That classic bottom-up emphasis on individual demand launched an industrial revolution and stoked the colonial expansion of the West. Then, in the mid-nineteenth century, an opposing view—that labor, not capital, is the essence of value, and that economies should be steered from the top down by government—arose with Karl Marx and Friedrich Engels. In the 1917 birth of the Soviet state, that idea found an application that would shape human affairs for much of the twentieth century.

Economic theory drives modern human history. Using concepts from Smith and others, early capitalists threw off the harness of an older system based on farming and the landed gentry. Then the brutal free market of the colonial era reached its own end point with the Great Depression and the two world wars that roughly bracketed it. Under guidance from

Keynes and his University of Cambridge colleagues, and with the rising influence of socialism, the classical model was then tweaked to accept limited government intervention as a way of stimulating and fine-tuning economies. That view gained support through the middle of the century, culminating, in America, with the Great Society programs begun in the late 1960s and guided by theorists from MIT and Harvard. The energy price shocks of the 1970s brought widespread economic malaise, accompanied by sharpened social polarities from the expanding Sino-Soviet threat. In response there was an institutional lurch in the West back to classic fundamentals, as called for by an academic movement developed in Austria and driven by Chicago. This neoclassical school—with its calls for reducing government and deregulating business—sparked the economic expansion of the 1980s and oversaw the end of the Soviet Union. As commentator George Will later remarked, "The Cold War is over and the University of Chicago won."

Truth or Consequences

When the wall separating East and West Berlin came down in 1989, it was a breakwater event. In addition to freeing millions from political oppression, it signaled collapse for the most powerful theory opposed to free market capitalism. Within a decade a new term would enter the popular lexicon: "globalization."

The Western global plan employs a daunting array of intellectual firepower and seems a major leap toward the future—with trillions of dollars in digital cash each day now washing through a global web of computers, fiber-optic links, and the hundreds of communications satellites suddenly orbiting earth. But at heart it remains the expression of an economic theory from the mid-eighteenth century. That theory looks to nature but is grounded in the even older view that nature itself is a big machine, which implies that linear equations and reducing things to their parts can tell us how everything works.

The formulas of that time were historic breakthroughs and remain true within limited contexts. Since then, however, we've learned more about how nature works. For instance, while in one sense energy does have linear qualities—that is, it flows only from the sun and is always thinning out from a concentrated state into random dissolution—that same energy also drives matter in recirculating loops that have no beginnings or ends, as feedback at every level links them into intercon-necting webs. This is where classical, linear, 1+2=3 logic falls short. For it fails to capture the larger reality that every action in a biological equa-tion gives rise to not just one but numerous other reactions, and that each of those in turn connects to many more, which then reach back to affect the first.

And unlike machines, as solar energy stirs matter into new biologi-cal forms, the living things that arise are a great deal more than the sum of their parts. We understand now that complex and dynamic new qual-ities emerge as atoms join to form molecules, which then connect to form cells, which in turn combine into new and diverse organisms that themselves link up in the interactive webs and cycles of ecology.

Using solar energy to stir matter into new form is the basic economic act. Natural flows of energy and matter underlie every economy, and we're tied to them no less than are algae, snails, and all other life forms. There is one big difference, though, and therein lies a problem. In our economy we let money represent the natural feedback from energy and material flows. Natural feedback rigorously connects other life forms to real limits in those flows, but money links first to economic theory. To the extent that theory misrepresents the workings of nature, it distorts our basic link to reality.

So it is with classical economics. As a result, the expansion of that system to worldwide scale has brought unforeseen consequences.

Living Large

If the heart of the problem is simple, its ramifications are not. The mod-ern global economy began just after World War II. It was then that the Bretton Woods agreement among the industrial powers led to formation of the World Bank, with its mission to end poverty; of the International Monetary Fund (IMF), which at first just helped sustain the then-prevailing fixed exchange rates; and of the General Agreement on Tariffs and Trade (GATT), providing a framework of international law. The global economy that existed prior to all this was reformed and powerfully enhanced by the Bretton Woods system. But trade remained limited by differing national approaches to tariffs and by the differing la-bor, environmental, and other business regulations then allowed.

In the modern era that large and unwieldy trading system has been modified through a series of large and unwieldy global meetings called "rounds," each of which goes on for years. From the Tokyo Round, beginning in 1973, came the call for fast-track approval of international trade agreements—giving governments no more than a pass or fail say in their confirmation. During the 1986 Uruguay Round, today's approach to globalization began to take form when a new function was added to the IMF. It effectively gained the power to impose free market structures on the internal laws of countries seeking aid. Then, in 1994, GATT was subsumed by the newly created World Trade Organization (WTO), with the authority to penalize any member nations—even the richest—whose trade laws impede the free flow of goods, services, and cash across international borders. As one exuberant CEO proclaimed at the time, globalization now meant "a worldwide business environment that's unfettered by government interference."

If all this sounds like a neoclassical pipe dream, the benefits have been nonetheless real. The global infant mortality rate has been cut nearly in half, and billions of people now live longer, eat better, and have more income. In 1950, South Korea and Singapore were just two among many poor Asian nations, and the world's total exports stood at $380 billion (in 2000 dollars). Now that amount is traded every three weeks. South Korea's per capita income today is twenty times India's. Singapore's is above that of some Western nations, and incomes in India and China are rising dramatically.

While global trade advocates wave their flag high, they're fighting rearguard actions, too. NGOs—nongovernmental organizations representing social concerns—are among globalization's harshest critics. They point out that billions of dollars in World Bank loans have helped machine age forms of development gain global reach, expanding the environmental problems that go with them. Another objection being raised concerns the IMF's "structural-adjustment" program, which imposes free trade structures on the laws of countries seeking aid. That program makes it easier for global firms to move polluting industries into the developing world, with the IMF and WTO suppressing health, environmental, and labor protections by asserting that they hamper open markets. Exporting free trade laws and shop-till-you-drop culture to poor nations is also said to cause major cultural disruptions there. Meanwhile, labor groups in the industrialized North grew restive. In just over two decades, 20 percent of U.S. manufacturing jobs migrated overseas. White-collar jobs are now being outsourced, too. And average income is in decline.

The growing objections first came to a head in a week of tumultuous street protests at the WTO's 1999 meeting in Seattle. Those raucous demonstrations brought concerns about globalization to the world's attention while marrying two longtime opponents: labor and environmentalists. News reports focused on the crowds of chanting hard hats, idealistic students, cavorting pagans, men wearing sea turtle costumes, and women with foam rubber trees on their heads. But behind all that lay a larger if less colorful story.

Writing in a 1998 op-ed piece for *The Wall Street Journal*, former Republican secretary of state George Shultz, former Republican Treasury secretary William Simon, and Walter Wriston, past chairman of one of the world's largest banks, called on Congress to stop funding the IMF. Alluding to its role in the disastrous Asian financial meltdown of the late 1990s (to be followed shortly by a similar collapse in Latin America), they accused the IMF of being "ineffective, unnecessary, and obsolete" because it encouraged unsound investments and management. During the Asian crisis Joseph Stiglitz, then chief economist for the World Bank and now a Nobel laureate, resigned, throwing bricks. He was "appalled," he said, at how the IMF and World Bank handled it, even made things worse. Complaining about the mechanistic, cookie-cutter approach used in the structural-adjustment plans imposed on borrower nations, he described how those plans were typically put together in just a few weeks, sometimes even days, and often with little knowledge of the countries being restructured.

In U.S. congressional hearings at the time—concerned with funding for these agencies—a variety of witnesses denounced the IMF. Structural adjustments, it was said, not only brought hardship, in the form of higher taxes and reduced health and education budgets, but also added insult to injury by failing to bring growth. In the words of Njoki Njoroge Njehu, an NGO head testifying for Kenya:

> I'm not an economist. But in the economics courses I took, I did grasp one idea—the law of supply and demand. My experience with structural adjustment, however, makes me wonder if the IMF and World Bank really understand it. One of the central, unchanging strategies of [those] programs is an orientation to export production. If we can sell goods to richer countries, we can earn hard currency to make debt payments, buy foreign goods, and perhaps develop our own economies. So our young people work unskilled jobs for low wages in assembly factories and our

best land is used not to grow food for ourselves but cash crops like cotton, coffee, tobacco, and flowers. We end up buying food that we used to grow. But when we go to sell our goods on the world market, we find that for commodity after commodity, prices are at all-time lows. It doesn't take much research or thought to discover that with most of the countries of Africa, Latin America, and Asia taking IMF advice, everyone is producing the same goods. So the market is glutted and the price drops. It shouldn't be a surprise, and yet so many governments the IMF is advising have ended up having to take loans to provide food for people who used to grow their own. Economics does indeed seem an odd science sometimes.

Illinois House Republican Judy Biggert appeared before the same committee. While she conceded that the structural-adjustment program—referred to officially as ESAF—did reduce inflation and so help stabilize income, its effect on gross domestic product was another story. For the record, she stated that in an IMF internal review, "it was reported that annual real per capita GDP growth rate averaged zero percent for all ESAF countries whereas non-ESAF countries experienced a one percent real per capita GDP growth rate." She then went on to point out that not only did the economies of ESAF countries fail to grow but in the decade from 1986 to 1996, the external debts they owed had doubled.

When Republican policy makers, international bankers, Nobel Prize–winning economists, labor leaders, NGO reformers, and people dressed up to look like sea turtles all find themselves on common ground, things have gotten out of hand.

While those factions would argue over details, the core problem remains that in our global economic system, crucial feedbacks are being distorted or are missing altogether. First, the World Bank, IMF, and WTO give global reach to a machine age economic theory, one whose pricing feedbacks misrepresent natural flows of energy and material. Second, a one-size-fits-all approach to structural adjustment ignores feedback from the many different kinds of parts in our macroeconomic whole, even as it stalls or distorts the local inputs that should steer regional economies. Finally, the big global trade agencies themselves lack another crucial kind of feedback. Being among the world's most powerful agencies, they are also among its least democratic. A main lightning rod for protest is the secretive way their policies are formed. The president of the World Bank is simply appointed by the U.S., which also negotiates behind closed doors with Japan and Europe over who will direct the IMF. Those directors and their boards then answer to few others in their cloaked deliberations. Meanwhile, a small Western industrial nation like the Netherlands has more votes in the IMF than either India or China. The WTO is more democratic in design but conducts its main business—overruling tariffs and quotas as well as health, labor, and environmental laws—in secret tribunals held in Geneva.

That lack of transparency and feedback, critics contend, overlays the incompetence of bureaucracy with the arrogance of autocracy. Stiglitz, who as World Bank vice president was in a good position to know, said, "I was dismayed at how out-of-date—and how out-of-tune with reality—the models Washington economists employed were." In the Asian crises, for example, he notes that microphenomena like bankruptcy were at the center of the problem, yet the macroeconomic models used to analyze those crises "took no account of bankruptcy." At the end of a long and detailed analysis, the conclusion Stiglitz draws is that "bad economics was only a symptom of the real problem: secrecy. Smart people are more likely to do stupid things when they close themselves off from outside criticism and advice."

Although the global trade big three—the World Bank, the IMF, and the WTO—act in the name of free markets, their emphasis on secrecy, their lack of democratic input, their centralized power structure, and their massive effort to impose a single macroeconomic theory from the top down all echo another great global enterprise. As one Washington policy wonk put it, "There hasn't been a group this convinced they were right since the Bolsheviks."

To point this out is not to argue against the great promise of a global human economy. If nature can link seafaring algae, plate tectonics, and cliff-dwelling snails in a single interactive global system, we can surely create one that links the supplies and demands of people from different cultures. Unfortunately, the macroeconomic system we're now using doesn't do that. It's a machine age, highly standardized approach that doesn't mesh well with variable inputs, whose administration lacks democratic feedback, and which misstates the even more basic feedback from energy and material flows in nature. These problems don't rule out the rise of a more democratic form of globalization. They do suggest that the big global trade agencies could, as one writer notes, "stand a little structural adjustment of their own."

Money Talks

Among the ranks of neoclassical partisans, keeping markets free from government interference is a linchpin for success. Free markets, they assert, work best with free and open competition. To the extent that those partisans are right, their success has been limited. The fact is that today's global system is only free from influence by the governments of poor countries. The poor nations answer to the big industrial nations—Canada, France, Germany, Italy, Japan, the U.K., the U.S.—which largely steer the world economy.

These powerful governments are democracies, but the rapid rise of globalization has put new emphasis on another concern: If the global trading system is staffed and guided largely by a handful of industrial nations, to what degree do those nations answer to undemocratic powers? While it's hard to know what goes on behind closed doors, some practices in the new global trading system do raise questions about the influence of multinational corporations. For instance, the privatization of companies is mandated for all borrower nations during IMF restructuring. This has resulted in large numbers of companies in borrower nations being taken over by multinational firms. That may be no problem in theory, but in practice it has brought with it some tricky accounting. In a device called "transfer pricing," a multinational parent corporation sells materials and services to its new subsidiaries at inflated prices. This reduces the profits those subsidiaries report in their host countries, and with that the taxes they pay there as well. In this context it's worth noting that roughly a third of all world trade occurs among the internal parts of individual multinationals, either between subsidiaries or with the head office.

More important is the little-noted shift in 1991—from GNP (gross national product) to GDP (gross domestic product)—that altered how global prosperity is tracked. For most of us, the switching of those letters meant little, if it registered at all. In reality it signaled a change with global consequences. Under the old GNP system, any earnings by the subsidiary of a multinational were reported in the country where its parent firm is based. After all, that's where the money ends up. Under the new GDP approach, those profits are now reported as an economic gain for the country where a subsidiary is located—*even though the actual money still flows back to the parent.* This bit of accounting smoke and mirrors has, as one report puts it, "turned many struggling nations into statistical boomtowns" as rises in the developing world's GDP numbers support the call for more globalization even while, in many cases, they conceal the fact that multinationals are raiding its resources.

Accounting sleight of hand is hardly confined to the international stage. Due to a recent wave of tricky-accounting scandals at home, Americans now view business leaders with the same doubts they show politicians. Those scandals were the tipping point in the long and hard-fought battle over campaign finance reform. U.S. legislation has now sought to address the $500 million in soft-money campaign contributions each year, which came mostly from corporations and were seen as corrupting electoral feedback loops. But while those campaign dollars do purchase access, by opening the doors of Congress, that amount is small beer compared with the $3 billion spent annually to finance the lobbyists who walk through those doors.

In another dubious move by global firms, they have repeatedly pressed governments around the world to ratify the Multilateral Agreement on Investment. It would require developing countries to repay multinational corporations should any new labor, health, or environmental laws result in a loss of their anticipated income (not actual income but money they only expect to make, as projected on paper). That raises a fundamental question: Are these corporations just big players in a free market, adapting to changing demand, or are they entrenched bureaucracies pushing from the top down to compel profits?

In light of all this, critics view the insistent corporate call for "free" global markets as little more than a public relations strategy meant to further quite a different end—as they knock down traditional border protections in developing nations, reach in to take control of businesses there, use cheap labor to produce goods for export without constraint by unions or environmental laws, avoid taxes through bookkeeping tricks that mask true profits, then siphon whatever profits they do declare back to the North while more accounting finesse presents them as prosperity for the very countries being plundered.

By 2003, the protesters in the streets at world economic summits were being joined by protests from member nations. Major unrest had already occurred following the Pacific Rim and Latin American catastrophes of the late nineties. Countries like China, Malaysia, New Zealand, Brazil, and Argentina were opting out of IMF policy prescriptions. Many, especially in Asia, felt their faith in the process had been betrayed as an IMF-forced devaluation of their assets was followed by a wave of "vulture capitalists" swooping in to buy up those assets at bargain-basement rates. The next wave of protests grew from the heavily biased mandates of the Uruguay Round. According to Stiglitz, this "forced developing countries to open up their markets to the products of the developed countries, while leaving in place protections and subsidies for many of the goods produced by the developed world." That policy was, he says, "so unbalanced that sub-Saharan Africa, the poorest region of the world, actually ended up worse off." At the world trade talks in Cancún, Mexico, delegates from twenty-one nations in Africa, Asia, and Latin America walked out in protest, mainly over the large agricultural subsidies being paid to farmers in rich countries.

Agriculture had by then also become an issue between the U.S., which led the push for genetically modified crops, and the European Union. Other countries also found themselves being pressured by free trade laws to accept GM crops they didn't want. Says the writer, philosopher, and historian John Ralston Saul:

> This . . . approach toward agriculture as an industry rather than as a food source—toward the implications of everything from fertilizers, herbicides, and insecticides to genetics, hormones, antibiotics, labeling, and sourcing—became the flash point for a far broader concern among citizens. This was the context in which a growing percentage of people judged the handling of key issues as different as mad cow disease, the availability of pharmaceuticals in the developing world, and global warming. They were beginning to feel that what was presented as an argument of Globalism versus protectionism was often just a confused opposition of personal choice and abstract corporate interests. So Globalism, put forward as a metaphor for choice, was organizing itself around not consumers but corporate structures, structures that sought profits by limiting personal choice.

The widespread standardization of today's American-style, which is to say corporate, globalization accelerates trade and the international flow of capital. But it's a brilliant answer to the wrong question. The real question is not how to increase profits at any cost. Rather, it is how can separate and distinctly different economies benefit without abandoning their own characters and priorities—just as infinitely diverse organisms flourish within global ecology. Journalist Thomas Friedman has seen firsthand the benefits of global trade for many small countries and is an ardent supporter. Still, he warned against the loss of cultural identity in his book *The Lexus and the Olive Tree*. Paraphrasing a colleague, he wrote that the angry opponents of American globalization see it as an uninvited guest:

> You try to shut the door and it comes in through the window. You try to shut the window and it comes in on the cable. You cut the cable, and it comes in on the Internet over the phone line. When you cut the phone line, it comes in over the satellite. When you throw away the cell phone, it's out there on the billboard. When you take down the billboard, it comes in through the workplace and the factory floor. And it's not only in the room with you, this Americanization-globalization. You eat it. It gets inside you. And when it comes in, it often blows open a huge gap between fathers and sons, mothers and daughters, grandparents and grandchildren. It creates a situation where one generation sees the world radically different from their parents, and it's all America's fault. The constant theme, for instance, of the Saudi millionaire terrorist Osama Bin Laden is that America has to get out of . . . the Islamic world at large, because its way of life is "defiling the Islamic home."

Friedman goes on to say, "You cannot build an emerging society—which is so essential for dealing with the globalization system—if you are simultaneously destroying the cultural foundations that cement your society and give it the self-confidence and cohesion to interact properly with the world."

Billions of people clearly have benefited from the new global economy. It's also clear that many of the poorest have not. At a 2002 meeting in Monterrey, Mexico, leaders from fifty-eight nations met to address the fact that as rich nations grow richer, nearly half of the world's people still live on less than two dollars a day. Even within the United States, arguably the new world economy's top beneficiary, there is a widening income gap. Analysis of Congressional Budget Office data shows that in the period from 1979 to 2000, average yearly pretax income for the bottom 40 percent of Americans rose 13 percent, from $18,695 to $21,118 (adjusted for inflation). Meanwhile the top 1 percent saw their incomes more than triple during that period, from $286,300 to $862,700. By 2003, the top tenth of 1 percent had more income than fully a third of the poorest Americans. Just before the Berlin Wall came down in 1989, average annual income for each of the ten highest-paid CEOs in America was $19 million. By 2000 it had reached $154 million and it continues to rise.

Money talks. Throughout the global boom of the 1990s, while the world economy grew by 2 or 3 percent annually, the big multinational firms were expanding each year by 8 to 10 percent. As a result, more than half of the world's one hundred largest economies today aren't countries at all, they're corporations. That change stokes the fear that these huge companies are working behind the scenes to become a kind of global shadow government. Many now believe that "corporatism" has replaced communism as the great new global threat to democracy. Lack of transparency and of rigorous democratic feedbacks at the IMF, the WTO, and the World Bank only enhances that concern. These early decades show that globalization can bring real benefits. They also show that vast new wealth has not changed the historical tendency of power to gather in a few hands, or the desire of those who hold it to cloak themselves in secrecy.

Can reformers bring glasnost to the world trade triumvirate? There has been progress. NGOs now sit in on some meetings. The bipartisan Meltzer Commission in Congress called for a shrinking of the IMF. The World Bank today mandates environmental considerations and devotes much less of its funding to huge dams, oil pipelines, and other big infrastructure projects. It has begun to focus instead on other aspects of human welfare, like eliminating malaria, and to look for ways to channel aid directly into villages, thereby avoiding the misdirection of funds that can occur at the hands of authoritarian governments. The growth of micro lending as an aid tool now puts small but crucial loans in the hands of local entrepreneurs. In general, more attention is being paid to cultural differences among nations.

But while reformers hammer at the big agencies, the essential problem remains. Even if they become more democratic, the economic system they promote is still out of touch with reality. That situation stems from what might be called our false economy. By distorting the feedback from natural flows of energy and materials, our machine age system achieves the curious end of divorcing us from the ultimate foundation for all economics—the natural flows of energy and matter. Fixing that is no small task.

Many critics see a good start in revising our system of national accounts. Today's global economy is in large part an extension of those GNP—now GDP—statistics, which the U.S. and other industrial economies have employed for half a century. In that time, the periodic release of GDP numbers has acquired the stature of a report card for public well-being. When those indicators dip, news reports turn somber. Should the numbers fall too far for too long we are said to be in recession as people worry about their jobs, the stock market tumbles, and politicians dive for cover. Central banks, which create our money in the first place, use them to help guide how much money to create. But while governments and the media treat GDP numbers as essential news, those numbers are better seen as the most obvious example of the problem—of how the money created by our central banks, and which we work so hard to earn, is out of touch with the real world.

The False Economy

Two guys sit in a bar, solving the world's problems. One of them turns to his friend and says, "The way I see it, there are always going to be trade-offs. If we want to keep our high standard of living, we'll just have to settle for a lower quality of life."

During the past three decades, while economic indicators have risen, it's become clear that we have traded something away in exchange for the abundant food supply and deluge of consumer products the industrial world now takes for granted. As we used energy from the sun (stored in fossil fuel) to draw more and more matter from the earth to make those new goods, we've progressively had less of other things our parents took for granted: freshwater, fresh air, deep topsoil, plentiful fuel and minerals, intact communities, open land, teeming wildlife. Maintaining a high GDP has also come for many at the cost of constant stress and longer work hours, and with that less time for family and leisure. Is it possible to have more money and less wealth?

That's not just possible, it has already happened. In their 1989 book, *For the Common Good*, former World Bank economist Herman Daly and theologian John Cobb, Jr., showed that the real quality of life in industrial nations peaked during the mid-seventies and has been declining ever since. That decline is not reflected in GDP indicators, because of the inaccurate way they define our standard of living. Several years later an insightful critique of the GDP was offered by three prominent analysts—economist Clifford Cobb, political philosopher Ted Halstead, and attorney Jonathan Rowe—from the economic reform group Redefining Progress. (Halstead has since gone on to form the influential New America Foundation, a "new centrist" think tank.) In their article they described GDP as follows:

> The GDP is simply a gross measure of market activity, of money changing hands. It makes no distinction whatsoever between the desirable and the undesirable, or costs and gain. On top of that it looks only at the portion of reality that economists choose to acknowledge—the part involved in monetary transactions. As a result the GDP not only masks the breakdown of the social structure and the natural habitat on which the economy—and life itself—ultimately depend; worse, it actually portrays such breakdown as economic gain.

Classical economic theory first viewed people as producers—farmers, factory workers, business executives—and *production* as the keystone of value. As the industrial revolution expanded from manufacturing into finance and trade, that view was modified to include services—the use of lawyers, for instance. As a result, anything people would pay for became endowed with official value. With that shift—from an emphasis on production to an emphasis on *utility*—the economic status of people changed, too. We became "consumers."

This view was enshrined in the gross national product system, which was originally an accounting method used in the United States to track industrial throughput. The GNP approach helped end the Depression and win World War II. With that success it became official policy, to be guided by newly minted government bodies like the Council of Economic Advisers. But GNP only tracked industrial activity. It took no notice that the energy and material inputs for all that production are drawn from natural systems, or of the crucial service they provide by absorbing the outputs we call wastes. Social cohesion was also treated as a given. That meant the important work contributed by family members at home, or by volunteers in communities, got no recognition. In short, if people weren't getting paid, their contributions didn't count. Over time, as GNP became GDP and took on the glow of doctrine, a broad political consensus arose that the environment and social cohesion were not as important, not as "valuable."

When it comes to measuring anything like real quality of life, GDP misses on two important fronts. First, the consumer theory of wealth, on which it is based, fails to count those important aspects of well-being. Second, in that theory, whatever people will pay for is viewed as good news. So in addition to overlooking things of value, GDP counts things as fortunate that clearly are not. If rising divorce rates mean families now need two households instead of one, even as they spend billions on legal fees, it's a big plus for GDP. Terrorism causes billions to be spent on security, another gain. And then there is the depletion of resources. When an oil company pumps its reserves from the ground, it deducts a depletion allowance from its taxes, because it's drawing down future reserves. But the GDP counts that depletion as pure growth, just as it did with ocean cod stocks as they were overfished to the brink of extinction. Money for waging war to protect foreign oil sources brings double-digit advances for the defense sector. Environmental waste means new billions spent on cleanups, and on the medical bills brought about by pollution. Do both parents have to work in order to cover the bills? Still more good news on the economic front: now they pay for services that once were provided at home—meals, child rearing, care for the elderly. As Cobb and his coauthors note, "It is as if a business kept a balance sheet by merely adding up all the 'transactions,' without distinguishing between income and expenses, or between assets and liabilities."

Most people find it hard to believe our system could contain such a howler. Their reluctance only helps perpetuate the problem. Meanwhile, our false economy pits us against many of our own best interests. It fosters a sense that unpaid services at home and volunteer work in communities have comparatively little value. It paints efforts to conserve energy, resources, and the health of natural systems—the foundation for all economies—as being uneconomic. Is it any wonder, ask Cobb and his coauthors, that these are the areas now in decline? "Politicians can no longer get away with glib assurances that the nation can grow its way out of family breakdown and environmental decay, inequity and debt," they conclude, "when in many cases the nation has been growing its way into them."

As the old Chinese proverb has it, "Even good news is bad news when it's false."

Long Green

The gold standard went out with mechanical cash registers. In the worldwide computer networks that make globalization possible, money is now largely a software artifact, akin to the Web-based avatars that circulate through virtual worlds. In that digital flux, national currency values are constantly changing, the shifts often turning on little more than belief. As one financier has described it, "Today the main currencies float and crush together like continental plates." This has prompted concern about the wild currency-value swings that occur, and the damaging speculation that often accompanies and even abets them. But the new digital, computer-based economy can also be seen as part of a positive transformation. It opens the way to a more realistic basis for value—a transition of human economics from the gold standard to the green standard.

Robert Costanza sits at a computer in the cluttered office where he works to derive economic principles from the study of natural systems. A former colleague of Herman Daly's at the University of Maryland, Costanza is one of a new breed of scientists with training in both ecology and economics. The International Society for Ecological Economics, which he helped to found, has fifteen hundred members in more than fifty countries.

To study ecology, Costanza points out, is to study complex systems. As he describes them, these are made up of strong—usually nonlinear—relations between the parts, along with intricate feedback loops that make it hard to tell cause from effect. Then there are time and space lags as well as other dynamic factors. So the old scientific method of just adding up small-scale behaviors to get large-scale results doesn't work. What Costanza finds interesting, he says, is that ecological dynamics drive economic systems, too. In fact the links between ecosystems and economic systems are so intimate, and so numerous, that treating them as separate is what he calls "a poor choice of boundary."

Even so, Costanza admits that plotting those links can be "devilishly complex." Powering up a computer, he clicks to a Web site that he describes as an overview of the Florida Everglades. No aerial photos of marshes and glades appear. Instead, brilliant colors cascade across the screen in intricate oil-on-water patterns. He explains that they map the effect of phosphorus runoff from surrounding sugar plantations as it moves into the system. The flowing colors and patterns show the nutrient working its way through Everglades food chains, from burgeoning macrophyte populations to the growing colonies of cattails now displacing saw grass marsh. As Costanza's living map tracks the progress of those changes, it also charts the ways they alter water flow.

More clicks call up a related site for the Patuxent River basin, which bisects Washington, D.C., and Baltimore before connecting to the Chesapeake Bay. As more colors and patterns pulse across the screen, Costanza says, "In this case we're not doing urban and agricultural impacts *on* a natural system, we're saying all of this *is* the system. So we want to understand it in a more integrated way . . . to include the dynamics of both the economic and ecological components."

Another big Costanza project has estimated the dollar value of services provided by nature worldwide. What would it cost to replace the work that honeybees do in pollinating plants, for instance, or for that matter the oxygen-generating work of the plants? How about the creation of new topsoil and freshwater? Or the absorption of wastes? Costanza and a dozen colleagues took the first comprehensive look at such questions in a paper published by the journal *Nature* in the spring of 1997. Reviewing contributions by seventeen biomes ranging from oceans to forests to wetlands, they estimated the value of nature's overall services at somewhere between $16 trillion and $54 trillion per year (by comparison, the World Bank estimated total global GDP at the time at about $23 trillion yearly). While he is the first to admit that these numbers are provisional, Costanza also feels they are an important step in reestablishing this "natural capital" to its rightful place as the basis for human economics.

If Costanza's numbers seem surprising, it's only because an awareness of ecology and how it works is so rare. Says Gretchen Daily of the Center for Conservation Biology at Stanford University:

> If asked to identify all that goes into making a fine cake, a baker would probably identify its ingredients, and the skill required to transform them . . .
> She might also describe the oven, pan, and kitchen gadgets needed. If pressed further, she might point out the need for capital infrastructure and human services to process, store, and transport the ingredients. However, the chances of the baker touching directly upon the importance of the natural renewal of soil fertility, the pollination of crops, natural pest control, the role of biodiversity in maintaining crop productivity—or, indeed,

upon any ecosystem service involved—are extremely remote. Ecosystem services are absolutely essential to civilization, but modern life obscures their existence.

Costanza and his colleagues stand at a historic crossroads. *Economic ecologists* are developing monetary values for nature. Meanwhile, from the other side of the equation, *ecological economists* work to develop pricing systems that incorporate those numbers.

The differences revealed by such full-cost accounting can be striking. One study found that the real cost of a pack of cigarettes to the U.S. economy is roughly twice its shelf price when lost productivity, health care costs, and the nearly half a million premature deaths that cigarette smoking causes each year are factored in. In another case, shortly after the first Persian Gulf War, the World Resources Institute found that if the war's cost were included in the price of gasoline, U.S. consumers would have paid something like four times what they were then spending at the pump. The practice of externalizing such real costs is pervasive, and inevitable in an economic system that fails to count them in its profit-and-loss statements. A German report found that in the two decades before the Berlin Wall came down, while West German GNP rose by 50 percent, externalized costs for such things as hazardous waste cleanup and erosion control grew by more than 300 percent. Paul Hawken and William McDonough describe the effect of such artificial efficiencies:

> Simply stated, the present market is giving us the wrong information. It tells us that flying across the country on a discount ticket is cheap when it is not. It tells us that our food is inexpensive when its method of production [is costly and unsustainable]. Whenever an organism gets the wrong information, it's a form of toxicity. In fact, that's how pesticides work. An herbicide is a hormone that kills by telling the plant to grow faster than its capacity to absorb nutrients. It literally grows itself to death. Sound familiar?

Misguided subsidies and tax policies only heighten the problem. According to economist David Pearce, $750 billion is spent each year by governments around the world to subsidize destructive or unsustainable business practices. Those subsidies encourage water use where water tables are falling. They expand the world's fishing fleets while catches decline. They accelerate mining of irreplaceable minerals and the clear-cutting of forests. Fossil fuel use gets billions in subsidies even as the atmosphere saturates with CO_2 and global temperatures rise.

Where does all that money come from? In the U.S. and Europe, the lion's share of it comes from income tax. Of the more than $1.5 trillion in federal taxes collected each year by the U.S. government, 80 percent comes from the tax on personal incomes. That's another policy that new biologists question. Some point out that an income tax drives up the salary levels that business has to pay. Compounding the problem, tax revenue then flows into subsidies that make energy and raw materials available for less than they really cost. The awkward child of that union is a business "productivity" revolution based on machines that use scarce or declining resources, purchased at below actual cost, to displace people from their jobs because the income tax add-on makes labor too expensive.

With our expanding populations and global industries, the many weaknesses of the machine metaphor as a guide for economic policy have become a lot harder to ignore. Environmentalists often focus blame on companies. While there are problematic companies, and curbing their abuses is essential, that's not where the problem begins. Just like everyone else—from households to national governments to global agencies—they answer to the economic system by which we all earn our daily bread.

For two centuries now we've been living like someone who spends $30 apiece to make counterfeit $20 bills. No matter how cleverly we make them, there's not much future there. If the goal of economics is to ensure human well-being both now and in the future, we need a more realistic model.

The Green Standard

All capital, says Robert Costanza, is "a stock that yields a flow of valuable goods or services." In that sense natural capital could be a "stock or population of trees or fish" that supplies an "annual yield of new trees or fish." The stock that yields those flows is capital. The flows themselves are income. So are the many services nature provides, such as waste recycling and erosion control. Since all those forms of natural income are generated by natural capital, Costanza compares it to the principal holdings in an investment portfolio—such as stocks, bonds, or some other security. Extending the metaphor, he compares natural income to the interest given off by that principal.

His larger point is that real conservatives never draw on principal to pay for daily needs. They spend only the income (the interest, or yield) generated by that principal. Costanza and Daly are just a few among the rising chorus of voices now arguing that nature's endowment, built up over nearly four billion years, is a form of principal. In their view that principal, that asset base, should be protected by the rules that govern financially conservative investment practice. How many fish can we take from the sea, they ask, without depleting principal stocks? How many trees can we log without destroying the systems that generate not only new trees but wildlife, oxygen, and much of our freshwater? And what of the natural capital lost when we squander energy resources and other materials, a cost now being externalized from their market prices?

Past efforts to address those problems through government, while effective at one level, have typically involved imposing bureaucratic rules on business from the top down. Those "command-and-control" regulations are expensive and inefficient, hamper innovation, and create resentment. But so long as industry and its allies in government could offer no other principle to use in steering policy—beyond a call for profit and free markets—the political process was little more than a tangle of competing special interests.

There's no question that free markets do the best job of setting prices, but only if they're realistic about the manufacturing costs that determine those prices. For us, just as for the rest of nature, accurate feedback is the key. Every day billions of people around the world make buying decisions based on price. Those decisions add up to the larger demands our system puts on nature. If we want a future in which our prosperity continues and even expands around the globe, and if we want business to better serve that goal, we have to feed accurate data into the process. An economy is an information system. All information systems work by the same rule: garbage in, garbage out.

In their book, *Natural Capitalism*, Paul Hawken, Amory Lovins, and Hunter Lovins describe how a feedback system with goals should function. First it "measures the difference between what is and what should be." Then it sends an error signal that, when fed back, "tells the system how to change in order to get better." Systems without good feedback, they say, are "by definition, stupid." But with it those systems get smart in a hurry. By way of illustration the authors ask, "How clean a car would you buy if its exhaust pipe, instead of being aimed at pedestrians, fed directly into the passenger compartment?"

The effort to build a smarter feedback system includes private sector initiatives like the green investment funds now springing up. On the policy side, the rising "green standard" is guiding work on a new generation of indicators aimed at replacing our flawed GDP. Another policy change, one being tried in small ways in Europe, is the "green tax shift" pioneered by eco-economist Ernst von Weizsäcker. By charging companies for costs that are now being externalized—like resource depletion—green taxes bring business ledgers back to reality. The plan is called a "shift" because the green tax add-ons are offset by payroll tax reductions. This creates jobs because a company can then lower the salaries it pays to workers without affecting the amount they actually get to take home. "That," says von Weizsäcker, "is good for employment and good for the environment. It seems they are harvesting a double dividend."

Many of today's problems stem from a dilemma called "the tragedy of the commons" (meaning common assets like fresh air, freshwater, wild fish stocks, and the like). The dilemma is that because there are no clear private interests there to defend, market demands on a common asset don't meet with the kind of cost resistance needed to maintain it. For example, this happens when a popular fish species is brought near to extinction by the uncoordinated acts of many individual fishing operations, also when regional underground aquifers are drained dry by the separate irrigation of thousands of private farms. In a similar vein, since there is no charge for releasing pollutants in the air, industries have long poured CO_2 into the sky. The quandary is that in each case, the free market is responding to the needs of private interests without reflecting the actual cost of exhausting a community asset.

The fact that community members benefit, too, with income from the jobs created, is the usual defense for that. But as the number of industries has grown, along with the impact of their waste streams and resource demands, things have become paradoxical—giving rise to the joke that to have a higher standard of living we should accept a lower quality of life. More income won't truly mean more wealth until money does a better job of representing the real world.

Green taxes are just one way of dealing with that. Another is the "cap-and-trade" system now gaining favor. That approach auctions pollution permits to industry; they can then be sold or traded on the open market. This averages the amounts of pollution released by participating companies (that is, the number of permits, combined with the amount of pollution that each permit allows, adds up to a larger "cap"—a regional, national, or international level of emissions considered acceptable). At the same time it allows each company some leeway in deciding how to deal with the problem. Cap-and-trade is a central element of the 1997 international Kyoto accords aimed at reducing global emissions of CO_2 and other pollutants into the sky.

Peter Barnes, a prominent business activist prone to market-based solutions, applauds the rise of cap-and-trade to the world stage. But he points out what he feels is an oversight in how the system is designed. His question is: If use of the sky becomes a profit center, and the sky is an asset for everyone, why shouldn't everyone get a share? In his book *Who Owns the Sky?* Barnes describes how such a setup might work by pointing to a system that has been in place since the 1970s in Alaska. Each year an equal share of Alaska's oil revenue flows directly into the hands of every man, woman, and child in the state. Those annual dividend checks have at times approached $2,000 apiece—money that then gets put away for school or placed in other investments, or flows into the state economy in a yearly surge of buying.

Barnes foresees benefits like those being distributed to much larger populations. In his view, cap-and-trade systems could manage a variety of common assets, including the atmosphere, aquifers, the airwaves used by broadcasters, even noise pollution and billboards. A percentage of the revenue from permit sales would then flow to everyone, with all shares being equal and nontransferable. Over time, says Barnes:

> all babies would become trust fund babies. When they enter adulthood, their parents would have small nest eggs to give them. No longer will poverty be passed from one generation to the next. [All players] of the game of capitalism would start out, if not equally endowed, at least with a modest sum of assets behind them.

In 2003, Steven Clemons, of the new-centrist think tank New America Foundation, proposed a system similar to Alaska's for the people of Iraq. He said, "It would go a long way to curbing the cynical belief that Americans want Iraqi oil for themselves, and it would give more Iraqis a stake in the success of their new country. It would be the equivalent of redistributing land to Japanese farmers after World War II, which was the single most important democratizing reform during the American occupation."

Creative Tension

There's a tension between the supporters of green taxes and those who favor cap-and-trade. Peter Barnes doubts that government will get the numbers right in setting green taxes. And he knows how government policies can change with the wink of a political eye. From the other side, green tax shifters doubt the enforceability of cap-and-trade permits. They also criticize that approach as just one more way for industrial economies to continue polluting, by buying permits from poor nations.

Bringing yet another perspective to the debate, Michael Braungart questions the whole effort to put economic values on nature. "If you can destroy a nightingale by paying so much money, then you basically don't accept a right for that species to exist," he says. But by that Braungart doesn't mean to argue for continuing down the path we're on. As things stand today, he points out, the billions in taxpayer dollars spent on cleanups are a huge distortion of the market. "Right now you are privatizing the profit and socializing the risk." Instead, he says, we should extend a company's responsibilities to include the wastes it releases, and with that any impact they have. "We say, if you want to have some profit, please, here is the risk that goes with it. The risk is yours, too." In the end, he believes, the best solution is to "eliminate the concept of waste."

The debate over how to achieve a green standard will be working its way through the media, business, academia, and the political system for years to come. Meanwhile, the fact that thoughtful, well-meaning people can argue over methods says something about the size and complexity of the challenge. It also shows how hard it will be to free ourselves from the intellectual biases of the past century. As Princeton economist Paul Krugman writes, on political difficulties faced by the market-based approach to protecting nature:

> A generation ago, many influential people were simply hostile to markets in general; furthermore, there was a tendency on the part of some groups to regard environmental protection as a moral issue . . . Meanwhile, conservatives have tended to oppose any policy, such as pollution taxes or the

auction of environmental licenses, which might yield revenue, fearing that it would simply be used to expand government.

But now, Krugman adds, ideologues of all stripes seem a bit shaken in their certainties, while the need to act on global environmental issues grows more obvious with each passing month.

The new biology retires many of the vestigial twentieth-century debates by redefining them. For instance, conscience is a valuable motive but by itself can do little as long as our economy misrepresents the stocks and flows of energy and materials in nature. Our vast global economic system now drives the daily purchases of billions of individuals in the wrong direction. In the face of it, appeals to conscience alone are little more than hollering into the wind. Moreover, in the ongoing battles between left and right, or between top-down and bottom-up approaches, finally it's not a question of choosing one or the other. The belief that we can, or even should, stems from misconceptions over how whole systems work.

One of the central lessons of nature is that we can't just pick one side and eliminate the other (idealists take note). As the twenty-first century opens before us, we begin to see how top-down and bottom-up are two faces of the same phenomenon, and that the old notion of communal versus individual (as a clear, either-or choice) is unrealistic too. For instance, nature does link everything into interacting webs of mutual support, but that doesn't make the natural world a communal peaceable kingdom. Far from it. Nor is rampant competition the only rule. Life is a balancing act, shot through with competing tensions. All we can do is tip the balance a little, and for a time, in a necessary tension forever pulsing between chaos and order, figure and ground, competition and cooperation, decentralized and centralized, bottom-up and top-down, micro and macro.

Maintaining that tension is a focus of the feedbacks guiding life, as it uses solar energy to stir matter into ever-more-complex forms. The question for the coming century is whether we can link our culture into those feedbacks, and by doing so drive it to a higher and more vibrant level of organization. In the meantime, as activists and policy makers argue over how to restructure the global economy, entrepreneurs are racing ahead of the pack to form individual companies that take up these ideas.

The New Company

"Show me the chairman of the board of the forest," says Dee Hock, founder and CEO emeritus of Visa International. "Show me the chief financial fish of the pond. Show me [tapping his head] the chief executive neuron of the brain!" Visa is one of the world's most successful bank cards. It's also the world's most successful case study in how to structure a company using nature as a model.

Visa was designed to be what Hock calls "chaordic"—a combination of chaos and order, competition and cooperation, centralization and decentralization that he describes as a "complex, self-organizing, nonlinear, self-governing, adaptive system." That litany of concepts from the new biology sounds like an approach lost in theory. Hock sees it as a survival guide for the evolving information age. And with it Visa has done more than survive. In the roughly three decades since he founded the company, it has sailed past its main competitor, MasterCard, on its way to becoming the world's largest commercial enterprise.

Along the way Hock's self-organizing, nonlinear, adaptive company pioneered such things as the first electronic authorization system, the debit card system, and the electronic funds transfer system, as well as electronic point-of-sale terminals and those magnetic stripes now found on the backs of all cards. Today, with hundreds of millions of cardholders, Visa processes over $3 trillion in transactions each year in what Hock has called "the largest single block of consumer purchasing power in the world economy." The company has a potential market capitalization of hundreds of billions—if it could be sold, that is. Because of its peculiar structure it cannot. Nor can it be raided.

The Visa organization is a significant step away from the linear, hierarchical structures of the machine age. Remove the engine from a train, Hock notes, and the whole enterprise grinds to a halt. But take any one bird from a flock and it quickly readjusts, then goes flapping merrily on its way. In much the same manner the Visa card links twenty-three thousand financial institutions into a polycentric, self-organizing web controlled by no one, an outside-in structure where "no part knows the whole, the whole does not know the parts, and none has any need to." That organization, Hock points out, is made possible by computers. Its development parallels the evolution of money into pure data—codified electrons and photons flashing around the world through global computer networks "at the speed of light, at minuscule cost, by infinitely diverse paths."

According to Michael Rothschild, in his insightful book *Bionomics*, "The human brain amounts to just 3 percent of total body weight but burns up about 20 percent of all the energy derived from food. The cost of keeping our brains fed would be far higher if the body's information processing were not decentralized." So, too, with companies. "Because conditions in every market niche keep changing," Rothschild says, "no organizational design is permanent. Large firms are reorganized endlessly, to find the right balance between the benefits of coordinated corporate action and the cost savings that flow from decentralization." By forever moving back and forth between centralized and decentralized, he says, "companies seek but never find the perfect organizational structure." Now linked by nine million miles of fiber-optic cable, the decentralized, computerized Visa global network does that as effortlessly as a living system. The outcome: at a rate of some eleven hundred transactions per second, it clears more electronic financial transactions each week than the wire system for the Federal Reserve clears in a year.

Hock is still not satisfied with the system he designed. "I don't think we got Visa 30 percent right," he says, and since his retirement he has warned about the dangers of a "creeping recentralization of power." As a defense against the old mistake of confusing control for order, he advocates looking at the world through the eyes of nature, viewing collapse or chaos "not as horrible disasters, but as the only agents powerful enough to force open the door to change." Ultimately, he says, it's about "learning to trust that there is order in chaos—and that together we can find it." To that end he offers some basic rules for the new generation of business leaders. Among those rules are:

Everything has both intended and unintended consequences. The intended consequences may or may not happen; the unintended consequences always do.

Simple, clear purpose and principles give rise to complex and intelligent behavior. Complex rules and regulations give rise to simple, stupid behavior.

Everything is its opposite, particularly competition and cooperation. Neither can rise to its highest potential unless both are seamlessly blended. Either without the other quickly becomes dangerous and destructive.

As Hock sees it, adopting these methods isn't optional; it's unavoidable. What's more, time is short. "When was the last time evolution rang your number and asked your consent?" he asks, then advises today's corporate leaders: "If your organization is not actively involved in reconceiving, you are already in a state of dissolution and decay."

For many, the process of reconceiving is well under way. Starting in the late 1980s, writes Rothschild, "well-managed large firms began flattening and decentralizing their traditional vertical hierarchies." And as in so many other areas involving the new biology, computers were the key:

> Before the microprocessor . . . large organizations had no choice but to bear heavy costs of coordination. Ever since large-scale industrial organizations first emerged in the nineteenth century, passing papers up and down the chain of command had been the only practical way to keep complex organizations under control. Suddenly, the microprocessor allowed firms to boost the sophistication of their products and accelerate their responses to customer demands by decentralizing and slashing the costs of coordination.

Among those firms was the corporate giant 3M, where the mandate today is to earn 15 percent of revenue from new products—a high degree of creativity for any large organization. It has accomplished that by loosening its structure. Project teams, working with little restraint from management, move between divisions or labs at will, forming to accomplish a task and then disbanding when their work is done. In another innovation, 3M supervisors bring new employees to seminars on risk taking. There, the recruits are taught to challenge supervisors, and encouraged with tales of innovations that came about in that way. Even though all organizations have an innate tendency to resolve tensions, at 3M and elsewhere the new management ideal views tension as a "goal" and sees maintaining it within healthy bounds as the key to any creative and dynamic system.

In other developments, companies such as GM and Deere & Company now employ complexity-based software to develop smarter manufacturing programs. Top consulting firms like McKinsey, Coopers and Lybrand, and Ernst & Young have dispatched staffers to the Santa Fe Institute (SFI)—complexity's reigning heartland—to explore the use of that approach in their practices. Ernst & Young even sent its clients fifteen thousand copies of *At Home in the Universe*, a weighty volume by Stuart Kauffman, the SFI biologist. Kauffman's theories of complexity at the boundary region between chaos and order, and of the emergence of "order for free" in chaotic systems, have sparked calls for a correction to Darwin and were an inspiration to Hock.

Meanwhile SFI extension professors J. Doyne Farmer and Norman Packard—who as kids tried using hidden computers with controllers in their shoes to beat the odds in Vegas—joined forces in 1991 to form the Prediction Company. The study of chaos has spawned powerful new mathematical tools that find order where none was expected in the turbulent flows and tangled workings of the natural world. Packard and Farmer have applied those tools to find orderly patterns in the tangled workings and turbulent flows of financial markets, in those trillions of dollars now streaming through global computer networks.

"We're not basing our predictions on a fundamental theory about human nature," says Farmer, "but rather on patterns and data." As he describes it:

> We gather data about financial markets, like currency exchange rates. We apply our learning algorithms to the data, looking for patterns that seem to persist through time. We build models that make trades based on these patterns, and implement them. Every day, data flows into Santa Fe from around the world, [and] triggers our computer programs to make predictions and trades, which are then sent around the world to the appropriate financial markets.

Their company now operates under an exclusive agreement with the investment-banking arm of UBS—the world's third-largest bank—to provide it with automated trading systems and "predictive signals."

"For the first time in history, we're starting to get a predictive economics," says Stewart Brand. "It's only mildly predictive, but mildly is a whole lot better than what it was." Brand is a notable figure, a kind of universal intellectual catalyst. He founded the *Whole Earth Catalog* and the WELL—an early public forum on the Internet. He is the author of numerous books and is a board member at the Santa Fe Institute. He currently spends a lot of his time with the Global Business Network (GBN), a consulting firm he cofounded and that specializes in "scenario planning." For clients ranging from labor unions to national governments to multinational corporations, GBN forecasters use a method very different from the linear extrapolations employed by most consultants. That approach—of just projecting a current trend forward at the same linear rate into the future—has given rise to famous blunders like IBM's ten-year forecast that the market for its newly introduced PC would not exceed 250,000, and AT&T's feeble projection that the world market for cell phones would top out at 900,000. Says Lawrence Wilkinson, who with Brand and Peter Schwartz was the company's third cofounder, "Most forecasting is about conquering uncertainty. But what we do is in a sense to celebrate uncertainty. We don't forecast. We look at a variety of nonlinear, unextrapolated futures that could exist, and then use them as a kind of wind tunnel for making decisions."

A variety of futures? As Brand explains it, "Part of what scenario planning forces you to do is to get out of the foresight business and into what are various plausible scenarios—divergent situations that could occur—and then project your mind out into them. You ask, How did this come to pass? What are the important forks in the path that are coming along? And then, once you're there, Wait a minute, how does this make sense when you look backward and what's the lesson here? So scenario planning is kind of a virtual forward evolution of varying paths. You're trying to develop a strategy that is robust against various scenarios.

"And the terminology that's used is straight out of biology," he adds. "Businesses are getting out of military metaphors, sports metaphors, and are increasingly comfortable with biological metaphors, just because that's how things work. Both the military and the sports metaphors were basically—you identified your competition and focused on them, and then tried to beat them, or at least not get beaten too badly by them. Biological metaphors let you think in terms like niches, and parasites, and symbionts, which are generally more useful ideas."

As with Hock's talk of a nonlinear, self-organizing company, Brand's language sounds exotic. Still, the proof lies in results. And like Visa, GBN has shown itself to be more effective than systems that have long defined its area of expertise. To name just two examples of that: It predicted a drop in oil prices during the late 1970s and early '80s, when oil companies expected them to rise. It also anticipated the fall of the Iron Curtain, something the U.S. Central Intelligence Agency missed.

Economic Evolution

Brian Arthur sits in an office at the Santa Fe Institute, looking out on the dry, sunbaked hills northeast of town. Arthur is a thoughtful, soft-spoken man with the buttoned-down appearance and manner one expects of a leading academic. But the former Stanford University professor is anything but a conventional economist. Like Hock's work and Brand's, and along with that of a growing number of economists around the world, Arthur's work is not just about bringing biology into the equation. It says that biology *is* the equation. "Certainly in the last twenty years, but more specifically in the last ten," he says, "you have a sudden mushrooming of thought that can be described as biological in economics." Arthur should know. He worked closely here for many years with biologist Stuart Kauffman in tracking similarities between their fields.

"We're beginning to get more sophisticated theoretically about what an ecology is," Arthur notes. That's due, he says, in no small part to the development of powerful computers and new math tools, which make it possible to model ecosystem dynamics such as feedback loops and adaptive behavior. "In all the sciences," he adds, "we're moving away from the mechanistic, static approach, where you take a butterfly, for example, and you put it in chloroform, or whatever, and pin it to a board; then you study it under a microscope. We're moving from that approach—of looking at things as static and in equilibrium—to actually trying to investigate what happens when things are in process, when the butterfly is in motion."

The SFI view of living process goes well beyond the flight of a butterfly. It begins at the most basic levels of life. As Doyne Farmer explains it:

> Many of us believe that self-organization is a general property—certainly of the universe, and even more generally of mathematical systems that might be called "complex adaptive systems." Complex adaptive systems have the property that if you run them . . . they'll naturally progress from chaotic, disorganized, undifferentiated, independent states to organized, highly differentiated, and highly interdependent states. Organized structures emerge spontaneously, just by letting the system run. Of course, some systems do this to a greater degree than others, or to higher levels than others, and there will be a certain amount of flukiness to it all. The progression from disorder to organization will proceed in fits and starts, as

it does in natural evolution, and it may even reverse itself from time to
time, as it does in natural evolution. But in an adaptive complex system,
the overall tendency will be toward self-organization.

In Kauffman's theory of how molecules first self-organized into the
structures that then self-organized into life, Arthur sees an economic
metaphor. "You can start to think about what leads to what," he says. "You
know, working up, say, from stone and obsidian and axe handles you can
see that, given that, you might have some possibilities for digging and
for shaping, and, given that, other possibilities start to open up. So you
can start to see economic possibilities as having bootstrapped their way
up—from nothing or from very little into this entire, sophisticated pole-
vaulting array of technologies and products." That explains a great deal
of what we see around us today. "If you look at the new technologies
that are out there, you start to see what look like dependence webs. One
technology is possible if other technologies already exist."

As new niches in a market arise, they feed on one another in what
he and Kauffman see as a coevolving system. Says Arthur, "We're more
aware now that products and firms and so on are not just in competition
with each other—which would give you a very simplistic Darwinian
view—but that they form an ecology that is mutually supportive and
mutually coevolving." By coevolving he means, "When you talk about
complexity, you start to talk about individual elements creating an overall pattern that the individual elements are adapting to. That's my working definition. I drive downtown. My actions in the traffic are adapting
to the traffic, but the traffic consists of individuals whose actions are also
adapting to the rest of the traffic and me. We are an ongoing coevolving
system of individuals."

Kauffman breaks that interaction down in a scenario reminiscent of
game theory. "I have a theory about what you're going to do," he says.
"But in due course you're going to do something that disconcerts my
theory. So I can either keep my theory or eventually I might change my
theory. But when I create a new theory about you I'm going to change
my actions, because I'm using my theory about you to guide what I do.
At that point my behavior patterns change, and so your theory about me
no longer fits what I'm doing. Now you change your theory, and that
drives you to change your actions. Then my theory about you is no
good any longer, and I change my theory about you. So now we're in a

state of coevolving theories about one another, where our theories in turn are coupled with our actions."

As Arthur sees it, coevolution is at work in every area of the economy. "Be it the oil market, the stock market, government policy—you're talking about decisions, sometimes you're talking about actions, sometimes you're talking about agreements, like trade agreements, sometimes you're talking about strategies. Those individual elements are usually locked together as elements adapting to a world that those elements are cocreating."

All this doesn't rule out the need for government policy. It still has relevance because "there are no guarantees that an evolving system will reach the best outcome for all concerned." One area ripe for government concern is the so-called "law of increasing returns," an idea originally proposed by the economist Alfred Marshall and now being actively explored on separate fronts by Arthur and by Princeton economist Paul Krugman. Increasing returns stands on its head the old axiom of "diminishing returns." In that older concept it's understood, for instance, that while putting twice as many people to work on a given piece of farmland can double its production, adding still more workers can fail to bring a commensurate rise. For instance, doubling farmhands from two to four might easily double crop yield, while doubling the number of hands once again, to eight, might bring only a further 25 percent increase—a diminishing return on investment.

But in the evolving global technosphere, examples of the opposite—of increasing returns—are now common. In a phenomenon called "lock in," a company's early command of an emerging market feeds a rising technological learning curve, which springboards its returns ever higher as its market share expands and competitors are squeezed out. Over the past two decades, to take the most notable example, that has been the story of Microsoft, which in the software market is now akin to a keystone species in an ecosystem.

How far can biological metaphors help in redefining economics? "It's not so much that we're directly borrowing from biology," Arthur says, "but rather that this is the way all complex adaptive systems work." In his view, that points to why the new biological metaphors are so vital. "I think we underemphasize the importance of mental models in Western thought. We tend to believe that we have a good picture of reality, that the way we see things corresponds exactly to what's out there.

What we don't get is that whatever is out there is being interpreted by us all the time in mental models. In other words, our tastes, our attitudes, what we do with the environment, how we think about dealing with each other—those are primarily decided by cultural beliefs."

Witness how the world economy—and with it the lives of billions of people—has been distorted by the machine metaphor. Says Arthur, "We don't know much about managing the economy because the standard theory says you don't have to manage it. And the socialist economy basically says, well, 'Steer it like you drive a car.' And yet you find that the steering wheel is very loose, and when you steer it to the right, it swerves to the left. So we're finding a lot of the deficiencies in economics are that we really don't understand adaptation, learning, and so on." That in turn, he adds, "gives you the implication that it's not clear how much progress we can make by slapping on carbon and pollution taxes or subsidies. I'm not objecting to any of these; some of them are good ideas. But it's not clear how much progress we're going to make unless the underlying beliefs start to change."

Money and the 2nd Law
Perhaps the first and most fundamental of those changes is developing an economic theory that recognizes there's only so much energy to go around. The sun, our ultimate source, throws off fantastic amounts of the stuff—some 10^{13} Q each year, with a single Q itself being equal to 10^{18} BTUs. Despite that, only 5,300 Q of solar energy strikes the earth's atmosphere, and half of that is reflected back into space. Then, of the sunlight actually reaching the ground, no more than 1.2 Q is absorbed by photosynthesis, the process that makes it available to other living things like us. Adding to that, we clever humans have figured out how to use the solar energy stored in fossil fuels, the underground storage battery of rotted biomass, which before we got to it held just over 200 Q. Putting that amount in perspective, the total global reserve of fossil fuels never equaled more than two months' worth of the energy that reaches earth in sunlight every year.

Photosynthesis makes all life possible. That's why the Greek historian Xenophon called agriculture "the mother and the nurse of all other arts." As a modern observer writes of ancient China, "Had it not been possible to obtain a . . . rice plant from a single seed, it would never have been possible to maintain the peasant, the landowner, the [monk] or the mandarin." His point is that without that surplus from nature, there would be no monetary surplus. It emerges first from plants, then "spreads in numberless streams through the whole production system via the price mechanism." In the end this means that with all our striving and creativity, our grand economic theories and spreading global industries, we can do no more than transform the energy and matter that nature makes available—just like algae forming snowflake shells, or like snails on the White Cliffs of Dover.

And as we use solar energy to stir matter into new form, whether we like it or not, we come up against the 2nd Law of Thermodynamics. The 1st Law states that the amount of energy in the universe never changes. That sounds like good news, until the 2nd Law shows that while the amount never changes, useful energy density is always thinning out from concentrated form into random dissipation. Think here of the sun radiating heat into the emptiness of space. The sun's heat never disappears; it just becomes diluted.

Because of the 2nd Law, our bodies have to take in large amounts of the solar energy stored in food to produce the refined chemical energy we need to live, just as power plants focus large amounts of the solar energy stored in coal to make the refined energy we call electricity. A piece of coal burning in a power plant is an extension of what happens in the sun, as fire releases solar energy from coal to produce ashes and heat. At a higher level of organization, our bodies do something similar when the mitochondria in our cells use solar energy from food to stoke a cold chemical fire by which energy is released to run our bodies.

In either case—through cells or through power plants—the amount of useful energy we can draw from the process will always be less than the total amount we feed into it. That's because no process is completely efficient. At every step some of energy's valuable concentration—and thus its ability to perform work—is lost to the universe forever. This constant dissipation is prescribed by the 2nd Law and is why life forms have to keep eating all the time, why we have to keep taking in fresh concentrated energy and matter from our environment. It's also why we release diluted heat and degraded matter back to it.

Farms, industries, and waste treatment facilities are just extensions of this process. We and the cultures we create are no different from seagoing algae and cliff-dwelling snails. We're all examples of what the poet

Goethe long ago called nature's "moving order"—coherent patterns through which energy and materials are transformed and then passed along. And the 2nd Law is key. Without the fresh input of energy that comes each morning with the sunrise, all of life would soon fade away.

Bioeconomics

Why that has yet to dawn on mainstream economics is a puzzle. There was a time when we understood all this without having to think about it, back before fossil fuels made it possible to accelerate our uptake of energy from the sun. Back then, it went without saying that value was tied to the flow of solar energy through living plants—through trees for building or to make fire, through crops to feed livestock or fuel our labor. But with the fossil-fueled machine age, utility (determined by the exchange of cash) became the sole gauge of value. As we ceased to be farming-based producers and instead became fossil-fueled consumers, we broke our intuitive bond with nature. With that break came a great sense of release. Suddenly we were free from the ancient constraints of throughput—from the limited flow of the sun's energy through living plants, and the limited amount of material that that solar energy could be used to mobilize. That break is now reflected in theory. Economic textbooks depict the flow of goods and services running from firms to households as being an even exchange for the flow of labor and money that runs from households to firms, as if to say their interaction is just a closed loop (a system reminiscent of Dr. Johnson's South Sea islanders, who eked out a perilous living by taking in one another's laundry). In this model there's no recognition that the inputs of energy and material needed to keep the cycle running come from depletable resources, no provision for outputs of waste and pollution, and no notion of the 2nd Law. Instead, the closed-loop flows of current theory are described as feeding one another, an unending cycle in which, as former World Bank economist Herman Daly puts it, "the concept of throughput is only dimly visible in the shadows."

There's just one problem with this. Well, two actually. First, in reality, our industrial culture throughputs fossil fuel waste to the sky at a rate that's overheating the planet. Second, of course, is that we never really freed ourselves from dependence on the sun. The fossil fuels we take from the ground are still solar energy; it's just been stored in rotted plants. By emptying those reserves, we only get to spend it quickly for a while.

Members of the very first school of economics, the preindustrial Physiocrats, knew that sunlight captured by growing plants is at the heart of things. That's why they felt only agriculture should be taxed, saying it's the one economic activity to yield a surplus. Moreover, by the mid-nineteenth century the 2nd Law was widely acknowledged to be unavoidable, so much so that it was seen as a challenge by Darwin. Within a short time, all the sciences had come to grips with it. All, that is, except economics.

Even so, as the mainstream walked an unrealistic path, in the background a bioeconomic theory was taking form. And it was forming around the 2nd Law, around an effort to make that a first principle for economics. Bioeconomics starts there. It recognizes that the amount of dense, concentrated energy in the universe is always diluting—always dissipating from each and every plant, and from each and every animal that feeds on those plants. So every day, life on earth dilutes forever some of nature's limited store of concentrated energy. That loss is replenished daily by the sun, which is dissipating, too. But since it will go on delivering fresh energy to earth each morning for another few billion years, its depletion is something that even the most ardent long-term planners can overlook. So the good news is that if we eat only those foods that grow naturally, they're essentially free—the bounty of nature. An apple on a tree is there for the picking.

Farms change that equation. They concentrate the solar energy being captured in life forms we like to eat (crops, livestock), but farms also require us to work in order to tend them. So if the amount of work energy needed to maintain them is more than the food energy we get from them, we're better off hunting and gathering. Viewed in this way, farming is an energy technology. And it's clear that for much of the past century we've skewed that energy equation by using fossil fuels, saying in essence that because mechanized farming means less labor for us personally, the vast new amounts of energy being spent to fuel our machines, and to create the fertilizers and pesticides we use, don't really count. That's why new biologists like Kansas farmer Wes Jackson are working to develop realistic "energy budgets" for farms.

It's not a new idea. The concept of tracking all the energy going into a farm—in order to make sure there's a genuine gain in the amount of food energy coming out of it—was first proposed more than 120 years ago by economist Sergei Podolinsky. A socialist, he criticized Marx and Engels for their belief that "scientific socialism" could somehow overcome the limits of natural resources and offer unlimited material expansion. Podolinsky rejected their view that labor is the only meaningful factor in increasing the bounty of the natural world. He urged them to consider the central role of energy flows, and with that the effect of the 2nd Law. To their discredit they refused, and proceeded down a road that pointedly ignored the 2nd Law (Engels misunderstood it, thinking it contradicted the 1st) and environmental considerations in general.

The bioeconomic concern for energy and the 2nd Law would find itself expressed in various ways as it was developed and refined. At the start of the twentieth century, it surfaced in the calculations of Silvio Gesell, a European businessman living in Argentina. What Gesell noticed was that the recurring boom-and-bust cycles affecting his business seemed to reflect rises and falls in interest rates, rather than any real shortages of supply or demand. Gesell saw interest as violating the laws of physics. Unlike everything else in nature, he said, money doesn't rot or degrade with age. On the contrary, money can go on growing endlessly through the accumulation of interest. Gesell called that a form of growth contrary to the 2nd Law, and thus at odds with what happens to the real wealth of nature—which money is supposed to represent. He considered that schism a great danger to human economies. For instance, the growth of debt from accumulating interest, he argued, could surpass the growth of real wealth and cause the banking system to collapse. Gesell believed that many of the world's financial problems could be solved by eliminating interest payments and by devising a currency that loses value in accordance with the 2nd Law. In his book *The Natural Economic Order*, published in 1916, he compared the flow of money to blood flow and talked of the "metabolic exchange" of transactions in the "social organism."

During the 1920s Frederick Soddy, a Nobel laureate in chemistry, turned his attention to economics. Soddy joined Gesell in pointing out the dangers of interest and the need for an economics based on the 2nd Law. All wealth, he said, grows from the solar energy captured by plants, which he described as "the original capitalists." Since we get our energy solely from them (whether as food or from fuels like coal and oil, created by ancient biomass), he argued that any realistic economics has to begin there, too. Writing at about the same time, ecologist Alfred Lotka raised another idea that would guide the emerging view. He defined evolution as a "general scrimmage for available energy."

In the second part of the twentieth century, another ecologist, Howard Odum, built on Lotka to define the fitness that evolution selects for as the ability to use energy more effectively. Whether the competition for survival is between organisms or whole ecosystems, he said, the essential contest is always between strategies for energy optimization. Looking to economics, he argued that any system aimed at the survival of humans has to be measured by the same yardstick.

During this time the basic argument for what is now called "energy economics" assumed modern form. As conceived by Odum and refined today: "Money circulates in a closed loop, whereas energy moves in from the outside, is used for economic tasks and then leaves the economic system as degraded heat [per the 2nd Law]." This means that, since energy from sunlight is the only meaningful input, the energy embodied in a good or service is an irreducible part of its economic value.

The 1970s saw an upsurge of interest in bioeconomic insights. A new generation brought with it sophisticated tools like computers and a growing body of knowledge. The implications of the 2nd Law figured in the work of Robert Ayres, who was among the first to stress how widespread the problem of economic externalizations had become. Another voice of protest was Wassily Leontief, who called his fellow economists to task for their "preoccupation with imaginary, hypothetical, rather than observable reality." After receiving a Nobel award early in the decade, Leontief went on to survey four years of articles from the prestigious journal *The American Economic Review*. He found that more than half of them used no supporting data at all. The models presented were purely mathematical.

During this period, as U.S. oil production fell and dependence on foreign sources grew, the importance of energy to economics was driven home by two great oil price shocks as OPEC—the Organization of Petroleum Exporting Countries—demanded steep hikes in the price of crude. News accounts at the time talked of "stagflation," reflecting a general bewilderment at how economic stagnation and price inflation could happen at the same time. Mainstream economics not only didn't foresee what happened in the seventies, it couldn't explain it. To those focused on bioeconomics, the cause was less mysterious. The economic models that held the field then, and in modified form still do, were not connected to the real world.

It's the Energy, Stupid!

In the creation of bioeconomics, one figure stands out: Nicholas Georgescu-Roegen. G-R, as he is often called, coined the term. He was a blunt, acerbic man who openly mocked the Western neoclassical model while at the same time labeling Marxists "commodity fetishists"—a practice that did little to endear him in academia. From his modest position at Vanderbilt University he nonetheless made his opinions felt throughout his field.

Georgescu-Roegen's magnum opus is titled *The Entropy Law and the Economic Process*, and its impact continues to grow. Paul Samuelson, CFO of American economists, has called him "a scholar's scholar, an economist's economist," and described him as a great mind living far ahead of his time. In the context of G-R's work, "ahead of his time" is a judicious phrase, which might be interpreted to mean: "He's right, but things today are so far from right that no one knows where to begin the task of fixing them."

G-R largely dismissed Marxism and branded the Western model half-smart. He had no problem with utility, or with the neoclassical view that capital (that is, expertise and natural resources, somewhat erratically represented by money) can be substituted for labor (as when machines replace employees at a factory). He embraced the reverse of that equation, too, in which labor can be substituted for capital. But the Western model holds that access to labor and capital is the entire basis for economies. That idea G-R rejected.

Bringing us up to par with the algae and the snails, he began from the view that any energy we spend, even when it's transformed outside our bodies, is an extension of human metabolism. This includes what Brian Arthur has termed our "entire, sophisticated pole-vaulting array of technologies and products." In that light G-R saw labor and capital—which he labeled "funds"—as only half of the economic equation. The other half he called the "flows." Flows are the rates at which energy and materials move through the system. He explained the need to distinguish funds from flows with a simple example. The energy of the sun is for all practical purposes an unlimited fund of natural capital, but its flow rate to earth's surface, the rate at which it's available for our use, is strictly limited. On the other hand, energy stored in fossil fuels is a limited fund, but its flow rate is virtually unlimited. For him those differences were routine common sense. Any theory that didn't take them into account was hopelessly unrealistic.

As far back as the 1960s, when most economists thought we could feed the world by using fossil-fueled machines to farm more crops, G–R's view of funds and flows led him to ridicule that view and predict the reverse. We would soon, he grumbled, be using crops that harvest energy from the sun to fuel our machines. That process is now under way. In Brazil, sugarcane grown for fuel is already displacing food crops, and biofuel subsidies are being offered to U.S. farmers.

Leaving no stone un–thrown, Georgescu-Roegen also went after energy economists. "Matter matters too," he admonished them. This is because the energy we use on earth doesn't exist in a pure state; it's always embodied in matter. Since matter is the vehicle for energy, he said, and since no work can be done without the use of matter, that hand-in-glove relationship means that as energy dissipates via the 2nd Law, matter dissipates, too.

This is one of those subtle but controversial points that G–R seemed to relish. As such it calls for clarification. According to the 2nd Law, when we release a large amount of concentrated energy (for instance, by burning coal) in a power plant, we generate an even more concentrated form of energy we call electricity. But that comes at a cost. In the end, the total amount of energy contained in the electricity we make is always going to be less than the total amount of energy that was in the coal to start with. If the 1st Law says that the amount of energy in the universe never changes, the obvious question is, What happened to the difference, what happened to the energy that got lost? The 2nd Law answers that question. The difference didn't just disappear; it was thrown off as energy in diluted form, as what we call waste heat. As a practical matter, while no energy ever disappears, it does lose some of its concentration.

So, too, G–R said, with materials. Even though matter is recycled endlessly on earth, we have to contend with something like a 2nd Law for the erosion and scattering of concentrated materials. In a familiar example, we shape various kinds of rubber into tires. Then, as millions of tires roll down roads around the globe, they shed uncounted billions of particles of rubber microdust. Industrial ecology aims to make a tire whose core can be recycled at the end of its useful life, and whose materials won't poison nature with the dust they shed. But that dust is nonetheless lost to us. Although it's still rubber, it is no longer available in a concentrated, useful form. If we try to reconcentrate it, the effort will cost us more energy and material than it yields.

Energy economists have understandably jumped on this argument. Unlike what happens to solar energy, they point out, nature eventually reconcentrates matter in recycled form, with or without our help. This is true, but G-R's argument nonetheless holds value for economics. While all matter on earth—beyond the occasional outgoing space probe—is eventually recycled, nature has endless amounts of time to do the job. If it takes a million years for algae to put the calcium back into undersea beds of limestone, it's no more than the blink of an eye for nature. How do we relate that to a human economy that views ten years as a long-term forecast?

It's a question of funds and flows. Given the very slow flow rate at which most natural funds of concentrated matter—metal ores, for example—become available to us, there is a virtual 2nd Law at work on them as they pass through our industries and economy. Even the most scrupulous recycling loops will lose some material along the way. In that, for all practical purposes, the gradual erosion and scattering of material parallels the 2nd Law's dilution of energy.

While bioeconomists work to clarify these views, the larger concern remains: Will they be able to drag our antiquated economy out of the eighteenth century and into the twenty-first? For now, things seem to be looking up. Their arguments have moved beyond the academic tempests that G-R took such delight in stirring, to inform the beginnings of a truly bioeconomic system. For instance, there is now a crucial effort under way to reinvent money. As the digital global economy replaces the old cash-based one that has guided development for so long, it is raising questions about what money really is, and providing some controversial new answers.

Buying Power

Money is a medium of exchange. When we pick an apple from a tree, we can trade it for an orange. But we first have to find someone who not only has an orange but also wants to trade it for an apple. And if apples and oranges ripen at different times of the year, or in different parts of the world, it's even harder to make the trade. Barter was the first economy, and it represents natural capital well, because the only things changing hands in a barter exchange are the goods themselves. The problem with barter has always been its inefficiency. Money solved that problem. Suddenly apple traders could skip the complex and time-consuming process of finding orange traders who wanted apples. All they needed was someone with ready cash.

That's because money is a promise to pay. Its holders receive a promise that they'll be given something tangible—labor, goods, gold—from someone else at some other time. This flexibility makes trading with cash more efficient and gives rise to specialization, which is a key to building complex cultures. Cash economies also differ from barter in another important way. Money gets passed along from hand to hand indefinitely. Everyone accepts it, so, unlike barter—where each exchange is separate and unique—money generates long flows of transactions. In those flows, each individual exchange makes another one possible, as being paid supplies the money to then pay someone else. The result is that once money enters the picture, people need to be transactors first, before they can be producers or consumers. In the history of trade, that was a big shift. Suddenly money became the thing that makes production and consumption possible, that makes the world go round.

While theorists argue about whether the key for adding value to nature is energy, utility, or some other factor, that dispute often misses something of equal importance. In the end, the circulation of money determines who actually gets to receive that added value. We all need money. For most of us the act of getting it involves constant struggle. So much so that we tend to see that struggle as one of life's basic and most challenging realities. But it has become clear in recent years that, in numerous ways, the money we work so hard to get has only a tenuous link to reality. With that awareness deeper questions arise. If money isn't real capital, what is it? Where does it come from? If it doesn't work like nature, how does it work?

By making human economies more efficient and diverse, the invention of money brought unprecedented wealth. It also brought something altogether new. Since money didn't rot, rust, or wear out like the fruits of nature, people with surplus cash were free to hold on to it.

They soon found that doing so was like putting a dam across a river. In that simple act they could block the flow of economic transactions downstream from them, making it harder for everyone else in the economy to get money. For instance, if consumers who like apples and oranges can't get their hands on cash, fruit stand operators are soon affected. That in turn affects the fruit distributors. Eventually, growers feel the pinch, too. In every step of the chain, where getting paid once supplied the money needed to then pay someone else, suddenly now the whole business grinds to a halt. Then, as the incomes of everyone linked to apples and oranges dry up, that reduction extends in all the directions money once took as it passed through their hands. Through the whole interlinking web of exchange, transactions that might otherwise have happened suddenly don't. Although there may be just as many apples and oranges for sale, and just as many consumers eager to have them, suddenly no one is buying because there isn't enough cash in circulation.

Once it was understood that money could be held indefinitely—without degrading as natural capital does—that awareness brought with it a new economic practice. Like a central water authority releasing water to drought-starved farmers, holders of surplus cash found they could charge a fee for releasing money. They still do. We call that fee interest.

Today, money begins in the headwaters of central banks like the Federal Reserve. For the most part, each nation in the global economy has one, and they work in much the same way to ensure economic stability. One way of doing that is by adjusting interest rates, to speed or slow activity. At the U.S. Fed, for instance, interest rates are adjusted with the familiar announcement of a change in the prime rate. This is just a target for what banks will have to pay when borrowing from each other to resupply their reserves—a widespread nightly event. And that announcement has a broader effect, since it's accepted by the financial community as a signal of Fed intentions for the future. Another way the Fed ensures stability is by making sure the amount of money in circulation roughly parallels the growth of real wealth in the economy. According to a publication of the Federal Reserve Bank of Chicago:

> Control of the *quantity* of money is essential if its value is to be kept stable . . . [I]f the volume of money grows more rapidly than the rate at which the output of real goods and services increases, prices will rise . . . But if, on the other hand, growth in the supply of money does not keep

pace with the economy's current production, then prices will fall, the nation's labor force, factories, and other production facilities will not be fully employed, or both.

Because the world is always changing, the amount of real wealth that needs to be represented by money is always changing, too, as is the need to speed or slow growth. So the economy is measured periodically with an array of indicators (prominent among them the seriously flawed GDP).

After deciding on a policy, the Fed shoots for that target through a series of actions that add to or subtract from the cash reserves being held by its member banks. The minimum required size of those reserves is fixed by national policy. So when the Fed shrinks or expands the money in them, that spurs banks to be more conservative or liberal. Adding cash to a bank's reserve frees it to inject more money into the economy. Shrinking its cash reserve causes it to draw money out of the economy (for instance, by no longer making new loans, and then waiting for old ones to be paid off). Such moves also help to push interest rates down or up. The most interesting thing about this is that the Fed works these transactions with money created out of thin air. In the nice phrase of one observer, it "lends it into existence." The member banks then pass it along to their customers. Nevertheless, each recipient of that money has to pay the piper.

As newly created money flows from central banks like the Fed to regional and then local banks, each in turn buys it by paying interest, and then tacks on some more before passing it along. Harry Truman notwithstanding, the buck stops with the hapless consumer at the end of that flow, the one who has to borrow money for the basic needs of life. To him or her falls the burden of actually paying back all that accumulating interest. As a result, even as money flows outward from central banks into general circulation, there is a constant undertow of profit running back upstream to those involved in the lending process. And in real terms, that profit is generated by the consumer who is the ultimate borrower. When a local bank lends a young couple $100,000 to buy a home, it expects to be paid back $200,000 over the next twenty years. But the bank doesn't create the second $100,000. Home buyers have to go out and battle for it against everyone else.

In that way the scramble for cash among consumers is made more competitive, even as interest payments siphon part of their income back into banks. And banks aren't the only ones extracting interest from them. Credit card debts, car payments, household furnishing loans, and a host of other devices from a host of other lenders all draw income from consumers. Businesses borrow, too, which adds interest payments to their labor and other expenses. That added cost gets passed along, once again, to consumers in the form of higher prices. As interest charges overlap and multiply, a gradual inflation of costs drives up the salaries people need in order to live—leading to an overall, systemic inflation in the economy.

Central banks are aware of this, and of how their actions can affect it. They've learned the hard way that they can boost inflation by creating too much money, in an attempt to paper over government debts, for example. Conversely, they can damp inflation by shrinking the money supply, but only to a point. Wherever there is interest, some inflation is unavoidable.

Seen through the eyes of nature, a little inflation is actually a good thing. Money that loses value slowly and *across the board* is in tune with the 2nd Law (in which concentrated, useful energy gradually dilutes from a system). The problem with our own system is that—once all our interest payment transfers have been factored in—the gradual devaluation of our money is anything but across the board. In fact it's actually reversed for some people, becoming a gain, while it serves to accelerate the loss for most others. The fact that consumers get to spend the money they borrow doesn't change this equation. That's because money has value only insofar as it translates into buying power. Since currency that's borrowed comes with interest payments owed, it conveys less buying power than currency that's lent, which benefits from interest payments received. So even though inflation devalues money evenly, interest payments change that equation as they siphon actual buying power away from those who borrow and into the hands of those who lend. In the words of one writer, the critic Margrit Kennedy, interest is a "redistribution mechanism." Her phrase is apt. Interest is a private tax. Through it, our monetary system constantly redistributes buying power from the poor to the rich, from small firms to large firms, from poor nations to rich nations. That process drives a monopolization of money and resources that distorts the free market.

The other problem with large payments of compound interest is that they're impossible. There is an old story about the Persian emperor who was introduced to chess by a clever mathematician. In appreciation, the emperor offered to grant him a wish. The mathematician asked for a single grain of rice on the first square of his chessboard, with the amount doubling on each of the following squares. The emperor was pleased by the modesty of this wish until it became clear that the yield of his entire realm was not enough to fulfill it. In fact, it would take more than four hundred times the yield of planet Earth to provide the amount of rice required on the sixty-fourth square of the board. Compound interest has the same effect on money. The return from a single penny invested at 5 percent interest at the birth of Jesus Christ would have bought a gold ball equal in weight to the whole earth by the time Christopher Columbus sailed to America. Today the return on that penny would be worth more than two trillion of those gold balls.

Like compound interest, living populations also grow exponentially. Algae, for instance, will expand rapidly to fill a pond. But they soon hit the wall of ecological limits, and when they do, the die-off can be severe. Algae have a simple outlook on life: they just eat and reproduce as fast as they can. Human economists seem to share that outlook. We're a more sophisticated life form, with a much larger awareness of the world. But rather than build that awareness into each transaction, our economists have designed a system that lets exponential interest cycles grow until—like populations of algae dying off—billions of human lives are caught up in a destructive adjustment. As is increasingly clear, the initial rise of these cycles has a less-than-rigorous connection to the growth of real wealth. Paradoxically, it has more to do with staying ahead of the returns required on the money that has been borrowed to fuel them. So debt expands faster than wealth, until the amount of money owed no longer bears any sensible relationship to the amount of real wealth needed to pay it. With that, it's only a matter of time before it hits a wall.

Interest rates can drive cycles in a second way, too. This happens when rising rates encourage lenders to release investment money—to let it flow out from their dams of fiscal parsimony. As a cycle builds, the amount of money in circulation gradually swells to flood proportions. That flood makes it easier for borrowers to get funds, which causes rates to fall. With that, lenders once again raise their dams, shutting off the flow of investment money until interest rates rise again.

Often these two interest-related dynamics work in tandem to drive the same boom-and-bust cycle. Either way, financiers who once fed the cycle inevitably find themselves competing to withdraw their cash—which quickly dries it up. And when the flow of investment money dries up, all those downstream feel the effect. Because there's no longer enough cash to go around, sellers of apples and oranges, along with other businesses, file for bankruptcy and people lose their jobs.

Typically, government central banks act to counter such a decline by lowering their prime interest rates, in order to inject new cash into circulation. But the central banks are so much smaller than the private economy that they can do no more than soften its great surges and retreats. The history of modern economics is written in recurring boom-and-bust cycles caused by the growth of compound interest rates, by the profit expectations that they breed, and by the real world's inability to meet them. Wars and pestilence, storms and drought—those bellwethers of the barter economy—today take second position behind interest as a source of economic instability.

Into the Mist

The dangers from that were themselves compounded when money was unhooked from the gold standard in 1971. Not that there was any real choice in the matter. At the time, global economics ran on a system dating from the famous Bretton Woods conference. Shortly after World War II, under the guidance of leading economists like John Maynard Keynes, that meeting harmonized trade and treasury policies of the major industrial powers. Looking back, we can see how some of the practices that emerged then have gone wrong. For instance, the gross national product yardstick (now GDP) used by central banks to gauge real wealth is flawed by externalizations. And big global trade agencies like the World Trade Organization and the International Monetary Fund lack transparency and democratic inputs. They also promote an unsustainable approach to industry. Still, the Bretton Woods system was a tremendous improvement over what came before, and one of its schemes turned out to be remarkably effective. Other national currencies were linked to U.S. dollars at fixed rates of exchange. Then a price of $35 per ounce for gold was set by law (with the loose understanding that not all those dollars would be redeemable at any one time). In that way the world's leading currencies were supported by a credible standard of value, and at the same time they avoided a too-rigid link to the gold standard, which many felt had contributed to the Depression. Largely as a result of the new system, the postwar era of the 1950s and '60s was an extended time of low interest rates, low inflation, and stable prices.

What undermined that system was the burden it put on America as the world's police force and financial administrator. For nearly three decades following Bretton Woods, dollars flowed steadily out of the U.S. treasury and into other nations via foreign aid and through the hands of American soldiers stationed overseas. With the war in Vietnam, overseas expenses soared. Adding to the problem, Presidents John Kennedy and Richard Nixon actually lowered taxes as their spending rose, then made up the difference with borrowed funds or by telling the Fed to just print more money. By 1971 financial catastrophe loomed. Some $300 billion had migrated overseas, with the assurance that it was redeemable in gold. Meanwhile, total U.S. gold reserves stood at just $14 billion. Something had to give. With the war dragging on, allies growing testy, international confidence in the dollar waning, rampant inflation at home, and an election coming, Nixon announced he was "closing the gold window."

That move sent shudders through the world economy and set off a decade of wild instability. Exchange rates began to gyrate, then interest seesawed and prices floated skyward. By the mid-seventies, with the war lost to the communists and Nixon mired in scandal, the United States had fallen from grace in the world's eyes. Topping things off, OPEC took that opportunity to give a lesson on the importance of energy to economics.

As serious as those events were, their impact would soon be overshadowed by another development from that period. In 1971, as part of the new economic order, the United States deposited $300 billion overseas, mostly in Europe. These "Eurodollars" were meant to back up U.S. Cold War commitments, but they differed radically from the other money issued and controlled by central banks. These were placed entirely in private hands. For instance, the Fed put no reserve requirements on them; the banks that received them could lend 100 percent of their holdings. In essence, the U.S. handed the money over and said, "Do what you like with it." Multinationals, the World Bank, even nations were soon borrowing and lending Eurodollars at a furious pace, and every time those dollars changed hands, more compound interest charges were added.

The Eurodollars weren't based on gold; they weren't really based on anything. They were the first major example of digital seed capital. And they quickly thinned out into a spreading mist of numbers based on little more than wildly compounding interest rates. As Eurodollars became vapor-dollars and filtered through the world economy, the stable, solid dollars of the postwar era were diluted. The buying power of consumers was diluted, too. Throughout the 1950s and '60s, average salaries remained around $7,000 to $9,000, and one salary was enough to buy a home and support a family of four. By 1982, people were working three times as long as they had in 1950 to buy an equivalent piece of property.

Then came the neoconservative revolution. Through big tax cuts President Ronald Reagan set off a prolonged economic expansion in the U.S. But Congress refused to also cut spending. Like presidents Kennedy and Nixon before him, Reagan simply borrowed the difference. As a result, over the span of just a few years, the United States went from its position as the world's leading lender to being the world's biggest debtor. In the roughly two decades dating from the decision to quit the gold standard—while average salaries, the gross national product, and government income grew by some 400 percent—government interest payments grew by 1,300 percent. (As this book goes to press, the U.S. government is once again borrowing to pay for tax cuts. Leaving aside Social Security, fully one-third of all federal spending today is paid for with borrowed money, most of it from Asian trading partners like China, Japan, and Taiwan. Add to this the nation's $600 billion foreign trade deficit, a subject of growing concern among its allies.)

Throughout the go-go years of the 1980s, the misty haze of Eurodollars continued to expand. As computers made lightning-fast global transactions possible, traders increasingly turned to speculation in currency shifts and options, or in other derivatives like those based on interest rates. The effect was dramatic. Borrowed and lent, and then lent again, swapped and arbitraged, and with no ecological limits to restrain them, the numbers kept multiplying. Then something unprecedented happened.

By 1987 there were rising concerns in the world's financial capitals. When, in an unhappy coincidence, several big players sold off holdings at the same time, the combined effect brought stock prices low enough to engage the new computerized trading programs. Suddenly computers all over the world triggered massive sell orders, and a financial panic ensued. In a single day—October 19, 1987—$500 billion simply evaporated. In percentage terms it was a financial collapse twice the size of the 1929 crash that set off the Great Depression. And it would become a loss of $1 trillion by the time it finished falling. But the truly unprecedented thing was that, unlike in 1929, the crash of 1987 had little effect on the everyday lives of most working people.

The difference was that the money lost in 1987 no longer represented real capital; most of it existed only on computer screens. As interest rates had multiplied, and then multiplied again, and profit expectations marched in lockstep with them; as arbitrage and other investment instruments grew ever more distant from the natural capital that is the basis for all real economics; Eurodollars had drifted into the realm of pure abstraction. Their value was guaranteed by little more than a willingness by those involved in passing them along to go on doing so, and most of those trading Eurodollars were professionals with a stake in the new status quo. Remarkably, a year after the crash, the whole vast, wildly expanding system was off and running again. By the early nineties, Nixon's original $300 billion in Eurodollars had become something like $2 trillion and is still growing. In 1971 an ounce of gold cost $35. By 2001 it cost $350. In just three decades the U.S. dollar had lost 90 percent of its value. Today, no one knows exactly how much money is out there. It is clear that whatever the quantity, only a very small part any longer represents natural capital. Instead, the great bulk of money in circulation today is a product of what one critic calls "the speculative global cyber-casino."

The world's current economic situation is quite serious, regardless of whether the latest cycle is up or down. The separation of the human economy from its natural foundations began a long time ago, with the advent of the machine age. Depletion of the world's resources has been growing ever since. Now compound interest rates have been freed to further distance our system from reality. They are a main factor in why today it takes two working adults to support a family. And they propel the increasingly hard-edged competition among consumers scrambling for money that buys less and less. They also make the larger economy volatile. Our recurring boom-and-bust cycles are fueled by interest rates. And because of them, the difference in size between the real economy and our financial economy is now so great that global financial stability turns on little more than belief. Along with that dilemma, the loss of fixed exchange rates has added another kind of volatility. Constantly shifting currency values are a problem for companies trying to make long-term plans. As financial writer Joel Kurtzman puts it in his book *The Death of Money*, "It is completely absurd to have a globally-linked economy where companies manufacturing on a global basis are wired together with currencies that shift in value minute by minute." He concludes, "A short-term, take-what-you-can-while-you-can-get-it attitude is rational in an environment where upheaval is the rule."

But the larger problem remains that the whole vast system is expanding headlong into uncharted territory. While no one knows the quantity of money in circulation, the trading volumes are enormous. Numbers equal to America's entire annual GDP now change hands globally every few days. The ability of government central banks to exert discipline on that is scant; they're just not big enough. A reserve requirement on Eurodollars was imposed after the 1987 crash, but by and large the "speculative global cyber-casino" continues to run on its own steam.

This is where the intersection of free market theory with the failure to bring natural capital into economics is most troubling. Champions of the free market quite rightly fight to keep it as free as possible. But because our system is divorced from the workings of nature, our distorted free market actually undermines real growth. So the freer we make it, the more we weaken our economy. In today's paradoxical world, capitalists are that in name only. The legal tender they use has only a tenuous link to real capital. Meanwhile, our global economy—on which turn the lives of billions of people and other living things—is not governed by nations, by nature, or even by the market in any rigorous sense. It is quite literally out of control.

At the heart of that problem lies interest. As Kurtzman wrote, "By abandoning gold, Nixon enlarged the size of the finance economy by several orders of magnitude. He also moved the world onto a new standard: the interest-rate standard. From that point of view all investment, finance and real, has a single benchmark: interest rates. And all investors have one simple goal: to earn more than the cost of money." That, he says, has given rise to a strange system in which "interest rates determine the value of the dollar instead of the other way around." As one economist has described it, "The dollar has become a circular argument. It is still a promise to pay. But to pay what to whom?"

A return to the gold standard, even the loosely fixed standard of Bretton Woods, is no longer practical or even desirable. But computerization of the global economy has made a new alternative possible—the transition from a gold standard to "the green standard."

Real Money

Most of today's economic problems were foreseen a century ago by Silvio Gesell, one of the earliest bioeconomists. It was Gesell who first pointed out the flawed nature of the money now in use, which allows the damming of cash flow to dry up transactions downstream. He was the first to talk of how that makes the charging of interest possible, and to point out that interest is contrary to the 2nd Law. Gesell also called for replacing that system with one in which financial redistribution by interest rates is banned and all money loses value, gradually and evenly across the board.

In 1918, just after World War I—while most observers talked of peace and of the new agencies designed to protect it, and as the world economy gathered itself for the great expansion of the 1920s—Gesell made this extraordinary prediction:

> If the present monetary system, based on interest and compound interest, remains in operation, I dare to predict today, that it will take less than 25 years for us to have a new and even worse war. I can foresee the coming development clearly. The present degree of technological advancement will quickly result in a record performance of industry. The buildup of capital will be rapid in spite of the enormous losses during the war, and through its over-supply will lower the interest rate. Money will then be hoarded. Economic activities will diminish and increasing numbers of unemployed persons will roam the streets . . . within the discontented masses, wild, revolutionary ideas will arise and also the poisonous plant called "Super-Nationalism" will proliferate. No country will understand the other, and the end can only be war again.

Gesell's forecast proved eerily on target. Within little more than a decade the Great Depression had begun, and a decade more would bring the start of World War II.

The Depression era was fertile ground for economic experiments. Marxism and other alternate theories flourished as people sought a way, any way, out of prolonged and wasting poverty. During that time Gesell's ideas were also put in play. The most successful test took place in the

Austrian town of Wörgl. With thousands out of work and tax funds declining, the town decided to issue its own currency. The new bills were backed by conventional Austrian schillings, but then differed in one important way. Instead of being able to gain buying power through the accumulation of interest, they were designed to lose it. Each month, any holder of a new bill had to purchase a stamp equal to 1 percent of the bill's face value and paste it on the back. Bills without all their stamps were invalid. By that means, Wörgl's stamp scrip automatically lost 12 percent of its value each year.

Since the town sold the stamps, that 12 percent in fees went to replenish its shrunken treasury. What's more, people knew their money would lose value if they held on to it, so no one did. Instead, they spent it as quickly as possible. With official Austrian schillings nearly impossible to come by in the Depression, the new stamp scrip quickly gained acceptance. Within a year it was circulating through the town's economy at a rate equal to more than twenty times that of official schillings. With ready cash once again in circulation, the effect was dramatic. The town's water system was rebuilt. Streets were paved. New houses went up, then a new bridge, a ski jump. While unemployment was growing steadily across Europe and around the world, in Wörgl it declined by 25 percent in a single year. Money is a promise to pay. As such, it is just a reliable means of keeping score. In Wörgl there was no shortage of people willing to work, or willing to employ them. The only thing missing was the way to keep score. By issuing its own currency, one that couldn't be profitably withheld from circulation, the town had solved its problem.

Meanwhile, curiosity about that solution was developing in other countries. The French prime minister even came to view the "miracle of Wörgl" for himself. But when hundreds of Austrian towns began to talk of adopting the new model, the government central bank took action. In a case that went to the Austrian Supreme Court, the sole right of the central bank to issue currency was affirmed. Wörgl's stamp scrip was outlawed, the economic boomlet subsided, and unemployment there returned to its previously high levels. Plans in other towns throughout Europe soon met with similar opposition, and no repeat of the experiment has been tried since.

In the U.S. a Depression-era stamp scrip proposal, based on Gesell's ideas and backed by the prominent economist Irving Fisher, was entertained at the cabinet level in Washington, D.C. It was rejected in the end as too fundamental a change. Still, support for the concept endured at high levels. John Maynard Keynes, in his *General Theory*, reviewed it and concluded:

> Thus those reformers, who look for a remedy by creating artificial carrying-costs for money through the device of requiring legal-tender currency to be periodically stamped at a prescribed cost . . . have been on the right track; and the practical value of their proposals deserves considerations.

An echo of Gesell even turned up in Keynes' postwar proposal for an International Clearing Union; in it countries running trade surpluses would have paid a liquidity charge of 1 percent per month. That proposal was submitted by the British delegation at Bretton Woods and was blocked by the U.S.

Although a socialist, Gesell was even less popular with Marxists. They took umbrage at his claim that human exploitation was due not to private ownership of the means of production but to structural defects in the monetary system. The Soviets condemned him as "an apologist of the monopoly bourgeoisie," and after World War II, organizations supporting his views were banned.

While Gesell's call for depreciating currency failed its political test, the advantages of interest-free trade did find expression in the many barter clubs begun during the Depression. One of the oldest and largest of these is the Swiss WIR (for Wirtschaftsring, or "economic circle"). The WIR was founded in 1934 as a local exchange network for businesses. It continues to play an important role in the Swiss economy today, with a yearly exchange of goods and services equaling more than $1 billion. Similarly, JAK (signifying "land, work, and capital") was set up by farmers in Denmark during the Depression. That system has lately undergone rapid growth in Scandinavia and is spreading to other regions. There are now hundreds more exchanges, among them LETS, IRTA, ROCS, and Time Dollar in North America. And they have been joined by e-start-ups like swap.com—all of which points to a central fact: today's renaissance in barter stems largely from the advent of computers and the Internet.

An economist explains how the Internet has made bartering apples and oranges more flexible and efficient:

One of the principal barriers opposing barter up until now—the difficulty in finding suitable partners for any exchange—has disappeared with the internet, since this medium can resolve, in an optimal manner, the problem of identifying potential trade partners. Using the internet, each supplier can present his or her offers to the entire world with minimal difficulty, at any hour of the day or night.

Money began with goldsmiths. Since they had the most secure means of storing gold, people often used them to store private bullion. In return, those depositors got paper receipts from the goldsmith. It wasn't long before, instead of going back to get more gold each time they wanted to buy something, holders of those receipts began simply exchanging the receipts for goods. Because money originated as gold, which evolved into scrip, we tend to view it as a substance. That's a basic misunderstanding. Money is a scorecard, a way of keeping track of how much people owe or are owed. We don't need bank money per se. All we need is a flexible, efficient, stable means of keeping score. Bank money has long served that purpose, if in a less than ideal manner. Because of that, the monopoly that central banks have on the creation and movement of money has been a historic force. But things are changing, and rapidly.

The Harvard economist Benjamin Friedman recently raised international eyebrows with his assertion that bank money "has become increasingly irrelevant to legal, domestic transactions," and by marshaling a tally of sophisticated arguments about why that means the death of central banks. In a paper that served as a lead topic during a World Bank conference held in 2000, he acknowledged the role of central banks in maintaining stability but doubted their ability to survive the coming era. Friedman referred to the globalization of financial markets, the private securitization of credit, and the growth of private markets relative to the shrinking size of influence exerted on them by central banks. Their monopoly on the creation of money can't last, either, he said. Friedman's comments about the growing irrelevance of bank control over cash are on the money, so to speak. "Being a monopoly is of little value," he concluded, "if no one needs, or even wants, to have whatever the monopoly is of."

Early experiments with Gesell's stamp scrip were blocked by the monopoly that central banks have on printing money. With electronic currencies, that barrier has been sidestepped. Digital money in such forms as points, rewards, frequent-flier miles, and e-money is now routinely issued by airlines, hotel chains, car rental agencies, credit card companies, and pretty much any other business with a computer. E-gold is an Internet currency backed 100 percent with gold bullion, which books $1.6 million worth of transactions daily. In addition, the Internet as a medium of exchange has proved fertile ground for the growing number of barter clubs.

All of the cashless new means of electronic exchange are flexible and efficient, and they promise real change. Still, if the influence of central banks wanes, what will become of one of their primary reasons for being? What will become of stability? Gesell claimed that falling interest rates prompt lenders to dam their cash until rates rise again. That practice, he said, is a major cause of economic downturns. When money is held back from the market, for instance, there may be just as many apples and oranges for sale, and just as many people eager to have them, but no one can buy because there's no cash around to use for keeping track of transactions. If Gesell was right, then during economic downturns the only thing missing is a way to keep score. Which would mean that barter clubs should undergo a surge of activity during those times as people adopt cashless alternatives.

That effect was verified in a careful 2000 study by the economist James Stodder of the highly regarded Rensselaer Polytechnic Institute, which has made the cultural impact of the Internet a special research area. Stodder looked at two large barter clubs, the Swiss WIR and the American IRTA (International Reciprocal Trade Association, which dates from the 1970s). He found that "the economic activity of both exchanges is counter-cyclical, rising and falling against, rather than with, the business cycle." Or, as Tobias Studer, an economist at the University of Basel, summarized those findings on WIR, "In periods of economic boom, it has tended to grow more slowly than the economic average, while in periods of recession, it has tended to grow more quickly than average. Thus it contributes to the stability of the Swiss economy."

By counterbalancing boom-and-bust cycles caused by interest, the spread of barter clubs is a small but relevant counter to the instability of today's global economy. That instability has also prompted calls for the return of fixed exchange rates. The euro is by default a fixed exchange rate for the many national currencies it replaced, and some would like to link the euro to the dollar. Stanford economist Ronald McKinnon has called for a fixed rate between the U.S. and Japan. Benjamin Friedman points to the interesting fact that even as the world splinters into more and more independent countries, the number of currencies in use is declining. The experiment with variable exchange rates is losing ground.

As that process plays out on the world's stage, the need for a suitable standard of value remains. The purpose of a standard—like the gold standard—is to make a currency credible. With it, money is grounded in something that has a stable and commonly agreed value. But if the gold standard is too narrow for today's economy, what alternatives are there? Some suggest linking the dollar to a market basket of goods, including gold, silver, grain, and other currencies. Ecological economists—with their efforts now to bring the energy and material flows of nature into pricing structures—have opened the door to broader measures. As their work becomes more sophisticated, and as computers become more powerful and universal, these developments raise the possibility of a global economy based on a true green standard.

Finally, though, even if money becomes a stable and reliable marker of value, there is the question of how to keep it circulating. The good news here is that while interest charges are not likely to go away anytime soon, they don't have to in order for reform to occur. In fact reform is under way, and will likely continue without government shake-ups, international conferences, or clashes between great powers. WIR, JAK, LETS, and the many other interest-free barter exchanges have been showing for decades how separate economic systems can work side by side—even complement one another. Now that money is becoming electronic, and so moving beyond the control of central banks, all this could have larger ramifications.

As Internet barter clubs proliferate, some see a chance to combine their best features with Gesell's call for a depreciating currency that parallels the 2nd Law. Earlier efforts to do that were blocked because they relied on stamp scrip, which could be outlawed by central banks. Today it can all be done electronically. Web-based groups and firms are now free to test these concepts under various conditions, to see if they provide benefits that can be adopted elsewhere.

Blue-Sky Concept

The postwar period of the 1950s and '60s was a time of political and cultural upheaval as people came to grips with the atomic bomb, the

Cold War, the advent of television, civil rights struggles, and political as-
sassinations. Looking back, we also see that the prosperity of that era was
based on unsustainable methods. But the economic system then was in
some ways doing what a good economic system should. It remained stable, quiet, and in the background, promoting long-term planning and a
simple, unquestioning confidence in the future. When people today wax
nostalgic about that time, while they may talk of style or music or the
simplicity of life, at the heart of that yearning lies the bedrock faith that
people had then in the future. We've lost some of that optimism as the
hidden weaknesses in our industrial system have come to light, and as
our currency has vaporized. Interest rates today are low, but dependent
on huge overseas national debts. What's more, with no realistic standard
of value, our money bears little relation to the underlying flows of energy and material that are its real foundation. And so it floats ever further into the realm of abstraction.

The bioeconomists are suggesting ways to address those problems. It
is no longer idle dreaming to imagine what a world with realistic money
might be like. First, the economy would be more stable, with a leveling
of the boom-and-bust cycles now caused by compound interest. That
could mean less government intrusion in free markets. Real money
would circulate more equitably. And unlike in the interest-based economy, the buying power lost from real money could flow into government coffers to reduce taxes.

Those who wished to save could do so. Banks wouldn't pay interest
on savings, but money placed in long-term savings accounts would not
lose value, either. Only money in checking accounts would depreciate.
Banks in turn would invest their funds for profit, just as they do now.
But instead of being able to put them out at interest, they would have
to invest them in assets that undergo real economic growth. Denied interest, private investors would have to do the same. Economist Dieter
Suhr, one of the more exacting advocates of money reform, sees another benefit. In his view, today's problematic distribution of funds,
based on the cost of getting money (the cost of interest), would be replaced with a "more efficient allocation by the prices of the goods
themselves," just as in barter.

All of that would steer investments in the direction of a sounder
economy. So governments and the degree of their interference in
free markets could shrink without adverse consequences—as economist Werner Onken points out, "Long-term positive interest rates . . .

disturb the balance of profit and loss necessary for the decentralized self-regulation of markets." It might also end the curious cycle in which the wealthy impoverish the poor through interest charges, only to have huge and inefficient government bureaucracies take money back from the wealthy through taxes and distribute it once again to the poor.

At the start of this transition, for companies in nations employing real money, the absence of interest costs would translate into lower prices. In world markets this would give them a competitive edge over those economies still tied to interest-bearing currency. It would also encourage sustainable approaches in energy, farming, industry, and other fields that are only marginally profitable under the present system. So rivers could become cleaner and skies bluer without government regulation. And it could profoundly impact global aid. Margit Kennedy points to the hundreds of millions of dollars in interest paid each day by developing nations for aid loans, up to a third of which are now taken just to cover the interest payments due on prior loans. How different might the world be, she asks, if international aid focused instead on setting up regional electronic exchanges that use depreciating currency? In such a world, local economies could act as a counterbalance, to stabilize and invigorate the global system.

It's difficult to get our minds around the notion that a more equitable and sustainable economy can come with less government and lower taxes. But they can and do belong together. The key lies in making our economy true to life. All energy in nature dissipates. That's the law—the 2nd Law—and there is no court of appeals. Those who challenge that fundamental rule are not wise or hard-nosed or realistic. Most of all, they are not conservative. They might more accurately be called "corporate conservatives," since their intemperate views are shaped largely by the interests of big multinational firms.

Real conservatives, by contrast, are those who work to fit human culture to the real world—to the basic systems from which it emerges, and on which it depends.

Humans are unique. Most living things don't think the way we do. We have ideas: some bad, some good, some great. Until now, money has been a good idea with an unrealized potential for greatness. As we begin to understand it better, we see how less money can mean more wealth, and why that possibility is worth pursuing. John Maynard Keynes once predicted that the future would "learn more from the spirit of Gesell than from Marx." With the aid of computers, that future has arrived.

Real Conservatives

When we talk of economics, we speak about creating wealth. But it all begins by using energy from the sun to stir matter from the earth into new forms—just like seafaring algae or snails on white cliffs. At its core, our economic system answers to the same laws that govern all of life.

Through the medium of industrialized farming, we now use energy from the sun to transform atoms from the earth into approximately ten thousand new people per hour. That expanding population then requires the use of more energy to transform more matter into homes. With that, industry grows, too, using still more energy to stir yet more matter into the machines that provide additional goods and services. As this huge new global flow approaches 500 billion tons per year, its sources are being exhausted at one end while the capacities of natural systems to absorb its wastes are flooded at the other. The reasons for that are numerous, but for humans, with our conscious designs and goal-driven culture, economics is the bottom line, a basic guiding force.

The brutal free markets of the nineteenth century and oppressive bureaucracies of the mid-twentieth can't tell us much about the future, because both of them grew from a machine age view of nature; they were only superficially realistic. As we move now to a different model, political categories like right and left become vestigial. Even notions of top-down and bottom-up have limited relevance in a naturalistic scheme where both are seen as interactive parts of a single coevolving whole. Nature fosters constant tensions within and between its systems, as a way of maintaining its dynamism. Those tensions—between figure and ground, bottom-up and top-down, micro and macro, impulse and restraint—are sustained and guided by what we call feedback.

Economic theory admits a push and pull between the stability of existing patterns and their "creative destruction" by innovation. It's a principle with deep roots in nature. But many now feel we're pushing the balance too quickly and too far toward change, a concern that has spawned unusual alliances. Those working on the right, to conserve family and community values, and those working on the left, to conserve nature, are finding themselves on new and unfamiliar common ground: they both want to temper the global economic fast-forward now being orchestrated by multinational corporations.

"Americans are conditioned to see ecology and social conservatism as occupying opposite ends of the political spectrum," write Clifford Cobb, Ted Halstead, and Jonathan Rowe. But they suggest that divide is caused largely by our outdated economic system. They also note that adherents from both ends of the spectrum have begun to see how heedless pursuit of GDP growth can undermine everyone's aims. Just as that chase "turns ancient forests into lumber and beaches into sewers, so it turns families into nodes of consumption and the living-room into a marketing free-fire zone. Both camps speak from the standpoint of *values* against the moral relativism and opportunism of the market."

The growing ranks of corporate conservatives like to dismiss such concerns with Darwinian terms like "competition" and "evolution," saying that whatever comes from them is for the best. But evolution works because accurate natural feedback links the wants and needs of individuals to the limits of their habitats. Our economic system no longer does that. The leaders of great corporations are supposed to be our ultimate realists, hard-nosed proponents of the bottom line. But in recent decades, and especially in the past few years, they sound like pie-in-the-sky academics, holed up in their high-rise ivory towers, defending outmoded theories from the ever-mounting realities that challenge them.

Those who oppose a more realistic system, one based on principles developed and proven over nearly four billion years, can no longer claim the mantle of "conservative." Just opposing change is not conservative if the change being called for is a shift back to basics. For centuries we have been insulating ourselves from reality by drawing down the energy stored in a fossil fuel storage battery for solar energy. This epic windfall has fostered an illusion, now consecrated at every level in culture, that the rules have somehow changed. Split off from answering directly to nature, we no longer have an instinctive feel for fundamentals. But nature's rules are inviolable. And the idea that we can change them isn't heroic; it's foolish. It is above all not conservative.

No board of directors made up of real conservatives would accept a continuous drawing down of capital—as we do now with irreplaceable resources—in order to maintain operations. The hard truth is that our business leaders aren't being tough enough. It's time for them to insist that our economic system adopt realistic principles for the use of energy and matter. Those who don't are playing fast and loose. They are champions of a radical view, and should be identified as such.

Back when the industrial revolution was gearing up, artists and poets raised concerns about the rift it was creating with nature. Among them was Samuel Taylor Coleridge. His ancient mariner symbolizes that rift when he kills the albatross, winged symbol of nature's goodwill. Shipmates label him the culprit by hanging the dead bird around his neck, but the forces of nature soon come crushing down on them all. Then, one day, his ship becalmed—lost, desolate, and in lonely isolation—the mariner looks into the sea and spies a writhing mass of water snakes twisting and gleaming like "a flash of golden fire." In that moment, as he reconnects with the beauty and mystery of nature, the albatross falls from his neck and his trial comes to an end.

Real conservatives work to reconnect human economics with nature. Their efforts lay the foundation for a system in which the products we buy in billions of individual transactions become an accurate form of feedback. With that, today's machine age, corporate globalization can be transformed into a more equitable and sustainable global economy.

When an ecosystem expands to its habitat limits, it begins a transition to what naturalists call a climax culture. As the system's resources grow scarcer, living forms within it become more efficient, diverse, and complex. Human culture is now entering that stage, and to the extent that our system is true to nature, our economic system is evolving to both mirror and encourage that. While this means dramatic change on many fronts, it is business leaders who will have to make some of the largest adjustments. The economy of the future will no longer be the zero-sum game of who gets the last drop of fossil fuel pumped from the ground. Instead it will be a much livelier contest between higher, smarter, more efficient, and more complex new forms as they jostle and adapt for a place in the interconnecting loops and webs of material and energy flows.

"If the workings of the economy parallel the functions of the ecosystem, if organizations follow the same principles of form and function that govern the evolution of organisms," writes Michael Rothschild in *Bionomics*, "then there is but one natural mode of economic organization."

With the rise of real conservatives, schooled in the hard economic lessons of nature, it's possible now to imagine a new kind of global economy, one that integrates diverse cultures—and the businesses and institutions within them—in much the same way that nature unifies its uncounted multitudes large and small. Like those calcium atoms that flow from seafaring algae through plate tectonics into snails on white cliffs; or like the myriad links between microscopic DNA and the large-scale dynamics of a forest; cells, organisms, and whole systems all run on the same ecological scheme. They share common means of processing energy and material flows, and are linked together at every scale by accurate feedback. Can we balance bottom-up and top-down as effectively as nature does—uniting individual needs and global flows, micro and macro, figure and ground into a seamless whole that in turn meshes well with nature?

The idea that business and the environment might be symbiotic is a revolution in itself. Still, it's only part of the overall picture. With the emergence of civilization have also come concepts like public education, a free and informed media, and democracy. These are feedback, too. Like money, like economic indicators, they provide information about the world around us. And all of them feed into another novel development: the rule of law as a means of upholding fair play. An economic system that doesn't recognize that as a standard for human welfare risks losing its franchise. Competition is part of all natural systems, but as a sole guiding principle it's half-baked ideology. Unhindered competition devolves society back toward a preconscious animal state. Anyone who sees that as a strategy for the future clearly hasn't thought the problem through.

As arguably the most complex life form yet, humans have figured out how to harvest more solar energy from photosynthesis by organizing plants into farms. That in turn gave rise to the higher and more complex organizations we call cities. From them came industry, which now spans the globe—affecting billions of people and virtually all life on earth. Now, as computers move us toward an information economy, the integrity of all our cultural feedbacks will be more important than ever before.

twelve

feedback culture

A strict law bids us dance.
—KWAKIUTL TEACHING

We are made of matter forged in stars, and powered by their fire. Everything alive brings those two realms together. Then, as energy from sunlight flows through living things on earth, layers of complexity evolve—each emerging out of those that came before. Nature's wild diversity grows from this ageless probe of earth's capacity for life. Just one hundred thousand years ago we arrived: conscious beings who can rise above instinct, prize communicators, builders of great cultures, odd new organisms who wonder about the future. But even as we reach out toward that future we remain part of the world from which we came, tied to nature's grand design.

A pulse is a rhythm. All of nature dances to a beat. The turning seasons flood the earth with energy each spring, then see it fade come fall, just as our own pulse is a vital sign of life. In us and all the living world, countervailing tendencies pulse one against the other. Bodies broadcast alternating hormones that promote opposing trends: some that spur excitement, others for subsidence. Predators and prey lock into coevolving dances as their populations wax and wane by turns. However we advance, reciprocating pulses and the gentle lift of rhythms within rhythms hold the stage. They have always been with us, reaching back through time beyond human memory.

A pulse is also a seedhead, carrier of patterns that inform new generations. All living bodies—zebras, lilies, starfish, people—are defined by information, the genetic patterns through which matter and energy flow. As a body pulses into existence, reproduces, and dies away, its main drive is to carry that pattern into the future. Now we've developed cultures. They carry patterns that inform new generations, too, in this case the knowledge and traditions we use to shape our world. At every level of life—from the growth of algae in a pond to the rise of a skyscraper in New York—this same basic process is at work: patterns of inherited information draw energy from the sun to stir matter from the earth into new forms.

We have been around now for one hundred thousand years, and human culture has existed for just half that time. Ten thousand years ago it put down roots with farming, which let us settle in one place. From farms grew cities, and the intellectual ferment that in turn advanced technology. With time the need for group decisions brought democracy. Then, some two centuries ago, the machine age began its dramatic ascent.

As the twenty-first century debuts, human culture enters yet another great transition. Where culture once shaped just our thoughts, now it offers means to alter life's most basic plans—to change our own genetic patterns and those of other life forms. And today we make machines that act like living things. All this marks a breakthrough in the course of evolution. Conscious thought and human tools can now affect the process.

Of those tools, computers are the key. They've been crucial to unlocking life's most basic rules. They're also vital in the effort to ingrain those rules in culture. And just as culture brought computers into being—and used them to forge better links with nature—in the future it will shape the benefits we draw from that new symbiosis.

At the start of another age, explorers from a distant land stood at the shore of a vast new world, looking out upon a landscape filled with unknown promise and peril. Like them, we find ourselves on an unfamiliar shore, with new dangers and opportunities at every side. Yet the challenge we face is greater. Those pioneers surveyed a world whose features, once discovered, would remain familiar. In the landscape we now enter—with the rise of genetic engineering and artificial evolution; of nanotechnology, biomimetic robots, neural net intelligence, artificial life, and virtual worlds; and with radical changes coming to broad fields like industry and economics—our world has begun to flux around us.

What would it be like to live in a time when communities reintegrate with nature, as industries behave like ecosystems and the value of money keys to the 2nd Law—a world in which we assemble molecules to "grow" solid objects, where robotic life forms mingle with "real" life forms, and virtual online realities shape "real" reality? What would it mean if our brains were wired to computers, computers had emotions, and new species were designed and turned loose to compete with those born in nature? In fact, that world is already taking shape. It becomes more apparent each year.

For us to imagine where all this will lead is, to borrow the phrase of one observer, "like a dog trying to imagine general relativity." When it comes to the truly big questions, our limited intellects and senses leave us with little more than a feeling of wonder. We do know that while the typical life of species on earth runs to millions of years, we've been around for only a hundred thousand. By comparison we are just getting started.

Given that, our notion of long-term planning could do with some adjustment. We need to plan not only for the next decade, or even the next century, but for the next one hundred thousand years and beyond. How is that possible in a world where the future is unknowable? Our best chance lies in working with the dynamics that have always sustained life. Whatever our intellectual limits, we see clearly now why nothing alive lasts outside the rules of nature. We also see that as human culture, and those patterns of knowledge and tradition it conveys, have spread across the globe, we have become major actors in natural systems. All of this points us toward a culture grounded in the new biology.

Machine age optimists have long dismissed environmentalists and their concerns with a stock refrain: "Don't worry. The combination of market forces and technical innovation will come up with a better solution to meet those problems." The new biology is that solution. And the implications are clear: They mandate learning all we can about how nature works, then using those lessons in designs for biocentric systems. They mean deciding where machine age methods can still serve, even as we purge them from those systems where they now wreak widespread havoc.

Above all, we'll need a way to manage such a huge and complex change. For the industrial populations now spreading over earth, that means feedback culture. What is feedback culture? It is ecological dynamics in play at a new and higher level of complexity. It's culture that engages with the basic rules of life, by morphing natural logic into social forms. It's complex and technological, harnessing the power and widespread distribution of computers. Feedback culture links their power to deeper investigations of nature. It then uses their pervasiveness, with the flexibility that brings, to help ingrain the lessons being learned into our daily lives. Feedback culture secures its energy inputs—food, for instance. It recognizes farming as a vital link to the ecological base from which all living matter comes; so farms respect the natural feedbacks from that base. And as in nature, power generation is sustainable, nonpolluting, and decentralized—securing it from broad disruptions. By looking to a green standard in economics, feedback culture evolves in these directions organically as real money and realistic pricing send real feedback to free markets, which do the same for farms, homes, industries. All of this spurs energy and resource efficiency, accompanied by closed-loop material flows.

Feedback culture means computerized and densely interactive communication webs. These convey a ripe mix of ideas, spawned by decentralized free media and by a schooling based on truer apprehension of the basic rules of life. Feedback culture reintegrates communities and, in what may be its central trait, is democratic. In democracies, it is feedback from the bottom up that guides the top-down acts of government. And since all of the above are shaped by government, its first and foremost job is to ensure that voter feedback loops aren't warped—not by undue influence, not by machine age ideologies, nor by any others yet to come.

One hundred thousand years ago, who could conceive the world we inhabit today? And as we prepare for an active role in evolution, who will guess at what the next one hundred thousand years may bring?

A feeling of wonder indeed. We stand at a critical juncture. How we deal with the challenges ahead will define what we become. And chief among them is the effort to design a technological culture that works within the basic rules of life. The machine age was a heroic effort to do just that, but we got it only half right. Much of the backlash against modern agriculture, industry, genetic engineering, suburban planning, and the global economy stems from how these fields are being shaped by old, machine age thinking. And because that old approach has spread so far, the culture it produced has had a vastly destructive impact on nature, as well as on the natural qualities of human community. Now we have a better plan. With the new biology we secure a realistic grounding in the world, and by doing that secure a future well beyond our view.

The Basic Rules of Life

No one knows for sure how life began. So far all pronouncements on that question come down to acts of faith. But compared with the machine age, with its clockwork notions of the world, we know a good deal more today about how nature works.

We see now that for every action there is not just one reaction. Instead, each action produces multiple reactions that in turn give rise to countless more, as they pulse and cycle back through living systems—cells, organs, bodies, ecosystems. A pulsing interactivity also lies behind the stolid face of that reality once known as the inanimate world. As the physicist Max Born put it, "We have sought for firm ground and found none. The deeper we penetrate, the more restless becomes the universe; all is rushing about and vibrating in a wild dance." Just as nearly four billion years ago that dance was elevated into living form, we now seek to amplify it into large-scale human culture. The machine age isn't obsolete because it's wrong, or the embodiment of dark and unnatural forces. With its simple, mechanistic explanations, the machine age is obsolete because it's incomplete.

Today we know that life is an ongoing integration of energy from the sun and materials from earth—an energetic impulse cloaked in matter. And while solar power drives all living systems, the 2nd Law means energy is always diluting, thinning out from concentrated form into useless dissipation. Due to that, it moves through life in one-way flows. That's not the case with matter, though. It recycles endlessly through living systems in closed loops. Energy and matter work together to incorporate and reproduce the third main element that makes life possible: information, encoded in genetic plans. By combining all three factors, the dynamic patterns we call species—from every kind of butterfly to every kind of ape—take form and adhere to the underlying ecological base, even as their individual bodies pulse in and out of existence. In this sense living things are "dissipative structures," constantly evolving patterns through which energy and matter flow.

We living patterns, human or otherwise, convert solar power to an internal chemical flame, a cold fire used to pump matter and energy through us. We also insulate our selves from the outside world by forming boundaries. Those boundaries are ubiquitous. Genes can exist without organisms (we call them viruses), but all organisms are in essence bounded genes, and like so much else in nature, life's boundaries are rarely strict or static. From the microscopic nucleus cupping and protecting its genes to the cell body that shelters the nucleus, and on up from there—to those organs that cells combine to form, and then to the organisms organs join to form—each system is encased in a semipermeable membrane. That barrier sets it apart from its larger context while at the same time letting vital flows of matter, energy, and information pass through.

Bodies have two material purposes in nature. They serve as metabolic buffers, protecting and preserving the genetic plans they hold. They also reproduce those plans (which is another kind of buffer, since making extra copies helps preserve them from extinction). While all organisms reproduce, their strategies can differ. One-celled forms just clone, with each cell splitting into two, then four, and so on, rapidly and endlessly, in a scheme that might be called "divide and conquer." More complex forms invest resources into making seeds and eggs—genes contained in cases filled with nutrients, which then help each new body get its start. A human being, in the simplest sense, is just an egg that grew arms and legs, a head, eyes, ears, a brain. The design for those extensions is found in our genetic plan, which employs them to acquire the fresh energy and matter that we channel through our bodies (so they can shield and reproduce that plan).

As organisms have emerged and reproduced and adapted through some four billion years of evolution, the parts that deal with fundamental processes are standardized and shielded from change. The genes controlling cell division and cell wall synthesis are the same throughout the living world, and have been for billions of years—we share genes with lettuce. So, too, for the energy carrier ATP. The nervous systems linking brains to senses also tend to be alike. The tiny mitochondria making power for our cells do that for everything from amoebas to whales.

Even parts that aren't so elementary are standardized, if they offer good solutions. The basic structure of the vertebrate limb was arrived at some 300 million years ago and has changed but little since. A like-proportioned spiral can be found in plants, snail shells, and mammal horns. Self-similar branching structures turn up in arteries, lungs, plant vascular systems, and insect tracheal tubes (not to mention river deltas). The poet Goethe, an accomplished naturalist, touched on this in his theory that all the parts of a plant are expressions of a single deeper pattern, one that transforms itself through various stages of the plant's growth—becoming leaves, flower petals, and other forms as they emerge.

Naturalist D'Arcy Thompson pointed to something like that with his famous "transformations." Drawing the skull of a rabbit on a grid, for instance, he then distorted it to show how the rabbit's skull can be stretched to resemble the skull of a horse. With that transformation he also showed how the patterns of the skull parts and the relations among them are essentially the same for both rabbits and horses, just as they are in comparisons among numerous other species.

Standardized, redundant patterns are in play throughout the living world. As microbes divide, as seeds grow to plants, and as embryos become animals and reproduce, life reuses proven patterns and insulates them from change. But change does occur: When organisms reproduce, background radiation mutates a few percentage points of each genetic plan. Accidents in development—the failure of a hormone to release, altered timing in a gene cascade—can affect the offspring. Change also occurs when male and female mating mixes genes. And just as life joins standardized genetic parts in making up new genomes, it also joins different kinds of life to make up whole new forms.

This symbiogenesis takes place among organisms that find mutual benefit in working closely. For instance, it was the absorption of one-celled mitochondria (which give off useful energy) into larger cells (which offer food and protection) that made complex organisms like us possible. As Lynn Margulis—who proposed the theory of symbiogenesis—and her son Dorion Sagan state in their book *Slanted Truths*, "It makes more sense now to think of beetles, rose bushes, and baboons as communities of bacteria than it does to think of bacteria as tiny animals or plants."

Another kind of coming together is described by biologist Stuart Kauffman of the Santa Fe Institute. He suggests a natural tendency for molecules to self-organize into cells, which tend to self-organize into organisms, which in turn self-organize into ecosystems.

Kauffman points out how living systems survive only by negotiating a balance between order and chaos. In much the same way, all organisms have to balance the need for stability against the need for change. Life's answer to this challenge starts with genomes, relatively stable platforms that nonetheless allow for innovation. Any modifications then get passed on or edited out with the success or failure of the organisms they produce—when they go out in the world to interact with members of their own kind, with other species, and with the availability of water, land, and energy. As they do that, their drive to reproduce encounters limits.

Those whose innovations better suit them to compete for scarce resources flourish; they have successfully adapted. The rest die out. In this respect, competition is a key factor in life. We call that competition "natural selection," survival of the fittest. (Philosopher of biology William Wimsatt argues that an ability to self-organize is among the things that natural selection "selects for.")

Reproduction is another basic fact of life, an element in successful competition. It ensures that the genetic pattern of an individual, and of its species, gets widely dispersed. With that, its rising numbers may spread to other habitats, where available resources differ. In the course of this "evolutionary search," the genome's ability to innovate and change comes into play. As adaptation builds on adaptation over time, new species emerge that are better fitted to those locales. Zoologist Richard Dawkins writes of how that process has shaped animals like camels into the form we recognize today:

> Like sandbluffs carved into fantastic shapes by the desert winds, like rocks shaped by ocean waves, camel DNA has been sculpted by survival in ancient deserts, and even more ancient seas, to yield modern camels. Camel DNA speaks—if only we could read the language—of the changing worlds of camel ancestors. If only we could read the language, the DNA of tuna and starfish would have "sea" written into the text. The DNA of moles and earthworms would spell "underground."

Cooperation is basic to life as well. As the tendencies to self-organize, reproduce, disperse, compete, and adapt all work together, they give rise to increasingly diversified systems, where broad varieties of species cooperate in highly integrated ways. But "cooperation," as biologists use the term, doesn't mean everyone shakes hands and agrees to get along. It more often means eating one another, or eating each other's waste, or evolving to eat something no one else can. Still, it's hard to overstate the importance of that cooperation. For instance, here is ecologist Paul Shepard describing predator-prey relations:

> The well-being of prey species is as much at stake as that of predators in food chain systems. The "struggle" of the individual prey to elude the predator has to do with sorting out particular sets of genes for continuation, not for the escape of the prey as a species. By eating certain individ-

uals and not others the predator becomes the prey's instrument for filtering the information to be transmitted to its own succeeding generations . . . it cannot be asserted that the hawk "uses" the mouse or rabbit any more than the mouse uses the hawk or the ecosystem uses them both.

In this and countless other ways, each member of a living system plays some role in creating or shaping the others. So as individuals jostle, the evolution of a single species stems from the coevolution of many. This is why, as one observer puts it, "sustained life is a property of an ecological system rather than of a single organism or species." Susan Oyama, the philosopher of biology, states the paradox nicely: "Organisms organize their surroundings as much as they are organized by them."

An ecosystem is a complex and highly integrated whole made up of other living systems—myriad dissipative structures ranging from micro to macro—each with its own genetic pattern, all bounded by semipermeable membranes, and all nested together and within one another. Those many different patterns interact through the food chains and webs that link them to the inorganic world. They are networks of networks, inherently unstable yet continuously pushed toward a rough and dynamic balance by the feedbacks looping through them. In all this the myriad flows coursing through an ecosystem are, in the words of science writer Fritjof Capra, "a continuation of the metabolic pathways through organisms."

While energy, material, and genetic information ripple through living systems—cascading and rebounding and seeking new expression—the efficiency of their energy use improves as they grow larger and more complex. Gram for gram, the body of an elephant is some seven times more efficient than the body of a mouse. So, too, a mature, complex ecosystem is more efficient than a simple, primitive one (think here of an old-growth forest versus algae expanding headlong in a pond). This means of improving efficiency seems to draw living systems toward larger and more complex forms, in a process that could be called "natural seduction."

Ecosystems are not, as some would have it, big loose organisms. On the other hand, organisms clearly are well-integrated ecosystems. As they coalesce in stable form, they grow boundaries to seclude themselves from the larger scheme, even as they code into their genes the data they will need to process energy and matter in their own distinctive ways.

Then, as they reproduce, they release still more adaptive, dissipative patterns into the world, to assume their role in the larger web of coevolving forms.

At heart, evolution is a ruthlessly effective process by which vast numbers of copies are made and the less successful ones simply deleted. Viewed from a linear perspective this seems wasteful but it's not, because as resources loop through webs of producers, consumers, and finally decomposers, all waste becomes food. In a healthy biological system "dead" just means "recycled," and that some genetic information has been edited. Realizations like this are part of a major shift in our thinking. Philosophers and scientists once worked to classify the "great chain of being"—a linear hierarchy of life forms progressing from primitive to the most advanced (that being us). Today a countermovement seeks to replace this with a lateral view, in which no real hierarchy exists (that is, bacteria are just as likely to be evolution's end). The problem is that both are true, or perhaps neither. In fact, life presents us with something we are only now beginning to perceive: a "circular hierarchy."

In that arrangement, energy drives matter to continuously cycle from simple, primitive systems up through larger, more complex systems, and then back once more through primitive ones. Here again is Shepard:

> Regardless of food habits, everything from protozoa to tigers incorporates other life to live . . . All are hunted in turn. The great predatory carnivores demonstrate it most plainly, but even they, in the end, are pursued by microbes, fungi, and plant roots . . . To be kindred does not mean that we should treat animals as our babies. It means instead a sense of many connections and transformations—us into them, them into us, and them into each other from the beginning of time.

What is the meaning of "cause and effect" when all causes are effects? What is the meaning of "predator" when all predators are prey? Such questions leave us pondering the uroborus, the ancient symbol of a snake swallowing its own tail. When we use mundane terms like "recycle" or "feedback loop," this is the wondrous process underlying those words.

As organisms fit themselves into natural flows—taking in fresh energy and material as food, and then expelling waste back to the environment—they must always walk the line between chaos and order. Too much chaos means death; too much order means death. Sensing and re-maining in the zone between those two opposing tensions is one of the challenges they face in dealing with the larger world.

Biology thrives on tensions. In fact, if life has a single, central dynamic, it's the push and pull of opposing trends. Wherever there's an impulse, life matches it to a restraint—chaos and order, figure and ground, linear and lateral, competition and cooperation, bottom-up and top-down, local and global, change and stability, structure and process. There is no easy equilibrium in these incompatible sets. Instead, they are pushed together by feedback loops that continuously drive them toward a balance they by nature can't achieve—and yet which, due to constant pressure from those feedbacks, never quite fails either. When we attempt to define that process, our habit of separating out such things as competition from cooperation turns out to be an artifact, a by-product of linear thinking. In strict terms, nature doesn't just compete, and it doesn't just cooperate. It unifies those incompatible opposites in a loose and dynamic coupling that we don't yet fully understand.

This makes life at once both stable and creative. Things don't even out, there is no lasting compromise, just the reciprocating dance of opposing forces and tendencies—forever repelling but forever being pushed back together by feedback—a dance in which too much or too little of either means death. And where life flourishes in the pulsing sweet spot at their heart.

In this way, natural selection "keeps complex genetic systems within the dynamic range between freedom and fixity, in which alone significant evolution can take place," say writer David Depew and biochemist Bruce Weber in their book *Darwinism Evolving*. That gives rise to another deep property of life, what they and others call "evolvability." It's a property that can vary. One-celled creatures, for example, easily shift their genes around to deal with new conditions. On the other hand, an elephant's genes have to orchestrate so many interacting systems and subsystems that big changes are ruled out.

The same holds true for all large complex systems. Primitive types, like the ponds filled with algae, evolve through time, eventually giving rise to more complex expressions. As those diverse, highly integrated ecosystems arise, they do a better job of capturing and using the three most basic elements of life: energy, information, and matter. In that process, though, they also become less congenial to change. So in the face of major perturbations—storms, fires, droughts, disease—they can collapse. Their components are then broken down and recycled back through more primitive forms, as what naturalists call the "ecological pulse" repeats.

Can evolution evolve? A comment from Peter Allen, head of the Complex Systems Management Centre at Cranfield University in Bedford, England, has bearing. Says Allen, "Evolution is shown to select for populations with an ability to learn, rather than for populations with optimal behavior." Enter humans.

Cars, movies, discos, phone lines, cities, smoking coal-fired power plants—all are products of evolution. As we look to the challenges ahead while searching out lessons from the past, we need to bear in mind that life enjoys taking chances. It continually tries new things and just runs the system to see what will happen. Then, if that system doesn't fit the larger scheme, life deletes it without comment and moves on. There's a hard lesson there: Just because we've built all this stuff does not mean that's how it was meant to be. Nor should we suppose that the machine age culture we've created is our omega. Assuming we get through the problems we face today, time will show the machine age as little more than a halting first step. With a near horizon populated by genetic engineering, nanotechnology, artificial intelligence, increasingly lifelike robots, and the many other ways computers are linking our imaginations to biology, we now face what may be the single most important fact in our brief and turbulent history: through us, evolution is accelerating.

To acknowledge that is not to argue predestination. Can we blow it, miss our chance, and end up like the many other complex systems that have risen and crashed before us since the dawn of time? Of course we can. History is littered with the debris of overconfident human cultures. As we put the evolutionary pedal to the metal, the chance for catastrophic failure parallels that of epic promise.

This brings new meaning to the phrase "a daunting prospect." Given our limited intellect, limited senses, and limited understanding, how can we hope to steer this rough new beast toward Bethlehem? The answer lies in feedback culture. We're going to need diversity, to generate the beneficial tensions that make a living system smart and dynamic. And we'll need clear and undistorted feedbacks to realistically monitor where we stand—to tell us where we've overtipped the balance too far toward chaos or too far toward order, too far toward competition or too far toward cooperation—before a downward trend takes hold. In that basic process lies our best way forward.

Process and Structure

Steps are being taken to achieve that. Working from the top down, the United Nations now offers a host of agencies, programs, and conferences advancing everything from new-urbanist housing to farming and energy alternatives. In addition, individual countries, led by the Netherlands and New Zealand, are developing national green plans. Separate cities have green plans, too. Brazil is rapidly becoming an open-source culture, and Iceland aims to become the world's first hydrogen economy.

Working from the bottom up, activist organizations ranging in outlook from Greenpeace to the Sierra Club rally support for environmental issues while bringing lawsuits and other actions to press their views. Academia sponsors conferences and conducts crucial research on every facet of the new biology. Professional groups of energy producers, computer programmers, industrial designers, and people from other disciplines meet to address the advances and problems common in their fields. Shirtsleeve groups have jumped in, too. Jakob von Uexküll, Jr.'s Right Livelihood awards—the alternate Nobels—have recognized new biologists. A nonprofit educational organization called the Bioneers attracts scientists, designers, businesspeople, farmers, activists, and assorted new age partisans to a lively annual conference in San Raphael, California. Bill McDonough and Michael Braungart set up the nonprofit GreenBlue, aimed at advancing cradle-to-cradle (C2C) principles in a variety of projects.

Still, big obstacles remain. The dangers of genetic research are becoming known, but there are no policies addressing other major questions, such as what problems may arise from proliferating "smart dust" or other ambitious new nanotech molecules. Nor do we have any clear sense of where letting machines develop their own intelligence will lead, or of how to deal with that when it comes. With the blossoming of Internet-based worms, viruses, spam, identity theft, and now government-sanctioned intrusions into privacy for the sake of fighting terrorism, we have become a little less sanguine about hooking into the Web.

In other areas—agriculture, town planning, industrial design, global economics—the new biology offers solutions while facing complex challenges to deploying them. Still elsewhere, the way forward is simply unclear: the generous impulse to feed all people on earth has produced more people, which runs up against the fact that industrial farming has already created a global human population that is well above sustainable levels.

A functional democracy is a dynamic feedback system: the ballot box, the media, the market, and other cultural institutions channel realistic information from the bottom up, as a means of guiding the top-down policies of government, or of deciding when and if government even needs to be involved. In all of this, the hardest thing to get our minds around is that there are few policies of enduring value, and that those few may have little to do with the usual political concerns.

Most policies are legal structures. They in turn are shaped by a legal feedback process. The distinction between *structure* and *process* is key. In nature, it's ecological process that transforms energy, matter, and information into the structures we call living things. Now we seek to mirror that process, to stir energy, matter, and information into equally vibrant cultural structures. This means turning one of our most basic beliefs on its head. In ecology, structures—which we're inclined to view as anchors of stability—are actually malleable, adapting and changing over time. Ecological process—which we think of as dynamic—is what remains unchanged. Viewing process as more stable than structure is paradoxical. It also underlies one of our primary errors. We've worked hard to build a culture on the belief that stable and lasting structures are the guarantors of permanence. In reality it's the other way around. Ecological process is stable. Structures tend to flux and shift, to appear and disappear as the world around them changes. By trying to hold them steady, we divorce ourselves from life.

This book is dense with policy suggestions. But because they are legal structures, most policies are and should be transient, changing as conditions change. In the end what counts is being true to the process— true to the interface by which a living system negotiates the ever-changing dictates of the larger world. And no adaptive system—whether it's algae, elephants, old-growth forests, or human culture—can last if the feedback it receives from the larger world is unrealistic. If we want civilization to endure and prosper for one hundred thousand years to come, we need to fix our cultural feedbacks first.

Corporations Are People, Too

In a healthy feedback culture the depletion of resources and the mounting accumulation of waste would drive our markets along more realistic lines. Sustainability would not have taken this long to become an issue. Machine age logic is the problem, just as all those cultural and legal structures that have institutionalized it are the embodiment of that problem. Of them, one legal structure that we've mistakenly made permanent is a special source of trouble. It's the one defining U.S. corporations. Corporations drive our modern economy. And their insulation from the real world—not just by incomplete financial feedback but in legal ways as well—impairs their ability to see what's coming and adjust before we hit the wall.

To say this is not to condemn the millions of people who work in corporations. Many of them quite reasonably believe the present corporate way of doing business will continue making the world a better place, just as it has in so many ways in the past. Even those who don't believe that find they're in a global system so pervasive there are few real alternatives. That the corporate system also serves people moved by little more than greed is nothing new. All human schemes are corruptible; the ancient effort to contain that fact remains far from success. The larger problem is the advent of a global stage on which that greed can easily perform, along with the fact that most laws geared to restricting it can't reach beyond national boundaries.

The corporate drive to expand is only natural, and generally speaking healthy. The extent to which that drive today distorts our cultural feedbacks is not. It stems in large part from a single U.S. law giving corporations—those vast and powerful tools of our devising—a legal status equal to our own. Due to that, our authority as individuals, even our collective authority in government, no longer stands above theirs. As a result, we are rapidly losing our ability to control them.

Few people realize that a drive to further weaken our control informs the current push to "get government off the backs of people." In theory, that's as it should be. If our media, education, and free market pricing conveyed accurate feedback from the world, there would be little need for overweening corrections from big government. Unfortunately, getting government off the backs of the people has now also come to mean getting it off the backs of huge multinational corporations.

And that strategy is working. The move in the past century toward a socialist agenda has been dramatically reversed. In many ways that was a necessary adjustment. But now government protections put in place even before socialism existed—laws and practices meant simply to protect community interests, or to ensure fair competition—are being dismantled in the name of individual freedom. Since corporations, under a

curious twist of U.S. law, are defined as actual, individual "people," having most of the same rights and protections as human beings, there's a
kind of legal truth in that. The problem is that multinationals have vast
resources and unmatched political sway. Giving them rights equal to
ours—free speech, for instance, or protection from government interference—makes these huge communal "individuals" a good deal more
equal than the rest of us.

As media infiltrate every aspect of our lives—public and private—
these corporate super-citizens have developed ways to use free speech
and other rights of individual citizens to distort our media feedback,
even convert it to their ends, as they buy up and take control of the
once-diverse and independent media outlets whose job it is to provide
us with accurate information about the world. Conservative columnist
William Safire decried this, saying, "Why do we have more channels
but fewer real choices today? Because the ownership of our means of
communication is shrinking." It is also worth asking why the Federal
Communications Commission (FCC), which is charged with preventing that consolidation, has lately taken to supporting it. Not long ago,
the Center for Public Integrity conducted a study of the relationship
between FCC officials and the telecom and media industries they regulate. It found that over the course of eight years, FCC staffers and officials took twenty-five hundred trips primarily paid for by those industries,
at a cost of $2.8 million. During the months leading up to a recent ma-
jor policy decision on allowing more media mergers, the FCC held seventy closed-door meetings with top broadcast executives. During that
same period it met with citizens' groups opposing the issue five times.

As the saying goes, "Freedom of the press belongs to those who
own one," and the press—TV, newspapers, magazines, radio stations,
and ancillary media like movies and music—is increasingly owned by a
short list of large corporations that, not incidentally, is also increasing its
dominance over government. How long the Internet will remain free
from corporate or government controls has now become a matter for
speculation.

Meanwhile, the old wall protecting scientific research from commercial interest is also being breached. For instance, with the advent of
patented life forms, an enormous flow of corporate funds is now pouring into private and academic labs (handily replacing the shrinking funds
from government). As a flood of corporate advertising and PR is joined

with fawning news reports and distorted research to justify corporate aims, our communal corporate individuals then spend billions of dollars on campaign finance and lobbying efforts to make sure those distorted messages fall on congressional ears that have been carefully attuned to hear them.

Any effort to stop this barrage comes up against the same legal stumbling block—corporations are "natural persons" by law. While corporate advertising can be regulated as a commercial form of expression, efforts to control the rest of their activities infringe on the right that every American citizen has to free speech, or on our other protections from government intrusion.

The odd thing about all this is that there is no actual law giving corporations the same rights as human beings. The U.S. Supreme Court precedent allowing that dates from one of the most corrupt periods of American history. But no decision was ever handed down making corporations into "natural persons" with free speech or the other rights of living individuals. That so-called right exists solely because the Court back then just started acting as though it did. Which then enshrined it in the halls of legal precedent. So today we are faced with ruinous consequences from a law with no real basis. Nevertheless, it has created a legalized life form (one much more primitive than we are, also much larger and more powerful), then given it the same protections from government control that we have, then turned it loose to compete with us. No wonder we have problems.

Multinationals in their present form won't last. They are machine age offspring that consume massive quantities of irreplaceable resources and leave behind great piles of indigestible waste—primitive forms that just expand like algae growing in a pond. Sooner or later they will hit the wall of habitat limits. In the process, though, in their mad scramble for growth, they are chewing through human cultural institutions we have built up over centuries.

I Heard the News Today, Oh Boy

Our communications media have long been an effective watchdog in the effort to contain corporate influence, providing critical feedback when all else failed. Now, even as "the mainstream media" reaches into every aspect of our lives, it is also becoming a corporate tool.

Columnist Donella Meadows, a thoughtful media critic, refers to "the powerful, enticing information stream that bathes us from birth." Science fiction writer William Gibson states simply, "The mediated world has become *the* world." The effect on us is profound. The average American five-year-old watches three and a half hours of TV each day. By the time that child enters school, he or she will have seen some thirty thousand ads. As adults, most people will see another twenty thousand, year in and year out, every year until they die. The money that advertisers spend on us per capita to convey those messages equals more than half the total U.S. outlay for education. And—not unlike the relationship between artificial fertilizer and industrialized crops—since the 1950s ad expenditures have been growing one-third faster than the economy. In response to this troublesome development, advertisers have developed "neuromarketing." It uses cognitive science and brain scans of people watching ads, looking for ways to project those ads more deeply into our minds.

Members of earlier cultures gathered around fires at night to initiate their children into the mysteries and meanings of the world, and to instruct them on what it takes to live a good life. Today, as one observer puts it, "advertisements are where our children receive their basic grasp of the world's meaning." Advertisements, or the programming that advertisers deem acceptable.

Former ad exec Jerry Mander describes just how powerful that has become:

> By its ability to implant identical images into the minds of millions of people, TV can homogenize perspectives, knowledge, tastes, and desires, to make them resemble the tastes and interest of the people who transmit the imagery.

As critic David Korten points out, "When the control of our cultural symbols passes to corporations, we are essentially yielding to them the power to define who we are." In this light, it's significant that 75 percent of all television ads are paid for by just one hundred giant firms.

And how are those corporations using their power? There are of course public service ads. Also corporate identity ads—like the "green-wash" productions lush with flowers shot in hazy light, assuring us of how much some oil company or timber harvester loves nature, letting us know that corporations have feelings, too. But those are too infrequent to count. At heart, virtually all ads carry the same message: "Buying things will make you happy."

> In the propaganda of the ad the ideal people are relaxed and carefree—drinking Pepsis around a pool—unencumbered by powerful ideas concerning the nature of goodness, undisturbed by visions of suffering that might be relieved . . . The ultimate meaning for human existence is getting all this stuff.

Joined at the hip to advertising is public relations, or PR. And just as the independent media outlets of yore are being conglomerated, advertising and PR agencies have also grown more interconnected. Today, two of the world's largest PR agencies—Burson-Marsteller and Hill & Knowlton—are subsidiaries respectively of Young & Rubicam and the WPP Group, two even bigger ad agencies. And this convergence is occurring around the world, creating huge firms that specialize in "media-feedback management." These firms bring into ever-fewer hands the power exercised by the influence of PR, as well as by the annual purchase of billions of dollars' worth of online and print media space, and radio time, and television time.

While advertising costs billions to get its message across, good PR doesn't have to buy space or time. Its aim is to occupy for free the media space and time not already occupied by ads. If the effect of a constant ad blitz is pernicious, that is nonetheless a known quantity. Public relations at its best is covert—we never know what hit us. One of the founding fathers of PR was Edward Bernays, a nephew of Sigmund Freud. Bernays maintained, "If we understand the mechanism and motives of the group mind, it is now possible to regiment the masses according to our will without their knowing it." He referred to that as the "engineering of consent."

It was Bernays who pulled off one of the great early PR stunts, one still taught in schools. On a spring day in 1929, a group of attractive young debutantes joined New York City's annual Easter Parade to make a statement for "female emancipation." As they paraded down Fifth Avenue in front of the assembled crowds and news photographers, they were lighting and waving cigarettes they proclaimed as "torches of liberty"—a shocking display for the time, when most Americans had never seen a woman smoking. Most Americans also didn't realize the demonstration was set up by Bernays, on behalf of the American Tobacco Company. The stunt worked. Pictures of the demonstration appeared in newspapers around the country, and the taboo against women smoking was soon broken, opening a whole new market for Bernays' client.

No one knew back then that cigarettes are harmful. And many PR pros, both then and today, have confined their efforts to promoting products and cultural events. That practice remains within the time-honored American tradition of rowdy and wholehearted salesmanship. Also, in Bernays' time, when companies had claims to make in Washington, they did so through staid lobbying groups like the National Coal Association and the Beer Institute. Things are different now. Today, with widespread protest movements to deal with and a huge media nervous system always hungry for news, corporations have developed PR into a sophisticated political tool. The "engineering of consent" and the ability of big interests to "regiment the masses according to our will without their knowing it" are being used by growing numbers of PR professionals to help warp and block the fundamental processes of democracy. These PR campaigns transform politics into a hall of media fun house mirrors in which little is as it seems.

In that illusory new world, the National Wetlands Coalition, with its logo of a duck flying blithely over a marsh, is backed by oil companies, gas companies, and real estate developers that aim to shoot down wetland protections. The industry-sponsored Consumer Alert opposes product safety laws. Citizens for the Right to Know, which fights drug price controls, has links to the Pharmaceutical Research and Manufacturers of America. As David Korten writes, the statements released by these and dozens of other such groups "are regularly reported in the press as the views of citizen advocates. The sole reason for their existence is to convince the public that the corporate interest *is* the public interest and that concerns about labor, health, and the environment are 'special' interests."

Groups like those are often created by big PR firms such as Burson-Marstteller, Hill & Knowlton, or Ketchum. Demand by corporations for fake-grassroots work is so common now that industry professionals have an insider term for it; they call it "astroturf." In *Toxic Sludge Is Good for You!*—a gleeful polemic romp through corporate media manipulation—

activists John Stauber and Sheldon Rampton persuaded PR astroturf specialists to talk about their work.

John Davies, for instance, has billed himself as "one of America's premier grassroots consultants." He has given out promotional literature that warns, "Traditional lobbying is no longer enough . . . To outnumber your opponents call Davies Communications." It touts his ability to "make a strategically planned program look like a spontaneous explosion of community support." Davies explained how he uses telemarketers to give Congress the impression that sympathetic listeners are actually angry citizens with enough fire in their bellies to write letters. First his phone bank callers get someone on the line who responds well to their pitch. Then the Davies rep offers to write a letter for him or her, which another employee quickly does. Davies: "If they're close by we hand deliver it. We hand-write it out on 'little kitty-cat stationery' if it's a little old lady. If it's a business we take it over to be photocopied on someone's letterhead. [We] use different stamps, different envelopes . . . Getting a pile of personalized letters that have a different look to them is what you want to strive for." Davies' client roster has included major oil companies as well as Hyatt, American Express, and Pacific Gas and Electric.

Mike Malik, speaking as a senior officer of Optima Direct, described how that firm offers "grassroots mobilizations" to its corporate clients via phone bank "patch-throughs." When Optima telemarketers get sympathetic responses from people being called on an issue, they are instantly switched through to their legislators. If properly managed, Malik said, their calls can appear to be spontaneous outbreaks of popular feeling. "Space the calls out throughout the day," he counseled. "Make it look as real as possible."

"Real Grass Roots—Not Astroturf," trumpeted one ad headline in *Campaigns & Elections* magazine. The ad was for a company called National Grassroots & Communications, which handles "new market entries" like Wal-Mart. National Grassroots' CEO, Pamela Whitney, said they like to hire local ambassadors to head their grassroots efforts. She prefers women who either are retired or have been active in their communities, such as former PTA presidents. Then a National Grassroots professional travels there to work with her in setting up the movement. Going in, Whitney said, her firm's representatives are always careful about how they look, adding, "When I go into a zoning board meeting I wear absolutely no makeup, I comb my hair straight back in a ponytail, and I wear my kids' old clothes. You don't want to look like you're someone from Washington, or someone from a corporation."

The work of smaller companies like these is often stirred into broad strategic campaigns, run by big PR firms, which then coordinate their work with advertising from the even bigger ad agencies that own them. As political PR work has increased, these combined enterprises have reached out in another direction, too, contracting with or buying powerful lobbying firms. Coordinated action is now the rule. The new triple-threat players in the market of ideas have tremendous reach and sway. In his book *The Corporate Planet*, Josh Karliner notes a case of that in which Burson-Marsteller was the pivot. "During the NAFTA negotiations," he says, "BM served as the Mexican government's top lobbyist, leading the twenty-four lobbying, PR, and law firms Mexico had hired." The Mexican government spent more than $25 million on that effort in the United States alone.

One of the more extraordinary efforts by an American PR firm on behalf of a foreign government was that of Hill & Knowlton, for the Kuwaiti royal family in its bid to provoke U.S. military action in what would become the first Gulf War. According to Stauber and Rampton, H&K steered a campaign that included some twenty PR, law, and lobbying firms. In the course of that, millions were funneled from the royal family into astroturf front groups like Citizens for a Free Kuwait (to be accurate: just $11.9 million of the group's funding came from the Kuwaiti royal family; another $17,861 was raised from other contributors). And of the total amount raised, $10.8 million then went directly to Hill & Knowlton. The firm took all the usual steps. It set up National Free Kuwait Day and a national day of prayer; it organized public rallies; it released hostage letters to the media. A book titled *The Rape of Kuwait* appeared, which was then sent out in press kits by Citizens for a Free Kuwait. The book garnered mentions on TV talk shows and in *The Wall Street Journal* and was even distributed to U.S. troops.

But all that was prologue to Hill & Knowlton's boldest move—the Nayirah affair. A few months before the vote by Congress on whether the U.S. would go to war, hearings on Capitol Hill were called by two politicians with links to H&K. Those hearings were held before the Congressional Human Rights Caucus, an unofficial group later revealed to be a Hill & Knowlton front. The drama began when Nayirah—a fifteen-year-old Kuwaiti girl—gave her testimony. Nayirah's full name could not be revealed, the committee was told, for fear of reprisals against her family back at home. Between sobs the girl described an awful scene she had witnessed while volunteering in a Kuwait City hospital. "While I was there," she said, "I saw the Iraqi soldiers come into the hospital with guns, and go into the room where . . . babies were in incubators. They took the babies out of the incubators, took the incubators, and left the babies on the cold floor to die."

Nayirah's story burned through the news media. It was repeated by the president. It was recited in congressional testimony and at the UN. As John MacArthur, the publisher of *Harper's Magazine*, would note—in *Second Front*, his book on media manipulation during that war—"Of all the accusations made against [Iraq], none had more impact on American public opinion than the one about Iraqi soldiers removing 312 babies from their incubators and leaving them to die on the cold hospital floors of Kuwait City."

From a news angle it was a great story, an important story. The only problem is that it was also a made-up story. Nayirah was eventually shown to be a member of the Kuwaiti royal family. In fact, she was the daughter of the Kuwaiti ambassador, Saud Nasir al-Sabah, who was there in the room with her when she appeared. Also close by was the Hill & Knowlton vice president who had coached her on her false testimony. And since Nayirah's testimony was given before a caucus, there were no legal ramifications. As MacArthur would later remark, "Lying under oath in front of a congressional committee is a crime, lying from under the cover of anonymity to a caucus is merely public relations."

Three months after the Nayirah testimony, the U.S. Senate narrowly approved the use of troops in Iraq. The measure passed by just five votes. Whether her story turned the tide is a question for history. But more than a decade later, U.S. forces are once again in Iraq. And questions are once again being raised about the reasons given for going to war.

Impure Research

The future will bring even more distortion of cultural feedbacks. In the United States, public relations employees now outnumber real news reporters by an ever-widening margin. Corporate PR firms work hard to sway reporters, and often do. Those firms can also now make news while skipping reporters altogether, with a new tool called a video news release. The VNRs are mock news clips, PR dressed up to look like actual reportage. They're distributed free to local television stations, which are typically hungry for footage and short of the cash needed to produce it. So VNRs get downlinked from a satellite and plugged into the six o'clock news. People watching that "news" at home have no idea where it came from. (The current White House administration was reprimanded for preparing and releasing these, with help from the giant PR firm Ketchum, as a way of propagating favorable media reports on its policies. It also accredited a fake reporter for White House news conferences, who then asked softball questions. Meanwhile, cabinet-level agencies secretly paid established journalists to promote their agendas.) Some TV and radio stations now carry whole programs that resemble news shows but promote hidden agendas without informing their audiences of that.

Corporations also use their financial power to distort the science that so often serves as basis for the news. Science done in-house by corporations, or paid for by them, is often viewed with skepticism, and for good reason. Studies funded by cigarette makers, by petroleum companies, by the chemical industry, by drugmakers, by firms designing genetically modified crops often seem to prove their products do no harm—even when there's overwhelming outside evidence to the contrary. Countering that, the research gold standard has long been academic science. By the disinterested pursuit of knowledge, universities stood apart.

That began to change in 1980, when the U.S. Supreme Court sanctioned the patenting of living things. The change accelerated as universities were faced with shrinking funds from government, and so turned to the money flooding into research for biotech, nanotech, cybertech, and other growing fields. American universities garnered ninety-five patents back in 1965. In 2000 they received thirty-two hundred. This trend is a growing concern, as documented in a recent book by Harvard University's former president Derek Bok: *Universities in the Marketplace: The Commercialization of Higher Education*. In 2000, Bok notes, U.S. universities also received more than $1 billion from those patents.

Another critic is Tufts University professor Sheldon Krimsky. He points out, "Today, biotechnology and pharmaceutical companies regularly give universities multimillion-dollar grants . . . At the same time, universities and their professors are plunging into the business world themselves, creating companies to sell products discovered in academic laboratories." Krimsky is concerned about what he calls "the funding effect in science"—the well-known phenomenon by which research outcomes tend "to favor the financial interests of their sponsors." In his book *Science in the Private Interest*, he argues that the funding effect has now arrived at universities, and as a result they are no longer disinterested sources of reliable information.

But what if results are monitored by federal advisory boards? Says Krimsky, "There are two rules that guide federal advisory committees. Rule No. 1 is that no scientist with a substantial conflict of interest should be permitted to serve on an advisory committee. Rule No. 2 is that Rule No. 1 can be waived. And the number of waivers is extraordinary."

A recent study at the Yale University School of Medicine confirmed the funding effect on drug studies. It looked at eleven hundred English-language research papers published since 1980. In studies where no pharmaceutical industry funding was involved, 53 percent had positive results. Where there was industry funding, positive evaluations increased to 80 percent. This problem is exacerbated by the fact that one in three researchers, and now two out of three universities, also have equity stakes in the research being done. Moreover, few of the journals publishing drug research require disclosure of those ties.

Greenback Feedback

The funding effect on science is pernicious because it's covert. So is the funding effect on legislators. The enormous media costs for election campaigns today mean politicians are always scouting cash. And big companies provide it, in ever-increasing amounts: over $500 million in soft money alone was spent in the most recent U.S. election cycle. At the same time, corporations spend six times that amount lobbying those same politicians, reminding them of what their corporate patrons expect. Howard Hughes reportedly once claimed that his relations with Richard Nixon and Lyndon Johnson were conducted on "a hard-cash, adult" basis. When Charles Keating, the notorious 1980s savings and loan exec, was asked if the $1.3 million he gave to five senators had influenced them, he replied, "I certainly hope so."

When a legislator, thus obliged, is faced with an oil company lobby-ist who downplays the importance of emissions controls, who provides corporate-funded science to prove that view, and who sees that the leg-islator's office is deluged by calls from astroturf constituents who support it, as PR and ad campaigns sell voters the same story, democracy has be-come a hollow shell—a carefully orchestrated charade.

Why does government policy encourage our dependence on oil, even as our need for foreign sources inflames the gravest security threat we face? How did drugmakers persuade the U.S. to veto a UN plan for letting poor nations acquire less expensive generic drugs? Why would Congress make it illegal for the government Medicare program to bar-gain for lower drug prices, and then outlaw any U.S. citizens who try to buy the same drugs for less through Canada? Why is it that corporations paid 40 percent of all U.S. taxes in the 1950s but now pay roughly 10 percent? How can Congress justify making bankruptcy protection much harder for Americans to obtain—in order to help out credit card com-panies that are already awash in profits, and which charge an average of 15 percent interest, and which mail out four billion new credit solicita-tions each year? Why is Congress trying to overrule state laws protecting individual financial privacy? How did the gene modifier Monsanto gain such influence with a Democratic administration that its agriculture de-partment was known as the "Department of Monsanto"? How is it that the venal and corrupt energy trader Enron—which helped to bankrupt California's public utilities before itself becoming one of the largest bankruptcies in U.S. history—had the members of a Republican ad-ministration at its beck and call? And just before that scandal surfaced, why did a group of senators threaten the Securities and Exchange Commission with budget cuts if it imposed tough conflict-of-interest standards on the accounting firms that were instrumental in causing the problem? Why would the federal Election Assistance Commission create a group to propose electronic voting standards to Congress, and then staff it with supporters of voting machines that leave no paper trails while barring experts who oppose those machines? For the answers to all these questions, try asking the more than twelve thousand lobbyists swarming over Capitol Hill these days (there are now twenty-two professional lobbyists for every actual member of Congress).

Statistics like this, and the bizarre policies they breed, are no doubt why musician Frank Zappa once remarked, "Politics is the entertain-

ment branch of industry." If so, the cost to the producers is high. One
big contributor noted, while speaking with *Common Cause Magazine*
some years back, how every corporate board he'd ever sat on required
that "you recuse yourself when an issue comes up where you have a
vested financial self-interest. The amazing thing about the way business
is done in Washington," he complained, "is not only do you not recuse
yourself, but you'd better get your ass up there and pay everyone you
possibly can."

In the end, about the only good thing to be said for the system of
legalized bribery now passing as a political process in Washington is that
it's an equal opportunity employer. There is no shortage of blame to go
around. Warren Buffett, one of the world's wealthiest men, warns that
America is changing into a nation governed by the wealthy. "We are on
the way to becoming a plutocracy," he says, adding, "That is not just
wrong. It is destabilizing." Because the competition to buy favor in the
capital is so intense, he also sees the price of entry rising, restricting access to a constantly shortening list of ever larger corporations.

Just as there are many corporate CEOs who resent having to do
business in a system that makes environmental degradation a linchpin of
success, there is no shortage of CEOs who object to the parade of greed
and folly in Washington. But they find themselves muzzled by their
responsibilities, a situation best described by the old Middle Eastern
proverb "The tongue is the neck's enemy." Execs who complain openly
risk having their companies cut off from a system on which they are
now dependent. In retirement, however, some are raising their voices.
For instance, Jerome Kohlberg—the famed takeover artist—is a leading
advocate of campaign finance reform. In his retirement he has pulled together a roster of other such execs, including former heads of Capital
Cities/ABC, Ford, GTE, Merck, Random House, and Quaker Oats,
along with powerful individuals like Buffett. The international financier
George Soros has made the issue a chief objective of his foundation, the
Open Society Institute.

A major campaign finance reform bill was finally passed by Congress
in 2002 after a long and heroic effort by Senators John McCain and
Russell Feingold and Representatives Christopher Shays and Martin
Meehan. Their labor was rewarded by constant ambushes by corporate
agents from the floors of both houses, by court challenges, with efforts
to gut it by the Federal Election Commission, by the appearance of

"shadow groups" to receive and disperse funds the law would block, by the sudden rise of nonprofit committees the law doesn't cover, and with a surge of new corporate funding to state political parties, where the laws are looser and money is less carefully tracked. A subsequent effort now aims to close big money access to the 527 committees that arose to poison the 2004 U.S. elections, but as any savvy fund-raiser knows, when one door closes, another opens. Like algae growing mindlessly in a pond, the machine age economic system churns on in its headlong consumption of our institutions and values.

Free Market Slamdown

Just the free market at work, we are reliably informed. In the end—if we can only be patient—it will serve the greater good. It was the brilliant economist Adam Smith who, in his 1776 book *The Wealth of Nations*, first described how free markets could work. Smith's theory of a market economy is one of the great insights of human history. Although ideas such as cybernetics and complex systems lay far in the future, he grasped the essence of those principles and gave them life in an economic model that is as efficient and self-organizing as any ecosystem.

In Smith's vision of a free market, no central power is required, or desired. He opposed the whole idea of powerful, centralized governments. Although it's rarely talked about today, he also opposed large concentrations of economic power, and for the same reason. He argued that big government and big business both had reason to suppress the diversity and turbulence of free markets. Referring to the low prices derived from open competition, he wrote, "It is to prevent this reduction of price, and consequently of . . . profit, by restraining that free competition which would most certainly occasion it, that all corporations, and the greater part of corporation law, have been established."

Today's corporate conservatives exalt Smith's theory and laud tough competition, but seem to have missed the part about keeping oversize opponents out of the ring. More precisely, they spend a lot of time attacking the effects of big government, then turn a blind eye toward the growing list of multinational corporations that are bigger than all but the largest governments.

What's more, because those multinationals grew from half-smart machine age models, and pay their bills with a currency divorced from reality, the global economy no longer has any rigorous connection to the free market of Smith's theory. After an initial surge of half a century—in which success followed on success and global economic output soared by nearly $30 trillion—the corporate model for globalization is faltering. Green revolution super-crops, which led to higher standards of living around the world, have reached their productive limit, but populations are still growing. The result is that world per capita food output is officially in decline. Worse still: Freshwater, topsoil, and fisheries are depleting at a rapid rate. Industrial toxins create health hazards for humans and other life forms, and fossil fuel combustion fills the air with CO_2, spurring concerns about the global warming that has brought a disastrous rise in floods, storms, and droughts and that is now melting the North Pole ice cap.

There is more than one way to have a global economy. The model in use today is best described as "corporate globalization." And the leaders of corporate globalization clearly have much to answer for. So who are those leaders? In formal terms the United Nations sanctions the World Bank and IMF as "special agencies," although their administration is largely walled off from public view, and any power the UN has over them is pretty much symbolic. The WTO has a few agreements with the UN but is virtually autonomous, too. Leaders of those three big trade agencies are effectively picked by the member nations with the most economic muscle, in a process that is thoroughly lobbied and vetted by large corporations. Many of the officials appointed, along with the politicians doing the appointing, are alumni of elite groups like the Council on Foreign Relations, the Bilderberg, the World Economic Forum, and the Trilateral Commission—arenas where corporate and government leaders meet away from public view. As these international corporate connections have worked their way through the system, the big three agencies best placed to promote competitive free trade and global economic well-being have been turned to other ends.

Adam Smith knew monopolies were a danger to free markets. In 1776 he wrote, "People of the same trade seldom meet together, even for merriment and diversion, but the conversation ends in a conspiracy against the public, or in some contrivance to raise prices." That's no less true today. One of the more prominent critics of corporate globalization is David Korten. He has worked with the U.S. Agency for International Development and the Ford Foundation's development programs; he has also taught at Harvard University Business School. In his forcefully argued book *When Corporations Rule the World*—which this section largely summarizes—he writes, "A favorite . . . argument for globalization is that opening national markets introduces greater competition and leads to increased efficiency. This neglects the larger reality that when markets are global, the forces of monopoly transcend national borders to consolidate at a global level." Korten knows whereof he speaks. According to *The Economist*, whenever more than half of a global industry is controlled by just five corporations, it is considered highly monopolistic. This formula, says the publication, now describes the auto, aerospace, electronic components, electrical and electronics, steel, and consumer durables industries. In addition—for personal computers, media, and oil—the proportion has reached 40 percent.

Writes Korten, "The public is encouraged to believe that the corporate titans of Japan, North America, and Europe are battling it out toe-to-toe in international markets. This image is increasingly a fiction that obscures the extent to which a few core corporations are strengthening their collective monopoly market power through joint ventures and strategic alliances with their major rivals." For those who would doubt that, *The Economist* suggests an exercise:

> Take a really big international industry such as cars, in which the products are complicated and fairly expensive. Write down all the manufacturers' names (there are more than 20 large ones for cars) along the four sides of a square. Now draw lines connecting manufacturers that have joint ventures or alliances with one another, whether in design, research, components, full assembly, distribution or marketing, for one product or for several, anywhere in the world. Pretty soon, the drawing becomes an incomprehensible tangle; just about everyone seems to be allied with everyone else, and the car industry is not an exception. It is a similar story in computer hardware, computer software, aerospace, drugs, telecommunications, defense and many others.

Business executive Cyrus Freidheim, when he was vice chairman of the management consulting firm Booz Allen Hamilton, predicted that the world economy will one day be controlled by what he calls "the relationship-enterprise." His phrase describes a vast web of interacting companies linked by strategic alliances that reach across different industries and countries while behaving almost as if they were a single firm. According to Freidheim, these monsters will one day dwarf today's big multinationals. Some relationship enterprises, he said, will even amass revenues in the trillion-dollar range—overshadowing all but a few national economies.

The point here is that the large corporations now running the global economy don't want free markets and open competition. They want just the opposite. They want monopolies and markets they can control, just as they have since the time of Adam Smith. Korten writes that today "the world's corporate giants are creating a system of managed competition by which they actively limit competition among themselves while encouraging intensive competition among the smaller firms and localities that constitute their periphery. The process forces the periphery to absorb more of the costs . . . so that the core can produce greater profits."

He then goes on to describe how this system has replaced Adam Smith's decentralized market of diverse, independent competitors with a very different structure:

> Those who work in the core are well compensated, with full benefits and attractive working conditions to assure their loyalty and commitment . . . The peripheral functions—farmed out either to subordinate units within the corporation or to outside suppliers dependent on the firm's business— are performed by low-paid, often temporary or part-time "contingent" employees who receive few or no benefits and to whom the corporation has no commitment. The result is a two-tiered structure that is highly differentiated with regard to competitive pressures . . . The peripheral units . . . function as independent small contractors pitted in intense competition with one another for the firm's continuing business. They are thus forced to cut their own costs to the bone.

Because they lack independent access to the market, he says, the smaller firms that orbit core corporations are not so much independent businesses as dependent appendages. A good example is agriculture, the world's largest market, which is now ruled by global combines like Cargill and Archer Daniels Midland. The result is that individual farmers, who once got 41 percent of every dollar consumers spent on food, now get just 9 percent. In this, as in so many corporate global markets today, the actual producer gets less and the consumer pays more than either would if the market were based on real competition—with the nicely increased difference going to some powerful multinational core.

Small companies aren't the only ones answering to that core. "Global corporations," says Dee Hock, former head of Visa International, "hold government . . . to ransom for use of land, for reprieve from taxation, for access to natural resources far below cost, for direct monetary subsidization, and for use of land, air, and water as a repository for refuse; all by the simple expedient of bargaining one government against another." An ad once placed by the Philippine government in *Fortune* magazine read:

> To attract companies like yours . . . we have felled mountains, razed jungles, filled swamps, moved rivers, relocated towns . . . all to make it easier for you and your business to do business here.

In all this, a fundamental balance has shifted. By the magic of multinational monopolies, global combines are no longer competing for our patronage. We are now competing for theirs.

This translates into more than just a concentration of profit. It's also a concentration of power. Democratic revolutions in the West—and in nations around the world now—have managed to defeat the centralized control of monarchs and despots, and the centralized control of communism. It should come as no surprise that wealth and power have now found another way to centralize their control. But it's ironic that the theorists of this latest assault legitimize it with a free market theory specifically warning against it.

Nature's economy integrates systems ranging from the microscopic to the global in a decentralized interactive system. Are we to believe that for humans to have a global economy, we must answer to huge, centrally controlled corporations?

In all centralized control systems, says Korten, "The power of the center stems from a number of interrelated sources: its power to create money, its ownership of the productive assets on which each locality depends, and its control of the institutional mechanisms that mediate relationships among localities." Those powers, he then goes on to say, "reside increasingly in global financial markets and corporations, which have established themselves as the de facto governance institutions of the planet."

American survivalists, who raise concerns that the UN will infringe on U.S. sovereignty, have the right feeling in their bellies. But the threat is not from the UN, which is comparatively powerless. The real threat lies in the rising corporate global regime, dressed in the benevolent sheep's clothing of the three big trade agencies it has taken as cover: the World Bank, WTO, and IMF. We have beat back international communism only to be confronted with yet another communal movement toward oppressive, centralized, mechanistic power—international corporatism.

Both democracy and free markets are born of what Korten calls "a deep distrust of large institutions and their concentrations of unaccountable power." To the extent that global corporatism gains power, both democracy and free markets are at risk.

As if that weren't enough to occupy our concern, all the familiar environmental problems remain. So as we lose ground to expanding corporate influence, most big corporations are themselves feeling a loss of essential staying power. That problem is due in part to our false economy, in which legal tender has only the vaguest relationship with real capital. It is also due to the narrow logic of machine age ways and means, which continue to exhaust our resource base as they pile up waste. Like algae expanding in a pond, corporate globalization now carries billions of people in a headlong rush toward the wall of ecological limits.

It bears stating and restating that corporations are largely staffed and run by people of goodwill. The problem lies not in them but in how our most basic notions of common sense and conventional wisdom are distorted by the machine metaphor. Dee Hock calls that "a false metaphor, a wrong concept of organization, an internal model of reality that is flawed." We created corporations and the ways they do their business. All this grew from a flawed mental construct, which became a flawed legal structure, which has since achieved unnatural power. Now, via that structure, even the simplest acts of conventional wisdom are channeled into mechanistic mode, to then be writ large on history and the lives of other species.

People who work at corporations are like everyone else in another way, too. They're concerned about their jobs. The number of people on earth who need to be supported by some kind of work now stands at six billion—a fact that serves as a frequent argument for globalization. But are multinationals helping? Korten notes that the two hundred largest corporations control 28.3 percent of world economic output but employ just one-third of 1 percent of the world's population. "The global trend," he writes, "is clearly toward greater concentration of the control of markets and productive assets in the hands of a few firms that make a minuscule contribution to total global employment." And now, he adds, "having gained control of the institutions that once served our needs, and intent on eliminating inefficiency to increase profits, the system has found that people are the primary source of inefficiency."

Events bear him out. In the rich nations, jobs are migrating offshore or being lost to false efficiencies that externalize true costs. For the first time in recent memory, the U.S. workweek is getting longer, even as most households feature two working adults and consumer debt roars past $10 trillion (since 1976 it has gone from being less than two months of annual average income to equaling almost four). Once-ascendant Japan has experienced several years of deflation, and formerly expanding Southeast Asian and Latin American economies are struggling. Only the cheapest labor markets are gaining jobs in significant numbers. China and India (two countries that have mostly ignored IMF-style advice) are currently booming, although the inflow of Western jobs and methods has brought with it Western problems as water supplies disappear and pollution grows. Overall, even through the boom years of the 1990s, average per capita income declined in fifty countries around the world.

Korten counts down the growing list of jobs no longer requiring real people: "In Mexico, small farmers are displaced to make way for mechanized agriculture. In India, they are forced off their lands by massive new dams needed to produce electricity so that factory workers can be replaced by more efficient machines. On Wall Street, the human traders who key decisions into computer terminals to execute trades in global money markets are replaced by more efficient computer programs. Small-town merchants are driven out by superstores run by mega-retailers, who in turn are threatened by dot.com retailers. Voice-recognition devices and automated answering devices replace telephone operators. Multimedia education replaces teachers. Corporate downsizing is eliminating redundant workers and middle managers. Corporate mergers and consolidation eliminate middle, and even top, managers." Blue-collar industrial jobs and now white-collar information age jobs in the U.S. are being outsourced to developing economies, an outflow that has begun replacing high-wage American consumers with low-wage ones.

The owners of capital seem safe for the moment, but as management analyst William Dugger has suggested, that, too, could change. "The corporation is a true Frankenstein's monster," he exclaims, "an

artificial person run amok." With that in mind he makes a fanciful prediction:

> Corporations have already begun to buy up their own stock, holding it in
> their treasuries. Taken to the logical conclusion, when 100 percent of the
> stock is treasury stock the corporation will own itself . . . Could a corpo-
> ration entirely dispense with not only human ownership but also human
> workers and managers? . . . What would it be then? . . . It would exist
> physically as a network of machines that buy, process, and sell commodi-
> ties, monitored by a network of computers. Its purpose would be to grow
> ever larger through acquiring more machines and to become ever more
> powerful through acquiring more computers to monitor the new ma-
> chines. It would be responsible to no one but itself in its mechanical drive
> for power and profit.

Dugger's story is more than a surreal fable. American corporations actually are Frankenstein monsters—"natural persons" under U.S. law, which
gives them the same freedom of speech and protection from government intrusion accorded to living American citizens. Corporations' unique
status as equals in rights, combined with their vastly more than equal financial standing, is a primary reason for their great power. Are they cor-
rupting legislators with hundreds of millions of dollars in campaign
finance contributions? They're just exercising free speech. Are they warping and twisting legislation to their advantage with billions spent on lobbying, questionable advertising, and deceptive PR? Free speech again.
After all, don't all individuals in America have the right to petition their
representatives and to express their opinions?

As noted earlier, this is a curious development, one made all the
more unusual because the elevation of U.S. corporations—from being just
handy tools of society to their current legal status as super-citizens—was
never passed by Congress and is grounded in no court decision. The
whole extraordinary edifice of corporate dealings in America, and by extension of the American multinationals now spreading across the globe,
is based on a law that never was.

Corporate Liberation and the Law That Never Was

Today's situation is actually an old problem expressed in new form. Around the world today, people find themselves in circumstances much like those of the colonists who began the American Revolution. Many of them had served as indentured servants to one or another of the great corporate charters used by European rulers then as instruments of colonial expansion. The British East India Company, the Hudson's Bay Company, the London Company, and the Massachusetts Bay Company held sway across great areas.

As a matter of course, they imposed trade practices benefiting them at the expense of local interests. (Every big European colonial charter did as much and sometimes worse). In the British American colonies, for instance, any goods coming to them first had to pass through England. Many exports leaving British colonies also had to pass through England on the way out. What's more, the colonists weren't allowed to make their own hats, woolens, or iron goods, even though they had the raw materials. Those materials had to be shipped to the home country, where the corporations had them manufactured into finished products and then sent back to the colonies for sale.

The famous Boston Tea Party wasn't just about taxes. The American Revolution was in large part a revolt against oppressive corporations.

Given its colonial experience—and with support from Adam Smith's free market theory (not incidentally published in 1776)—the early American republic kept corporations on a short leash. It was understood how they could serve public purposes, such as building turnpikes or canals, where combined resources were needed for large projects. But corporations were not allowed the constitutional or judicial right even to exist. They could be created only temporarily, only by state legislatures, and only for specific tasks. And they existed solely at the pleasure of those legislatures. Strict time limits were set by law for the expirations of their charters. Their charters were also subject to numerous provisions for cancellation at any time if a corporation's behavior was deemed contrary to the public good. Through the late eighteenth and early nineteenth centuries, various such laws were enacted in Rhode Island, Massachusetts, New York, New Jersey, Pennsylvania, Maryland, Delaware, Florida, Louisiana, and Michigan. Richard Grossman and Frank Adams, in their detailed and well-researched pamphlet *Taking Care of Business: Citizenship and the Charter of Incorporation*, note that the state legislatures dictated rules for issuing stock, for shareholder voting, for obtaining corporate information, for paying dividends, and keeping records. They limited capitalization, debts, land holdings, and sometimes profits. They required a company's accounting books to be turned over to a legislature upon request. The power of large shareholders was limited by scaled voting, so that large and small investors had equal voting rights. Interlocking directorates were outlawed. Shareholders had the right to remove directors at will.

Several states also made stockholders liable for all debts or harms caused by their corporations. And banks were especially singled out. Private banking corporations were actually illegal in Illinois and Indiana. In an editorial typical of the time, a New Jersey newspaper wrote:

> The Legislature ought cautiously to refrain from increasing the irresponsible powers of any corporations, or from chartering new ones, [lest citizens end up being] mere hewers of wood and drawers of water for jobbers, banks and stockbrokers.

Midway through the nineteenth century, a struggle emerged between the federal government—siding with corporations via the Supreme Court—and the states. The high court challenged the right of states to create and cancel corporate charters. The states fought back with a flurry of constitutional revisions. According to Grossman and Adams, "Starting in 1844, nineteen states amended their constitutions [to ensure their right] to make corporate charters subject to alteration or revocation by legislatures." But the worm turned with the Civil War. Flush with treasure from military contracts, corporations made their move on a federal government weakened and in disarray from the conflict.

By the late nineteenth century the railroads had distorted the political process at every level to secure new rights. They also procured huge public land grants and equally huge public subsidies. Corporations were growing into conglomerates and trusts. A new industrial class was emerging. And with its great wealth came a pervasive new influence on government. Shortly before his death, President Abraham Lincoln bemoaned that development, saying, "Corporations have been enthroned . . . An era of corruption in high places will follow and the money power will endeavor to prolong its reign by working on the prejudices of the people . . . until wealth is aggregated in a few hands . . . and the republic is destroyed."

Throughout the century, corporations had worked to release themselves from the tight leash held by state legislatures. Corporate agents attacked the power of any state charter that could create or dispel a corporation, deriding that as a special privilege. It was argued that setting up a national law of incorporation (translate: beyond the reach of the state legislatures) would be fairer and more efficient. Those agents also pressed the courts to take the control of corporate charters from state legislatures—a transfer that was eventually obtained.

Finally, they acquired the central tool that would make today's U.S. corporations the unassailable powers they've become. The victory was won in stages, through a combination of outright corruption and ineffable finesse. And in the end it would be founded on no law, no act of Congress, no legitimate basis of any kind. But it has reshaped and continues to reshape our world in ways perhaps no other one development has.

The groundwork for that was laid in Congress just after the Civil War. In 1868, the Fourteenth Amendment to the U.S. Constitution—intended to free the slaves and make all (in those days male) individuals equal before the law—was being framed in Congress. On the committee drafting that amendment was Republican senator Roscoe Conkling, a former railroad lawyer. Where the document noted who was to receive equal rights, Conkling shrewdly inserted the single word "person" instead of the proper legal term, "natural person." One of his Republican colleagues in the House, John A. Bingham, another former railroad lawyer, worked to make sure the same language passed in his chamber. That ambivalence opened the door to giving constitutionally protected equal rights not only to living, breathing "natural persons" but also to the corporations that had long been recognized in law as artificial persons. Both Conkling and Bingham later bragged of their ruse and, after leaving Congress, went on to cushy lives as railroad favorites.

The ensuing years were a time of rampant corruption in government. According to historian Matthew Josephson, in his classic book, *The Robber Barons*, "The halls of legislation were transformed into a mart where the price of votes was haggled over, and laws, made to order, were bought and sold." Even President Rutherford B. Hayes, who owed his office to insider deal making, was moved to complain, "This is a government of the people, by the people, and for the people no longer. It is a government of corporations, by corporations, and for corporations."

During this time, the sly wording palmed off by Conkling and Bingham served as the basis for a series of cases before the Supreme Court. In those, the Court was repeatedly asked to include corporations within the Fourteenth Amendment's definition of "persons." Doing so would have given them such rights as free speech and protection from government interference, just like real Americans. But in every instance the Court demurred. Then in 1886, in an otherwise minor tax case called *Santa Clara County v. Southern Pacific Railroad Company*, the question was raised again. Although the Court once more ducked the constitutional issue, today's status of corporations as real "persons" under the Fourteenth Amendment is, by an odd twist, founded on that case.

When it reached the Supreme Court, the *Santa Clara* case came before the court of Chief Justice Morrison Remick Waite. Waite was a former attorney who had spent his career defending railroads and other large corporations. He was appointed to the court by the alcoholic war-hero president Ulysses S. Grant (on his seventh try at finding a nominee Congress would approve). Before becoming the leading justice of the nation's most powerful court, Waite had not served as a judge. Even so, his court fittingly decided *Santa Clara* on a lesser point, and declined to consider the constitutional question of whether corporations were real "persons" under the Fourteenth Amendment. For the record its verdict stated, "If these [lesser points] are tenable, there will be no occasion to consider the grave questions of constitutional law . . . As the judgment can be sustained upon this [lesser] ground, it is not necessary to consider any other questions raised by the pleadings."

But just before the Court's verdict was announced, Waite made an aside to the attorneys for the case. He said that "The court does not wish to hear argument on the question whether the provision in the Fourteenth Amendment to the Constitution . . . applies to these corporations. We are of the opinion that it does."

His aside was also heard by the court reporter. Back then, before recordings or stenography, the court reporter was a highly paid and highly responsible part of the system, writing summaries that appeared in official records as a heading above the actual text of a decision. The court reporter at the time was J. C. Bancroft Davis, who had previously been assistant secretary of state and then acting secretary of state under

President Grant. Given that, it's hard to imagine Davis failing to grasp the importance of the summary he would write of *Santa Clara*, for volume 118 of *United States Reports: Cases Adjudged in the Supreme Court at October Term 1885 and October Term 1886*.

Turning the Court's decision on its head, Davis wrote an opening sentence that would alter the course of history:

> The defendant corporations are persons within the intent of the clause in section 1 of the Fourteenth Amendment to the Constitution of the United States, which forbids a State to deny to any person within its jurisdiction the equal protection of the laws.

So thanks to J. C. Bancroft Davis, from this point on whenever judges looked for a precedent in *Santa Clara*, vol. 118 of *United States Reports*, the first thing they saw was his summary informing them that the U.S. Supreme Court had decided corporations were now considered natural persons under the Fourteenth Amendment, with all the rights and protections it implies. In that brief passage he achieved what years of corporate pleading before the Court had not. It's worth noting here that Davis, in addition to his other career achievements, was a former president of the board of directors for the Newburgh and New York Railroad Company.

Once Davis had inserted their collective foot in the door, corporations ramped up their assault on the courts. Between the time of the *Santa Clara* decision and 1910, more than 300 Fourteenth Amendment cases were brought before the U.S. Supreme Court alone. Of them, 19 had to do with African Americans. The rest of those suits, 288 in all, were filed by corporations seeking to assert and define their rights as real "persons." As precedent built upon precedent, cementing the status of those new "persons" into law, American corporations were at long last liberated from their bondage.

What followed was as predictable as it is dire. According to writer and radio commentator Thom Hartmann—whose diligent research this account follows—subsequent high-court decisions "struck down minimum wage laws, workmen's compensation laws, utility regulation, and child labor laws," often using corporate personhood as their basis. The vicious, even fatal clashes between corporations and working people during this time created the political base for the New Deal reformations growing out of the Great Depression.

Through all those great events, and following on to the enormous problems facing the world today, the curious means by which U.S. corporations gained the same freedoms and protections as living people remain a constant shadow. Hartmann describes the law that never was:

No laws were passed by Congress granting that corporations should be treated the same under the constitution as living, breathing human beings, and none have been passed since then. It was not a concept drawn from older English law. No court decisions, state or federal, held that corporations were "persons" instead of "artificial persons." The Supreme Court did not rule, in this case or any case, on the issue of corporate personhood. In fact, to this day there has been *no* Supreme Court ruling that could explain why a corporation—with its ability to continue operating forever, a legal agreement that can't be put in jail and doesn't need fresh water to drink or clean air to breathe—should be granted the same Constitutional rights our Founders explicitly fought for, died for, and granted to the very mortal human beings who are citizens of the United States.

American corporations are now real people simply because they are real people. The persistent efforts of generations of corporate agents have spawned a legal "person" far larger and more powerful than any flesh-and-blood person can hope to be. And to this overwhelming power we have ceded the rights and protections our ancestors fought so hard to take away from it and give to us, rights intended as our chief defense against overwhelming power.

Fifty years later, Supreme Court justice Hugo Black would remark, "I do not believe the word 'person' in the Fourteenth Amendment includes corporations . . . Neither the history nor the language of the Fourteenth Amendment justifies the belief that corporations are included within its protection." Later still, Justice William O. Douglas made the same point. Writing of corporations as real persons, he said, "There was no history, logic or reason given to support that view."

What proverbial man on the corner, standing on his proverbial soapbox, could think to match the sway of a global corporation like General Electric, which has its own television network and two cable news channels plus assorted law firms, ad agencies, PR agencies, and a small army of lobbyists in Washington and around the world? As Justice William Brennan, Jr., wrote in 1986:

Direct corporate spending on political activity raises the prospect that resources amassed in the economic marketplace may be used to provide an
unfair advantage in the political marketplace . . . The resources in the
treasury of a business corporation . . . are not an indication of popular
support for the corporation's political ideas . . . The availability of these
resources may make a corporation a formidable political presence, even
though the power of the corporation may be no reflection of the power
of its ideas.

Corporations may lack the right to vote, says David Korten, but it's
"a minor inconvenience, given their ability to mobilize hundreds of
thousands of votes from among their workers, suppliers, dealers, customers, and the public, and to package millions of dollars in political
contributions."

Dee Hock, who headed one of the world's largest corporations, offers a telling denunciation:

The for-profit, monetized shareholder form of corporation has demanded
and received perpetual life. It has demanded and received the right to define its own purpose and act solely for self-defined self-interest. It has demanded and received release from the revocation of its charter for inept
or antisocial acts. The roles of giant, transnational corporations and government have slowly reversed. Government is now more an instrument of
such corporations than the corporations are instruments of government.
They are no longer, not even indirectly, an instrument of the populace
they affect, but an instrument of the few who control the ever-increasing
power and wealth they command. The inevitable tendency of wealth is to
acquire power. The inevitable tendency of power is to protect wealth.
The tendency of wealth and power combined is to acquire ever more
wealth and power. The use of a commercial corporate form for the purpose of social good has become incidental.

Real conservatives know the importance of free speech and of democratic process, along with personal responsibility, initiative, and freedom. The rise of corporations as "natural persons" under law threatens
all of these. What is the value of free speech when it's blocked or distorted or wholly reinvented by a vast and persuasive mediasphere controlled by a few large corporations? How democratic is a democracy

whose political feedbacks are thus controlled, one that routinely now betrays the public interest? If individual responsibility once was undermined by dependence on big government, what to make of the current effort to gull and coerce us into even greater dependence on big multinational corporations? What of individual initiative when small businesses are marginalized by and dependent on a multinational core? And where, in all this, does freedom lie? Do we still have the freedom to say no?

Once, we held the center and corporations were our creations, a means of doing things we wanted done. More and more now they hold the center, and we find ourselves on the periphery—increasingly dependent, and increasingly deprived of the means needed for reform.

Those who would block that reform are not necessarily forces from the dark side. By all accounts they're just corporate agents sitting in West Wing chairs, sitting in congressional chairs, sitting in judicial chairs, sitting in agency regulators' chairs, sitting in the chairs of newscasters and radio talk show hosts, just doing what they are paid to do—reciting the lines written for them at corporation-funded think tanks staffed by still more corporate agents who are sitting in the chairs of scholars. But despite what they may say, or how passionately they say it, these people are not conservatives. They're not liberals, either. They're agents of a system foreign to democracy, agents of a foreign power.

Against this onslaught, partisan solutions won't work. They miss the essential problem. It's no longer us Democrats against those Republicans, or us Republicans against those Democrats. In fact it could be argued that the hyped-up battle between those two distracts us from the true threat. The battle that matters most right now is we the people—at home, in business, or on whichever side of the political aisle—against those who would corrupt the processes that keep our system vital. "The more we cut our giant corporations down to human scale, the more we will be able to reduce the size of government," says David Korten. Perhaps it's time for those who fight big government and those who fight big business to claim their common ground. So they can work together to fight both.

A popular trend in Hollywood movies pits a small band of heroic and determined humans against an overwhelming alien force threatening to destroy civilization. This is generally treated as an entertaining fiction, but it's a fair reflection of our situation today. The alien force threatening our way of life is an out-of-control machine age corporate system—the all-consuming giant that the corporate person has become. The small, heroic band of humans thrown by fate into the path of this juggernaut are the nine members of the United States Supreme Court. Our fate, in a very real sense, lies in their hands.

Local Incentive

As independent media are swallowed and digested by conglomerates, the diversity of feedback needed for good democratic judgment wanes. As corporations reach into even our public schools, gearing children to corporate doctrines, local diversity and the perspectives that it brings to any democratic process are being massaged away, too. The same is happening in commerce as small businesses get bought up or bankrupted by huge, communal corporations. And in this bland new world, how long will the Web remain free?

One can't help wishing that the corporate conservatives forever touting a return to classical economics would get their wish. Those theories are often more in tune with nature. Nature's economy preserves diversity while integrating global and local elements, as with seafaring algae and tectonic plates, as with snails and white cliffs. For nature, local diversity is a key to global vitality. Adam Smith's ideas mirror that, with his stress on the dangers of concentrated power and on the importance of diverse local inputs in creating free markets. Freedom, if it means anything, means the right to say no. But as a price of admission, corporate globalization now rules out local diversity by removing the right of communities, regions, even whole nations to do so. With that we have such new frontiers in paradox as "free market monopolies" and "imposed benefits."

One reason local interests are suffering is that the corporate world trade system now in place is not really centered on trade; it's keyed instead to something called economic integration. Any discussion of why that matters begins with David Ricardo's theory of comparative advantage. In essence, it says nations should produce what they're best suited for: Portugal should make wine, England should make wool. Then each nation can trade what it makes best to the other. Ricardo is often cited to legitimize corporate globalization, but that assertion fails the laugh test.

Ricardo's theory rests on just a few basic notions: For instance, he assumed that there was full employment in each of the countries involved. He also said that trade between partners must be balanced. Finally, while his system assumes that trade goods move back and forth across international lines, it also assumes that capital does not. In Ricardo's vision of an international economy, investment capital stays put at home. This last informs the discussion at hand, and was outlined in his 1817 book, *On the Principles of Political Economy and Taxation* (see notes for detail).

Ricardo showed how international trade can encourage each nation to export the products that it's best able to produce, and in doing so distribute benefits among them fairly and on many levels. It's an elegant model. But while corporate agents often mention it as justification, they then ignore the above three ground rules: Where Ricardo calls for full employment in each trading nation, today's globalists are inclined to see a bright side in unemployment, since it keeps inflation down. Where he insists on balanced trade, they view trade imbalances as by and large irrelevant (the U.S. trade deficit is presently soaring north of $600 billion). And far from containing capital within national borders, one of their canons is the free flow of capital across them.

Which brings the discussion back where it began. As David Korten points out, our global economy today is less about trade than about global economic integration. That difference is important because, "although the theory of comparative advantage applies to balanced *trade* between otherwise independent national economies, a very different theory—the theory of downward leveling—applies when national *economies* are integrated [emphasis added]."

The problem lies in where investment capital flows. "When capital is confined within the national borders of trading partners," he says, "it must flow through the industries in which its home country has a comparative advantage." Contrast this with what happens when whole national economies are integrated with one another, as they are in today's model.

When capital is free to flow across borders, its international expression is no longer tied to the interests of any one nation. This then alters how nations interrelate. Instead of competing through the value of trade goods that they can swap—as they do in Ricardo—they now compete to attract money from outside investors. And that money is not guided by the need to make products that are beneficial to one country or another. Instead, writes Korten, it just "flows to whatever locality offers the maximum opportunity to externalize costs through cash subsidies, tax breaks, substandard pay and working conditions, and lax environmental standards." As a result, he concludes, "income is thus shifted from workers to investors, and costs are shifted from investors to the community." Thomas Friedman, a staunch supporter of global trade, nevertheless notes how "for many workers around the world, oppression by the unchecked commissars has been replaced with oppression by the unregulated capitalists, who move their manufacturing from country to country, constantly in search of those who will work for the lowest wages and the lowest standards."

Ricardo's not the only prominent economist to disavow the international flow of capital. John Maynard Keynes once said, "Ideas, knowledge, art, hospitality, travel—these are the things which should of their nature be international. But let goods be homespun whenever it is reasonably and conveniently possible, and above all, let finance be primarily national."

The inequities and weaknesses of modern corporate globalization are many. But despite all, the larger point here is that it's just one approach to structuring world trade. Its problems aren't common to all global models. Given the stormy climate of ideas on this subject, it also bears constant restating that the call to reform globalization need not be an objection to the existence of world trade or of free markets. Ideological hostility toward all business is a vestige of twentieth-century thinking, the product of an old feud no longer relevant. Nor should globalization be a problem in theory. Nature integrates local and planetary dynamics with ease and seamless efficiency. The real question for a global economy is "By what means?"

This subject warrants more attention than Congress gave it in 1994, before voting to sanction the World Trade Organization. At that time the organization Public Citizen offered to donate $10,000 to any charity selected by members of Congress who would sign an affidavit saying they had read the five-hundred-page agreement, and then answer ten simple questions about it. There were no takers. Months passed before one senator finally read it and answered the questions. Although a free trade advocate, he promptly changed his vote to nay, based on that agreement's lack of any meaningful guarantees for due process. To no avail. With little evidence they even knew what was in it, 68 senators and 235 representatives soon voted it into law.

There must be a better way to manage world affairs. Clearly no sudden and dramatic restructuring is possible in today's vast, complex system. But even without the sanction of Ricardo or Keynes, it's possible to imagine how global economic integration could better serve the interests of all people in our networked modern world. There is, for instance, no compelling reason (beyond the objections of multinationals) why the big three global trade agencies can't mandate across-the-board standards for health, labor, educational, and environmental protections as the price of entry into the global economy. WTO tribunals in Geneva enforce an across-the-board absence of those protections now. Why not turn that practice on its head? After all, the broad effect on competition—whether nobody has those protections or everyone has them—is neutral, essentially a wash. And a shift of this kind could occur organically in a world economy that's more transparent, more subject to due process, and guided by realistic feedback. Can there be a globalization in which the expansion of trade assures people of poor nations those same rights and protections long enjoyed in the West (instead of the current system, in which the West is gradually losing them, too)?

Capitalism doesn't have to be a tool of corporatism. Imagine a world where a truly democratic capitalism is the spearhead of human rights, where the kind of practice more common in Europe and once typical of the U.S.—in which community stakeholders have a greater say in corporate decision making—becomes the global norm.

If we can move beyond corporate globalization, the effort to bring developing nations into the world economy offers other opportunities as well. It opens the way for methods and technologies drawn from the new biology. Emerging nations could then take the lead in a gradual transition to a very different world—an economic ecology of diverse local inputs employing new monetary models, new models for energy, new models for industry, new standards for cultural feedbacks. The big three trade agencies could administer that system if they became more democratic. And that can happen if public awareness and participation grow. Pressure on them may also come from within. If the World Bank, IMF, and WTO in present form have problems, they are nonetheless staffed with thousands of admirable men and women working to make the world a better place. What's lacking is not the will to do good work, but a system that doesn't hamstring and distort their best efforts.

A Pulse Is a Rhythm

The tension between local and global is natural. We don't have to choose
one or the other. In fact, to do so, in the large sense, is a form of error.
As physicist Niels Bohr once said, "The opposite of a correct statement
is a false statement. But the opposite of a profound truth may well be another profound truth."

Looked at as a whole system, nature centers on incompatible tensions.
They're at the heart of life's vitality. Structure and process, figure and
ground, individual and communal, bottom-up and top-down, linear and
lateral, competition and cooperation, chaos and order, adaptable and stable, local and global: those dualities can't be blended into peaceful harmony. They seem designed by nature to prevent that. Rather, they are like
hormones that by turn promote excitement and subsidence (as excitement moves toward death by chaos, and then subsidence moves toward
death from too much order). They are opposites but they're linked. And
so those pairs dance to and fro; each one's trend stopped short of its extreme by feedbacks pressing it back in toward the center—back to where
those counteracting opposites can push each other outward once again.

That is a pulse. By pulsing one way, then another, with feedback as
its guide, life navigates the shifting ground between opposing trends to
find the sweet spot at their heart.

If we want to extend our civilization for the next one hundred
thousand years, there are just two basic rules, both of which merge culture with the rest of life. They are (*a*) preserve opposing tensions, and
(*b*) make sure feedback loops are strong and true. Rendered into feedback culture, this means (*a*) maintaining free speech and free markets,
which allow a diversity of local views and practices, in order to help opposing tensions flourish; and then (*b*) making sure that media, scientific,
economic, and democratic feedback loops are true, to ensure that they
can hold those rambunctious players together and moderate extreme or
unreal tendencies, so the dancers don't veer off the floor.

All this involves a different view of partisanship. Seen through the
lens of feedback culture, disagreement is what drives the system. Different
needs, different beliefs, ideological rivalries, all propel the process. But
to the extent that that is true, it's equally true that ideology can't control
the process. Because for either side to win, finally and completely—as
utopians, by definition, want to do—also means to fail the larger design
that keeps a living system vital. In feedback culture, the best way forward

lies not in choosing one side over the other, nor in smoothing their differences away. Instead, making the world a better place means maintaining a lively tension between those adversaries while wrapping them in a nest of realistic feedbacks—which keep the whole pulsing, dancing, sexy, hungry, constantly evolving enterprise intact.

Staying Power

Historians say planning for the future without learning from the past is like trying to plant cut flowers. As we identify the problems born of the machine age, we can begin to address that concern. It's also time to move beyond the anger and ideological cant of twentieth-century thinking. This means accepting that the machine age is not the opposite of nature. In fact, it's an example of how much benefit there is in getting things half right. The new biology doesn't reject the machine age. It builds on and incorporates that by stirring its classic logic into the larger complexities and dynamics of living systems.

Just knowing all this, though, won't repair the legacy of our long reliance on machine age methods. The last century was defined by the great conflict between machine age capitalism and machine age socialism. With the benefit of hindsight we can see now that both were large, centralized, communal, mechanistic forms of organization, and how both freed themselves to pillage natural systems by distorting or denying basic cultural feedbacks. The victory of the West in that contest was a Pyrrhic one. With the international resource wars that have now begun, awareness of the deeper threat is rising. Sharp religious conflict and the terrorism accompanying it have been inflamed by war over oil in the Middle East. Water is a growing source of regional disputes.

Contests over food will come, as topsoil disappears and per capita food production continues to fall. Machine age strategies for growing more food involve genetically engineering plants for higher productivity, and to help those plants survive ever-higher doses of herbicides and pesticides (no doubt there are optimistic gene modifiers who will one day seek to reengineer us to withstand those higher doses, too). But there are physical limits to how much actual food a plant can produce. And that leaves aside the problem of what a rising tide of toxic industrial-farm runoff is doing to the earth's water, or to the topsoil base needed to grow our crops.

A Cornell University study says the earth can sustainably support one or two billion people in the style to which industrial nations are accustomed. Through machine age methods of farming and manufacturing we have managed to grow the world's human population to six billion.

What the Cornell study points to is more than a problem; it is an epochal misstep. Because the main and crucial thing machine age systems lack is staying power. To borrow a phrase, "What can't last won't last." Beyond all political innuendo, the word "sustainable" means simply that this or that way of doing things has staying power. We are now one hundred thousand years old. There remains a vast way to go, and it's clear the machine metaphor can't take us there. By depleting resources too quickly and piling up too much waste, we have already begun to hit the wall of ecological limits. That we are smarter than algae is a given. Whether we are wiser remains an open question.

On Certainty

It's not as hard to do the right thing as it is to know what the right thing is to do. The machine age wasn't developed by people who meant to cause problems. They began with a premise they believed was sound. Only time and application showed its weakness. So how can we be sure now? How to know when we are working from a stable foundation? It's not a simple question. Western philosophers have labored for twenty-five hundred years without finding answers beyond challenge. Theologians have done no better; as Paul Tillich acknowledged, "Doubt isn't the opposite of faith, doubt is an element of faith." Science has probed the inner heart of matter without finding solid ground. Physicist Richard Feynman allowed that science is "a body of statements of varying degrees of certainty—some most unsure, some nearly sure, none absolutely sure." Darwin insisted his theory offered no certainties, just plausible explanations. What about the pure logic of mathematics? Albert Einstein said, "Insofar as mathematics is about reality, it is not certain, and insofar as it is certain, it is not about reality."

Our limited intelligence and senses leave us always wondering at a larger reality we assume is out there yet never fully comprehend. Kansas agriculturalist Wes Jackson states the dilemma: "How do we operate knowing we're fundamentally ignorant? What kind of a science comes out of that? What kind of philosophy comes out of that? What kind of political structure comes out of that?"

Law and Order

Perhaps the closest thing to certainty we have is reflected in another Feynman remark: "Nature cannot be fooled." Most people accept that nature imposes certain laws on us. The problem lies in figuring out what they are. Newtonian physics uncovered principles that medieval thinkers missed. It turns out that those principles are just approximations. Still, by showing how each action in the physical world brings a predictable reaction, they opened our eyes to a new aspect of natural law and revolutionized human culture. Now we begin to see how—in living systems—the rules of classical physics are subsumed by another set of natural laws we can't fool with, those of ecological process.

While we can run from the basic rules of life, we can't hide. Biological feedback prevails in the end. The machine age offered only a brief illusion of freedom from those rules. Moreover, whether we try to live within them or not has no bearing on nature. Those who complain of ecological damage, with its threat to other species (and humans), do so for good reasons. But what we destroy are life's current structures—its flora, fauna, and other forms. We should regret their loss, and will pay for it in ways large and small. But life itself is a process. Once set in motion it just keeps working with whatever energy, information, and materials come to hand.

That process—with its looping dynamics and mysterious complexities—is hard for us to fully grasp. It will nonetheless decide if modern humans are a successful experiment. "It is impossible for us to break the law. We can only break ourselves against the law," said movie director Cecil B. DeMille. He was talking about another set of commandments but the phrase is apt. Resistance to nature is not so much futile as irrelevant.

Nothing can live outside the basic rules of life, at least not for long. Any attempt to do so brings the extraordinary confluence of paybacks nature reserves for those who try. As Feynman's remark suggests, there is a kind of certainty in that. Ultimate answers may well lie beyond our reach, but they are also not required. Death marks an obvious boundary. Short of death, natural feedback is a nudge from the deeps of ecological process, like a backseat driver saying, "Turn here," or "Stop!" If we intend to stick around for the next one hundred thousand years, we can't escape the process. Listening to those signals is the only means we have.

Notes Stuart Kauffman, the Santa Fe Institute biologist, "As we talk about a sustainable world, you have to understand what 'sustainable' means. The biosphere has been sustainable for 3.5 billion years or whatever. That doesn't mean there hasn't been vast and constant change. Our image of what stability means is wrong . . . it's stationary. The real world may not be stable in those kinds of ways." His remark points back to the central paradox: it's ecological process that is stable, life's structures that are always changing. As city planner Richard Levine puts it, "Sustainability is not a goal; it's a process."

Through the Looking Glass

Ecological *process* remains stable through time. This process then gives rise to living forms, to *structures* that adapt and change. As a model for feedback culture, this suggests that the first job of government is not national defense or guarding the environment or protecting the weak from the strong. Rather, its first job is defining and stabilizing basic processes. If we get those right, the rest will follow—healthy and adaptive legal structures will grow from them.

Given that, government in a feedback culture would distinguish between primary and secondary policies. Those called primary would safeguard basic process: for instance, feedbacks like electoral procedures and economic indicators, along with the diversity of free media and free markets, among other things. Those primary policies would then underlie the formation of secondary policies: the evolving legal structures that address our day-to-day concerns. It's a nice coincidence that in democracy, the policies here dubbed primary are what we call "constitutional," which acknowledges their primacy by insulating them from change. Also like nature, as secondary, legal structures arise from the workings of a stable constitutional process, it reflects the creation and adaptation of living forms as they arise from ecological process. In this sense democracy is an intuitive mirror of nature.

Looking to biology helps determine what should be a primary policy. For instance, it suggests that diversity, decentralization, property rights, and privacy are just different ways of looking at the same thing (in this sense "privacy" means information is contained within a local boundary, which protects it from disturbance by the larger system). All those concepts aid the beneficial tensions we obtain from true diversity, and so are matters for primary policy. In the new world dawning, primary policy should also carefully define what is or is not an organic life form—in agriculture, in robotics and AI, and to avoid granting rights of citizenship to nonliving entities.

Because citizenship for organizations wasn't literally ruled out by the Constitution, corporations got around it to create an artificial person with greater powers than living Americans have. "You are my creator," said the monster to Dr. Frankenstein, "but I am your master." The advent of corporate personhood was a primary error, one now affecting the world in countless ways. And just as it has broad impacts, correcting it would bring equally widespread benefits. It would free us to address the legalized bribery of today's lobbying and campaign finance systems; to restrain the "engineering of consent" in democratic process via PR and ads; to make a start at reforming globalization; to halt the rise of what columnist William Safire has called "media giantism," with its feedback homogenization; and to restrain the undue corporate influence now rearing its head in scientific and educational fields. All this would help rein in the most forceful promoters of those mechanistic farming, industrial, and economic practices now eating away at the environment. Community designer Mike Corbett once remarked that when he solved one problem and it solved several others, he knew he was getting somewhere.

In a healthy feedback culture, primary policies maintain stable processes, which then guide the creation of secondary policies—ever-changing legal structures that adapt to meet our day-to-day concerns. Looking to biology helps define and clarify those as well. A good example of that lies in an emerging concern: as the twentieth-century battle between capitalism and communism wanes, elements of that struggle are morphing into a more fundamental contest—between a libertarian push toward chaotic, unfettered individuality and the communal push toward stifling, highly ordered bureaucracy.

It's an old custom to think of a safe path as a corridor of order through chaotic surroundings (or for those in the arts, perhaps, the obverse). But armed with deeper insights from nature, we see now that the best way forward is one that's neither too underconnected nor too overconnected—that is not altogether chaotic, not rigidly ordered, but also not just a bland averaging of the two. Instead it's more like a valley with, on the one side, a gradually rising hill of order and, on the other, a gradually rising hill of chaos. In this sense our day-to-day legislative challenge is to remain roughly in the zone between them—as we by turns first wander one way, then are pushed by feedback toward the other.

This kind of thinking calls for new ideas. Especially now that old notions of conservative and liberal are breaking down. The once fiscally prudent members of the right have been pushed aside by a new generation of spendthrift, credit card conservatives with no reply to tax-and-spend liberals but their own even more expensive borrow-and-spend approach. In their push to get government off the backs of individuals (and off the backs of big corporations), they now routinely brand even the most basic community interests as remnants of socialism. Meanwhile, their anything-goes, libertarian support for business has rendered them the leading allies of machine age methods and global corporate dominion. But real conservatives distrust *all* concentrations of power. They also see the value of husbanding resources, both financial and natural. Still, if today's conservatives are losing sight of their roots, liberals have fared little better. Many of the corporate initiatives now causing problems were passed with support from liberals. Long a party grounded in blue-collar labor, they have encouraged the migration of those jobs offshore, and made no broad effort to fix the false economy accelerating that trend. It was a liberal administration that aggressively promoted the spread of genetically modified life forms across the globe. And though liberals have in other ways been champions of conservation and the environment, they've lagged in stepping away from bureaucratic end-of-pipe regulation and toward a nature-based approach. Real conservatives know that the key to good solutions lies in mirroring ecological process.

Just as the left brought us under the sway of large centralized bureaucracies, and the right now brings us under the sway of large centralized multinational corporations, both in their own way have undermined free markets and decentralization. Separately or together, they have also weakened privacy, private property, and media diversity. All of this in turn endangers cultural diversity.

William Safire expressed the problem well:

The *concentration* of power—political, corporate, media, cultural—should be anathema to conservatives. The *diffusion* of power through local control, thereby encouraging individual participation, is the essence of federalism and the essence of democracy.

Real conservatives understand how localized diversity is the basis for system-wide vitality in a culture—that the two are one—so long as media, scientific, economic, and democratic feedbacks are true.

The Missing Link

From nanotechnology to democratic processes and in virtually every field between, the same revolution is under way. Because the new biology affects so many different fields at once, there is no longer any question that it's significant. So why, then, has it taken this long to make its mark? After all, when Newton codified classical physics in the late seventeenth century, it very quickly transformed natural science, dynamics, astronomy, and philosophy. The machine age was founded on those principles. Yet though Darwin published his insight into ecological process in 1859, it languished in the scientific cheap seats until the 1980s. Economist Brian Arthur suggests why. As he explains it:

> [Philosopher] Daniel Dennett has become famous for saying that the best idea of all time was Darwin's idea . . . that Darwin is dangerous. It's like a universal solvent. Any discipline that tries to contain it, it just eats through the discipline. Be it anthropology, our understanding of economies, our understanding of computer algorithms—the discipline is never the same . . . This is the theme of the next century. The base reasoning throughout all disciplines is becoming Darwinian. So why wasn't that true a hundred years ago? How come there wasn't an enlightenment in the 1900s coming out of Darwin, parallel to the enlightenment coming out of Newton and Descartes? My answer is . . . Darwin couldn't be mechanized, could not be reduced to equations. It turns out that way of thinking didn't really catch on until we got desktop computers. Then we could look at whole patterns evolving. This has meant that in all of the sciences there has been a heavy step back to an organic view. Suddenly we are able to look at highly interactive, coevolving systems directly—not by pencil and paper, but by computer. So what the telescope did for astronomy and what the microscope did for biology . . . the computer is doing for this ecological metaphor.

Computers have another impact on philosophy, too. When the machine age implanted reductionism into culture, it broke human fields of endeavor into isolated specialties. Ecological thought now seeks to overlay them with interconnecting webs. The Nobel physicist Murray Gell-Mann, the Santa Fe Institute paterfamilias, says, "We think specialization is necessary and good, but we believe it has to be supplemented with integrative thinking, and that right now there's an imbalance—that there's a great need for competent integrative thinking." And just as computers turned out to be the missing link in the effort to "see" ecological processes, they have also proved instrumental in the cross-disciplinary movement led by SFI. A-Life progenitor Chris Langton describes how: "Physicists speak a different language from economists, and have different bodies of theory," he says. So too for biologists. "The fact that we all have to speak the same language to get ourselves on the computer has allowed us to compare very different systems. We now have this common linguistic territory, and we've found commonality among things we would have thought were different otherwise."

Thinking Machines

As computers help transform the way we think, they also—through their widespread distribution—help ingrain those new ideas in every facet of our lives. In nanotechnology and materials science, robotics and AI; in complexity theory, the study of ecology, and agriculture; for decentralized energy microgrids and virtual community planning; in industrial ecology and bioeconomic theory; as well as in media, education, and the democratic process—with its voter databases and number-crunching opinion poll analysis, and now electronic voting booths—all have been profoundly affected by, in some cases are little more than elaborations of, computers.

They're no less involved now in the myriad outputs of our consumer economy. Computers are often instrumental in the research leading to a new product. Then they're used to design the product. The product is manufactured on a computerized assembly line, promoted over media that use computerized production and transmission systems, and sold to customers who have been targeted through the use of computerized databases. Life cycle analysis computers track the flow of energy and materials into the product, even as computerized checkout and accounting systems track its distribution and sale. And, increasingly, computer chips are embedded in the product itself (by one reckoning, in the U.S. today there are sixty thousand computer chips for every person).

From video games to virtual flight training for pilots, from space programs to all the global positioning and communications and spy satellites they launch, computers are the key. The World Wide Web has become a reality unto itself. With its e-mail, instant messaging, search engines, and proliferating chat rooms, dating services, smart mobs, podcasts, wikis, VoIPs, blogs, vlogs, and evolving artificial life forms; and with sites for buying everything from stocks and bonds to pop tunes to pickup trucks (Web-based commerce is already a $50 billion sector), the Internet has become a new kind of ecosystem. There are Web sites to raise money for politicians and Web sites for the muckrakers who decry them. There are Internet-mediated procedures for conducting lab research or medical operations at a distance. People from all walks of life interact in multiplayer games and through their avatars in virtual worlds. Businesses and schools explore virtual reality conferencing. Grid computing links computing centers or vast numbers of desktops to form virtual supercomputers that analyze global climate, model the complexities of protein folding, or scan huge databases to aid in drug discovery.

But there are problems, too. Without computers, the genetic engineering of new and fearsome bioweapons would never have come to pass. Our growing reliance on computers brings other security problems, too, as when companies let outsiders code their software, and in the vulnerabilities of open-source designs. Spam and Trojan horses are pandemic. Crime on the Net is surging, both in frequency and in complexity. According to the London-based computer security firm mi2g, a recent single month saw a record twenty thousand "successful and verifiable" hacker incidents. Internet reach and anonymity help terrorists to organize. Computerized voting booths proliferate while critics point to the inevitability of cyber-tampering. Privacy, a keystone of civil culture, is everywhere under assault by these and other factors, ranging from the cookies in our desktops to the secret codes now printed onto laser color printouts to the electronic tracking chips that will soon be embedded in everything from product packaging to the tires on our cars. Thomas Friedman notes, "Every phone call you make, every bill you charge, every prescription drug you buy, every video you rent, every plane ride you take, every cash machine you use, gets logged somewhere in a computer . . . and you have no idea when it may come back to haunt you." Adding to that concern, new laws like the Digital Millennium Copyright Act and the Patriot Act make it easier for corporations and government agencies to track online activities without our knowledge or consent.

On a related front, as economies and national defense establishments grow dependent on computer webs, the specter of cyberwar looms. Hack attacks are a constant threat. The GPS satellites that guide everything from military ops to commercial shipping, and that set the crucial time stamps for Internet routing, can be knocked out with existing arms. They're also vulnerable to the new electromagnetic pulse weapons, which emit powerful microwave bursts that burn out electronic circuitry. Virtually all private sector computer systems and most government systems are vulnerable to these "e-pulse" bombs. That's a special concern in the modern, data-rich battlefield, but it also opens the way for new kinds of terrorist assaults on our highly networked infrastructure. Time was, "infrastructure" meant harbors, airports, factories, and bridges. Today it includes the computer circuits that run everything from telecommunications to nuclear power plant fail-safe systems. There is now a White House special adviser on cyberspace security to address this threat. The Defense and Commerce departments, along with the FBI, also each have "critical infrastructure" boards devoted to cyber security.

New vulnerabilities aren't the only drawback. Because decentralized data networks like the Web amplify every kind of information, they also enhance the spread of poorly founded rumors and trends. This includes machine age outlooks. In the case at hand, they have globalized an economic system grounded in a partial understanding of reality. In the process they helped carry to every corner of the earth an unsustainable approach to farming and manufacturing.

Given all that, there's a tendency to blame the messenger. But computers are a tool. Like most tools they can serve in various ways. Even as they are used to harm the natural world, they're also being used to protect it. Writing for *Mother Jones* magazine, Walter Truett Anderson outlined that role:

> An enormous environmental information system has grown, spreading and connecting around the world. The living Earth is now inseparable from this ever-expanding complex of satellites, transmitters, relay towers, computers,

and software. With these devices, people observe the condition of the ozone, speculate on the future of the world's climate, study tectonic movements deep below the surface, brood over the oceans, track the migrations of wild animals and the changes in forests and deserts. This is technology that doesn't fit into any simplistic pro vs. con debate. It is neither the malevolent cause of our problems nor their magical solution—just an essential means of acquiring information. And it will play a larger part in bringing greater environmental awareness than the collected works of all the writers and philosophy professors who push deep ecology and bioregionalism.

One thing that computers have always been about is the growth of data, and of the innovation rising from it. By improving and clarifying the information we draw from nature, they deepen our understanding. As communications tools, they accelerate that knowledge through all the wide variety of human interests. As design and manufacturing tools, they accelerate its conversion into innovations. And as marketing and accounting tools, they then accelerate those innovations into general use, with all its impacts on the natural world.

This new loop—of information taken up from nature, massaged through computerized human culture, and then downloaded back to nature—in no way alters ecological process. In fact, it's where the new biology comes from. But it does increase the rate at which innovations large and small, benign and problematic, are fed into the process. With that has come a rapid increase in complexity, and the speeding up of evolution.

Artificial Life in the Balance

All living things carry information about how they can use energy to stir matter into new forms. Until modern humans came along, though, genomes were the only medium evolution had for storing and transmitting that information. Through the medium of culture, we can now store and transmit complex information genes don't hold. This has evolutionary impact. The diversity of human interests expands the complexity of information. And culture, just by its existence, also magnifies complexity, since it replicates data so much faster than organic reproduction can, and because its copying fidelity is lower. Computers have accelerated all that. Now scientists aim to up the stakes still further.

Marshall McLuhan once called computers an extraordinary extension of the human nervous system. He may have been too cautious. As science moves to develop computers with minds of their own, cultural evolution could detach from exclusively human wants and needs.

Of self-organizing systems in general, SFI physicist Murray Gell-Mann writes, "Not everything keeps increasing in complexity . . . Rather, the highest complexity to be found has a tendency to increase." For some analysts, that insight, joined with progress in robotics, AI, the Web, and now the grid, suggests the means by which some networked meta–life form could arise, one that would absorb and supersede humanity. Is that a real concern?

Our civilization insulates us from the hard edge of ecological process. In this, we're like those mitochondria that once took residence in the larger cells now feeding and sheltering them. Just as the human body is a kind of civilization for the symbiotic bacteria inhabiting us, our own civilization is a larger body in which we humans live our lives with more security and comfort. It's conceivable that that system in some distant time might coalesce into a new and larger organism. And in the end it could subsume us, just as we subsume mitochondria. Computers make it at least plausible. The more meaningful question is whether it's a cause for worry.

From an evolutionary standpoint it is not. Symbiogenesis—in which two or more organisms gradually meld into one—is not a form of capture. Rather, it's a mutually beneficial partnership that verges into permanence with time. If the partnership doesn't work, the partners don't integrate. One need only look at our failing symbiosis with the machine age to see how true that is, as growing numbers of feedbacks now push us not toward further integration but away from it.

There may be near-term problems with robots, or with other artificially intelligent systems. The worst of them are less likely to be grounded in ecological process than in machine age thinking. No one can know for sure, but the odds are that we serve our interest by giving them an evolutionary intelligence (and perhaps—for the long run—by making sure they feed on something we don't need).

In a footnote to history, it bears noting that Santa Clara County in California—which gave us the Supreme Court case used to create our corporate Frankenstein monsters—is now the home of Silicon Valley, that prolific source of parts and software for a new generation of would-be artificial life forms.

Machine Genes

If there's an area of immediate concern, it's not the push to make machines that work like life. It is the effort by radical corporations using machine age ideas to modify existing life. The potential benefits of genetic engineering can't be argued away. The risks involved are nonetheless great.

Some who promote the genetic revolution hold humanity apart, suggesting there are cases where we can do better than nature. They argue, for example, that nature didn't invent the wheel. But nature did invent the wheel, through us. That we also invented disco doesn't mean we are unnatural. As Thomas Edison used to say, "In order to have a lot of good ideas, you have to have a lot of bad ideas." That is nature's way, and it should continue to be ours, assuming we can make our cultural feedbacks strong and true. Until then, though, it may be wise to err on the side of caution where huge and powerful corporations with machine age points of view are tinkering with elemental life processes.

Ultimately, the genetic genie is out of its bottle and won't be stopped. Those who spend their best efforts trying to deny it altogether will just be unprepared to deal with it when it finally comes full force. One suggestion for how to proceed comes from the genome itself. Nature favors genetic stability in some regions, mutability in others, with change allowed in those less crucial to survival. For instance, cell energy conversion is standardized across broad areas of life; it hasn't changed for billions of years. On the other hand, limb length in mammals varies constantly, even from one individual to the next.

This simple wisdom suggests encouraging pure research while restraining its application where fundamental impacts are likely, a policy that is also in line with nature's urge to maintain a tension between impulse and restraint. That approach, for instance, would sanction most existing medical procedures but resist germ-line modification, which brings permanent change to the human genome. It would also curb the spread of genetically modified organisms into natural systems around the globe, a practice that changes them inalterably.

Their spread, through industrial farming, is part of a half-smart solution. With the best of intentions we set out fifty years ago to feed the world. The unanticipated outcome was that world population quickly grew to billions more people than industrial farms can continue to support, and that the farms themselves caused major environmental damage. In response to those impacts we are setting off to make that mistake again, now on a new front, by applying the same half-smart logic to genetic modification of crops. This is a classic case of learning the wrong lesson. Artificial intelligence pioneer Marvin Minsky tells a story about a dog he had that liked to chase cars. Eventually it was hit by one. In response, the dog continued chasing cars but on a different street.

Civilized Behavior

In the broadest sense, life on earth is adjusting to the entry of conscious deliberation and volition into the system—through the medium of human culture. What that will mean in the next one hundred thousand years is anyone's guess. Still, the future is not beyond our influence. We may be unable to change ecological process, and precise control of complex systems is not an option. But just how deeply we can affect the birds and trees and other life forms is clear in the environmental havoc we've already wreaked with machine age thinking. And to the extent we can cause problems for life, we can also play a beneficial role.

Consciousness and the civil cultures it has wrought are not unnatural. They are a higher level of ecological expression, nature's grandest experiment so far in social competition and cooperation. But new levels of complexity bring with them the emergence of new qualities. As our shift to an ecological model becomes plausible, this is a key distinction. Primal nature is a useful guide for handling flows of energy and materials, and for certain underlying principles in our basic institutions. But absent the restraints of civil culture, life's methods can be brutal: anger, fear, dominance, violence, and greed are natural impulses first. Nature's solution for unemployment is to kill the weak. Civilization is more than just automatic instincts and drives.

In a similar vein, civilization also means more than just letting free markets work. If our most compelling bases for judgment, the cumulative high points of our knowledge, are the needs of five-year economic plans, we are by definition unwise. And contrary to the spin of corporate conservatives, support for the civil institutions of government is not a form of socialism. Free markets are created by people, as are democratic governments. Both are modeled on nature, and neither is meant to "win." Maintaining a healthy tension between them is consistent with nature's fondness for balancing impulse and restraint. George Soros, though one of the world's most aggressive and successful capitalists, notes:

Every society needs some shared values to hold it together. Market values on their own cannot serve that purpose . . . Markets reduce everything, including human beings (labor) and nature (land), to commodities. We can have a market economy but we cannot have a market society. In addition to markets, society needs institutions to serve such social goals as political freedom and social justice.

Human concerns may be diverse, but we all want a society that provides us with secure and meaningful lives (and better ones for our children, and so on for theirs, for as far into the future as possible). That impulse drives the development of civil communities, and neither markets nor raw nature offers a guide to civil conduct. For that we have philosophers, religious leaders, and now radio talk show hosts. But beyond all of these, for that we have education.

A Pulse Is a Seedhead

Cultural feedbacks are remote sensory systems, transmitting information back to us from the larger world. As that data drives our culture, it also flows through our awareness into libraries, databases, and other storehouses—the cultural equivalent of genes. Education draws on those genes; it is a distillation of our feedbacks. While feedbacks bring data to us, education is information we feed forward to the future—in a mirror of the genetic information carried by seedheads—to create a new generation of civilized humans.

Education is cultural reproduction, and just as in sexual reproduction, it carries change. We consciously change our culture in response to new information, new philosophies—as now with our growing insights into natural process and into what those insights mean. As that knowledge filters into grade schools, and is taken up by university programs, an emerging generation then helps carry it forward.

By using the rules that shape biology to also shape our culture, we maintain our best guide to the future. For it unites us to the ongoing process of transformation that is a central fact of life. Like all living systems, human cultures can evolve.

The poet Goethe long ago suggested that when a plant grows, a deep and unchanging pattern shapes the emerging parts, transforming itself from leaves to petals to stamens as they appear. That change, he said, is like the change an insect undergoes in metamorphosis. Writer

John Elkington, in his book *The Chrysalis Economy*, makes a similar case for our situation now. "The global economy," he says, "is entering a pro-tracted period of . . . dramatic technological, corporate and market trans-formation" with strong parallels to "the natural process of metamorphosis."

Will industrial revolution give way to industrial evolution? We are living through a fundamental change, the rise of a new cultural philos-ophy. And when philosophy changes, everything changes. The novelist Vladimir Nabokov—a keen entomologist—once said the metamorphosis "from larva to pupa or from pupa to butterfly is not a particularly pleas-ant process for the subject involved." Still, it can be rewarding:

> There comes for every caterpillar a difficult moment when he begins to feel pervaded by an odd sense of discomfort. It is a tight feeling—here about the neck and elsewhere, and then an unbearable itch . . . You will ask—what is the feeling of hatching? Oh, no doubt, there is a rush of panic to the head, a thrill of breathless and strange sensation, but then the eyes see, in a flow of sunshine, the butterfly sees the world.

Moving Toward the Light

"Wonder is the feeling of a philosopher," said Aristotle, "and philoso-phy begins in wonder." We want to understand, to perceive the larger world beyond our reach. In a fine passage, the naturalist Joseph Wood Krutch describes that impulse:

> Both Wordsworth and Thoreau knew that when the light of common day seemed no more than common it was because of something lacking in them, not because of something lacking in it, and what they asked for was eyes to see a universe they knew was worth seeing. For that reason theirs are the best of all attempts to describe what real awareness consists of . . . that the rare moment is not the moment when there is something worth looking at but the moment when we are capable of seeing it.

In a deep sense the whole, long evolution of intelligence is a gradual ex-pansion of awareness, and of the greater understanding that it brings. Vision itself grew from a dim awareness of the light. Next came eyes, to distinguish shapes and then, as eyes moved close together, depth. With each of those advances, understanding grew, as life forms came to see things they had never seen before. Consciousness expanded our awareness further. It brought another kind of seeing, and with that came still more new revelations. Among them was discovery of the natural laws that led to farming. That transformed our way of life. Farms then spawned cities, with all the ferment and sophisticated feedbacks they produce. They continued to expand our understanding and awareness—this time with science, which spurred a revolution called the machine age.

In each case the same essential process was at work: new awareness led to greater understanding, which then reshaped our world. Today finds us increasing our awareness again, this time through computers and their networks. We draw new insights from their power and precision, and from their ceaseless flows of data. We can also transfer, store, and process data now in quantities and at speeds that once were unthinkable. And in all this we see again more natural laws once hidden from our view—all those ecological patterns and processes that signal yet another transformation.

In *Darwinism Evolving*, its authors write, "The idea that there is a hidden order now revealed by our massive increase in computative ability produces" a "kind of awe." This revolution in our understanding of natural process, they say, also leads us "to suspect that we are only nibbling around the edges of deeper dimensions of pattern latent in the natural world." However far we've come, a great deal more lies ahead.

The long term is long. Life on earth has existed for nearly four billion years, and species tend to live for millions. Modern humans bring a new kind of awareness to life but are a mere one hundred thousand years old. We are still babies in evolutionary terms. We have only just opened our eyes. We are just beginning to see.

notes

A number of the interviews for this book were reviewed by their sources, to ensure currency, just prior to publication. In these cases the original year of the interview is listed in the note, followed by the month and year of the update. Footnoting with Web pages presents novel difficulties: Their content may be changed from time to time, even when the addresses remain the same. Also, fixing the dates of material accessed on the Web can be a challenge, as there are no widely accepted protocols for listing them. In these notes, where no other date was available, I have cited the date on which I accessed the Web page in question. Note that Web pages whose links are no longer active or whose information has since been changed can often be found on the Wayback Machine, the Internet archive, at http://www.archive.org. Finally, every effort has been made to credit the original sources of the information presented here. I regret any oversights and will correct for later editions any that are brought to my attention.

1. The New Biology

3 *Then a microbe with a novel skill*: Mitochondria.

9 *"the mechanical explanation of . . . nature"*: Alfred North Whitehead, *Science and the Modern World* (1925; New York: Free Press, 1967), p. 60.

10 *"self-organizing"*: Per Fritjof Capra, *The Web of Life: A New Scientific Understanding of Living Systems* (New York: Anchor Books, 1996), p. 22.

10 *"Nature," he wrote*: Quoted in David J. Depew and Bruce H. Weber, *Darwinism Evolving: Systems Dynamics and the Genealogy of Natural Selection* (Cambridge, Mass.: MIT Press, 1996), p. 46.

11 *By then the rancor*: Ibid., p. 50.

12 *Saint-Hilaire's adaptation*: Ibid., p. 43.

12 *"are much more universal"*: Walter J. Gehring, *Master Control Genes in Development and Evolution: The Homeobox Story* (New Haven, Conn.: Yale University Press, 1998), p. 50.

13 *"Learn from me"*: Mary Shelley, *Frankenstein* (London: Everyman's Library, 1985), p. 46.

13 *"All fire will die"*: Kevin Kelly, *Out of Control: The New Biology of Machines, Social Systems, and the Economic World* (Reading, Mass.: Addison-Wesley, 1994), p. 405.

14 *"Every organic being naturally"*: Charles Darwin, *On the Origin of Species*, pp. 61–62, quoted in John A. Moore, *Science as a Way of Knowing: The Foundations of Modern Biology* (Cambridge, Mass.: Harvard University Press, 1993), p. 132.

14 *Without environmental constraints*: This calculation was made by the mathematician Stephen Farrier.

15 *"As more individuals are produced"*: Darwin, *On the Origin of Species*, pp. 61–62, quoted in Moore, *Science as a Way of Knowing*, p. 131.

15 *"Owing to this struggle"*: Darwin, *On the Origin of Species*, pp. 61–62, quoted in Moore, *Science as a Way of Knowing*, p. 132.

15 *"Nature, red in"*: Alfred, Lord Tennyson, *In Memoriam*, sec. 56, stanza 4.

15 *"I should premise"*: Darwin, *On the Origin of Species*, p. 64, quoted in Bruce Mazlish, *The Fourth Discontinuity: The Co-evolution of Humans and Machines* (New Haven, Conn.: Yale University Press, 1993), p. 93.

15 *"the web and woof"*: Quoted in Anna Bramwell, *Ecology in the 20th Century: A History* (New Haven, Conn.: Yale University Press, 1989), p. 47.

15 *"that a finch"*: Mazlish, *Fourth Discontinuity*, p. 102.

16 *"There is no fundamental difference"*: Quoted in ibid., p. 102.

16 *"The change in species"*: Richard Milner, *The Encyclopedia of Evolution: Humanity's Search for Its Origins* (New York: Facts on File, 1990), p. 436.

16 *"no elegant equations"*: Michael Rothschild, *Bionomics: The Inevitability of Capitalism* (New York: Henry Holt, 1990), p. 41.

16 *Changes were afoot*: George B. Dyson, *Darwin Among the Machines: The Evolution of Global Intelligence* (Reading, Mass.: Perseus Books, 1997), p. 44. The author refers to the work of George Boole and, later, John von Neumann, saying that the lessons of Boole's work in particular have only partially been adopted by the scientific establishment.

16 *"The number of humble-bees"*: Darwin, *On the Origin of Species*, p. 75, quoted in Mazlish, *Fourth Discontinuity*, p. 93.

17 *the term "ecology"*: Haeckel's spelling was "oekologie."

17 *"the science of relations"*: Quoted in Bramwell, *Ecology in the 20th Century*, p. 40.

17 *"As the vegetable kingdom"*: Samuel Butler, "Luck, or Cunning, as the Main Means of Organic Modification? An Attempt to Throw Additional Light upon Darwin's Theory of Natural Selection," quoted in Dyson, *Darwin Among the Machines*, p. 15.

18 *"acquired as an adaptation"*: Quoted in Milner, *Encyclopedia of Evolution*, p. 460.

19 *"A hen is only"*: Quoted in Rothschild, *Bionomics*, p. 1.

19 *What was lacking*: Milner, *Encyclopedia of Evolution*, p. 460.

20 *the hall of the electric dynamos*: The dynamos were large early generators.

20 *"man had translated himself"*: Henry Adams, *The Education of Henry Adams* (New York: Modern Library, 1931), p. 381.

20 *"To Adams," he wrote of himself*: Ibid., p. 380.

20 *A popular echo*: My thanks to Chris Chang for suggesting this example.

22 *"hopeful monsters"*: The term was later coined by the geneticist Richard Goldschmidt.

23 *The formerly chaotic*: Capra, *Web of Life*, pp. 86–87.

24 *Those self-organizing hexagons*: D'Arcy Thompson, *On Growth and Form*, abr. ed. (Cambridge, U.K.: Cambridge University Press, 1961), p. 106.

24 *again becoming current*: Capra, *Web of Life*, p. 25.

24 *"The world"*: Quoted in ibid., p. 30.

25 *Work done earlier*: By Claude Bernard, the founder of modern experimental medicine. Ibid., p. 24.

25 *"homeostasis"*: Ibid., p. 43.

25 *"a continual migration of atoms"*: Quoted in Vaclav Smil, *Cycles of Life: Civilization and the Biosphere* (New York: Scientific American Library, 1997), p. 6.

25 *a "superorganism"*: Quoted in Kelly, *Out of Control*, p. 97.

25 *"general scrimmage for available energy"*: Kozo Mayumi and John M. Gowdy, eds., *Bioeconomics and Sustainability: Essays in Honor of Nicholas Georgescu-Roegen* (Cheltenham, U.K.: Edward Elgar, 1999), p. 130.

26 *For example, take the contest*: Milner, *Encyclopedia of Evolution*, p. 86.

26 *The biologist Ludwig von Bertalanffy*: Capra, *Web of Life*, p. 28.

26 *"At each level of complexity"*: Ibid., pp. 28–29.

28 *The rebels found*: Jan Sapp, *Beyond the Gene: Cytoplasmic Inheritance and the Struggle for Authority in Genetics* (New York: Oxford University Press, 1987), p. 231.

29 *"stripped to essentials"*: Quoted in ibid., p. 215.

29 *"I suspect that the cytoplasm"*: Quoted in ibid., p. 87.

31 *More generally, the AEC*: Stephen Bocking, "Visions of Nature and Society: A History of the Ecosystem Concept," *Alternatives*, July 1994, p. 12.

31 *In the late sixties*: Ibid.

33 *order "floats in disorder"*: Quoted in Capra, *Web of Life*, p. 190.

33 *"What we call organisms"*: David Sloan Wilson, review of *Darwinism Evolving*, by Depew and Weber, *Artificial Life* 2 (1995), pp. 261–67.

34 *Margulis sent her paper*: John Brockman, *The Third Culture: Beyond the Scientific Revolution* (New York: Simon & Schuster, 1995), p. 135.

34 *"biologists must begin"*: Ibid., p. 36.

34 *"We are not single"*: Quoted by Faye Flam, "An Enemy Within," *Philadelphia Inquirer*, April 28, 1997, p. C01.

35 *We understand that life*: Strictly speaking, there are some organisms that live entirely away from the sun's warmth, but they rely on stellar heat stored in the earth's core.

37 *As Bill Wimsatt asks*: Personal conversation with William Wimsatt, March 1997.

2. Building Blocks

42 *So everything is made of them*: Stars like our sun began as atoms that were superheated to form a plasma, in which their protons and electrons become disassociated. When they cool—billion of years from now—those atoms will re-form.

44 *Within four years*: U.S. Senate, *New Technologies for a Sustainable World: Hearing Before the Subcommittee on Science, Technology, and Space of the Committee on Commerce, Science, and Transportation*, 102nd Cong., 2nd sess., June 26, 1992 (Washington, D.C.: U.S. Government Printing Office, 1993).

44 *By then scientists*: From testimony by Eugene Wong, assistant director of the National Science Foundation for engineering, appearing before the House Committee on Science, Subcommittee on Basic Research, June 22, 1999. The hearings were published as *Nanoscale Science and Technology: Opportunities for the Twenty-first Century*.

44 *A million of them*: Ron Bailey, "The Revolution Has Begun," book review, *Wall Street Journal*, May 23, 2003, p. W14.

44 *"Atoms don't wear out"*: Personal conversation with K. Eric Drexler, May 1995.

44 *"break down materials"*: K. Eric Drexler and Chris Peterson with Gayle Pergamit, *Unbounding the Future* (New York: Quill/Morrow, 1991), p. 192.

45 *Instead of requiring*: Personal conversation with Julian Vincent, 1998; reviewed by him, Oct. 2003.

45 *One U.S. researcher*: Clive Thompson, "Nanoparticles Pop Up Everywhere," *Discover*, Jan. 2004, p. 58. The researcher cited is the neuroscientist Beverly Rzigalinski of the University of Central Florida.

45 *Japanese scientists*: Henry Fountain, "Nanomedicine," Observatory, *New York Times*, July 1, 2003, p. F1.

45 *"started to move"*: Niall McKay, "Honey, I Shrunk the HMO!" *Wired*, Jan. 2000, pp. 190–91. The scientists cited were Carlo Montemagno and George Bachand.

45 *Another group*: Anne Eisenberg, "A Sugar Cube, Please: I Need to Charge My Cellphone," *New York Times*, Sept. 18, 2003, p. G6. The scientists cited were Derek Lovley of the University of Massachusetts and Tayhas Palmore of Brown University.

46 *A diamond jet*: Ralph C. Merkle, "Whither Nanotechnology?" Nanotechnology: The Coming Revolution in Manufacturing, n.d., http://www.wtec.org/loyola/nano/us_r_n_d/08_06.htm.

46 *Smalley got his Nobel*: A buckminsterfullerene is sixty carbon atoms joined in a geodesic structure.

46 *He was director*: Smalley was also the cofounder and chairman of Carbon Nanotechnologies, a privately held company.

46 *With nanotube technology*: Rajat K. Paharia, "Forecasting the Future of Information Technology," March 20, 1998, http://www.stanford.edu/class/cs293/nano/.

46 *Make materials out of them*: Carl T. Hall, "Brave New Nano-World Lies Ahead," *San Francisco Chronicle*, July 19, 1999, P. A1.

47 *"The aim is not simply"*: Ralph C. Merkle, "Nanotechnology: The Coming Revolution in Manufacturing," testimony to the House Committee on Science, Subcommittee on Basic Research, June 22, 1999, http://www.house.gov/science/merkle_062299.htm.

47 *"Because of nanotechnology"*: Bailey, "Revolution Has Begun," p. W14.

47 *companies around the world*: Among the first commercial companies devoted exclusively to nanotechnology is Zyvex, based in Richardson, Texas, which was founded in 1997 with the express aim of making assemblers (Merkle left his job at Xerox PARC to join Zyvex). The myriad start-ups that have since come along show the flexibility that is a nanotech hallmark. A quick look through back issues of *Small Times*, an industry trade organ, reveals a growing list: in the United States it includes NanoMuscle, facial muscles for toy dolls; Nanomix, molecular hydrogen storage for fuel cells; Nanosphere and Nanosys, medical testing; NanoOpto, optical telecom components; Nucryst, nano-antimicrobials; Nanocor, nano-fillers that reinforce plastic; Quantum Dot, light-emitting nano-crystals for medical research; NanoVia, which employs lasers to shape molecular structures; and Arryx, a maker of "nano-tweezers" for picking up nano-parts and moving them around. There are trade groups, too, like the NanoBusiness Alliance and AtomWorks.

47 *The joint venture*: Paul Kallender, "Asia-Pacific Governments Invest in Nano Labs and Research Centers," *Small Times*, Jan. 22, 2004, http://www.smalltimes.com.

48 *For 2004, U.S. federal funding*: The 21st Century Nanotechnology Research and Development Act, S. 189, 10th Cong., 1st sess., sec. 6, Authorization of Appropriations (Congressional Budget Office, June 30, 2003), http://www.cbo.gov/showdoc.cfm?index=4390&sequence=0.

48 *U.S. officials see*: Barnaby J. Feder, "As Uses Grow, Tiny Materials' Safety Is Hard to Pin Down," *New York Times*, Nov. 3, 2003, p. C1.

48 *"a snapshot of an explosion"*: Barnaby J. Feder, "Tiny Technologies Slip Unseen into Daily Life," *New York Times*, March 3, 2002, p. C1.

48 Nanotechnology and Homeland Security: Written by the father-son team Mark and Daniel Ratner.

48 *One expert worries*: Erica Goode, "When Findings Aid an Enemy," *New York Times*, Sept. 25, 2001, p. F1. The expert cited is Glenn Reynolds of the University of Tennessee.

48 *there are parasites that lodge*: See extended reference in chapter 6.

48 *Other research*: Feder, "As Uses Grow, Tiny Materials' Safety Is Hard to Pin Down," p. C1.

48 *The animals soon began*: Ibid. The lead researcher cited is Vyvyan Howard.

48 *An alarm has also*: Barnaby J. Feder, "Research Shows Hazards in Tiny Particles," *New York Times*, April 14, 2003, p. C8.

49 *"Particles of that size"*: Thompson, "Nanoparticles Pop Up Everywhere," p. 58.

49 *Of the roughly*: Ibid.

49 *"Many might argue"*: Paul Marks, "What's Going to Happen?" review of *Our Molecular Future*, by Douglas Mulhall, *New Scientist*, April 20, 2002, p. 49.

49 *In fact a number of scientists*: Kenneth Chang, "Yes, They Can! No, They Can't: Charges Fly in Nanobot Debate," *New York Times*, Dec. 9, 2003, p. F3.

49 *"Assemblers can't just crawl"*: Michael Gross, "News from the Nanoworld," *Guardian*, May 20, 1999, p. 102.

49 *"The structural biology of the cell"*: Ibid.

50 *"The protein factory"*: Ibid.

50 *"would greatly limit"*: Quoted in Chang, "Yes, They Can! No, They Can't," p. F3.

50 *"The smaller the scale"*: Quoted in Philip Ball, "Life's Lessons in Design," *Nature*, Jan. 18, 2001, p. 413.

50 *"Fundamental research on"*: Ibid.

50 *"I think the brave new world"*: Gross, "News from the Nanoworld," p. 102.

51 *Nature, he says, has taught us . . .*: Ibid. The experimental work conducted by Leonard Adelman in 1994 at the University of Southern California was the first to use fragments of DNA to compute a problem. It produced the solution to a highly complex graph theory puzzle. Another scientist working with natural structures is Robert Birge of the University of Connecticut, who has used light-harvesting proteins typically found in swamps to produce a high-density optical memory. At Wayne State University in Detroit, Michael Conrad used enzymes as computing elements. MIT's Tom Knight and Gerald Sussman are developing what they call "amorphous computing," which works through modified *E. coli* cells in solution. They'll be powered with sugar. David Stenger, of the U.S. Naval Research Laboratory in Washington, D.C., and a colleague from industry are working with neurons to make a bioelectronic computer they expect to use for pattern-recognition tasks. Quantum computing, while outside the strict domain of this book, has enormous promise.

The DNA approach is fast. Biosystems are also massively parallel and energy efficient and can have great memory capacity. But there are challenges, too—with the limited range of problems an organic component may have evolved to address, and with the difficulty of getting input and output into and out of them. The source for this paragraph is Paharia, "Forecasting the Future of Information Technology."

52 *That scaffold serves*: Walter J. Gehring, *Master Control Genes in Development and Evolution: The Homeobox Story* (New Haven, Conn.: Yale University Press, 1998), p. 94.

53 *To their amazement*: Stephen Hart, "Test-Tube Survival of the Molecularly Fit: Darwinian Directed Molecular Evolution," *BioScience* 43, no. 11 (Dec. 1993), p. 738.

53 *After a few dozen cycles*: Ibid.

53 *When he graphed*: Peter Radetsky, "Speeding Through Evolution: Gerald Joyce's Directed-Evolution Experiments," *Discover*, May 1994, p. 82.

53 *"They were mutually exclusive"*: Quoted in ibid.

54 *By the twenty-seventh generation*: Ibid.

54 *"Today's loser may"*: Quoted in ibid.

54 *"Mother Nature at Warp Speed"*: Paul Jacobs, "Evolution's Test Tube Revolution," *Los Angeles Times*, April 6, 1999, p. A1.

54 *"Initial human trials"*: Quoted in ibid.

55 *The drug is currently*: Personal conversation with Jamie Lacey, MedImmune corporate communications, March 2004.

55 *"Now it's the standard"*: Personal conversation with Frances Arnold, Feb. 2004.

55 *"an important landmark"*: Quoted in Andy Coghlan, "Human Cells Adopt DIY Chromosome," *New Scientist*, April 5, 1997, p. 19. There are three basic regions of DNA in a chromosome. The type called origin of replication is the region from which the two spiral strands unwind, so they can be copied. During cell reproduction the centromere, which is at the center of the DNA, ensures that each daughter cell will get a full copy of the original. The telomeres cover the ends of DNA. Willard succeeded in synthesizing all three. Willard's human artificial chromosomes, or HACs, were loaded into cells by inserting them in lipids, which are fatty globules that pass easily through cell membranes. The hardest part of the synthesis was making the centromeres, which had not then been sequenced. Willard used what turned out to be a lucky guess. And he let the cells make their own histones.

56 *"germ-line engineered humans"*: Robert Taylor, "Like It or Not, in a Few Short Years We'll Have the Power to Control Our Own Evolution," *New Scientist*, Oct. 3, 1998, p. 24.

56 *"free market environment"*: Quoted in Michael Cross, "The Right to Choose?" review of *Redesigning Humans*, by Gregory Stock, *New Scientist*, May 25, 2002, p. 52.

57 *"a tragicomic creation"*: Andrew Kimbrell, *The Human Body Shop: The Cloning, Engineering, and Marketing of Life* (Washington, D.C.: Regnery Publishing, 1997), p. 210.

57 *"the changes we make"*: Brian Alexander, "The Remastered Race," *Wired*, May 2002, p. 68.

57 *"The human body and mind"*: Quoted in Nicholas Wade, "Should We Improve Our Genome?" *New York Times*, Nov. 11, 2003, p. F13.

57 *"If you genetically alter"*: Bill McKibben, "The Posthuman Condition," *Harper's Magazine*, April 2003, p. 20. The passage was excerpted from his book *Enough: Staying Human in an Engineered Age* (New York: Henry Holt, 2004).

58 *"How many glowing"*: James Gorman, "When Fish Fluoresce, Can Teenagers Be Far Behind?" *New York Times*, Dec. 2, 2003, p. F3.

58 *"Evolution is being superseded"*: Quoted in Taylor, "Like It or Not," p. 24.

58 *"It's what we want"*: Quoted in Alexander, "Remastered Race," p. 68.

58 *"that an artificial chromosome"*: Andy Coghlan, "We Have the Power," *New Scientist*, Oct. 23, 1999, p. 4.

58 *"We are in control"*: Personal conversation with Joseph Zendegui, March 2004.

59 *The article was authored*: Donald E. Ingber, "The Architecture of Life," repr. in *Scientific American*, Jan. 1998.

59 *"Viruses, enzymes, organelles"*: Ibid.

59 *"They're stabilized mainly by gravity"*: Personal conversation with Donald Ingber, 1998; reviewed by him, June 2004.

60 *"pre-stressed system"*: James Glanz, "Force-Carrying Web Pervades Living Cell," *Science*, May 2, 1997, p. 678.

60 *At the microscopic level*: Ingber, "Architecture of Life."

60 *"your skin stretches"*: Ibid.

60 *a tetrahedral shape*: A tetrahedron is a solid figure with four triangular surfaces.

60 *"Some of them have"*: Personal conversation with Ingber, 1998; reviewed by him, June 2004.

61 *"Left Leg Kit (Male)"*: In the MGI company literature.

61 *He also continues to publish*: Donald E. Ingber, "Tensegrity II: How Structural Networks Influence Cellular Information Processing Networks," *Journal of Cell Science* 116 (2003), p. 1397.

61 *That's 10 percent higher*: Robert Adler, "The Champions: When It Comes to Efficiency, Nothing Beats a Galloping Horse," *New Scientist*, Aug. 21, 1999, p. 6.

61 *That stored energy*: Ibid.

62 *The first is by stretching*: Ibid.

62 *Urry uses chemical*: Personal conversation with Daniel Urry, 1999; reviewed by him, June 2004.

63 *And when those molecules*: Philip Ball, "Living Factories," *New Scientist*, Feb. 3, 1996, p. 2.

63 *"This is what sustains life"*: Personal conversation with Urry, 1999; reviewed by him, June 2004.

63 *He scraped away*: Ibid.

63 *When he put a pulsing*: Ibid.

63 *"As the wall stretches"*: Ibid.

63 *"And that's what"*: Ibid.

64 *Their start-up company*: Ibid. (Urry had a seriously damaged disc when he was in medical school. But over the course of several years, by wearing a back brace and through careful exercise, he was able to avoid surgery and regrow it himself back into a state of health.)

65 *"What does it all mean"*: Cited by ibid.

65 *"but then people wander"*: Ibid.

66 *"For their ceramics"*: Personal communication with Julian Vincent, Dec. 2004.

66 *Summing up*: Ibid.

66 *Compare that, he says*: Ibid.

66 *"by dropping its bottom"*: Tim Radford, "Science and Technology: Mother of Invention," *Guardian*, March 26, 1998: Guardian Online Page Section, issue PSA-2061 (from the Northern Light database).

68 *"Under impact, weight for weight"*: Personal communication with Vincent, Dec. 2004.

68 *A study of the cockroach's*: That research comes primarily under the auspices of the Defence Evaluation and Research Agency and the Defence Clothing and Textiles Agency, and is being carried out at universities and government labs throughout Britain.

68 *Another looks at how insect wings*: Personal conversation with Vincent, 1998; reviewed by him, Oct. 2003.

69 *"To make this technology possible"*: "Buck Rogers, Watch Out!" http://science. nasa.gov/headlines/y2001/ast01mar_1.htm.

69 *"active aeroelastic" wing*: Paul Marks, "The Shape of Wings to Come," *New Scientist*, Dec. 13, 2003, p. 28.

70 *Looking in a linear way*: Delta Willis, *The Sand Dollar and the Slide Rule: Drawing Blueprints from Nature* (Reading, Mass.: Addison-Wesley, 1995), p. 63.

3. Figure and Ground

71 *But at the city's heart, like a sign of*: With apologies to Graham Greene.

72 *He calls his jungle retreat Terra Verde*: http://www.internext.com.br/terraverde/ ing/terraverde/htm.

73 *It is an area unique*: Sulistrowski is currently looking for partners who can help him set up a foundation to continue the work of preserving the twenty-seven-thousand-acre virgin forest when he is gone. Interested parties can contact him by e-mail at terraverde@internext.com.br.

73 *"a better knowledge"*: Personal conversation with Zygmunt Sulistrowski, 1998; reviewed by him, April 2004.

75 *But by the end of*: The notion that information flowed only outward from the nuclear DNA was convincingly debunked by Howard Temin, whose work in the late 1960s and early '70s established the existence of reverse transcriptase. He showed that in certain cases RNA could translate itself into new DNA. One of those cases is the HIV virus.

76 *"It is not birth"*: Quoted in Scott F. Gilbert, *Developmental Biology*, 5th ed. (Sunderland, Mass.: Sinauer Associates, 1997), p. 209.

77 *"A descriptive program"*: Lewis Wolpert, et al., *Principles of Development* (London: Current Biology, 1998), p. 21.

78 *That happens as the egg*: Ibid., p. 127.

78 *Conceptually, these come to resemble*: Ibid.

78 *Wherever it came*: Gilbert, *Developmental Biology*, p. 553.

78 *Those factors also*: Ibid., p. 197.

78 *the migration of cell zones*: Ibid., pp. 209–10.

78 *"a true communication channel"*: Mae-Wan Ho, quoted in "Environment and Heredity in Development and Evolution," in Mae-Wan Ho and Peter T.

Saunders, eds., *Beyond Neo-Darwinism: An Introduction to the New Evolutionary Paradigm* (London: Academic Press, 1984), pp. 284–85.

78 *"carrier of heredity"*: Quoted in ibid., p. 280.

78 *"it would be the only"*: Arthur Koestler, quoted in Kevin Kelly, *Out of Control: The New Biology of Machines, Social Systems, and the Economic World* (Reading, Mass.: Addison-Wesley, 1994), p. 370.

79 *A growing embryo*: Wolpert et al., *Principles of Development*, p. 5.

79 *human fetal brain neurons*: James P. Hogan, *Mind Matters: Exploring the World of Artificial Intelligence* (New York: Del Rey/Ballantine Books, 1997), p. 312.

79 *dynamic sequences cascade*: Susan Oyama, *The Ontogeny of Information: Developmental Systems and Evolution* (Cambridge, U.K.: Cambridge University Press, 1985), p. 159.

80 *"loose coupling"*: Ibid., p. 162, attributed to Howard E. Gruber, "History and Creative Work: From the Most Ordinary to the Most Exalted," *Journal of the History of the Behavioral Sciences* 19 (1983), pp. 4–14.

80 *"flexibility gives rise"*: Oyama, *Ontogeny of Information*, p. 162.

80 *"only by having"*: Ibid., p. 162.

80 *One of the new biologists*: Extensive work on fish propulsion has also been conducted at Duke University, including Hugh Crenshaw's Nekton project on flagellate swimming and the amazing Twiddlefish developed by Chuck Pell in the Bio-Design Studio.

80 *With his colleagues*: Michael Triantafyllou works with his brother George, who is also a naval engineer and is based at Athens University, in Greece, and with Mark Grosenbaugh, a marine engineer from the Woods Hole Oceanographic Institution in Massachusetts. The graduate student David Barrett helped model the tuna.

81 *Someday schools of swimming robofish*: Bennett Daviss, "Jet-Propelled Tuna," *New Scientist*, March 4, 2000, http://www.bluefish.org/jettuna.htm.

82 *"A fly has, on average"*: Quoted in James Gorman, "What Really Happens When Fruit Flies Fly?" *New York Times*, June 6, 2003, p. F1.

82 *They also use an exotic array*: Carl Zimmer, "Fly-O-rama!" *Popular Science*, Dec. 2002, p. 28.

82 *Dickinson is working*: Dickinson himself worked at UC Berkeley until his recent move to Caltech. Much of his basic work was done at Berkeley. His first experiments were performed working with Karl Götz of Germany's Max Planck Institute for Biological Cybernetics.

83 *Using dice to*: Personal conversation with Ingo Rechenberg, 1998; reviewed by him, May 2004.

84 *His colleague T. K. Mueller*: Mueller recently took a new position at the University of Zurich.

86 *He also has a line*: Personal conversation with Jerry Pratt of the MIT leg lab, March 1998.

86 *Scientists at Carnegie Mellon*: Robert Capps, "The Humanoids," *Wired*, July 2004, p. 123.

86 *There, one finds:* The AI Lab, now absorbed into CSAIL (Computer Science and Artificial Intelligence Laboratory), moved into new quarters as this book was going to press. Its new home is the Ray and Maria Stata Center. The unusual building was designed by the architect Frank Gehry.

86 *This is the leg lab:* The lab is now called the Media Lab's Biomechatronics Group.

86 *One of these, graduate student:* Jerry Pratt has since graduated and founded a business, Yobotics, which designs artificial limbs for robots and disabled people.

87 *That progress comes:* Raibert founded the lab at Carnegie Mellon in 1980. He moved it to MIT in 1987.

87 *It worked partly by:* Personal conversation with Hugh Herr, 1998; reviewed by him, March 2004.

87 *"From that single-legged machine":* Ibid. Herr is on the faculty at the Harvard–MIT Division of Health Sciences and Technology, where he teaches both biophysics and computer science.

87 *According to Herr:* Ibid.

87 *That's a fast pace:* Some of Raibert's concepts have been incorporated into M2, a life-size walking humanoid for reconnaissance in dangerous areas. It's being developed by Daniel Paluska and Allen Parseghian, with funding from DARPA. See Paul Bouton, "The Next Step," *Wired*, Sept. 2000, p. 181.

87 *"One thing we find":* Personal conversation with Pratt, March 1998.

87 *"Even though it was a funny wheel":* Herr has a special perspective on this field. In his teens, then a world-class mountain climber, he got caught in a storm and lost both legs to frostbite. He now holds half a dozen patents for new developments in prosthetic legs. Herr has shifted the lab's focus away from pure robotics and onto human physical augmentation.

88 *The incoming data:* Hogan, *Mind Matters*, p. 185.

88 *As that happens:* Enrico Coen, *The Art of Genes: How Organisms Make Themselves* (Oxford, U.K.: Oxford University Press, 1999), p. 225.

89 *"the more subtle types of response":* Ibid.

89 *"between computers and brains":* Personal conversation with Tomaso Poggio, 1998; reviewed by him, March 2004.

89 *One of the questions:* Ibid.

89 *"Monkeys":* Ibid.

90 *William Dobelle:* Of the Dobelle Laboratories in Commack, New York.

90 *Among them, Mark Humayun:* Steven Kotler, "Vision Quest: A Half Century of Artificial Sight Research Has Succeeded and Now This Blind Man Can See," *Wired*, Sept. 2002, p. 95.

91 *"When people sit down":* Personal conversation with Dean Santner, 2002; reviewed by him, March 2004. Anthropometry is the measurement of the various parts of the human body. Kinesiology is the science of body movement.

91 *"Our participants automatically":* Quoted in John Sutton, "Being Too Courteous to Madding Computers," *New Scientist*, Aug. 21, 1999, p. 6.

91 *"Associated Press newswire item":* Cited in Neil Gershenfeld, *When Things Start to Think* (New York: Henry Holt, 1999), p. 147.

92 *"between a person sitting"*: Ibid.

92 *"The speed of the computer"*: Ibid., p. 7.

92 *"Our senses are connected"*: Ibid., p. 135.

4. Thinking

93 *Another of the school's pioneers*: The 1993 Nobel Prize in Physiology or Medicine was awarded to Phillip A. Sharp, Richard J. Roberts, and their respective colleagues.

94 *"There's a growing awareness"*: Personal conversation with Phillip A. Sharp, March 1998.

94 *As evidence of that*: In 2004, the neuroscientist Susan Hockfield, formerly provost at Yale, became not only MIT's first woman president but also its first president to be drawn from the life sciences.

94 *"So the campus"*: Ibid.

94 *more costly structure*: It cost $350 million to build.

94 *its dramatic new home*: The Computer Science and Artificial Intelligence Laboratory, in the new Ray and Maria Stata Center.

94 *in 1956 at a legendary Dartmouth conference*: "The Dartmouth Summer Research Project on Artificial Intelligence." Two years later, Heinz Von Foerster would found the Biological Computer Laboratory at the University of Illinois.

95 *They took that name*: Andrew Leonard, *Bots: The Origin of New Species* (San Francisco: Hardwired, 1997), p. 33.

95 *"I am" became "you are"*: Ibid., p. 34.

95 *"Tell me more about that"*: Quoted in James P. Hogan, *Mind Matters: Exploring the World of Artificial Intelligence* (New York: Del Rey/Ballantine Books, 1997), p. 210.

95 *"Men are all alike"*: Ibid., p. 209.

96 *But he began to wonder*: Leonard, *Bots*, p. 33.

96 *"extremely short exposures"*: Quoted in ibid., p. 36.

96 *A physicist turned philosopher*: Hogan, *Mind Matters*, p. 291.

97 *In that report*: Ibid.

97 *There was also no tolerance*: Ibid., p. 295.

97 *Dreyfus condemned the failure*: Ibid.

97 *Among others, Herbert Simon*: Ibid., p. 291.

97 *It wasn't published officially*: Ibid.

98 *"Imagine yourself sitting"*: Quoted in Peter Baumgartner and Sabine Payr, eds., *Speaking Minds: Interviews with Twenty Eminent Cognitive Scientists* (Princeton, N.J.: Princeton University Press, 1995), p. 16.

98 *It was just as clear*: Ibid.

98 *"No machine will be able"*: Quoted in ibid., p. 308.

98 *"The main problem"*: Quoted in John Brockman, *The Third Culture: Beyond the Scientific Revolution* (New York: Simon & Schuster, 1995), p. 154.

98 *In the early 1990s DARPA*: Baumgartner and Payr, *Speaking Minds*, p. 291.

99 *"If we do not know how"*: Quoted in ibid., p. 28.

99 *"If you want to do things"*: Quoted in ibid., p. 39.

99 *"a complex architecture"*: Quoted in ibid., p. 290.

99 *"The brain is not just the hardware"*: Quoted in ibid., p. 217.

100 *"Until we try to emulate"*: Quoted in Hogan, *Mind Matters*, p. 188.

100 *By far the densest concentration*: Ibid., p. 311.

100 *In that eighth-inch-thick layer*: Ibid.

100 *If all the neurons*: Gordon Rattray-Taylor, *The Natural History of the Mind* (Harmondsworth, U.K.: Penguin Books, 1981), p. 42.

101 *Each neuron is excited or inhibited*: Ibid., p. 311.

101 *It converts that information*: Ibid.

101 *Some suggest it may*: Ibid.

102 *"Clearly," said Hillis*: Quoted in Dennis Shasha and Cathy Lazere, *Out of Their Minds: The Lives and Discoveries of 15 Great Computer Scientists* (New York: Copernicus, 1995), p. 188.

102 *By combining parallel*: The concept of neural net computing dates back to the 1940s (McClelland). In it software connections weaken or strengthen according to how often they are reinforced (reactivated). Although neural net software can be run on serial logic computers, PDP is a more effective fit.

102 *"Hillis's work demonstrates"*: Brockman, *Third Culture*, p. 378.

102 *"I have programs that have evolved"*: Quoted in ibid., p. 382.

103 *"Parallel algorithms"*: Quoted in Baumgartner and Payr, *Speaking Minds*, p. 221.

103 *A space probe to Venus*: Hogan, *Mind Matters*, p. 343.

103 *"Rather than spending uncountable hours"*: Kevin Kelly, *Out of Control: The New Biology of Machines, Social Systems, and the Economic World* (Reading, Mass.: Addison-Wesley, 1994), p. 309.

104 *Surely, they concluded*: Ibid., p. 199.

104 *But they work*: Ibid., p. 337.

104 *A DARPA bulletin*: "DARPA Technology Transition," from the introduction.

105 *One of Koza's programs*: James Bailey, *After Thought: The Computer Challenge to Human Intelligence* (New York: Basic Books, 1996), p. 142. Kepler's Third Law is the mathematical relationship between the distance of a planet from the sun and the planet's orbital period (how long it takes to go around). The square of the period is proportional to the cube of the distance.

105 *"result that is publishable"*: John R. Koza, "Scientific Research Interests," http://www.genetic-programming.com/johnkoza.html#anchor6009925 (accessed Sept. 6, 2004). Koza is consulting professor in the Department of Computer Science and the Symbolic Systems Program in the School of Engineering at Stanford University.

105 *"First, at some point"*: Hogan, *Mind Matters*, p. 326.

105 *They also do better at*: Ibid., p. 314.

105 *"Mary is having a sandwich"*: Ibid., p. 326.

106 *Thinking Machines stopped*: Its data-mining business continued under the name Darwin. Darwin was purchased by Oracle in 1999.

106 "*It was the Woodstock*": Larry Smarr, director of the California Institute for Telecommunications and Information Technology, quoted in Steve Lohr, "Teaching Computers to Work in Unison," *New York Times*, July 15, 2003, p. F1.

107 *Information Power Grid*: http://www.ipg.nasa.gov.

107 *NSF's Grid Physics Network*: http://www.griphyn.org.

107 *Germany's Unicore*: http://www.unicore.de.

107 *the U.K. National Grid*: http://www.grid-support.ac.uk.

107 *the European DataGrid*: http://www.startap.net/euro-link/APPLICATIONS/ CERN_datagrid.html.

107 *the International Virtual DataGrid Laboratory*: http://www.ivdgl.org.

107 *into one behemoth processing entity*: For all of the above, see M. Mitchell Waldrop, "Grid Computing Could Put the Planet's Information-Processing Power on Tap," *Technology Review*, May 2002, p. 31.

107 *TeraGrid*: http://www.teragrid.org.

107 *A project called Enabling Grids*: The Large Hadron Collider Computing Grid, designed to help in the search for the Higgs boson—a key but elusive ingredient of modern particle theory—may be even larger when it's fully operational.

107 *And the new power*: John Markoff and Jennifer L. Schenker, "Europe Exceeds U.S. in Refining Grid Computing," *New York Times*, Nov. 10, 2003, p. C1.

107 *It worked so well that*: The Novartis grid uses software by United Devices of Austin, Texas.

108 "*There are 100 million machines*": Quoted in Barnaby J. Feder, "Supercomputing Takes Yet Another Turn," *New York Times*, Nov. 20, 2000, p. C4 .

108 *Within eighty days*: Ibid.

108 "*seamless computational universe*": The phrase is Waldrop's, from "Grid Computing," p. 31.

108 "*The ultimate goal*": Quoted in Lohr, "Teaching Computers to Work in Unison," p. F1.

108 *With the grid, we now stand*: Ibid.

108 "*What we are seeing*": Quoted in Waldrop, "Grid Computing," p. 31.

108 "*The main problem area*": Quoted in Baumgartner and Payr, *Speaking Minds*, p. 295.

108 "*Just as one cannot*": Quoted in ibid., p. 211.

109 "*a nice day for a picnic*": Quoted in ibid., p. 209.

109 "*The world is its own best model*": Quoted in Hogan, *Mind Matters*, p. 195.

109 *By that he means*: According to Stefano Nolfi and Dario Floreano, the first work in this area was done by Valentino Braitenberg: *Vehicles* (Cambridge, Mass.: MIT Press, 1984). Footnote in Nolfi and Floreano, *Evolutionary Robotics: The Biology, Intelligence, and Technology of Self-Organizing Machines* (Cambridge, Mass.: MIT Press, 2000), p. 262.

109 "*I wish to build completely autonomous*": Rodney A. Brooks, "Intelligence Without Representation" (1991), repr. in John Haugeland, *Mind Design II*:

Philosophy, Psychology, Artificial Intelligence, rev. and enl. ed. (Cambridge, Mass.: MIT Press, 1997), p. 401.

109 *After Brooks became director*: Steven Levy, *Artificial Life: A Report from the Frontier Where Computers Meet Biology* (New York: Vintage Books, 1992), p. 291.

110 *"Evolution took three billion years"*: Brooks, "Intelligence Without Representation," p. 420.

110 *Once they were in place*: Hogan, *Mind Matters*, p. 195.

110 *"It is soon apparent"*: Brooks, "Intelligence Without Representation," p. 418.

110 *"Terrain structure"*: Paul Shepard, *Traces of an Omnivore* (Washington, D.C.: Island Press for Shearwater Books, 1996), p. 105.

110 *The coastal snail* Littorina: Levy, *Artificial Life*, pp. 295–96.

111 *Brooks and his students*: Brooks, "Intelligence Without Representation," p. 404.

111 *Rather than being a single*: Ibid.

111 *In particular, Connell*: Levy, *Artificial Life*, p. 295.

111 *Building on earlier work, Connell gave Herbert*: Brooks, "Intelligence Without Representation," p. 412.

111 *Many people in the lab*: Levy, *Artificial Life*, p. 295.

112 *But with nothing more*: Brooks, "Intelligence Without Representation," p. 413.

112 *Along the way they have also supplied*: On the West Coast, at the Neurosciences Institute (http://www.nsi.edu) in La Jolla, California, the institute's founder, Gerald Edelman, has been doing seminal work in a roughly corresponding research area for some time. His book *Wider Than the Sky: The Phenomenal Gift of Consciousness* is a lay account of that work.

112 *"When you have a complex set"*: Personal conversation with Rosalind Picard, 1998; reviewed by her, March 2004.

112 *In his thesis*: Christian Balkenius, "Natural Intelligence in Artificial Creatures" (Lund, Sweden), *Lund University Cognitive Studies* 37 (1995), ch. 6.2, http://asip.lucs.fil.lu.se/people/christian.balkenius/thesis.

113 Descartes' Error: Antonio Damasio, *Descartes' Error: Emotion, Reason, and the Human Brain* (New York: Putnam, 1994).

113 *"He clicks off his emotion chip"*: Personal conversation with Picard, 1998; reviewed by her, March 2004.

113 *"What we don't see"*: Ibid.

114 *"If chimpanzees had the atom bomb"*: Personal conversation with E. O. Wilson, 1996.

114 *"Yes, for sure," says Picard*: Personal conversation with Picard, 1998; reviewed by her, March 2004.

114 *"We model affect as a network"*: Juan D. Velasquez, "Modeling Emotions in Autonomous Agents" (MIT Artificial Intelligence Laboratory, Sept. 1997).

114 *Although her features are rudimentary*: Cynthia Breazeal, "Kismet: A Robot for Social Interactions with Humans," http://www.ai.mit.edu/projects/kismet/.

114 *"Kismet takes advantage"*: Quoted in Duncan Graham-Rowe, "Booting Up Baby," *New Scientist*, May 22, 1999, p. 43.

114 *But should her human companion*: Bruce Schechter, "A Man, a Plan, and a Robot That Makes Eye Contact," *New York Times*, Aug. 3, 1999, p. F1.

115 *"These drives are always changing"*: Quoted in ibid.

115 *"I want to help get these ideas"*: Personal conversation with Mitchel Resnick, 1998; reviewed by him, March 2004.

115 *"With traditional Legos"*: Ibid.

116 *"ideas about feedback and control"*: Ibid.

116 *"Now, again," he says*: Ibid.

116 *The headline read*: Katie Hafner, "What Do You Mean, 'It's Just Like a Real Dog'?" *New York Times*, May 25, 2000, p. G1.

117 *Following on the success*: Hackers have found a new outlet for their talents in the reprogramming of Aibos. There are now Aibos that can dance the hustle and that bark "Bite my shiny ass!" See Brendan I. Koerner, "'Bite My Shiny Ass!' Barks the Aibo," *Wired*, Feb. 2003, p. 28.

117 *Enter Mattel's Miracle Moves Baby*: In a distantly related development, Los Angeles–based Abyss Creations uses similar materials to make highly flexible and strikingly lifelike sex dolls. Called RealDolls, the life-size figures are handmade, come in male and female versions, and sell for several thousand dollars each. The company says it is working on an animatronic version.

117 *"The kind of software"*: Personal conversation with Helen Greiner, March 1998.

118 *The U.S. Congress has mandated*: Tim Weiner, "A New Model Army Soldier Rolls Closer to the Battlefield," *New York Times*, Feb. 16, 2005.

118 *"The Pentagon predicts that robots"*: Ibid.

118 *That effort is backed*: Ibid.

118 *Where the great majority*: Personal conversation with Mark Tilden, May 1995.

118 *"They crawled off the shelves"*: Quoted in Peter Menzel and Faith D'Aluisio, *Robo Sapiens: Evolution of a New Species* (Cambridge, Mass.: MIT Press, 2000), excerpted in *Discover*, Sept. 2000, p. 89.

118 *Back at iRobot*: Erik Davis, "Congratulations, It's a Bot!" *Wired*, Sept. 2000, p. 269.

119 *field-programmable gate array*: FPGAs were invented by Xilinx, Inc., of San Jose, California.

119 *These contain arrays*: Nolfi and Floreano, *Evolutionary Robotics*, p. 262.

120 *Then, providing it with plans*: Kenneth Chang, "Scientists Report They Have Made Robot That Makes Its Own Robots," *New York Times*, Aug. 31, 2000, p. A1.

120 *"They were not engineered"*: Ibid.

120 *"revives concerns that"*: Ibid.

120 *He envisions vegetation munchers*: Fred Hapgood, "Living Off the Land," *Smithsonian Magazine*, July 2001, www.smithsonianmag.si.edu/smithsonian/issues01/jul01/phenom_jul01.htm.

120 *A parallel effort*: The team is led by Chris Melhuish at the University of the West of England in Bristol.

120 *a robot that will feed on garden slugs*: Duncan Graham-Rowe, "Feed Me," *New Scientist*, July 22, 2000, http://www.newscientist.com/hottopics/ai/toytrain.jsp.

120 "*One of the most promising innovations*": Peter Bentley, "The Garden Where Perfect Software Grows," *New Scientist*, March 6, 2004, p. 28.

121 "*1—A robot may not injure*": Quoted in Bruce Mazlish, *The Fourth Discontinuity: The Co-evolution of Humans and Machines* (New Haven, Conn.: Yale University Press, 1993), p. 55.

121 "*It seems to me*": Personal conversation with Picard, 1998; reviewed by her, March 2004.

121 "*We're beginning to depend*": Quoted in Brockman, *Third Culture*, p. 386.

122 "*If we are to make further progress*": Quoted by Joseph Weizenbaum, in Baumgartner and Payr, *Speaking Minds*, p. 259.

122 "*by 2040, the robots*": Quoted in Kenneth Chang, "Can Robots Rule the World? Not Yet," *New York Times*, Sept. 12, 2000, p. F1.

122 "*Within thirty years*": Quoted in Hogan, *Mind Matters*, p. 351.

122 "*The emergence of life and intelligence*": George B. Dyson, *Darwin Among the Machines: The Evolution of Global Intelligence* (Reading, Mass.: Perseus Books, 1997), p. 9.

122 "*You can't know, because*": Personal conversation with Rodney Brooks, March 1998.

122 "*So mind you, once*": Ibid.

122 "*The intelligent robot*": Ibid.

122 *Toward that end*: Eric Niiler, "New Bio-Circuit Technology Presents Intriguing Medical and Military Possibilities," *San Diego Union-Tribune*, Jan. 19, 2000, p. E1.

122 *According to Abarbanel*: Ibid.

5. Interacting Parts

125 "*If we can discover*": Sandra Blakeslee, "Science's Elusive Realm: Life's Little Mysteries," *New York Times*, April 24, 2001, p. F3.

125 "*The miracles of nature*": R. B. Laughlin, et. al., "The Middle Way," *Proceedings of the National Academy of Science* 97, no. 1 (2000), pp. 32–37.

126 *But they disrupt*: Personal conversation with Robert Laughlin, 2002.

126 *Says Robert Laughlin*: Laughlin won the 1998 Nobel Prize in Physics.

126 "*We are blinded*": Ibid.

126 "*admitting it is a strength*": Ibid.

126 *Gell-Mann pushed for*: Personal conversation with Murray Gell-Mann, 1995. Reviewed by him, May 2005.

127 *Norman Packard*: Packard has now formed a new company—ProtoLife—to explore the creation of a living cell from nonliving materials.

127 *It was here that*: Langton left SFI in 1997. As this book went to press, he was not discussing his current work publicly.

127 "*crude look*": Personal conversation with Gell-Mann, 1997. Reviewed by him, May 2005.

127 "*Murray has developed*": Quoted in John Brockman, *The Third Culture: Beyond the Scientific Revolution* (New York: Simon & Schuster, 1995), p. 332.

127 "*Particle physicists*": Quoted in ibid., p. 331.

128 "*nothing would be uncertain*": Quoted in Fritjof Capra, *The Web of Life: A New Scientific Understanding of Living Systems* (New York: Anchor Books, 1996), p. 184.

128 "*Even if the initial condition*": Quoted in Brockman, *Third Culture*, p. 319.

128 *This suggests other effective organizing principles*: Personal conversation with Gell-Mann, 1997. Reviewed by him, May 2005.

128 "*function best in a regime*": Murray Gell-Mann, *The Quark and the Jaguar: Adventures in the Simple and the Complex* (New York: W. H. Freeman, 1994), p. 369.

129 "*Imagine a set of letters*": Personal conversation with Stephen Farrier, Feb. 2001.

129 "*To engage in the Darwinian saga*": Stuart Kauffman, *At Home in the Universe: The Search for Laws of Self-Organization and Complexity* (New York: Oxford University Press, 1995), p. 73.

129 "*If you have complex enough systems*": Quoted in Brockman, *Third Culture*, p. 338.

130 "*then some of the order*": Ibid.

130 "*Not only does metabolic life*": Kauffman, *At Home in the Universe*, p. 73.

130 "*Ant colonies, highway traffic*": Mitchel Resnick, *Turtles, Termites, and Traffic Jams: Explorations in Massively Parallel Microworlds* (Cambridge, Mass.: MIT Press, 1997), pp. 3–4.

131 *There, his adviser was*: Personal conversation with Christopher Langton, Feb. 2004.

132 "*bring together the study*": Steven Levy, *Artificial Life: A Report from the Frontier Where Computers Meet Biology* (New York: Vintage Books, 1992), p. 91.

132 *At Los Alamos two years later*: Ibid., p. 114.

133 "*It's like cellular automata*": Personal conversation with Langton, 1997; reviewed by him, Feb. 2004.

133 *As the situation evolves*: Lab demonstration at SFI by Langton, 1997; reviewed by him, Feb. 2004.

133 "*Stan Ulam said that calling*": Personal conversation with Langton, 1997; reviewed by him, Feb. 2004.

133 "*a strategy doesn't have*": Ibid.

133 "*Nature has learned how to bring*": Brockman, *Third Culture*, pp. 349–50.

134 The Ants, *a standard reference work*: Vaclav Smil, *Cycles of Life: Civilization and the Biosphere* (New York: Scientific American Library, 1997), p. 59.

134 "*An ant, viewed as a behaving system*": Herbert Simon, *The Sciences of the Artificial*, quoted in Levy, *Artificial Life*, p. 105.

134 *This begins to explain*: George Johnson, "Mindless Creatures, Acting 'Mindfully,'" *New York Times*, March 23, 1999, p. F1.

134 "*An army of ants too dumb*": Kevin Kelly, *Out of Control: The New Biology of Machines, Social Systems, and the Economic World* (Reading, Mass.: Addison-Wesley, 1994), p. 306.

135 *Examples like this have given rise*: Capra, *Web of Life*, p. 172.

135 *Moreover, a colony of social insects*: James P. Hogan, *Mind Matters: Exploring the World of Artificial Intelligence* (New York: Del Rey/Ballantine Books, 1997), p. 142.

135 *For instance, in many ant species*: Resnick, *Turtles, Termites, and Traffic Jams*, pp. 60–61.

135 *For the ants, disciplined following*: Ibid., p. 138.

135 *Perfect adherence*: Ibid.

136 *Their foraging strategies*: Eric Bonabeau and Guy Theraulaz, "Swarm Smarts," *Scientific American*, March 2000, p. 72.

136 *But if the ants find a clear channel*: Ibid.

136 *Some A-Life experts*: Ibid.

136 *The first predatory digital organisms*: Levy, *Artificial Life*, pp. 317–18.

137 *A computer theory and robotics major*: Ibid., p. 311.

137 *Cohen became the father*: Ibid., p. 314.

137 *the university's VAX 11/750 computer*: Ibid., p. 313.

137 *"a program that can 'infect' other programs"*: Ibid., p. 312.

137 *That's when a Cornell University student*: Ibid., p. 324.

137 *Congress mulled*: Andrew Ross, *Strange Weather: Culture, Science, and Technology in the Age of Limits* (New York: Verso, 1991), p. 75.

137 *In that single year the number*: Ibid.

137 *One late-night comedian*: Dennis Miller, *Saturday Night Live*, quoted in ibid., p. 76.

138 *He began his career in the tropical forests*: Kelly, *Out of Control*, p. 283.

138 *Ray watched in awe*: Ibid., p. 284.

138 *How, he wondered, did all those interacting parts*: Ibid.

138 *To a scientist*: George B. Dyson, *Darwin Among the Machines: The Evolution of Global Intelligence* (Reading, Mass.: Perseus Books, 1997), p. 125.

138 *"stopped reading novels"*: Quoted in Kelly, *Out of Control*, p. 285.

139 *Because it had less information*: Thomas S. Ray, "Parasites," ATR Human Information Processing Research Laboratories, Kyoto, Japan, July 15, 1996, http://www.his.atr.jp/~ray/pubs/fatm/node18.html.

139 *"The parasites cannot displace their hosts"*: Thomas S. Ray, "Lotka-Volterra Cycles," ATR Human Information Processing Research Laboratories, Kyoto, Japan, July 15, 1996, http://www.his.atr.jp/~ray/pubs/fatm/node19.html.

139 *And whenever the computer's memory*: Thomas S. Ray, "Immunity," ATR Human Information Processing Research Laboratories, Kyoto, Japan, July 15, 1996, http://www.hip.atr.co.jp/~ray/pubs/fatm/node20.html.

139 *These were in essence*: Kelly, *Out of Control*, p. 288.

140 *In that, there was a parallel*: Ibid., p. 289.

140 *"to engineer the proper conditions"*: Thomas S. Ray, "A Proposal to Create Two Biodiversity Reserves: One Digital and One Organic," ATR Human Information Processing Research Laboratories, Kyoto, Japan, March 18, 1994, http://www.construct.net/tierra/essay.html.

140 *Artificial Life*: The journal is published by MIT Press.

140 *"One thing happening now"*: Personal conversation with Mark A. Bedau, Feb. 2004.

140 *"the biosphere—as reflected in the fossil record"*: Ibid.

140 *"We still are missing"*: Mark A. Bedau, "Artificial Life: Organization, Adap-

tation and Complexity from the Bottom Up," *Trends in Cognitive Sciences* 7 (2003), pp. 505–12.

141 *A recent international conference*: The Workshop on Bridging Nonliving and Living Matter.

141 *"spontaneous formation"*: Steen Rasmussen et al., "Transitions from Nonliving to Living Matter," *Science*, Feb. 13, 2004, www.sciencemag.org.

141 *at the Institute for Biological Energy Alternatives*: In Rockville, Maryland.

141 *"They're basically gutting"*: Personal conversation with Norman Packard, March 2004.

141 *For that purpose they have chosen*: Rasmussen et al., "Transitions from Nonliving to Living Matter."

141 *Its aim is to develop*: Personal conversation with Bedau, Feb. 2004.

142 *If any local system of molecules*: Rasmussen et al., "Transitions from Nonliving to Living Matter."

142 *One paper*: By Stirling Colgate (LANL), David Krakauer (SFI), Harold Morowitz (George Mason University), and Eric Smith (SFI). Cited in ibid.

142 *This insight follows on*: Humberto Maturana and Francisco Varela, "Autopoiesis: The Organization of the Living" (1973), cited in ibid.

142 *who in the 1970s made the case for*: Bedau, "Artificial Life."

142 *In fact it was Brooks*: Rodney A. Brooks, "The Relationship Between Matter and Life," *Nature* 409 (2001), pp. 409–11, cited in Rasmussen et al., "Transitions from Nonliving to Living Matter."

142 *"If Brooks is right"*: Bedau, "Artificial Life."

143 *Virtual worlds were born*: Some would also include here the real-time-rendered 3-D games, such as Wolfenstein 3D and Doom, from the early 1990s.

143 *two London graduate students*: Roy Trubshaw and Richard Bartle of the University of Essex.

144 *But he was surprised to find*: Andreas Frew, "Washington Diary," *New Scientist*, Jan. 29, 2000, p. 49.

144 *There the "avatars"—rapidly evolving*: Bruce Damer, Stuart Gold, and Jan de Bruin, assisted by Dirk-Jan de Bruin, "Steps Toward Learning in Virtual World Cyberspace: TheU Virtual University and BOWorld," Contact Consortium paper, http://www.ccon.org/papers/twltpaper.html.

144 *For them cyberspace*: Ibid.

145 *"community of worlds"*: ThePalace.com, http://www.thepalace.com:8000/perl/palsearch.pl?Terms=avatar&Match=All&Sort=Pop&Page=2.

145 *"If You Can Dream It, You Can Do It"*: Site directory, ibid.

145 *proliferating AI bots and biots*: Biots are bots that can learn and reproduce and evolve.

146 *In recognition, Funcom*: Seth Schiesel, "Voyager to a Strange Planet," *New York Times*, June 12, 2003, p. G1.

146 *A recent study estimates that the current economic productivity*: Mark Ward, "Virtual Gaming Worlds Overtake Namibia," BBC News Online, Aug. 19, 2004, http://news.bbc.co.uk/2/hi/technology/3570224.stm.

146 *A twenty-two-year-old gamer known as Deathifier*: "Gamer Buys $26,500 Virtual Land," BBC News Online, Dec. 17, 2004, http://news.bbc.co.uk/2/hi/technology/4104731.stm.

146 *"The intent," says the center's director*: Amy Harmon, "More Than Just a Game, but How Close to Reality?" *New York Times*, April 3, 2001, p. G1.

146 *"personalized online representations"*: Steve G. Steinberg, "HypeList: Deflating This Month's Overblown Memes," *Wired News*, Nov. 11, 1997, http://www.wired.com/news/cultural/0,1284,8431,00.html.

146 *"visible alter egos"*: Bruce Damer, http://www.ccon.org/conf99/about.html.

147 *In another the prizewinning Chrome Angel*: All of this paragraph is per Contact Consortium, "About Avatars99," http://www.ccon.org/conf99/about.html.

147 *Virtual worlds pioneer*: That year they also founded Digital Space, which supports the technical side of Contact Consortium projects and creates commercial, industrial, and research virtual worlds for many clients, including NASA and Adobe.

147 *"is a place, not just an interface"*: DigiGardener's Album—Background, http://www.ccon.org/theu/album-background.html.

147 *"Little kids are building enormous 3D cityscapes"*: Bruce Damer talking with Karen Lake, "Internet Strategy You Can Use Today!" StrategyWeek.com, http://interviews. strategyweek.com/rs.nsf/interviews/bruce+damer?open document.

147 *"know they are true pioneers"*: DigiGardener's Album—Background.

148 *"We have hundreds of square miles"*: Personal conversation with Bruce Damer, March 2004.

148 *They interact in virtual conference rooms*: A conversation between Damer and Lake, quoted in "Internet Strategy You Can Use Today!"

148 *In 1996, Stuart Gold*: A link to the now-inactive site for TheU can be found at the Contact Consortium's home page, http://www.ccon.org/theu/index.html.

148 *"a learning space appropriate to"*: Damer et al., "Steps Toward Learning in Virtual World Cyberspace."

148 *a Canadian school*: Simon Fraser University.

148 *Students made conventional 2-D*: The students also produced virtual portfolios of their work, allowing them online global access to potential collaborators and customers.

148 *There, students wore real versions*: Personal conversation with Galen Brandt, March 2004. The Ratava's Line project is at http://www.digitalspace.com/content/atmosphere/2003/fitsfu/.

148 *In another educational display*: The Virtual High School, http://www.vhs.ucsc.edu/.

149 *LinkWorld*: http://www.borderlink.org/technologies/lw.php.

149 *Teachers also arrange sessions*: Ibid.

149 *So the Drive on Mars*: The Drive on Mars project is documented and available at http://www.driveonmars.com.

149 *As the sun passed overhead*: A Mars day is called a "sol." It is twenty-four hours and thirty-nine minutes long. NASA scientists operating the Mars rover were shut up in lighttight rooms so they could live in Mars time.

150 "*In a typical virtual world . . . material world*": Thomas S. Ray, "The Burden of Preconception," http://www.his.atr.jp/~ray/pubs/fatm/node45.html.

150 "*with us into cyberspace*": The term "cyberspace" was coined by William Gibson, in his classic science fiction novel *Neuromancer* (1984).

150 "*Our primitive ancestors would gather*": Personal conversation with Damer, March 2004.

151 "*Professional synergist*": The phrase is Damer's, from his book *Avatars!* The reference is on the Web page "21st Century Online," http://www.biota.org/ostman/charles1.htm.

151 "*There is a state of change at hand*": Charles Ostman, "Charles Ostman—the Far Frontier," http://www.futureguru.com/charles1.htm.

151 "*We are becoming immersed*": Charles Ostman, "Synthetic Sentience on Demand," http://www.biota.org/ostman/synthsn2.htm.

151 "*children born today*": James Bailey, *After Thought: The Computer Challenge to Human Intelligence* (New York: Basic Books, 1996), p. 12.

152 *Now there were too many*: Kelly, *Out of Control*, p. 399.

152 *The lesson*: Ibid.

152 "*In the long run*": Ibid.

152 "*We own the technology*": Ibid., p. 401.

152 "*Evolution is the consequence*": Neil Gershenfeld, *When Things Start to Think* (New York: Henry Holt, 1999), p. 212.

152 "*As a thought exercise*": Thomas S. Ray, "Limits of Imagination," http://www.his.atr.jp/~ray/pubs/fatm/node43.html.

6. Ecology

157 *One strikes an ancient, mossy log . . . her young huddle in a shady gap*: This depiction is a re-creation based on Dwight R. Kuhn, photographer, "The Tree Is Dead! Long Live the Tree!" *Audubon*, Nov. 1990, p. 100.

157 *Some need more than*: Alan Rike Drengson and Duncan MacDonald Taylor, *Ecoforestry: The Art and Science of Sustainable Forest Use* (Gabriola Island, B.C.: New Society Publishers, 1997), p. 94.

157 *Since nurse logs offer habitat*: Ibid.

158 "*Complex mineral substances*": Quoted in Kevin Kelly, *Out of Control: The New Biology of Machines, Social Systems, and the Economic World* (Reading, Mass.: Addison-Wesley, 1994), p. 82.

160 *The myriad life forms*: Drengson and Taylor, *Ecoforestry*, p. 104.

160 *The freshwater that nurse logs absorb*: Ibid., p. 66.

161 *That water then flows from wooded slopes*: Providing two-thirds of all freshwater in the forty-eight contiguous American states. See Mike Dombeck, "The Forgotten Forest Product: Water," *New York Times*, Dec. 3, 2003, p. A21.

161 *In nature, most of the nitrogen*: It also comes from decaying organic matter, which has already absorbed nitrogen through them.

162 *Those microbes make their homes*: In forests, some nitrogen fixation also takes place on the roots of plants that aren't legumes. There are just a few types of these, with alder being the most significant.

162 *In a year's time*: Ninety to 270 pounds of fixed nitrogen per acre, or 100 to 300 kilograms per hectare. See Judith D. Soule and Jon K. Piper, *Farming in Nature's Image: An Ecological Approach to Agriculture* (Washington, D.C.: Island Press, 1992), p. 91.

164 *"chaos emerges from order"*: C. S. Holling, "The Renewal, Growth, Birth, and Death of Ecological Communities," *Whole Earth* (Summer 1998), p. 32.

164 *"There is a continual migration"*: Quoted in Vaclav Smil, *Cycles of Life: Civilization and the Biosphere* (New York: Scientific American Library, 1997), p. 6.

164 *"are engaged in a kind of choreography"*: Paul Shepard, *Traces of an Omnivore* (Washington, D.C.: Island Press for Shearwater Books, 1996), p. 114.

165 *For instance, researchers studying*: Sim Van der Ryn and Stuart Cowan, *Ecological Design* (Washington, D.C.: Island Press, 1996), p. 20.

166 *This is why top predators*: Soule and Piper, *Farming in Nature's Image*, p. 88.

166 *It takes a hundred kilograms*: Ibid.

166 *Gram for gram, hawks*: Ruth A. Eblen and William R. Eblen, eds., *The Encyclopedia of the Environment* (Boston: Houghton Mifflin, 1994), p. 173.

166 *"continuation of the metabolic pathways"*: Fritjof Capra, *The Web of Life: A New Scientific Understanding of Living Systems* (New York: Anchor Books, 1996), p. 35.

167 *They also contain whole populations*: Ibid., p. 34.

167 *But because individuals both*: David J. Depew and Bruce H. Weber, *Darwinism Evolving: Systems Dynamics and the Genealogy of Natural Selection* (Cambridge, Mass.: MIT Press, 1996), p. 473.

168 *In one five-hundred-mile stretch*: William K. Stevens, "Search for Missing Otters Turns Up a Few Surprises," *New York Times*, Jan. 5, 1999, p. F1.

168 *"For them, switching from seals to otters"*: Paul K. Dayton, a marine biologist with the Scripps Institution of Oceanography in La Jolla, California, quoted in Newhouse News Service, "Marine Biologists Identify Kink in Food Chain," *Syracuse Herald American*, Oct. 18, 1998, p. A8.

169 *Researchers from the U.S. Geological Survey*: The lead researcher was Dr. James A. Estes, a marine ecologist. He and his team are based at the University of California at Santa Cruz.

169 *With fewer seals and sea lions to eat*: Stevens, "Search for Missing Otters Turns Up a Few Surprises," p. F1.

169 *This in turn affects fish-eating predators*: Ibid.

169 *The eggs are eaten by horn snails*: Matt Walker, "A Taste for Tadpole," *New Scientist*, Aug. 28, 1999, p. 14.

170 *"Could we have so many birds"*: Quoted in ibid.

170 *In Panama, for example*: This research was conducted over a ten-year period by Allen Herre of the Smithsonian Tropical Research Institute in Panama. Cited in Laurie Garrett, *The Coming Plague: Newly Emerging Diseases in a World Out of Balance* (New York: Farrar, Straus and Giroux, 1994), p. 588.

171 *Cholera spreads in two ways*: Michael S. Tempesta and Steven King, "Tropical Plants as a Source of New Pharmaceuticals," in Pamela A. Barnacal, ed., *Pharmaceutical Manufacturing International 1994: The International Review of Pharmaceutical Technology Research and Development* (London: Sterling, 1994), p. 47.

171 *He tested his notion*: Ibid.

171 *"The ones that are left"*: Ibid.

172 *In 1942, virtually all strains*: Gershom Zajicek of Hebrew University–Hadassah Medical School, writing in *The Cancer Journal* in 1993, cited in Gil Friend, "Surprise! The World Works Exactly as We Know It Does," *The New Bottom Line: Strategic Perspectives on Business and Environment*, Sept. 28, 1998, http://www.igc.org/eco-ops/nbl/nbl.7.7.html.

172 *While the emergence of a penicillin-resistant bacterium*: Garrett, *Coming Plague*, p. 582.

172 *That helps explain why today*: Zajicek, writing in *The Cancer Journal* in 1993, cited in Friend, "Surprise!"

173 *"evolutionary pressure"*: Ibid.

174 *It was Caporale who some twenty years ago*: Lynn Helena Caporale, "Is There a Higher Level Genetic Code That Directs Evolution?" *Molecular and Cellular Biochemistry* 64, no. 1 (1984), pp. 5–13.

174 *And it was Caporale who opened*: Caporale was acknowledging a comment made by the University of Chicago microbiologist James A. Shapiro.

174 *"Standard theories are still framed"*: James A. Shapiro, "Barbara McClintock, 1902–1992," *BioEssays* 14, no. 11 (Nov. 1992), p. 791.

175 *"It really isn't correct"*: Lynn Helena Caporale, *Darwin in the Genome: Molecular Strategies in Biological Evolution* (New York: McGraw-Hill, 2003), p. 41.

175 *"rapid genome restructuring"*: James A. Shapiro, "Genome System Architecture," in Lynn Helena Caporale, ed., *Molecular Strategies in Biological Evolution*, Annals of the New York Academy of Sciences, vol. 870 (New York: New York Academy of Sciences, 1999), p. 32.

175 *"plasticity"*: Matthew I. Bellgard et al., "Dynamic Evolution of Genomes and the Concept of Genome Space," in Caporale, *Molecular Strategies in Biological Evolution*, p. 293.

175 *They've begun to study*: Sandra Blakeslee, "Some Biologists Ask 'Are Genes Everything?'" *New York Times*, Sept. 2, 1997, p. C1.

175 *"the entire set of genomes"*: Bellgard et al., "Dynamic Evolution of Genomes," p. 293.

176 *Over the course of some four billion years*: Takashi Gojobori, "Part VI. Summary," in Caporale, *Molecular Strategies in Biological Evolution*, p. 340.

176 *"a rich kind of design competence"*: Van der Ryn and Cowan, *Ecological Design*, p. 20.

176 *The following is a homework assignment*: Claire Kinnell, science assignment, third grade, Bridgeport Elementary School, Bridgeport, N.Y., Nov. 9, 1998.

177 *"Out of the mouth of babes"*: Psalms 8:2.

7. Growing Problems

181 *When inflation and interest rates*: Bill McKibben, "What Good Is a Forest?" *Audubon*, May–June 1996, p. 54.

181 *By the mid-nineties Maine forests*: Ibid.

181 *Thirty percent of the remainder*: Figures are from the World Resources Institute, cited in Janet N. Abromovitz, "Forest Loss Unchecked," in Lester R. Brown

et al., eds., *Vital Signs 2002: The Trends That Are Shaping Our Future* (New York: W. W. Norton, 2002), p. 104.

182 *"It is more profitable to clearcut"*: Quoted in Alan Rike Drengson and Duncan MacDonald Taylor, *Ecoforestry: The Art and Science of Sustainable Forest Use* (Gabriola Island, B.C.: New Society Publishers, 1997), p. 233.

182 *We also didn't know*: Ibid., p. 66.

183 *"The grass was the country"*: Willa Cather, *My Ántonia*, quoted in Wes Jackson, *Altars of Unhewn Stone: Science and the Earth* (San Francisco: North Point Press, 1987), p. 77.

183 *Today the number of us eating*: Charles C. Mann, "Crop Scientists Seek a New Revolution," *Science*, Jan. 15, 1999, p. 310.

183 *That historic feat is due*: Among them, the plant breeder Norman Borlaug won a Nobel Peace Prize in 1970 for his leadership in the development of high-yield crops.

183 *Consultative Group on International Agricultural Research (CGIAR)*: Ibid.

184 *When dwarf strains of maize (corn)*: Ibid.

184 *Nitrogen is key*: Phosphorus is another key ingredient in chemical fertilizers. Due to space considerations it is not discussed in detail here.

185 *It also turned out that a wide range*: P. A. Matson et al., "Agricultural Intensification and Ecosystem Properties," *Science*, July 25, 1997, p. 504.

185 *The net result*: Ibid.

185 *Peter Kenmore*: Kenmore is now senior officer of the FAO Plant Protection Service in Rome.

185 *"like pouring kerosene on a fire"*: Quoted in Kristin Dawkins, "Bucking Biotech: The Global Threat of the New Agribusiness," *Dollars & Sense*, May 15, 1997, p. 26. Kristin Dawkins is director of research at the Institute for Agriculture and Trade Policy in Minneapolis.

185 *Where once they got just 7 percent*: Paul Hawken, Amory Lovins, and L. Hunter Lovins, *Natural Capitalism: Creating the Next Industrial Revolution* (Boston: Little, Brown, 1999), p. 196.

185 *All of the fruit fly populations*: James Randerson, "Resistance to Pesticides Goes Global in a Flash," *New Scientist*, Oct. 5, 2002, p. 15.

185 *In the Philippines, for example*: Matson et al., "Agricultural Intensification and Ecosystem Properties," p. 504.

186 *Annual world use of pesticides overall*: David Donaldson, Timothy Kiely, and Arthur Grube, "Pesticides Industry Sales and Usage: 1998 and 1999 Market Estimates," U.S. Environmental Protection Agency report, Aug. 2002.

186 *Fully 70 percent of the antibiotics*: Union of Concerned Scientists, "SSI Alert: Antibiotic Use in US Agriculture," Jan. 19, 2001, http://www.ucsusa.org/food/hogging_exec.html.

186 *The amount of land*: Mann, "Crop Scientists Seek a New Revolution," p. 310.

186 *some two-thirds of all the freshwater*: Hawken, Lovins, and Lovins, *Natural Capitalism*, p. 193.

186 *Fertilizer use has also risen*: Ibid., p. 191.

186 *"The revolution in agriculture"*: Cutler Cleveland, speaking at "Investing in Natural Capital," a conference in Stockholm, Sweden, 1992 (Griesinger Films, 1993).

186 *Current estimates*: Hawken, Lovins, and Lovins, *Natural Capitalism*, p. 192.

186 *By midway through the 1990s*: Vaclav Smil, *Cycles of Life: Civilization and the Biosphere* (New York: Scientific American Library, 1997), p. 122.

186 *In 1900, when an American farmer*: Janine M. Benyus, *Biomimicry: Innovation Inspired by Nature* (New York: Morrow, 1997), p. 19.

186 *Today, Peter Henry*: Personal conversation with Peter Henry, 2002.

187 *"In some years, if it wasn't"*: Ibid.

187 *Ten companies now control*: Jeremy Rifkin, "Genetic Blueprints Aren't Mere Utilities," *Los Angeles Times*, July 8, 1998, p. B7.

187 *Six handle 85 percent*: John Madeley, *Big Business, Poor Peoples: The Impact of Transnational Corporations on the World's Poor* (London: Zed Books, 1999), p. 36.

187 *"Too bad 'save the dirt'"*: The ad ran in the science section of the Aug. 24, 1999, *New York Times*.

187 *What the ad didn't say*: The ad also didn't mention that another reason for Monsanto's development of the new seeds is that its patent on Roundup was expiring and it needed to protect the market for a product that accounted for some 40 percent of its profits. See Dawkins, "Bucking Biotech," p. 26.

188 *"Now imagine . . . tribes of mites"*: Douglas H. Chadwick, "What Good Is a Prairie?" *Audubon*, Nov.–Dec. 1995, p. 36.

188 *Some 20 percent of irrigated farmland*: Brian Halweil, "Farmland Quality Deteriorating," in Brown et al., *Vital Signs 2002*, p. 103.

188 *Even with real improvements*: Ibid., p. 102.

188 *One-third of its original topsoil*: Hawken, Lovins, and Lovins, *Natural Capitalism*, p. 192.

189 *In his book* Grassland: Cited in Benyus, *Biomimicry*, p. 15.

189 *"Modern agriculture has failed"*: Judith D. Soule and Jon K. Piper, *Farming in Nature's Image: An Ecological Approach to Agriculture* (Washington, D.C.: Island Press, 1992), p. 12.

189 *So even as the amount of water*: Ibid., p. 15.

189 *U.S. tests have found residues*: As this book goes to press, this information is the latest available. It's from the EPA's National Pesticide Survey Project, conducted in 1990. Available from the National Technical Information Service, fact sheet PB93115988.

189 *the herbicide atrazine*: Associated Press, "Weed Killer Deforms Frogs in Sex Organs, Study Finds," *New York Times*, April 17, 2002, p. A19.

190 *A University of North Carolina study*: Marcia E. Herman-Giddens et al., "Secondary Sexual Characteristics and Menses in Young Girls Seen in Office Practice: A Study from the Pediatric Research in Office Settings Network," *Pediatrics* 99, no. 4 (April 1997), pp. 505–12.

190 Our Stolen Future: Theo Colborn, Dianne Dumanoski, and John Peterson Myers, *Our Stolen Future: Are We Threatening Our Fertility, Intelligence, and Survival? A Scientific Detective Story* (New York: Dutton, 1996).

190 *In waterways it becomes*: Smil, *Cycles of Life*, p. 134.

191 *In a memorable nineteenth-century example*: Richard Milner, *The Encyclopedia of Evolution: Humanity's Search for Its Origins* (New York: Facts on File, 1990), p. 189.

191 *"perhaps incapable at present"*: "Report on the State of the World's Plant Genetic Resources for Food and Agriculture, Prepared for the International Technical Conference on Plant Genetic Resources, Leipzig, Germany, 17–23 June 1996" (Rome: Food and Agriculture Organization of the United Nations, 1996), p. 24.

192 *"It revealed that most varieties"*: Ibid., p. 14.

192 *Clive Stannard*: Stannard is assistant secretary of the Commission on Plant Genetic Resources for Food and Agriculture at the Food and Agriculture Organization.

192 *"food security depends"*: From notes for a presentation on plant genetic resources developed by Clive Stannard and communicated by him to the author in April 2004.

192 *"Maximum rice yields"*: Quoted in Mann, "Crop Scientists Seek a New Revolution," p. 310.

192 *"Recent data on crop yields"*: Quoted in Hawken, Lovins, and Lovins, *Natural Capitalism*, p. 191.

193 *In fifty years our reserves of phosphate*: Luther Tweeten, "Phosphate Supply a Threat to Sustainable Agriculture" (University Communications, Ohio State University, Feb. 22, 1996). Tweeten is a professor of agricultural marketing, policy, and trade.

193 *In the American West*: Hawken, Lovins, and Lovins, *Natural Capitalism*, p. 215.

193 *They are presented here in order of appearance:*

    Ross E. Milloy, "A Rift over Rio Grande Water Rights," *New York Times*, Sept. 18, 2001, p. A14.

    William Finnegan, "Leasing the Rain," *The New Yorker*, April 8, 2002, p. 43.

    Fred Pearce, "Water War," *New Scientist*, May 18, 2002, p. 18.

    Douglas Jehl, "Atlanta's Growing Thirst Creates Water War," *New York Times*, May 27, 2002, p. A1.

    John Tagliabue, "As Multinationals Run the Taps, Anger Rises over Water for Profit," *New York Times*, Aug. 26, 2002, p. A1.

    Eric Eckholm, "China Will Move Waters to Quench Thirst of Cities," *New York Times*, Aug. 27, 2002, p. A1.

    Jeff Howe, "The Great Thirst," *Wired*, Aug. 2002, p. 118.

    Serge Schmemann, "Israel Waits for Sea of Galilee's Low Tide to Turn," *New York Times*, Sept. 10, 2002, p. A4.

    Dean E. Murphy, "20,000 Fish Are Dead in River Where Water Flow Is Disputed," *New York Times*, Oct. 3, 2002, p. A25.

    Douglas Jehl, "Arkansas Rice Farmers Run Dry, and U.S. Remedy Sets Off Debate," *New York Times*, Nov. 11, 2002, p. A1.

    Michael Wines, "Grand Soviet Scheme for Sharing Water in Central Asia Is Foundering," *New York Times*, Dec. 9, 2002, p. A14.

    "U.S. to Cut California's Share of Water from Colorado River," *New York Times*, Dec. 28, 2002, p. A12.

Dean E. Murphy, "Failed Deal in California Cuts Water for Nevada," *New York Times*, Jan. 2, 2003, p. A10.

Douglas Jehl, "A New Frontier in Water Wars Emerges in East," *New York Times*, March 3, 2003, p. A1.

"Millions Face Water Shortage in North China, Officials Warn," *New York Times*, June 6, 2003, p. A7.

Dean E. Murphy, "Accord in West Will Give Cities Farmers' Water," *New York Times*, Oct. 17, 2003, p. A1.

Ralph Blumenthal, "West Texans Sizzle over a Plan to Sell Their Water," *New York Times*, Dec. 11, 2003, p. A28.

195 *"padding the statistics"*: Personal conversation with Wes Jackson, 1997; reviewed by him, May 2004.

195 *It forecasts that within the next quarter century*: Mann, "Crop Scientists Seek a New Revolution," p. 310.

195 *"Three large countries"*: Sandra Postel, "Water Stress Driving Grain Trade," in Brown et al., *Vital Signs 2002*, p. 134.

195 *"When you add up everything"*: Quoted in Mann, "Crop Scientists Seek a New Revolution," p. 310.

196 *And in fact, according to a recent UN report*: Ben J. Wattenberg, "It Will Be a Smaller World After All," *New York Times*, March 8, 2003, p. A17.

196 *When anthropologist Napoleon Chagnon*: Napoleon A. Chagnon, *Yąnomamö: The Fierce People*, 2nd ed. (New York: Holt, Rinehart and Winston, 1977), p. 1. The extent of their range is depicted on a frontispiece map.

197 *That means it has been used*: Smil, *Cycles of Life*, p. 123.

197 *But the oil needed*: The Cornell University physicist Thomas Gold argued that life first appeared underground, in warm seas of hydrocarbons welling up from deep in the earth. This means, he said, that our petroleum reserves—commonly referred to as fossil fuels—are not rotted biomass in origin, as is presently believed. He maintained that those underground hydrocarbon seas were a preexisting chemical resource, one that primitive life forms have simply inhabited—thus accounting for their dense presence in petroleum, and for the modern theory that it originated from living biomass. (See *Wired* magazine, "Fuel's Paradise," issue 8.07, July 2000: http://www.wired.com/wired/archive/8.07/gold_pr.html. See also Gold's 1999 book, *The Deep Hot Biosphere*.)

In deference to Gold's stature as both a scientist and a preeminent contrarian, his comments deserve reply here. On the question of where hydrocarbons come from, I have followed prevailing science. In any event, while Gold's argument holds interest for geologists and life scientists, philosophically it just defers the question. Whether hydrocarbon energy comes to us by rotted biomass or by some deep earth chemistry, ultimately all energy is stellar in origin. With regard to life's beginning, this book makes no case for how life first took shape, arguing "No one knows for sure how life began" (p. 395). Whether it initially took form on the surface or below ground is beyond my scope. As before, I've followed prevailing science for the opening of this book.

197 *"Every single calorie we eat"*: Richard Manning, "The Oil We Eat: Following the Food Chain Back to Iraq," *Harper's Magazine*, Feb. 2004, p. 37.

198 *If, starting in 1984, energy use*: Soule and Piper, *Farming in Nature's Image*, p. 24.

198 *human consumption of freshwater*: "Water in the Year 2000," *Tomorrow* (Fall 1996), p. 64.

198 *"They are offering"*: Jackson, *Altars of Unhewn Stone*, p. 55.

199 *"adopt a framework that would operate"*: Bill Lambrecht, "World Recoils at Monsanto's Brave New Crops," *St. Louis Post-Dispatch*, Dec. 27, 1998, p. A1.

199 *"biotechnology shills"*: "A Cheerleader Steps Back," *St. Louis Post-Dispatch*, June 9, 1999, p. B6.

199 *Of the forty thousand field tests*: Andrew Pollack, "Report Says More Farmers Don't Follow Biotech Rules," *New York Times*, June 19, 2003, p. C5.

199 *In addition, the study concluded*: Cornell ecologists report, "Alien Animals, Plants, and Microbes Cost US $123 Billion a Year," *Cornell News Release: Cost of Alien Species*, Feb. 11, 1999.

199 *"We now have biotechnologists"*: Andrew Kimbrell, "The Gene Rush: Genetic Engineers or Bioneers?" speaking at the Bioneers conference "Practical Solutions for Restoring the Earth," Oct. 31–Nov. 1, 1997, San Francisco. Transcript by TUC Radio, San Francisco, http://www.tucradio.org/contact.html.

200 *But a recent study based on USDA information*: Pollack, "Report Says More Farmers Don't Follow Biotech Rules," p. C5.

200 *Lab research has shown*: James Randerson, "Modified Crop Breeds Toxic Hybrid," *New Scientist*, Nov. 30, 2002, p. 7.

200 *The same transfer has been demonstrated*: Bob Holmes, "Dangerous Liaisons," *New Scientist*, Aug. 31, 2002, p. 38.

200 *In the area around the rapeseed*: Ibid.

200 *Now much more powerful herbicides*: "Resistance Is Useless," *New Scientist*, Feb. 19, 2000, p. 21.

200 *In the U.S. between 2001 and 2003*: C. M. Benbrook, "Impacts of Genetically Engineered Crops on Pesticide Use in the United States: The First Eight Years," *BioTech InfoNet*, technical paper no. 6, Nov. 2003, http://www.biotech-info.net/technicalpaper6.html.

201 *"The genes that catch my attention"*: Quoted in Holmes, "Dangerous Liaisons," p. 38.

201 *Elaine Ingham*: Dr. Elaine Ingham's testimony before the New Zealand Royal Commission on Genetic Modification, Executive Summary, Feb. 2001, http://www.biotech-info.net/EI_testimony_NZ.html.

201 *"It is inadequate"*: Ibid.

202 *"You can't look at the genome"*: Quoted in Marina Chicurel, "We Can't Understand Cells by Taking Them Apart Piece by Piece," *New Scientist*, Dec. 11, 1999, p. 39.

202 *"Gene families should be analyzed as systems"*: Lynn Helena Caporale, *Molecular Strategies in Biological Evolution*, Annals of the New York Academy of Sciences, vol. 870 (New York: New York Academy of Sciences, 1999), p. 10.

202 *Sydney Brenner*: Brenner is at the Molecular Sciences Institute in Berkeley.

202 *how those genes are arranged*: Sandra Blakeslee, "Some Biologists Ask 'Are Genes Everything?'" *New York Times*, Sept. 2, 1997, p. C1.

202 *Scott Gilbert*: Gilbert is at Swarthmore College in Pennsylvania.

202 *"depends on the context"*: Scott F. Gilbert, *Developmental Biology*, 5th ed. (Sunderland, Mass.: Sinauer Associates, 1997), p. 209.

202 *"the leading supplier of directed evolution technologies"*: "Molecular Breeding," Maxygen official Web site, n.d., http://www.maxygen.com/webpage_templates/site_index.php3?page_name=site_index.

203 *"cutting them all into small pieces"*: John Sutherland, "Enzyme Evolution," *Chemistry & Industry*, Oct. 4, 1999, p. 745.

203 *The company was founded in 1997*: "Vaccines," Maxygen official Web site, n.d., http://www.maxygen.com/webpage_templates/secondary.php3?page_name=vaccines.

203 *Just in time for New Year's 2000*: "Agriculture," Maxygen official Web site, n.d., http://www.maxygen.com/webpage_templates/secondary.php3?page_name=agriculture_intro.

203 *during a $110 million initial public offering*: Peter Fairley, "Directed Evolution Enzymes Enter the New Economy," *Chemical Week*, April 5, 2000, p. 29.

203 *In an interview*: "Sex in a Bottle," *Economist*, June 26, 1999, p. 94.

203 *"to rapidly develop"*: "Research," Maxygen official Web site, n.d., http://www.maxygen.com/webpage_template/secondary.php3?page_name=research_intro.

204 *"Multinational corporations"*: Quoted in Nancy Beth Jackson, "Through Politicking for Plants, He Made His Garden Grow," *New York Times*, Aug. 4, 1998, p. F3.

8. The Even Greener Revolution

206 *Within each commercial timber stand*: Alan Rike Drengson and Duncan MacDonald Taylor, *Ecoforestry: The Art and Science of Sustainable Forest Use* (Gabriola Island, B.C.: New Society Publishers, 1997), p. 149.

206 *Others reach down*: Ibid., pp. 64–65.

207 *The famed anthropologist Gregory Bateson*: This story was relayed to me by the architect William McDonough, a pioneer in the design of green buildings and in urban ecology. He credits Bateson.

207 *Forests once covered*: Ibid., p. 129.

207 *It's why they leave a few dead trees*: Ibid., p. 56.

208 *And rotations—how soon trees are recut*: Ibid., p. 46.

208 *It uses many of the practices*: Peter N. Duinker and Reino E. Pulkki, "Magnifica Comunità di Fiemme: One Thousand Years of Community Forestry in the Alps," http://www.greendesign.net/understory/sum99/MagnificaDuinker.html (accessed April 1, 2000).

208 *In Germany today*: Drengson and Taylor, *Ecoforestry*, p. 149.

208 *a tract that size in Switzerland*: Ibid., p. 157.

209 *"the decrease in land values, soil erosion"*: Ibid., p. 233.

209 *"The information of nature"*: Personal conversation with Tom Eisner, 1995.

210 *INBio*: Instituto Nacional de Biodiversidad.

210 *When she mentioned a hepatitis treatment*: Joan Conrow, "Medicine Man," *National Wildlife*, June/July 2001, http://www.nwf.org/nationalwildlife/2001/medmanjj01.html.

210 *In later tests*: David Briscoe, "Agreement Would Share Profits from AIDS Drug with Samoan Healers," Associated Press, Imdiversity.com, http://www.imdiversity.com/villages/asian/Article_Detail.asp?Article_ID=8398 (accessed Dec. 21, 2001).

210 *Because of the molecule's structure*: Some phorbol esters are used to cause tumors in cancer research.

210 *"Chemists at the bench"*: Conrow, "Medicine Man."

211 *"Talking to them about the plants"*: Ibid.

211 *"It's important to be able to sift"*: Potter Wickware, "Data Explosion Fuels Search for Drugs," *Nature*, Aug. 19, 1999, p. 799.

211 *"Look at insects"*: Personal conversation with Tom Eisner, 1995.

211 *"Agricultural plants are not natural"*: Kenny Ausubel, speaking on the "Theft of the Ark: Restoring Biodiversity in Agriculture" panel, at the Bioneers conference "Practical Solutions for Restoring the Earth," Oct. 31–Nov. 1, 1997, San Francisco. Transcript by TUC Radio, San Francisco, http://www.tucradio.org/contact.html.

211 *Kenny Ausubel*: Ausubel is an award-winning journalist, filmmaker, and social entrepeneur. He is the founder and co-executive director of the annual Bioneers conference. Now held each fall in San Raphael, California, it is arguably the most advanced public forum for environmental and new age perspectives on the new biology.

212 *A joint European program*: Those research centers are the Louis Bolk Institute in Driebergen, the Netherlands; the Elm Farm Research Centre near Newbury, England; and Switzerland's Research Institute of Organic Agriculture in Frick, near Basel.

212 *"Mother Earth never attempts to farm"*: Cited in Judith D. Soule and Jon K. Piper, *Farming in Nature's Image: An Ecological Approach to Agriculture* (Washington, D.C.: Island Press, 1992), p. xiv.

213 *"Instead of trying to feed plants with fertilizer"*: Robert Frenay, "Envirotech: Notes from the Underground," *Audubon*, May/June 1995, p. 26.

213 *"Anything having an effect on root distribution"*: Lady Eve Balfour, "Towards a Sustainable Agriculture—the Living Soil," an address given to an IFOAM conference in Switzerland in 1977 (reproduced with permission by the Organic Gardening & Farming Society of Tasmania, Inc.), http://www.netspeed.com.au/cogs/cogbal.htm.

214 *"alternative farmers often produce"*: Board of Agriculture, National Research Council, *Alternative Agriculture: Committee on the Role of Alternative Farming Methods in Modern Agriculture* (Washington, D.C.: National Academy Press, 1989), p. 8.

214 *"many federal policies discourage"*: Ibid., p. 10.

214 *"relatively little help"*: Ibid., p. 8.

214 *"federal programs be restructured"*: Ibid., p. 17.

214 *In the following decade the journal*: Cited in Robert Frenay, "Envirotech: Gaining Ground," *Audubon*, July–Aug. 1994, p. 23.

214 *"about 50 percent higher"*: L. E. Drinkwater, P. Wagoner, and M. Sarrantonio, "Legume-Based Cropping Systems Have Reduced Carbon and Nitrogen Losses," *Nature*, Nov. 19, 1998, pp. 262–65.

214 *A 2001 report*: John P. Reganold et al., "Sustainability of Three Apple Production Systems," *Nature*, April 19, 2001, pp. 926–30.

214 *"This is one of the first well-replicated"*: Quoted in Tom Clarke, "Policy: Green Apples Upset Cart," *Nature Genetics*, April 19, 2001, http://www.nature.com/nature/links/010419/010419-1.html.

214 *In 2002, a study*: Cited in Rob Edwards, "The Natural Choice," *New Scientist*, March 16, 2002, p. 10. The study was conducted by Patterson and his colleagues from Dumfries and Galloway Royal Infirmary, along with a team from the University of Strathclyde.

215 *Avery's Center for Global Food Issues receives*: Marian Burros, "Is Organic Food Provably Better?" *New York Times*, July 16, 2003, p. F1.

215 *"I don't think there is any question"*: Ibid.

215 *After what might be called*: Philip Brasher, "USDA Proposes New National Standards for Organic Food," Associated Press, March 8, 2000.

216 *McDonald's, the global fast-food burger chain*: David Barboza with Sherri Day, "McDonald's Seeking Cut in Antibiotics in Its Meat," *New York Times*, June 20, 2003, p. C1.

216 *"Sales of organic and natural foods"*: Quoted in "Organic Methods Boost Profits on Farms, Lead to Company Mergers," *In Business*, Jan./Feb. 2000, p. 7.

217 *When it left the hive*: Martin P. Waterman, "The Good, the Bad, and the Ugly: Insect Research Doesn't Discriminate," *Growing Edge* 7, no. 3 (Spring 1996), p. 21.

217 *Beetle bait isolated*: Andy Coghlan, "Double-Crossed: A Potato Pest's Favorite Fragrance Could Be Its Undoing," *New Scientist*, Feb. 19, 2000, p. 14.

218 *"The battle of the bugs"*: Waterman, "The Good, the Bad, and the Ugly," p. 21.

218 *"The goal should be to suppress"*: Allison A. Snow and Pedro Moran-Palma, "Commercialization of Transgenic Plants: Potential Ecological Risks," *BioScience* 47, no. 2 (Feb. 1997), p. 86.

218 *"An adult insect"*: Soule and Piper, *Farming in Nature's Image*, p. 108.

218 *Cornell scientists*: The team was led by Bernd Blossey, director of Cornell University's Biological Control of Non-indigenous Plants Species Program.

219 *Some 50 percent*: Fred Pearce, "Green Harvest," *New Scientist*, Feb. 23, 2002, p. 16.

219 *Sweet potatoes are planted*: Donella Meadows, "Natural Pest Control Working in Cuba," *Charleston Gazette*, June 16, 1997, p. 4A.

219 *In only three years the overall use*: John Madeley, *Big Business, Poor Peoples: The Impact of Transnational Corporations on the World's Poor* (London: Zed Books, 1999), p. 44.

219 *In that test, thousands of rice farms*: Carol Kaesuk Yoon, "Simple Method Found to Increase Crop Yields Vastly," *New York Times*, August 22, 2000, p. F1.

219 *Since rice blast travels*: Ibid.

220 *According to their report*: Youyong Zhu et al., "Genetic Diversity and Disease Control in Rice," *Nature*, Aug. 17, 2000, p. 718, http://www.nature.com/cgi–taf/DynaPage.taf?file=/nature/journal/v406/n6797/full/406718a0_fs.html.

220 *"Resistant plants did block"*: Yoon, "Simple Method Found to Increase Crop Yields Vastly," p. F1.

220 *"shows how we've lost sight of"*: Ibid.

220 *"People have said"*: Quoted in ibid.

220 *Scientists are testing intercropping*: Ibid.

220 *An Iowa farmer who alternated*: "Beyond Organics," *New Scientist*, May 18, 2002, p. 33.

220 *Another study, done in Mexico*: Ibid. The study was conducted by Miguel Altieri of the University of California at Berkeley.

221 *"they get more rain"*: Joel Salatin, "Rotational Grazing," speaking at the Bioneers conference "Practical Solutions for Restoring the Earth," Oct. 31–Nov. 1, 1997. Quotations in this text were reviewed by Salatin, April 2004.

221 *It supports more humans, too*: Ibid.

221 *"when you mob the animals up"*: Ibid.

222 *"so it doesn't die maintaining those centimeters"*: Ibid.

222 *"the fresh tillers are yellowish"*: Ibid.

222 *"pulsing the pasture"*: Ibid.

222 *"Farmers all the time are complaining"*: Ibid.

223 *"that much of the rangeland"*: Paul Hawken, Amory Lovins, and L. Hunter Lovins, *Natural Capitalism: Creating the Next Industrial Revolution* (Boston: Little, Brown, 1999), p. 208.

223 *Between 1993 and 1997*: Ibid.

223 *Nitrogen runoff*: Ibid.

223 *Methane is a potent*: Ibid., p. 207.

223 *Since 1960, some 25 percent*: "The Hamburger Connection," Rainforest Action Network, Aug. 14, 2000, http://www.ran.org/info_center/factsheets/04e.html.

224 *"The problem is that we don't"*: Salatin, "Rotational Grazing."

224 *"There is lots of water in the desert"*: Personal conversation with Wouter van Dieren, 1998. Reviewed by him, April 2004.

225 *the Hamburg Environmental Institute*: Hamburger Umweltinstitut.

225 *Many of them have been in operation*: Personal conversation with Michael Braungart, April 2004.

226 *"If farmers would stop using"*: Masanobu Fukuoka, *The One-Straw Revolution: An Introduction to Natural Farming* (Emmaus: Rodale Press, 1978), p. 70.

226 *"an elegantly conceived sequence of plantings"*: Hawken, Lovins, and Lovins, *Natural Capitalism*, p. 210.

226 *"In early October"*: Janine M. Benyus, *Biomimicry: Innovation Inspired by Nature* (New York: Morrow, 1997), p. 36.

226 *"five to ten people"*: Fukuoka, *One-Straw Revolution*, p. 103.

226 *The yield is comparable*: Ibid., p. xxii.

228 *"The idea of environment"*: Personal conversation with Wes Jackson, 1997; reviewed by him, May 2004.

228 *He quotes ecologist*: Stan Rowe is a professor emeritus at the University of Saskatchewan.

228 *"just sort of loose stuff lying around"*: Personal conversation with Jackson, 1997; reviewed by him, May 2004.

228 *"the spaces between plants"*: Ibid.

228 *"In all, let Nature never be forgot"*: from "An Epistle to the Right Honourable Richard, Earl of Burlington."

228 *"There's something very powerful"*: Personal conversation with Jackson, 1997; reviewed by him, May 2004.

229 *The eventual result of that effort*: Another early source of guidance was Arnold Schultz, a professor of forestry at UC Berkeley. His paper "The Ecosystem as a Conceptual Tool for the Management of Natural Resources" cites Stan Rowe as well.

231 *"We need economic models"*: Wes Jackson, *Altars of Unhewn Stone: Science and the Earth* (San Francisco: North Point Press, 1987), p. 96.

232 *"Economics can change"*: Personal conversation with Marty Bender, Aug. 1997.

232 *"Marty is looking at energy"*: Personal conversation with Jackson, 1997; reviewed by him, May 2004.

232 *"expand our boundary"*: Ibid.

233 *"The major environmental problems"*: Personal conversation with Jackson, May 2004.

233 *"In natural systems agriculture"*: Personal conversation with Jackson, 1997; reviewed by him, May 2004.

233 *"It took endangered-species conservationists"*: Gary Nabhan, speaking on the "Theft of the Ark" panel, at the Bioneers conference "Practical Solutions for Restoring the Earth," Oct. 31–Nov. 1, 1997.

233 *A farmer isn't a separate unit*: Jackson, *Altars of Unhewn Stone*, p. 75.

233 *"launders government money"*: Ibid., p. 104.

233 *More than a decade ago*: Gail Feenstra, "Agricultural Systems Incorporate Social, Environmental Concerns," University of California Sustainable Agriculture Research and Education Program (Spring 1992), http://www.sarep. ucdavis.edu/NEWSLTR/v4n3/sa-2.htm.

234 *Then, where the size of surrounding farms*: Ibid.

234 *"function best in a regime intermediate"*: Murray Gell-Mann, *The Quark and the Jaguar: Adventures in the Simple and the Complex* (New York: W. H. Freeman, 1994), p. 369.

234 *"Then, between them, the works"*: Personal conversation with Stephen Farrier, Feb. 2001.

234 *"Not the autocracy of a single"*: Charles M. Johnston, *Necessary Wisdom: Meeting the Challenge of a New Cultural Maturity* (Seattle: ICD Press in association with Celestial Arts of Berkeley, Calif., 1991), p. 199.

236 *"The criteria for a sustainable agriculture"*: Balfour, "Towards a Sustainable Agriculture—the Living Soil."

9. Town and Country

237 *As it has for centuries*: Most of the descriptions in this paragraph were drawn from Richard Kauffman, photographs, and Carol Field, text, *The Hill Towns of Italy* (San Francisco: Chronicle Books, 1997), pp. 3, 68–69, 74. Those descriptions were confirmed during a personal visit to the area in May 2004.

238 *"narrow streets flow into public squares"*: Richard Levine, "Un Medioevo nel nostro futuro?" *Spazio e societa* 10 (April–June), p. 18.

238 *"Many small connecting streets"*: Ibid.

238 *"is the way they grew organically"*: Kauffman and Field, *Hill Towns of Italy*, p. 70.

238 *"fabric of city space"*: Levine, "Un Medioevo nel nostro futuro?" p. 18.

238 *"internal energy and information flows"*: Ibid.

238 *"the warmth and the sense of identity"*: Kauffman and Field, *Hill Towns of Italy*, p. 15.

238 *It was then, too, that Todi*: Personal conversation with Richard Levine, May 2004.

239 *"The town is able to change"*: Ibid.

240 *"It was a society in which"*: Levine, "Un Medioevo nel nostro futuro?" p. 21.

240 *"disorder, conflict, and mistakes"*: Personal conversation with Levine, 1995; reviewed by him, May 2004.

241 *"would enjoy all the advantages"*: Quoted in Judy Corbett and Michael Corbett, *Designing Sustainable Communities: Learning from Village Homes* (Washington, D.C.: Island Press, 2000), p. 5.

241 *"you will live under trees"*: Quoted in François Spoerry, *A Gentle Architecture, from Port-Grimaud to Port Liberté*, trans. Madeleine Masson (Chichester, U.K., and New York: Pheon Books in association with John Wiley & Sons, 1991), pp. 25–26.

242 *"replaced the slow and continuous"*: Ibid., p. 27.

244 *"cultural centers that are unable"*: Quoted in Bernard J. Frieden and Lynne B. Sagalyn, *Downtown: How America Rebuilds Cities* (Cambridge, Mass.: MIT Press, 1991), p. 58.

244 *"A lot of our problems"*: Corbett and Corbett, *Designing Sustainable Communities*, p. 4.

244 *And during those fifteen years*: Elizabeth Becker, "2 Acres of Farm Lost to Sprawl Each Minute, New Study Says," *New York Times*, Oct. 4, 2002, p. A22.

244 *Today, for every minute*: Ibid.

244 *According to the Oakland*: http://www.urbanecology.org.

244 *"Just as the elevator made the skyscraper"*: Richard Rogers, "Looking Forward to Compact City," *Independent*, Feb. 20, 1995, p. 18.

245 *"My ambition has been to produce"*: Spoerry, *Gentle Architecture,* frontispiece.

245 *"brutal" and "aggressive"*: Ibid., p. 28.

246 *"beauty" and "overall effect"*: Ibid., p. 60.

246 *As a student in the 1930s*: Ibid., p. 22.

246 *"a whole arsenal of"*: Ibid., p. 49.

246 *"classic urban forms"*: Ibid., p. 120.

246   A Pattern Language, *first published in 1977*: Patricia Leigh Brown, "A Design Controversy Goes Cozy.com," *New York Times*, Nov. 23, 2000, p. F1.

247   *"a wise old owl of a book"*: Ibid.

247   *along with several colleagues*: Christopher Alexander, Sara Ishikawa, and Murray Silverstein, with Max Jacobson, Ingrid Fiksdahl-King, and Shlomo Angel, *A Pattern Language: Towns, Buildings, Construction* (New York: Oxford University Press, 1977).

247   *"If there is a beautiful view"*: Ibid., p. 311.

247   *"A town needs public squares"*: Ibid., p. 311.

247   *"The life of a public square"*: Ibid., p. 600.

248   *"Outdoors, people always try"*: Ibid., p. 558.

248   *"building set-backs from the street"*: Ibid., p. 593.

248   *"Wherever there is action"*: Ibid., p. 604.

248   *"A public space without a middle"*: Ibid., pp. 607–608.

248   *Given its hyperlinked structure*: Emily Eakin, "Architecture's Irascible Reformer," *New York Times*, July 12, 2003, p. B7.

248   *In all of that it serves*: In 2003, Alexander released a four-volume opus, *The Nature of Order: An Essay on the Art of Building and the Nature of the Universe*, which outlines the properties that he believes inform beauty in nature, art, craft, and great buildings.

248   *"the effective dissolution"*: Léon Krier, *Architecture: Choice or Fate* (Windsor, Berks, U.K.: Andreas Papadakis, 1998), p. 94.

249   *"second nature"*: Personal conversation with Léon Krier, 1998; reviewed by him, April 2004.

249   *"resulting in very low densities"*: Krier, *Architecture*, p. 89.

249   *They're agrarian centers*: Personal conversation with Levine, 1998; reviewed by him, May 2004.

249   *"Just like a family of individuals"*: Krier, *Architecture*, p. 124.

250   *"Maturity is the end goal"*: Ibid., p. 89.

251   *"extremely complex and wasteful"*: Ibid., p. 93.

251   *"density, function, location"*: Ibid., p. 108.

251   *"leads only to uniformity"*: Personal conversation with Krier, 1998; reviewed by him, April 2004.

251   *According to the trade journal*: Sidebar to Robert Steuteville, "Key Findings of the Annual Survey: New Urbanism Rocks, Despite Sluggish Economy," *New Urban News* 7, no. 6 (Dec. 2002), p. 1.

251   *"You can count on Americans"*: Quoted by Andres Duany at "The Technique of Traditional Town Planning" conference, Jan. 28–31, 1998, Biltmore Hotel, Coral Gables, Fla.

252   *With rush hour*: According to the Tri-State Transportation Campaign, in 2003 the population of Manhattan was 1,564,798; in 2000 the daily incoming commuters numbered 1,458,790, and the daily "backward" commuters (from Manhattan and return) numbered 121,982.

252   *Congressional Medal of Honor winners*: The highest American decoration for valor.

253 *Traditionally styled ballparks*: Baltimore's beautiful, traditionally styled ballpark, Camden Yards, was completed in 1992 and has inspired a host of related city stadiums around the United States. Looking beyond ballparks, Syracuse, New York, now has its Armory Square; Pasadena, California, its Plaza Pasadena; San Diego its Horton Plaza; and Seattle its Pike Place Market. Boston has the renowned Faneuil Hall Marketplace. Playa Vista, in Los Angeles, is a major urban infill development of more than a thousand acres. At Harbor Point in Boston, a partly abandoned inner-city housing project has been transformed into a traditional mixed-use neighborhood. The Hope VI program is currently set to tackle one of the largest and most infamous of the modernist American "projects," the Robert Taylor Homes—two and a half miles of bleak high-rises along Chicago's South Side. They will be replaced by human-scale, affordable housing arrayed in traditional neighborhoods. Major efforts of various kinds are also under way in cities like Chattanooga, Milwaukee, Atlanta, Seattle, San Francisco, Baltimore, Minneapolis–St. Paul, Pittsburgh, and Washington, D.C. Nor is that trend confined to the United States. Quinlan Terry's Richmond Riverside development in London is widely admired. It created a full city block of distinguished, traditional commercial structures along with retail, apartments, and underground parking on a prominent riverfront site. Throughout much of Europe—where the suburban outflow was less pronounced—the revival of city centers has preceded American efforts.

253 *A recent study shows that nearly 20 percent*: The study was conducted by PricewaterhouseCoopers. Cited in Robert Davis, "Valuing Real Estate," *New Urban News* 7, no. 1 (Jan.–Feb. 2002), p. 21.

253 *"As investors admit"*: Ibid.

254 *He notes the emergence*: Cited in "The Future Belongs to Town Centers," *New Urban News* 7, no. 1 (Jan.–Feb. 2002), p. 1.

254 *Gibbs sees the creation*: Ibid.

254 *More than half of all miles*: Jane Holtz Kay, "Without a Car in the World," *Technology Review*, July 1997, p. 56.

254 *"New urbanists do work"*: Andres Duany, "Our Urbanism," *Architecture Magazine*, Dec. 1998, p. 37.

254 *Rather than spreading*: In rural areas, environmentalists call for new-urban planners to expand on existing population centers rather than despoil more open land.

254 *"We measure our wealth"*: Andres Duany, speaking at "The Technique of Traditional Town Planning" conference.

255 *Krier's master plan for Florence-Novoli*: Krier, *Architecture*, p. 111.

255 *Instead a national search scouted out*: New-urbanist developments are now being monitored and evaluated by a nonprofit organization, the Congress for the New Urbanism, and reported by start-up publications like *New Urban News* and *The Town Paper*.

255 *"The masterplan is to the construction"*: Krier, *Architecture*, p. 113.

255 *"The International Style built many beautiful buildings"*: Vincent Scully, "The Architecture of Community," in *The New Urbanism: Toward an Architecture of Community* (New York: McGraw-Hill, 1994), p. 223.

256 *"When buildings share a common vernacular"*: Duany, "Our Urbanism," p. 38.

257 *a growing list of planners*: The roster of new-urbanist planners currently in-
cludes, in the United States alone, Duany and Plater-Zyberk, Peter Calthorpe,
Elizabeth Moule and Stefanos Polyzoides, Robert A.M. Stern, Daniel Solo-
mon, and such firms as Cooper, Robertson & Partners; Peterson/Littenberg,
Dover, Kohl & Partners; Looney Ricks Kiss; Moore Ruble Yudell; Lennertz,
Coyle & Associates; Torti Gallas and Partners; and Urban Design Associates.

257 *"Kids love high density"*: Todd Zimmerman, of the new-urbanist market analysts Zimmerman/Volk Associates, based in Clinton, New Jersey, speaking at
"The Technique of Traditional Town Planning" conference.

257 *"While they do not necessarily cost more"*: Duany, "Our Urbanism," p. 39.

258 *"The prince wanted this to be a showcase"*: Personal conversation with Andrew
Hamilton. He was also the developer of London's Richmond Riverside.

259 *Those principles call for an "ecosystemic" approach*: Quoted in Robert Frenay,
"Chattanooga Turnaround," *Audubon*, Jan.–Feb. 1996, p. 85. Reviewed by
Levine, May 2004.

259 *"natural capital"*: E. F. Schumacher pioneered the notion of natural capital in
his 1973 book *Small Is Beautiful: Economics as if People Mattered*.

259 *Levine is currently working with Vienna-based*: Oikodrom promotes urban ecology internationally. Levine's partner there is the group's president, Heidi
Dumreicher.

260 *"Design must always have"*: Richard Neutra, *Survival Through Design* (New
York: Oxford University Press, 1954), p. 171.

260 *"The proper gauge of value"*: Ibid., pp. 370–71.

260 *"community planning is"*: Ibid., p. 337.

261 *"Solar technology was very new"*: Corbett and Corbett, *Designing Sustainable
Communities*, p. 27.

261 *The only economically secure strategies*: In the U.S., the evolving state of urban
ecology ranges in its manifestations from James Rouse's Columbia, Maryland,
an early environmentally sensitive new town in the "garden city" tradition, to
the visionary architect Paolo Soleri's Arcosanti, rising from the Arizona desert
like some fantastic hive. Near Eugene, Oregon, the twenty-five-year-old
community of Cerro Gordo is based on permaculture—a farming technique
that integrates soil analysis, wind patterns, and water flows with the design of
settlements. South Carolina has Dewees Island, near Charleston; Illinois has
Prairie Crossing, near Grayslake. The federal government, in a program aimed
at reducing disaster relief costs, helped move Pattonsburg, Missouri, from the
Mississippi River floodplain to higher ground, and to rebuild it along sustainable lines. Coffee Creek Center in Indiana preserves the local watershed.
Civano, near Tucson, began as a "solar village." In Ithaca, New York, EcoVillage
was developed in cooperation with Cornell University. Existing cities from
Chattanooga to Pittsburgh to Austin, Texas; and from Denver to Santa Monica,
California, also have advanced programs in place. Mayor Jerry Brown has
worked to transform Oakland into what he calls an "ecopolis."

262 *The Rocky Mountain Institute*: It can be found on the Web at http://www.rmi.org.

262 *The home near Seattle*: Julie V. Iovine, "Muscle Houses Trying to Live Lean," *New York Times*, Aug. 30, 2001, p. F1.

262 "*A building is not something*": Stewart Brand, *How Buildings Learn: What Happens After They're Built* (New York: Viking, 1994), p. 188.

262 *Mindful of that, the designers*: In this, Audubon went through one of those learning experiences common to pioneers. A while after the building opened, staffers began noticing occasional small white shapes fluttering in and out of their fields of vision. These were at first considered isolated cases, but with time it became clear that the wool carpets, free as they were from pesticides, had become infested with a tiny white species of moth. The society responded by carefully screening available pesticides to find one benign to humans. But it soon became clear that not only was it benign to humans; it was also benign to the moths. Repeated applications failed, and eventually large new patches of replacement carpet began appearing on floors throughout the building. When Jan Beyea departed Audubon, there were joking references to his ducking the moth problem. At his going-away party, Beyea confronted the issue head-on. He said he had heard the rumors and was prepared to offer a solution. He suggested introducing predators into the building, possibly reptiles.

263 *In the book* Natural Capitalism: Paul Hawken, Amory Lovins, and L. Hunter Lovins, *Natural Capitalism: Creating the Next Industrial Revolution* (Boston: Little, Brown, 1999), p. 88. Hawken coined the phrase "natural capitalism" in 1994, in a speech by that name for the California Institute of Science.

263 "*constantly vary temperatures*": Ibid.

264 *What is the value of a 15 percent increase*: New tools to help in such decisions are now appearing. RMI consults with developers around the world and makes its standards and practices, along with case studies, available to subscribers on a Web site. *Environmental Building News* is an online trade journal. The Green Building Council offers a rating system. The Sustainable Buildings Industry Council makes a software design tool called Energy-10. It helps architects tailor buildings to specific climates and needs, as does the *Environmental Resource Guide*, developed in a joint effort by the American Institute of Architects and the U.S. Environmental Protection Agency.

264 *There, productivity gains*: Diane Wintroub Calmenson, "Let the Sun Shine," *Interiors & Sources*, April 1997, p. 40.

264 "*This building is about connections*": Quoted in ibid.

264 *McDonough wrote the preface*: David Gissen, ed., *Big & Green: Toward Sustainable Architecture in the 21st Century* (New York: Princeton Architectural Press; Washington, D.C.: National Building Museum, 2002), Commerzbank, p. 90; Condé Nast, p. 22; Ventiform, p. 20.

265 *which also served as the catalog*: Big & Green was published in conjunction with the exhibition of the same name, presented at the National Building Museum in Washington, D.C., Jan. 17–June 22, 2003.

265 "*The Earth's natural communities*": William McDonough, preface to ibid., p. 8.

266 *"when songbirds return to the site"*: The details listed here of McDonough's career come from various interviews the author conducted with him over several years, and were supplemented with Andrea Truppin's story "William
McDonough: 1999 Designer of the Year," *Interiors*, Jan. 1999, p. 2.

267 *"You don't have to be a member"*: Personal conversation with David Crockett,
1995; reviewed by him, Oct. 2004.

268 *"the city is doing a magnificent job"*: Personal conversation with Milton Jackson,
1995; updated with him in Sept. 2002.

269 *"If you look at the industrial age"*: Personal conversation with Crockett, 1995;
reviewed by him, Oct. 2004.

270 *Within twenty-five years*: James D. Wolfensohn, president of the World Bank
Group, "Remarks on the Comprehensive Development Framework," speaking in Hanoi, Vietnam, Feb. 23, 2000, http://web.worldbank.org/WBSITE/
EXTERNAL/NEWS/0,,contentMDK:20040925~menuPK:34475~pagePK:
34370~piPK:34424~theSitePK:4607,00.html."

270 *Like Chattanooga, this city of 1.6 million*: The population of the combined city
and metro area is 2.4 million.

270 *by 2002, after the World Trade Center attack*: Per a New York Times/CBS News
poll conducted in late August 2002. It found that 57 percent of New Yorkers
still wanted to be living in New York in four years. Cited in Janny Scott and
Marjorie Connelly, "For Many New Yorkers, a Tentative Normality," *New
York Times*, Sept. 11, 2002, p. G10.

270 *More than 99 percent of Curitibans*: Hawken, Lovins, and Lovins, *Natural
Capitalism*, p. 307.

271 *Like Lerner, his successor*: Mayor Taniguchi's second term ended in the fall of
2004, due to a mandatory term limit.

271 *An electronic sign in midtown*: More than one thousand trees are saved each day.

271 *"Urban diversity is the key"*: Personal conversation with Cassio Taniguchi,
1998; reviewed by his office, March 2004.

272 *"reproduction and multiplication" of urban centers*: Krier, *Architecture*, p. 124.

272 *"I would rather fight with the sheep"*: Personal conversation with Laudelino
Matoso, 1998.

272 *Each year the city has its herds shorn*: Personal conversation with Taniguchi,
1998; reviewed by his office, March 2004.

273 *"are distinctly cooler than cities"*: Ian L. McHarg, *Design with Nature* (Garden City,
N.Y.: Natural History Press, 1969), p. 64.

273 *It has also surrounded itself with an urban boundary*: Robert Freilich, editor of
Urban Lawyer, speaking at the "Smart Growth" conference in Albany, New
York, on March 3, 1999.

273 *More than thirty governors*: Harriet Tregoning, director of the EPA's Urban and
Economic Development Division, speaking at ibid.

273 *"Agriculture pays $3"*: Ed Thompson, speaking at ibid.

274 *"Even if the power they produce"*: "The Dawn of Micropower," *Economist*, Aug. 5,
2000, p. 75.

274 *That surge is fed by predictions*: Ibid.

274 *But how secure is an Internet*: This occurred in August 2003. Fifty million people were without power for several days.

274 *One such park is already up and running*: Steve Silberman, "The Energy Web," *Wired*, July 2001, p. 115.

275 *"The smarter energy network of the future"*: Ibid.

275 *"Our society is changing more rapidly"*: Ibid.

275 *"may now allow many countries"*: "The Electric Revolution," *Economist*, Aug. 5, 2000, p. 19.

277 *Meanwhile, a seedling of their concept*: With Levine and Yanarella, Dennis Marshall was the third member of the team that developed Emerald City.

278 *hyperlinking structure*: The concept of hyperlinked pages was first articulated in 1945, by computing pioneer Vannevar Bush.

278 *His interest in sustainable planning*: James Hrynyshyn, "City of Dreams," *New Scientist*, July 27, 2002, p. 38.

278 *"As long as your city can provide"*: Quoted in ibid.

278 *"a way of looking into the future"*: Christina DeMarco, a senior Vancouver planner, quoted in ibid.

279 *"Sustainability," he says*: Personal conversation with Levine, May 2004.

279 *"It's a utility, one that will let us"*: Ibid.

10. Industrial Ecology

285 *These blue-water rivers*: Vaclav Smil, *Cycles of Life: Civilization and the Biosphere* (New York: Scientific American Library, 1997), p. 50.

286 *It pulls a warm oceanic river*: William H. Calvin, "The Great Climate Flip-Flop," *The Atlantic Monthly*, January 1998, p. 47.

286 *This is the source of Europe's*: Jonathan Adams et al., "Sudden Climate Transitions During the Quaternary," *Progress in Physical Geography* 23 (1999), pp. 1–36, http://www.esd.ornl.gov/projects/qen/transit.html.

286 *"is effectively a suburb of Beijing"*: Tom Cahill, at the University of California at Davis, quoted in Associated Press, "Researchers Trace Seattle Pollutants to China," *Syracuse Post-Standard*, March 5, 1999, p. A6.

286 *Once there, they form transparent layers*: Robert L. Park, *Voodoo Science: The Road from Foolishness to Fraud* (New York: Oxford University Press, 2000), p. 32.

286 *But global industries now release*: There are many greenhouse gases. For the sake of brevity, this chapter focuses on carbon dioxide, which is the largest by volume.

286 *Scientists now believe*: Walter Gibbs, "Research Predicts Summer Doom for Northern Icecap," *New York Times*, July 11, 2000, p. F2.

286 *in fifteen million years*: Andrew C. Revkin, "Under All That Ice, Maybe Oil," *New York Times*, Nov. 30, 2004, p. F1.

287 *And with that, it draws less water*: W. S. Broecker, "What if the Global Conveyor Were to Shut Down? Reflections on a Possible Outcome of the Great Global Experiment," *GSA Today* 9, no. 1 (Jan. 1999), pp. 1–7. See also http://www.geosociety.org/pubs/gsatoday/gsat9901.htm.

287 *What if the weather in Berlin*: Calvin, "Great Climate Flip-Flop," p. 47.

287 *The response by a group*: Ibid.

287 *A sudden cooling of Europe's climate*: Ibid.

287 *At least twice, that cooling*: William K. Stevens, "Arctic Find May Jolt Sea's Climate Belt," *New York Times*, Dec. 7, 1999, p. F3.

287 *The so-called Little Ice Age*: William K. Stevens, "Scientists Studying Deep Ocean Currents for Clues to Climates," *New York Times*, Nov. 9, 1999, p. F5.

288 *"This is the largest change"*: Quoted in Rob Edwards, "Freezing Future," *New Scientist*, Nov. 27, 1999, p. 6.

288 *"Feedbacks are what determine thresholds"*: Calvin, "Great Climate Flip-Flop," p. 47.

288 *"The number of really big weather disasters"*: Quoted in Fred Pearce, "Insurers Count Cost of Global Warming," *New Scientist*, July 27, 2002, p. 7.

289 *"contributed substantially to the observed warming"*: Andrew C. Revkin, "A Shift in Stance on Global Warming Theory," *New York Times*, Oct. 26, 2000, p. A22.

289 *"It's time to take the filters out"*: Personal conversation with William McDonough, 1999; reviewed by him, Aug. 2004.

290 *"the power and magic"*: Ed Cohen-Rosenthal, "What Is Eco-Industrial Development?" (unpublished manuscript, Cornell University, Ithaca, N.Y., n.d.), ch. 1.

290 *The waste heat*: Ernest Lowe, John L. Warren, and Stephen R. Moran, *Discovering Industrial Ecology: An Executive Briefing and Sourcebook* (Columbus, Ohio: Battelle Press, 1997), p. 41.

290 *Now each American uses*: Hardin Tibbs, "Humane Ecostructure: Can Industry Become Gaia's Friend?" *Whole Earth Review* (Summer 1998), p. 61.

291 *"More than 90 percent"*: Quoted in Diane Wintroub Calmenson, "From Generation to Generation: A Conversation with William McDonough," *Interiors & Sources*, April 1997, p. 25.

291 *Each year Americans handle*: Paul Hawken, Amory Lovins, and L. Hunter Lovins, *Natural Capitalism: Creating the Next Industrial Revolution* (Boston: Little, Brown, 1999), p. 52.

291 *With the aluminum America wastes*: Ibid., p. 50.

291 *"Over the course of a decade"*: Ibid., p. 53.

291 *We have already run out of places*: Tibbs, "Humane Ecostructure," p. 61.

292 *"Because of the increasingly tight coupling"*: Brad Allenby, "Earth Systems Engineering and Management," *Technology and Society* 19, no. 4 (Winter 2000/2001), pp. 10–23.

292 *A hard-nosed realism*: My thanks to Ted Williams for the information in this passage. Ted is the Incite columnist for *Audubon* magazine and editor of *Fly Rod & Reel Magazine*. We spoke in September 2004.

293 *three more planet Earths to support everyone*: Anne Simon Moffat, "Ecologists Look at the Big Picture," *Science*, Sept. 13, 1996, p. 1490.

293 *"How do we save business?"*: Hawken is a well-known activist and popular speaker at conferences and workshops around the world. This quotation and the others that appear here without notes are catchphrases used in his talks.

293 *The pace of growth is quickening*: Tibbs, "Humane Ecostructure," p. 61.

293 *That is industrial ecology*: The term "industrial ecology" was coined by Robert Frosch and Nicholas Gallopoulos, two General Motors engineers, for a 1989 pa-

per that built on earlier work by the economist Robert Ayres. In it they recommended that an industrial system be viewed as "analogous in its functioning to a community of biological organisms," in which "each process and network of processes must be viewed as a dependent and interrelated part of a larger whole."

293 *"Sustainable development will constitute"*: Stewart L. Hart, "Beyond Greening: Strategies for a Sustainable World," *Harvard Business Review* (Jan.–Feb. 1997), p. 66.

294 *"the total amount of energy"*: Personal conversation with Wouter van Dieren, 1998; reviewed by him, April 2004.

294 *McDonough cites*: Personal conversation with McDonough, 1999; reviewed by him, Aug. 2004.

294 *"The world is moving from an era"*: Speaking on the "Natural Design" panel, at the Bioneers conference "Practical Solutions for Restoring the Earth," Oct. 31–Nov. 1, 1997, San Francisco. Transcript by TUC Radio, San Francisco, http://www.tucradio.org/contact.html.

295 *Working behind the scenes*: Huisingh is a senior scientist in the Energy, Environment, and Resources Center at the University of Tennessee in Knoxville. As a private consultant, he works with industry and with international agencies ranging from UNEP (United Nations Environment Programme) to the World Bank. He also holds part-time faculty positions at three other schools—in the United States, Sweden, and Mexico.

295 *As described in the book*: *Lean Thinking* was authored by the industrial experts James Womack and Daniel Jones.

295 *is now being taken up in the West*: Hawken, Lovins, and Lovins, *Natural Capitalism*, p. 125.

295 *"What happens if cars become"*: Personal conversation with van Dieren, 1998; reviewed by him, April 2004.

295 *once the easy efficiency gains*: Personal conversation with Richard Levine, 1995; reviewed by him, May 2004.

295 *"If they make twice as many boxes"*: Personal conversation with McDonough, 1999; reviewed by him, Aug. 2004. The concept of "dematerialization" was first articulated by Buckminster Fuller.

295 *"You are continuing a system"*: Personal conversation with van Dieren, 1998; reviewed by him, April 2004.

296 *"It makes thousands of blossoms"*: William McDonough and Michael Braungart, "The NEXT Industrial Revolution," *Atlantic Monthly*, Oct. 1998, p. 82.

296 *"Cradle-to-grave analysis"*: Personal conversation with McDonough, 1999; reviewed by him, Aug. 2004.

296 *Water flowing out of the production plant*: McDonough and Braungart, "The NEXT Industrial Revolution," p. 82.

296 *toss it in the backyard to feed the soil*: Personal conversation with McDonough, 1995; reviewed by him, Aug. 2004.

296 *The Zero Emissions Research and Initiatives*: The ZERI team includes George Chan of Mauritius, who has had an influential role in the formation of these

concepts. Chan also worked with Braungart's group on the farming system mentioned in chapter 9. More specifically, he worked on development of the farm in Brazil.

296　*"advanced process engineering"*: Gunter Pauli, *Breakthroughs: What Business Can Offer Society* (Surrey, U.K.: Epsilon Press, 1996), p. 206.

297　*The algae are then channeled*: ZERI Systems: "Beer Bakes Bread and Feeds Fish," ZERI Web site, http://www.zeri.org/systems.htm#draw (accessed Sept. 6, 2004). According to Pauli, a ZERI brewery generates "food, fuel and fertilizer . . . And what is most critical is that the system, without waste, generates up to four times more jobs." See *Breakthroughs*, p. 217.

297　*And a U.S. textbook*: Sherwood C. Reed, E. Joe Middlebrooks, and Ronald W. Crites, *Natural Systems for Waste Management and Treatment* (New York: McGraw-Hill, 1988).

297　*Natural Systems International*: Personal conversation with Michael Ogden, 2002.

298　*As water is drawn up*: Christopher Hallowell, "Plants That Purify: Nature's Way to Treat Sewage," *Audubon*, Jan.–Feb. 1992, p. 76. "A small group of plants with large leaf structure surfaces, such as the African calla lily, can suck up water at a prodigious rate—about 1,000 gallons per day, depending on sunlight—and release it into the air through evapotranspiration."

298　*He went on to design systems*: He describes those projects in his book: B. C. Wolverton and John D. Wolverton, *Growing Clean Water: Nature's Solution to Water Pollution* (Picayune, Miss.: WES, Inc., 2001).

298　*an early Wolverton system*: In Denham Springs, Louisiana.

298　*"One early summer morning"*: Hallowell, "Plants That Purify," p. 76.

299　*It has become a tourist draw*: Sim Van der Ryn and Stuart Cowan, *Ecological Design* (Washington, D.C.: Island Press, 1996), p. 118.

299　*And once wastewater has passed*: Ibid., p. 119.

299　*"We and the plants both speak"*: Personal conversation with Robert Socolow, 1995. Socolow heads Princeton University's Center for Energy and Environmental Studies.

299　*"The ability of complex, interdependent"*: McDonough and Braungart, "The NEXT Industrial Revolution," p. 82.

300　*"There is one emission"*: Personal conversation with Jens Soth, 1998.

300　*"get awards for being clean"*: Personal conversation with Socolow, 1995.

300　*Polyvinyl chloride—commonly called PVC*: The film *Blue Vinyl*—a "toxic comedy" by Judith Helfand—details the process, risks, and true costs embodied in vinyl siding. The Web site is http://www.bluevinyl.org.

300　*One problem with it*: "Polyvinyl Chloride White Paper," HDR Sustainable Design Services, Aug. 12, 1999, http://www.hdrinc.com/search/.

300　*"You need to eliminate everything"*: Personal conversation with Michael Braungart, 1998; reviewed by him, Aug. 2004.

301　*he heads a group*: Hamburger Umweltinstitut.

301　*"Today . . . shoes are relatively nice"*: Personal conversation with Braungart, 1995; reviewed by him, Aug. 2004.

302 *While PVC and other major toxins*: Sneaker maker Nike, double-teamed by McDonough and Braungart, has pledged to stop using PVC in its shoe soles.

302 *Then make sure*: Personal conversation with McDonough, 1995; reviewed by him, Aug. 2004.

302 *Their "industrial ecosystem"*: In Kalundborg, it is generally referred to as an "industrial metabolism." The term "industrial ecosystem" is more common elsewhere. According to Suren Erkman, the first use of the term "industrial ecosystem" was apparently in a paper given at the 1977 meeting of the German Geological Association. The paper was dedicated to the economist Nicholas Georgescu-Roegen (deviser of an economic theory based on the 2nd Law of Thermodynamics). But by that time the general concept had been around for a decade in one form or another. Howard Odum and other systems ecologists had sensed that industry might be a subsystem of nature. The nuclear physicist Ted Taylor wrote about industry and natural process in the late 1960s and formed a company with the economist Robert Ayres—who would go on to articulate the concept of "industrial metabolism." Various UN agencies after 1972 were involved in formalizing ideas like "zero pollution" and "non-waste technology and production." According to Lowe, Warren, and Moran, in *Discovering Industrial Ecology*, p. 136, at about the same time Nelson Nemerow, the industrial-waste specialist, proposed an "environmentally balanced industrial complex" in which different companies would use each other's material and energy wastes for feedstocks. Erkman states that as the two great oil price shocks of the 1970s rippled through Western economies, Japan, with no oil reserves of its own, was the first nation to make the use of ecological principles in manufacturing official. Erkman's paper "Industrial Ecology: A Historical View" appeared in the *Journal of Cleaner Production*, 1997, vol. 5, pp. 1–10.

303 *For instance, one has been identified*: Lowe, Warren, and Moran, *Discovering Industrial Ecology*, p. 135.

304 *along the Houston, Texas, ship channel*: Ibid., p. 131.

304 *"Industrial Ecology and Global Change"*: Robert Socolow, Clinton Andrews, Frans Berkhout, and Valerie Thomas, eds., *Industrial Ecology and Global Change* (Cambridge, U.K.: Cambridge University Press, 1994).

304 *The governor of the surrounding province*: Personal conversation with Ernest Lowe, 2002.

304 *Donald Huisingh worked*: Lowe, Warren, and Moran, *Discovering Industrial Ecology*, p. 154.

304 *In Nova Scotia, Raymond Côté*: Personal conversation with Marian Chertow, 2002.

304 *"I find communities are very receptive"*: Personal conversation with Lowe, 2002.

304 *The Southern Waste Information eXchange*: The Southern Waste Information eXchange (SWIX) can be found at http://www.wastexchange.org/.

305 *Pauli believes it can now help*: Pauli, *Breakthroughs*, pp. 216–17.

305 *They simply add waste exchange*: Hardin Tibbs, "Industrial Ecology: An Environmental Agenda for Industry," GBN, pdf, June 1993, http://www.gbn.com/ArticleDisplayServlet.srv?aid=235.

305 *"Where tall hierarchies served growth"*: Tachi Kiuchi and William K. Shireman, *What I Learned in the Rainforest: A CEO Explores Creativity, Innovation, and Profit in the New Economy* (prepublication MS draft, Sept. 10, 1998), p. 16.

305 *"ecologies of scale"*: Ibid.

306 *"Complexity comes naturally"*: Personal conversation with Soth, 1998.

306 *These "trees" can feature several hundred lines*: From LCA's beginnings under SETAC—the Society of Environmental Toxicology and Chemistry—there have now evolved some thirty individual systems. Two in wide use are the Ecopoints method, from Switzerland, and the Eco-Indicator, developed in the Netherlands.

307 *EPS can take into account*: Personal conversation with Sven Ryding, 1995.

307 *Wouter van Dieren's organization*: Van Dieren's organization is IMSA (Instituut voor Milieu-en Systeemanalyse, Amsterdam). See the IMSA Web site at http://www.imsa.nl.

307 *the pages of their book* Cradle to Cradle: William McDonough and Michael Braungart, *Cradle to Cradle: Remaking the Way We Make Things* (New York: North Point Press, 2000).

307 *Although it looks and feels like paper*: Their book *Cradle to Cradle* is a "Durabook," a concept developed by Charles Melcher. His New York–based company, Melcher Media, has a patent pending on his system.

307 *"creates a financial incentive"*: Walter Stahel, "From Products to Services: Selling Performance Instead of Goods," *IPTS Report* 27 (Sept. 1998), http://www.product-life.org/publications.htm.

308 *That's why decomposers outnumber*: Lowe, Warren, and Moran, *Discovering Industrial Ecology*, p. 25.

308 *"We need to design industrial ecosystems"*: Tibbs, "Humane Ecostructure," p. 61.

308 *"design for reincarnation"*: Personal conversation with Braungart, April 2004.

309 *their company MBDC*: McDonough Braungart Design Chemistry.

309 *It featured an interior*: Ibid.

309 *It reclaims tens of thousands*: Hawken, Lovins, and Lovins, *Natural Capitalism*, p. 184.

309 *this new category of "green collar" jobs*: *Green-Collar Jobs* is the title of a book by Alan Thein Durning.

309 *"productivity can go* down": Paul Hawken, *The Ecology of Commerce* (New York: HarperBusiness, 1993), p. 69.

310 *molecules called ATP*: Adenosine triphosphate. In plants, ATP is produced by the chloroplasts.

311 *Our industries have evolved*: Fuelwood is roughly 9 percent hydrogen; coal is 50 percent, oil 75 percent, and natural gas 80 percent hydrogen.

312 *Various fuels can be extracted*: Hydropower produced by dams has long been used. But concerns over the destruction of spawning fish populations have increased, even as the diversion of water for irrigation drains the lakes and rivers that are its source.

312 *Where it's breezy, windmills*: Early models of wind power generators had blades that turned rapidly and were a hazard to flying birds. Recent models are larger,

with blades that turn very slowly, posing less danger. Due to pressure from environmentalists, they are also less likely to be sited in bird flyways.

312 *By comparison, today's fossil fuel plants*: Fusion power, a nuclear process that mimics what happens to hydrogen in the sun, is still in the research stage.

313 *In the roughly twenty years*: For a detailed description of their work, see Janine M. Benyus, *Biomimicry: Innovation Inspired by Nature* (New York: Morrow, 1997), pp. 63–86.

314 *And according to the marketing consulting group*: Frost & Sullivan news release, "Millennium to Dawn with 'Green Power' Sunrise" (Jan. 2000).

315 *Many of the world's carmakers*: Ballard fuel cells are of the "proton exchange membrane" type generally referred to as PEMs.

316 *One Chicago newspaper*: Robert Frenay, "Water Power," *Audubon*, May–June 1996, p. 25.

316 *open-source prototype called the Hypercar*: RMI is releasing the engineering innovations it develops during the car's design phase to all interested parties, in order to encourage the uptake of those developments into auto design and manufacturing worldwide.

316 *"Very exciting things are happening"*: Amory Lovins, speaking on the "Natural Design" panel at the Bioneers conference "Practical Solutions for Restoring the Earth," Oct. 31–Nov. 1, 1997.

317 *"Fuel cells begin to look very attractive"*: Robert Nowak, quoted in Anne Eisenberg, "What's Next: Fuel Cell May Be the Future Battery," *New York Times*, Oct. 21, 1999, p. G13.

317 *Their solution was to evolve fats*: Ruth A. Eblen and William R. Eblen, eds., *The Encyclopedia of the Environment* (Boston: Houghton Mifflin, 1994), p. 353.

317 *It should be noted here*: Addison Bain, former manager of NASA's hydrogen program, spent a decade researching the *Hindenburg* disaster. He found that the craft's outer skin had been painted with a coating nearly identical with a compound used today as a flame accelerator in rocket fuel. Although the ship's builders let hydrogen take the blame, he notes that they rectified the coating problem in the next airship they built. From Brad Lemley, "The Hindenburg Revisited," sidebar to "Lovin' Hydrogen," *Discover*, Nov. 2001, p. 55.

318 *They could be paid for*: Ford has a major initiative in the works exploring this option. In 2001 BMW toured the United States with a fleet of fifteen hydrogen-powered internal combustion hybrids (they could also run on gasoline).

318 *Teams in England and the U.S.*: Chris Melhuish at the University of the West of England in Bristol; Stuart Wilkinson of the University of South Florida in Tampa; Randy Cortright at the University of Wisconsin in Madison.

319 *Since 1986 a public/private effort*: The station is in Neunburg vorm Wald.

319 *"We would like to use"*: Personal conversation with Elias Greenbaum, May 2002.

319 *Agriculture was our first*: Personal conversation with Armin Reller of the University of Hamburg's Institute of Inorganic and Applied Chemistry, March 1998.

319   *Since the early 1980s*: Personal conversation with Ingo Rechenberg, 1998; reviewed by him, March 2004.

320   *"live in sulfur-poor anaerobic conditions"*: "Anaerobic" means "devoid of oxygen."

320   *"The cell culture can go"*: "Common Algae Can Be Valuable Source for Hydrogen Fuel" (news release, University of California at Berkeley, Feb. 21, 2000).

320   *Someday we may even see*: Smil, *Cycles of Life*, p. 11. "Water is . . . by far the most important donor of hydrogen in photosynthesis."

321   *"can take its place in a larger system"*: Personal conversation with Levine, 1995; reviewed by him, May 2004.

321   *"Let's say we've got this planet"*: Personal conversation with McDonough, 1999; reviewed by him, Aug. 2004.

322   *"is shifting from being"*: Brad Allenby, "Earth Systems Engineering," *Green Business Letter*, Dec. 1999, p. 8.

323   *"It's not about respecting biodiversity"*: Personal conversation with Braungart, April 2004.

323   *"The unique attribute"*: Kiuchi and Shireman, *What I Learned in the Rainforest*, p. 12.

11. The Real Conservatives

325   *algae that eat calcium*: In the form of calcium carbonate. The calcium enters into many different compounds as it passes through the cycles described in this section.

325   *runoff from onshore*: According to Christopher Guay (Jan. 10, 2003), a researcher at the Earth Sciences Division of Lawrence Berkeley National Laboratory, in Berkeley, California, roughly 1 percent of the falling shells reach the ocean floor at any given time, with the rest dissolving into solution and being reabsorbed by the algae or other life forms. Over millions of years, however, the cumulative loss of that 1 percent would amount to total depletion of calcium from the system if it weren't for the tectonic recycling effect of ocean floor limestone being thrust up on land, and then the dissolving effect on that limestone of rainwater, with its subsequent runoff back into the sea.

325   *In the ongoing cycles*: The snowflake analogy used here takes poetic license with the shell of the coccolithophore, which is an accretion of microscopic geometric discs.

327   *"Outside the circle"*: The University of Chicago economist Melvin Reder, quoted in a review of his book *Economics*. John Casti, "Prophet Warning," *New Scientist*, May 15, 1999, p. 44.

327   *"they sat on the platform with you?"*: Quoted in Sylvia Nassar, "The Sometimes Dismal Nobel Prize," *New York Times*, Oct. 13, 2001, p. C3.

327   *"Every government in the world"*: Casti, "Prophet Warning," p. 44.

327   *The Cold War*: No less extraordinary is the fact that the schools of thought behind that conflict were devised and adopted without any hard numbers to back them up.

327   *"The ideas of economists"*: Quoted in William R. Waters, "A Review of the

Troops: Social Economics in the Twentieth Century," *Review of Social Economy* 51, no. 3 (1993), p. 262.

329 *In response there was an institutional lurch*: Although the University of Chicago economists were the influential American voice for neoconservative economics, they and others built on the work of an Austrian group led by the Nobel laureate F. A. Hayek. See, for instance, his *Denationalisation of Money: The Argument Refined: An Analysis of the Theory and Practice of Concurrent Currencies.*

330 *the Bretton Woods agreement*: The conference that produced this agreement took place in Bretton Woods, New Hampshire.

331 *"a worldwide business environment"*: Harry Gary, CEO of United Technologies, quoted in Stephen G. Leahy, "Freer Trade Lets Industry Call the Shots," *Gazette of Montreal*, Nov. 16, 1993, p. B3.

332 *one of the world's largest banks*: Citicorp and Citigroup.

332 *"ineffective, unnecessary, and obsolete"*: George Shultz, William Simon, and Walter Wriston, "Who Needs the IMF?" *Wall Street Journal*, Feb. 3, 1998, p. A22.

332 *Joseph Stiglitz*: Stiglitz is now a professor at Columbia University. There he has formed the Initiative for Policy Dialogue, in order to widen the discussion on global trade and finance.

332 *Complaining about the mechanistic*: Joseph Stiglitz, "What I Learned at the World Economic Summit," *New Republic*, April 17, 2000, p. 56.

332 *"I'm not an economist"*: Njoki Njoroge Njehû, director of 50 Years Is Enough, U.S. Network for Economic Justice, appearing before the House Committee on Banking and Financial Services, Subcommittee on Domestic and International Monetary Policy, *The Administration's Fiscal Year 2000 Authorization Requests for International Financial Institutions*, 106th Cong., 1st sess., April 21, 1999, serial no. 106-15 (Washington, D.C.: U.S. Government Printing Office, 1999), p. 113.

333 *ESAF*: Enhanced Structural Adjustment Facility.

333 *"it was reported that annual real"*: Judy Biggert, testimony before the House Committee on Banking and Financial Services, Subcommittee on Domestic and International Monetary Policy, in op. cit., p. 62.

334 *the Netherlands has more votes*: Chalmers Johnson, *Blowback: The Costs and Consequences of American Empire* (New York: Henry Holt, 2000), p. 210.

334 *overruling tariffs and quotas*: Lori Wallach, "Corporate Protectionism: Recent Trade Agreements Value Profits over People," *Public Citizen News*, special anniversary issue (2001), p. 10, http://www.citizen.org/documents/globalization.pdf.

334 *"I was dismayed"*: Stiglitz, "What I Learned at the World Economic Summit," p. 56.

334 *"There hasn't been a group"*: Quoted in Jerry Useem, "There's Something Happening Here," *Fortune*, May 15, 2000, p. 232.

334 *"stand a little structural adjustment"*: Ibid.

335 *"turned many struggling nations"*: Clifford Cobb, Ted Halstead, and Jonathan Rowe, "If the GDP Is Up, Why Is America Down?" *Atlantic Monthly*, Oct. 1995, p. 59.

336 *Accounting sleight of hand*: As this book goes to press, the United Nations is being investigated for fraudulent financial practices involving kickbacks to UN officials from the former Iraqi dictator Saddam Hussein, relating to the UN-administered "oil for food" program.

336 *Due to a recent wave*: Followed by a wave of tricky-accounting scandals in Europe.

336 *Americans now view business leaders*: Paul Krugman, "Plutocracy and Politics," *New York Times*, June 14, 2002, p. A37.

336 *It would require developing countries*: Alice H. Amsden, "Why Are Globalizers So Provincial?" *New York Times*, Jan. 31, 2002, p. A25. This is also noted in John Madeley, *Big Business, Poor Peoples: The Impact of Transnational Corporations on the World's Poor* (London: Zed Books, 1999), p. 22, and was further described to me by Ernst von Weizsäcker in a personal conversation, March 1998.

337 *"forced developing countries"*: Joseph Stiglitz, "The Roaring Nineties," *Atlantic Monthly*, Oct. 2002, p. 75.

337 *"This . . . approach toward agriculture"*: John Ralston Saul, "The Collapse of Globalism and the Rebirth of Nationalism," *Harper's Magazine*, March 2004, p. 35.

338 *"You try to shut the door"*: Thomas L. Friedman, *The Lexus and the Olive Tree* (New York: Farrar, Straus and Giroux, 2000), p. 395.

338 *"You cannot build an emerging society"*: Ibid., p. 302.

339 *As a result, more than half*: "The Chips Are Down," *New Scientist*, April 27, 2002, p. 33. Specifically, the report states, "General Motors' annual sales amount to more than the GNP of Thailand or Norway, Ford's add up to more than the GNP of Poland, Walmart stores have a turnover that outstrips the GNPs of Saudi Arabia, Greece, Portugal, Venezuela and the Philippines. Although sales and GNP are far from identical measures, and nations and corporations are too different to compare simply, the figures illustrate the giant economic clout of big companies."

340 *In their 1989 book*: Herman E. Daly and John B. Cobb, Jr., *For the Common Good: Redirecting the Economy Toward Community, the Environment, and a Sustainable Future* (Boston: Beacon Press, 1989).

341 *Clifford Cobb*: Clifford Cobb is the son of John Cobb, Jr.

341 *"The GDP is simply a gross measure"*: Cobb, Halstead, and Rowe, "If the GDP Is Up, Why Is America Down?" p. 59.

341 *We became "consumers"*: Ibid.

341 *Over time, as GNP became GDP*: Ibid. Due to the Soviet Union's adherence to the "labor" theory of value, much the same thing was happening on the other side of the Iron Curtain.

342 *"It is as if a business"*: Ibid.

342 *"Politicians can no longer"*: Ibid.

343 *"Today the main currencies"*: George Soros, "The Capitalist Threat," *Atlantic Monthly*, Feb. 1997, p. 48.

343 *A former colleague of Herman Daly's*: Since this interview Costanza has moved to an endowed professorship in ecological economics at the University of

Vermont. He also directs the Gund Institute for Ecological Economics there (http://www.uvm.edu/giee).

343 "*a poor choice of boundary*": Robert Costanza et al., "Modeling Complex Ecological Systems: Toward an Evolutionary, Dynamic Understanding of People and Nature," *Bioscience* 43, no. 8 (Sept. 1993), p. 545.

344 "*In this case we're not doing urban*": Personal conversation with Robert Costanza, 1999.

344 *Reviewing contributions by seventeen biomes*: Costanza et al., "The Value of the World's Ecosystem Services and Natural Capital," *Nature*, May 15, 1997, p. 253.

344 "*If asked to identify*": Quoted in Peter Barnes, *Who Owns the Sky? Our Common Assets and the Future of Capitalism* (Washington, D.C.: Island Press, 2001), p. 40.

345 *One study found that the real cost*: "Cigarettes Cost U.S. $7 per Pack Sold, Study Says," *New York Times*, April 12, 2002, p. A20.

345 *A German report found*: Cited in Wouter van Dieren, ed., *Taking Nature into Account: Toward a Sustainable National Income: A Report to the Club of Rome* (New York: Copernicus/Springer-Verlag, 1995), p. 180.

345 "*Simply stated, the present market*": Paul Hawken and William McDonough, "Seven Steps to Doing Good Business," *Inc.*, Nov. 1993, p. 79.

345 *According to economist David Pearce*: He was speaking at the "Eco-Efficiency: A Modern Feature of Environmental Technology" conference, held in Düsseldorf, March 2–3, 1998. Another study was conducted in 1997 by the Earth Council. It's cited in Lester R. Brown, *Eco-Economy: Building an Economy for the Earth* (New York: W. W. Norton, 2001), p. 240. It estimated $700 billion.

346 "*a stock that yields a flow*": Robert Costanza, "Valuation of Ecological Systems," in Gary K. Meffe and C. Ronald Carroll, eds., *Principles of Conservation Biology* (Sunderland, Mass.: Sinauer Associates, 1994), p. 449.

347 "*measures the difference*": Paul Hawken, Amory Lovins, and L. Hunter Lovins, *Natural Capitalism: Creating the Next Industrial Revolution* (Boston: Little, Brown, 1999), p. 284.

348 *But with it those systems*: Ibid., p. 283.

348 "*How clean a car would you buy*": Ibid.

348 *private sector initiatives*: On the consumer side, market recognition for green products is being enhanced by eco-labels. Germany's Blue Angel was the first. The European Union now has the Flower eco-label, while the United States has Green Seal and Scandinavia the Swan. Dozens of other countries provide them as well. Then there are industry sanctions like Europe's Blue Flag Campaign for ecotourism and those of the Forest Stewardship Council and the Marine Stewardship Council, for forest products and seafood. Lisa Mastny, "Ecolabeling Gains Ground," in Lester R. Brown et al., eds., *Vital Signs 2002: The Trends That Are Shaping Our Future* (New York: W. W. Norton, 2002), pp. 124–25.

348 *On the policy side*: Those efforts include the Genuine Progress Indicator, championed by Redefining Progress. They also include the Human

Development Index, designed by the United Nations Development Programme; and the economist Hazel Henderson's Country Futures Indicators. The prominent European environmentalist Wouter van Dieren has joined others in calling for the assembly of an international working group to compare and refine the various new approaches into one system.

348 *Another policy change*: Using taxes to correct market "maladjustments" was first suggested in the 1920s by the British economist Arthur Pigou.

348 *"green tax shift"*: With a green tax shift, government revenue neither grows nor declines. But that shift does discourage the externalizations now common in most industries, even as it refocuses their constant drive to cut costs, steering them away from "labor productivity" and toward the new discipline of "resource productivity." Although no plan today shifts more than a few percent of federal revenue in this way, optimists believe green taxes could replace much of the income tax by mid-century. Sweden was the first country to try a green tax shift. It began cutting its income tax in 1991, offsetting it with new levies on carbon and sulfur emissions. Since then, tolls on energy use, water use, pollution, or waste disposal have been used to lower income taxes in Denmark, Spain, the Netherlands, the United Kingdom, Finland, Germany, Italy, and France. Some schemes would go further, allowing a reduction of the capital gains taxes paid by investors.

348 *"That," says von Weizsäcker*: Personal conversation with von Weizsäcker, 1998.

348 *"the tragedy of the commons"*: This concept was articulated by the ecologist Garrett Hardin.

349 *they can then be sold or traded*: Richard Sandor, who helped found the Chicago futures exchange, now heads the Chicago Climate Exchange, which trades those permits.

349 *Peter Barnes*: In 1988 Barnes founded Working Assets Long Distance. That company donates a percentage of its sales to social and environmental causes, which customers mark off on their bills.

349 *Barnes describes how such a setup*: Barnes, *Who Owns the Sky?*, pp. 50–53, 64, 127–29.

349 *"It would go a long way"*: John Tierney, "A Popular Idea: Give Oil Money to the People Rather Than the Despots," *New York Times*, Sept. 10, 2003, p. A11.

350 *"If you can destroy a nightingale"*: Personal conversation with Michael Braungart, 1998; reviewed by him, Aug. 2004.

350 *"A generation ago"*: Paul Krugman, in his introduction to the pamphlet "Tax Waste, Not Work: How Changing What We Tax Can Lead to a Stronger Economy and a Cleaner Environment," by M. Jeff Hamond et al. (San Francisco: Redefining Progress, April 1997), p. 4.

352 *"Show me the chairman"*: Bonnie Durrance, "The Evolutionary Vision of Dee Hock: From Chaos to Chaords," *Training & Development* 51, no. 4 (April 1997), p. 24. This passage reviewed by Dee Hock, Oct. 2004.

352 *"complex, self-organizing, nonlinear"*: Personal conversation with Dee Hock, Oct. 2004.

352 *In the roughly three decades*: Visa is a reformulation of the now-defunct BankAmerica card.

352 *the world's largest commercial enterprise*: Jeffrey Kutler, "Looking Beyond Cards, Visa's First Chief Has Found Wider Worlds to Conquer," *American Banker*, April 16, 1998, p. 1. This passage reviewed by Hock, Oct. 2004.

352 *Along the way Hock's self-organizing*: From the speaker biography of the Second Annual Bionomics Conference, Oct. 22, 1994, San Francisco. This passage reviewed by Hock, Oct. 2004.

352 *"at the speed of light"*: Personal conversation with Hock, Oct. 2004.

353 *"The human brain amounts"*: Michael Rothschild, *Bionomics: The Inevitability of Capitalism* (New York: Henry Holt, 1990), p. 96.

353 *Now linked by nine million miles*: Dee Hock, "Institutions in the Age of Mindcrafting," speaking at the Second Annual Bionomics Conference, Oct. 22, 1994, San Francisco. The transcript is credited to the Cascade Policy Institute, http://www.cascadepolicy.org/. This passage reviewed by Hock, Oct. 2004.

353 *"I don't think we got Visa"*: Quoted in Kutler, "Looking Beyond Cards," p. 1. This passage reviewed by Hock, Oct. 2004.

353 *"not as horrible disasters"*: Hock, "Institutions in the Age of Mindcrafting." This passage reviewed by Hock, Oct. 2004.

353 *"Everything has both intended"*: Ibid. This passage reviewed by Hock, Oct. 2004.

354 *"If your organization is not"*: Quoted in Kutler, "Looking Beyond Cards," p. 1. This passage reviewed by Hock, Oct. 2004.

354 *"Before the microprocessor"*: Rothschild, *Bionomics*, pp. 104–105.

354 *Even though all organizations*: Toby J. Tetenbaum, "Shifting Paradigms: From Newton to Chaos," *Organizational Dynamics* 6, no. 4 (1998), p. 21.

354 *Ernst & Young even sent*: Ibid.

355 *"We gather data about financial markets"*: Quoted in John Brockman, *The Third Culture: Beyond the Scientific Revolution* (New York: Simon & Schuster, 1995), p. 371.

355 *"predictive signals"*: "Company Profile," Prediction Company Web site, n.d., http://www.predict.com/html/company.htm (accessed Sept. 2004).

356 *cell phones would top out at 900,000*: It's now more than ten times that number.

356 *"Most forecasting is about"*: Personal conversation with Lawrence Wilkinson, 1997.

356 *"Part of what scenario planning"*: Personal conversation with Stewart Brand, 1997; reviewed by him, Oct. 2004.

356 *It also anticipated*: Personal conversation with Wilkinson, 1997.

357 *"Certainly in the last twenty years"*: This and the following are from personal conversations with Brian Arthur, ranging from 1995 to 2004. Reviewed by him, Oct. 2004.

357 *"Many of us believe that self-organization"*: Quoted in Brockman, *Third Culture*, p. 368.

358 *"I have a theory about what you're going to do"*: Personal conversation with Stuart Kauffman, 1995.

360 *equal to 10^{18} BTUs*: BTU (British thermal unit): "A measure of heat energy;

the amount needed to raise the temperature of one pound of water by one degree Fahrenheit." Per http://www.solarnow.org/glossary.htm.

360 *Putting that amount in perspective*: Nicholas Georgescu-Roegen, "Energy and Economic Myths," repr. from *Southern Economic Journal* 41, no. 3 (Jan. 1975), http://dieoff.com/page148.htm.

360 "*the mother and the nurse*": Quoted by Silvana De Gleria, "Nicholas Georgescu-Roegen's Approach to Economic Value: A Theory Based on Nature with Man at Its Core," in Kozo Mayumi and John M. Gowdy, eds., *Bioeconomics and Sustainability: Essays in Honor of Nicholas Georgescu-Roegen* (Cheltenham, U.K.: Edward Elgar, 1999), p. 85.

360 "*Had it not been possible*": Ibid.

361 *The sun's heat never disappears*: Physicists call that gradual but irreversible dilution "entropy." Thus, by an awkward inversion of language, they identify the concentrated heat energy in the sun as "low-entropy," meaning "undiluted."

362 "*the concept of throughput*": Quoted in Mayumi and Gowdy, *Bioeconomics and Sustainability*, p. 140.

363 *That's why they felt*: Mayumi and Gowdy, *Bioeconomics and Sustainability*, p. 126.

364 *A socialist, he criticized Marx*: Ibid., p. 128.

364 *Engels misunderstood it*: Ibid., p. 28. The 1st Law of Thermodynamics states that the total amount of energy in the universe never changes.

364 *Unlike everything else in nature*: Ibid., p. 129.

364 *In his book* The Natural Economic Order: Werner Onken, "A Market Economy Without Capitalism," *American Journal of Economics and Sociology* 59, no. 4 (Oct. 2000), pp. 609–22, http://userpage.fu-berlin.de/~roehrigw/onken/engl.htm.

364 "*the original capitalists*": Quoted in Mayumi and Gowdy, *Bioeconomics and Sustainability*, p. 129.

364 *Since we get our energy solely*: Ibid.

365 *Looking to economics*: Ibid., p. 134.

365 "*Money circulates in a closed loop*": Ibid., p. 135.

365 *The implications of the 2nd Law*: Ibid., p. 137.

365 *The models presented*: Ibid., pp. 52–53.

366 "*commodity fetishists*": Ibid., p. 85.

366 "*a scholar's scholar*": Paul A. Samuelson, quoted by Herman E. Daly, "How Long Can Neoclassical Economists Ignore the Contributions of Georgescu-Roegen?" in Mayumi and Gowdy, *Bioeconomics and Sustainability*, p. 13.

366 *Bringing us up to par*: This idea was first expressed by the ecologist Alfred Lotka, who articulated the link between what he called "endosomatic" and "exosomatic" energy outlays.

367 *We would soon, he grumbled*: Herman E. Daly and John B. Cobb, Jr., *For the Common Good: Redirecting the Economy Toward Community, the Environment, and a Sustainable Future*, 2nd ed. (Boston: Beacon Press, 1994), p. 197.

367 *Since matter is the vehicle*: Mayumi and Gowdy, *Bioeconomics and Sustainability*, p. 100.

367 *matter dissipates, too*: Ibid., p. 142.

367 *So, too, G-R said*: Ibid., p. 96.

367 *In a familiar example*: Ibid., p. 76.

368 *If we try to reconcentrate it*: Ibid., p. 96.

368 *G-R's argument nonetheless holds*: His styling of that as a 4th Law of Thermodynamics is widely regarded as overreaching.

369 *The result is that once money*: Dieter Suhr, "The Neutral Money Network: A Critical Analysis of Traditional Money and the Financial Innovation 'Neutral Money' " (University of Augsburg, Germany, 1990), http://userpage.fu-berlin.de/~roehrigw/suhr/nngengl.html.

369 *In the end, the circulation*: Margit Kennedy, *Interest and Inflation Free Money* (Okemos, Mich.: Seva International, 1995), http://userpage.fu-berlin.de/~roehrigw/kennedy/english/chap1.htm.

370 *In that simple act*: Suhr, "Neutral Money Network."

370 *"Control of the* quantity *of money"*: "Modern Money Mechanics: A Workbook on Bank Reserves and Deposit Expansion," Federal Reserve Bank of Chicago, posted by the Monques Index, a Web site with extensive links relating to the history and function of money, http:landru.i-link-2.net/monques/mmm2.html#Modern (accessed Sept. 2004).

371 *"lends it into existence"*: Sarah van Gelder, "An interview with Bernard Lietaer" (print rights reserved by *YES!* magazine, reproduced with permission), http://www.transaction.net/press/interviews/lietaer0497.html (accessed Jan. 9, 2003).

371 *Nevertheless, each recipient*: The Fed also lends new money to banks through its "discount window." The amounts involved are minor in comparison.

371 *When a local bank lends*: Ibid.

372 *"redistribution mechanism"*: Kennedy, *Interest and Inflation Free Money*.

373 *In fact, it would take more than four hundred times*: Ibid.

373 *Today the return on that penny*: Ibid.

373 *With that, lenders once again*: Suhr, "Neutral Money Network."

374 *In that way the world's leading currencies*: Joel Kurtzman, *The Death of Money* (New York: Simon & Schuster, 1993), pp. 52–53.

375 *Largely as a result*: Ibid., p. 54.

375 *For nearly three decades*: Ibid., p. 55.

375 *Exchange rates began to gyrate*: Ibid., p. 60.

376 *Throughout the 1950s and '60s*: Ibid., p. 59.

376 *By 1982, people were working*: Kennedy, *Interest and Inflation Free Money*.

376 *one-third of all federal spending today*: Paul Krugman, "Passing It Along," *New York Times*, July 18, 2003, p. A17.

376 *As computers made lightning-fast*: Kurtzman, *Death of Money*, pp. 92–93.

377 *By the early nineties, Nixon's*: Ibid., p. 87.

377 *In just three decades the U.S. dollar*: Ibid., p. 88.

377 *"the speculative global cyber-casino"*: Kennedy, *Interest and Inflation Free Money*.

378 *"It is completely absurd"*: Kurtzman, *Death of Money*, p. 230.

378 *"A short-term"*: Ibid., p. 236.

378   *The ability of government central banks*: Ibid., pp. 88–89, 91.

378   *"By abandoning gold"*: Ibid., p. 94.

378   *"interest rates determine"*: Ibid., p. 93.

378   *"The dollar has become"*: R. David Ransom of Wainwright Economics in Boston, quoted in ibid., p. 61.

379   *"If the present monetary system"*: Quoted in Kennedy, *Interest and Inflation Free Money.*

380   *With thousands out of work*: "The Chips Are Down: What Lies Ahead for a World Riven by Money?" *New Scientist*, April 27, 2002, p. 36.

381   *"Thus those reformers"*: Quoted in "The Ghost of Gesell," *Financial Times Information*, Global News Wire, Feb. 10, 1999.

381   *That proposal was submitted*: Onken, "Market Economy Without Capitalism."

381   *They took umbrage*: Ibid.

381   *"an apologist of the monopoly bourgeoisie"*: Ibid.

381   *the Swiss WIR*: The WIR Web site is http://www.wir.ch/.

381   *It continues to play*: Its exchange of goods and services in 2000 was equal in value to 1.833 billion Swiss francs. This figure is from James Stodder, "Reciprocal Exchange Networks: Implications for Macroeconomic Stability," *Proceedings of the 2000 IEEE Engineering Management Society: August 13–15, 2000, Albuquerque, New Mexico*, http://www.rh.edu/~stodder/RecX.htm.

382   *"One of the principal barriers"*: Tobias Studer, "The WIR System in the View of an American Researcher," trans. of "Le système WIR dans l'optique d'un scientifique américain," *WirPlus*, Oct. 2000, http://www.rh.edu/news/news01/stodderpub.html.

382   *"has become increasingly irrelevant"*: Benjamin M. Friedman, "The Future of Monetary Policy: The Central Bank as an Army with Only a Signal Corps?" *International Finance* 2, no. 3 (1999), p. 330.

382   *"Being a monopoly"*: Ibid., p. 327.

383   *E-gold is an Internet currency*: Julian Dibbell, "In Gold We Trust," *Wired*, Jan. 2002, p. 60.

383   *"the economic activity"*: Stodder, "Reciprocal Exchange Networks."

383   *"In periods of economic boom"*: Studer, "WIR System in the View of an American Researcher."

383   *The euro is by default*: Kurtzman, *Death of Money*, p. 236.

383   *Stanford economist*: Samuel Brittan, "Low Inflation Is Not Good Enough," *Financial Times*, Oct. 14, 1999, p. 23. The effort to link the Argentine peso to the dollar was undermined by policies of the international development agencies.

384   *Today it can all be done*: Kennedy, *Interest and Inflation Free Money.*

385   *"more efficient allocation"*: Suhr, "Neutral Money Network."

385   *"Long-term positive"*: Onken, "Market Economy Without Capitalism."

386   *It might also end the curious cycle*: Kennedy, *Interest and Inflation Free Money.*

386   *How different might the world be*: Ibid.

386   *the future would "learn more"*: Ibid.

387   *"Americans are conditioned"*: Clifford Cobb, Ted Halstead, and Jonathan Rowe,

"If the GDP Is Up, Why Is America Down?" (*Atlantic Monthly*, October 1995): 59.

389 *"a flash of golden fire"*: Samuel Taylor Coleridge, *The Rime of the Ancient Mariner* (New York: Reynal & Hitchcock, 1946), pp. 31–32.

389 *"If the workings of the economy"*: Rothschild, *Bionomics*, p. 107.

12. Feedback Culture

391 *"A strict law bids us dance"*: Quoted in T. C. McLuhan, *The Way of Earth: Encounters with Nature in Ancient and Contemporary Thought* (New York: Simon & Schuster, 1994), p. 430. (The Kwakiutl are a native tribe found on the west coast of Canada and in the American Northwest.)

393 *"like a dog trying"*: Doyne Farmer, quoted in John Brockman, *The Third Culture: Beyond the Scientific Revolution* (New York: Simon & Schuster, 1995), p. 370.

395 *"We have sought for firm ground"*: "Quotations in Physics" (Physics Department, Salt Lake Community College, July 2, 2001), http://sol.slcc.edu/schools/hum_sci/physics/whatis/quotations.html.

396 *The nervous systems linking*: John Gerhart and Marc Kirschner, *Cells, Embryos, and Evolution: Toward a Cellular and Developmental Understanding of Phenotypic Variation and Evolutionary Adaptability* (Malden, Mass.: Blackwell Science, 1997), p. 1.

396 *The basic structure of the vertebrate limb*: Scott F. Gilbert, *Developmental Biology*, 5th ed. (Sunderland, Mass.: Sinauer Associates, 1997), p. 898.

397 *it was the absorption*: Fully 10 percent of our dry body weight is composed of alien species of bacteria, without which we couldn't live. See Lynn Margulis and Dorion Sagan, *Slanted Truths: Essays on Gaia, Symbiosis, and Evolution* (New York: Copernicus, 1997), p. 77.

397 *"It makes more sense"*: Ibid., p. 78.

398 *Philosopher of biology*: William C. Wimsatt, "Developmental Constraints, Generative Entrenchment, and the Innate-Acquired Distinction," in William Bechtel, ed., *Integrating Scientific Disciplines* (Dordrecht: Martinus–Nijhoff, 1986), pp. 185–208.

398 *"Like sandbluffs carved into fantastic shapes"*: Richard Dawkins, quoting from his book *Unweaving the Rainbow*. The quotation appears in his essay "Son of Moore's Law," in John Brockman, ed., *The Next Fifty Years: Science in the First Half of the Twenty-first Century* (New York: Vintage Books, 2002), pp. 154–55.

398 *"The well-being of prey species"*: Paul Shepard, *Traces of an Omnivore* (Washington, D.C.: Island Press for Shearwater Books, 1996), p. 24.

399 *So as individuals jostle*: David J. Depew and Bruce H. Weber, *Darwinism Evolving: Systems Dynamics and the Genealogy of Natural Selection* (Cambridge, Mass.: MIT Press, 1996), p. 473.

399 *"sustained life is a property"*: Harold J. Morowitz, quoted in ibid., p. 403.

399 *"Organisms organize their surroundings"*: Susan Oyama, *The Ontogeny of Information: Developmental Systems and Evolution* (Cambridge, U.K.: Cambridge University Press, 1985), p. 150.

399 *"a continuation of the metabolic pathways"*: Fritjof Capra, *The Web of Life: A New Scientific Understanding of Living Systems* (New York: Anchor Books, 1996), p. 35.

399 *Gram for gram, the body*: Personal conversations with James Brown (University of New Mexico biologist) and Geoffrey West (Los Alamos National Laboratory physicist), 1997. See also Diane Banegas, "The Tree of Life: Scientists Model Nature's System of Fractal Branching Networks," *SFI Bulletin* (Summer 1997), p. 7:

> "A cat is roughly 100 times larger than a mouse, so you'd expect a cat's metabolic rate to be 100 times larger than a mouse's, but it isn't," West explained. "The metabolic rate is only about 30 times larger—a number predicted by Kleiber's Law."
>
> For their part, Brown and [Brian] Enquist were trying to solve the riddle of why the metabolic rate of plants exhibits the same quarter-power scaling phenomenon observed in animals.

400 *"circular hierarchy"*: In his book *Gödel, Escher, Bach: An Eternal Golden Braid*, Douglas R. Hofstadter called examples of this phenomenon "strange loops."

400 *"Regardless of food habits"*: Shepard, *Traces of an Omnivore*, p. 49.

401 *writer David Depew and biochemist Bruce Weber*: David J. Depew is a professor in the Department of Communication Studies and the Rhetoric of Inquiry at the University of Iowa. Bruce H. Weber is a professor of biochemistry and the chair of the Department of Chemistry and Biochemistry at California State University, Fullerton.

401 *"evolvability"*: Cited in Depew and Weber, *Darwinism Evolving*, p. 21. The zoologist Richard Dawkins described this concept as early as 1987.

402 *"Evolution is shown to select"*: Quoted in Delta Willis, *The Sand Dollar and the Slide Rule: Drawing Blueprints from Nature* (Reading, Mass.: Addison-Wesley, 1995), p. 203.

403 *A nonprofit educational organization called the Bioneers*: Founded in 1990, the Bioneers/Collective Heritage Institute is a nonprofit organization that promotes practical environmental solutions and innovative social strategies for restoring the earth and communities. They conduct research and education in the areas of biodiversity, cultural diversity, environmental restoration, and restorative farming. Contact Bioneers toll-free at 1-877-BIONEER; Web site: www.bioneers.org.

403 *GreenBlue*: http://www.greenblue.org.

406 *"Why do we have more channels"*: William Safire, "The Great Media Gulp," *New York Times*, May 22, 2003, p. A33.

406 *the Center for Public Integrity conducted a study*: Bob Herbert, "Cozy with the F.C.C.," *New York Times*, June 5, 2003, p. A35.

408 *"the powerful, enticing"*: Donella Meadows, "Spiritual Wonder No Match for Advertising," *Charleston Gazette*, May 5, 1997, p. 4A. Meadows is a biophysicist, a systems analyst, and an adjunct professor of environmental studies at Dartmouth College. She is a prolific writer and environmental activist and was principal author of the Club of Rome's 1972 report, *The Limits to Growth*.

408 *"The mediated world"*: Speaking in *No Map for These Territories* (2001 documentary), directed by Mark Neale, produced by Docurama.

408 *"neuromarketing"*: Gareth Branwyn, "Jargon Watch," *Wired*, March 2003, p. 34.

408 *It uses cognitive science*: Alissa Quart, "Cognitive Science Goes Commercial: A Smarter Way to Sell Ketchup," *Wired*, Dec. 2002, p. 37.

408 *"advertisements are where our children"*: From the physicist Brian Swimme's book *The Hidden Heart of the Cosmos*, cited in Meadows, "Spiritual Wonder No Match for Advertising," p. 4A.

408 *"By its ability to implant"*: Quoted in David Korten, *When Corporations Rule the World*, 2nd ed. (San Francisco: Berrett-Koehler Publishers; and Bloomfield, Conn.: Kumarian Press, 2001), p. 154.

408 *"When the control"*: Ibid., p. 160.

409 *"In the propaganda of the ad"*: Quoted from Swimme's book *The Hidden Heart of the Cosmos*, cited in Meadows, "Spiritual Wonder No Match for Advertising," p. 4A.

409 *"If we understand the mechanism"*: Quoted in Mark Dowie's introduction to John Stauber and Sheldon Rampton, *Toxic Sludge Is Good for You! Lies, Damn Lies, and the Public Relations Industry* (Monroe, Maine: Common Courage Press for the Center on Media & Democracy, 1995), p. 1.

409 *It was Bernays who pulled off*: Ibid.

410 *Also, in Bernays' time*: Korten, *When Corporations Rule the World*, p. 144.

410 *The industry-sponsored Consumer Alert*: Ibid., p. 145.

410 *Pharmaceutical Research and Manufacturers of America*: Jeff Gerth and Sheryl Gay Stolberg, "With Quiet, Unseen Ties, Drug Makers Sway Debate," *New York Times*, Oct. 5, 2000, p. A1.

410 *"are regularly reported"*: David Korten, *When Corporations Rule the World*, p. 145.

411 *"one of America's"*: Stauber and Rampton, *Toxic Sludge Is Good for You!* pp. 90–91.

411 *"grassroots mobilizations"*: Ibid., pp. 84–85.

411 *"Real Grass Roots—Not Astroturf"*: Ibid., p. 79.

411 *"When I go into a zoning board meeting"*: Ibid., pp. 91–92.

412 *"During the NAFTA negotiations"*: Josh Karliner, *The Corporate Planet: Ecology and Politics in the Age of Globalization* (San Francisco: Sierra Club Books, 1997), p. 184.

412 *And of the total amount raised*: Stauber and Rampton, *Toxic Sludge Is Good for You!* p. 169.

412 *The book garnered mentions*: Ibid., pp. 170–71.

412 *Those hearings were held before*: As revealed in John MacArthur's book *Second Front*, on media manipulation during the war. See Stauber and Rampton, *Toxic Sludge Is Good for You!* p. 172.

413 *"While I was there"*: Quoted in Stauber and Rampton, *Toxic Sludge Is Good for You!* p. 173.

413 *"Of all the accusations"*: Quoted in ibid.

413 *"Lying under oath"*: Quoted in ibid., p. 172.

413 *The measure passed*: Ibid.

413 *In the United States, public relations employees*: Korten, *When Corporations Rule the World*, p. 148.

414 *The current White House administration*: Anne E. Kornblut, "Administration Is Warned About Its 'News' Videos," *New York Times*, Feb. 19, 2005.

414 *It also accredited*: Frank Rich, "The White House Stages Its 'Daily Show,'" *New York Times*, Feb. 20, 2005.

414 *This trend is a growing concern*: Melody Peterson, "A Conversation with Sheldon Krimsky: Uncoupling Campus and Company," *New York Times*, Sept. 23, 2003, p. F2.

414 *"Today, biotechnology and pharmaceutical companies"*: Ibid.

415 *"There are two rules"*: Quoted in ibid.

415 *A recent study*: Robert Matthews, "Researchers' Links with Biomed Industry Lead to Bias in Clinical Trials," *New Scientist*, Feb. 1, 2003, http://www.newscientist.com/article/mg17723801.000.html.

415 *This problem is exacerbated*: Patrick di Justo, "Under the Influence," *Wired*, May 2003, p. 58.

415 *And big companies provide it*: Advocacy Group Spending, 527 Committee Activity, Expenditure Breakdown, Federally Focused Organizations, Opensecrets. org, http://www.opensecrets.org/527s/527cmtes.asp?level=E&cycle=2004 (accessed Dec. 12, 2004).

415 *"a hard-cash adult" basis*: Quoted in Michael Drosnin, *Citizen Hughes: In His Own Words, How Howard Hughes Tried to Buy America* (New York: Broadway Books, 2004), p. 211. More precisely, Hughes used this term to describe his relationship with Johnson. Hughes referred to Nixon—whose entire career was haunted by shady financial dealings with Hughes—as "my man," and said of him, "He I know for sure knows the facts of life" (Drosnin, p. 42). Drosnin argues that Nixon's concerns about his covert dealings with Hughes are what led to the Watergate break-ins.

415 *"I certainly hope so"*: Quoted in "You Pays Your Money . . . ," *Economist*, July 29, 1999, http:www.economist.com/displaystory.cfm?story_id=323783.

416 *And just before that scandal surfaced*: Stephen Labaton, "Auditing Firms Exercise Power in Washington," *New York Times*, Jan. 19, 2002, p. A1.

416 *For the answers to all these questions*: Who Gives, Influence Inc 2000: Summary, Opensecrets.org, http://www.opensecrets.org/pubs/lobby00/summary.asp (accessed Dec. 12, 2004).

417 *"you recuse yourself"*: Quoted in Vicki Kemper and Deborah Lutterbeck, "The Country Club," *Common Cause Magazine*, March 22, 1996, p. 16.

417 *"We are on the way to becoming a plutocracy"*: Quoted in "Plutocrats Against Plutocracy," *Economist*, April 1, 1999, http://www.economist.com/displaystory. cfm?story_id=195284.

417 *In his retirement he has pulled together*: Ibid.

418 *self-organizing as any ecosystem*: Korten, *When Corporations Rule the World*, p. 119.

418 *"It is to prevent this reduction"*: Quoted in ibid., p. 62.

419 *"People of the same trade"*: Quoted in ibid., p. 206.

420 *"A favorite . . . argument for globalization"*: Ibid., pp. 206–207.

420 *This formula, says the publication*: Cited in ibid., p. 207.

420 *"Take a really big international industry"*: Quoted in ibid., p. 209.

420 *"the relationship-enterprise"*: Quoted in ibid.

421 *"the world's corporate giants"*: Ibid.

421 *"Those who work in the core"*: Ibid., pp. 212–13.

421 *Because they lack*: Ibid., p. 213.

421 *The result is that individual farmers*: Ibid., pp. 212–13.

421 *"Global corporations"*: Dee Hock, "Dee Hock's Vision of Today's Deformed and Tomorrow's Transformed Corporations," *Chautauqua Sages: Dee Hock*, http://www.nancho.net/newchau/hock.html (accessed Dec. 2002).

422 *"To attract companies like yours"*: Quoted in Korten, *When Corporations Rule the World*, p. 161.

422 *"The power of the center"*: Ibid., p. 241.

423 *"a deep distrust"*: Ibid., p. 19.

423 *"a false metaphor, a wrong concept"*: Hock, "Dee Hock's Vision of Today's Deformed and Tomorrow's Transformed Corporations."

423 *"The global trend"*: Korten, *When Corporations Rule the World*, p. 210.

424 *"having gained control"*: Ibid., p. 219.

424 *even through the boom years*: Ibid., p. 298.

424 *"In Mexico, small farmers are displaced"*: Ibid., p. 221.

425 *"Corporations have already begun to buy"*: Quoted in ibid., p. 223.

426 *As a matter of course, they imposed*: This and the following paragraph are from ibid., p. 62.

427 *"dictated rules for issuing stock"*: Richard L. Grossman and Frank T. Adams, *Taking Care of Business: Citizenship and the Charter of Incorporation* (Cambridge, Mass.: Charter Inc., Program on Corporations, Law & Democracy, 1993), pp. 8–13.

427 *"The Legislature ought cautiously to refrain"*: Quoted in ibid., p. 14.

427 *"Starting in 1844, nineteen states"*: Ibid., p. 13.

427 *"Corporations have been enthroned"*: Quoted in Korten, *When Corporations Rule the World*, p. 64.

428 *It was argued that setting up*: Grossman and Adams, *Taking Care of Business*, p. 16.

428 *Those agents also pressed*: Ibid., pp. 18–19.

428 *On the committee drafting that amendment*: Thom Hartmann, "Unequal Protection: The Rise of Corporate Dominance and the Theft of Human Rights" (2002), p. 12, http://www.thomhartmann.com/theft.shtml.

428 *"The halls of legislation"*: Quoted in Korten, *When Corporations Rule the World*, p. 65.

428 *"This is a government of the people"*: Quoted in ibid.

429 *"If these [lesser points] are tenable"*: Quoted in Hartmann, "Unequal Protection," p. 10.

429 *"The court does not wish to hear"*: Ibid., p. 8.

430 *"The defendant corporations are persons"*: Quoted in ibid., p. 10.

430 *It's worth noting here*: Ibid., p. 18.

430 *The rest of those suits, 288 in all*: Ibid., p. 9.

430 *Thom Hartmann*: Hartmann is a bestselling author and nationally syndicated radio talk show host who espouses what he describes as "the radical middle." His books include *We the People*, *Unequal Protection*, and *What Would Jefferson Do?* For more information see http://www.thomhartmann.com/.

430 *"struck down minimum wage laws"*: Hartmann, "Unequal Protection," p. 12.

431 *"No laws were passed by Congress"*: Ibid., p. 3.

431 *"I do not believe the word 'person'"*: Quoted in ibid., p. 9.

431 *"There was no history"*: Quoted in ibid.

432 *"Direct Corporate spending on political activity"*: See *Federal Election Commission v. Massachusetts Citizens for Life Inc.*

432 *"a minor inconvenience"*: Korten, *When Corporations Rule the World*, p. 105.

432 *"The for-profit, monetized shareholder"*: Hock, "Dee Hock's Vision of Today's Deformed and Tomorrow's Transformed Corporations." This passage reviewed by Dee Hock, Oct. 2004.

433 *"The more we cut"*: Korten, *When Corporations Rule the World*, p. 275.

434 *Ricardo's theory rests on just a few basic*: Korten, *When Corporations Rule the World*, p. 84.

435 On the Principles of Political Economy and Taxation: Ricardo begins by noting, "If the profits of capital employed in Yorkshire, should exceed those of capital employed in London, capital would speedily move from London to Yorkshire." But even so, he adds, "it would not follow that capital and population would necessarily move from England to Holland, or Spain, or Russia, where profits might be higher." Ricardo attributes this to "the difficulty with which capital moves from one country to another," a fact of life in his time. He then offers another reason for why his theory does not include the international movement of capital:

> The fancied or real insecurity of capital, when not under the immediate control of its owner, together with the natural disinclination which every man has to quit the country of his birth and connexions, and intrust himself with all his habits fixed, to a strange government and new laws, checks the emigration of capital. These feelings, *which I should be sorry to see weakened*, induce most men of property to be satisfied with a low rate of profits in their own country, rather than seek a more advantageous employment for their wealth in foreign nations [emphasis added].

The above excerpt is taken from David Ricardo, "On Foreign Trade," in *On the Principles of Political Economy and Taxation* (London: John Murray, 1817; 3rd ed., 1821), http://faculty.washington.edu/krumme/readings/ricardo7.html.

436 *"flows to whatever locality"*: Korten, *When Corporations Rule the World*, p. 85.

436 *"for many workers around the world"*: Thomas L. Friedman, *The Lexus and the Olive Tree* (New York: Farrar, Straus and Giroux, 2000), pp. 206–207.

436 *"Ideas, knowledge, art"*: Quoted in Korten, *When Corporations Rule the World*, p. 262.

436 *the organization Public Citizen*: Ralph Nader and Lori Wallach, "GATT, NAFTA, and the Subversion of the Democratic Process," in Jerry Mander and Edward Goldsmith, eds., *The Case Against the Global Economy: And for a Turn Toward the Local* (San Francisco: Sierra Club Books, 1996), pp. 92–93.

437 *After all, the broad effect on competition*: Special exemptions from them could protect small business start-ups.

439 *Historians say planning for the future*: David McCullough, quoted in George Will, "NEH, Bush Defend Culture," *Syracuse Post-Standard*, Dec. 27, 2002, p. A8.

440 *A Cornell University study*: David Pimental, Rebecca Harmon, Matthew Pacenza, Jason Pecarsky, and Marcia Pimental, "Natural Resources and an Optimal Human Population," *Population and Environment* 15, no. 5 (1994), p. 352.

440 *"What can't last won't last"*: David Brooks, "In the Midst of Budget Decadence, a Leader Will Arise," *New York Times*, Feb. 19, 2005.

440 *"How do we operate knowing"*: Personal conversation with Wes Jackson, 1997; reviewed by him, May 2004.

442 *"As we talk about a sustainable world"*: Personal conversation with Stuart Kauffman, May 1995.

442 *"Sustainability is not a goal"*: Personal conversation with Richard Levine, 1995; reviewed by him, May 2004.

443 *Community designer Mike Corbett*: Hunter Lovins, speaking on the "Natural Design" panel at the Bioneers conference "Practical Solutions for Restoring the Earth," Oct. 31–Nov. 1, 1997, San Francisco.

444 *"The concentration of power"*: Safire, "Great Media Gulp," p. A33.

445 *"[Philosopher] Daniel Dennett"*: Personal conversation with Brian Arthur, 1997; reviewed by him, Nov. 2004.

446 *"We think specialization"*: Murray Gell-Mann, "Quarks & Jaguars," *Talk of the Nation*, National Public Radio, Aug. 26, 1994.

446 *"Physicists speak a different language"*: Personal conversation with Christopher Langton, 1997; reviewed by him, March 2004.

447 *Crime on the Net*: Larry Ponemon, chair of the Ponemon Institute, an information management group and consultancy, cited in Bob Tedeschi, "Crime Is Soaring in Cyberspace but Many Companies Are Keeping It Quiet," *New York Times*, Jan. 27, 2003, p. C4.

447 *"successful and verifiable"*: Ibid., p. C4.

447 *"Every phone call you make"*: Friedman, *Lexus and the Olive Tree*, p. 427.

448 *"An enormous environmental information system"*: Walter Truett Anderson, "There's No Going Back to Nature," *Mother Jones*, Sept./Oct. 1996, p. 77.

450 *"Not everything keeps increasing"*: Murray Gell-Mann, *The Quark and the Jaguar: Adventures in the Simple and the Complex* (New York: W. H. Freeman, 1994), p. 371.

452 *Support for the civil institutions of government*: The call by corporate conservatives to privatize government services in order to make them more efficient is

equally questionable. While it's true that private companies are more efficient at minimizing their costs, that's only the first stage of a two-stage process. The second stage involves maximizing their profits. When government privatizes services, it has to pay for both of those stages.

453 *"Every society needs some shared values"*: George Soros, "Toward a Global Open Society," *Atlantic Monthly*, Jan. 1998, p. 20.

453 *an emerging generation then helps carry it forward*: The fact that media feedbacks bypass education to have a direct and largely uncontrolled impact on children—the principal subjects of education—is not evidence against this comparison. Rather, it points to the need for discussion of whether immature humans (that is, those below the age of constitutional consent) should be better insulated from media feedbacks.

454 *"The global economy"*: John Elkington, *The Chrysalis Economy: How Citizen CEOs and Corporations Can Fuse Values and Value Creation* (Oxford: Capstone, 2001), p. xi.

454 *"There comes for every caterpillar"*: Vladimir Nabokov, *Nabokov's Butterflies: Unpublished and Uncollected Writings*, ed. and annotated by Brian Boyd and Robert Michael Powell, new trans. by Dmitri Nabokov (Boston: Beacon Press, 2000), pp. 472, 473.

454 *"Both Wordsworth and Thoreau"*: Joseph Wood Krutch, *The Desert Year*, quoted in John K. Terres, *Things Precious & Wild: A Book of Nature Quotations* (Golden, Colo.: Fulcrum, 1991), p. 111.

456 *"The idea that there is a hidden order"*: Depew and Weber, *Darwinism Evolving*, p. 16.

index

a note about the author

Robert Frenay is a freelance writer living in New York. He is a former contributing editor for *Audubon* magazine, where he covered positive developments along the interface of nature and technology. He left there to work on this book, his first.